FOUNDATIONS OF SECURE COMPUTATION

NATO Science Series

A Series presenting the results of activities sponsored by the NATO Science Committee.
The Series is published by IOS Press and Kluwer Academic Publishers in conjunction with the NATO Scientific Affairs Division.

General Sub-Series

A Life Sciences	IOS Press
B Physics	Kluwer Academic Publishers
C Mathematical and Physical Sciences	Kluwer Academic Publishers
D Behavioural and Social Sciences	Kluwer Academic Publishers
E Applied Sciences	Kluwer Academic Publishers
F Computer and Systems Sciences	IOS Press

Partnership Sub-Series

1 Disarmament Technologies	Kluwer Academic Publishers
2 Environmental Security	Kluwer Academic Publishers
3 High Technology	Kluwer Academic Publishers
4 Science and Technology Policy	IOS Press
5 Computer Networking	IOS Press

The Partnership Sub-Series incorporates activities undertaken in collaboration with NATO's Partners in the Euro-Atlantic Partnership Council - countries of the CIS and Central and Eastern Europe - in Priority Areas of concern to those countries.

NATO-PCO-DATA BASE

The NATO Science Series continues the series of books published formerly in the NATO ASI Series.
An electronic index to the NATO ASI Series provides full bibliographical references (with keywords and/or abstracts) to more than 50 000 contributions from international scientists published in all sections of the NATO ASI Series.
Access to the NATO-PCO-DATA BASE is possible in two ways:
- via online FILE 128 (NATO-PCO-DATA BASE) hosted by ESRIN, Via Galileo Galilei, I-00044 Frascati, Italy;
- via CD-ROM "NATO-PCO-DATA BASE" with user-friendly retrieval software in English, French and German (© WTV GmbH and DATAWARE Technologies Inc., 1989).

The CD-ROM of the NATO ASI Series can be ordered from PCO, Overijse, Belgium.

Series F: Computer and Systems Sciences – Vol. 175 ISSN: 1387-6694

Foundations of Secure Computation

Edited by

Friedrich L. Bauer
Institut für Informatik, Technische Universität München, München, Germany

Ralf Steinbrüggen
Institut für Informatik, Technische Universität München, München, Germany

IOS Press
Ohmsha

Amsterdam • Berlin • Oxford • Tokyo • Washington, DC

Published in cooperation with NATO Scientific Affairs Division

Proceedings of the NATO Advanced Study Institute on
Foundations of Secure Computation
Marktoberdorf, Germany
27 July – 8 August, 1999

ISBN 1 58603 015 9 (IOS Press)
ISBN 4 274 90350 8 C3041 (Ohmsha)
Library of Congress Catalog Card Number: 00-101057

Publisher
IOS Press
Van Diemenstraat 94
1013 CN Amsterdam
The Netherlands
fax: +31 20 620 3419
e-mail: order@iospress.nl

Distributor in the UK and Ireland
IOS Press/Lavis Marketing
73 Lime Walk
Headington
Oxford OX3 7AD
England
fax: +44 1865 75 0079

Distributor in the USA and Canada
IOS Press, Inc.
5795-G Burke Centre Parkway
Burke, VA 22015
USA
fax: +1 703 323 3668
e-mail: iosbooks@iospress.com

Distributor in Germany
IOS Press
Spandauer Strasse 2
D-10178 Berlin
Germany
fax: +49 30 242 3113

Distributor in Japan
Ohmsha, Ltd.
3-1 Kanda Nishiki-cho
Chiyoda-ku, Tokyo 101
Japan
fax: +81 3 3233 2426

PRINTED IN THE NETHERLANDS

The κ-Calculus (NCκC)*

David von Oheimb et al.
MOD ⊆ Bavaria, Pred(MM)

* `http://hophophop.kangaroo.oz`, see also `http://www.in.tum.de/~oheimb/MOD1999/Kangaroo.html`

Preface

A global computational infrastructure has been established in recent years. This, and the advent of programming languages like Java supporting mobile distributed computing, has posed a great challenge to the computer science community. The capability of securing the infrastructure rests on mathematical foundations for programming languages and communication systems.

This volume focuses on security aspects of Communication and Mobility, Specification and Verification, Extraction and Realizability, Logic and Domains, Complexity and Feasibility.

Mobile computing on wide area networks must face the barriers of local conditions, of physical distances, bandwidth fluctuations, and intermittent connectivity. The combination of mobility, security, communication, and dynamic binding has to be explored under the language-design and semantic-unification perspectives. – In this volume, LUCA CARDELLI presents a calculus of *ambients* covering the various aspects.

Security protocols play a central role. Formal methods are required for analyzing assertions and deriving properties of protocols concerning authenticity and secrecy. There is still great demand for applying known techniques to important protocols and for analyzing these techniques for enabling the comparison of results. Furthermore, protocols should not only be studied in isolation but also as part of entire systems. – MARTIN ABADI gives an informal overview and discusses specifications of security protocols and their properties, keeping a calculus for access control and the *spi* calculus in the background.

Programs based on program algebra invoke services offered by coprograms. – J. A. BERGSTRA and M. E. LOOTS analyze the interaction between programs and coprograms and use coprograms for projection semantics.

In order to secure software and hardware, system designers and developers seek for appropriate methods and tools. It is an ongoing process to meet their requests of natural and expressive formal languages. – ROBERT L. CONSTABLE and JASON HICKEY use type theory as a fundament and define records and dependent records in *Nuprl*. The machinery can be seen at work with algebra and communication systems.

This also provides a basis for treating object-oriented concepts such as classes and inheritance. Regarding languages like Java, these are the main issues of language analysis. – TOBIAS NIPKOW and his group verify type safety of Java classes and of the corresponding part of the Java Virtual Machine, i.e. the absence of this kind of run time type errors. They explain how to represent and how to solve tasks like this in *Isabelle/HOL*.

In order to achieve correctness, the simplest possible formalization of the concepts involved is desirable and also essential to cope with large applications. Program extraction is a competitive alternative to program verification. – HELMUT SCHWICHTENBERG gives an exposition of the logic and introduces a refined approach of extracting programs from classical proofs.

Can we find a suitable combination of a logic and a realizability universe such that we can extract interesting concurrent programs from proofs of their specification? – SAMSON ABRAMSKY explores the possibilities for broadening the scope of realizability to Linear Logic and to concurrent and non-deterministic computation.

The incorporation of time into logic and the development of Game Semantics gave rise to a purely combinatorial understanding of logic. – JEAN-YVES GIRARD organizes some kind of tunnel between syntax and semantics, with a meeting in the middle: The syntax is replaced by a game-theoretic variant and an abstract notion of game is elaborated which can be specialized to deliver just this variant. A new logic named *ludics* is under development.

Is there a general method or a general class of structures which captures computations via approximations as in the example of real numbers? – VIGGO STOLTENBERG-HANSEN elaborates that the method of domain representability is a general way of studying effectivity on topological algebras in terms of true computations on concrete approximations.

Proof Theory is concerned with the connection between recursive programs and computational complexity, moreover with the connection between termination proofs and logical complexity. The bounds for the provably terminating functions can be reduced reasonably if a two-sorted re-interpretation of the usual primitive recursion scheme is used. – S. S. WAINER and his co-authors characterize the provably terminating functions in a first-order proof theoretic context.

Partial evaluation is a program transformation that specializes programs in order to achieve efficiency. – OLIVIER DANVY presents programming techniques for writing generating extensions.

The contributions emerged from lectures of the 20th International Summer School on Foundations of Secure Computation, held at Marktoberdorf from July 27 to August 8, 1999. More than 100 persons, counting participants, lecturers, and staff, attended. With people from more than 20 countries all over the world discussing, learning, and further developing this exciting topic, the summer school was a unique event both from a professional and from a social point of view. It is our privilege to thank all those people who helped to make the summer school a big success. These are the participants, the lecturers, our hosts in Marktoberdorf, people helping in the staff, and especially Mrs. Ingrid Luhn, who took care of a smooth course of events. We feel obliged to David von Oheimb for the K-Calculus which accompanies the five parts of the book illuminating main subjects of the respective contributions. Finally, we thank the people from IOS who managed printing carefully.

The Marktoberdorf Summer School was arranged as an Advanced Study Institute of the NATO Science Committee with financial aid from the Commission of the European Communities and from the National Science Foundation, Washington.

Munich, January 2000 — The editors

Contents

Part 0
Communication and Mobility

L. Cardelli

M. Abadi

J. A. Bergstra

0. Kangaroo Ambients

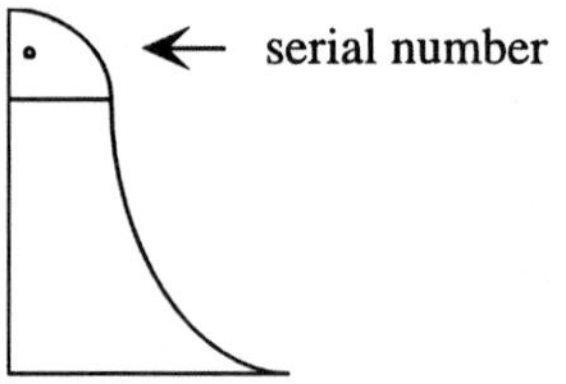

Nesting:

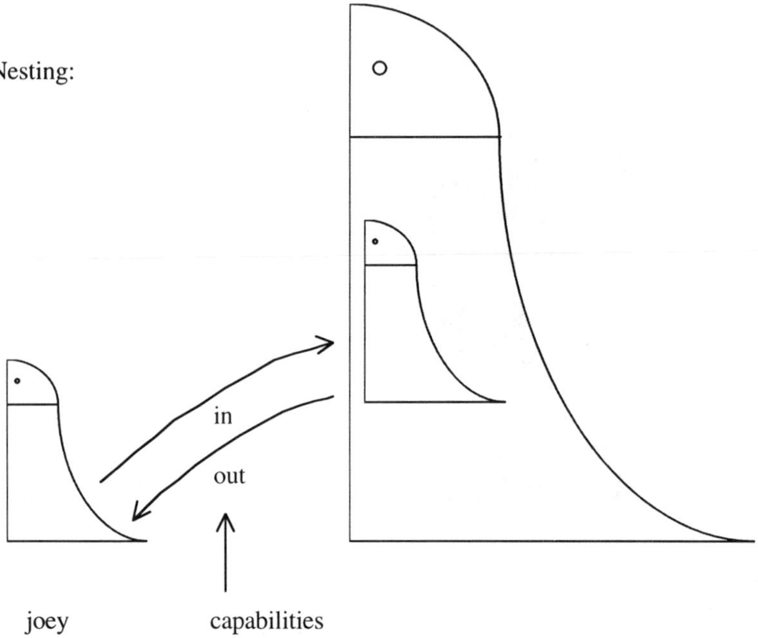

Interpretation of other notions ??

Perhaps with an improved type system ...

Foundations of Secure Computation
F.L. Bauer and R. Steinbrüggen (Eds.)
IOS Press, 2000

Mobility and Security

Luca Cardelli

Microsoft Research

Lecture Notes for the Marktoberdorf Summer School 1999,
from works by Luca Cardelli and Andrew D. Gordon

Abstract. We discuss the computational aspects of wide area networks, and we describe various facets of a process calculus devised to embody mobility, security, and wide area network semantics. These lecture notes are an abridged version of [8, 11, 27, 12, 13].

Part I: Wide Area Computation

1 Introduction

The Internet and the World-Wide-Web provide a computational infrastructure that spans the planet. It is appealing to imagine writing programs that exploit this global infrastructure. Unfortunately, the Web violates many familiar assumptions about the behavior of distributed systems, and demands novel and specialized programming techniques. In particular, three phenomena that remain largely hidden in local area network architectures become readily observable on the Web:

- ***(A) Virtual locations***. Because of the presence of potential attackers, barriers are erected between mutually distrustful administrative domains. Therefore, a program must be aware of where it is, and of how to move or communicate between different domains. The existence of separate administrative domains induces a notion of virtual locations and of virtual distance between locations.
- ***(B) Physical locations***. On a planet-size structure, the speed of light becomes tangible. For example, a procedure call to the antipodes requires at least 1/10 of a second, independently of future improvements in networking technology. This absolute lower bound to latency induces a notion of physical locations and physical distance between locations.
- ***(C) Bandwidth fluctuations***. A global network is susceptible to unpredictable congestion and partitioning, which result in fluctuations or temporary interruptions of bandwidth. Moreover, mobile devices may perceive bandwidth changes as a consequence of physical movement. Programs need to be able to observe and react to these fluctuations.

These features may interact among themselves. For example, bandwidth fluctuations may be related to physical location because of different patterns of day and night network utilization, and to virtual location because of authentication and encryption across domain boundaries. Virtual and physical locations are often related, but need not coincide.

In addition, another phenomenon becomes unobservable on the Web:

- ***(D) Failures***. On the Web, there is no practical upper bound to communication delays. In particular, failures become indistinguishable from long delays, and thus undetectable. Failure recovery becomes indistinguishable from intermittent connectivity. Furthermore, delays (and, implicitly, failures) are frequent and unpredictable.

These four phenomena determine the set of *observables* of the Web: the events or states that can be in principle detected. Observables, in turn, influence the basic building blocks of computation. In moving from local area networks to wide area networks, the set of observables changes, and so does the computational model, the programming constructs, and the kind of programs one can write. The question of how to "program the Web" reduces to the question of how to program with the new set of observables provided by the Web.

At least one general technique has emerged to cope with the observables characteristic of a wide area network such as the Web. *Mobile computation* is the notion that running programs need not be forever tied to a single network node. Mobile computation can deal in original ways with the phenomena described above:

- ***(A) Virtual locations***. Given adequate trust mechanisms, mobile computations can cross barriers and move between virtual locations. Barriers are designed to impede access, but when code is allowed to cross them, it can access local resources without the impediment of the barriers.
- ***(B) Physical locations***. Mobile computations can move between physical locations, turning remote calls into local calls, and thus avoiding the latency limit.
- ***(C) Bandwidth fluctuations***. Mobile computations can react to bandwidth fluctuations, either by moving to a better-placed location, or by transferring code that establishes a customized protocol over a connection.
- ***(D) Failures***. Mobile computations can run away from anticipated failures, and can move around presumed failures.

Mobile computation is also strongly related to recent hardware advances, since computations move implicitly when carried on portable devices. In this sense, we cannot avoid the issues raised by mobile computation: more than an avant-garde software technique, it is an existing hardware reality.

2 Three Mental Images

We begin by comparing and contrasting three *mental images*; that is, three abstracted views of distributed computation. From the differences between these mental images we derive the need for new approaches to global computation.

2.1 Local Area Networks

The first mental image corresponds to the now standard, and quickly becoming obsolete, model of computation over local area networks.

When workstations and PCs started replacing mainframes, local networks were invented to connect autonomous computers for the purpose of resource sharing. A typical local area network consists of a collection of computers of about the same power (within a couple of hardware generations) and of network links of about the same bandwidth and latency. This environment is not always completely uniform: specialized machines may operate as servers or as engineering workstations, and specialized subnetworks may offer special services. Still, by and large, the structure of a LAN can be depicted as the uniform network of nodes (computers) and links (connections) in Mental Image 1.

A main property of such a network is its predictability. Communication delays are bounded, and processor response time can be estimated. Therefore, link and process failures can be detected by time-outs and by "pinging" nodes.

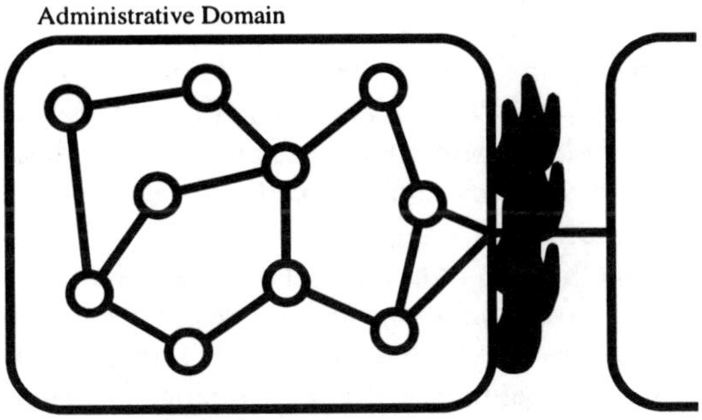

Mental Image 1: Local Area Network

Another important property of local area networks is that they are usually well-administered and, in recent times, protected against attack. Network administrators have the task of keeping the network running and protect it against infiltration. In the picture, the boundary line represents an *administrative domain*, and the flames represent the protection provided by a *firewall*. Protection is necessary because local area networks are rarely completely disconnected: they usually have slower links to the outside world, which are however enough to make administrators nervous about infiltration.

The architecture of local area networks is very different from the older, highly centralized, mainframe architecture. This difference, and the difficulties implied by it, resulted in the emergence of novel distributed computing techniques, such as remote-procedure-call, client-server architecture, and distributed object-oriented programming. The combined aim and effect of these techniques is to make the programming and application environment stable and uniform (as in mainframes). In particular, the network topology is carefully hidden so that any two computers can be considered as lying one logical step apart. Moreover, computers can be considered immobile; for example, they usually preserve their network address when physically moved.

Even in this relatively static environment, the notion of mobility has gradually acquired prominence, in a variety of forms. Control mobility, found in RPC (Remote Procedure Call) and RMI (Remote Method Invocation) mechanisms, is the notion that a thread of control moves (in principle) from one machine to another and back. Data mobility is achieved in RPC/RMI by linearizing, transporting, and reconstructing data across machines. Link mobility is the ability to transmit the end-points of network channels, or remote object proxies. Object mobility is the ability to move objects between different servers, for example for load balancing purposes. Finally, in Remote Execution, a computation can be shipped for execution to a server (this is an early version of code mobility, proposed as an extension of RPC [41]).

In recent years, distributed computing has been endowed with greater mobility properties and easier network programming. Techniques such as Object Request Brokers have emerged to abstract over the location of objects providing certain services. Code mobility has emerged in Tcl and other scripting languages to control network applications. Agent mobility has been pioneered in Telescript [43], aimed towards a uniform (although wide area) network of services. Closure mobility (the mobility of active and connected entities) has been investigated in Obliq [7].

In due time, local area network techniques would have smoothly and gradually evolved towards deployment on wide area networks, e.g. as was explicitly attempted by the CORBA effort. But, suddenly, a particular wide area network came along that radically changed the fundamental assumptions of distributed computing and its pace of progress: the Web.

2.2 *Wide Area Networks*

Global computing evolved over the span of a few decades in the form of the Internet. But it was not until the emergence of the Web that the peculiar characteristics of the Internet were exposed in a way that anybody could verify with just a few mouse clicks. For clarity and simplicity we will refer to the Web as the primary global information infrastructure, although it was certainly not the first one.

We should remember that the notions of a global address space and of a global file system have been popular at times as extensions of the mainframe architecture to wide area networks. The first obvious feature of the Web is that, although it forms a global computational resource, it is nothing like a global mainframe, nor an extension of it. The Web does not support a global (updatable) file system and, although it supports a global addressing mechanism, it does not guarantee the integrity of addressing. The Web has no single reliable component, but it also has no single failure point; it is definitely not the centralized all-powerful mainframe of 1950's science fiction novels that could be shut off by attacking its single "brain".

The fact that the Web is not a mainframe is not a big concern; we have already successfully tackled distributed computing based on LANs. More distressing is the fact that the Web does not behave like a LAN either. Many proposals have emerged along the lines of extending LAN concepts to a global environment; that is, in turning the Internet into a distributed address space, or a distributed file system. However, since the global environment does not have the stability properties of a LAN, this can be achieved only by introducing redundancy (for reliability), replication (for quality of service), and scalability (for management) at many different levels. Things might have evolved in this direction, but this is not the way the Web came to be. The Web is, almost by definition, unreliable, unpredictable, and unmanageable as a whole, and was not designed with LAN-like guarantees of service.

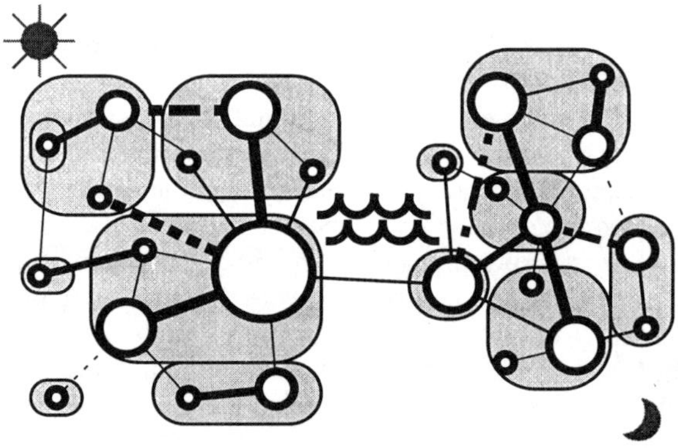

Mental Image 2: Wide Area Network (for example, the Web)

Therefore, the main problem with the Web is that it is not just a big LAN, otherwise, modulo issues of scale, we would already know how to deal with it. There are several ways in which the Web is not a big LAN, and we will describe them shortly. But the fundamental reason is that, unlike a LAN, the Web is not centrally administered. Instead, it is a dynamic collection of countless independent administrative domains, all widely different and mutually distrustful. This is represented in Mental Image 2.

In that picture, computers differ greatly in power and availability, while network links differ greatly in capacity and reliability. Large physical distances have visible effects, and so do time zones. The architecture of a wide area network is yet again fundamentally different from that of a local area network. Most prominently, the network topology is dynamic and non-trivial. Computers become intrinsically mobile: they require different addressing when physically moved across administrative boundaries. Techniques based on mobility become more important and sometimes essential. For example, mobile Java applets provided the first disciplined mechanism for running code able to (and allowed to) systematically penetrate other people's firewalls. Countless projects have emerged in the last few years with the aim of supporting mobile computation over wide areas, and are beginning to be consolidated.

At this point, our architectural goal might be to devise techniques for managing computation over an unreliable collection of far-flung computers. However, this is not yet the full picture. Not only are network links and nodes widely dispersed and unreliable; they are not even liable to stay put, as we discuss next.

2.3 Mobile Computing

A different global computing paradigm has been evolving independently of the Web. Instead of connecting together all the LANs in the world, another way of extending the reach of a LAN is to move individual computers and other gadgets from one LAN to another, dynamically.

We discussed in the Introduction how the main characteristics of the Web point towards mobile comput*ation*. However, that is meant as mobile computation over a fixed (although possibly flaky) network. A more interesting picture emerges when the very components of the network can move about. This is the field of mobile comput*ing*. Today, laptops and personal organizers routinely move about; in the future entire networks will go mobile (as in IBM's Personal Area Network). Existing examples of this kind of mobility include: a smart card entering a network computer slot; an active badge entering a room; a wireless PDA or laptop entering a building; a mobile phone entering a phone cell.

We could draw a picture similar to Mental Image 1, but with mobile devices moving within the confines of a single LAN. This notion of a dynamic LAN is a fairly minor extension of the basic LAN concepts, and presents few conceptual problems (wireless LANs are already common). A much more interesting picture emerges when we think of mobile gadgets over a WAN, because administrative boundaries and multiple access pathways then interact in complex ways, as anybody who travels with a laptop knows all too well.

Mental Image 3 focuses on two domains: the United States and the European Union, each enclosed by a political boundary that regulates the movement of people and computers. Within a political boundary, private companies and public agencies may further regulate the flow of people and devices across their doors. Over the Atlantic we see a third domain, representing Air France flight 81 travelling from San Francisco to Paris. AF81 is a very active mobile computational environment: it is full of people working with their laptops and possibly connecting to the Internet through airphones. (Not to mention the hundreds of computers that control the airplane and let it communicate with a varying stream of ground stations.)

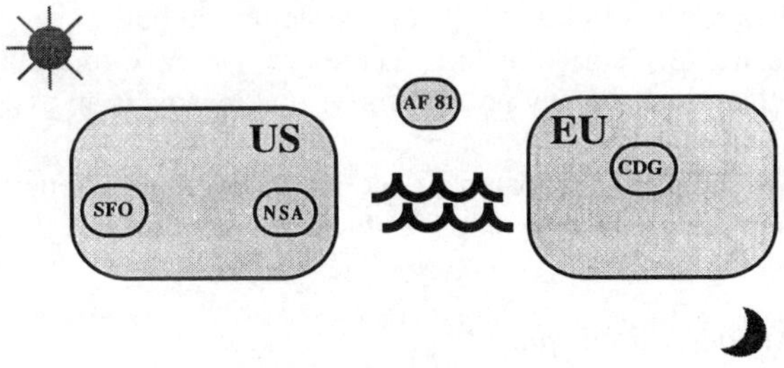

Mental Image 3: Mobile Computing

Abstracting a bit from people and computation devices, we see here a hierarchy of boundaries that enforce controls and require permissions for crossing. Passports are required to cross political boundaries, tickets are required for airplanes, and special clearances are required to enter (and exit!) agencies such as the NSA. Sometimes, whole mobile boundaries cross in and out of other boundaries and similarly need permissions, as the mobile environment of AF81 needs permission to enter an airspace. On the other hand, once an entity has been allowed across a boundary, it is fairly free to roam within the confines of the boundary, until another boundary needs to be crossed.

2.4 General Mobility

We have described two different notions of mobility. The first, *mobile computation*, has to do with virtual mobility (mobile software). The second, *mobile computing*, has to do with physical mobility (mobile hardware). These two fields are today almost disconnected, the first dominated by a software community, and the second dominated by a hardware community. However, the borders between virtual and physical mobility are fuzzy, and eventually we will have to treat all kinds of mobility in a uniform way. Here are two examples where the different forms of mobility interact.

The first example is one of virtual mobility achieved by physical means. Consider a software agent in a laptop. The agent can move by propagating over the network, but can also move by being physically transported with the laptop from one location to another. In the first case, the agent may have to undergo security checks (e.g., bytecode verification) when it crosses administrative domains. In the second case the agent may have to undergo security checks (e.g., virus detection) when the laptop is physically allowed inside a new administrative domain. Do we need two completely separate security infrastructures for these two cases, or can we somehow find a common principle? A plausible security policy for a given domain would be that a physical barrier (a building door) should provide the same security guarantees as a virtual barrier (a firewall).

The second example is one of physical mobility achieved by virtual means. Software exists that allows remote control of a computer, by bringing the screen of a remote computer on a local screen. The providers of such software may claim that this is just as good as moving the computer physically, e.g. to access its local data. Moreover, if the remote computer has a network connection, this is also equivalent to "stringing wire" from the remote location, since the remote network is now locally accessible. For example, using remote control over a phone line to connect from home to work where a high-bandwidth Internet connection is available, is almost as good as having a high-bandwidth Internet connection brought into the home.

The other side of the coin of being mobile is of becoming disconnected or intermittently connected. Even barring flaky networks, intermittent connectivity can be caused by physical movement, for example when a wireless user moves into some form of Faraday cage. More interestingly, intermittent connectivity may be caused by virtual movement, for example when an agent moves in and out of an administrative domain that does not allow communication. Neither case is really a failure of the infrastructure; in both cases, lack of connectivity may in fact be a desirable security feature. Therefore, we have to assume that intermittent connectivity, caused equivalently by physical or virtual means, is an essential feature of mobility.

In the future we should be prepared to see increased interactions between virtual and physical mobility, and we should develop frameworks where we can discuss and manipulate these interactions.

2.5 Barriers and Action-at-a-Distance

The unifying difficulty in both mobile computing and mobile computation is the proliferation of barriers, and the problems involved in crossing them. This central difficulty implies that we must regard barriers as fundamental features of our computational models.

In general, we can forget about the notion of *action-at-a-distance computing*: the idea that resources are available transparently at any time, no matter how far away. Instead, we have to get used to the notion that movement and communication are step-by-step activities, and that they are visibly so: the multiple steps involved cannot be hidden, collapsed, or rendered atomic.

The action-at-a-distance paradigm is still prevalent within LANs, and this is another reason why LANs are different from WANs, where such an assumption cannot hold.

2.6 WAN Postulates

We summarize this section by a collection of postulates that capture the main properties of the reality we are interested in modeling:

- Separate locations exist.
- Different locations have different properties, hence both people and programs will want to move between them.
- Barriers to mobility will be erected to preserve the properties of certain locations.
- Some people and some programs will still need to cross those barriers.

The point of these postulates is to stress that mobility and barrier crossing are inevitable requirements of our current and future computing infrastructure.

The observables that are characteristic of wide area networks have the following implications:

- Distinct virtual locations are observed because of the existence of distinct administrative domains, which are produced by the inevitable existence of attackers. Distinct virtual locations preclude the unfettered execution of actions across domains, and require a security model.
- Distinct physical locations are observed, over large distances, because of the inevitable latency limit given by the speed of light. Distinct physical locations preclude instantaneous action at a distance, and require a mobility model.
- Bandwidth fluctuations (including hidden failures) are observed because of the inevitable exercise of free will by network users, both in terms of communication and movement. Bandwidth fluctuations preclude reliance on response time, and require an asynchronous communication model.

3 Modeling Wide Area Computation

Section 2 was dedicated to showing that the reality of mobile computation over a WAN does not fall into familiar categories. Therefore, we need to invent a new model that can help us in understanding and eventually in taking advantage of this reality.

3.1 Barriers

We believe that the most fundamental new notion is that of barriers; this is the most prominent aspect of post-LAN computing environments.

Many of the basic features of WANs have to do with barriers: ***Locality*** (the existence of different virtual or physical locations, and the notion of being in the same or different locations) is induced by a topology of barriers. ***Mobility*** is barrier crossing. ***Security*** has to do with the ability or inability to cross barriers. ***Communication*** is partitioned by barriers: local communication happens within barriers, while long-distance communication is a combination of local communication and movement across barriers. ***Action at a distance*** (immediate interaction across many barriers) is forbidden.

We have chose barriers as the most important feature of an abstract model of computation for wide area networks, the Ambient Calculus [11], which we briefly outline here and investigate in the remaining sections.

3.2 Ambients

The current literature on wide area network languages can be broadly classified into agent-based languages (e.g., Telescript [43]), and place-based languages (e.g., Linda [14]). An ambient is a generalization of both notions. Like an agent, an ambient can move across places (also represented by ambients) where it can interact with other agents. Like a place, an ambient supports local undirected communication, and can receive messages (also represented by ambients) from other places. Ambients can be arbitrarily nested, generalizing the limited place-agent-data nesting of most agent languages, and the nesting of places allowed in some Linda dialects.

Briefly, an *ambient* is a place that is delimited by a boundary and where multi-threaded computation happens. Each ambient has a *name*, a collection of local *processes*, and a collection of *subambients*. Ambients can move in and out of other ambients, subject to *capabilities* that are associated with ambient names. Ambient names are unforgeable, this fact being the most basic security property.

In further detail, an ambient has the following main characteristics.

- An ambient is a *bounded* place where computation happens.

  If we want to move computations easily we must be able to determine what parts should move. A boundary determines what is inside and what is outside an ambient, and therefore determines what moves. A boundary implies some flexible addressing scheme that can denote entities across the boundary; examples are symbolic links, URLs (Uniform Resource Locators) and Remote Procedure Call proxies. Flexible addressing is what enables, or at least facilitates, mobility. It is also, of course, a cause of problems when the addressing links are "broken".

- Ambients can be nested within other ambients, forming a tree structure.

  As we discussed, administrative domains are (often) organized hierarchically. Mobility is represented as navigation across a hierarchy of ambients. For example, if we want to move a running application from work to home, the application must be removed from an enclosing (work) ambient and inserted in a different enclosing (home) ambient.

- Each ambient has a collection of local running processes.

  A local process of an ambient is one that is contained in the ambient but not in any of its subambients. These "top level" local processes have direct control of the ambient, and in particular they can instruct the ambient to move. In contrast, the local processes of a subambient have no direct control on the parent ambient: this helps guaranteeing the integrity of the parent.

- Each ambient moves as a whole with all its subcomponents.

  The activity of a single local process may, by causing movement of its parent, influence the location, and therefore the activity, of other local processes and subambients. For example, if we move a laptop and reconnect it to a different network, then all the threads, address spaces, and file systems within it move accordingly and automatically, and have to cope with their new surrounding. Agent mobility is a special case of ambient mobility, since agents are usually single-threaded. Ambients, like agents, automatically carry with them a collection of private data as they move.

- Each ambient has a name.

  The name of an ambient is used to control access (entry, exit, communication, etc.). In a realistic situation the true name of an ambient would be guarded very closely, and only specific capabilities based on the name would be handed out.

3.3 *Ideas for Wide Area Languages*

Ambients represent our understanding of the fundamental properties of mobile computation over wide area networks. Our final goal, though, is to program the Internet in some convenient high-level language. Therefore, we aim to find programming constructs that are semantically compatible with the ambient principles, and consequently with wide area networks.

These compatibility requirements include (A) *WAN-soundness*: a wide area network language cannot adopt primitives that entail action-at-a-distance, continued connectivity, global consensus, or security bypasses, and (B) *WAN-completeness*: a wide area network language must be able to express the behavior of web surfers and of mobile agents and users, and of any other entities that routinely roam those networks.

More specifically, we believe the following are necessary ingredients of wide area languages.

- ***Naming***. Names are symbolic ways of referring to entities across a barrier. Names are detached from their corresponding entities; one may possess a name without having immediate access to any entity of that name. To enable mobility and disconnected operation, all entities across a barrier should be denoted by names, not by "hard" pointers.
- ***Migration***. Active hardware and software components should be able to migrate. Migration of certain active hardware components is possible today, but the ability to automatically disconnect and reconnect those components to surrounding (possibly multiple) networks is not currently available. Migration of active software components is even harder, typically for lack of system facilities for migrating live individual threads and groups of threads.
- ***Dynamic connectivity***. A wide area network cannot be started or stopped all at once. Therefore, it is necessary to dynamically connect components. This is contrary to the current prominence in programming languages of static binding, static module composition, and static linking. The ambient calculus provides an example of a novel mixture of ordinary static scoping of names (which enables typechecking) with dynamic binding of operations to names (which enables dynamic linking).
- ***Communication***. Communication on wide area networks must in general be asynchronous. However, local communication (within or even across a single barrier) can usefully be synchronous. Moreover, in the presence of mobility, it is necessary to have some level of synchronization between communication and movement operations. This remains an interesting design area for mobile languages.
- ***Security***. Security abstractions should be provided at the programming-language level, that is, above the fundamental cryptographic primitives. Programmers need to operate with reliable high-level abstractions, otherwise subtle security loopholes can creep in. We believe that barriers are one such high-level security abstraction, which can be supported by programming constructs that can be mechanically analyzed (e.g., via type systems [10]).

Summary

The ambient semantics naturally suggests unusual programming constructs that are well-suited for wide area computation. The combination of mobility, security, communication, and dynamic binding issues has not been widely explored yet at the language-design level, and certainly not within a unifying semantic paradigm. We hope our unifying foundation will facilitate the design of such new languages.

Part II: Ambient Calculus

4 Mobility

We describe a minimal calculus of ambients that includes only mobility primitives. Still, this calculus is already quite expressive. In Section 5 we then introduce communication primitives that allow us to write more natural examples.

4.1 Mobility Primitives

We first introduce a calculus in its entirety, and then we comment on the individual constructions. The syntax of the calculus is defined in the following table. The main syntactic categories are processes (including both ambients and agents that execute actions) and capabilities.

Table 1: Mobility Primitives

n	names
$P,Q ::=$	processes
$(\nu n)P$	restriction
$\mathbf{0}$	inactivity
$P \mid Q$	composition
$!P$	replication
$n[P]$	ambient
$M.P$	action
$M ::=$	capabilities
$in\ n$	can enter n
$out\ n$	can exit n
$open\ n$	can open n

Table 2: Free names

$fn((\nu n)P)$	$\triangleq$	$fn(P) - \{n\}$	$fn(in\ n)$	$\triangleq$	$\{n\}$
$fn(\mathbf{0})$	$\triangleq$	$\emptyset$	$fn(out\ n)$	$\triangleq$	$\{n\}$
$fn(P \mid Q)$	$\triangleq$	$fn(P) \cup fn(Q)$	$fn(open\ n)$	$\triangleq$	$\{n\}$
$fn(!P)$	$\triangleq$	$fn(P)$			
$fn(n[P])$	$\triangleq$	$\{n\} \cup fn(P)$			
$fn(M.P)$	$\triangleq$	$fn(M) \cup fn(P)$			

We write $P\{n\leftarrow m\}$ for the substitution of the name m for each free occurrence of the name n in the process P. Similarly for $M\{n\leftarrow m\}$.

Table 3: Syntactic conventions

$(\nu n)P \mid Q$	is read	$((\nu n)P) \mid Q$	
$!P \mid Q$	is read	$(!P) \mid Q$	
$M.P \mid Q$	is read	$(M.P) \mid Q$	
$(\nu n_1 ... n_m)P$	$\triangleq$	$(\nu n_1)...(\nu n_m)P$	
$n[]$	$\triangleq$	$n[\mathbf{0}]$	
M	$\triangleq$	$M.\mathbf{0}$	(where appropriate)

The first four process primitives (restriction, inactivity, composition and replication) are commonly found in process calculi. To these we add ambients, $n[P]$, and the exercise of capabilities, $M.P$. Next we discuss these primitives in detail.

4.2 Explanations

We begin by introducing the semantics of ambients informally. A reduction relation $P \longrightarrow Q$ describes the evolution of a process P into a new process Q.

Restriction

The restriction operator:

$$(\nu n)P$$

creates a new (unique) name n within a scope P. The new name can be used to name ambients and to operate on ambients by name.

As in the π-calculus [35], the (νn) binder can float outward as necessary to extend the scope of a name, and can float inward when possible to restrict the scope. Unlike the π-calculus, the names that are subject to scoping are not channel names, but ambient names.

The restriction construct is transparent with respect to reduction; this is expressed by the following rule:

$$P \longrightarrow Q \;\Rightarrow\; (\nu n)P \longrightarrow (\nu n)Q$$

Inaction

The process:

$$\mathbf{0}$$

is the process that does nothing. It does not reduce.

Parallel

Parallel execution is denoted by a binary operator that is commutative and associative:

$$P \mid Q$$

It obeys the rule:

$$P \longrightarrow Q \;\Rightarrow\; P \mid R \longrightarrow Q \mid R$$

This rule directly covers reduction on the left branch; reduction on the right branch is obtained by commutativity.

Replication

Replication is a technically convenient way of representing iteration and recursion. The process:

$$!P$$

denotes the unbounded replication of the process P. That is, $!P$ can produce as many parallel replicas of P as needed, and is equivalent to $P \mid !P$. There are no reduction rules for $!P$; in particular, the term P under ! cannot begin to reduce until it is expanded out as $P \mid !P$.

Ambients

An ambient is written:

$$n[P]$$

where n is the name of the ambient, and P is the process running inside the ambient.

In $n[P]$, it is understood that P is actively running, and that P can be the parallel composition of several processes. We emphasize that P is running even when the surrounding ambient is moving. Running while moving may or may not be realistic, depending on the nature of the ambient and of the communication medium through which the ambient moves, but it is consistent to think in those terms. We express the fact that P is running by a rule that says that any reduction of P becomes a reduction of $n[P]$:

$$P \rightarrow Q \;\Rightarrow\; n[P] \rightarrow n[Q]$$

In general, an ambient exhibits a tree structure induced by the nesting of ambient brackets. Each node of this tree structure may contain a collection of (non-ambient) processes running in parallel, in addition to subambients. We say that these processes are running in the ambient, in contrast to the ones running in subambients. The general shape of an ambient is, therefore:

$$n[P_1 \mid ... \mid P_p \mid m_1[...] \mid ... \mid m_q[...]] \qquad (P_i \neq n_i[...])$$

To emphasize structure we may display ambient brackets as boxes. Then the general shape of an ambient is:

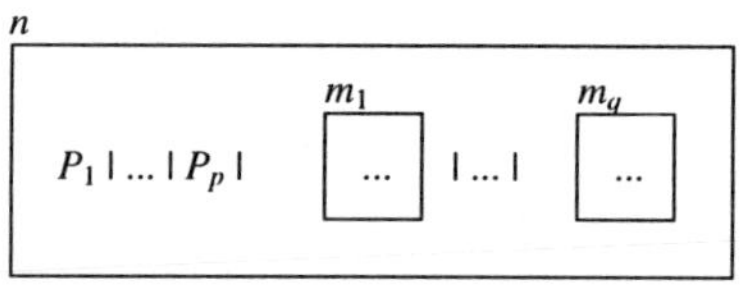

Nothing prevents the existence of two or more ambients with the same name, either nested or at the same level. Once a name is created, it can be used to name multiple ambients. Moreover, $!n[P]$ generates multiple ambients with the same name. This way, for example, one can easily model the replication of services.

Actions and Capabilities

Operations that change the hierarchical structure of ambients are sensitive. In particular such operations can be interpreted as the crossing of firewalls or the decoding of ciphertexts. Hence these operations are restricted by *capabilities*. Thanks to capabilities, an ambient can allow other ambients to perform certain operations without having to reveal its true name. With the communication primitives of Section 5, capabilities can be transmitted as messages.

The process:

$$M.\, P$$

executes an action regulated by the capability M, and then continues as the process P. The process P does not start running until the action is executed. For each kind of capability M we have a specific rule for reducing $M.\, P$. These rules are described below case by case.

We consider three kinds of capabilities: one for entering an ambient, one for exiting an ambient and one for opening up an ambient. Capabilities are obtained from names; given a name m, the capability *in m* allows entry into m, the capability *out m* allows exit out of m and the capability *open m* allows the opening of m. Implicitly, the possession of one or all of these capabilities is insufficient to reconstruct the original name m from which they were extracted.

Entry Capability

An entry capability, *in m*, can be used in the action:

$$in\ m.\, P$$

which instructs the ambient surrounding *in m. P* to enter a sibling ambient named m. If no sibling m can be found, the operation blocks until a time when such a sibling exists. If more than one m sibling exists, any one of them can be chosen. The reduction rule is:

$$n[in\ m.\ P \mid Q] \mid m[R] \longrightarrow m[n[P \mid Q] \mid R]$$

Or, by representing ambient brackets as boxes:

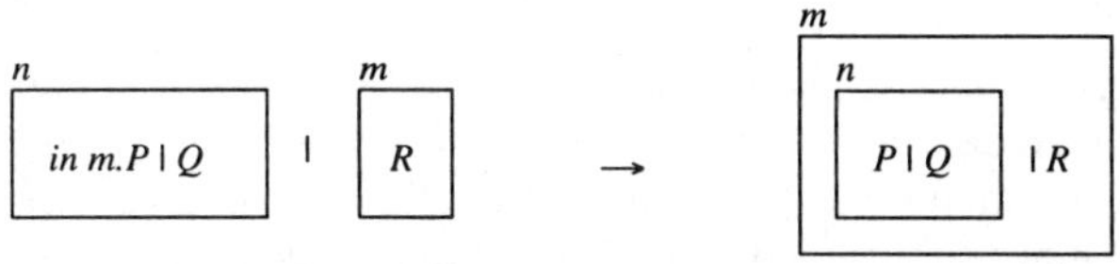

If successful, this reduction transforms a sibling *n* of an ambient *m* into a child of *m*. After the execution, the process *in m. P* continues with *P*, and both *P* and *Q* find themselves at a lower level in the tree of ambients.

Exit Capability

An exit capability, *out m*, can be used in the action:

$$out\ m.\ P$$

which instructs the ambient surrounding *out m. P* to exit its parent ambient named *m*. If the parent is not named *m*, the operation blocks until a time when such a parent exists. The reduction rule is:

$$m[n[out\ m.\ P \mid Q] \mid R] \longrightarrow n[P \mid Q] \mid m[R]$$

That is:

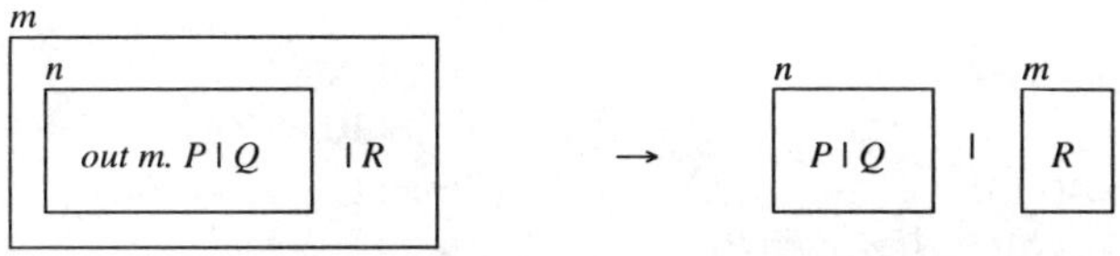

If successful, this reduction transforms a child *n* of an ambient *m* into a sibling of *m*. After the execution, the process *in m. P* continues with *P*, and both *P* and *Q* find themselves at a higher level in the tree of ambients.

Open Capability

An opening capability, *open m*, can be used in the action:

$$open\ m.\ P$$

This action provides a way of dissolving the boundary of an ambient named *m* located at the same level as *open*, according to the rule:

$$open\ m.\ P \mid m[Q] \longrightarrow P \mid Q$$

That is:

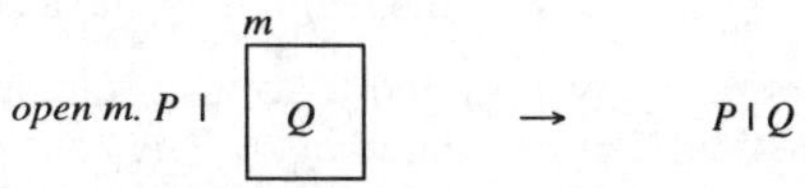

If no ambient *m* can be found, the operation blocks until a time when such an ambient exists. If more than one ambient *m* exists, any one of them can be chosen.

An *open* operation may be upsetting to both *P* and *Q* above. From the point of view of *P*, there is no telling in general what *Q* might do when unleashed. From the point of view of *Q*, its environment is being ripped open. Still, this operation is relatively well-behaved because: (1) the dissolution is initiated by the agent *open m. P*, so that the appearance of *Q* at the same level as *P* is not totally unexpected; (2) *open m* is a capability that is given out by *m*, so *m*[*Q*] cannot be dissolved if it does not wish to be (this will become clearer later in the presence of communication primitives).

4.3 Operational Semantics

We now give an operational semantics of the calculus of section 4.1, based on a structural congruence between processes, $\equiv$, and a reduction relation $\longrightarrow$. We have already discussed all the reduction rules, except for one that connects reduction with equivalence. This is a semantics in the style of Milner's reaction relation [34] for the π-calculus, which was itself inspired by the Chemical Abstract Machine of Berry and Boudol [3].

Processes of the calculus are grouped into equivalence classes by the following relation, $\equiv$, which denotes structural congruence (equivalence up to trivial syntactic restructuring).

Table 4: Structural Congruence

$P \equiv P$	(Struct Refl)
$P \equiv Q \;\Rightarrow\; Q \equiv P$	(Struct Symm)
$P \equiv Q,\, Q \equiv R \;\Rightarrow\; P \equiv R$	(Struct Trans)
$P \equiv Q \;\Rightarrow\; (\nu n)P \equiv (\nu n)Q$	(Struct Res)
$P \equiv Q \;\Rightarrow\; P \mid R \equiv Q \mid R$	(Struct Par)
$P \equiv Q \;\Rightarrow\; !P \equiv\, !Q$	(Struct Repl)
$P \equiv Q \;\Rightarrow\; n[P] \equiv n[Q]$	(Struct Amb)
$P \equiv Q \;\Rightarrow\; M.P \equiv M.Q$	(Struct Action)
$P \mid Q \equiv Q \mid P$	(Struct Par Comm)
$(P \mid Q) \mid R \equiv P \mid (Q \mid R)$	(Struct Par Assoc)
$!P \equiv P \mid\, !P$	(Struct Repl Par)
$(\nu n)(\nu m)P \equiv (\nu m)(\nu n)P$	(Struct Res Res)
$(\nu n)(P \mid Q) \equiv P \mid (\nu n)Q \quad \text{if } n \notin fn(P)$	(Struct Res Par)
$(\nu n)(m[P]) \equiv m[(\nu n)P] \quad \text{if } n \neq m$	(Struct Res Amb)
$P \mid \mathbf{0} \equiv P$	(Struct Zero Par)
$(\nu n)\mathbf{0} \equiv \mathbf{0}$	(Struct Zero Res)
$!\mathbf{0} \equiv \mathbf{0}$	(Struct Zero Repl)

In addition, we identify processes up to renaming of bound names:

$$(\nu n)P \;=\; (\nu m)P\{n \leftarrow m\} \quad \text{if } m \notin fn(P)$$

By this we mean that these processes are understood to be identical (for example, by choosing an appropriate representation), as opposed to structurally equivalent.

Note that the following terms are distinct:

$!(\nu n)P \not\equiv (\nu n)!P$	replication creates new names
$n[P] \mid n[Q] \not\equiv n[P \mid Q]$	multiple n ambients have separate identity

The behavior of processes is given by the following reduction relation. The first three rules are the one-step reductions for *in*, *out* and *open*. The next three rules propagate reductions across scopes, ambient nesting and parallel composition. The final rule allows the use of equivalence during reduction. Finally, $\longrightarrow^*$ is the chaining of multiple reduction steps.

Table 5: Reduction

$n[in\ m.\ P \mid Q] \mid m[R] \longrightarrow m[n[P \mid Q] \mid R]$	(Red In)
$m[n[out\ m.\ P \mid Q] \mid R] \longrightarrow n[P \mid Q] \mid m[R]$	(Red Out)
$open\ n.\ P \mid n[Q] \longrightarrow P \mid Q$	(Red Open)

$P \longrightarrow Q \;\Rightarrow\; (\nu n)P \longrightarrow (\nu n)Q$		(Red Res)
$P \longrightarrow Q \;\Rightarrow\; n[P] \longrightarrow n[Q]$		(Red Amb)
$P \longrightarrow Q \;\Rightarrow\; P \mid R \longrightarrow Q \mid R$		(Red Par)
$P' \equiv P,\, P \longrightarrow Q,\, Q \equiv Q' \;\Rightarrow\; P' \longrightarrow Q'$		(Red $\equiv$)
$\longrightarrow^*$		reflexive and transitive closure of $\longrightarrow$

5 Communication

Although the pure mobility calculus is powerful enough to be Turing-complete, it has no communication or variable-binding operators. Such operators seem necessary, for example, to comfortably encode other formalisms such as the λ-calculus and the π-calculus.

Therefore, we now have to choose a communication mechanism to be used to exchange messages between ambients. The choice of a particular mechanism is to some degree orthogonal to the mobility primitives: many such mechanisms can be added to the mobility core. However, we should try not to defeat with communication the restrictions imposed by capabilities. This suggests that a primitive form of communication should be purely local, and that the transmission of non-local messages should be restricted by capabilities.

To focus our attention, we pose as a goal the ability to encode the asynchronous π-calculus. For this it is sufficient to introduce a simple asynchronous communication mechanism that works locally within a single ambient.

5.1 Communication Primitives

We again start by displaying the syntax of a whole calculus. The mobility primitives are essentially those of section 4, but the addition of communication variables changes some of the details. More interestingly, we add input ($(x).P$) and output ($\langle M \rangle$) primitives and we enrich the capabilities to include paths.

Table 6: Mobility and Communication Primitives

$P,Q ::=$	processes
$(\nu n)P$	restriction
$\mathbf{0}$	inactivity
$P \mid Q$	composition
$!P$	replication
$M[P]$	ambient
$M.P$	capability action
$(x).P$	input action
$\langle M \rangle$	async output action
$M ::=$	messages
x	variable
n	name
in M	can enter into M
out M	can exit out of M
open M	can open M
ε	null
$M.M'$	path

Table 7: Free names (revisions and additions)

$fn(M[P]) \triangleq fn(M) \cup fn(P)$		$fn(x) \triangleq \emptyset$	
$fn((x).P) \triangleq fn(P)$		$fn(n) \triangleq \{n\}$	
$fn(\langle M \rangle) \triangleq fn(M)$		$fn(\varepsilon) \triangleq \emptyset$	
		$fn(M.M') \triangleq fn(M) \cup fn(M')$	

Table 8: Free variables

$fv((\nu n)P) \triangleq fv(P)$	$fv(x) \triangleq \{x\}$
$fv(\mathbf{0}) \triangleq \emptyset$	$fv(n) \triangleq \emptyset$
$fv(P \mid Q) \triangleq fv(P) \cup fv(Q)$	$fv(in\ M) \triangleq fv(M)$
$fv(!P) \triangleq fv(P)$	$fv(out\ M) \triangleq fv(M)$
$fv(M[P]) \triangleq fv(M) \cup fv(P)$	$fv(open\ M) \triangleq fv(M)$
$fv(M.P) \triangleq fv(M) \cup fv(P)$	$fv(\varepsilon) \triangleq \emptyset$
$fv((x).P) \triangleq fv(P) - \{x\}$	$fv(M.M') \triangleq fv(M) \cup fv(M')$
$fv(\langle M \rangle) \triangleq fv(M)$	

We write $P\{x \leftarrow M\}$ for the substitution of the capability M for each free occurrence of the variable x in the process P. Similarly for $M\{x \leftarrow M'\}$.

Table 9: New syntactic conventions

$(x).P \mid Q$	is read	$((x).P) \mid Q$

5.2 Explanations

Messages

The entities that can be communicated are either names or capabilities. In realistic situations, communication of names should be rather rare, since knowing the name of an ambient gives a lot of control over it. Instead, it should be common to communicate restricted capabilities to allow controlled interactions between ambients.

It now becomes useful to combine multiple capabilities into *paths*, especially when one or more of those capabilities are represented by input variables. To this end we introduce a path-formation operation on capabilities ($M.\ M'$). For example, ($in\ n.\ in\ m$). P is interpreted as $in\ n.\ in\ m.\ P$.

Note also that, for the purpose of communication, we have added names to the collection of messages. A communicated name can be used as a capability to create ambients of that name.

We distinguish between ν-bound names and input-bound variables. Variables can be instantiated with names or capabilities. In practice, we do not need to distinguish these two sorts lexically, but we often use n, m, p, q for names and w, x, y, z for variables.

Ambient I/O

The simplest communication mechanism that we can imagine is local anonymous communication within an ambient (ambient I/O, for short):

$(x).P$	input action
$\langle M \rangle$	async output action

An output action releases a message into the local ether of the surrounding ambient. An input action captures a message from the local ether and binds it to a variable within a scope. We have the reduction:

$$(x).P \mid \langle M \rangle \longrightarrow P\{x \leftarrow M\}$$

This local communication mechanism fits well with the ambient intuitions. In particular, long-range communication, like long-range movement, should not happen automatically because messages may have to cross firewalls.

Still, this simple mechanism is sufficient to emulate communication over named channels, and more generally to provide an encoding of the asynchronous π-calculus [11].

A Syntactic Anomaly

To allow both names and capabilities to be output and input, there is a single syntactic sort that includes both. Hence, a meaningless term of the form $n.\ P$ can arise, for instance, from the process $((x).\ x.\ P) \mid \langle n \rangle$. This anomaly is caused by the desire to denote movement capabilities by variables, as in $(x).\ x.\ P$, and from the desire to denote names by variables, as in $(x).\ x[P]$. We permit $n.\ P$ to be formed, syntactically, in order to make substitution always well defined. In sections 8, 9, and 10, we develop a type system that distinguishes names from capabilities, and that solves this anomaly.

5.3 Operational Semantics

For the extended calculus, the structural congruence relation is defined as in section 4.3, with the understanding that P and M range now over larger classes, and with the addition of the following equivalences:

Table 10: Structural Congruence

$P \equiv Q \;\Rightarrow\; M[P] \equiv M[Q]$	(Struct Amb)
$P \equiv Q \;\Rightarrow\; (x).P \equiv (x).Q$	(Struct Input)
$\varepsilon.P \equiv P$	(Struct ε)
$(M.M').P \equiv M.M'.P$	(Struct .)

We now also identify processes up to renaming of bound variables:

$$(x).P \;=\; (y).P\{x \leftarrow y\} \quad \text{if } y \notin fv(P)$$

Finally, we have a new reduction rule for communication:

Table 11: Reduction

$(x).P \mid \langle M \rangle \longrightarrow P\{x \leftarrow M\}$	(Red Comm)

Part III: Equivalence

6 A Theory of Equivalence

Morris-style contextual equivalence [36] (otherwise known as may-testing equivalence [19]) is a standard way of saying that two processes have the same behavior: two processes are contextually equivalent if and only if they admit the same elementary observations whenever they are inserted inside any arbitrary enclosing process. In the setting of the ambient calculus, we shall define contextual equivalence in terms of observing the presence, at the top-level of a process, of an ambient whose name is not restricted.

We say that a process P *exhibits an ambient named* n, and write $P{\downarrow}n$, just if P is a process containing a top-level ambient named n, that is not restricted. We say that a process P *converges to a name* n, and write $P{\Downarrow}n$, just if after some number of reductions, P exhibits an ambient named n. Formally, we define:

$$P{\downarrow}n \;\triangleq\; P \equiv (\nu\, m_1 ... m_i)\,(n[P'] \mid P'') \quad \text{for some } m_1...m_i, P', P'' \text{ where } n \notin \{m_1...m_i\}$$
$$P{\Downarrow}n \;\triangleq\; \text{either } P{\downarrow}n \text{ or } P \longrightarrow P' \text{ for some } P' \text{ and } P'{\Downarrow}n$$

Next we define contextual equivalence in terms of the predicate $P\Downarrow n$. Let a context $C()$ be a process containing zero or more holes. We write holes as (). For any process P, let $C(P)$ be the process obtained by filling each hole in C with a copy of P. Names free in P may become bound; for example, if $P = n[\langle x\rangle]$ and $C() = (\nu n)(x).()$, the variable x and the name n have become bound in $C(P) = (\nu n)(x).n[\langle x\rangle]$. Hence, we do not identify contexts up to renaming of bound variables and names.

Let *contextual equivalence* be the relation $P \simeq Q$ defined by:

$$P \simeq Q \quad \triangleq \quad \text{for all } n \text{ and } C(),\ C(P)\Downarrow n \Leftrightarrow C(Q)\Downarrow n$$

The following two propositions state some basic properties enjoyed by contextual equivalence. Let a relation $\mathcal{R}$ be a precongruence if and only if, for all P, Q, and $C()$, if $P \mathrel{\mathcal{R}} Q$ then $C(P) \mathrel{\mathcal{R}} C(Q)$. If, in addition, $\mathcal{R}$ is reflexive, symmetric, and transitive, we say it is a congruence. For example, the structural congruence relation has these properties. Moreover, by a standard argument, so has contextual equivalence:

6-1 Proposition

Contextual equivalence is a congruence.

Structural congruence preserves exhibition of or convergence to a name, and hence is included in contextual equivalence:

6-2 Lemma

Suppose $P \equiv Q$. If $P\downarrow n$ then $Q\downarrow n$. Moreover, if $P\Downarrow n$ then $Q\Downarrow n$ with the same depth of inference.

6-3 Proposition

If $P \equiv Q$ then $P \simeq Q$.

7 Examples

In [27] we present convenient proof techniques for contextual equivalence, and we give a proof of the "perfect firewall equation" described in this section.

7.1 Simple examples

Here are some easy inequivalences:

$p[]$ and $q[]$	are distinguished by the context ()
$open\ p.\mathbf{0}$ and $open\ q.\mathbf{0}$	are distinguished by the context $p[n[]] \mid ()$
$in\ p.\mathbf{0}$ and $out\ p.\mathbf{0}$	are distinguished by the context $m[n[() \mid out\ p.\ out\ m] \mid p[]]$

As in most process calculi, reduction does not imply equivalence:

$$n[] \mid open\ n.\mathbf{0} \longrightarrow \mathbf{0} \quad \text{but} \quad n[] \mid open\ n.\mathbf{0} \not\simeq \mathbf{0}$$

Finally, a general law:

$$(\nu n)(n[] \mid open\ n.P) \simeq (\nu n)P$$

7.2 Example: Perfect firewalls

Consider a process $(\nu n)n[P]$, where n is not free in P. Since the name n is known neither inside the ambient $n[P]$, nor outside it, the ambient $n[P]$ is a "perfect firewall" that neither allows another ambient to enter nor to exit. Such a process could be used to abstractly model an internet firewall named n enclosing a group of machines P, or a sandbox named n enclosing a group of applets P.

The intended property of a perfect firewall can be expressed as an equation; the *Perfect Firewall Equation* below, which expresses the fact that nobody can externally observe a perfect firewall, even though the processes inside the firewall may be active and even cause the firewall to move around.

$$n \notin fn(P) \;\Rightarrow\; (\nu n)n[P] \simeq \mathbf{0} \qquad \text{(Alternatively: } (\nu n)n[(\nu n)P] \simeq \mathbf{0}.\text{)}$$

7.3 *Example: Perfect encryption*

An ambient of the form $k[\langle M\rangle]$ can be used to abstractly model a ciphertext $\{M\}_k$ obtained by encrypting a plaintext M with a key k (we assume that k does not occur in M). The idea is that the key k (or, more precisely the capability *open k*) is needed to access the plaintext M. The intuition that a ciphertext is incomprehensible if one does not know the key can be expressed as the following *Perfect Encryption Equation*. This equation says that any two ciphertexts are indistinguishable (equally unusable) if one does not know their keys. Knowledge of the keys by the context is prevented by the restrictions.

$$(\nu k)k[\langle M\rangle] \simeq (\nu k')k'[\langle M'\rangle]$$

The equation simply follows from the perfect firewall equation, because $(\nu k)k[\langle M\rangle] \simeq \mathbf{0} \simeq (\nu k')k'[\langle M'\rangle]$ if $k \notin fn(M)$ and $k' \notin fn(M')$. It should be compared with the equation $(\nu k)c\langle\{M\}_k\rangle \simeq (\nu k')c\langle\{M'\}_{k'}\rangle$ from the spi calculus [1].

7.4 *Example: An agent crossing a firewall*

A perfect firewall is not very useful, since it does not let anything pass through. In general we want permeable firewalls that filter traffic according to some security policy. Even these permeable firewalls can be described by equations, although the equations need to become more sophisticated.

In this example, we describe a protocol that allows a "friend" agent to enter a firewall. We assume that the agent and the firewall share some prearranged passwords k, k', k''; these could have been privately generated during a previous visit of the agent to the firewall.

$$\begin{aligned} \mathit{Firewall} &\triangleq (\nu w)w[k[\mathit{out}\ w.\ \mathit{in}\ k'.\ \mathit{in}\ w] \mid \mathit{open}\ k'.\ \mathit{open}\ k''.P] \\ \mathit{Agent} &\triangleq k'[\mathit{open}\ k.k''[C]] \end{aligned}$$

Assuming k, k', k'' do not occur in C or P and w does not occur in C, we get the following safety property, expressed as an equation:

$$(\nu k\ k'\ k'')\ (\mathit{Agent} \mid \mathit{Firewall}) \simeq (\nu w)w[C \mid P]$$

Contextual equivalence here means that the agent may successfully cross the firewall (the residual C of the agent may end up inside w). In addition, the agent may successfully cross the firewall under any attack, since equivalence "in every context" includes both "in parallel with any attacking process" and "inside any attacking environment".

The main caveat is that only high level attacks by ambient calculus processes are covered by this analysis, not low-level attacks such as disassembling the agent in transit. Still, the analysis holds in situation such as applet-to-applet interactions within a trusted server.

Part IV: Types

8 Type Systems

Java has demonstrated the utility of type systems for *mobile code*, and in particular their use and implications for security. Security properties rest on the fact that a well-typed Java program (or the corresponding verified bytecode) cannot cause certain kinds of damage.

We now provide a type system for *mobile computation*, that is, for computation that is continuously active before and after movement. We show that a well-typed mobile computation cannot cause certain kinds of run-time fault: it cannot cause the exchange of values of the wrong kind, anywhere in a mobile system.

In the previous sections we have introduced the (untyped, monadic) *ambient calculus*, a process calculus for mobile computation and mobile devices. That calculus is able to express, via encodings, standard computational constructions such as channel based communication, functions, and agents [11].

The type system presented here is able to provide typings for those encodings, recovering familiar type systems for processes and functions. In addition, we obtain a type system for mobile agents and other mobile computations [12,10]. The type system is obtained by decorating the untyped calculus with type information.

Our type system tracks the typing of messages exchanged within an ambient. For example, the following system consists of two ambients, named a and b:

$$a[(x{:}Int).P \mid open\ b] \mid b[in\ a.\ \langle 3\rangle]$$

The ambient named a contains a process $(x{:}Int).P$ that is ready to read an integer message into a variable x and proceed with P, and a process *open b* that is ready to open (dissolve the boundary) of an ambient b found within a. The ambient named b contains a process $in\ a.\ \langle 3\rangle$ that moves the ambient b inside a (by executing *in a*) and then outputs the message 3. The ambient b is opened after moving into a, so the output comes into direct contact with the reading process within a. The result is the binding of an integer message to an integer variable, yielding the state:

$$a[P\{x \leftarrow 3\}]$$

The challenge of the type system is to verify that this exchange of messages is well-typed. Note that in the original system the input and the output were contained in separate locations.

Our ambient calculus is related to earlier distributed variants of the π-calculus, some of which have been equipped with type systems. The type system of Amadio [2] prevents a channel from being defined at more than one location. Sewell's system [40] tracks whether communications are local or non-local, so as to allow efficient implementation of local communication. In Riely and Hennessy's calculus [38], processes need appropriate permissions to perform actions such as migration; a well-typed process is guaranteed to possess the appropriate permission for any action it attempts. Other work on typing for mobile agents includes a type system by De Nicola, Ferrari, and Pugliese [18] that tracks the access rights an agent enjoys at different localities; type-checking ensures that an agent complies with its access rights.

9 The Polyadic Ambient Calculus

We slightly extend the ambient calculus of section 5. In that calculus, communication is based on the exchange of single values. Here we extend the calculus with communication based on tuples of values (polyadic communication), since this simple extension greatly facilitates the task of providing an expressive type system. The process $\langle M_1, ..., M_k\rangle$ represents the output of a tuple of values, with no continuation. The process $(n_1{:}W_1, ..., n_k{:}W_k).P$ represents the input of a tuple of values, with continuation P. In addition, we annotate bound variables with type information.

Communication is used to exchange both names and capabilities, which share the same syntactic class M of messages. One of the main tasks of our type system is to distinguish the Ms that are names from the Ms that are capabilities, so that each is guaranteed to be used in an appropriate context. In general, the type system might distinguish other kinds of messages, such as integer and boolean expressions, but we do not include those in our basic calculus.

Table 12: Polyadic Ambient Calculus

$P,Q ::=$	processes
$(\nu n{:}W)P$	restriction
$\mathbf{0}$	inactivity
$P \mid Q$	composition
$!P$	replication
$M[P]$	ambient
$M.P$	action
$(n_1{:}W_1, ..., n_k{:}W_k).P$	input
$\langle M_1, ..., M_k\rangle$	async output
$M ::=$	messages
n	name
$in\ M$	can enter into M
$out\ M$	can exit out of M
$open\ M$	can open M
ε	null path
$M.M'$	composite path

The following tables describe the operational semantics of the extended calculus. The type annotations present in the syntax do not play a role in reduction; they are simply carried along by the reductions and will be explained in the next section.

Table 13: Free names

$fn((\nu n{:}W)P) \triangleq fn(P) - \{n\}$		$fn(n)$	$\triangleq \{n\}$
$fn(\mathbf{0}) \triangleq \emptyset$		$fn(in\ M)$	$\triangleq fn(M)$
$fn(P \mid Q) \triangleq fn(P) \cup fn(Q)$		$fn(out\ M)$	$\triangleq fn(M)$
$fn(!P) \triangleq fn(P)$		$fn(open\ M)$	$\triangleq fn(M)$
$fn(M[P]) \triangleq fn(M) \cup fn(P)$		$fn(\varepsilon)$	$\triangleq \emptyset$
$fn(M.P) \triangleq fn(M) \cup fn(P)$		$fn(M.M')$	$\triangleq fn(M) \cup fn(M')$
$fn((n_1{:}W_1, ..., n_k{:}W_k).P) \triangleq fn(P) - \{n_1, ..., n_k\}$			
$fn(\langle M_1, ..., M_k\rangle) \triangleq fn(M_1) \cup ... \cup fn(M_k)$			

Table 14: Structural Congruence

$P \equiv P$	(Struct Refl)
$P \equiv Q \Rightarrow Q \equiv P$	(Struct Symm)
$P \equiv Q, Q \equiv R \Rightarrow P \equiv R$	(Struct Trans)
$P \equiv Q \Rightarrow (\nu n{:}T)P \equiv (\nu n{:}T)Q$	(Struct Res)
$P \equiv Q \Rightarrow P \mid R \equiv Q \mid R$	(Struct Par)
$P \equiv Q \Rightarrow !P \equiv !Q$	(Struct Repl)
$P \equiv Q \Rightarrow M[P] \equiv M[Q]$	(Struct Amb)
$P \equiv Q \Rightarrow M.P \equiv M.Q$	(Struct Action)
$P \equiv Q \Rightarrow (n_1{:}T_1, ..., n_k{:}T_k).P \equiv (n_1{:}T_1, ..., n_k{:}T_k).Q$	(Struct Input)
$P \mid Q \equiv Q \mid P$	(Struct Par Comm)
$(P \mid Q) \mid R \equiv P \mid (Q \mid R)$	(Struct Par Assoc)
$!P \equiv P \mid !P$	(Struct Repl Par)
$(\nu n{:}T)(\nu m{:}U)P \equiv (\nu m{:}U)(\nu n{:}T)P$ if $n \neq m$	(Struct Res Res)
$(\nu n{:}T)(P \mid Q) \equiv P \mid (\nu n{:}T)Q$ if $n \notin fn(P)$	(Struct Res Par)
$(\nu n{:}T)m[P] \equiv m[(\nu n{:}T)P]$ if $n \neq m$	(Struct Res Amb)

$P \mid \mathbf{0} \equiv P$	(Struct Zero Par)
$(\nu n{:}Amb[T])\mathbf{0} \equiv \mathbf{0}$	(Struct Zero Res)
$!\mathbf{0} \equiv \mathbf{0}$	(Struct Zero Repl)
$\varepsilon.P \equiv P$	(Struct ε)
$(M.M').P \equiv M.M'.P$	(Struct .)

Table 15: Reduction

$n[in\ m.\ P \mid Q] \mid m[R] \longrightarrow m[n[P \mid Q] \mid R]$	(Red In)
$m[n[out\ m.\ P \mid Q] \mid R] \longrightarrow n[P \mid Q] \mid m[R]$	(Red Out)
$open\ n.\ P \mid n[Q] \longrightarrow P \mid Q$	(Red Open)
$(n_1{:}W_1, ..., n_k{:}W_k).P \mid \langle M_1, ..., M_k\rangle \longrightarrow P\{n_1{\leftarrow}M_1, ..., n_k{\leftarrow}M_k\}$	(Red Comm)
$P \longrightarrow Q \;\Rightarrow\; (\nu n{:}W)P \longrightarrow (\nu n{:}W)Q$	(Red Res)
$P \longrightarrow Q \;\Rightarrow\; n[P] \longrightarrow n[Q]$	(Red Amb)
$P \longrightarrow Q \;\Rightarrow\; P \mid R \longrightarrow Q \mid R$	(Red Par)
$P' \equiv P, P \longrightarrow Q, Q \equiv Q' \;\Rightarrow\; P' \longrightarrow Q'$	(Red ≡)

10 Exchange Types

An ambient is a place where other ambients can enter and exit, and where processes can exchange messages. The first aspect, mobility, is regulated by run-time capabilities and will not be restricted by our type system (but see [10]). The second aspect, communication, is what we now concentrate on.

10.1 Topics of Conversation

Within an ambient, multiple processes can freely execute input and output actions. Since the messages are undirected, it is easily possible for a process to utter a message that is not appropriate for some receiver. The main idea of our type system is to keep track of the *topic of conversation* that is permitted within a given ambient, so that talkers and listeners can be certain of exchanging appropriate messages.

The range of topics is described in the following table by *message types*, *W*, and *exchange types*, *T*. The message types are *Amb*[*T*], the type of names of ambients that allow exchanges of type *T*, and *Cap*[*T*], the type of capabilities that when used may cause the unleashing of *T* exchanges (as a consequence of opening ambients that exchange *T*). The exchange types are *Shh*, the absence of exchanges, and $W_1 \times ... \times W_k$, the exchange of a tuple of messages with elements of the respective message types. For k=0, the empty tuple type is called **1**; it allows the exchange of empty tuples, that is, it allows pure synchronization. The case k=1 allows any message type to be an exchange type.

Table 16: Types

W ::=	message types
$Amb[T]$	ambient name allowing T exchange
$Cap[T]$	capability unleashing T exchange
T ::=	exchange types
Shh	no exchange
$W_1 \times ... \times W_k$	tuple exchange

For example:

- A quiet ambient: *Amb*[*Shh*]
- A harmless capability: *Cap*[*Shh*]

- A synchronization ambient: $Amb[\mathbf{1}]$
- An ambient that allows the exchange of harmless capabilities: $Amb[Cap[Shh]]$
- A capability that may unleash the exchange of names of quiet ambients: $Cap[Amb[Shh]]$

10.2 Intuitions

Before presenting the formal type rules, we discuss the intuitions that lead to them.

Typing of Processes

If a message M has message type W, then $\langle M \rangle$ is a process that outputs (exchanges) W messages. Therefore, we will have a rule stating that:

$$M : W \;\Rightarrow\; \langle M \rangle : W$$

If P is a process that may exchange W messages, then $(x{:}W).P$ is also a process that may exchange W messages. Therefore:

$$P : W \;\Rightarrow\; (x{:}W).P : W$$

The process $\mathbf{0}$ exchanges nothing, so it naturally has exchange type Shh. However, we may also consider $\mathbf{0}$ as a process that may exchange any type. This is useful when we need to place $\mathbf{0}$ in a context that is already expected to exchange some given type.

$$\mathbf{0} : T \qquad \text{for any } T$$

If P and Q are processes that may exchange T, then $P \mid Q$ is also such a process. Similarly for $!P$.

$$P : T,\, Q : T \;\Rightarrow\; P \mid Q : T$$
$$P : T \;\Rightarrow\; !P : T$$

Therefore, by keeping track of the exchange type of a process, T-inputs and T-outputs are tracked so that they match correctly when placed in parallel.

Typing of Ambients

An ambient $n[P]$ is a process that exchanges nothing at the current level, so, like $\mathbf{0}$, it can have any exchange type, and can be placed in parallel with any process.

$$n[P] : T \qquad \text{for any } T$$

There needs to be, however, a connection between the type of n and the type of P. We give to each ambient name a type $Amb[T]$, meaning that only T exchanges are allowed in any ambient of that name. Ambients of different names may permit internal exchanges of different types.

$$n : Amb[T],\, P : T \;\Rightarrow\; n[P] \text{ is well-formed (and can have any type)}$$

By tagging the name of an ambient with the type of exchanges, we know what kind of exchanges to expect in any ambient we enter. Moreover, we can tell what happens when we open an ambient of a given name.

Typing of Open

Tracking the type of I/O exchanges is not enough by itself. We also need to worry about *open*, which might open an ambient and unleash its exchanges inside the surrounding ambient.

If ambients named n permit T exchanges, then the capability *open n* may unleash those T exchanges. We then say that *open n* has a capability type $Cap[T]$, meaning that it may unleash T exchanges when used:

$$n : Amb[T] \quad \Rightarrow \quad open\ n : Cap[T]$$

As a consequence, any process that uses a $Cap[T]$ must be a process that is already willing to participate in exchanges of type T, because further T exchanges may be unleashed.

$$M : Cap[T],\ P : T \quad \Rightarrow \quad M.P : T$$

The capability types $Cap[T]$ do not keep track of any information concerning *in* and *out* capabilities; only the effect of *open* is tracked.

10.3 Typing Rules

We base our type system on three judgments. The main judgment tracks the exchange type of a process, that is the type of the I/O operations of the process, and of the I/O operations that the process may unleash by opening other ambients.

Judgments

$E \vdash \diamond$	good environment
$E \vdash M : W$	good expression of message type W
$E \vdash P : T$	good process of exchange type T

Based on the discussion in the previous section, we can formalize the type system as described in the following table. Convention: a list of assumptions $E \vdash J_1 \ldots E \vdash J_k$ for k=0 means $E \vdash \diamond$.

Table 17: Rules

(Env $\emptyset$)
$$\frac{}{\emptyset \vdash \diamond}$$

(Env n)
$$\frac{E \vdash \diamond \quad n \notin dom(E)}{E, n{:}W \vdash \diamond}$$

(Exp n)
$$\frac{E', n{:}W, E'' \vdash \diamond}{E', n{:}W, E'' \vdash n : W}$$

(Exp ε)
$$\frac{E \vdash \diamond}{E \vdash \varepsilon : Cap[T]}$$

(Exp .)
$$\frac{E \vdash M : Cap[T] \quad E \vdash M' : Cap[T]}{E \vdash M.M' : Cap[T]}$$

(Exp In)
$$\frac{E \vdash M : Amb[S]}{E \vdash in\ M : Cap[T]}$$

(Exp Out)
$$\frac{E \vdash M : Amb[S]}{E \vdash out\ M : Cap[T]}$$

(Exp Open)
$$\frac{E \vdash M : Amb[T]}{E \vdash open\ M : Cap[T]}$$

(Proc Action)
$$\frac{E \vdash M : Cap[T] \quad E \vdash P : T}{E \vdash M.P : T}$$

(Proc Amb)
$$\frac{E \vdash M : Amb[T] \quad E \vdash P : T}{E \vdash M[P] : S}$$

(Proc Res)
$$\frac{E, n{:}Amb[T] \vdash P : S}{E \vdash (\nu n{:}Amb[T])P : S}$$

(Proc Zero)
$$\frac{E \vdash \diamond}{E \vdash \mathbf{0} : T}$$

(Proc Par)
$$\frac{E \vdash P : T \quad E \vdash Q : T}{E \vdash P \mid Q : T}$$

(Proc Repl)
$$\frac{E \vdash P : T}{E \vdash !P : T}$$

(Proc Input)
$$\frac{E, n_1{:}W_1, \ldots, n_k{:}W_k \vdash P : W_1 \times \ldots \times W_k}{E \vdash (n_1{:}W_1, \ldots, n_k{:}W_k).P : W_1 \times \ldots \times W_k}$$

(Proc Output)
$$\frac{E \vdash M_1 : W_1 \quad \ldots \quad E \vdash M_k : W_k}{E \vdash \langle M_1, \ldots, M_k \rangle : W_1 \times \ldots \times W_k}$$

- Example: A process that outputs names of quiet ambients:

$\emptyset \vdash !(\nu n{:}Amb[Shh])\langle n\rangle : Amb[Shh]$

- Example: A capability that may unleash *S*-exchanges. Note that the *in n* action contributes nothing to the type of the path; only the *open m* action does:

$\emptyset, n{:}Amb[T], m{:}Amb[S] \vdash in\ n.\ open\ m : Cap[S]$

The correctness of the type system is expressed by the following proposition:

10-1 Proposition (Subject Reduction)
If $E \vdash P : U$ and $P \rightarrow Q$ then $E \vdash Q : U$.
□

Certain "run-time error" expressions are allowed in the syntax but are nonsensical because they confuse names with capabilities. Examples are $in\ n[P]$, $(\nu n{:}Amb[T])n.P$, and $\langle in\ (in\ n)\rangle$. Such expressions are not initially typeable, and they cannot be produced by well-typed processes because Proposition 10-1 says that the evolution of well-typed processes leads only to well-typed processes.

Part V: Logic

11 Modal Logics for Mobile Ambients

In the course of our ongoing work on mobility, we have often struggled to express precisely certain properties of mobile computations. Informally, these are properties such as "the agent has gone away", "eventually the agent crosses the firewall", "every agent always carries a suitcase", "somewhere there is a virus", or "there is always at most one agent called *n* here". There are several conceivable ways of formalizing these assertions. It is possible to express some of them in terms of equations, as in sections 6 and 7, but this is sometimes difficult or unnatural. It is easier to express some of them as properties of computational traces, but this is very low-level.

Modal logics (particularly, temporal logics) have emerged in many domains as a good compromise between expressiveness and abstraction. In addition, many modal logics support useful computational applications, such as model checking. In our context, it makes sense to talk about properties that hold at particular locations, and it becomes natural to consider *spatial modalities* for properties that hold at a certain location, at some location or at every location. For example, we have the following correspondence between spatial constructs in the ambient calculus and certain formulas:

Processes		*Formulas*	
$\mathbf{0}$	(void)	$\mathbf{0}$	(there is nothing here)
$n[P]$	(location)	$n[\mathcal{A}]$	(there is one thing here)
$P \mid Q$	(composition)	$\mathcal{A} \mid \mathcal{B}$	(there are two things here)

We have a logical constant $\mathbf{0}$ that is satisfied by the process $\mathbf{0}$ representing void. We have logical propositions of the form $n[\mathcal{A}]$ (meaning that $\mathcal{A}$ holds at location n) that are satisfied by processes of the form $n[P]$ (meaning that process P is located at n) provided that P satisfies $\mathcal{A}$. We have logical propositions of the form $\mathcal{A}' \mid \mathcal{A}''$ (meaning that $\mathcal{A}'$ and $\mathcal{A}''$ hold contiguously) which are satisfied by contiguous processes of the form $P' \mid P''$ if P' satisfies $\mathcal{A}'$ and P'' satisfies $\mathcal{A}''$, or vice versa.

Spatial modalities have an intensional flavor that distinguishes our logic from other modal logics for concurrency. Previous work in the area concentrates on properties that are invariant up to strong equivalences such as bisimulation [29,17], while our properties are invariant only up to simple spatial rearrangements. Some of our techniques can be usefully applied to other process calculi, even ones that do not have locations, such as CCS.

Starting from a solid computational intuition, a process calculus, we derive logical inference rules, including the rules of modalities for time, space, and satisfiability, and novel rules for locations and process composition. In [13], based on the satisfaction relation between processes and formulas, we investigate model checking of mobile programs.

12 The Ambient Calculus with Public Names

We consider only ambients having public names; that is we do not deal with name restriction and scope extrusion. Handling of private names in a logic is a very interesting topic, but we leave it for future work.

12.1 Ambients

We modify the basic ambient calculus of section 5. The changes consist in removing name restriction, and in strengthening the definition of structural congruence so that it characterizes the intended equivalence of spatial configurations. We also remove the distinction between names and variables (particularly since we no longer have name binders), and we use a single predicate to characterize free names.

The following table summarizes the syntax of processes. We have separated the process constructs into *spatial* and *temporal*; this is similar to the distinction between static and dynamic constructs in CCS [32].

Table 18: Processes

$P,Q,R ::=$	processes		$M ::=$	messages
$\mathbf{0}$	void	spatial	n	name
$P \mid Q$	composition	spatial	$in\ M$	can enter into M
$!P$	replication	spatial	$out\ M$	can exit out of M
$M[P]$	ambient	spatial	$open\ M$	can open M
$M.P$	capability action	temporal	ε	null
$(n).P$	input action	temporal	$M.M'$	path
$\langle M \rangle$	output action	temporal		

The set of free names of a process P, written $fn(P)$, is defined as usual; the only binder is in the input action.

12.2 Structural Congruence and Reduction

Structural congruence is used heavily in the logic, as well as in the reduction semantics.

Table 19: Structural Congruence

$P \equiv P$	(Struct Refl)
$P \equiv Q \Rightarrow Q \equiv P$	(Struct Symm)
$P \equiv Q, Q \equiv R \Rightarrow P \equiv R$	(Struct Trans)
$P \equiv Q \Rightarrow P \mid R \equiv Q \mid R$	(Struct Par)
$P \equiv Q \Rightarrow !P \equiv !Q$	(Struct Repl)
$P \equiv Q \Rightarrow M[P] \equiv M[Q]$	(Struct Amb)
$P \mid Q \equiv Q \mid P$	(Struct Par Comm)
$(P \mid Q) \mid R \equiv P \mid (Q \mid R)$	(Struct Par Assoc)
$P \mid \mathbf{0} \equiv P$	(Struct Par Zero)
$!(P \mid Q) \equiv !P \mid !Q$	(Struct Repl Par)
$!\mathbf{0} \equiv \mathbf{0}$	(Struct Repl Zero)

$!P \equiv P \mid !P$	(Struct Repl Copy)
$!P \equiv !!P$	(Struct Repl Repl)
$P \equiv Q \;\Rightarrow\; M.P \equiv M.Q$	(Struct Action)
$P \equiv Q \;\Rightarrow\; (n).P \equiv (n).Q$	(Struct Input)
$\varepsilon.P \equiv P$	(Struct ε)
$(M.M').P \equiv M.M'.P$	(Struct .)

Spatial configurations are ambient configurations consisting only of spatial operators. For example, $a[b[\mathbf{0}] \mid !c[\mathbf{0} \mid \mathbf{0}] \mid !\mathbf{0}]$ is a spatial configuration. These configurations have a natural interpretation as edge-labeled finite-depth trees, where replication introduces infinite branching. The rules for structural congruence are sound and complete for equivalence of these trees. We do not elaborate this further, but it suffices to say that this completeness result motivated the choice of axioms for structural congruence, and particularly the new axioms for replication (which are the same as in Engelfriet's work on the π-calculus [21]).

Table 20: Reduction

$n[in\ m.\ P \mid Q] \mid m[R] \longrightarrow m[n[P \mid Q] \mid R]$	(Red In)
$m[n[out\ m.\ P \mid Q] \mid R] \longrightarrow n[P \mid Q] \mid m[R]$	(Red Out)
$open\ n.\ P \mid n[Q] \longrightarrow P \mid Q$	(Red Open)
$(n).P \mid \langle M \rangle \longrightarrow P\{n \leftarrow M\}$	(Red Comm)
$P \longrightarrow Q \;\Rightarrow\; n[P] \longrightarrow n[Q]$	(Red Amb)
$P \longrightarrow Q \;\Rightarrow\; P \mid R \longrightarrow Q \mid R$	(Red Par)
$P' \equiv P,\ P \longrightarrow Q,\ Q \equiv Q' \;\Rightarrow\; P' \longrightarrow Q'$	(Red ≡)

$\longrightarrow^*$ is the reflexive and transitive closure of $\longrightarrow$

13 The Logic

In a modal logic, the truth of a formula is relative to a state (or world). In our case, the truth of a *space-time* modal formula is relative to the *here and now*. Each formula talks about the current time, that is, the current state of execution, and the current place, that is, the current location. For example, the formula $n[\mathbf{0}]$ is read: *there is here and now an empty location called n.* The operator $n[\mathcal{A}]$ represents a single step in space, allowing us to talk about the place one step down into n. Another operator, $✧\mathcal{A}$, allows us to talk about an arbitrary number of steps in space; this is akin to the temporal eventuality operator, $\Diamond\mathcal{A}$.

13.1 Logical Formulas

The syntax of logical formulas is summarized below. This is a modal predicate logic with classical negation. As usual, many standard connectives are interdefinable. The meaning of the formulas will be given shortly in terms of a satisfaction relation. Informally, the first three formulas (true, negation, disjunction) give propositional logic. The next three (void, location, composition) capture spatial configurations, as we discussed. Then we have quantification over names, the two spatial and temporal modalities, and two further operators that we explain later. Quantified variables range only over names: these variables may appear in the location and location adjunct constructs.

The free names of a formula, $fn(\mathcal{A})$, are easily defined since there are no name binders. The free variables of a formula, $fv(\mathcal{A})$, are defined along standard lines: only quantifiers bind variables. A formula $\mathcal{A}$ is closed if $fv(\mathcal{A}) = \emptyset$.

Table 21: Logical Formulas

η is a name n or a variable x

$\mathcal{A}, \mathcal{B}, \mathcal{C}$ ::=

$\mathbf{T}$	true
$\neg\mathcal{A}$	negation
$\mathcal{A} \vee \mathcal{B}$	disjunction
$\mathbf{0}$	void
$\eta[\mathcal{A}]$	location
$\mathcal{A} \mid \mathcal{B}$	composition
$\forall x.\mathcal{A}$	universal quantification over names
$\Diamond\mathcal{A}$	sometime modality (temporal)
$\diamond\!\!\!\cdot\,\mathcal{A}$	somewhere modality (spatial)
$\mathcal{A}@\eta$	location adjunct
$\mathcal{A} \triangleright \mathcal{B}$	composition adjunct

13.2 Satisfaction

The satisfaction relation $P \models \mathcal{A}$ means that the process P satisfies the closed formula $\mathcal{A}$. This relation is defined inductively in the following table, where Π is the sort of processes, Φ is the sort of formulas, ϑ is the sort of variables, and Λ is the sort of names. We are very explicit about quantification and sorting of meta-variables because of subtle scoping issues, particularly in the definition of $P \models \forall x.\mathcal{A}$. We use the same syntax for logical connectives at the meta-level and object-level, but this is unambiguous.

The meaning of the temporal modality is given by reductions in the operational semantics of the ambient calculus. For the spatial modality, we need the following definition: the relation $P{\downarrow}P'$ indicates that P contains P' within exactly one level of nesting; that is, P' is one step away from P in space, in some downward direction.

$$P{\downarrow}P' \quad \text{iff} \quad \exists n, P''.\ P \equiv n[P'] \mid P''$$

Then, $P{\downarrow}^*P'$ is the reflexive and transitive closure of the previous relation, indicating that P contains P' at some nesting level. Note that P' consists of either the top level P, or the entire contents of an enclosed ambient.

Table 22: Satisfaction

$\forall P{:}\Pi.$	$P \models \mathbf{T}$		
$\forall P{:}\Pi, \mathcal{A}{:}\Phi.$	$P \models \neg\mathcal{A}$	$\triangleq$	$\neg\, P \models \mathcal{A}$
$\forall P{:}\Pi, \mathcal{A},\mathcal{B}{:}\Phi.$	$P \models \mathcal{A} \vee \mathcal{B}$	$\triangleq$	$P \models \mathcal{A} \vee P \models \mathcal{B}$
$\forall P{:}\Pi.$	$P \models \mathbf{0}$	$\triangleq$	$P \equiv \mathbf{0}$
$\forall P{:}\Pi, n{:}\Lambda, \mathcal{A}{:}\Phi.$	$P \models n[\mathcal{A}]$	$\triangleq$	$\exists P'{:}\Pi.\ P \equiv n[P'] \wedge P' \models \mathcal{A}$
$\forall P{:}\Pi, \mathcal{A},\mathcal{B}{:}\Phi.$	$P \models \mathcal{A} \mid \mathcal{B}$	$\triangleq$	$\exists P',P''{:}\Pi.\ P \equiv P' \mid P'' \wedge P' \models \mathcal{A} \wedge P'' \models \mathcal{B}$
$\forall P{:}\Pi, x{:}\vartheta, \mathcal{A}{:}\Phi.$	$P \models \forall x.\mathcal{A}$	$\triangleq$	$\forall m{:}\Lambda.\ P \models \mathcal{A}\{x \leftarrow m\}$
$\forall P{:}\Pi, \mathcal{A}{:}\Phi.$	$P \models \Diamond\mathcal{A}$	$\triangleq$	$\exists P'{:}\Pi.\ P \rightarrow^* P' \wedge P' \models \mathcal{A}$
$\forall P{:}\Pi, \mathcal{A}{:}\Phi.$	$P \models \diamond\!\!\!\cdot\,\mathcal{A}$	$\triangleq$	$\exists P'{:}\Pi.\ P{\downarrow}^* P' \wedge P' \models \mathcal{A}$
$\forall P{:}\Pi, \mathcal{A}{:}\Phi.$	$P \models \mathcal{A}@n$	$\triangleq$	$n[P] \models \mathcal{A}$
$\forall P{:}\Pi, \mathcal{A},\mathcal{B}{:}\Phi.$	$P \models \mathcal{A} \triangleright \mathcal{B}$	$\triangleq$	$\forall P'{:}\Pi.\ P' \models \mathcal{A} \Rightarrow P \mid P' \models \mathcal{B}$

We spell out some of these definitions. A process P satisfies the formula $n[\mathcal{A}]$ if there exists a process P' such that P has the shape $n[P']$ with P' satisfying $\mathcal{A}$. A process P satisfies the formula $\mathcal{A}' \mid \mathcal{A}''$ if there exist processes P' and P'' such that P has the shape $P' \mid P''$ with P' satisfying $\mathcal{A}'$ and P'' satisfying $\mathcal{A}''$. A process P satisfies the formula $\Diamond\mathcal{A}$ if $\mathcal{A}$ holds in the future for some residual P' of P, where "residual" is defined by $P \rightarrow^* P'$. A process P satisfies the formula $\diamond\mathcal{A}$ if $\mathcal{A}$ holds at some sublocation P' within P, where "sublocation" is defined by $P \downarrow^* P'$.

The last two connectives, @ and $\triangleright$, can be used to express context/system specifications; they were inspired by the wish to express security properties. A reading of $P \vDash \mathcal{A}@n$ is that P (together with its context) manages to satisfy $\mathcal{A}$ even when placed into a location called n. A reading of $P \vDash \mathcal{A} \triangleright \mathcal{B}$ is that P (together with its context) manages to satisfy $\mathcal{B}$ under any possible attack by an opponent that is bound to satisfy $\mathcal{A}$. Moreover, $P \vDash (\Box\mathcal{A}) \triangleright (\Box\mathcal{A})$ can be interpreted as saying that P preserves the invariant $\mathcal{A}$. We will see that these two connectives arise as natural adjuncts to the location and composition connectives.

The following table lists some derived connectives, and it illustrates properties that can be expressed in the logic. The informal meanings can be understood better by expanding out the definitions from the table above.

Table 23: Derived Connectives

$\mathbf{F}$	$\triangleq \neg\mathbf{T}$	false
$\mathcal{A} \wedge \mathcal{B}$	$\triangleq \neg(\neg\mathcal{A} \vee \neg\mathcal{B})$	conjunction
$\mathcal{A} \Rightarrow \mathcal{B}$	$\triangleq \neg\mathcal{A} \vee \mathcal{B}$	implication
$\mathcal{A} \Leftrightarrow \mathcal{B}$	$\triangleq (\mathcal{A} \Rightarrow \mathcal{B}) \wedge (\mathcal{B} \Rightarrow \mathcal{A})$	logical equivalence
$\mathcal{A} \parallel \mathcal{B}$	$\triangleq \neg(\neg\mathcal{A} \mid \neg\mathcal{B})$	decomposition (for every split, one part satisfies $\mathcal{A}$ or the other satisfies $\mathcal{B}$)
$\mathcal{A}^{\forall}$	$\triangleq \mathcal{A} \parallel \mathbf{F}$	every component satisfies $\mathcal{A}$. Ex., each n contains just m: $(n[\mathbf{T}] \Rightarrow n[m[\mathbf{T}]])^{\forall}$
$\mathcal{A}^{\exists}$	$\triangleq \mathcal{A} \mid \mathbf{T}$	some component satisfies $\mathcal{A}$. Ex., there is an n containing an m: $n[m[\mathbf{T}]^{\exists}]^{\exists}$
$\exists x.\mathcal{A}$	$\triangleq \neg\forall x.\neg\mathcal{A}$	existential quantification over names. Ex., $\exists x.x[x[\mathbf{T}]]$
$\Box\mathcal{A}$	$\triangleq \neg\Diamond\neg\mathcal{A}$	everytime modality. Ex., n is stable: $\Box n[\mathbf{T}]$
$⌑\mathcal{A}$	$\triangleq \neg\diamond\neg\mathcal{A}$	everywhere modality. Ex., there is no n: $⌑\neg(n[\mathbf{T}]^{\exists})$
$\mathcal{A} \propto \mathcal{B}$	$\triangleq \neg(\mathcal{B} \triangleright \neg\mathcal{A})$	fusion (there is a context satisfying $\mathcal{B}$ that helps ensuring $\mathcal{A}$)
$\mathcal{A} \mid\!\Rightarrow \mathcal{B}$	$\triangleq \neg(\mathcal{A} \mid \neg\mathcal{B})$	fusion adjunct (for every split, if one part satisfies $\mathcal{A}$ the other satisfies $\mathcal{B}$)

Some syntactic conventions: '$\triangleright$' and the modalities binds more strongly than '$\mid$'; they all bind more strongly than the standard logical connectives, which have standard precedences. Quantifiers extend to the right as far as possible.

The following is a fundamental property of the satisfaction relation; it states that satisfaction is invariant under structural congruence of processes. In other words, logical formulas can only express properties that are invariant up to structural congruence.

13-1 Proposition (Satisfaction is up to ≡)

$(P \vDash \mathcal{A} \wedge P \equiv P') \Rightarrow P' \vDash \mathcal{A}$

The definition of satisfaction is based heavily on the structural congruence relation. This use of structural congruence may appear arbitrary: other equivalence relations could be used in its place. We have tried to motivate the choice of structural congruence by discussing in Section 12.2 how structural congruence precisely captures the intuition of ambients as spatial configurations. Moreover, structural congruence is easily decidable, which is useful in model-checking applications [13].

14 Validity

In this section, we study valid formulas, valid sequents, and valid logical inference rules. All these are based on the satisfaction relation given in the previous section. Once the definition of satisfaction is fixed, we are basically committed to whatever logic comes out of it. Therefore, it is important to stress that the satisfaction relation appears very natural to us. In particular, the definitions of $\mathbf{0}$, $n[\mathcal{A}]$, and $\mathcal{A} \mid \mathcal{B}$ seem inevitable, once we accept that formulas should be able to talk about the tree structure of locations, and that they should not distinguish processes that are surely indistinguishable (up to $\equiv$). The connectives $\mathcal{A}@n$ and $\mathcal{A}\triangleright\mathcal{B}$ have natural security motivations. The modalities $\Diamond\mathcal{A}$ and $\diamond\mathcal{A}$ talk about process evolution and structure in an undetermined way, which is good for mobility specifications. The rest is classical predicate logic, with the ability to quantify over location names.

Through the satisfaction relation, our logic is based on solid computational intuitions. We should now approach the task of discovering the rules of the logic without preconceptions. As we shall see, what we get has familiar as well as novel aspects.

14.1 The Meaning of Rules

A closed formula is valid if it is satisfied by every process. (For the moment, we consider only validity for closed formulas, i.e., propositional validity.) We use validity for interpreting logical inference rules, as described in the next definition. We use a linearized notation for inference rules, where the usual horizontal bar separating antecedents from consequents is written '$\}$' in-line, and ';' is used to separate antecedents.

Table 24: Validity, Sequents, and Rules

$\mathbf{vld}(\mathcal{A}) \triangleq \forall P{:}\Pi.\ P \vDash \mathcal{A}$ ($\mathcal{A}$, closed, is valid)

$\mathcal{A} \vdash \mathcal{B} \triangleq \mathbf{vld}(\mathcal{A} \Rightarrow \mathcal{B})$

$\mathcal{A}_1 \vdash \mathcal{B}_1; \ldots; \mathcal{A}_n \vdash \mathcal{B}_n \,\}\, \mathcal{A}_0 \vdash \mathcal{B}_0 \triangleq \mathcal{A}_1 \vdash \mathcal{B}_1 \wedge \ldots \wedge \mathcal{A}_n \vdash \mathcal{B}_n \Rightarrow \mathcal{A}_0 \vdash \mathcal{B}_0$ $(n \geq 0)$

$\mathcal{A}_1 \vdash \mathcal{B}_1 \,\{\}\, \mathcal{A}_2 \vdash \mathcal{B}_2 \triangleq \mathcal{A}_1 \vdash \mathcal{B}_1 \,\}\, \mathcal{A}_2 \vdash \mathcal{B}_2 \wedge \mathcal{A}_2 \vdash \mathcal{B}_2 \,\}\, \mathcal{A}_1 \vdash \mathcal{B}_1$

$\mathcal{A}_1 \vdash \mathcal{B}_1; \ldots; \mathcal{A}_n \vdash \mathcal{B}_n \,\}\, \mathcal{A} \dashv\vdash \mathcal{B} \triangleq$
$\quad \mathcal{A}_1 \vdash \mathcal{B}_1; \ldots; \mathcal{A}_n \vdash \mathcal{B}_n \,\}\, \mathcal{A} \vdash \mathcal{B} \wedge \mathcal{A}_1 \vdash \mathcal{B}_1; \ldots; \mathcal{A}_n \vdash \mathcal{B}_n \,\}\, \mathcal{B} \vdash \mathcal{A}$

We adopt a non-standard formulation of sequents, where each sequent has exactly one assumption and one conclusion: $\mathcal{A} \vdash \mathcal{B}$. Our intention in doing so is to avoid pre-judging the interpretation of the structural operator "," in standard sequents. In our logic, by taking $\wedge$ on the left and $\vee$ on the right of $\vdash$ as structural operators (i.e., as ","), all the standard rules of sequent and natural deduction systems with multiple premises/conclusions can be derived. Instead, by taking $\mid$ on the left of $\vdash$ as a structural operator, all the rules of intuitionistic linear logic can be derived. Finally, by taking nestings of $\wedge$ and $\mid$ on the left of $\vdash$ as structural "bunches", we obtain a bunched logic [37].

14.2 Rules of the Logic

In the sequel, we organize our results into tables of Rules, which are validated in the model, and into tables of Corollaries, which are derived purely logically from the inference rules.

Propositions

The following is a non-standard presentation of the propositional sequent calculus [26], based on our single-assumption single-conclusion sequents. In this presentation, the rules of propositional logic become very symmetrical, and many proofs become more regular, having to consider only single formulas instead of sequences of formulas.

Table 25: Propositional Rules

(A-L)	$\mathcal{A}\wedge(\mathcal{C}\wedge\mathcal{D}) \vdash \mathcal{B} \;\{\}\; (\mathcal{A}\wedge\mathcal{C})\wedge\mathcal{D} \vdash \mathcal{B}$	(W-R)	$\mathcal{A} \vdash \mathcal{B} \;\}\; \mathcal{A} \vdash \mathcal{C}\vee\mathcal{B}$
(A-R)	$\mathcal{A} \vdash (\mathcal{C}\vee\mathcal{D})\vee\mathcal{B} \;\{\}\; \mathcal{A} \vdash \mathcal{C}\vee(\mathcal{D}\vee\mathcal{B})$	(Id)	$\}\; \mathcal{A} \vdash \mathcal{A}$
(X-L)	$\mathcal{A}\wedge\mathcal{C} \vdash \mathcal{B} \;\}\; \mathcal{C}\wedge\mathcal{A} \vdash \mathcal{B}$	(Cut)	$\mathcal{A} \vdash \mathcal{C}\vee\mathcal{B};\; \mathcal{A}'\wedge\mathcal{C} \vdash \mathcal{B}' \;\}\; \mathcal{A}\wedge\mathcal{A}' \vdash \mathcal{B}\vee\mathcal{B}'$
(X-R)	$\mathcal{A} \vdash \mathcal{C}\vee\mathcal{B} \;\}\; \mathcal{A} \vdash \mathcal{B}\vee\mathcal{C}$	(T)	$\mathcal{A}\wedge\mathbf{T} \vdash \mathcal{B} \;\}\; \mathcal{A} \vdash \mathcal{B}$
(C-L)	$\mathcal{A}\wedge\mathcal{A} \vdash \mathcal{B} \;\}\; \mathcal{A} \vdash \mathcal{B}$	(F)	$\mathcal{A} \vdash \mathbf{F}\vee\mathcal{B} \;\}\; \mathcal{A} \vdash \mathcal{B}$
(C-R)	$\mathcal{A} \vdash \mathcal{B}\vee\mathcal{B} \;\}\; \mathcal{A} \vdash \mathcal{B}$	(¬-L)	$\mathcal{A} \vdash \mathcal{C}\vee\mathcal{B} \;\}\; \mathcal{A}\wedge\neg\mathcal{C} \vdash \mathcal{B}$
(W-L)	$\mathcal{A} \vdash \mathcal{B} \;\}\; \mathcal{A}\wedge\mathcal{C} \vdash \mathcal{B}$	(¬-R)	$\mathcal{A}\wedge\mathcal{C} \vdash \mathcal{B} \;\}\; \mathcal{A} \vdash \neg\mathcal{C}\vee\mathcal{B}$

The standard deduction rules of propositional logic, both for the sequent calculus and for natural deduction (interpreting "," as $\wedge$ on the left and $\vee$ on the right), are derivable from the rules in the table.

Composition

The composition rules apply not only to our calculus but also, for example, to CCS.

Table 26: Composition Rules

(| **0**)	$\}\; \mathcal{A} \mid \mathbf{0} \dashv\vdash \mathcal{A}$	**0** is nothing
(| ¬**0**)	$\}\; \mathcal{A} \mid \neg\mathbf{0} \vdash \neg\mathbf{0}$	if a part is non-**0**, so is the whole
(A |)	$\}\; \mathcal{A} \mid (\mathcal{B} \mid \mathcal{C}) \dashv\vdash (\mathcal{A} \mid \mathcal{B}) \mid \mathcal{C}$	| associativity
(X |)	$\}\; \mathcal{A} \mid \mathcal{B} \vdash \mathcal{B} \mid \mathcal{A}$	| commutativity
(| ⊢)	$\mathcal{A}' \vdash \mathcal{B}';\; \mathcal{A}'' \vdash \mathcal{B}'' \;\}\; \mathcal{A}' \mid \mathcal{A}'' \vdash \mathcal{B}' \mid \mathcal{B}''$	| congruence
(| ∨)	$\}\; (\mathcal{A}\vee\mathcal{B}) \mid \mathcal{C} \vdash \mathcal{A} \mid \mathcal{C} \vee \mathcal{B} \mid \mathcal{C}$	|-∨ distribution
(| ||)	$\}\; \mathcal{A}' \mid \mathcal{A}'' \vdash (\mathcal{A}' \mid \mathcal{B}') \vee (\mathcal{B}' \mid \mathcal{A}'') \vee (\neg\mathcal{B}' \mid \neg\mathcal{B}'')$	decomposition
(| ▷)	$\mathcal{A} \mid \mathcal{C} \vdash \mathcal{B} \;\{\}\; \mathcal{A} \vdash \mathcal{C}\triangleright\mathcal{B}$	|-▷ adjunction

The converse of |-∨ distribution, $\mathcal{A} \mid \mathcal{C} \vee \mathcal{B} \mid \mathcal{C} \vdash (\mathcal{A}\vee\mathcal{B}) \mid \mathcal{C}$, is derivable, and so is a |-∧ distribution rule, $(\mathcal{A}\wedge\mathcal{B}) \mid \mathcal{C} \vdash \mathcal{A} \mid \mathcal{C} \wedge \mathcal{B} \mid \mathcal{C}$. However, the converse of that, namely $\mathcal{A} \mid \mathcal{C} \wedge \mathcal{B} \mid \mathcal{C} \vdash (\mathcal{A}\wedge\mathcal{B}) \mid \mathcal{C}$, is not sound. (Take $\mathcal{A} = n[m[\mathbf{T}]]$, $\mathcal{B} = n[p[\mathbf{T}]]$, $\mathcal{C} = n[\mathbf{T}]$, and $P = n[m[]] \mid n[p[]]$; then $P \vDash \mathcal{A} \mid \mathcal{C}$ and $P \vDash \mathcal{B} \mid \mathcal{C}$, but $\neg\, P \vDash (\mathcal{A}\wedge\mathcal{B}) \mid \mathcal{C}$.) As a consequence, one cannot always "push | inside ∧" on the left-hand side of a sequent. In particular, after an application of (| ⊢) one cannot in general renormalize a sequent to bring ∧'s to the top level.

The decomposition axiom, (| ||), can be used to analyze a composition $\mathcal{A}' \mid \mathcal{A}''$ with respect to arbitrarily chosen $\mathcal{B}'$ and $\mathcal{B}''$. An easy consequence of it is $\neg(\mathcal{A} \mid \mathcal{B}) \vdash (\mathcal{A} \mid \mathbf{T}) \Rightarrow (\mathbf{T} \mid \neg\mathcal{B})$, which means that if a process cannot be decomposed into parts that satisfy $\mathcal{A}$ and $\mathcal{B}$, but can be decomposed in such a way that a part satisfies $\mathcal{A}$, then it can also be decomposed in such a way that a part does not satisfy $\mathcal{B}$. An even simpler consequence is that $\neg(\mathbf{T} \mid \mathcal{B}) \vdash \mathbf{T} \mid \neg\mathcal{B}$, which is one of the few cases in which one can push ¬ across |.

The rule (| ▷) states that $\mathcal{A}\triangleright\mathcal{B}$ and $\mathcal{A} \mid \mathcal{B}$ are adjuncts. This has a large number of interesting consequences, most of them deriving from the adjunction along standard lines, for example:

Table 27: Some Composition Corollaries

(▷ ⊢)	$\mathcal{A}' \vdash \mathcal{A};\; \mathcal{B} \vdash \mathcal{B}' \;\}\; \mathcal{A}\triangleright\mathcal{B} \vdash \mathcal{A}'\triangleright\mathcal{B}'$	(▷▷)	$\}\; (\mathcal{A}\triangleright\mathcal{B}) \mid (\mathcal{B}\triangleright\mathcal{C}) \vdash \mathcal{A}\triangleright\mathcal{C}$
(▷ |)	$\}\; (\mathcal{A}\triangleright\mathcal{B}) \mid \mathcal{A} \vdash \mathcal{B}$	(▷-L)	$\mathcal{D} \vdash \mathcal{A};\; \mathcal{B} \vdash \mathcal{C} \;\}\; \mathcal{D} \mid (\mathcal{A}\triangleright\mathcal{B}) \vdash \mathcal{C}$

It is worth pointing out that some composition rules produce interesting interactions between the ∧ and | fragments of the logic. For example, $(\mathcal{A} \mid \mathcal{B}) \wedge \mathbf{0} \vdash \mathcal{A}$ is derivable using (| ||) and (| ¬**0**).

Locations

The location rules are very specific to the ambient calculus.

Table 28: Location Rules

$(n[]\ \neg\mathbf{0})$	$\}\ n[\mathcal{A}] \vdash \neg\mathbf{0}$	locations exist
$(n[]\ \neg\mid)$	$\}\ n[\mathcal{A}] \vdash \neg(\neg\mathbf{0} \mid \neg\mathbf{0})$	locations are not decomposable
$(n[]\vdash)$	$\mathcal{A} \vdash \mathcal{B}\ \{\}\ n[\mathcal{A}] \vdash n[\mathcal{B}]$	$n[]$ congruence
$(n[]\ \wedge)$	$\}\ n[\mathcal{A}]\wedge n[\mathcal{B}] \vdash n[\mathcal{A}\wedge\mathcal{B}]$	$n[]$-$\wedge$ distribution
$(n[]\ \vee)$	$\}\ n[\mathcal{A}\vee\mathcal{B}] \vdash n[\mathcal{A}]\vee n[\mathcal{B}]$	$n[]$-$\vee$ distribution
$(n[]\ @)$	$n[\mathcal{A}] \vdash \mathcal{B}\ \{\}\ \mathcal{A} \vdash \mathcal{B}@n$	$n[]$-@ adjunction
$(\neg\ @)$	$\}\ \mathcal{A}@n \dashv\vdash \neg((\neg\mathcal{A})@n)$	location adjunct is self-dual

The rule $(n[]\ @)$ states that $\mathcal{A}@n$ and $n[\mathcal{A}]$ are adjuncts. Note that $(n[]\vdash)$ holds in both directions, and that the inverse directions of $(n[]\ \wedge)$ and $(n[]\ \vee)$ are derivable; hence, the location fragment of the logic is particularly simple to handle. Some consequences are: $n[\mathcal{A}@n] \vdash \mathcal{A}$, and $\mathcal{A} \dashv\vdash n[\mathcal{A}]@n$, and $\neg n[\mathcal{A}] \dashv\vdash \neg n[\mathbf{T}] \vee n[\neg\mathcal{A}]$.

Time and Space Modalities

The "somewhere" modality was our starting point in developing our logic. We can now investigate its properties.

Table 29: Time and Space Modality Rules

$(\Diamond)$	$\}\ \Diamond\mathcal{A} \dashv\vdash \neg\Box\neg\mathcal{A}$	$(✧)$	$\}\ ✧\mathcal{A} \dashv\vdash \neg¤\neg\mathcal{A}$
$(\Box\ \mathrm{K})$	$\}\ \Box(\mathcal{A}\Rightarrow\mathcal{B}) \vdash \Box\mathcal{A} \Rightarrow \Box\mathcal{B}$	$(¤\ \mathrm{K})$	$\}\ ¤(\mathcal{A}\Rightarrow\mathcal{B}) \vdash ¤\mathcal{A} \Rightarrow ¤\mathcal{B}$
$(\Box\ \mathrm{T})$	$\}\ \Box\mathcal{A} \vdash \mathcal{A}$	$(¤\ \mathrm{T})$	$\}\ ¤\mathcal{A} \vdash \mathcal{A}$
$(\Box\ 4)$	$\}\ \Box\mathcal{A} \vdash \Box\Box\mathcal{A}$	$(¤\ 4)$	$\}\ ¤\mathcal{A} \vdash ¤¤\mathcal{A}$
$(\Box\ \mathbf{T})$	$\}\ \mathbf{T} \vdash \Box\mathbf{T}$	$(¤\ \mathbf{T})$	$\}\ \mathbf{T} \vdash ¤\mathbf{T}$
$(\Box\vdash)$	$\mathcal{A} \vdash \mathcal{B}\ \}\ \Box\mathcal{A} \vdash \Box\mathcal{B}$	$(¤\vdash)$	$\mathcal{A} \vdash \mathcal{B}\ \}\ ¤\mathcal{A} \vdash ¤\mathcal{B}$
$(✧\Diamond)$	$\}\ ✧\Diamond\mathcal{A} \vdash \Diamond✧\mathcal{A}$		
$(\Diamond\ n[])$	$\}\ n[\Diamond\mathcal{A}] \vdash \Diamond n[\mathcal{A}]$	$(✧\ n[])$	$\}\ n[✧\mathcal{A}] \vdash ✧\mathcal{A}$
$(\Diamond\mid)$	$\}\ \Diamond\mathcal{A} \mid \Diamond\mathcal{B} \vdash \Diamond(\mathcal{A} \mid \mathcal{B})$	$(✧\mid)$	$\}\ ✧\mathcal{A} \mid \mathcal{B} \vdash ✧(\mathcal{A} \mid \mathbf{T})$

The operators $\Diamond$ and $✧$ obey the rules of S4 modalities (the first 5 rules in each column); these follow simply from reflexivity and transitivity of $\longrightarrow^*$ and $\downarrow^*$. These operators, however, are not S5 modalities, that is, $\Diamond\mathcal{A} \vdash \Box\Diamond\mathcal{A}$ is not valid (if $\mathcal{A}$ may happen along some reduction branch, it will not necessarily happen starting from every reduction point), and neither is $✧\mathcal{A} \vdash ¤✧\mathcal{A}$ (if $\mathcal{A}$ holds in some sublocation, it does not necessarily hold in some sublocation of every sublocation).

The two modalities permute in one direction (somewhere sometime implies sometime somewhere), but the other direction is not sound. (Consider $P = (open\ n.\ m[p[]]) \mid n[]$. Then $P \vDash \Diamond✧p[\mathbf{0}]$, but $P \nvDash ✧\Diamond p[\mathbf{0}]$). The modalities differ prominently in the way they distribute over compositions and locations, as seen in the bottom rules.

Satisfiability

Validity and satisfiability can be reflected into the logic by means of the $\mathcal{A}^{\mathbf{F}}$ operator (here we use $\mathcal{A}^{\neg}$ for $\neg\mathcal{A}$):

$\mathcal{A}^{\mathbf{F}} \triangleq \mathcal{A}\triangleright\mathbf{F}$	$P \vDash \mathcal{A}^{\mathbf{F}}$ iff $\forall P'{:}\Pi.\ \neg P' \vDash \mathcal{A}$	$\mathcal{A}$ is unsatisfiable
$Vld\,\mathcal{A} \triangleq \mathcal{A}^{\neg\mathbf{F}}$	$P \vDash Vld\,\mathcal{A}$ iff $\forall P'{:}\Pi.\ P' \vDash \mathcal{A}$	$\mathcal{A}$ is valid
$Sat\,\mathcal{A} \triangleq \mathcal{A}^{\mathbf{F}\neg}$	$P \vDash Sat\,\mathcal{A}$ iff $\exists P'{:}\Pi.\ P' \vDash \mathcal{A}$	$\mathcal{A}$ is satisfiable

From the definitions of $\triangleright$ and **F**, we obtain that $P \vDash \mathcal{A}^{\mathbf{F}} \Leftrightarrow (\forall P':\Pi.\ P' \vDash \mathcal{A} \Rightarrow P|P' \vDash \mathbf{F}) \Leftrightarrow (\forall P':\Pi.\ \neg P' \vDash \mathcal{A})$, i.e., iff $\mathcal{A}$ is unsatisfiable independently of P.

One of the main properties of $\mathcal{A}^{\mathbf{F}}$ is that $\mathcal{A} \mid \mathcal{A}^{\mathbf{F}} \vdash \mathbf{F}$, by ($\triangleright$ |). That is, $\mathcal{A}$ cannot be both satisfiable and unsatisfiable. In addition we obtain, from the model, the following rules, from which it is possible to show within the logic that *Vld* and *Sat* obey the rules of S5 modal operators:

Table 30: Satisfiability Rules

($\triangleright\mathbf{F}\,\neg$)	$\}\ \mathcal{A}^{\mathbf{F}} \vdash \mathcal{A}^{\neg}$	if $\mathcal{A}$ is unsatisfiable then $\mathcal{A}$ is false
($\neg\,\triangleright\mathbf{F}$)	$\}\ \mathcal{A}^{\mathbf{F}\neg} \vdash \mathcal{A}^{\mathbf{FF}}$	if $\mathcal{A}$ is satisfiable then $\mathcal{A}^{\mathbf{F}}$ is unsatisfiable

Predicates

So far we have considered only propositional validity; when considering quantifiers, we need to extend our notion of validity. If $fv(\mathcal{A})=\{x_1, ..., x_k\}$ are the free variables of $\mathcal{A}$ and $\varphi \in fv(\mathcal{A}) \to \Lambda$ is a substitution of variables for names, we write $\mathcal{A}_\varphi$ for $\mathcal{A}\{x_1 \leftarrow \varphi(x_1), ..., x_k \leftarrow \varphi(x_k)\}$, and we define:

$$\mathbf{vld}(\mathcal{A}) \triangleq \forall \varphi \in fv(\mathcal{A}) \to \Lambda.\ \forall P:\Pi.\ P \vDash \mathcal{A}_\varphi$$

This definition of predicate validity generalizes the previous definition of **vld**, which was restricted to the case of $fv(\mathcal{A}) = \emptyset$. It similarly generalizes the definitions of sequents and rules. (Remark: the rules of propositional logic extend to predicate logic.)

Table 31: Quantifier Rules

($\forall$-L)	$\mathcal{A}\{x \leftarrow \eta\} \vdash \mathcal{B}\ \}\ \forall x.\mathcal{A} \vdash \mathcal{B}$	where η is a name or a variable
($\forall$-R)	$\mathcal{A} \vdash \mathcal{B}\ \}\ \mathcal{A} \vdash \forall x.\mathcal{B}$	where $x \notin fv(\mathcal{A})$

As an example, $\diamond\!\!\!\cdot\ \forall x.\neg(x[\mathbf{T}]^{\exists})$ is the formula for "somewhere there are no ambients". Since there are no infinite spatial paths $P_1 \downarrow P_2 \downarrow P_3 \downarrow ...$, we can show in the model that this formula is valid. On the other hand, its temporal dual, "sometime there are no ambients", $\diamond \forall x.\neg(x[\mathbf{T}]^{\exists})$, is invalid; for instance, it is not satisfied by $n[]$.

Name Equality

It is possible to encode name equality within the logic in terms of location adjuncts, by taking $\eta = \mu \triangleq \eta[\mathbf{T}]@\mu$. We obtain that for all $\varphi \in fv(\eta,\mu) \to \Lambda$ and all $P:\Pi$, $P \vDash (\eta = \mu)_\varphi \Leftrightarrow \varphi(\eta) = \varphi(\mu)$. As an example, the following formula means "any two ambients here have different names", which can be read as a no-spoofing security property:

$$\forall x.\ \forall y.\ x[\mathbf{T}] \mid y[\mathbf{T}] \mid \mathbf{T} \Rightarrow \neg\, x = y$$

15 Conclusions

The global computational infrastructure has evolved in fundamental ways beyond standard notions of sequential, concurrent, and distributed computational models. The notion of *ambients* captures the structure and properties of wide area networks, of mobile computing, and of mobile computation. The ambient calculus [11] formalizes these notions simply and powerfully, supporting reasoning about mobility and security. On this foundation, we can envision new programming methodologies, libraries and languages for wide area computation.

References

[1] Abadi, M. and A.D. Gordon, **A calculus for cryptographic protocols: the spi calculus**. *Proc. of the Fourth ACM Conference on Computer and Communications Security,* 36-47, 1997.

[2] Amadio, R.M., **An asynchronous model of locality, failure, and process mobility**. *Proc. COORDINATION 97*, Lecture Notes in Computer Science 1282, Springer Verlag. 1997.

[3] Berry, G. and G. Boudol, **The chemical abstract machine.** *Theoretical Computer Science* **96**(1), 217-248, 1992.

[4] Bharat, K. and L. Cardelli: **Migratory applications**, *Proc. of the ACM Symposium on User Interface Software and Technology '95.* 133-142. 1995.

[5] Boudol, G., **Asynchrony and the π-calculus.** *Technical Report 1702, INRIA, Sophia-Antipolis,* 1992.

[6] Bracha, G. and S. Toueg, **Asynchronous consensus and broadcast protocols**. *J.ACM* **32**(4), 824-840. 1985.

[7] Cardelli, L., **A language with distributed scope**. *Computing Systems,* **8**(1), 27-59. MIT Press. 1995.

[8] Cardelli, L., **Abstractions for mobile computation**, in *Secure Internet Programming: Security Issues for Distributed and Mobile Objects*, Jan Vitek and Christian Jensen (Eds.). Springer. 1999.

[9] Cardelli, L. and R. Davies. **Service combinators for web computing.** *Proc. of the First Usenix Conference on Domain Specific Languages, Santa Barbara.* 1997.

[10] Cardelli, L., Ghelli, G., Gordon, A.D.: **Mobility types for mobile ambients.** ICALP'99. LNCS 1644, 230-239, Springer, 1999.

[11] Cardelli, L. and A.D. Gordon, **Mobile ambients**, in *Foundations of Software Science and Computational Structures*, Maurice Nivat (Ed.), LNCS 1378, Springer, 140-155. 1998

[12] Cardelli, L., and A.D. Gordon, **Types for mobile ambients.** *Proc. 26th Annual ACM Symposium on Principles of Programming Languages*, 79-92. 1999.

[13] Cardelli, L., and A.D. Gordon, **Anytime, anywhere. Modal logics for mobile ambients**. *Proc. 27th Annual ACM Symposium on Principles of Programming Languages*, 2000. (To appear.)

[14] Carriero, N. and D. Gelernter, **Linda in context**. *Communications of the ACM*, **32**(4), 444-458. 1989.

[15] Carriero, N., D. Gelernter, and L. Zuck, **Bauhaus Linda**, in *Object-Based Models and Languages for Concurrent Systems*, P. Ciancarini, O. Nierstrasz and A. Yonezawa (Ed.), Lecture Notes in Computer Science 924, Springer Verlag, 66-76. 1995.

[16] Chandra, T.D., S.Toueg, **Unreliable failure detectors for asynchronous systems.** *ACM Symposium on Principles of Distributed Computing*, 325-340. 1991.

[17] Dam, M.: **Relevance logic and concurrent composition**. LICS'88, 178-185, 1988.

[18] De Nicola, R., G.-L. Ferrari and R. Pugliese, **Locality based Linda: programming with explicit localities**. *Proc. TAPSOFT'97.* Lecture Notes in Computer Science 1214, 712-726, Springer Verlag. 1997.

[19] De Nicola, R., and M.C.B. Hennessy. **Testing equivalences for processes**. *Theoretical Computer Science*, **34**, 83-133, 1984.

[20] Engberg, U.H., Winskel, G.: **Linear logic on Petri nets**. BRICS Report RS-94-3, 1994.

[21] Engelfriet, J.: **A multiset semantics for the π-calculus with replication**. TCS (**153**)65-94, 1996.

[22] Fischer, M.J., N.A. Lynch, and M.S. Paterson, **Impossibility of distributed consensus with one faulty process.** *J.ACM* **32**(2), 374-382. 1985.

[23] Fournet, C. and G. Gonthier, **The reflexive CHAM and the join-calculus**. *Proc. 23rd Annual ACM Symposium on Principles of Programming Languages*, 372-385. 1996.

[24] Fournet, C., G. Gonthier, J.-J. Lévy, L. Maranget, D. Rémy, **A calculus of mobile agents**. *Proc. 7th International Conference on Concurrency Theory (CONCUR'96)*, 406-421. 1996.

[25] Girard, J-Y., Lafont, Y.: **Linear logic and lazy computation**. TAPSOFT 87, LNCS 250 vol 2, 53-66, Springer, 1987.

[26] Girard, J.-Y., Lafont, Y., Taylor, P.: **Proofs and types**. Cambridge University Press, 1989.

[27] Gordon, A.D, and L. Cardelli, **Equational properties of mobile ambients**. *Proc. FOSSACS'99*, Lecture Notes in Computer Science 1578, 212-226, Springer Verlag, 1999.

[28] Gosling, J., B. Joy and G. Steele, **The Java language specification**. Addison-Wesley. 1996.

[29] Hennessy, H., Milner, R.: **Algebraic laws for nondeterminism and concurrency**. JACM, **32**(1)137-161, 1985.

[30] Honda., K. and M. Tokoro, **An object calculus for asynchronous communication.** *Proc. ECOOP'91,* Lecture Notes in Computer Science 521, 133-147, Springer Verlag, 1991.

[31] Lafont, Y.: **The linear abstract machine**. TCS (**59**)157-180, 1988.

[32] Milner, R.: **Flowgraphs and flow algebras**. JACM **26**(4), 1979.

[33] Milner, R., **A calculus of communicating systems**. Lecture Notes in Computer Science 92. Springer Verlag. 1980.

[34] Milner, R., **Functions as processes**. *Mathematical Structures in Computer Science* **2**, 119-141. 1992.

[35] Milner, R., J. Parrow and D. Walker, **A calculus of mobile processes, Parts 1-2**. *Information and Computation*, **100**(1), 1-77. 1992

[36] Morris, J.H., **Lambda-calculus models of programming languages.** Ph.D. Thesis, MIT, Dec 1968.

[37] O'Hearn, P.W., Pym, D.: **The logic of bunched implications**. Bulletin of Symbolic Logic. To appear, 1999.

[38] Riely, J., and M. Hennessy, **A typed language for distributed mobile processes**. *Proc. 25th Annual ACM Symposium on Principles of Programming Languages*, 378-390, 1998.

[39] Sander, A. and C. F. Tschudin, **Towards mobile cryptography**, *ICSI technical report 97-049*, November 1997. *Proc. IEEE Symposium on Security and Privacy*, Spring 1998.

[40] Sewell, P., **Global/local subtyping and capability inference for a distributed π-calculus**. *Proc. ICALP'98*. Lecture Notes in Computer Science 1443, 695-706, Springer, 1998.

[41] Stamos, J.W. and D.K. Gifford, **Remote evaluation**. *ACM Transactions on Programming Languages and Systems* **12**(4), 537-565. 1990.

[42] Urquhart, A.: **Semantics for relevant logics.** Journal of Symbolic Logic **37**(1)159-169, 1972.

[43] White, J.E., **Mobile agents**. In *Software Agents*, J. Bradshaw, ed. The MIT Press. 1996.

Foundations of Secure Computation
F.L. Bauer and R. Steinbrüggen (Eds.)
IOS Press, 2000

Security Protocols and their Properties*

Martín Abadi
Bell Labs Research
Lucent Technologies

Abstract. Specifications for security protocols range from informal narrations of message flows to formal assertions of protocol properties. This paper discusses those specifications, emphasizing authenticity and secrecy properties. It also suggests some gaps and some opportunities for further work. Some of them pertain to the traditional core of the field; others appear when we examine the context in which protocols operate.

1 Introduction

The method of "security by obscurity" dictates that potential attackers to a system should be kept from knowing not only passwords and cryptographic keys but also basic information about how the system works, such as the specifications of cryptographic algorithms, communication protocols, and access control mechanisms. It has long been argued that "security by obscurity" is usually inferior to open design [64, 34]. Of course, the value of writing and publishing specifications is greater when the specifications are clear, complete, and at an appropriate level of abstraction.

Current specifications of security mechanisms and properties vary greatly in quality, scope, purpose, and vocabulary. Some specifications are informal narrations that mix natural language and ad hoc notations. For example, the documents that describe the functioning of security protocols such as SSL [33], SSH [74], and IKE [38] often have this style. Other specifications are precise mathematical statements, sometimes expressed in formal calculi. These specifications have played a particularly significant role in cryptography and cryptographic protocols, but also appear in other areas, for example in information-flow analysis (e.g., [24, 34, 51, 56]).

Many of these specifications serve as the basis for reasoning, with various degrees of rigor and effectiveness, during system design, implementation, and analysis. In recent years, there has been much progress in the development of techniques for stating and proving properties about small but critical security components. For example, a substantial and successful body of work treats the core messages of security protocols and the underlying cryptographic functions. In this area, theory has been relevant to practice, even in cases where the theory is simplistic or incomplete. There seems to have been less progress in treating more complex systems [65], even those parts in the vicinity of familiar security mechanisms. For example, we still have only a limited understanding of many of the interfaces, prologues, and epilogues of practical security protocols.

*This paper is largely based on two previous papers, "Two facets of authentication" [3] (©1998 IEEE) and "Security protocols and specifications" [4] (©1999 Springer-Verlag), which were written at Compaq's Systems Research Center.

In this paper, we discuss specifications in the field of security, focusing on protocol specifications. We examine specifications of several sorts:

- In section 3, we consider specifications that concern the step-by-step behavior of a protocol. Such specifications can be largely independent of any assumptions or intended effects of the protocol.
- In sections 4, 5, and 6, we consider properties of protocols, in particular authenticity and secrecy properties.
- In section 7, we view protocols in context by discussing their boundaries. These boundaries include programming interfaces, protocol negotiation, and error handling.

This paper is an informal, partial overview, and does not advocate any particular methods for specification and verification. Occasionally, however, a calculus for access control [45, 6] and the spi calculus [8] serve in explanations. In addition, the paper suggests some gaps and some opportunities for further work. The subject of this paper seems to be reaching maturity, but also expanding. There is still much scope for applying known techniques to important protocols, for developing simpler techniques, for exploring the foundations of those techniques, and also for studying protocols in context, as parts of systems.

2 An example

This section sketches a first example of a security protocol, as background for the rest of the paper. Although there are many kinds of security protocols, examples like this one are both common and useful.

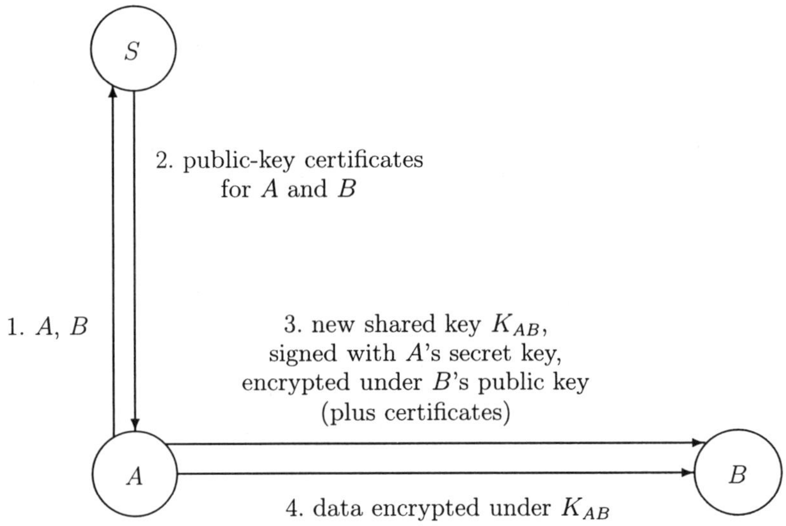

The protocol relies on a symmetric cryptosystem, such as DES, and on an asymmetric one, such as RSA [26, 62, 56]. With DES, a message encrypted under a key can be decrypted using the same key. Therefore, keys are typically known to several protocol participants, and are called shared keys; they are also called session keys when they protect the messages of a session. In RSA, on the other hand, keys come in pairs. In each pair, one key is used for decryptions and for signatures, and the other is used for encryptions and for signature verifications. The former key may be known to only one participant, while the latter may be widely known. They are therefore called the secret key and the public key, respectively. In addition to symmetric and asymmetric cryptosystems, many protocols rely on one-way hash functions (roughly, functions that are hard to invert and collision-free) [56]. In this protocol, for example, applying a one-way hash function may reduce the size of the data to be signed. Despite these distinctions, we need not be concerned with the details of cryptosystems; we treat them rather abstractly (as black boxes) as in much of the literature.

In the figure, A and B represent principals (users or computers); S is a server. The objective of the protocol is the secure communication of some data between A and B. First, A contacts the server by sending its name and B's. The server replies with certificates that associate the names to public keys, which A can forward to B. In addition, A invents a shared key K_{AB} and sends it to B, signed with A's secret key and encrypted under B's public key; B can decrypt this message and check its signature, obtaining K_{AB}. Finally, A sends encrypted data to B under K_{AB}. Although the figure does not show it, B can send encrypted data to A under K_{AB} as well, in the opposite direction.

For instance, the data that A and B exchange may represent file-system operations or electronic-commerce transactions. Thus, this protocol (and similar ones) can serve a variety of purposes. In contrast, some other protocols are intended for a narrower range of applications, sometimes with application-specific techniques and objectives. They seem to be less important at present. At any rate, this paper does not discuss particular applications in depth.

This first protocol description is somewhat vague and incomplete. The rest of the paper explains protocols in greater depth and detail.

3 Protocol narrations

The most common protocol specifications are mere narrations of protocol executions. These narrations focus on the "bits on the wire": they say what data the various participants in a protocol should send in order to communicate. They are sometimes simple, high-level descriptions of message flows (like the figure of section 2), sometimes more detailed documents that permit the construction of interoperable implementations.

3.1 *Informal protocol narrations*

Following Needham and Schroeder [60], we may write a typical pair of messages of a protocol thus:

$$\begin{array}{lll} \text{Message 1} & A \rightarrow B: & \{N_A\}_{K_{AB}} \\ \text{Message 2} & B \rightarrow A: & \{N_A, N_B\}_{K_{AB}} \end{array}$$

In Message 1, A sends to B an encrypted message, with key K_{AB} and cleartext N_A. In Message 2, B responds with a similar message, including N_B in the cleartext. The braces represent the encryption operation, in this case using a symmetric cryptosystem such as DES. The subscripts on K_{AB}, N_A, and N_B are merely hints. It may be understood that A and B both know the key K_{AB} in advance and that A and B freshly generate N_A and N_B respectively, as nonces (quantities generated for the purpose of being fresh).

As Bob Morris has pointed out [9], the notation "Message n $X \rightarrow Y : M$" needs to be interpreted with care, because security protocols are not intended to operate in benign environments. The network between X and Y may be unreliable and even hostile. Needham and Schroeder's model is standard:

> We assume that an intruder can interpose a computer in all communication paths, and thus can alter or copy parts of messages, replay messages, or emit false material. [...]
>
> We also assume that each principal has a secure environment in which to compute, such as is provided by a personal computer or would be by a secure shared operating system.

Furthermore, the principals X and Y themselves may not deserve total trust. So we may interpret "Message n $X \rightarrow Y : M$" only as "the protocol designer intended that X send M as the nth message in the protocol, and for it to be received by Y". One may want additional properties of this message, for example that only Y receive it or that Y should know that this message is part of a particular protocol execution; however, such properties cannot be taken for granted.

A sequence of messages is not a complete description of a protocol; it must be complemented with explanations of other forms. Protocol narrations often give some but not all of these explanations.

- As done above, a specification should say which pieces of data are known to principals in advance and which are freshly generated.

- A specification should also say how principals check the messages that they receive. For example, after receipt of Message 2, principal A may be expected to check that it is encrypted under K_{AB} and that the first component of its cleartext is the nonce N_A sent in Message 1. If this check fails, A may ignore the message or report an error. (Section 7 discusses errors further.) Checks are an essential part of protocols. For example, the absence of a check in the CCITT X.509 protocol [20] allowed an attack [18]; other attacks arise when principals assume that the messages that they receive have particular forms [11].

- The emission of Message n+1 follows the reception of Message n only in the simplest protocols. In general, a protocol may allow multiple messages belonging to the same session to be in flight simultaneously. The constraints on the order of messages in SSL have often been misunderstood [71]. Other complex protocols may be similarly confusing.

- As a convention, it is generally assumed that many protocol executions may happen simultaneously, and that the same principal may participate in several such executions, possibly playing different roles in each of them. This convention has exceptions, however. For example, some protocols may restrict concurrency in order to thwart attacks that exploit messages from two simultaneous executions. In addition, some roles are often reserved for fixed principals—for example, the name S may be used for a fixed authentication server. A complete specification should not rely on unclear, implicit conventions about concurrency and roles.

These limitations are widely recognized. They have been addressed in approaches based on process calculi (e.g., [49, 55, 8, 46, 66]) and other formal descriptions of processes (e.g., [61, 68]). The process calculi include established process calculi, such as CSP, and others specifically tailored for security protocols. Next we sketch how protocols are described in the spi calculus [8]; descriptions in other process calculi would have similar features.

3.2 Formal protocol narrations

The spi calculus is an extension of the pi calculus [58] with primitives for cryptographic operations. Spi-calculus processes can represent principals and sets of principals. For example, the process:

$$(\nu K_{AB})(P_A \mid P_B)$$

may represent a system consisting of two principals, playing the roles of A and B as described above, in a single execution of the protocol. The construct ν is the standard restriction binder of the pi calculus; here it binds a key K_{AB}, which will occur in P_A and P_B. The construct $\mid$ is the standard parallel-composition operation of the pi calculus. Finally, P_A and P_B are two processes. The process P_B may be:

$$c(x).\mathit{case}\ x\ \mathit{of}\ \{y\}_{K_{AB}}\ \mathit{in}\ (\nu N_B)\overline{c}\langle\{y, N_B\}_{K_{AB}}\rangle$$

Informally, the components of this process have the following meanings:

- c is the name of a channel, which we use to represent the network on which the principals communicate.
- $c(x)$ awaits a message on c. When a message is received, the bound variable x is instantiated to this message. The expected message in this example is $\{N_A\}_{K_{AB}}$.
- $\mathit{case}\ x\ \mathit{of}\ \{y\}_{K_{AB}}\ \mathit{in}\ (\nu N_B)\overline{c}\langle\{y, N_B\}_{K_{AB}}\rangle$ attempts to decrypt x using the key K_{AB}. If x is a term of the form $\{M\}_{K_{AB}}$, then the bound variable y is instantiated to the contents M, and the remainder of the process $((\nu N_B)\overline{c}\langle\{y, N_B\}_{K_{AB}}\rangle)$ is executed.
- (νN_B) generates N_B.
- $\overline{c}\langle\{y, N_B\}_{K_{AB}}\rangle$ sends $\{M, N_B\}_{K_{AB}}$ on c, where M is the term to which y has been instantiated.

The syntax of the spi calculus distinguishes names (such as c, K_{AB}, and N_B) from variables (x and y), and processes (active entities) from terms (data that can be sent in messages). We refer to previous papers for details of this syntax and its semantics. We also omit a definition of P_A; it is similar in style to that of P_B.

Since the spi calculus is essentially a programming language, it is a matter of programming to specify the generation of data, checks on messages, concurrency, and replication. For these purposes, we can usually employ standard constructs from the pi calculus, but we may also add constructs when those seem inadequate (for example, for representing number-theoretic checks). In particular, we can use the ν construct for expressing the generation of keys, nonces, and other data. For example, the name N_B bound with ν in P_B represents the piece of data that B generates. On the other hand, the free names of P_B (namely c and K_{AB}) represent the data that B has before the protocol execution.

Thus, specifications in the spi calculus and other formal notations do not suffer from some of the ambiguities common in informal protocol narrations. Moreover, precise specifications need not be hard to construct: in recent work, Lowe, Millen, and others have studied how to turn sequences of messages into formal specifications [55]. To date, however, formal specifications do not seem to have played a significant role for protocol implementations. Their main use has been for reasoning about the properties of protocols; those properties are the subject of the next section.

4 Protocol properties

Although the execution of a protocol may consist in sending bits on wires, the bits have intended meanings and goals. These meanings and goals are not always explicit or evident in protocol narrations [9].

There is no universal interpretation for protocols. Two usual objectives are to guarantee authenticity and secrecy of communications: only the intended principals can send and receive certain pieces of data. Other objectives include forward secrecy [28], non-repudiation, and availability. Some objectives contradict others. For example, some protocols aim to guarantee anonymity rather than authenticity, or plausible deniability [63] rather than non-repudiation. Moreover, many definitions have been proposed even for such basic concepts as authenticity (e.g., [13, 36, 50]).

Nevertheless, there are some common themes in the treatment of protocol properties.

- The participants in security protocols do not operate in a closed world, but in communication with other principals. Some of those principals may be hostile, and even the participants may not be fully trusted. Thus, interaction with an uncertain environment is crucial.

- Security properties are relative to the resources of attackers. Moreover, it is common to attempt to guarantee some properties even if the attackers can accomplish some unlikely feats. For example, following Needham and Schroeder, it is common to assume that an attacker can interpose a computer in all communication paths. In addition, although precautions may be taken to avoid the compromise of session keys, an attacker might obtain one of those keys. A good protocol design will minimize the effect of such events. In particular, certificates for keys should expire [25]; and when one key is expiring, it should not be used for encrypting the new key that will replace it.

- It is common to separate essential security properties from other properties such as functional correctness and performance. For example, one may wish to establish that messages between a client and a server are authentic, even if one cannot prove that the server's responses contain the result of applying a certain function to the client's requests.

Protocol properties have been expressed and proved in a variety of frameworks. Some of these frameworks are simple and specialized (e.g., [18]), others powerful and general. A frequent, effective approach consists in formulating properties as predicates on the behaviors (sequences of states or events) of the system consisting of a protocol and its environment (e.g., [73, 13, 37, 49, 59, 61, 16, 66]). For example, in the simple dialogue between A and B shown in section 3, the authenticity of the second message may be expressed thus:

> If A receives a message encrypted under K_{AB}, and the message contains a pair N_A, N_B where N_A is a nonce that A generated, then B has sent the message sometime after the generation of N_A.

Once properly formalized, this statement is either true or false for any particular behavior. Such predicates on behaviors have been studied extensively in the literature on concurrency (e.g., [10, 44]).

A richer view of authenticity also takes into account concepts such as authority and delegation [35, 45]. Those concepts appear, for example, when we weaken the authenticity statement by allowing B to delegate the task of communicating with A and the necessary authority for this task. However, it is still unclear how to integrate those concepts with predicates on behaviors. The next section discusses some of those concepts informally. (Papers by Gollmann and Lowe also elaborate on the definition of authenticity [36, 50], in other directions.)

The following section, section 6, presents two definitions of secrecy. Only one of them is based on predicates on behaviors.

5 Two facets of authentication

Authentication can serve both for assigning responsibility and for giving credit. An "authenticated" message M from a principal A to a principal B may be used in at least two distinct ways:

- B may believe that the message M is being supported by A's authority. For example, suppose that B is a file server, A a client, and M a request to delete a file f. Then B may use A's identity as an argument to the access control decision of whether to delete f.

- B may attribute credit for the message M to A. For example, suppose that B is running a contest, offering a prize to the principal that mails the factors for a large number. When B receives the message M as an entry, B may give credit for the entry to A.

These two uses are sharply different. Furthermore, some natural protocols are adequate for assigning responsibility but not for giving credit, and vice versa. When a new authentication protocol is designed, it is therefore prudent to state whether the protocol is intended to establish responsibility, credit, or both. Similarly, when an authentication protocol is analyzed, it is prudent to clarify whether its properties suffice for establishing responsibility or credit.

This section explains the distinction between responsibility and credit, through several examples, and discusses the role of this distinction in the design and analysis of protocols. The two facets of authentication are most clearly separate in protocols that rely on asymmetric cryptosystems. We therefore take such protocols as examples. Although our list of examples is not meant to be comprehensive, we illustrate the distinction between responsibility and credit through several protocols of different styles. Our emphasis is not on classifying cryptographic techniques. (See [56, Chapter 12] for a helpful classification.) Rather, we focus on the higher-level guarantees that protocols provide to the applications that may rely on them.

The direct author of a message need not always be held responsible for the message or be given credit for it. In particular, a principal may delegate some part of its authority to another principal, taking responsibility for messages sent by the delegate (much like one can let a friend withdraw from one's bank account). Similarly, a principal may legitimately divert credit for its messages to another principal (much like one can deposit into a friend's bank account). Therefore, even when it is proved beyond a reasonable doubt that a principal sent a message, responsibility and credit may not follow. Responsibility and credit are thus distinct from non-repudiation of origin and other related concepts [75, 63].

5.1 *Four examples*

Next we consider four examples. They all concern techniques that appear in published, useful protocols. In all four examples, responsibility and credit for the messages between two parties is assigned by the parties themselves. For simplicity, we do not consider scenarios where a third party (for example, a judge) may assign responsibility or credit, but such scenarios could be interesting too.

Signing a public key As a first example, we consider a simple protocol where a principal A creates a short-term key pair, sends the short-term public key to a principal B, signing it with its long-term secret key, then uses the short-term secret key for signing further messages:

$$\begin{array}{lll} \text{Message 1} & A \rightarrow B: & A,\ B,\ \{K,\ A,\ B,\ T\}_{K_A^{-1}} \\ \text{Message 2} & A \rightarrow B: & A,\ B,\ \{\{M\}_{K^{-1}}\}_{K_B} \end{array}$$

Here M is an arbitrary message, T is a timestamp, K_A is A's long-term public key, K_A^{-1} is the corresponding secret key, K is A's short-term public key, and K^{-1} is the corresponding secret key. We use braces for signatures, as in $\{M\}_{K^{-1}}$, and for encryptions, as in $\{\{M\}_{K^{-1}}\}_{K_B}$. Message 1 is the core of the protocol; Message 2 appears only as an example of the use of K.

In one interpretation of this protocol, Message 1 conveys that A takes responsibility for the key K, so B can blame A for any message signed with K^{-1}. Thus, the protocol fits applications that require responsibility for a message (or for a connection). For example, the protocol seems adequate for the situation where B is a file server, A a client, and M a request to delete a particular file. It seems adequate even if A gives K^{-1} to a delegate, allowing the delegate to make requests on A's behalf (although delegation mechanisms where B knows the identity of the delegate may be preferable [45]).

In a second interpretation of this protocol, B would assign credit to A for every message that is signed with K^{-1}. This interpretation is not justified, as the following would constitute an attack:

$$\begin{array}{llll} \text{Message 1} & A \rightarrow B: & A,\ B,\ \{K,\ A,\ B,\ T\}_{K_A^{-1}} & \text{(intercepted by } C\text{)} \\ \text{Message 1'} & C \rightarrow B: & C,\ B,\ \{K,\ C,\ B,\ T\}_{K_C^{-1}} & \\ \text{Message 2} & A \rightarrow B: & A,\ B,\ \{\{M\}_{K^{-1}}\}_{K_B} & \text{(intercepted by } C\text{)} \\ \text{Message 2'} & C \rightarrow B: & C,\ B,\ \{\{M\}_{K^{-1}}\}_{K_B} & \end{array}$$

Here C is an attacker who signs the public key generated by A. On receipt of M, we would have B give credit for M to C rather than to A. This sequence of messages constitutes an attack with the second interpretation, since it may result in erroneous credit to C. On the other hand, with the first interpretation, this sequence of messages may result in erroneous blame to C; it may also result in denial of service to A and B, but has no other direct negative impact on them.

The protocol can be strengthened in a variety of ways. In particular, A may sign its own name with the secret key K^{-1}, for example as in:

$$\begin{array}{lll} \text{Message 1} & A \rightarrow B: & A,\ B,\ \{K,\ A,\ B,\ T\}_{K_A^{-1}},\ \{A\}_{K^{-1}} \\ \text{Message 2} & A \rightarrow B: & A,\ B,\ \{\{M\}_{K^{-1}}\}_{K_B} \end{array}$$

or

$$\begin{array}{lll} \text{Message 1} & A \rightarrow B: & A,\ B,\ \{K,\ A,\ B,\ T\}_{K_A^{-1}} \\ \text{Message 2} & A \rightarrow B: & A,\ B,\ \{\{A,\ M\}_{K^{-1}}\}_{K_B} \end{array}$$

These modification do not prevent an attacker C from signing the key K with its key K_C^{-1}; however, C cannot sign its own name with K^{-1}, since C does not have K^{-1}. Therefore, the protocol becomes adequate for giving credit for M to A.

We may say that, with these modifications, A proves possession of the secret key K^{-1} [56, Definition 12.7]. However, this statement should not be taken literally. For example, suppose that A is a user with a smart-card and that B is a server. The smart-card may sign a short-term key K generated by the workstation to which the smart-card is connected, and the workstation may sign the name A, while the user and the smart-card may never have access to the secret key K^{-1}.

Protocols similar to this one may be used for registering public keys. In this application, B is a certification authority and A is a client that enters a new public key K into B's registry. It has been argued that, whenever a client is associated with a public key K, the client should prove possession of the corresponding secret key K^{-1} [56, Remark 13.23]. However, this view is not universal—it is not shared, in particular, in some recent public-key-infrastructure designs [31].

Encrypting a session key While the first example shows that a signature may lead to responsibility, the second example shows that an encryption may lead to credit, and that a decryption may lead to responsibility.

We consider the situation where a principal A transmits a session key K (say, a DES key) to another principal B, encrypting K under B's public key K_B, and including the name A along with K:

$$\begin{array}{lll} \text{Message 1} & A \rightarrow B: & \{A,\ K\}_{K_B} \\ \text{Message 2} & A \rightarrow B: & \{M\}_K \\ \text{Message 3} & B \rightarrow A: & \{M'\}_K \end{array}$$

Messages 2 and 3 simply illustrate the use of the session key K for sending some messages, M and M'. We assume that both principals have means for recognizing and ignoring their own messages, so for example A will not mistake a replay of $\{M\}_K$ for a message from B.

This protocol is adequate for applications that require responsibility for B, and perhaps for applications that require credit for A:

- Only B can extract K from Message 1. Therefore, B can take responsibility for the use of K. Whenever A receives a message encrypted under K, if A did not generate the message itself, then A can be certain that B generated the message, or that some principal to which B gave K generated the message. So A can hold B responsible for the message.

- Since Message 1 yields no proof of A's identity, B does not know who else has K. Therefore, B should not send any secrets under K. We do not consider the issue of credit for B for lack of a compelling example where B would claim credit for public data. (Perhaps only secrets are worth claiming credit for.)
- Since any principal could have produced Message 1, B cannot hold anyone responsible for messages from A encrypted under K.
- Nevertheless, by including its name in Message 1, A claims credit for messages encrypted under K. Of course, if A chooses K incompetently or maliciously, then another principal C might have K as well, and might also produce messages encrypted under K. Still, since A has K, and assuming that C sends those messages to A or that A is capable of intercepting them, A can read and produce those same messages. Therefore, (some) credit to A is justified.

The last of these points indicates that this protocol may not be a solid basis for unqualified credit to A. The following alternative protocol provides a clearer case for credit to A and preserves the responsibility of B:

$$\begin{array}{lll} \text{Message 1} & A \rightarrow B: & \{J_A\}_{K_B} \\ \text{Message 2} & B \rightarrow A: & J_B \\ \text{Message 3} & A \rightarrow B: & \{M\}_K \\ \text{Message 4} & B \rightarrow A: & \{M'\}_K \\ & (K = H(J_A, J_B, A, B)) & \end{array}$$

where J_A and J_B are random quantities invented by A and B, respectively, and K is computed by applying a one-way hash function H to the concatenation of J_A, J_B, and the names A and B. With this alternative protocol, A can still forward a message M received from another principal, of course, but A cannot pick a session key K in use by other principals.

Making a session key from encrypted shares As a third example, we consider a protocol for obtaining a shared key from encrypted shares. The protocol has been applied in several contexts. It appears in the work of Lampson et al. [45], and it also appears as a component of Krawczyk's SKEME protocol [42]. We adopt Krawczyk's name for this protocol: SHARE.

SHARE enables two principals A and B to obtain a shared key, assuming that initially each knows the public key of the other (K_A or K_B). Much as in the previous example, each of the principals invents a random quantity (J_A or J_B), as a "half key". Then the following exchange takes place:

$$\begin{array}{lll} \text{Message 1} & A \rightarrow B: & \{J_A\}_{K_B} \\ \text{Message 2} & B \rightarrow A: & \{J_B\}_{K_A} \end{array}$$

After this exchange, the two principals A and B compute a shared key K by applying a one-way hash function to the concatenation of the half keys J_A and J_B.

In his explanation of SHARE, Krawczyk says:

> If A follows the protocol then she is assured that the shared key [...] is not know to anyone except B (though A does not have the assurance that B knows the key). And analogously for B.

These properties should not be interpreted literally (and it is not Krawczyk intention that they be interpreted literally [43]). In fact, in their literal interpretation, these properties do not hold. Consider, for example, the following message sequence:

$$\begin{array}{lll} \text{Message 1} & A \rightarrow B: & \{J_A\}_{K_B} \\ \text{Message 1'} & B \rightarrow C: & \{J_A\}_{K_C} \\ \text{Message 2} & C \rightarrow A: & \{J_C\}_{K_A} \end{array}$$

In this sequence, A sends a half key to B, who then sends the same half key to C. By whatever means, B makes C believe that Message 1' comes from A. Therefore, C replies to A with another half key. As a result of this exchange, both A and C compute a shared key; C believes that it is shared with A, while A believes that it is shared with B.

Whether this scenario constitutes an attack depends on the use of the protocol. It constitutes an attack in applications where it can result in harm to the principals A and C, which follow the protocol.

- In some situations, this scenario may cause some confusion, but no clear harm. As a result of B's behavior, A may attribute C's requests to B, and lend them the weight of B's authority. Moreover, A may inadvertently reveal some of B's secrets to C. Thus, B's behavior may harm B, but would not directly harm A or C.

  Note that B does not obtain the key that A and C compute. Therefore, B cannot learn C's secrets by decrypting the subsequent messages from C to A. (In this respect, this scenario is quite different from Lowe's attack on the Needham-Schroeder public-key protocol [49], although its structure is reminiscent of that attack.)

- More concretely, A may be a file server, and B and C two of its clients. In this case, the confusion may result in some immediate damage to B's files as a result of C's requests. Moreover, C may be able to read some of B's files.

  Indirectly, however, there can also be some harm to C if C's requests are not sufficiently explicit. Because of the confusion, A may write some of C's data into B's files. In a later session B can read these files, obtaining C's data.

- Finally, if A is running a contest, then it may think that a winning entry that arrives under K came from B when in fact it came from C.

In short, SHARE is adequate for some applications that require responsibility but not necessarily for applications that give credit.

With some additional precautions, SHARE can be used in applications that give credit. For example, each message that an application encrypts under the shared key could include (bound in the encryption) the name of its source, who expects credit for this message if any credit is to be had at all. The inclusion of this name is a prudent measure; it agrees with Principle 3 of [9]:

> If the identity of a principal is essential to the meaning of a message, it is prudent to mention the principal's name explicitly in the message.

Thus, the issue of credit can be separated from the protocol for agreement on a key, and shifted to the use of the key.

Alternatively, we can easily strengthen SHARE, preventing the scenario described above. One possible modification is to let K be the result of applying a one-way hash function to the concatenation of J_A, J_B, and the names A and B, as in the previous example. Another one is to add messages where the two parties A and B prove knowledge of K, as in SKEME.

Krawczyk does not view SHARE as a complete protocol, but only as a phase of SKEME:

> To be really meaningful this phase [SHARE] needs to be combined with the other phases of the protocol [SKEME].

One may instead argue that SHARE is meaningful on its own, although precautions are needed for its use, and elucidating its meaning requires separating credit from responsibility.

The Station-to-Station protocol As a last example, we consider the Station-to-Station protocol [28]. This protocol is fairly well known, so we do not reproduce it or discuss it in detail.

Basically, the Station-to-Station protocol consists of a signed Diffie-Hellman exchange [27], where both parties sign the Diffie-Hellman shares, and where they confirm possession of the resulting session key by using it to encrypt the signed Diffie-Hellman shares. Without the key confirmation, the protocol suffices for establishing responsibility: each party may hold the other responsible for messages under the session key. With the key confirmation, the protocol is also suitable for establishing credit.

Although the Station-to-Station protocol may be rather attractive, it is not without alternatives. Other techniques for key confirmation could replace the encryption of the signed Diffie-Hellman shares. Furthermore, the key confirmation could be postponed or avoided altogether if, whenever credit is wanted, each message encrypted under the session key would contain the name of its source.

5.2 Views on responsibility and credit

We close this section with a discussion of views on responsibility and credit in the design and analysis of protocols.

Design In the literature on protocol design, there seems to be a consensus that an authentication protocol should at least establish responsibility, probably because responsibility is crucial for access control. In the context of access control, the fundamental property of a secure channel from a principal is that the channel "speaks for" the principal [45, 6]. In essence, a channel C speaks for a principal A if A's authority backs every message on C. This semantics justifies the following axioms:

- If A says that C speaks for A, then C does speak for A.
- If C speaks for A and C says s, then A says s.

These axioms are useful and sensible when "A says s" entails that A takes responsibility for s; but they would be unreasonable if "A says s" was meant to imply that A deserves credit for s. In access control, responsibility is largely separate from credit.

There does not seem to be a consensus that an authentication protocol should also establish credit. Although the literature does not seem to contain an explicit, articulate debate about this issue, we can propose likely arguments for both sides.

- We may argue that, once a protocol has set up a channel that speaks for a principal, it is easy to use the channel for establishing credit whenever the need arises. (For example, the principal may send its name on the channel; see section 5.1.) So it is not essential that an authentication protocol establish credit.

- On the other hand, we may say that stronger guarantees are better than weaker guarantees, particularly when protocols may be applied carelessly or in ways not fully anticipated by their designers. Establishing credit is a matter of prudence.

The latter argument may be prevailing. Popular Internet protocols (such as the SSL protocol) probably establish credit, although one may conjecture that applications rarely take advantage of this feature.

Analysis Formal analyses seldom highlight the distinction between responsibility and credit, and the effect of a proof of possession of a secret key. There are some exceptions, for example in the work of van Oorschot and Syverson [69, 67]. Elsewhere, the distinction between responsibility and credit seems to be made through decisions in the modelling of protocol participants.

- Honest protocol participants are expected to follow the rules of the protocol faithfully, and not to try to obtain credit for messages that they did not generate themselves. A proof about honest protocol participants may show that a protocol establishes responsibility, but not credit.

- When an attacker is included as protocol participant, the attacker is not forced to follow the rules of the protocol, and may attempt to get undue credit. A proof that concerns such an attacker can show that a protocol establishes credit.

The protocols described in this section should make good examples for future work on protocol analysis. While these protocols do not present any challenges of scale, they exhibit common subtleties.

6 Two notions of secrecy

Continuing the explanation of protocol properties, this section presents and compares two definitions of secrecy. One relies on equivalences between processes. The other one is based on an inductive characterization of the knowledge of the environment in the behaviors of protocols.

6.1 Secrecy and equivalences

Some security properties—such as noninterference—are not predicates on behaviors [52, 53]. For instance, suppose that we wish to require that a protocol preserve the secrecy of one of its parameters, x. The protocol should not leak any information about x—in other words, the value of x should not interfere with the behavior of the protocol that the environment can observe. The parameter x may denote the identity of one of the participants or the sensitive data that is sent encrypted after a key exchange. In general, we cannot express this secrecy property as a predicate on behaviors.

On the other hand, representing the protocol as a process $P(x)$, we may express the secrecy property by saying that $P(M)$ and $P(N)$ are equivalent (or indistinguishable), for all possible values M and N for x [8, 46] (see also [32, 70, 39]). Here we say that two processes P_1 and P_2 are equivalent when no third process Q can distinguish running in parallel with P_1 from running in parallel in P_2. This notion of process equivalence (testing equivalence) has been applied to several classes of processes and with several concepts of distinguishability, sometimes allowing complexity-theoretic arguments (e.g., [23, 17, 8, 46]).

Now focusing on the spi calculus, we obtain one definition of secrecy:

Definition 1 (One definition of secrecy) *Suppose that $P(x)$ is a process with at most x as free variable. Then $P(x)$* preserves the secrecy *of x if $P(M)$ and $P(N)$ are equivalent for all terms M and N without free variables.*

Previous papers on the spi calculus [8, 1] contain some substantial examples to which this concept of secrecy applies, with proofs. Here we discuss examples only briefly.

- $\overline{c}\langle\{x\}_K\rangle$, which sends x encrypted under a key K on a channel c, does not preserve the secrecy of x. An environment that has c and K can distinguish $\overline{c}\langle\{M\}_K\rangle$ and $\overline{c}\langle\{N\}_K\rangle$ when M and N are different terms.

- In contrast, $(\nu K)\overline{c}\langle\{x\}_K\rangle$, which sends x encrypted under a fresh key K on a channel c, preserves the secrecy of x. However, $(\nu K)(\overline{c}\langle\{x\}_K\rangle \mid \overline{c}\langle\{n\}_K\rangle)$, which sends both x and n encrypted under a fresh key K on a channel c, does not preserve the secrecy of x, because the environment can detect when x is n by comparing two ciphertexts.

- $\mathit{case}\ x\ \mathit{of}\ \{y\}_K\ \mathit{in}\ \overline{c}\langle m\rangle$, which sends a message on a channel c only if x is of a certain form ($\{y\}_K$), does not preserve the secrecy of x, because it leaks some information about x. This leak is an implicit information flow [24].

- In a typical example, $P(x)$ describes a protocol for establishing a session key K and for sending x encrypted under K. Proving that $P(x)$ preserves the secrecy of x may require lemmas about the auxiliary key K. The final result, though, concerns x rather than K.

6.2 Secrecy and inductive definitions

Approaches based on predicates on behaviors rely on a rather different definition of secrecy, which can be traced back to the influential work of Dolev and Yao [30] and other early work in this area [41, 57, 54]. According to that definition, a process preserves the secrecy of a piece of data M if the process never sends M in clear on the network, or anything that would permit the computation of M, even in interaction with an attacker.

Next we show one instantiation of this general definition, again resorting to the spi calculus, with a symmetric cryptosystem. For this purpose, we introduce the following notation from the operational semantics of the spi calculus; throughout, P and Q are processes, M is a term, m, m_1, ..., m_k are names, and x is a variable.

- $P \xrightarrow{\tau} Q$ means that P becomes Q in one silent step (a τ step).

- $P \xrightarrow{m} (x)Q$ means that, in one step, P is ready to receive an input x on channel m and then to become Q.

- $P \xrightarrow{\overline{m}} (\nu m_1, \ldots, m_k)\langle M\rangle Q$ means that, in one step, P is ready to create the new names $m_1, \ldots, m_k$, to send M on channel m, and then to become Q.

We represent the state of knowledge of the environment of a process by a set of terms S with no free variables (intuitively, a set of terms that the environment has). Given a set S, we define $C(S)$ to be the set of all terms computable from S, with the properties that $S \subseteq C(S)$ and $C(C(S)) = C(S)$; thus, C is a closure operator. The main rules for computing $C(S)$ concern encryption and decryption. For a symmetric cryptosystem, where the same key is used for encryption and decryption, we have:

- if $M \in C(S)$ and $N \in C(S)$ then $\{M\}_N \in C(S)$;
- if $\{M\}_N \in C(S)$ and $N \in C(S)$ then $M \in C(S)$.

More generally, for an asymmetric cryptosystem, the second rule should instead say that if $\{M\}_N \in C(S)$ and $N^{-1} \in C(S)$ then $M \in C(S)$, where N is an encryption key and N^{-1} is the corresponding decryption key. Straightforward rules concern terms of other forms, for example pairs:

- if $M \in C(S)$ and $N \in C(S)$ then $(M, N) \in C(S)$;
- if $(M, N) \in C(S)$ then $M \in C(S)$ and $N \in C(S)$.

Given a set of terms S_0 and a process P_0, we let R be the least relation such that:

- $R(P_0, S_0)$.
- If $R(P, S)$ and $P \xrightarrow{\tau} Q$ then $R(Q, S)$.
- If $R(P, S)$ and $P \xrightarrow{m} (x)Q$ and $m \in C(S)$ and $M \in C(S)$ then $R(Q[M/x], S)$.
- If $R(P, S)$ and $P \xrightarrow{\overline{m}} (\nu m_1, \ldots, m_k)\langle M\rangle Q$ and $m \in C(S)$ and $m_1, \ldots, m_k$ do not occur free in P_0 and S then $R(Q, S \cup \{M\})$.

Intuitively, $R(P, S)$ means that, if the environment starts interacting with process P_0 knowing S_0, then the environment may know S (and all terms computable from it, $C(S)$) when P_0 evolves to P. The environment may know some names initially, but it does not create more names along the way.

- The first clause in this definition sets the initial state of the interaction.
- The second one is for silent steps.
- The third one deals with a message from the environment to the process. The environment must know the message's channel name m and contents M.
- The fourth one deals with a message in the opposite direction. Assuming that the environment knows the message's channel name m, it learns the message's contents M. Some new names $m_1, \ldots, m_k$ may occur in M. (The names are new with respect to P_0 and S, and a fortiori with respect to S_0 since $S_0 \subseteq S$.)

We arrive at the following alternative view of secrecy:

Definition 2 (Another definition of secrecy) *Suppose that P is a process, S a set of terms, and M a term, all without free variables, and that the free names of M are among those of P and S. Let R be the relation associated with P and S. Then P* may reveal *M from S if there exist P' and S' such that $R(P', S')$ and $M \in C(S')$; and P* preserves the secrecy *of M from S otherwise.*

This definition is a translation of definitions proposed in other settings. We do not have much experience with this definition in the spi calculus. However, it is easy to apply to examples:

- $\overline{c}\langle\{m\}_K\rangle$ may reveal m from $\{c, K\}$.
- In contrast, $\overline{c}\langle\{m\}_K\rangle$ and $(\nu K)\overline{c}\langle\{m\}_K\rangle$ both preserve the secrecy of m from $\{c\}$. So does $(\nu K)(\overline{c}\langle\{m\}_K\rangle \mid \overline{c}\langle\{n\}_K\rangle)$.
- $(\nu K)(\overline{c}\langle K\rangle \mid c(x).\mathit{case}\ x\ \mathit{of}\ \{y\}_K\ \mathit{in}\ \overline{c}\langle\{m\}_K\rangle)$ may reveal m from $\{c\}$: after the environment learns K from the first message, it can send a ciphertext under K, triggering the emission of $\{m\}_K$, which it can decrypt by using K again.
- Although we could say, informally, that $(\nu K)\overline{c}\langle K\rangle$ may reveal K from $\{c\}$, the definition does not justify it, because of the requirement on the free names of M. This requirement is sensible: omitting it, we could say (without saying much!) that $(\nu K)\overline{c}\langle K\rangle$ may reveal m from $\{c\}$ for every name m different from c, since bound names are subject to renaming.
- Suppose that $P(x)$ describes a protocol for establishing a session key K and for sending x encrypted under K, using a public channel c. If the protocol is sound and n is a fresh name, we should obtain that $P(n)$ preserves the secrecy of n from $\{c\}$.

  On the other hand, we cannot obtain that $P(x)$ preserves the secrecy of x from $\{c\}$ for every x, because the environment may know some possible values of x. In particular, the value of x might be c; it might also be the name of one of the protocol participants that is transmitted in clear on c.

6.3 Comparisons

By presenting both definitions of secrecy in the same framework, we are in a position to compare them and understand them better. We can immediately see that, unfortunately, neither definition of secrecy implies the other: the first one concerns a process with a free variable x, while the second one concerns a process and some terms with no free variables. There are also deeper differences between them. In particular, the first definition rules out implicit information flows, while the second one does not. The first definition can express that a piece of data x is protected even if some of the possible values of x are known to the environment; the second definition cannot deal with such general statements, and seems to work best when the piece of data is a fresh name, such as a fresh key.

We leave for further work explaining when one definition is appropriate and when the other, and finding useful relations between them. In practice, however, they may be roughly equivalent in many examples: the secrecy of a piece of data x and the secrecy of a fresh key that protects x are often closely related.

Both of these definitions of secrecy rely on a simple, abstract representation of cryptographic functions. More detailed accounts of cryptography may include complexity-theoretic assumptions about those functions (e.g., [51]). Another, challenging subject for further work is bridging the gap between those treatments of cryptography. For instance, we may wonder whether the complexity-theoretic assumptions justify our definitions of secrecy. Analogous questions arise for definitions of authenticity.

7 Protocol boundaries

Often the specification of a protocol and its verification focus on the core of the protocol and neglect its boundaries. However, these boundaries are far from trivial; making them explicit and analyzing them is an important part of understanding the protocol in context. These boundaries include:

(1) interfaces and rules for proper use of the protocol,

(2) interfaces and assumptions for auxiliary functions and participants, such as cryptographic algorithms and network services,

(3) traversals of machine and network boundaries,

(4) preliminary protocol negotiations,

(5) error handling.

We discuss these points in more detail next.

(1) Whereas narrations may say what data the various principals in a protocol should send, they seldom explain how the principals may generate and use that data. On the other hand, the good functioning of the protocol may require that some pieces of data be unrelated (for example, a cleartext and the key used to encrypt it). Other pieces of data (typically session keys, but sometimes also nonces) may need to remain secret for some period of time. Furthermore, as a result of an execution of the protocol, the participants may obtain some data with useful properties. For instance, the protocol may yield a key that can be used for signing application messages. Application program interfaces (or even programming languages) should allow applications to exploit those useful properties, with clear, modular semantics, and without revealing tricky low-level cryptographic details (e.g., [14, 48, 47, 72, 2, 7, 12]).

(2) Some protocols rely on fixed suites of cryptosystems. In other cases, assumptions about the properties of cryptographic operations are needed. For example, in the messages of section 3, it may be important to say whether B can tell that A encrypted N_A using K_{AB}. This property may hold because of redundancy in N_A or in the encryption function, and would not hold if any message of the appropriate size is the result of encrypting some valid nonce with K_{AB}. It may also be important to say that B is not capable of making $\{N_A, N_B\}_{K_{AB}}$ from $\{N_A\}_{K_{AB}}$ and N_B without K_{AB}. This property is a form of non-malleability [29]. In recent years, the literature on protocols has shown an increasing awareness of subtle cryptographic issues; it may be time for some principled simplification.

Similarly, protocols often rely on network time servers, trusted third parties, and other auxiliary participants. Detailed assumptions about these servers are sometimes absent from protocol narrations, but they are essential in reasoning about protocols.

(3) Protocol messages commonly go across network interfaces, firewalls with tunnels, and administrative frontiers (e.g., [14, 72, 22, 21, 5]). In some contexts (e.g., [19]), even the protocol participants may be mobile. These traversals often require message translations (for example, marshaling and rewriting of URLs). They are subject to filtering and auditing. Furthermore, they may trigger auxiliary protocols. Some of these traversals seem to be a growing concern in protocol design.

(4) Systems often include multiple protocols, each of them with multiple versions and options. Interactions between protocols can lead to flaws; they can be avoided by distinguishing the messages that correspond to each protocol (e.g., [9, 40]). Before executing a protocol (in a particular version, with particular options) the participants sometimes agree to do so by a process of negotiation in which they may consider alternatives. The alternatives can vary in their levels of security and efficiency. In protocols such as SSL, this process of negotiation is rather elaborate and error-prone [71]. Despite clear narrations, it offers unclear guarantees.

(5) As discussed in section 3, protocol specifications often do not explain how principals react when they perceive errors. Yet proper handling of errors can be crucial to system security. For example, in describing attacks on protocols based on RSA's PKCS #1 standard [15], Bleichenbacher reported that the SSL documentation does not clearly specify error conditions and the resulting alert messages, and that SSL implementations vary in their handling of errors. He concluded that even sending out an error message may sometimes be risky and that the timing of the checks within the protocol is crucial.

The intrinsic properties of a protocol, such as the secrecy of session keys, are worthy of study. However, these intrinsic properties should eventually be translated into properties meaningful for the clients of the protocol. These clients may want security, but they may not be aware of internal protocol details (such as session keys) and may not distinguish the protocol from the sophisticated mechanisms that support it and complement it. Therefore, specification and reasoning should concern not only the core of the protocol in isolation but also its boundaries, viewing the protocol as part of a system.

Acknowledgements

Discussions with Mike Burrows, Hugo Krawczyk, and Butler Lampson led to most of the material of section 5. I believe that the arguments "for credit" and "against credit" of section 5.2 approximately reflect the views of Krawczyk and Lampson, respectively. (So they deserve some credit for these arguments but are not responsible for them.) Comments by referees of [3] suggested the mentions of non-repudiation and of third-party judgement. Comments by Andy Gordon and Marcelo Fiore led to improvements in the second definition of secrecy, which differs slightly from that of [4]. Also helpful were discussions with Ross Anderson, Dieter Gollmann, Paul Kocher, Gavin Lowe, John Mitchell, Roger Needham, Ron Rivest, Mike Roe, Phil Rogaway, and Adi Shamir.

References

[1] Martín Abadi. Secrecy by typing in security protocols. In *Theoretical Aspects of Computer Software*, volume 1281 of *Lecture Notes in Computer Science*, pages 611–638. Springer-Verlag, 1997.

[2] Martín Abadi. Protection in programming-language translations. In *Proceedings of the 25th International Colloquium on Automata, Languages and Programming*, volume 1443 of *Lecture Notes in Computer Science*, pages 868–883. Springer-Verlag, July 1998. Also Digital Equipment Corporation Systems Research Center report No. 154, April 1998.

[3] Martín Abadi. Two facets of authentication. In *Proceedings of the 11th IEEE Computer Security Foundations Workshop*, pages 27–32, 1998.

[4] Martín Abadi. Security protocols and specifications. In *Foundations of Software Science and Computation Structures: Second International Conference, FOSSACS '99*, volume 1578 of *Lecture Notes in Computer Science*, pages 1–13. Springer-Verlag, March 1999.

[5] Martín Abadi, Andrew Birrell, Raymie Stata, and Edward Wobber. Secure web tunneling. *Computer Networks and ISDN Systems*, 30(1–7):531–539, April 1998. Proceedings of the 7th International World Wide Web Conference.

[6] Martín Abadi, Michael Burrows, Butler Lampson, and Gordon Plotkin. A calculus for access control in distributed systems. *ACM Transactions on Programming Languages and Systems*, 15(4):706–734, October 1993.

[7] Martín Abadi, Cédric Fournet, and Georges Gonthier. Secure implementation of channel abstractions. In *Proceedings of the Thirteenth Annual IEEE Symposium on Logic in Computer Science*, pages 105–116, June 1998.

[8] Martín Abadi and Andrew D. Gordon. A calculus for cryptographic protocols: The spi calculus. *Information and Computation*, 148(1):1–70, January 1999. An extended version appeared as Digital Equipment Corporation Systems Research Center report No. 149, January 1998.

[9] Martín Abadi and Roger Needham. Prudent engineering practice for cryptographic protocols. *IEEE Transactions on Software Engineering*, 22(1):6–15, January 1996.

[10] Bowen Alpern and Fred B. Schneider. Defining liveness. *Information Processing Letters*, 21(4):181–185, October 1985.

[11] Ross Anderson and Roger Needham. Robustness principles for public key protocols. In *Proceedings of Crypto '95*, pages 236–247, 1995.

[12] Mihir Bellare, Ran Canetti, and Hugo Krawczyk. A modular approach to the design and analysis of authentication and key exchange protocols. In *Proceedings of the 30th Annual ACM Symposium on Theory of Computing*, pages 419–428, May 1998.

[13] Mihir Bellare and Phillip Rogaway. Entity authentication and key distribution. In *Advances in Cryptology—CRYPTO '93*, volume 773 of *Lecture Notes in Computer Science*, pages 232–249. Springer Verlag, August 1993.

[14] Andrew D. Birrell. Secure communication using remote procedure calls. *ACM Transactions on Computer Systems*, 3(1):1–14, February 1985.

[15] Daniel Bleichenbacher. Chosen ciphertext attacks against protocols based on the RSA encryption standard PKCS #1. In *Advances in Cryptology - CRYPTO'98*, volume 1462 of *Lecture Notes in Computer Science*, pages 1–12. Springer-Verlag, 1998.

[16] Chiara Bodei, Pierpaolo Degano, Flemming Nielson, and Hanne Riis Nielson. Control flow analysis for the π-calculus. In *CONCUR'98: Concurrency Theory*, volume 1466 of *Lecture Notes in Computer Science*, pages 84–98. Springer Verlag, September 1998.

[17] Michele Boreale and Rocco De Nicola. Testing equivalence for mobile processes. *Information and Computation*, 120(2):279–303, August 1995.

[18] Michael Burrows, Martín Abadi, and Roger Needham. A logic of authentication. *Proceedings of the Royal Society of London A*, 426:233–271, 1989. A preliminary version appeared as Digital Equipment Corporation Systems Research Center report No. 39, February 1989.

[19] L. Cardelli and A. D. Gordon. Mobile ambients. In *Foundations of Software Science and Computation Structures, First International Conference (FoSSaCS '98)*, volume 1378 of *Lecture Notes in Computer Science*, pages 140–155. Springer Verlag, 1998.

[20] CCITT. *Blue Book (Recommendation X.509 and ISO 9594-8: The directory-authentication framework)*. CCITT, 1988.

[21] Pau-Chen Cheng, Juan A. Garay, Amir Herzberg, and Hugo Krawczyk. Design and implementation of modular key management protocol and IP secure tunnel on AIX. In *Proceedings of the 5th USENIX UNIX Security Symposium*, pages 41–54, June 1995.

[22] William Cheswick and Steven Bellovin. *Firewalls and Internet Security*. Addison-Wesley, 1994.

[23] Rocco De Nicola and Matthew C. B. Hennessy. Testing equivalences for processes. *Theoretical Computer Science*, 34:83–133, 1984.

[24] Dorothy E. Denning. *Cryptography and Data Security*. Addison-Wesley, Reading, Mass., 1982.

[25] Dorothy E. Denning and Giovanni Maria Sacco. Timestamps in key distribution protocols. *Communications of the ACM*, 24(7):533–535, August 1981.

[26] Data encryption standard. Fed. Inform. Processing Standards Pub. 46, National Bureau of Standards, Washington DC, January 1977.

[27] W. Diffie and M. Hellman. New directions in cryptography. *IEEE Transactions on Information Theory*, IT-22(6):644–654, November 1976.

[28] Whitfield Diffie, Paul C. van Oorschot, and Michael J. Wiener. Authentication and authenticated key exchanges. *Designs, Codes and Cryptography*, 2:107–125, 1992.

[29] Danny Dolev, Cynthia Dwork, and Moni Naor. Non-malleable cryptography. In *Proceedings of the Twenty Third Annual ACM Symposium on Theory of Computing*, pages 542–552. ACM, 1991.

[30] Danny Dolev and Andrew C. Yao. On the security of public key protocols. *IEEE Transactions on Information Theory*, IT-29(12):198–208, March 1983.

[31] Carl M. Ellison. SPKI certificate documentation. Web pages at `http://www.clark.net/pub/cme/html/spki.html`, 1997.

[32] Riccardo Focardi and Roberto Gorrieri. A classification of security properties. *Journal of Computer Security*, 3:5–33, 1994/1995.

[33] Alan O. Freier, Philip Karlton, and Paul C. Kocher. The SSL protocol: Version 3.0. Available at `http://home.netscape.com/eng/ssl3/ssl-toc.html`, March 1996.

[34] Morrie Gasser. *Building a Secure Computer System*. Van Nostrand Reinhold Company Inc., New York, 1988.

[35] Morrie Gasser and Ellen McDermott. An architecture for practical delegation in a distributed system. In *Proceedings of the 1990 IEEE Symposium on Security and Privacy*, pages 20–30, May 1990.

[36] Dieter Gollmann. What do we mean by entity authentication? In *Proceedings of the 1996 IEEE Symposium on Security and Privacy*, pages 46–54, May 1996.

[37] James W. Gray III and John McLean. Using temporal logic to specify and verify cryptographic protocols (progress report). In *Proceedings of the 8th IEEE Computer Security Foundations Workshop*, pages 108–116, 1995.

[38] D. Harkins and D. Carrel. RFC 2409: The Internet Key Exchange (IKE). Available at `ftp://ftp.isi.edu/in-notes/rfc2409.txt`, November 1998.

[39] Nevin Heintze and Jon G. Riecke. The SLam calculus: programming with secrecy and integrity. In *Proceedings of the 25th ACM Symposium on Principles of Programming Languages*, pages 365–377, 1998.

[40] John Kelsey, Bruce Schneier, and David Wagner. Protocol interactions and the chosen protocol attack. In *Security Protocols: 5th International Workshop*, volume 1361 of *Lecture Notes in Computer Science*, pages 91–104. Springer Verlag, 1997.

[41] Richard A. Kemmerer. Analyzing encryption protocols using formal verification techniques. *IEEE Journal on Selected Areas in Communications*, 7(4):448–457, May 1989.

[42] Hugo Krawczyk. SKEME: A versatile secure key exchange mechanism for internet. In *Proceedings of the Internet Society Symposium on Network and Distributed Systems Security*, February 1996. Available at `http://bilbo.isu.edu/sndss/sndss96.html`.

[43] Hugo Krawczyk. Private communication. 1997.

[44] Leslie Lamport. A simple approach to specifying concurrent systems. *Communications of the ACM*, 32(1):32–45, January 1989.

[45] Butler Lampson, Martín Abadi, Michael Burrows, and Edward Wobber. Authentication in distributed systems: Theory and practice. *ACM Transactions on Computer Systems*, 10(4):265–310, November 1992.

[46] P. Lincoln, J. Mitchell, M. Mitchell, and A. Scedrov. A probabilistic poly-time framework for protocol analysis. In *Proceedings of the Fifth ACM Conference on Computer and Communications Security*, pages 112–121, 1998.

[47] John Linn. Generic interface to security services. *Computer Communications*, 17(7):476–482, July 1994.

[48] Jonn Linn. RFC 1508: Generic security service application program interface. Web page at `ftp://ds.internic.net/rfc/rfc1508.txt`, September 1993.

[49] Gavin Lowe. Breaking and fixing the Needham-Schroeder public-key protocol using FDR. In *Tools and Algorithms for the Construction and Analysis of Systems*, volume 1055 of *Lecture Notes in Computer Science*, pages 147–166. Springer Verlag, 1996.

[50] Gavin Lowe. A hierarchy of authentication specifications. In *Proceedings of the 10th IEEE Computer Security Foundations Workshop*, pages 31–43, 1997.

[51] Michael Luby. *Pseudorandomness and Cryptographic Applications.* Princeton University Press, 1996.

[52] John McLean. Security models. In John Marciniak, editor, *Encyclopedia of Software Engineering.* Wiley & Sons, 1994.

[53] John McLean. A general theory of composition for a class of "possibilistic" properties. *IEEE Transactions on Software Engineering*, 22(1):53–66, January 1996.

[54] Catherine Meadows. A system for the specification and analysis of key management protocols. In *Proceedings of the 1991 IEEE Symposium on Research in Security and Privacy*, pages 182–195, 1991.

[55] Catherine Meadows. Panel on languages for formal specification of security protocols. In *Proceedings of the 10th IEEE Computer Security Foundations Workshop*, page 96, 1997.

[56] Alfred J. Menezes, Paul C. van Oorschot, and Scott A. Vanstone. *Handbook of Applied Cryptography.* CRC Press, 1996.

[57] Jonathan K. Millen, Sidney C. Clark, and Sheryl B. Freedman. The Interrogator: Protocol security analysis. *IEEE Transactions on Software Engineering*, SE-13(2):274–288, February 1987.

[58] Robin Milner, Joachim Parrow, and David Walker. A calculus of mobile processes, parts I and II. *Information and Computation*, 100:1–40 and 41–77, September 1992.

[59] John C. Mitchell, Mark Mitchell, and Ulrich Stern. Automated analysis of cryptographic protocols using Murϕ. In *Proceedings of the 1997 IEEE Symposium on Security and Privacy*, pages 141–151, 1997.

[60] Roger M. Needham and Michael D. Schroeder. Using encryption for authentication in large networks of computers. *Communications of the ACM*, 21(12):993–999, December 1978.

[61] L. C. Paulson. The inductive approach to verifying cryptographic protocols. *Journal of Computer Security*, 6(1–2):85–128, 1998.

[62] R. L. Rivest, A. Shamir, and L. Adleman. A method for obtaining digital signatures and public-key cryptosystems. *Communications of the ACM*, 21(2):120–126, February 1978.

[63] Michael Roe. *Cryptography and Evidence.* PhD thesis, University of Cambridge Computer Laboratory, 1997. Available as a technical report of the Centre for Communications Systems Research at `http://www.ccsr.cam.ac.uk/techreports/`.

[64] Jerome H. Saltzer and Michael D. Schroeder. The protection of information in computer system. *Proceedings of the IEEE*, 63(9):1278–1308, September 1975.

[65] Fred B. Schneider, editor. *Trust in Cyberspace.* National Academy Press, prepublication copy edition, 1998. Report of the Committee on Information Systems Trustworthiness, Computer Science and Telecommunications Board, National Research Council.

[66] Steve Schneider. Verifying authentication protocols in CSP. *IEEE Transactions on Software Engineering*, 24(9):741–758, September 1998.

[67] Paul F. Syverson and Paul C. van Oorschot. On unifying some cryptographic protocol logics. In *IEEE Computer Society Symposium on Research in Security and Privacy*, pages 14–28, 1994.

[68] F. Javier Thayer Fábrega, Jonathan C. Herzog, and Joshua D. Guttman. Strand spaces: Why is a security protocol correct? In *Proceedings 1998 IEEE Symposium on Security and Privacy*, pages 160–171, May 1998.

[69] Paul C. van Oorschot. Extending cryptographic logics of belief to key agreement protocols. In *Proceedings of the first ACM Conference on Computer and Communications Security*, pages 232–243, 1993.

[70] Dennis Volpano, Cynthia Irvine, and Geoffrey Smith. A sound type system for secure flow analysis. *Journal of Computer Security*, 4:167–187, 1996.

[71] David Wagner and Bruce Schneier. Analysis of the SSL 3.0 protocol. In *Proceedings of the Second USENIX Workshop on Electronic Commerce Proceedings*, pages 29–40, November 1996. A revised version is available at `http://www.cs.berkeley.edu/~daw/me.html`.

[72] Edward Wobber, Martín Abadi, Michael Burrows, and Butler Lampson. Authentication in the Taos operating system. *ACM Transactions on Computer Systems*, 12(1):3–32, February 1994.

[73] Thomas Y. C. Woo and Simon S. Lam. A semantic model for authentication protocols. In *Proceedings of the 1993 IEEE Symposium on Research on Security and Privacy*, pages 178–194, 1993.

[74] Tatu Ylönen. SSH—Secure login connections over the Internet. In *Proceedings of the Sixth USENIX Security Symposium*, pages 37–42, July 1996.

[75] Jianying Zhou and Dieter Gollmann. A fair non-repudiation protocol. In *Proceedings of the 1996 IEEE Symposium on Security and Privacy*, pages 55–61, May 1996.

Foundations of Secure Computation
F.L. Bauer and R. Steinbrüggen (Eds.)
IOS Press, 2000

Program Algebra and Coprogram Calculus

J.A. Bergstra* & M.E. Loots†

Abstract. On the basis of the program notation PGLD of program algebra, a program notation PGLDg (PGLD with goto's) is proposed with indirect absolute jumps. An indirect absolute jump, also called a goto instruction, instructs the agent executing a program to move to an occurrence of a label catch instruction. The semantics of PGLDg is determined by a projection back to PGLD. An interpretation of flow charts into PGLDg is given, thus demonstrating the expressive strength of PGLDg.

PGLDg turns out to be a useful point of departure for further language extensions, the meaning of more involved languages being determined by a projection back to PGLDg. This semantic method (paradigm) is introduced as projection semantics. As an example a language extension of PGLDg with a conditional construct is discussed.

Coprograms are introduced to model the working memory of a machine executing a program. Projection semantics as a paradigm must provide the possibility to translate a program into a PGLDg program together with an appropriate coprogram. A rigorous definition of coprograms is provided. Two modes of cooperation between programs and coprograms are introduced: 'use' and 'apply'. Coprograms give rise to a natural calculus, which is studied in some detail.

The use of coprograms in projection semantics is exemplified in the case of a language extension with recursion.

1 Introduction

The point of departure for this paper is the program notation PGLD which was described in [4]. By providing a complete introduction of PGLD we will make it possible for this paper to be read as a self-contained unit.

We view PGLD as a manifest program notation in the sense of [7]. In doing so we take it for granted that the PGLD programs comprise lists of instructions amenable to execution by a computer, needing no further argument either from experience, from experiment, from convention or from convenience.

Our view on programming, at least on how the subject can be introduced from first principles, is very similar to the ideas proposed in connection with the toy robot programming system KAREL (and its OO enhancement KAREL++) from [1]. Programming for KAREL starts from the same primitives as those introduced in the program algebra. These primitives are restricted to actions, tests and control commands. Programming for KAREL may be seen as an instance of programming in a structured version of one of the program-algebra-based languages. Because the structured control features used in [1] can easily be formulated via flow charts, we aim at a similar expressive power.

*University of Amsterdam, Programming Research Group, & Utrecht University, Department of Philosophy, Applied Logic Group, email: Jan.Bergstra@phil.uu.nl. Jan Bergstra acknowledges substantial support by Alban Ponse.

†Tilburg University, Faculty of Philosophy, email: M.E.Loots@kub.nl.

The first purpose of this paper is to extend the development of program notations based on program algebra with features that allow the linearized representation of flow charts. Thus, a program notation PGLDg is developed that is significant in its own right. For PGLDg a projection semantics is given by means of a translation into PGLD. By translating flow charts into PGLDg, a projection semantics for flow charts is obtained.

1.1 Three arguments in favor of PGLDg

As PGLDg is not a structured language its introduction may need some motivation. PGLDg naturally emerges if one intends to model flow charts in a program algebra setting. Flow charts being quite important for the methodology of programming, this point is significant. Secondly, one may view PGLDg (and also PGLD) as a technique for encoding finite transition systems in the notational style of program algebra. It is hard to imagine any program notation for digital computers that significantly moves outside the realm of finite transition systems. The importance of finite transition systems being undisputed, this counts as an important rationale for PGLDg. Thirdly, it turns out that PGLDg admits many interesting extensions that can be translated back into PGLD. Although PGLDg may not be a helpful vehicle for programmers, PGLDg is a very useful tool for semantic work.

1.2 Applications of PGLDg

Flow charts are projected onto PGLDg, providing a projection semantics for flow charts. PGLDg will be extended with a conditional construct for which a projection semantics is found by translating the extension back into PGLDg. An extension of PGLDg with recursion is projected back to PGLDg combined with a coprogram containing a natural number stack. Coprograms are introduced in full detail as a preparation for this application.

1.3 Four extensions of PGLA; a brief survey

In order to represent the basis of the program algebra underlying this paper a short description of PGLA and its extensions leading upto PGLD is given. This information is not essential for understanding the technical details of the rest of the paper, providing no more than a context for the design of PGLD.

PGLA contains atomic instructions, atomic instructions with positive and negative test (like PGLD), concatenation (like PGLD), repetition and forward jump instructions. PGLB extends PGLA with backward jumps on top of the forward jumps of PGLA. However, PGLB leaves out repetition, which can be simulated by means of a backward jump. The semantics of PGLB is determined by a mapping, called a program algebra projection, `pglb2pgla` from PGLB to PGLA. The meaning of PGLB program X can be determined as $|X|_{pglb} = |\texttt{pglb2pgla}(X)|_{pgla}$. Following [4] a program notation can in general be defined as a pair of a collection of syntactic objects L and a mapping (program algebra projection) φ from L to PGLA.

PGLC is a modification of PGLB, which has more standard termination conventions and leaves out PGLB's explicit successful termination. The semantics of PGLC is given via a translation `pglc2pglb`, which maps a PGLC program X to a (by definition equivalent) PGLB program $\texttt{pglb2pgla}(X)$. The meaning $|X|$ of X is given by:

$|X| = |\texttt{pglb2pgla}(\texttt{pglc2pglb}(X))|$. Writing $f \circ g(X)$ for $f(g(X))$ we can say that the semantics of a PGLC program X is given by $\texttt{pglb2pgla} \circ \texttt{pglc2pglb}$. The program notation PGLC offers a very simple format for assembly-like programs with control jumps based on offsets.

PGLD is yet another modification of these languages and will be the point of departure for the present paper. It replaces the relative jumps of PGLC by absolute jumps. An absolute jump takes as its parameter a natural number, which is interpreted as the program counter in the instruction list. The semantics is determined by a mapping `pgld2pglc`, which was outlined in [4].

2 Program Expression Syntax for PGLD

The program notation PGLD was introduced in [4]. That paper also contains the description of a transformation (projection) which allows one to translate a PGLD program back to a PGLA program. Because we will need PGLD, we will focus on an introduction of that notation per se. The detour along the more elementary forms of program algebra being ignored, a behavioral semantics can be provided in a direct fashion.

The syntax of program expressions in PGLD is generated from five constants (or kinds of constants) and one composition mechanism. The constants can be viewed as basic instructions. The composition mechanism is the structuring 'feature' of the programming language: text-sequential composition of X and Y, written $X;Y$. The rationale of this syntax is based on the Program Algebra that we have outlined in [4]. As a parameter we need a collection Σ of so-called atomic actions. These actions are considered boolean returning. This means that every execution of the actions produces a boolean value. That value is returned to the calling program in the case of test instructions and is omitted in the case of void instructions.

void atomic instruction. All elements $a \in \Sigma$ serve as atomic actions or instructions; when executed these actions may modify (have a side-effect on) a state. The attribute void indicates that a returned boolean value is not used by the program. After having performed an atomic instruction a program must enact its subsequent instruction. If that instruction fails to exist termination occurs.

positive test instruction. For all actions $a \in \Sigma$ there is the positive test instruction $+a$. If $+a$ is performed by a program, the state is affected according to a, whereafter the sequence of remaining actions is performed in case true was returned. If there are no remaining actions program execution will terminate. If false was returned after a was performed, the next action is skipped and execution proceeds with the instruction following that skipped instruction.

negative test instruction. For all actions $a \in \Sigma$ there is the negative test instruction $-a$. If $-a$ is performed by a program, the state is affected according to a, whereafter the sequence of remaining actions is performed in case false was returned. If the test is the last action of the program the execution will terminate after its execution. If true was returned after a was performed, the next action is skipped and execution proceeds with the instruction following that skipped instruction.

absolute jump instructions. For any natural number k in NN (we use NN for the set of natural numbers and PNN for the set of positive natural numbers) there is an action $\#\#k$ which denotes a jump to the k-th instruction of the program. We call k the counter of the (absolute) jump instruction. If $k = n$, with n the position in the sequence of instructions at which the jump is placed, the jump is to the very instruction itself (zero steps forward). In this case a loop or divergence will result. If the counter of the jump equals $n + 1$ the instruction is a skip (i.e. it skips itself). If $k = 0$ or k exceeds the number of instructions of its program then termination of the program execution will take place upon execution of that jump instruction.

abort instruction. The jump without counter (#) serves as a notation for an instruction resulting in the unsuccessful termination (abort) of the program.

Examples of PGLD programs (or rather program expressions) are:

- $a; b; c$
- $b; +a; \#\#5; \#\#2; -c; +c$
- $\#\#1$

2.1 An algebra of program objects for PGLD

The closed expressions in PGLD constitute an algebra of programs objects after dividing out the congruence generated by the associativity of concatenation. It follows that each program can be seen as a sequence of instructions: $X = u_1; ...; u_k$. As we have stated in [4] the program objects are the elements of a program algebra, whereas the semantic constructions that are assigned to these program objects need not constitute a program algebra. We will use behavior extraction as a semantics for the program objects. In principle the semantics of PGLD programs is to be obtained via the projection pgld2pgla as follows: $|X|_{pgld} = |\texttt{pgld2pgla}(X)|_{pgla}$. This equation expresses the underlying assumption that, as far as semantics is concerned, the projection pgld2pgla takes priority over other considerations.

We will not repeat the details of the program algebra projection pgld2pgla at this point, these matters having been documented in [4]. No familiarity with these transformations is needed for a proper understanding of the remainder of this paper. Avoiding projection, the behavior assigned to a PGLD program X can be described directly in terms of a system of recursion equations associated with the structure of X. This will be done in the following paragraph. It can help the reader to obtain an intuition for the meaning of PGLD expressions. It should be noticed, however, that whenever another semantic assignment is used for PGLA, that semantic modification will automatically entail a modification in the semantics used for PGLD, projection having priority over any other semantic consideration.

A direct description of the behavior of programs in a program notation, following the intuitive understanding of its execution model, is called an operational semantics. Next we will present an operational semantics for PGLD.

Two methods to extract the behavior of a program can be distinguished. The preferred way to obtain this behavior is via a program algebra projection into PGLA following [4]. Therafter the behavior extraction for PGLA can be applied. Alternatively a direct definition for the behavior extraction operator can be given. Such a direct definition is often called a (structural) operational semantics. Here we will provide a direct description of that behavior. Projection semantics and operational semantics have advantages and disadvantages. The advantages for projection semantics are: (i) the interface between the theory of programs and the theory of behaviors is localized at the simple level of PGLA. Consequently, if one chooses to use a different theory of behaviors only the behavior extraction for PGLA is affected, all projections remaining valid. (ii) chains of intermediate projections may be easier to 'manage' than complex definitions for operational semantics. The complexity of each of these intermediate projections may be kept simple whereas a direct operational semantics may involve an unreadable amount of bookkeeping.

2.2 Operational semantics for PGLD

For each closed program expression of PGLD a behavior can be defined. We will use an auxiliary operator $|-,-|_d$ and we have $|X|_{pgld} = |1, X|_d$. This way an independent description of the behavior of PGLD programs is obtained.

With $|i, X|_d$ we denote the behavior of X if its execution is started up with its i-th instruction. Here i can be an arbitrary natural number. Let $X = u_1; ...; u_k$. The semantic equations for $|-,-|_d$ are:

$$|j, X|_d = ||!|| \texttt{ if } j > k \texttt{ or } j < 1$$

$$|j, X|_d = ||a|| \cdot |j+1, X|_d \texttt{ if } u_j = a$$

$$|j, X|_d = ||a|| \cdot |j+1, X|_d \texttt{ if } u_j = +a \texttt{ and } Y(a) \texttt{ holds}$$

$$|j, X|_d = ||a|| \cdot |j+2, X|_d \texttt{ if } u_j = +a \texttt{ and } Y(a) \texttt{ is false}$$

$$|j, X|_d = ||a|| \cdot |j+1, X|_d \texttt{ if } u_j = -a \texttt{ and } Y(a) \texttt{ is false}$$

$$|j, X|_d = ||a|| \cdot |j+2, X|_d \texttt{ if } u_j = -a \texttt{ and } Y(a) \texttt{ holds}$$

$$|j, X|_d = M \texttt{ if } u_j = \#$$

$$|j, X|_d = |l, X|_d \texttt{ if } u_j = \#\#l$$

Here $||!||$ is the irreducible behavior of the successful termination instruction, $||a||$ denotes the primitive behavior that describes the execution of a single atomic action, and $Y(a)$ is a predicate that predicts whether action a will return `true` or `false`. Additionally, $P \cdot Q$ represents the sequential composition of P and Q. If repeated application of these equations leads to no primitive behavior, the divergent behavior D is assigned as a meaning to a program. This happens only in case there is a loop in the program. M is the meaningless program which denotes the semantics of the abort instruction. For a theory of behaviors with D and M we refer to [6].

We notice that pairs of equations can be combined as follows, be it at the cost of readability. The 3-th and the 4-th equation together are equivalent to:

$$|j, X|_d = (||a|| \cdot |j+1, X|_d) \triangleleft Y(a) \triangleright (||a|| \cdot |j+2, X|_d) \texttt{ if } u_j = +a$$

Similarly equations 5 and 6 can be combined into:

$$|j, X|_d = (||a|| \cdot |j+2, X|_d) \triangleleft Y(a) \triangleright (||a|| \cdot |j+1, X|_d) \texttt{ if } u_j = -a.$$

3 Labels and goto's in PGLDg

We will outline an important modification of the language PGLD. First the syntax is given, together with an intuitive account of the meaning of its control mechanisms. Secondly a program algebra projection into PGLD is provided.

3.1 Program expression syntax for PGLDg

As in PGLD, the only composition mechanism of programs in PGLDg is concatenation. PGLDg differs from PGLD in containing labels and goto's. Because they can be emulated by means of labels and goto's, absolute jumps have been deleted, the language becoming more homogeneous as a result. Incorporation in PGLDg of absolute jumps will not introduce any conceptual or semantic difficulties, however, and can under circumstances be quite practical.

As labels we will use the natural numbers. $\pounds k$ denotes a label with name k with $\#\#\pounds k$ a jump towards a label is denoted. Such jumps are also called goto's and for some reason they have a bad reputation. There is a convincing literature about unfortunate use of labels and goto's. We fail to grasp, however, how such observations can substantially reflect on the value or even the perception of the value of such extremely clear-cut mechanisms as labels and goto's. All that can be said is that labels and goto's may be too low level mechanisms for 'end programmer expression'.

The argument in favor of labels and goto's coincides with the argument against absolute or relative jumps. Absolute jumps depend strongly on the sequential numbering of instructions. Every modification of a program that affects this numbering may have as a side-effect that many jump instructions have to be changed. This is very impractical for a programmer (and for an author of software transformation programs). Now the key observation is that what is really meant by an absolute jump is a jump to a position in a program.

A survey of the actions of PGLDg is listed below:

- Actions and tests like in PGLD. These comprise: void atomic instruction (a), positive test instruction ($+a$), negative test instruction($-a$) and the abort instruction ($\#$).
- Label catch instruction. The instruction $\pounds k$, for k a natural number, represents a visible label. As an action it is a skip in the sense that it will not have any effects on a state space. (L-occurrence)
- Absolute goto instruction. For each non-zero natural number k the instruction $\#\#\pounds k$ represents a jump to the (beginning of) the first label catch instruction in the program which is labeled by the label k. If no such instruction can be found termination of the program execution will occur. (G-occurrence)

An example of a PGLDg program is:

$$\pounds 0; -a; \#\#\pounds 1; \#\#\pounds 0; \pounds 1$$

In this program a is repeated until it returns value `false`. That is also the functionality of the simpler program $\pounds 0; +a; \#\#\pounds 0$.

3.2 A projection from PGLDg to PGLD

We take it for granted that the reader has an intuitive grasp of the meaning of these programs. Nevertheless we will determine their meaning by providing the details of a projection from PGLDg into PGLD. Given the familiar program algebra projection for PGLD (from [4]) a program algebra projection for PGLDg results. Using the direct behavioral semantics provided for PGLD above, the mapping from PGLDg to PGLD also brings about a behavioral semantics for PGLDg without any reference to [4]. This can be summarized with the following equation:

$$|X|_{pgldg} = |\texttt{pgldg2pgld}(X)|_{pgld}.$$

The projection `pgldg2pgld` from PGLDg to PGLD is quite simple. For a program X, the following steps have to be taken:

1. Replace for each label k, the goto instruction $\#\#\pounds k$ by $\#\#n$ with n equal to the smallest j such that the j-th instruction contains an L-occurrence of the label k, if that instruction exists, or replace it by $\#\#0$ otherwise.
2. Each label catch instruction $\pounds k$ is replaced by $\#\#j+1$ with j the instruction number of that label catch instruction. (This is a slightly cumbersome way to produce a skip instruction.)

More formally the projection `pgldg2pgld` works as follows on a program $u_1; ...; u_k$:

$$\texttt{pgldg2pgld}(u_1; ...; u_k) = \psi_1(u_1); ...; \psi_k(u_k)$$

where the auxiliary operation ψ_j reads as follows:

$$\psi_j(\#\#\pounds k) = \#\#\texttt{target}(k)$$
$$\psi_j(\pounds k) = \#\#j + 1$$
$$\psi_j(u) = u \ \texttt{otherwise}$$

The auxiliary function `target`(k) produces for k the smallest number j such that the j-th instruction of the program is of the form $\pounds k$, if such a number exists and 0 otherwise. Example: `pgldg2pgld`$(\pounds 0; +a; \#\#\pounds 1; \#\#\pounds 0; \pounds 1) = \#\#2; +a; \#\#5; \#\#1; \#\#6$.

3.3 Embedding PGLD into PGLDg

In the direction opposite to that of projections we have language embedding (also called coprojections). The embedding from PGLD into PGLDg makes clear that moving from PGLD to PGLDg implies no loss of expressive power. The embedding `pgld2pgldg` of PGLD into PGLDg works as follows: let $X = u_1; ...; u_k$, then the embedded version is defined as

$$\texttt{pgld2pgldg}(u_1; ...; u_k) = \pounds 0; \vartheta_1(u_1); ...; \vartheta_k(u_k); \pounds k + 1.$$

Here $\vartheta_j(u)$ reads as follows:

$$\vartheta_j(\#\#l) = \pounds j; \#\#\pounds k + 1 \ \texttt{if} \ l \geq k + 1$$
$$\vartheta_j(\#\#l) = \pounds j; \#\#\pounds l \ \texttt{if} \ l < k + 1$$
$$\vartheta_j(+a) = \pounds j; +a; \#\#\pounds j + 1; \#\#\pounds j + 2$$
$$\vartheta_j(-a) = \pounds j; -a; \#\#\pounds j + 1; \#\#\pounds j + 2$$
$$\vartheta_j(u) = \pounds j; u \ \texttt{otherwise}.$$

3.4 A rule for extending PGLDg

Extending PGLDg can be done by means of the introduction of additional actions outside the atomic action parameter set Σ. Such actions will be called *advanced control instructions.* Care should be taken not to use advanced control instructions immediately after a positive or negative test. The reason for imposing this restriction on extensions of PGLDg is that in most cases a semantic projection of the language extension will transform its advanced control instructions into sequences of PGLDg instructions (perhaps in a context-dependent way). This may then lead to a difficulty in the intuitive understanding of the test instruction. If an advanced control instruction must be skipped, it is not clear whether it is the entire translated sequence of actions or just their first element that is skipped. To avoid this question the aforementioned restriction will suffice. As a goto instruction is not considered an advanced control instruction, the expressive power of the program notations is not influenced by this restriction.

4 Linearization of flow charts in PGLDg

In this section we will discuss flow charts in detail, the discussion culminating in a translation (linearization) of flow charts into PGLDg. The translation demonstrates the expressive power of PGLDg but may be of independent interest as well.

4.1 Flow Charts

Flow charts constitute a classical graphical device for denoting manifest software. We will not discuss the history of flow charts at this point. However, we will make an exception for [8, 9] and [10], since they too add an algebraic flavor to the formalization of flow charts. In [5], a connection is made with a more operational algebra.

It is safe to state that the flow chart notation is quite old, be it that different notational styles have emerged. The well-known Petri nets may be viewed as a very mature form of flow charts. In the case of flow charts, one visualizes the flow of control through a computation roadmap, to be distinguished from the case of data flow systems where the flow of data is being visualized. A flow chart consists of a collection of cells and a collection of flows. A cell contains an action. Actions are taken from a collection Σ serving as a parameter. These actions are boolean returning in the sense that an environment executing the actions will return a boolean value to the cell calling the action. There are two kinds of cells: void cells and test cells. A void cell ignores the returned boolean value. A test cell uses the returned boolean to decide how to proceed.

A flow is a connection, either between two cells or between a cell and the external context. We take the collection of flows to be a subset of the natural numbers. In the flow collection of a flow chart, 0 will represent the entry flow or incoming flow, along which control initiates computation, and 1 will represent the exit flow or outgoing flow, along which control leaves the computation of the chart after its completion. All other flows are called internal. These flow charts correspond to entire programs or systems.

For every cell there is one entry flow, given by the entry flow function $entry(-)$. For every void action node there is an exit flow given by the exit flow function $exit(-)$. For every test cell there is a positive exit flow given by the function $+exit(-)$ and a negative exit flow written $-exit(-)$. All entry flows and exit flows are taken from the collection of flows that is a parameter of the flow chart.

There is a fundamental constraint: for every flow f different from the incoming flow 0 there is exactly one cell k (be it void or boolean returning) for which $entry(k)$ equals f.

Computation of a flow chart works as follows: start in the incoming flow 0. Set the current flow cf to 0. Repeat the following steps until the outgoing flow is eventually reached, upon which the computation terminates: from current flow cf selects the unique cell k such that $entry(k) = cf$; then if this cell is a void action cell, perform its action (i.e. perform atomic behavior $||a||$ with a the label of k) and proceed (i.e. set cf equal) to flow $exit(k)$; otherwise, if it is a test cell perform its action, and depending on whether `true` (positive) or `false` (negative) was returned, set cf to $+exit(k)$ or $-exit(k)$ respectively. At termination the behavior corresponding to termination, denoted with $||!||$ is performed, whereafter the behavior stops.

The representation of flow charts as programs can easily be done at the level of the program notation PGLDg that is introduced above. For that reason we view PGLDg as a manifest program notation. It was conceived in order to be able to represent flow charts, which are definitely manifest. PGLDg may be seen as a language that offers a bare minimum of features needed for the representation of flow charts as linear program texts. That linearization being an important aspect of programming per se, we conclude that these linearized flow charts as well as the underlying flow charts are themselves manifest software.

4.2 Graphical display of flow charts

Flow charts probably owe most of their fame to the attractive possibilities of visualization they offer. We will not draw any flow charts so as to avoid the question how to formalize a picture. That question may lead us to 2-dimensional grammars or to handwaving. We maintain that a flow chart is best seen as a mathematical entity which can, but need not, be depicted in a drawing. In the process of drawing up a flow chart several important transformations are usually carried out, which we will briefly describe. We will then outline how a picture can be formalized and may give rise to a flow chart in the sense as we previously defined it.

First of all the void cells will appear as squares with their action label written inside. The difference between cells simply emerges from their different positions in the picture. Cells are traditionally depicted as non-overlapping icons. For void actions one often uses a square with the entry incoming from above and the exit outgoing below. Similarly, test cells are often depicted as triangles, again with their action label written inside. For the sake of simplicity we will assume, however, that the test cells are also depicted as squares. Then flows take the form of curved lines. The entry flow of a cell 'flows into' it from above. In the case of a void action cell, the unique exit flow leaves the square from below. In the case of test cells, two lines will leave the square from below, one labeled with '$+$' the other with '$-$'. The incoming flow enters the picture from above and leads into exactly one icon, the outgoing flow leaves the picure from below. All flows have a direction. Flows may join but cannot fork. The outgoing lines from two icons may join and then become entry lines for another icon. The logical flows as they occurred in the formalized description of flow charts above can be recovered as sets of lines that join into the same entry or that join into the outgoing flow. The numbering of the flows in the picture is of course superfluous for the purpose of distinction. Indeed, different flows are separated by one or more cells. In the formalization of a depicted flow chart some numbering of the flows must be introduced arbitrarily, before the cells are mapped onto a set. At that stage the cell classification (void action or test action), the cell labeling, the entry mapping and the various exit mappings can be determined.

4.3 Linearization

The description of flow charts that was provided in paragraph 4.1 provides no immediate clue as to how to embed flow charts into a program notation. We will now indicate that PGLDg has exactly the adequate expressive power to do so. To each flow chart (in the formal sense) FC we will assign a program $\texttt{ffcs2pgldg}(FC)$ in PGLDg which represents that flow chart and can be taken as a program notation for it. We consider the connection between the setting of formalized flow charts FFCS and PGLDg to be so close that it justifies extending the classification of FFCS as manifest software to PGLDg. We will need a technical notion concerning the structure of programs in PGLDg. A normal control flow segment is a program in which normal flow of control can lead to an execution from the start to the end without any goto being executed (except the last action, which is allowed to be a goto). NFCS, the class of normal flow of control segments, is defined inductively as follows:

- a, $+a$, $-a$, $\pounds k$, and $\#\#\pounds k$ are in NFCS,
- if X is in NFCS then so are:
  1. $a; X$ for all atomic actions a,
  2. $\pounds k; X$ for all k,
  3. $+a; u; X$ and $-a; u; X$ for all atomic actions a and for all instructions u,
- No other PGLDg programs are in NFCS.

A program is in segmented form if it has the form $X_1; \#; X_2; \#; ...; \#; X_n$ with each of the X_j in NFCS. For a given flow chart FC we will define a program $\texttt{ffcs2pgldg}(FC)$ in segmented form representing the flow chart FC. Let $C_1, ..., C_n$ be an enumeration of the cells of the flow chart. For every cell C_j the program P_j is as follows:

- if C_j is a void action cell with label a and $entry(C_j) = f, exit(C_j) = g$ then $P_j = \pounds f; a; \#\#\pounds g$,
- if C_j is a test action cell with label a and $entry(C_j) = f, +exit(C_j) = g, -exit(C_j) = h$ then: if $g = h$ we take $P_j = \pounds f; a; \#\#\pounds g$ and if $g \neq h$ we write $P_j = \pounds f; +a; \#\#\pounds g; \#\#\pounds h$.

Having these programs available per cell, we find:

$$\texttt{ffcs2pgldg}(FC) = \#\#\pounds 0; \#; P_1; \#; P_2; \#; ...; \#; P_n; \#; \pounds 1.$$

We recall that the entire flow chart will have 0 as its incoming and 1 as its only outgoing flow.

In most cases it will be possible to find a shorter representation of a flow chart using larger segments. Such a representation will use normal flow of control to move from the code of one cell to that of another one. The more efficient representation will be behaviorally equivalent to the one given here We will not pursue that matter any further here as it seems to be of little practical interest. Most likely a compiler optimization utility would be able to generate the transformation to more compact code for a flow chart from the present representation.

5 Projection semantics for conditional constructs

On top of PGLDg it is easy and for the job of denoting programs clearly helpful to offer the conventional conditional constructs. These can be viewed as design patterns from the point of view of PGLDg programming. We will now provide a syntax PGLDgc allowing conditional instructions. The extension gc indicates the simultaneous presence of goto's and conditionals. Then a projection is given from PGLDgc into PGLDg.

5.1 Syntax for conditional instructions

The syntax for conditional constructs takes the form of three new (advanced control) actions (see paragraph 3.4):

if-instruction. For an action $a \in \Sigma$ the instructions $\texttt{if}\ +a\{$ and $\texttt{if}\ -a\{$ initiate the text of a conditional construct.

then/else separator. The instruction '}{' connects two program sections that are enclosed in braces.

end brace. The instruction '}' serves as a closing brace in connection with its complementary opening brace.

An example clarifies the intended meaning of (this rendering of) conditional instructions. The subsequent program algebra projection into PGLDg formalizes the same. The program

$$\texttt{if} + a\{; b; +c; \#\#\pounds 0; \#\#\pounds 1; \}\{; e; f; \pounds 0; g; \pounds 1; h; \}; -a; \#; b$$

will start with the execution of a. If that yields `true` the first branch is taken. Execution of the first branch will unavoidably lead to a jump into the second branch. It depends on the yield of c at which position in the second branch the computation proceeds. If the yield of the action a mentioned before is `false` then the second branch (beginning just after the separator instruction '}{') is executed.

5.2 A projection operator

The mapping `pgldgc2pgldg` determines the semantics of these constructs. It simultaneously removes all occurrences of `if-{;-;}` and of `if-{;-;}{;-;}`. All labels that occur in the program before transformation are multiplied by 3. This will guarantee that labels of the form $3 \cdot i + 1$ and $3 \cdot i + 2$ are new and cannot interfere with existing labels. Let $X = u_1; ...; u_k$. Then we read:

$$\texttt{pgldgc2pgldg}(X) = \psi_1(u_1); ...; \psi_k(u_k)$$

with the auxiliary operations ψ_i determined by the following rewrite rules (with positive conditions, negative conditions and priorities):

$$\psi_i(\#\#\pounds l) = \#\#\pounds 3 \cdot l$$

$$\psi_i(\pounds l) = \pounds 3 \cdot l$$

$$\psi_i(\texttt{if} + a\{) = -a; \#\#\pounds 3 \cdot i + 1$$

$$\psi_i(\texttt{if} - a\{) = +a; \#\#\pounds 3 \cdot i + 1$$

$$\psi_i(\}) = \# \texttt{ if coind}(i) = 0$$

$$\psi_i(\}) = \pounds 3 \cdot j + 1 \texttt{ if } j = \texttt{coind}(i) \neq 0 \texttt{ and kind}(j) = \texttt{single}$$

$$\psi_i(\}) = \pounds 3 \cdot j + 2 \texttt{ if } j = \texttt{coind}(i) \neq 0 \texttt{ and kind}(j) = \texttt{double}$$

$$\psi_i(\}\{) = \#\#\pounds 3 \cdot j + 2; \pounds 3 \cdot j + 1 \texttt{ if } j = \texttt{coind}(i) \neq 0 \texttt{ and kind}(j) = \texttt{double}$$

$$\psi_i(u) = u \texttt{ otherwise}$$

The auxiliary function coind has type $\{1,...,k\} \rightarrow \{0,1,...,k\}$. coind($i$) equals 0 if u_i is not '}' or '}{', or if u_i = '}' and u_i is not the closing brace of an if-instruction, or of u_i = '}{' and u_i is not the intermediate separator of an if-instruction. Otherwise coind(j) equals the index of the if-instruction of which it is a closing brace or an intermediate separator. The auxiliary function kind has domain $\{1,...,k\}$ and codomain {single,double,noif}. kind(i) = single if u_i is an if-instruction that begins a conditional construct without separator, and it equals double if u_i begins an if-statment with a separator instruction inside; otherwise kind(i) = noif.

5.3 Compile time data left unspecified

We will not formally specify the auxiliary operations that have been used in the description of the projection pgldgc2pgldg in more detail. For instance computing coind is just a matter of finding the corresponding opening brace ignoring the separator instructions. In order to determine kind(i) one views the separators as brace pairs, and starts looking for the corresponding closing brace for the opening brace in the if-instruction. If it is a solitary closing brace, the if-instruction (or rather its index) is single (armed), if it happens to be a brace included in a separator instruction the if-instruction is double (armed) and in all other cases the index is 'noif'.

It should be noticed that the information contained in the operators just mentioned must be discovered and used at compile time. It will not play a role during the run-time execution of the translated program.

5.4 Examples

Unfortunately the definition of pgldgc2pgldg is not easy to read and hard to memorize. Examples are needed to understand what is going on.

$$\texttt{pgldgc2pgldg}(\texttt{if} + a\{; b; \}\{; c; \}; d) = -a; \#\#\pounds 4; b; \#\#\pounds 5; \pounds 4; c; \pounds 5; d$$

$$\texttt{pgldgc2pgldg}(\texttt{if} - a\{; b; \}\{; c; \}) = +a; \#\#\pounds 4; b; \#\#\pounds 5; \pounds 4; c; \pounds 5$$

$$\texttt{pgldgc2pgldg}(\texttt{if} + a\{; b1; -b; \#\#\pounds 4; b2; \}\{; c; \}; d; \pounds 4) =$$
$$-a; \#\#\pounds 4; b1; -b; \#\#\pounds 12; b2; \#\#\pounds 5; \pounds 4; c; \pounds 5; d; \pounds 12$$

6 Coprograms

Coprograms consume and process actions complementary to programs issuing actions. Coprograms maintain a state and reply with a boolean response to each action in their interface. As coprograms offer a service to other units, their interface is also called a service interface. Coprograms can be combined with several natural operators, thus giving rise to a coprogram calculus. Abstract data type coprograms are used for abstract data type modeling.

Coprograms are used to represent data structures and data types in a context focussing on their role within programs. Data types are given a secondary role. Although programs are given the lead and data types are considered auxiliary in nature, the formalization of data types is still of major importance for program understanding.

Data type modeling requires as much care as the analysis of programs and programming concepts. Coprograms admit several interesting operators, so there is an algebra of coprograms as well as there is an algebra of programs.

We prefer to call the former a calculus of coprograms. The reason for this choice is that identity in the program calculus is defined in terms of set-theoretic constructions rather than directly or indirectly by means of equational reasoning. We will provide an informal introduction to the operational intuition of coprograms. Subsequently we discuss a pedestrian classification of specification techniques for coprograms, followed by an equally informal classification of interfaces. The calculus of coprograms is discussed in some detail and examples are provided.

6.1 Coprograms: a rigororous definition

A coprogram is a pair consisting of an interface and a reply function. The interface in turn consists of a collection of actions (also called instructions), the reply function being a mapping that gives for each finite sequence of interface actions (i.e. actions from the interface) the reply produced by the coprogram. This reply is a boolean value (`true` or `false` unless an error has occurred (M) or divergence occurs (symbolized by D).

6.2 Operational intuition of coprograms

The intuition is as follows: an agent outside the coprogram makes use of the service offered by the coprogram. These services are listed as instructions in the service interface of the coprogram. Each instruction in this interface can be processed by the coprogram. The coprogram updates its state and produces a reply in the form of a boolean value which is returned to the agent that invoked the service. Two errors can occur: abort (M) or divergence (D). In both cases the coprogram replies with a corresponding error value rather than an ordinary boolean. Further, it will not process any subsequent requests after having run into an error. It is assumed that the agent starts the operation of the coprogram with its first request for a service. The coprogram is always initialized from the same initial state.

6.2.1 The role of coprograms

Coprograms emerge first of all as a tool for the description of data structures. Well-known data structures such as memory registers, stacks, queues and tables can all be modeled as coprograms. Although the terminology of coprograms seems to be novel, the concept of coprograms is not new. In [2] they appear under the name of processes, a phrase that is currently used for a far more general kind of behavior. We refer to [3] for a discussion of abstract data type behavior motivating the role coprograms in this paper. An extensive literature on observability in data types relates to very similar notions. If one forgets the use of divergence (D) and error (M), it turns out that a coprogram is simply a formal language, perhaps based upon an unusual alphabet of symbols.

6.2.2 *Abstract data type coprograms*

Abstract data coprograms describe abstract data types in such a way that they can be used as part of an abstract machine. There is no implication that the abstract data type, or its coprogram must be realized either in hardware or in software if it is used in a system description. Its role is restricted to specification. In many cases specifications involving abstract data type coprograms can be transformed into implementations in a fully automatic and an algorithmically satisfactory way. The transformation used for that purpose, however, need not generate a system that has the same or virtually the same architecture as the given specification. Only the externally visible behavior must comply with the specification, all of its internal details in fact being private to the specification.

6.2.3 *Program components and coprogram components*

A program component is a pair of an interface Σ and a program such that all basic instructions used by the program are in Σ. We use 'program component' independently of the phrase 'software component'. There is no implication that a program component contains a program in binary form. This definition is meaningful for all program notations in program algebra. A coprogram has a definite interface and coprogram components will be identified with coprograms.

We propopose the phrase i-program (interfaced program) for a program component. We write X^i for interfaced programs. The interface is extracted by an application of the operator Σ_l to X^i.

6.3 *Coprogram details*

A coprogram H is a pair (Σ, F), where Σ is a collection of actions constituting the service interface of H, and F is the so-called reply function. F takes as arguments the non-empty sequences of actions in Σ and has outputs in $\{\texttt{true}, \texttt{false}, D, M\}$. The requirement is that for $a \in \Sigma$ and $w \in \Sigma^*$ if $F(w) = D$ then also $F(w,a) = D$ and if $F(w) = M$ then also $F(w,a) = M$. Here w, a indicates the extension of list w with a and Σ^* denotes as usual the family of (empty and non-empty sequences) of elements of Σ. We will use the convention that sequences of interface actions are separated by commas.

For a set Σ the collection of all coprograms with service interface Σ is denoted with $\texttt{Coprog}(\Sigma)$. This collection can be considered the semantics of the service interface Σ. We will not discuss the set-theoretic size of this collection. It is quite large but only a fraction of its conceivable elements has some relevance for computer programming.

7 System components and polarized interfaces

We will use system component to denote any kind of component. The phrase software component, unfortunately, has become charged with a technical meaning, thus making it less useful for general purposes. The phrase system component should be protected from being given a specific technical meaning.

7.1 *Interfaces and polarization*

An interface is a set of (names of) instructions (or actions). Interfaces have an independent status. Interfaces can be associated with system components in various ways. It is often the case that a component 'has' one or more interfaces. The precise technical meaning of 'has' may vary. We will always assume that for something to be called a component, it must at least be clear which interfaces it has.

Familiarity with the range of services offered by the interface of a system component enables another component to interact with it via the instructions in the interface.

7.1.1 *Interface polarization*

Program algebra, coprogram calculus, projection semantics and related topics are based upon polarized interfaces. The polarity of an interface determines whether it contains requests or services.

Interface polarization refers to the assumption that all interfaces can be split into the following two polarities: service versus co-service. We will assume that all interfaces are polarized until further notice. Non-polarized interfaces are the point of departure for process algebra and trace theory. Non-polarized interfaces are instrumental for the description of parallel systems.

7.1.2 *Upper interface and lower interface*

A service interface is an interface containing only actions that can be called by another component. The upper interface of a component equals the union of its service interfaces. In other words: the upper interface of a component is its maximal service interface. A co-service interface of a component is an interface containing only actions which may be requested from another component. An action in a lower interface of a component must be performed (executed) by another component which offers the action as a service in its upper interface. The lower interface of a component equals the union of its co-service interfaces. In other words: the lower interface of a component is its largest co-service interface.

Co-operation between two system components will, as a rule[1], involve an action in the lower interface of an initiating component[2] and in the upper interface of a called component.[3]

[1]This asymmetry can be dropped if interface polarization is not assumed.

[2]Note: program components have no upper interface and coprogram components have no lower interface.

[3]If the upper interface of a component is empty, the component is said to lack an upper interface. The symmetric convention holds for lower interfaces.

7.1.3 Service interfaces and co-service interfaces

Service interfaces and co-service interfaces have been introduced above. Formally each subset of the upper interface of a component is a service interface for it and each subset of the lower interface of a component is a co-service interface for it. A more sophisticated definition of the concept of a component will allow one to take a family of service and co-service interfaces as a constituent of a componenent (rather than merely the unions of service interfaces and co-service interfaces respectively). Service versus co-cervice expresses a complementarity in the following sense: given an interface that offers instructions as an external service, the complementary co-interface is an interface along which another system component may call these services. Co-operation between components requires an appropriate match between service interfaces and co-service interfaces. Service interfaces are included in the upper interface of a component. Co-service interfaces are included in the lower interface of a component.

7.2 Interface roles

Both service interfaces and co-service interfaces can be connected with different purposes. We will present some important roles. Being a target interface is a possible role of a co-service interface. Similary being a co-target interface is a possible role of a service interface.

7.2.1 Target interfaces and co-target interfaces

A target interface of a system component is a co-service interface that is used to issue requests for external action. The processing of requests from a target interface will lead to the production of a boolean reply value, the main reason for the request being connected with other expected effects.

A co-target interface (often also called API, for Application Programmer Interface) is a service interface through which another component can enact services with external effects.

7.2.2 Reply service interfaces and reply co-service interfaces

A reply service interface is a service interface containing instructions that exclusively invoke state transitions within the component to prepare for the adequate delivery of boolean replies. Coprogram components have a reply service interface only.

A reply co-service interface is a co-service interface containing actions whose only role it is to ask for a reply or to update the state of the recipient of the instruction as a preparation for future actions from the reply co-service interface.

7.3 Interface notation

For a system component C, the union of all of its service interfaces is denoted by $\Sigma_u(C)$, and the union of all its coservice interfaces is written: $\Sigma_l(C)$. If there is at most one service interface, $\Sigma_u(C)$ is also called the service interface of the component C, and if there is at most one lower interface, $\Sigma_l(C)$ is also called the co-service interface of C.

7.3.1 *Pseudo co-service interfaces*

Programs as such do not have an interface, the difficulty being that it is not clear which superset of the collection of actions featuring in a program behavior should be considered the correct interface. The minimal collection Σ of atomic actions containing all actions that are present in the text of X is denoted with $\Sigma_l^{ps}(X)$, the collection being called a pseudo interface.

To see why $\Sigma_l^{ps}(X)$ is a pseudo interface rather than a proper one consider this example:

$$X = a(124); +b(358); \#\#67; -a(98); a(358).$$

Now $\Sigma_l^{ps}(X) = \{a(98), a(124), a(358), b(358)\}$ which is very implausible as an interface. A reasonable interface might be: $\{a(n), b(n) \mid 0 < n < 1000\}$. This leads to the introduction of the program component $< \{a(n) \mid n < 1000\}, X >$.

7.3.2 *Behavior pseudo co-service interfaces*

Just as it is reasonable to associate a pseudo co-service interface with a program, it is meaningful to associate a pseudo co-service interface with a program behavior. It simply contains all actions that the behavior performs. We omit the precise definions. For a behavior P we denote its pseudo co-interface with $\Sigma_l^{ps}(P)$. Let PGLZ denote an 'arbitrary' program notation, under the condition that a behavioral semantics in the style of program algebra does exist. If X is a PGLZ program with behavior $|X|_{pglz}$ then $\Sigma_l^{ps}(|X|_{pglz}) \subseteq \Sigma_l^{ps}(X)$. A strict inclusion may hold, e.g. consider the PGLA program $X = !; a$.

The interface condition for program components can be stated as follows: for $< \Sigma, X >$ to be a component (with X a PGLZ program) it is required that $\Sigma_l^{ps}(|X|_{pglz}) \subseteq \Sigma$.

7.4 *Comment: stratified objects*

Of course, unlike a program component or a coprogram component, a system component can have both non-empty upper and lower interfaces. If the two are disjoint the component is called a stratified object; if there is an overlap between the two interfaces, the component is called a recursive (or non-stratified) object.

In particular, if $\Sigma_u(C) \cap \Sigma_l(C) \neq \emptyset$, it makes sense to assume that instructions in $\Sigma_u(C) \cap \Sigma_l(C)$ are to be processed by the component proper, that interpretation constituting a form of recursion.

8 A coprogram library and coprogram calculus

In this section a small collection (library) of important coprograms is presented as well as the operator set of coprogram calculus.

8.1 *Four abstract data type coprograms*

The examples below are considered fundamental because they are useful in a number of circumstances. The examples and their names may be considered the initial segment of a library of useful coprograms. Coprograms carrying names starting with cp have a public status. The specifications are informal, but can of course be formalized in much more detail.

Boolean register: `cpbr`. The service interface of `cpbr` consists of:
{`cpbr.setc(true)`, `cpbr.setc(false)`,
`cpbr.eqc(true)`, `cpbr.eqc(false)`}.
The reply function will reply `false` to the test instructions
`cpbr.eqc(true)` and `cpbr.eqc(false)`
until the first `cpbr.setc(true)` instruction is called. Thereafter the state of the register starts initialized with `true`. At each request of the form `cpbr.setc(true)` or `cpbr.setc(false)` the reply function replies `true`. This is an arbitrary default reply for an action that only serves to update the register. The state of the coprogram is flipped whenever it receives a set instruction to the opposite truth value. The test instructions do not change the state but will return a reply `true` whenever the test instruction mentions the current value of the register.

NN register: `cpnr`. The NN register can contain arbitrary natural numbers: its service interface is:
{`cpnr.setc(i)`, `cpnr.eqc(i)` | `i` ∈ NN}. The reply function is self-evident. It generalizes the reply function of `cpbr` to NN instead of {`true,false`}.

NN counter: `cpnc` The NN counter `cpnc` has the following service interface:
{`cpnc.succ(),cpnc.pred(),cpnc.isZero()`}. Again the reply function is clear from the mnemonics of the interface actions, as is the convention to reply `true` as a default, on the assumption that the counter is initialized in the empty condition. In particular it is assumed that, having become zero, the action `cpnc.pred()` leaves its argument at zero.

NN stack: `cpns` The NN stack `cpns` has the following instruction set as its service interface: {`cpns.pushc(i),cpns.pop(),cpns.topEqc(i)` | `i` ∈ NN}. The reply function is clear from the mnemonics of the interface actions, as is the convention to reply `true` as a default, on the assumption that the stack is initialized in the empty condition.

8.2 Coprogram calculus

Five operators and a constant for coprograms are useful in many cases: service interface (Σ_s), non-interfering combination ($H_1 \oplus H_2$), name refinement ($\texttt{f}.H$), restriction ($\Sigma \triangle H$), export ($\Sigma \square H$), which is complementary to restriction, and the empty coprogram ($\emptyset$). The discussion of restriction and export is postponed to the following section.

8.2.1 Service interface operator

If the coprogram H consists of the pair $< \Sigma, F >$ then $\Sigma_s(H) = \Sigma$. The service interface of a coprogram is an upper interface, because the coprogram will not take the initiative in carrying out an instruction from the interface, but will leave that to other parties. Furthermore, it is a reply service interface, the calling party only having an interest in the returned boolean values.

8.2.2 Name refinement

Name refinement ($\texttt{f}.H$) prefixes all names of a coprogram (H) with `f.` for some name `f`. As an example consider the boolean register (`br`) from paragraph 8.1. If several copies of this coprogram are needed one may use:

`f1.cpbr,f2.cpbr,f3.cpbr.`

The interface actions of `f1.cpbr` are

{`f1.cpbr.setc(true)`,`f1.cpbr.setc(false)`,...,

`f3.cpbr.setc(true)`,`f3.cpbr.setc(false)`}.

8.2.3 Non-interfering combination

The non-interfering combination operator takes two coprogram arguments, say H_1 and H_2. The upper interface consists of those actions occurring in only one of the two service interfaces:

$$\Sigma_u(H_1 \oplus H_2) = (\Sigma_u(H_1) \cup \Sigma_u(H_2)) - (\Sigma_u(H_1) \cap \Sigma_u(H_2)).$$

Let F_i be the reply function for H_i. The reply function F for $H_1 \oplus H_2$ inspects the last instruction of its argument list. If that instruction is from H_i all instructions of H_{3-i} (i.e. in $\Sigma_u(H_{3-i})$ are removed and the reply is computed by means of an application of F_i to the remaining list.

8.2.4 Empty coprogram

The empty coprogram is denoted with $\emptyset$. This is the unique coprogram H with $\Sigma_u(X) = \emptyset$, playing but a formal role in the calculus of coprograms.

8.2.5 Calculation rules

Several identities concerning non-interfering combination are valid:

$$H \oplus \emptyset = H, H \oplus H = \emptyset$$

$$H_1 \oplus H_2 = H_2 \oplus H_1$$
$$\texttt{f}.(H_1 \oplus H_2) = (\texttt{f}.H_1) \oplus (\texttt{f}.H_2)$$
$$(H_1 \oplus H_2) \oplus H_3 = H_1 \oplus (H_2 \oplus H_3) \texttt{ if } \Sigma_u(H_1) \cap \Sigma_u(H_2) \cap \Sigma_u(H_3) = \emptyset$$

8.2.6 Comment

The non-interfering combination provides a disjoint combination of the facilities of the two coprograms, provided their service interfaces are disjoint. If the service interfaces overlap an ambiguity must be avoided and for that reason actions in the overlap are not offered by the non-interfering combination. The facilities of several copies of the same coprogram can be combined after preparatory name refinement, for instance:

$$\texttt{f1.cpbr} \oplus \texttt{f2.cpbr} \oplus \texttt{f3.cpbr}.$$

8.3 Restriction and export for coprogram calculus

The restriction $(\Sigma \triangle H)$ of coprogram H is obtained by removing all interface actions in Σ from the interface of H and by dropping all input streams featuring an action in Σ. The export operator does the converse: it drops all interface actions outside Σ. For restriction and export there are several universally valid identities.

8.3.1 Distribution identities

$$\Sigma \triangle (H_1 \oplus H_2) = (\Sigma \triangle H_2) \oplus (\Sigma \triangle H_1)$$

$$\Sigma \square (H_1 \oplus H_2) = (\Sigma \square H_2) \oplus (\Sigma \square H_1)$$

8.3.2 Special cases

$$\Sigma_u(H) \square H = H, \quad \emptyset \triangle H = H, \quad \emptyset \square H = \emptyset$$

$$\Sigma_u(H_1) \square (H_1 \oplus H_2) = H_1 \ \texttt{if} \ \Sigma_u(H_1) \cap \Sigma_u(H_2) = \emptyset$$

8.3.3 Interaction with the service interface operator

$$\Sigma_u(\Sigma \triangle H) = \Sigma_u(H) - \Sigma, \quad \Sigma_u(\Sigma \square H) = \Sigma \cap \Sigma_u(H)$$

$$\Sigma \triangle H = (\Sigma_u(H) - \Sigma) \square H$$

$$\Sigma \square H = (\Sigma_u(H) - \Sigma) \triangle H$$

9 Interfacing programs and coprograms

Program components have a co-service interface and coprograms have a service interface. Whenever there is a non-empty overlap between the co-service interface of a program component and the service interface of a coprogram, the two components can be interfaced.

The subject of interfacing being open-ended in nature, our discussion focusses on two especially important cases. Let X^i be a program component (with program X and lower interface $\Sigma_l(X^i)$) and let H be some coprogram.

- Use. If $\Sigma_l(X^i) \not\subseteq \Sigma_u(H)$, we may regard $\Sigma_l(X^i) - \Sigma_u(H)$ as a target interface for X^i, $\Sigma_l(X^i) \cap \Sigma_u(H)$ as a reply co-service interface for X^i and also as a reply service interface for H.

  The task of H is to support X^i in its operation, which will express its value by calling actions through the target interface $\Sigma_l(X^i) - \Sigma_u(H)$. Upon termination of the execution of X, H is forgotten and so is the state it is in.

- Apply. If $\Sigma_l(X^i) \subseteq \Sigma_u(H)$, we may regard $\Sigma_l(X^i)$ as a target interface for X^i. At the same time $\Sigma_l(X^i)$ plays the role of a co-target interface of H.

  Upon termination of the execution of X, the result of the computation materializes in the state of H. The task of X is to transform the state of H.

Both cases 'use' and 'apply' will be captured by means of a special purpose operator. In the case of 'use', the special operator produces the behavior of the program alongside its co-target interface. In the case of 'apply', the special operator determines the state in which the program leaves the coprogram after termination.

9.1 The use-operator and the apply-operator

The use-operator combines a program behavior P and a coprogram H producing a behavior, written P/H. Use refers to the fact that the program issues instructions to the coprogram only for the sake of getting replies returned.

The apply-operator connects a program behavior and a coprogram in an alternative fashion (and under different conditions). It requires $\Sigma_l^{ps}(P) \subseteq \Sigma_l(H)$. The apply-operator is written $P \bullet H$, for a behavior P and a coprogram H. The apply-operator yields a coprogram (or in case of divergence or error D and M respectively).

Both the use-operator and the apply-operator are extended to take progams rather than behaviors as their first arguments. We will only use that extension in combination with the behavioral abstraction operator $|-|$. A subscript will then indicate the program notation of the program and the notation works as follows:

$$|X/H|_L = |X|_L/H$$

$$X \bullet_L H = |X|_L \bullet H.$$

The difference between the use-operator and the apply-operator is a matter of perspective: the use-operator considers the coprogram a transformer of behaviors (or programs) and determines another behavior, whereas the apply-operator considers the program a transformer of coprograms and therefore produces a coprogram (unless some error occurs). In the perspective of the apply-operator the coprogram is input and the modifications that are applied to it during a computation are the essence. The use-operator simply drops the coprogram after program termination. Use-operators are meaningful only for programs using basic actions that are not contained in the co-service interface of the component.

9.2 Repeated use and apply

It is reasonable to repeatedly use the use-operator. If $\Sigma_u(H_1) \cap \Sigma_u(H_2) = \emptyset$, one may write:

$$(X/H_1)/H_2 = X/(H_1 \oplus H_2).$$

Similarly a repreated application of the apply-operator is possible. Under strict conditions demanding that ';' represents sequential composition between X_1 and X_2, the following is valid:

$$X_1 \bullet (X_2 \bullet H) = (X_2; X_1) \bullet H.$$

9.3 Semantic equations for use and apply

Behaviors suitable for the semantics of program algebra expressions have been discussed earlier. Recall that M denotes the behavior shown by a program in error. This will be caused by the evaluation of an abort instruction. D is the behavior of a non-terminating or divergent program. A diverging program may not even perform tests while diverging.

The most typical source of divergence is a cyclic succession of jump or goto instructions. $||!||$ is the irreducible behavior of the successful termination instruction, $||a||$ denotes the primitive behavior describing the execution of a single atomic action, and $Y(a)$ is a predicate (or condition) predicting whether the boolean-returning action a will return `true` or `false`. Further $P \cdot Q$ represents the sequential composition of behaviors P and Q. Conditions are used to combine behaviors as follows: if P and Q are behaviors, and if a is a boolean-returning atomic instruction, $P \triangleleft Y(a) \triangleright Q$ behaves like P if $Y(a)$ holds true and like Q if it does not. Program behaviors will always end (if at all) with M, D or $||!||$.

9.3.1 Coprogram effect notation

Let P be a program behavior and let H be a coprogram. We wish to define P/H as the behavior of P using H. The actions in the lower interface of P that are also in the upper interface of H will be processed by H. An auxiliary notation has to be introduced beforehand. For a coprogram $H =< \Sigma, F >$ and an action a in its upper interface the coprogram $H_{\partial a}$ is defined by

$$H_{\partial a} =< \Sigma, F' >$$

with $F'(w) = F(a, w)$ for all interface action sequences w.

9.3.2 Semantic equations for the use-operator

The defining rules for P/H are these:

$$||!||\,/H = ||!||$$
$$M\,/H = M,\ \ D\,/H = D$$
$$(||a||\ \cdot P)/H = ||a|| \cdot (P/H) \texttt{ if } a \notin \Sigma_u(H)$$
$$(||a||\ \cdot P)/H = (P/H_{\partial a}) \texttt{ if } a \in \Sigma_u(H)$$
$$(P \triangleleft Y(a)) \triangleright Q)/H = (P/H) \triangleleft Y(a) \triangleright (Q/H) \texttt{ if } a \notin \Sigma_u(H)$$
$$(P \triangleleft Y(a) \triangleright Q)/H = (P/H) \triangleleft F(a) \triangleright (Q/H) \texttt{ if } a \in \Sigma_u(H).$$

These equations determine a behavior by means of a step-wise processing of the actions of the program. Only the actions and tests outside $\Sigma_u(H)$ will contribute to the resulting behavior. If such an action cannot be found, this may be due to non-termination. Non-termination is then expressed by means of the equation: $P/H = D$.

9.3.3 Equations for the apply-operator

D and M are considered coprograms as well. If the reply function yields D or M this is represented by the resulting coprogram being identified with D or M respectively. (D and M have all possible actions in their upper interface and always return D resp. M.)

$$||!|| \bullet H = H$$
$$M \bullet H = M,\ \ D \bullet H = D$$
$$(||a||\ \cdot P) \bullet D = D,\ \ (||a||\ \cdot P) \bullet M = M$$
$$(||a|| \cdot P) \bullet H = (P/H_{\partial a}) \texttt{ provided } H \neq D \text{ and } H \neq M$$
$$(P \triangleleft Y(a) \triangleright Q) \bullet H = (P \bullet H) \triangleleft F(a) \triangleright (Q \bullet H)$$

If application of these rules fails to lead to a converging computation, the computation of P on H is said to diverge, which is written as $P \bullet H = D$.

9.4 *How use is used and how apply is applied*

The use-operator can play an key role in projection semantics. In some cases a projection for a program notation can only be found at the cost of the introduction of an auxiliary coprogram which the projected program may use.

The apply-operator plays a key role in the description of batch processing. In the formalization of batch processing both inputs and outputs of programs are packed in a coprogram. A batch program is seen as a coprogram transformer, semantically captured by the apply-operator.

9.5 *Concluding remarks on coprograms*

The symmetry and complementarity of programs and coprograms is based upon the adoption of polarized interfaces. Polarized interfaces are to program algebra what arbitrary interleaving is to process algebra, a hypothesis which is speculative and productive at the same time.

Just as ACP-style process algebra can be understood as a project designed to exploit the arbitrary interleaving hypothesis, program algebra may be regarded as a theory committed to the exploitation of the conceptual limits of the interface polarization hypothesis.

If the interface polarization hypothesis is refuted, programs and coprograms can be regarded as instances of the same category: processes.

10 Projection semantics for recursion

The present objective is to design primitives for recursion on the basis of PGLDg and to provide a projection semantics for this extension of PGLDg.

10.1 *Extensions of PGLDg*

PGLDgr is an extension of PGLDg with two primitives capturing the essence of recursion. PGLDgμ will be needed as an intermediate stage for the projection semantics of PGLDgr. It being the simplest of the two by far, its details are presented first. Subsequently PGLDgr is introduced.

10.2 *Advanced control instructions*

Some general properties of PGLDg extensions should be discussed in order to motivate certain design decisions for the new primitives.

10.2.1 *PGLY$_\Sigma$, instruction sequences with basic actions*

PGLY will stand for any extension of PGLDg. Its programs consist of finite sequences of instructions. These instructions can be a, $+a$, $-a$, with a taken from the basic action parameter Σ of the language. However, they can also be PGLDg control instructions (in particular: $\#$, $\pounds k$, $\#\#\pounds k$), instructions specific to PGLY, or instructions in specified coprogram service interfaces. The instructions specific to PGLY are called advanced control instructions, control because they are not basic actions or tests, advanced because they are not in PGLDg. For each parameter set Σ there is an instance PGLY$_\Sigma$

of the language PGLY. All extensions of PGLDg involve additional instructions. Each instruction which is not in the parameter set Σ of atomic actions and not in the syntax of PGLDg is called an advanced control instruction. We will assume that basic actions from Σ are always different from the advanced control instructions.

10.3 Coprogram control instructions

Often it is important to permit a language to make use of the actions in the service interface $\Sigma_u(H)$ of some coprogram H. Although such actions are best regarded as part of the parameter set Σ, bookkeeping concerns suggest having them outside Σ in their own class of basic actions: coprogram control actions. These actions together constitute a reply co-service interface in the terminology of section 7.2.2. We will use some coprograms below (the stack and the thread vector), collecting all of their interface actions in $\Sigma_{l_{max}}$. Parameter sets Σ are kept disjoint from $\Sigma_{l_{max}}$.

10.4 Coprogram based language extensions

For a program notation PGLY and a coprogram CPZ, the program notation PGLY/CPZ allows PGLY programs to contain instructions from the service interface of CPZ (denoted with cpz inside formulas.) Under the assumption that coprogram service interface instructions are outside Σ, PGLY/CPZ$_\Sigma$ denotes all programs of this extension of PGLY containing basic instructions from Σ. The behavior of PGLY/CPZ program X is derived from its behavior as a PGLY program as follows:

$$|X|_{pgly/cpz} = (|X|_{pgly})/\texttt{cpz}$$

Here P/H is the use-operator of 9.1, instantiated with $P = |X_{pgly}|$ and $H = \texttt{cpz}$. It follows that if the behavior of PGLY programs is known, then the behavior of PGLY/CPZ programs is known as well. We will make use of this observation for PGLX = PGLDg and for CPZ = cpns, the coprogram containing a natural number stack.

10.5 Two stage projection semantics

We will outline in abstract terms how the projection semantics of PGLDgr is organized before giving any further details of the notation PGLDgr. In this way the method of projection semantics is illustrated most clearly. Assume that a reasonably clear intuitive account for the meaning of a language PGLY (for which we will take PGLDgr below) has been provided along with the description of its syntax (in particular its advanced control instructions). Projection semantics is given by means of the construction of:

- a coprogram cpz (in the case of recursion: cpns), and
- a transformation pgly2pgldg/cpz (called a projection), transforming arbitrary PGLY$_\Sigma$ programs to PGLDg$_\Sigma$ programs making use of actions from the interface of cpz.

in such a way that the following identity can be considered an adequate formal definition of the behavior of a PGLY program X:

$$|X|_{pgly} = |\texttt{pgly2pgldg/cpz}(X)|_{pgldg/cpz}$$

$$(= (|\texttt{pgly2pgldg/cpz}(X)|_{pgldg})/\texttt{cpz})$$

10.5.1 Using an intermediate program notation

The description of a projection from PGLY to PGLDg being hard to write down directly, we will make use of an extension PGLDgμ of PGLDg and its projection `pgldgmu2pgldg`. Given this projection, the task of finding a projection `pgly2pgldg/cpz` is reduced to the task of finding a projection `pgly2pgldgmu/cpz` such that

$$|X|_{pgly} = |\mathtt{pgly2pgldgmu/cpz}(X)|_{pgldgmu/cpz}$$

The projection `pgldgmu2pgldg` then provides a semantics for `pgldgmu/cpz` programs Y in the following way:

$$|Y|_{pgldgmu/cpz} = (|\mathtt{pgldgmu2pgldg}(Y)|_{pgldg})/\mathtt{cpz}$$

Of course, the more expressive the language one uses as a target of the projection, the easier it becomes to define it.

10.6 A design rule

The general design rule is to avoid test actions being immediately followed by advanced control instructions. The rationale for this restriction, imposed on all language extensions PGLX of PGLDg, is to avoid confusion when a transformation expands the advanced control instruction to a sequence of instructions, the confusion being about where to resume computation after a negative outcome of the test.

10.7 Two extensions of PGLDg

We will now discuss the syntax of two extensions of PGLDg, beginning with the extension with the goto/search instruction. This advanced control instruction initiates a search, leading to the identification of a natural number which then can be used as the target label of a goto instruction.

10.7.1 A notation with dynamic goto's: PGLDgμ

For technical reasons a simple extension of PGLDg is very useful. This extension introduces a single new advanced control instruction,on the assumption that a certain family of instructions may be used. The construction is called 'goto/search instruction', appearing in two forms: positive and negative. Let $\varphi(j)$ be a test instruction dependent on a natural number j. Then $+\varphi(0), -\varphi(0), +\varphi(1), -\varphi(1), +\varphi(2), -\varphi(2), \ldots$ are test instructions. The positive and negative goto/search instructions for $\varphi(j)$ are:

- $\#\#\pounds[\mu j. + \varphi(j)]$
- $\#\#\pounds[\mu j. - \varphi(j)]$

The language PGLDgμ permits the use of positive and negative goto/search instructions, in addition to the instructions of PGLDg.

10.7.2 Projection semantics for PGLDgμ

Of course, intermediate language PGLDgμ needs a projection semantics. The translation of programs works statement by statement. Only the (new) advanced control instructions are modified: in particular, if k is the numerical value of the largest label occurring in a program to be translated, the transformation of the positive goto/search instruction is as follows: **pgldgmu2pgldg**$(\#\#\pounds[\mu j. + \varphi(j)]) =$

$$+\varphi(0); \#\#\pounds 0; +\varphi(1); \#\#\pounds 1; \cdots; +\varphi(k); \#\#\pounds k.$$

In words: decide whether $\varphi(0)$ holds; if so, goto $\pounds 0$, if not, consider $\varphi(1)$, etc. For the negative case we find: **pgldgmu2pgldg**$(\#\#\pounds[\mu j. - \varphi(j)]) =$

$$-\varphi(0); \#\#\pounds 0; -\varphi(1); \#\#\pounds 1; \cdots; -\varphi(k); \#\#\pounds k.$$

The projection **pgldgmu2pgldg** translates goto/search instructions in a context-depending way. The more different label catches a program contains, the more tests the translated goto/search instruction will have to perform. If needed, different translations of goto search can be mapped onto a single occurrence of the sequence, thus ensuring better code compactness after projection. For this reason the trailing # has been added. Failing that abort instruction, code sharing cannot always be achieved. If processing speed matters and additional coprograms can be used, a binary search can replace the linear search, thus making the program larger in size but faster at work.

The general nature of the projection **pgldgmu2pgldg** implies that it will work in the presence of arbitrary coprograms. It induces a projection

`pgldgmu/cpns2pgldg/cpns`, and **pgldgmu/cptv2pgldg/cptv**.

10.8 Primitives for recursion: PGLDgr

The introduction of recursion on top of PGLDg can be achieved by introducing two new instructions: the returning goto instruction and the return instruction. The syntax proposed for these instructions is as follows:

- $\rho\#\#\pounds k$
- ρ

The returning goto instruction '$\rho\#\#\pounds k$' implies a goto together with the command to jump to the instruction immediately following itself whenever a return instruction is reached in the computation following $\pounds k$. The return instruction 'ρ' must be executed by jumping back to the the control point just after the last returning goto instruction to which a return has not yet taken place.

Of course, PGLDgr allows the instructions of PGLDg (including some actions from a collection A of atomic instructions) and the two instructions '$\rho\#\#\pounds k$' and 'ρ'. The latter instructions are considered advanced control instructions.

A better explanation can be found by using a stack. There is a stack of control points (labels or instruction numbers). A returning goto instruction first puts the control point just following it on the stack and then issues a goto. A return instruction performs a look-up on the stack and finds the return label on top of the stack, then it issues a goto towards this return label. After that goto has been performed the stack is popped.

10.8.1 Projection semantics for recursion primitives

We will translate PGLDgr into PGLDg, with the help of the coprogram NN stack (**cpns**) from 8. The projection is named **pgldgr2pgldgmu/cpns** and its definition is given by $\texttt{pgldgr2pgldgmu/cpns}(u_1; ...; u_n) = \psi_1(u_1); ...; \psi_n(u_n)$, where the auxiliary functions ψ_i read as follows:

$$\psi_i(\#\#\pounds l) = \#\#\pounds 2 \cdot l$$

$$\psi_i(\pounds l) = \pounds 2 \cdot l$$

$$\psi_i(\rho\#\#\pounds k) = \texttt{cpns.pushc}(2 \cdot k + 1); \#\#\pounds 2 \cdot k; \pounds 2 \cdot k + 1; \texttt{cpns.pop()}$$

$$\psi_i(\rho) = \#\#\pounds[\mu j. + \texttt{cpns.topEqc}(j)]$$

$$\psi_i(u) = u \ \texttt{otherwise}$$

The first and second equation ensure that all labels occurring in the source program are renamed so that no confusion with new labels will arise. This renaming is achieved by doubling the numerical value of the label. Odd labels will be new ones, introduced by the translation. The semantics of a PGLDgr program X is thus determined by:

$$|X|_{pgldgr} = |\texttt{pgldgr2pgldgmu/cpns}(X)|_{pgldgmu/cpns}.$$

11 Concluding remarks

The novelty of the paper lies in the precise analysis of the interaction between programs and coprograms and in the use of coprograms for the purpose of projection semantics. Further it extends the language hierarchy of program algebra with several notations interesting in their own right. Many further extensions can be conceived of, some of which have been worked out in detail. In particular a projection semantics for multi-threaded programs and for mobile programs has been developed in a satisfactory way. It is still an open question, however, which coprograms are needed to provide a projection semantics for a substantial part of object-oriented programming.

References

[1] J. Bergin, M. Stehlik, J. Roberts, and R. Pattis. *Karel++, a gentle introduction to the art of object-oriented programming.* John Wiley and Sons, 1997.

[2] J.A. Bergstra. Datatypen bezien vanuit de recursietheorie. In J.C. van Vliet, editor, *Colloquium Capita Datastructuren*, pages 157–170. Mathematisch Centrum, Amsterdam, 1978.

[3] J.A. Bergstra. What is an abstract data type? *Information Processing Letters*, 7(1):42–43, 1978.

[4] J.A. Bergstra and M.E. Loots. Program algebra for component code. Technical Report P9811, Programming Research Group, University of Amsterdam, 1998.

[5] J.A. Bergstra, C.A. Middelburg, and Gh. Ştefănescu. Network algebra for asynchronous dataflow. *International Journal of Computer Mathematics*, 65:57–88, 1997.

[6] J.A. Bergstra and A. Ponse. Process algebra with five-valued conditions. In C.S. Calude and M.J. Dinneen, editors, *Combinatorics, Complexity, and Logic, Proceedings of DMTCS'99 and CATS'99, Australian Computer Science Communcations*, volume 21, pages 128–143. Springer-Verlag, Singapore, 1999.

[7] J.A. Bergstra and S.F.M. van Vlijmen. *Theoretische Software-Engineering.* ZENO-Institute, Leiden, Utrecht, The Netherlands, 1998. In Dutch.

[8] V.E. Căzănescu and Gh. Ştefănescu. A formal representation of flowchart schemes I. *Analele Universităţii Bucuresti, Matematică - Informatică*, 37:33–51, 1988.

[9] V.E. Căzănescu and Gh. Ştefănescu. A formal representation of flowchart schemes II. *Studii si Cercetări Metematice*, 41:151–167, 1989.

[10] Gh. Ştefănescu. Algebra of flownomials. Part 1: Binary flownomials, basic theory. Technical Report I9437, Department of Computer Science, Technical University Munich, October 1994.

Part 1
Specification and Verification

R. L. Constable

J. Hickey

T. Nipkow

1. Operators for NCKC

- **Jumps**

: $\mathcal{L} \to \mathcal{L}$, atomic

(seqential) composition:  ∘  ≡  is associative

in-place jumps:  is identity

Caveat: jumps not transitive (see Hauptsatz),

i.e.  ⇏ 

- **Parallel Composition**

_ || _: $(\mathcal{L} \to \mathcal{L}) \to (\mathcal{L} \to \mathcal{L}) \to (\mathcal{L} \to \mathcal{L})$

 ||  [same direction, synchronized, e.g. holding hands]

shorthand: 

|| is not commutative, but assiciative,

even constructive: rather primitive recursive

cf. hyper-critical generous theorem spoofing system *Annabelle* (I ❤ *A*)

- **Kill Operator**

 : K → Void

Specification:  (K) =  (no jumps)

Implementation: exercise [hint: fast car]

Foundations of Secure Computation
F.L. Bauer and R. Steinbrüggen (Eds.)
IOS Press, 2000

Nuprl's Class Theory and its Applications

Robert L. Constable — *Cornell University*
Jason Hickey — *Caltech*

Abstract

This article presents a theory of classes and inheritance built on top of constructive type theory. Classes are defined using dependent and very dependent function types that are found in the Nuprl constructive type theory. Inheritance is defined in terms of a general subtyping relation over the underlying types. Among the basic types is the intersection type which plays a critical role in the applications because it provides a method of composing program components.

The class theory is applied to defining algebraic structures such as monoids, groups, rings, etc. and relating them. It is also used to define communications protocols as infinite state automata. The article illustrates the role of these formal automata in defining the services of a distributed group communications system. In both applications the inheritance mechanisms allow reuse of proofs and the statement of general properties of system composition.

1 Introduction

The results presented here were created as part of a broad effort to understand how to use computers to significantly automate the design and development of software systems. This is one of the main goals of the "PRL project" at Cornell[1]. One of the basic tenants of our approach to this task is that we should seek the most naturally expressive formal language in which to specify the services, characteristics and constraints that a software system must satisfy.

If the formal expression of services is close to a natural one, then people can more readily use it. We also want to allow very compact notations for concepts used to describe systems, and this effect is also a consequence of expressive richness. We have discovered that it is frequently the case that the system we have built to implement one formal language will support an even richer one. So we have come to see our work as also progressively improving the reach of our tools.

Achieving a rich formalism is an on-going task because we are quite far from understanding the full variety of mechanisms and concepts that are used by systems designers, and we discover new concepts in the context of any formalism built to capture what we have understood well enough to formalize. This paper reports on new results in this on going process. To understand our new ideas requires explaining the starting point; we do that in the section on types.

The new ideas are based on a definition of records and dependent records that we started exploring several years ago [11, 17, 22] and is related to recent work in Martin-Löf type theory [5]. This is the subject of section 3, Classes. Class theory provides the basis for formalizing object-oriented concepts such as classes and inheritance. The way we present these notions connects in an unexpected way to the basic ideas behind Girard's new logic, Ludics [19].

The most widely accessible applications of these ideas is to the basic structures and containment among them of algebra, e.g. relating monoids, groups, rings, algebras and so forth. Indeed for us, several of the ideas arose in the investigation of symbolic algebra in Nuprl. The first public discussion of these ideas came in the first author's lectures about this work to the symbolic algebra community (1997). We will see an especially elegant presentation of the algebraic concepts that is made possible by providing a uniform treatment of naming of the fields in a structure. This idea

[1] The scope of this project is defined at it's Cornell web site www.cs.cornell.edu/Info/Projects/NuPrl/nuprl.html. This work was supported by DARPA under grant F30602-98-2-0198.

arose in the context of formalizing a software system [6], and we describe the system applications in section 5, Applications to systems.

The concepts of record and subtyping allow us to express the basic ideas of object-oriented programming. What we observe is that although it has been difficult to provide a clean mathematical foundation for all aspects of object-oriented programming (see the attempts by Cardelli [8, 20, 21]), nevertheless we can account elegantly for the concepts of *class* and *method.*

2 Types

2.1 The Core Theory

Type theory is one of the most successful foundational theories for computer science [11, 10, 9]. It is a mathematical theory which has provided solutions to a large number of the practical problems. It is an excellent basis for the semantics of functional and procedural programming languages. [2] It provides guidlines for the design of such languages, as work on ML illustrates. Type theory also guides the compilation of languages such as ML, Haskell, and Java. It provides the basis for programming logics and program verification [14, 3, 36, 15]. These solutions are not "perfect", and there is more work to be done as better programming languages are designed.

One reason for the constant evolution of programming languages is that there is a fundamental compromise between expressiveness and compilation technology. As we come to understand compilation of rich languages such as ML, we learn to handle more features efficiently, so languages can be enriched. There is an unexpected contribution to this process from type theory. Namely, these theories define an internal programming language. In the case of Nuprl this language is very much like ML with a much richer type system. So Nuprl is an "idealized programming language" in the sense that if we could efficiently compile it, we would have achieved a local maximum in language technology. So we can judge the practical languages such as ML, Java, Modula and Haskell in terms of how few idosyncratic, compilation dictated restrictions there are in the language definition. The fewer there are, the closer the language approximates one of the ideal languages. This gives designers a target and a rough metric of success.

2.2 Primitive Types

void is a type with no elements
unit is a type with one element, denoted $\bullet$

There will be other primitive types introduced later. Notice, in set theory we usually have only two primitive sets, ϕ, the empty set, and some infinite set (usually ω).

Compound Types We build new types using *type constructors.* These tell us how to construct various kinds of objects. (In pure set theory, there is only one kind, *sets*).

The type constructors we choose are motivated both by mathematical and computational considerations. So we will see a tight relationship to the notion of *type* in programming languages. The notes by C.A.R. Hoare, *Notes on Data Structuring*, make the point well [23].

2.3 Cartesian products

If A and B are types, then so is their Cartesian product, written $A \times B$. There will be many *formation rules* like this, telling us how to construct new types from existing ones; so we adopt a simple convention for stating them in the style of inference rules. We write

$$\frac{A \text{ is a } Type \quad B \text{ is a } Type}{A \times B \ \text{ is a } Type.}$$

[2] The type theory we have in mind is one rich enough to include the theory of *domains* which accounts for partial objects, such as partial functions.

The elements of a product type are pairs, $\langle a, b\rangle$. Specifically if a belongs to A and b belongs to B, then $\langle a, b\rangle$ belongs to $A \times B$. We abbreviate this by writing rules for type membership as inference rules.

$$\frac{a \in A \quad b \in B}{\langle a, b\rangle \in A \times B.}$$

We say that

$$\langle a, b\rangle = \langle c, d\rangle \text{ in } A \times B \text{ iff } a = c \text{ in } A \text{ and } b = d \text{ in } B.$$

There is essentially only one way to decompose pairs. We say things like, "take the first element of the pair P," symbolically we might say $first(P)$ or $1of(P)$. We can also "take the second element of P," $second(P)$ or $2of(P)$.

In programming languages these types are generalized to n-ary products, say $A_1 \times A_2 \times \ldots \times A_n$.

In set theory, equality is uniform and built-in, but in type theory we define equality with each constructor, either built-in (as in Nuprl) or by definition as in this core theory.

Function Space

We use the words "function space" as well as "function type" for historical reasons. If A and B are types, then $A \to B$ is the type of *computable functions* from A to B. These are given by rules which are defined on each a in A and which produce a *unique value*. We summarize by

$$\frac{A \text{ is a } Type \quad B \text{ is a } Type}{A \to B \text{ is a } Type.}$$

One common informal notation for functions is seen in algebra texts, e.g. Bourbaki's *Algebra* [7]; namely, we write expressions like $x \mapsto b$ or $x \overset{f}{\mapsto} b$; the latter gives a name to the function. For example, $x \mapsto x^2$ is the squaring function on numbers.

If b computes to an element of B when x has value a in A for each a, then we say $(x \mapsto b) \in A \to B$. Formally we will use lambda notation, $\lambda(x.b)$ for $x \mapsto b$. The natural rule for typing a function $\lambda(x.b)$ is to say that $\lambda(x.b) \in A \to B$ provided that when x is of type A, b is of type B. We can express these *typing judgments* in the form $x : A \vdash b \in B$. The typing rule is then

$$\frac{x : A \vdash b \in B}{\vdash \lambda(x.b) \in A \to B.}$$

If f, g are functions, we define their equality as

$$f = g \quad \text{iff } f(x) = g(x) \quad \text{for all} \quad x \text{ in } A.$$

If f is a function from A to B and $a \in A$, we write $f(a)$ for the value of the function.

2.4 Disjoint Unions (also called Discriminated Unions)

Forming the union of two sets, say $x \cup y$, is a basic operation in set theory. It is basic in type theory as well, *but* for computational purposes, we also want to discriminate based on which type an element is in. To accomplish this we put tags on the elements to keep them disjoint and define the concept of a *disjoint* union. Later we define a more general union. Here we use *inl* and *inr* as the tags.

$$\frac{A \text{ is a } Type \quad B \text{ is a } Type}{A+B \text{ is a } Type.}$$

The membership rules are

$$\frac{a \in A}{inl(a) \in A+B} \qquad \frac{b \in B}{inr(b) \in A+B.}$$

We say that $inl(a) = inl(a')$ iff $a = a'$ and likewise for $inr(b)$.
We can now use a case statement to detect the tags and use expressions like

$$\begin{array}{lll} \text{if } x = inl(z) & \text{then} \ldots & \text{some expression in } z \ldots \\ \text{if } x = inr(z) & \text{then} \ldots & \text{some expression in } z \ldots \end{array}$$

in defining other objects. The test for $inl(z)$ or $inr(z)$ is computable. There is an operation called *decide* that discriminates on the type tags. The typing rule and syntax for it are given in terms of a typing judgment of the form $E \vdash t \in T$ where E is a list of declarations of the form $x_1 : A_1, \ldots, x_n : A_n$ called a *typing environment*. The A_i are types and x_i are variables declared to be of type A_i. The rule is

$$\frac{E \vdash d \in A+B \quad E, u : A \vdash t_1 \in T \quad E, v : B \vdash t_2 \in T}{E \vdash decide(d; u.t_1; v.t_2) \in T.}$$

2.5 Dependent Product

Suppose we wish to construct a type representing the date:

$$\begin{aligned} Month &= \{1, \ldots, 12\} \\ Day &= \{1, \ldots, 31\} \end{aligned}$$

$$Date = Month \times Day$$

We would need a way to check for valid dates. The pair, $\langle 2, 31 \rangle$ is a perfectly legal member of *Date*, although it is not a valid date. One thing we can do is to define

$$\begin{aligned} Day(1) &= \{1, \ldots, 31\} \\ Day(2) &= \{1, \ldots, 29\} \\ &\vdots \\ Day(12) &= \{1, \ldots, 31\} \end{aligned}$$

and now write our data type as a "dependent product"

$$Date = m : Month \times Day(m).$$

We mean by this that the second element of the pair belongs to the type indexed by the first element. Now, $\langle 2, 20 \rangle$ is a legal date since $20 \in Day(2)$, and $\langle 2, 31 \rangle$ is illegal because $31 \notin Day(2)$.

Many programming languages implement this or a similar concept in a limited way. An example is Pascal's *variant records*. While Pascal requires the indexing element to be of scalar type, we will allow it to be of any type.

We can see that what we are doing is making a more general type. It is very similar to $A \times B$. Let us call this type $prod(A; x.B)$. We can display this as $x : A \times B$. The typing rules are:

$$\frac{E \vdash a : A \quad E \vdash b \in B[a/x]}{E \vdash pair(a, b) : prod(A; x.B).}$$

$$\frac{E \vdash p : prod(A; x.B) \quad E, u : A, v : B[u/x] \vdash t \in T}{E \vdash spread(p; u, v.t) \in T.}$$

Note that we haven't added any elements. We've just added some new typing rules.

2.6 Dependent Functions

If we generalize the type $A \rightarrow B$ by allowing B to be a family of types indexed by A, then we get a new type, denoted by $fun(A; x.B)$, or $x : A \rightarrow B$. The rules are:

$$\frac{E, y : A \vdash b[y/x] \in B[y/x]}{E \vdash \lambda(x.b) \in fun(A; x.B)} \; new \; y$$

$$\frac{E \vdash f \in fun(A; x.B) \quad E \vdash a \in A}{E \vdash ap(f; a) \in B[a/x].}$$

Example 2 : Back to our example *Dates*, we see that $m : Month \rightarrow Day[m]$ is just $fun(Month; m.Day)$, where *Day* is a family of twelve types, and $\lambda(x.maxday[x])$ is a term in it.

2.7 Universes

A critical property of our type theory is that types are also objects. The collection of all types built from the atomic types by the operations we have defined form a type called a *universe.* A universe is an example of a "large type" — a type whose members include types. Following Martin-Löf [31] we consider a hierarchy of universes, $\mathbb{U}_1, \mathbb{U}_2, \ldots$ Each $\mathbb{U}_i$ belongs to all $\mathbb{U}_j$ with $j > i$, and the hierarchy is cumulative, i.e. $\mathbb{U}_i \sqsubseteq \mathbb{U}_{i+1}$.

We treat universe indexes ambiguously, writing U_i to denote any universe. We sometimes write *Type* when the universe level is not critical. Universes are discussed extensively by Allen [2] and Constable [11]. We use them later to define records and classes.

2.8 Propositions as types

One of the key distinguishing features of Martin-Löf type theory [30, 31, 32] and the Nuprl type theory [12, 10, 11] is that propositions are considered to be types, and a proposition is true iff it is inhabited. The inhabitants of a proposition are mathematical objects that provide evidence for the truth of the proposition.

This approach to propositions is related to the so-called *Curry-Howard isomorphism* [18, 24] between propositions and types. But the correspondance is elevated in our type theory to the status of a definition. The Curry-Howard isomorphism explains why the definition is sensible for Heyting's formalization of Browwer's constructive semantics for propositions. We briefly recall these semantics and state the Nuprl definitions for the logical operators. According to Browwer the logical operators have these constructive meanings:

$\bot$	is never true (read $\bot$ as "false").
$A \;\&\; B$	is true (provable) iff we can prove A and we can prove B.
$A \vee B$	is true iff either we can prove A or we can prove B, and we say which is proved.
$A \Rightarrow B$	is true iff we can effectively transform any proof of A into a proof of B.

$\neg A$	holds iff $A \Rightarrow \perp$.
$\exists x : A.B$	is true iff we can construct an element if type A, say a, and a proof of $B[a/x]$.
$\forall x : A.B$	is true iff we have an effective method to construct a proof of $B[a/x]$ for any a in A.

For an atomic proposition, P, with no logical substructure, we say it is true exactly when we have evidence, P, for it. The evidence can be taken to be atomic as well, e.g. unstructured. So we use the unit element, $\bullet$, as evidence.

We express Browwer's semantics by these definitions of the logical operators:

Definition	$A \ \& \ B$	$==$	$A \times B$
	$A \vee B$	$==$	$A + B$
	$A \Rightarrow B$	$==$	$A \rightarrow B$
	$\exists x : A.B$	$==$	$x : A \times B$
	$\forall x : A.B$	$==$	$x : A \rightarrow B$
	$\perp$	$==$	*void*
	$\top$	$==$	$\mathbf{1}$.

We can also define other logical operators that express shades of meaning not commonly expressed. For example, we will see later that intersection, $\cap x : A.B$, makes sense as a kind of universal quantifier.

We use $Prop_i$ as a synonym for $Type_i$. We also abbreviate $Prop$ as $\mathbb{P}$.

Classical Nuprl

Doug Howe [25, 26] has shown that Nuprl, as presented here, is consistent if we add the axioms $\forall P : Prop_i.(P \vee \neg P)$. He shows how to interpret types as sets and replace computable functions with set theoretic graphs. In Howe's semantics, the definitions given above for logical operators correspond to the usual classical logical operators.

2.9 Subset Types

According to the previous section, among the objects of mathematics we consider are *propositions.* For example, $0 =_N 0$ and $0 < 1$ are true propositions about the type N. We also consider *propositional forms* such as $x =_N y$ or $x < y$. These are sometimes called *predicates.*

The type of all (small) propositions is *Prop*. *Propositional functions* on a type A are elements of the type $A \rightarrow Prop$.

We also need types that can be restricted by predicates such as $\{x : N | x = 0 \text{ or } x = 1\}$. This type behaves like the *Booleans.*

The general formation rule for subset types is this. If A is a type and $B : A \rightarrow Prop$, then $\{x : A | B(x)\}$ is a *subtype* of A. The elements of $\{x : A | B(x)\}$ are those a in A for which $B(a)$ is true. Sometimes we state the formation in terms of predicates, so if P is a proposition for any x in A, then $\{x : A | P\}$ is a subtype of A.

2.10 Intersection types

Given two types A and B, it makes sense to consider the elements they have in common; we call that type the *intersection* of A and B, written $A \cap B$. We require that ($a = b$ in $A \cap B$) iff $a = b$ in A and $a = b$ in B. For example, it is clear that *void* $\cap$ A is *void* for any type A and $A \cap A$ is A.

It might be a suprise that $(1 \rightarrow 1) \cap (void \rightarrow void)$ is not *void* but contains the identity function, $\lambda(x.x)$. This is because the base objects of Nuprl are *untyped*, so $\lambda(x.x)$ is polymorphic, indeed belonging to all types $A \rightarrow A$. It is clear that $\{x : A | P(x)\} \cap \{x : A | Q(x)\}$ is $\{x : A | P(x) \ \& \ Q(x)\}$.

The intersection type is defined for a family of types as well. Let $B(x)$ be a family of types for $x \in A$, then $\cap \ x : A.B(x)$ is their intersection; and $b \in \cap \ x : A.B(x)$ iff $b \in B(a)$ for all $a \in A$. also

$b = b'$ in $\cap\, x : A.B(x)$ iff $b = b'$ in $B(a)$ for all $a \in A$. Notice that when A is empty, $\cap\, x : A.B(x)$ is not empty but has exactly one element. This element is denoted by any closed expression of the theory, e.g. $void = 1$ in $\cap\, x : void.B(x)$. Such equalities follow from the understanding that under the asumption that $x \in void$, we can infer anything.

Types such as $\cap\, x : void.B(x)$ are maximal in the sense that every type is a subtype and every closed term denotes the single member of the type. We pick one such type expression and call it the *top type*, denoted Top. For example, $\cap\, x : void.x$ can be Top.

Type equality follows the pattern for structural equality, namely

$$(\cap\, x : A.B(x) = \cap\, x : A'.B'(x)) \text{ iff } A = A' \text{ and } B(a) = B'(a).$$

Intersection types can express conditional typehood, which is useful in typing partial functions. If B does not depend on x, then $\cap\, x : A.B$ expresses the notion that *B is a type provided that A is inhabited.* We write this as *B given A*, following an analysis of this idea by Stuart Allen. Allen calls these *guarded types.*

Guarded types can specify the conditions under which $A \to B$ is a type in Nuprl. Namely, if A is nonempty, then B must be a type. So the typing is

$$\lambda(A, B.A \to B) \in (A : Type \to B : (\cap\, x : A.Type) \to Type).$$

Guarded types are also useful in expressing one-one correspondances between types. For example we know that mappings from pairs p in $x : A \times B(x)$ into $C(p)$ are isomorphic to curried mappings of the type $x : A \to y : B(x) \to C(\langle x, y\rangle)$. Similarly, mappings $x : \{y : A \mid B(y)\} \to C(x)$ are isomorphic to those in $x : A \to \cap\, y : B(x).C(x)$.

2.11 Subtyping

There is a natural notion of subtyping in this theory. We say that $A \sqsubseteq B$ iff $a = a'$ in A implies that $a = a'$ in B. For example, $\{x : A \mid P(x)\} \sqsubseteq A$ for any predicate $P(x)$. We clearly have $void \sqsubseteq A$ for any type A and $A \sqsubseteq Top$ for any type A, and $A \cap B \sqsubseteq A$ for any types A and B. It is easy to see that the following relationships hold.

	$A \sqsubseteq A'$	$B \sqsubseteq B'$	
1.	$A \times B$	$\sqsubseteq$	$A' \times B'$
2.	$A + B$	$\sqsubseteq$	$A' + B'$
3.	$A' \to B$	$\sqsubseteq$	$A \to B'$

The relation in 3 holds because functions in type theory are polymorphic. Given $f \in A' \to B$, we see that it belongs to $A \to B'$ as well because on inputs *restricted to* A it will produce results in B. In set theory this relationship would not hold.

3 Classes

3.1 Records

In the context of the type theory in section 2, there is more than one natural idea of a "class". We could borrow the idea from set theory that a class is a "large collection", one too large to be considered a set (see for example Bernays [4]). In our theory this corresponds to taking classes as "large types", i.e. types which contain types as members, in proper elements of universe, U_2.

We follow instead the idea from algebra and programming languages that classes are like algebraic structures, they are sets with operators. But classes are defined using signatures, and these are large types. Without the signature definition, as a large type, we could not have the definition of a class as a small type. The precise type we start with is a record type, these will also be classes.

Let F be a discrete type, the field names, and define a signature over F as a function from F into types, say $Sig \in F \to$ Types.

Definition: a *record type on discrete type F with signature $Sig \in F \to$* Types is the dependent type $i : F \to Sig(i)$.

Notation: If F is a finite type, say $\{x_1, \ldots, x_n\}$, then we write the record as $\{x_1 : Sig(x_1); \ldots; x_n$ $Sig(x_n)\}$. If we are given types $T_1, \ldots, T_n$ we can also write simply $\{x_1 : T_1; \ldots; x_n : T_n\}$ and this implies that we built the function assigning type T_i to name x_i.

Notice that if F_1 and F_2 are discrete types such that $F_1 \sqsubseteq F_2$ and $Sig_1 : F_1 \to$ Type, $Sig_2 : F_2 \to$ Type and $Sig_1(x) \sqsubseteq Sig_2(x)$ for $x \epsilon F_1$ then

$$i : F_2 \to Sig_2(i) \sqsubseteq j : F_1 \to Sig_2(j).$$

For example, if $F_1 = \{x_1, y\}$ and $F_2 = \{x, y, z\}$ then $\{x_1 : T_1; y : T_2; z : T_3\} \sqsubseteq \{x : T_1; y : T_2\}$, where $Sig_1(x) = T_1$, $Sig_1(y) = T_2$, $Sig_2(x) = T_1$, $Sig_2(y) = T_2, Sig_2(3) = T_3$. In this case $Sig_1(i) = Sig_2(i)$ for $i \epsilon \{x, y\}$, but we could allow $\{x : T_1'; y : T_2'\}$ where $T_1' \sqsubseteq T_1, T_2' \sqsubseteq T_2$.

Consider $\{0, 1\} = N_2 \subseteq N_3 = \{0, 1, 2\}$, then $N_3 \to B \sqsubseteq N_2 \to B$. For instance, consider f defined by this table,

x	$f(x)$
0	*tt*
1	*tt*
2	*ff*

Then, $f \epsilon N_3 \to B$ implies $f \epsilon N_2 \to B$ by ignoring arguments, e.g. ignore $f(2)$. In set theory $\{\langle 0, tt\rangle, \langle 1, tt\rangle, \langle 2, ff\rangle\}$ is clearly not a subset of $\{\langle 0, tt\rangle, \langle 1, tt\rangle\}$. If we used explicitly typed function terms, such as $\lambda x^A.b$, then $\lambda x^{N3}.b \not\epsilon N_2 \to b$ since $N_3 \not\subseteq N_2$.

An important specific example of these relationships will be discussed extensively in section 4. We consider it here briefly. Given a type M as the carrier of algebraic structure, we can define the structure of a monoid over M, $Monoid_M$, as $\{op : M \times M \to M; id : M\}$. By adding a component, we can extend this to a group structure, $Group_M$, as $\{op : M \times M \to M; op : M; inv : M \to M\}$. Notice that $Group_M \sqsubseteq Monoid_M$.

A monoid over a type M is a pair $\langle op, id\rangle$ where $op \epsilon M \times M \to M$ is associative and $id \epsilon M$ is an identity. A group over M is $\langle op, id, inv\rangle$ where $\langle op, id\rangle$ is a monoid and $inv \in M \to M$ is an inverse.

3.2 Uniform Records

Extending records is a basic operation, as in extending a Monoid structure to a Group structure. This can be done in a uniform way if we agree on a common set of names to be used as names of the components ("fields" as they are often called). Let us take *Label* as an infinite discrete type. Signatures *Sig* over *Label* are functions in $i : Label \to Type$, and records with this signature are $i : Label \to Sig(i)$. We call these *uniform records*, and also denote them $\{Sig\}$.

We generally consider records in which only finitely many labels are names of significant components. If we map the insignificant components to the type *Top*, then intersection of arbitrary uniform records makes sense and is defined as

$$(i : Label \to Sig_1(i)) \cap (j : Label \to Sig_2(j)) = i : Label \to Sig_1(i) \cap Sig_2(i).$$

Record intersection is an operation that extends records as we see if we assume that *op*, *id* and *inv* are elements of *Label* and assume that $MonSig_M(i) = Top$ if $i \neq op$ and $i \neq id$. Generally when we write $\{x_1 : Sig(x_1); \ldots; x_n : Sig(x_n)\}$ we will assume that $Sig(i) = Top$ for $i \neq x_j$. So now consider $\{op : M \times M \to M; id : M\} \cap \{inv : M \to M\}$.

The result is $Group_M$, $\{op : M \times M \to M; id : M; inv : M \to M\}$ because in the structure $\{inv : M \to M\}$, the components for *op* and *id* are *Top* and in Monoid the component for *inv* is *Top*. Thus for example, the type at *op* in the intersected structure is

$$op : (M \times M \to M) \cap Top \text{ and } (M \times M \to M) \cap Top = M \times M \to M.$$

When two records share a common field, the intersected record has the intersection of the types, that is $\{x : T\} \cap \{x : S\} = \{x : T \cap S\}$ So generally,

$$\{x : T\} \cap \{y : S\} = \begin{cases} \{x : T, y : S\} & if\ x \neq y \\ \{x : T \cap S\} & if\ x = y \end{cases}$$

3.3 Dependent Records

Records can be seen as (Cartesian) products with labels for the components. Can we define the record analogue of dependent products? The right notation would be $\{x_1 : T_1; x_2 : T_2(x_1); \ \ldots ; x_n : T_n(x_1, \ \ldots , x_{n-1})\}$ where $T_i(x_1, \ \ldots , x_{i-1})$ is a type depending on $x_1, \ \ldots , x_{i-1}$.

Can we define this structure in terms of a function $Sig : \{x_1, \ \ldots , x_n\} \to Type$? We see that $Sig(x_1)$ is just a type, but $Sig(x_2)$ uses a function $F \in Sig(x_1) \to Type$, and it is F applied to x_1. We might think of writing $F(x_1)$, but x_1 is a name and F wants an element of $Sig(x_1)$. Basically we need to talk about an arbitrary element of the type we are building. That is if $r \in i : \{x_1, \ \ldots , x_n\} \to Sig(i)$, then $Sig(x_2)$ is $F(r(x_1))$. So to define Sig we need r, and to type r we need Sig.

We see that an element of a type such as $\{x_1 : T_1; \ \ldots ; x_n : T_n(x_1, \ \ldots , x_{n-1})\}$ has the property that its type depends on its "previous values". That is, the type of $r(x_1)$ is $Sig(x_1)$, but the type of $r(x_2)$ is $Sig(x_2)(r(x_1))$.

We can encode this type using the *very-dependent function type* denoted $\{f \mid x : A \to B[f, x]\}$. We define it below. Now we use it to define the dependent records. We take A to be the finite type $\{0 \ldots (n-1)\}$. Let

$$T_f(n) \equiv \left\{ f \;\middle|\; i\!: \{0 \ldots (n-1)\} \to \left[\begin{array}{lll} case(i)\,of & & \\ 0 & \Rightarrow & T_0 \\ 1 & \Rightarrow & T_1(f\,(0)) \\ & \vdots & \\ n-1 & \Rightarrow & T_{n-1}(f\,(0))(f\,(1)) \cdots (f\,(n-2)) \end{array}\right] \right\}.$$

If we have a function F that returns the values T_i for $0 \leq i < n$ given the index i, we can give this type a more concise form. Let $fix(f.b)$ define the fixed point of the program b. That is, $fix(f.b) \equiv Y\lambda f.b$. Given functions F and f, and an index i we can define a function *napply* that applies F to $f(0), \ldots, f(n-1)$:

$$napply \equiv \lambda f.\lambda i.fix(g.\lambda G.\lambda j.\ \mathbf{if}\ j = i\ \mathbf{then}\ G\ \mathbf{else}\ g(G(f(j)))(j+1)).$$

The arguments to *napply* are as follows:

i is an integer that is the index of the final argument,

j is an integer that is the index of the first argument,

G is the value that will be applied to the arguments $f(j), f(j+1), \ldots, f(i-1)$,

f is a function returning the arguments.

Computing *napply* gives

$$napply\ (f)(i)(G)(j) \equiv G(f(j))(f(j+1)) \cdots (f(i-1)).$$

Using *napply*, the type $T_f(n)$ is then described as:

$$T_f(n) \equiv \{f|i : \{0 \ldots (n-1)\} \to napply(f)(i)(F(i))(0)\}.$$

The type function F can be defined in a similar manner. Given F, and an index i, we can compute the i-ary dependent function type with the term:

$$\begin{aligned} nfun \equiv \lambda F.\lambda i.fix(g.\lambda h.\lambda j.\ & \textbf{if } j = i \textbf{ then } \mathbb{U}_i \\ & \textbf{else } x : napply\ (h)(j)(F(j))(0) \rightarrow g(\lambda k.\ \textbf{if } k = j \textbf{ then } x \\ & \qquad\qquad\qquad\qquad\qquad\qquad\qquad\qquad \textbf{else } h(k))(j+1). \end{aligned}$$

The arguments are:

i is an integer that is the index of the last type in the function type being constructed,

j is an integer that is the index of the first type in the functin type being constructed,

F is the value that will be applied to get the argument type of the function type being constructed,

h is a function defined on $\{0\ldots(j-1)\}$ that returns the initial arguments of the dependent function type being constructed.

After computation, we have

$$\begin{aligned} nfun(F)(i)(h)(j) &\equiv x_j : F(j)(h(0))(h(1))\ldots(h(j-1)) \\ &\rightarrow x_{j+1} : F(j+1)(h(0))(h(1))\ldots(h(j-1))(x_j) \\ &\ \vdots \\ &\rightarrow x_{i-1} : F(i-1)(h(0))(h(1))\ldots(h(j-1))(x_j)\ldots(x_{i-2}) \\ &\rightarrow \mathbb{U}_i. \end{aligned}$$

In the normal case, $j = 0$ and the argument h is not used, and we have

$$\begin{aligned} nfun(F)(i)(h)(0) &\equiv x_0 : F(0) \\ &\rightarrow x_1 : F(1)(x_0) \\ &\ \vdots \\ &\rightarrow x_{i-1} : F(i-1)(x_0)(x_1)\cdots(x_{i-2}) \\ &\rightarrow \mathbb{U}_i. \end{aligned}$$

The type for F is then:

$$T_F(n) \equiv \{F|i : \{0\ldots(n-1)\} \rightarrow nfun(F)(i)(\lambda x.x)(0)\}.$$

If we parameterize these types over n, we have the types

$$\begin{aligned} S_f &\equiv n : \mathbb{N} \times T_f(n) \\ S_F &\equiv n : \mathbb{N} \times T_F(n). \end{aligned}$$

The type S_F specifies *descriptions* of dependent products of arbitrary finite arity, and the type S_f specifies the corresponding dependent product type. The inhabitants of S_f are pairs $\langle n, f\rangle$ where n is the arity of the product, and f is a function with domain $\{0\ldots(n-1)\}$ that serves as the projection function.

This finite arity dependent product type will be useful to define the type *Signature*. It can also be used to define the type of sequents in a constructive logic: the hypotheses of the sequents are defined as a dependent product of finite arity, and the goal is a type that may depend on all hypotheses. We will cover next a more formal treatment of the semantics of the function type.

3.4 Semantics of the very-dependent function type

Next we will discuss briefly a semantics for the very-dependent function type, restricted to non-cyclic definitions. There are interesting variations on the semantics that allow cyclic definitions, or definitions that derive the order from the computation in the range, or that allow the expression of partial function types. However, these semantics are an area of research—they do not fit in well with the current semantics of the type theory, and it seems likely that the semantics of the entire type theory would have to be modified to accomodate them. We don't discuss the extended semantics in this paper.

Simple semantics The simplest interpretation for the very-dependent function type $\{f|x : A \to B\}$ requires that there be no cycles in the type definition. That is, the term $B[f, i]$ must not evaluate f on i for any $i \in A$, and it must have a normal form. The simplest way to enforce this property is to require that A be well-ordered according to some relation $<: A \to A \to \mathbb{U}_i$, and to require that $B[f, i]$ be well-defined for f with domain $\{a : A \mid a < i\}$. This is a conservative restriction, since only the subtype of A that is used in defining the range need be well-ordered.

With this restriction, we can give a semantics for the type $\{f|x : A \to B\}$ as follows.

Semantics 1

The term $\{f|x : A \to B\}$ is a type with membership φ, if and only if:

1. A is a type with membership α,
2. A is well-founded with respect to some partial order $<$,
3. for any a such that $\alpha(a)$, there is a $\gamma_{a'}$ for all a' where $\alpha(a')$ and $a' < a$ and the following hold:
   (a) $\{f|x : \{a'' : A|a'' < a'\} \to B\}$ is a type with membership $\gamma_{a'}$,
   (b) $B[g; a']$ is a type with membership β_g for any g where $\gamma_{a'}(g)$,
   (c) for any f, $\varphi(f)$ if and only if, for all a where $\alpha(a)$ holds, $\gamma_a(f)$ and $\beta_f(f(a))$ also hold.

This semantics is well-founded because A is well-founded. The membership predicates γ and β can be constructed by induction. In the base case, the type $\{f|x : \{a'' : A|a'' < a'\} \to B\}$ reduces to $\{f|x : void \to B\}$ which is a type for any term B. Similarly, the semantics requires that at the base case that $B[g, a']$ be a type for the function g with domain *void*, which means that B cannot evaluate g on any argument. The definitions for γ and β are constructed mutually recursively for the entire domain A.

A. Kopylov has recently shown that we can define the dependent records in terms of a simple dependent intersection type $\cap\, x : A.B$ with a simple semantics.

4 Applications to Algebra

4.1 Skeletal Structures

We have seen that records parameterized by a type, the *carrier*, can represent skeletal algebraic structures. We have seen

$$Group_M \sqsubseteq Monoid_M.$$

With judicious choice of names we can add more structure, for instance to define a ring over M, we extend the Group with more operators and constants, say

$$Ring_M == \{op : M \times M \to M; id : M; inv : M \to M; op_2 : M \times M \to M; id_2 : M\}.$$

With this choice of names we have

$$Ring_M \sqsubseteq Group_M \sqsubseteq Monoid_M.$$

But we are not able to express yet that op_2 and id_2 form a second monoid. We would like $\{op_2 : M \times M \to M; id_2 : M\}$ to be a monoid and inherit properties about monoids. We will see that this can be done over uniform records by first relabeling the fields. We will have that

$$\{op_2 : M \times M \to M; id_2 : M\} \circ L \sqsubseteq Monoid_M.$$

4.2 Relabeling Uniform Structures

If $\{op_2 : M \times M \to M; id_2 : M\}$ is a uniform record over Label, then we can think of labelling the fields by composing a function $Label \to Label$ with the record function.

For example, if $L \in Label \to Label$ is defined by $L(op) = op_2, L(id) = id_2$, and if $r \in \{op_2 : M \times M \to M; id_2 : M\}$, then $r \circ L \in \{op : M \times M \to M; id : M\}$; so $r \circ L$ is an element of $Monoid_M$.

Let us define $\{op_2 : M \times M \to M; id_2 : M\} \circ L$ as $r \in \{f : (i : Label \to MonSig_M(i)) | \exists g : \{op_2 : M \times M \to M; id_2 : M\}.f = g \circ L\}$.

4.3 Full Algebraic Structure

The skeletal algebraic structures do not specify properties of the operations. To define a monoid we need to say that *op* is an associative binary operator and that *id* is an identity. Here are propositions that express these properties. We display *op* as an infix operator.

$$Assoc(M, op) == \forall x, y, z : M.((x \; op \; y) \; op \; z) = (x \; op(y \; op \; z) \text{ in } M),$$

$$Id(M, op) == \forall x : M.((id \; op \; x) = x \text{ in } M)\&((x \; op \; id) = x \text{ in } M).$$

The *full algebraic structure* for a monoid is

$$Monoid_M == \{op : M \times M \to M; id : M; assoc : Assoc(M, op); id\_prop : Id(M, id)\}.$$

To define a group we add

$$Inv(M, op, id, inv) == \forall x : M \; ((x \; op \; inv(x)) = id \text{ in } M) \; \&((inv(x) \; op \; x) = id \text{ in } M).$$

$$Group_M == Monoid_M \cap \{inv : M \to M; inv\_prop : Inv(M, op, id, inv)\}.$$

In this notation, we can assume that any labels that are not explicitly bound (call them free), such as *op* and *id* in the second record, are assigned the type Top.

We can continue to add properties by intersection. For example, to define *commutative (or Abelian) groups*, we first define

$$Comm(M, op) == \forall x, y : M.(x \; op \; y) = (y \; op \; x) \text{ in } M, \quad \text{then}$$

$$AbelianGroup_M == Group_M \cap \{comm : Comm(M, op)\}.$$

4.4 Colimits and Categorical Operations

There are categorical constructions, such as colimits, that can be used to unite theories. The Designware and Specware systems developed by Kestrel Inc are based on these concepts [34, 35]. We can mimic these constructions using our record calculus. Here is how we treat the basic example from the articles written by Doug Smith.

Consider two structures over E with a binary relation (decidable), one transitive and one reflexive,

say SR $==$ $\{r_1 : E \times E \rightarrow \mathbb{B}; refl : Reflexive(E, r_1)\}$,

and ST $==$ $\{r_2 : E \times E \rightarrow \mathbb{B}; trans : Transitive(E, r_2)\}$,

where $Reflexive(E, r)$ $==$ $\forall x : E.(x\ r\ x)$,

and $Transitive(E, r)$ $==$ $\forall x, y, z : E.((x\ r\ y\ \&\ y\ r\ z) \Rightarrow x\ r\ z)$.

In Specware, to write these theories, the binary relations are related to each other by defining morphisms from a common skeleton as follows:

$$\{r : E \times E \rightarrow \mathbb{B}\} \xrightarrow{f} \{r_1 : E \times E \rightarrow \mathbb{B}; refl : Reflexive(E, r_1)\}$$

$$\{r : E \times E \rightarrow \mathbb{B}\} \xrightarrow{g} \{r_2 : E \times E \rightarrow \mathbb{B}; trans : Transitive(E, r_2)\}.$$

Then a colimit, SRT, with respect to f and g is defined. It has the "universal property", and these components:

$$SRT == \{rr : E \times E \rightarrow \mathbb{B}; refl : Reflexive(E, rr); trans : Transitive(E, rr)\}.$$

If we let S be the skeletal structure, then the diagram is:

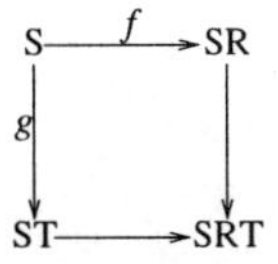

In our approach, we obtain the colimit as

$$SR \circ L_1 \ \cap\ ST \circ L_2,$$

where L_1 maps rr to r_1 and L_2 maps rr to r_2.

5 Applications to Systems

5.1 Labeled Transition Systems and IO Automata

The class concept and record calculus can be used to formally describe software systems by composition from components. We illustrate this by describing the service specifications for the Ensemble group communication systems [27]. These specifications are based on IO automata - a formalism extensively studied by Lynch and Tuttle [29]. We start with a formal specification of these automata as non-deterministic transition systems.

General IO automata are instances of *labeled transition systems*. An automaton consists of a set of states Q; a set of labels A, called *actions*, that label each of the transitions of the automaton; a set of *initial* states i; and a set of allowable transitions t. In type theory, an automaton is described by the following type:

$$\begin{aligned} Auto \equiv & \quad Q\colon Type \\ \times & \quad A\colon Type \\ \times & \quad i\colon Q \to \mathbb{P} \\ \times & \quad t\colon (Q \times A \times Q) \to Prop. \end{aligned} \tag{1}$$

This is similar to the definition used in our formalization of automata theory [13].

The initial states i are a subset of the possible states Q, defined using a predicate $Q \to \mathbb{P}$, where $\mathbb{P}$ is the set of propositions (for simplicity, this can be thought of as a Boolean value). The transition definition is similar. Note that the states and actions may be types with an infinite number of elements.

5.2 Notations for IO Automata

IO automata are often defined using stylized pseudo-code. The *actions* correspond to "significant" external events of the system being specified. For example, a simple specification of a FIFO protocol is shown below. The FIFO actions are SEND(m) and RECV(m), where m ranges over some message type $\mathcal{M}$. The automaton contains two queues called *sent* and *received* that save the messages. Sending a message corresponds to following a transition labeled SEND(m), the message is added to the *sent* list of messages. Receiving messages corresponds to following a transition labeled RECV(m). A message m can be received only when there are more messages in the *sent* queue than the *received* queue, and the next message in *sent* is m (this is a *precondition* of the transition); the effect is to add the message to the *received* queue.

FIFO	
Actions:	SEND(m), RECV(m), for $m \in \mathcal{M}$
State:	*sent* $\in \mathcal{M}$ *List*, initially empty,
	received $\in \mathcal{M}$ *List*, initially empty
SEND(m)	
Eff: append m to *sent*	
RECV(m)	
Pre: $\lvert received \rvert < \lvert sent \rvert$	
$sent[\lvert received \rvert - 1] = m$	
Eff: append m to *received*	

An automaton defines a set of *executions* $q_0, a_0, q_1, a_1, \ldots$, where each triple q_i, a_i, q_{i+1} is a valid transition of the automaton. It also defines a set of *traces*, which are the actions of the valid executions. If A and B are automata, and the traces of A are a subset of the traces of B, we say that A *implements* B. An *invariant* is a predicate that is true of all states in all executions of an automaton. The FIFO automaton defines that invariant that the *received* queue is always a prefix of the *sent* queue. We abbreviate this using the satisfaction relation of the form $A \models P$ where A is an automaton and P is a safety property on traces. In this case we write, FIFO $\models$ *always received* $\leq$ *sent.*

5.3 Composition of IO Automata

So far, this presentation of IO automata adheres to the original form of Lynch and Tuttle.[3] Next we wish to define a form of composition that preserves safety properties, that is state invariants and properties of individual traces of the automaton. Composition of automata is discussed extensively by Lynch [28], and she states a number of theorems that relate the traces of a composition to the traces of the components. Composition identifies actions with the same name in different

[3]Lynch and Tuttle also labels actions as being *input*, *output*, or *internal* to give a little more semantic content, but we find this labeling unnecessary.

component automata, so when any one component takes this action, so do all components with this name in their signature. The traces of a composition should be the intersection of the traces of the components. Basically the composition of two automata is their product. We define it precisely now. The obvious choice for composition is the *intersection* of their traces. If M and M' are automata, their intersection has states that are states both of M and M', and traces that belong both to M and M'. If $M = (Q, A, i, t)$ and $M' = (Q', A', i', t')$, we define their intersection as follows:

$$\begin{aligned} M \cap M' \equiv (\ & Q \cap Q', \\ & A \cap A', \\ & \lambda s.(i(s) \wedge i'(s)), \\ & \lambda q_1, a, q_2.t(q_1, a, q_2) \wedge t'(q_1, a, q_2)). \end{aligned} \tag{2}$$

With this definition, we have the following theorem, proved formally in Nuprl.

Theorem 1 *For any automata M and M', and state predicate P, if $M \models$ always P, then $M \cap M' \models$ always P.*

The proof is straightforward, since any execution of $M \cap M'$ is also an execution of M. In the degenerate case, if the state spaces Q and Q' do not have any elements in common, the intersection $M \cap M'$ is the empty automaton; it has no executions or traces. In our framework, we address this problem by including "all" state variables and actions in every automata, but leaving almost all of them unspecified, as shown in the following section.

The pseudo-code suggests a *style* of automata definition that can be used to guide their construction. In the pseudo-code, the actions have a *label* (like SEND or RECV), and a *value* (like $m \in \mathcal{M}$) that is associated with the label. Given a type of labels *Label*, the set of stylized actions can be defined as the dependent sum $Action == l : Label. \times F_A(l)$ where $F_A \in Label \rightarrow Type$ is a type-function that defines the type of the value associated with each label. For example, the actions of the FIFO automaton are defined by the following product:

$$l{:}\ Label. \times (\textbf{if}\ l = \text{"SEND"} \vee l = \text{"RECV"}\ \textbf{then}\ \mathcal{M}\ \textbf{else}\ Top).$$

If the action label is SEND or RECV, the action *value* belongs to the type of messages $\mathcal{M}$. Otherwise, the data part is totally unspecified.

The stylized states are defined similarly. A state has a set of named variables (we can use the *Label* type), and each variable has a value. The most natural type is the record type. For example, the FIFO state can be represented by the record $\{sent : \mathcal{M}\ List\ ;\ received : \mathcal{M}\ List\}$. $State = l : Label \rightarrow F_S(l)$ for some type-function $F_S \in Label \rightarrow Type$. The FIFO state has the following definition:

$$l : Label \rightarrow (\textbf{if}\ l = \text{"}sent\text{"} \vee l = \text{"}received\text{"}\ \textbf{then}\ \mathcal{M}\ List\ \textbf{else}\ Top).$$

Again, the state is *unspecified* on labels that are not in {"*sent*", "*received*"}. This results in the main type-theoretic principle we use to avoid degeneracy: record *intersection* corresponds to record *concatenation.*

$$\{l_1{:}\ T_1; l_2{:}\ T_{2a}\} \cap \{l_2{:}\ T_{2b}; l_3{:}\ T_3\} \equiv \{l_1{:}\ T_1; l_2{:}\ T_{2a} \cap T_{2b}; l_3{:}\ T_3\}.$$

Intersection for the product type also has the concatenation property, ie., when two automata are intersected, their state variables and action signatures are concatenated. This simple feature captures the object-oriented nature of our framework: the intersection of automata corresponds to *inheritance* in object-oriented languages.

The pseudo-code can be represented in the type-theory by separating it into the four parts of an automaton. The actions define a product type, the state variables define a record (a function type), and the initial values of the state variables specify the initial conditions. The transition definitions define a transition relation. For an automata with state type Q, the transition definition $L(x)$ `Pre` $P(q,x)$ `Eff:` $expr(q,x)$ for $x \in T$ defines a conjunctive clause in the transition definition as follows:

$$\forall x \in T.(a = L(x) \Rightarrow P(q_1, x) \wedge (q_2 = expr(q_1, x) \in Q)).$$

That is, the transition (q_1, a, q_2) is in the transition relation only if, whenever the action a is $L(x)$ for some $x \in T$, the precondition P holds on the initial state q_1, and the result of the effect is equal to the final state q_2 *on the variables specified in the state* Q. Other variables are unconstrained. The `Eff:` clause of a transition definition is optional; if it is omitted, the equality condition on q_2 is omitted in the type-theoretic interpretation, allowing the state to change arbitrarily. The formal definition of the FIFO automaton is the following program:

$$\begin{array}{l}
Q = l : \mathit{Label} \rightarrow (\textbf{if } l = \text{“}\mathit{sent}\text{”} \vee l = \text{“}\mathit{received}\text{”} \textbf{ then } \mathcal{M}\ \mathit{List} \textbf{ else } \mathit{Top}),\\
A = l.\mathit{Label} \times (\textbf{if } l = \text{“SEND”} \vee l = \text{“RECV”} \textbf{ then } \mathcal{M} \textbf{ else } \mathit{Top}),\\
i = \lambda q.(q.\mathit{sent} = [] \wedge q.\mathit{received} = []),\\
\begin{array}{lrcl}
t = \lambda q_1, a, q_2. & \forall m \in \mathcal{M}.(a = \text{SEND}(m) & \Rightarrow & (q_2.\mathit{sent} = m \text{ appended to } q_1.\mathit{sent}\\
& & \wedge & q_2.\mathit{received} = q_1.\mathit{received}))\\
& \wedge\ \ \forall m \in \mathcal{M}.(a = \text{RECV}(m) & \Rightarrow & (|q_1.\mathit{received}| < |q_1.\mathit{sent}|\\
& & \wedge & q_1.\mathit{sent}[|q_1.\mathit{received}| - 1] = m\\
& & \wedge & q_2.\mathit{received} = m \text{ appended to } q_1.\mathit{received}\\
& & \wedge & q_2.\mathit{sent} = q_1.\mathit{sent})).
\end{array}
\end{array}$$

There are some drawbacks to the automata we have just presented. First, every state machine shares the same state space—in essence, all state variables are global. We use this feature during composition (like the FINITE_FIFO example), but there is no notion of "public" or "private" variables, where private variables do not become shared during composition. Second, the action space is global as well, so it is not possible to re-use an automaton in multiple specifications with different action namings.

5.4 Uniform Automata and Relabeling

Both of these problems can be addressed by introducing *renaming* operations that we defined on uniform records. We use the following informal notation, given an arbitrary renaming function $R \in \mathit{Label} \rightarrow \mathit{Label}$ on *labels*, and an automaton M:

$$\begin{array}{l} M, \text{ renaming actions } l(x) \text{ to } R(l)(x)\\ M, \text{ renaming variables } v \text{ to } R(v). \end{array}$$

When actions are renamed, the action type and the transition definitions must be modified. Consider the following stylized machine M:

$$M = (Q = l : \mathit{Label} \rightarrow F_s(l), A = l : \mathit{Label} \times F_A(l, i, t)).$$

The action renaming "*M, renaming actions $L(x)$ to $R(L)(x)$*" defines the renamed machine M' shown below.

$$\begin{array}{rclcl}
M' & = & (& Q' & = & l : \mathit{Label} \rightarrow F_s(l)\\
& & & A' & = & l : \mathit{Label} \times \left(\bigcap_{\{l' \in \mathit{Label} \mid R(l') = l\}} .F_A(l')\right)\\
& & & i' & = & i,\\
& & & t' & = & \lambda q_1, l(x), q_2.\ \textbf{if}\quad \exists l' \in \mathit{Label}.(R(l') = l) \textbf{ then}\\
& & & & & \qquad\qquad\qquad t(q_1, l'(x), q_2)\\
& & & & & \qquad\quad \textbf{else}\\
& & & & & \qquad\qquad\qquad q_1 = q_2 \in Q').
\end{array}$$

Since R is an arbitrary renaming function, it may map several labels to a single value. The action type associated with label l in A' is the *intersection* of all the action types $F_A(l')$ for any label

l' in the inverse image $R^{-1}(l)$. If $R^{-1}(l)$ is nonempty, the transition definition allows *any* of the transitions $l'(x)$ for any $l' \in R^{-1}(l)$. Otherwise, the value type on label l in A' degenerates to *Top*, and a transition is allowed only if it leaves the state unchanged. From this definition, we get the following formal meta-theorem for safety properties P:

Theorem 2 *For any automaton M, renaming function R, and state predicate P, if $M \models$ always P then (M, renaming actions $l(x)$ to $R(l)(x)$) $\models$ always P.*

The state renaming operation is similar. The states, initial state predicate, and transition relation must be modified. The following machine defines the renamed machine "$M'' = m$, *renaming variables* v *to* $R(v)$":

$$\begin{array}{rcllcl} M'' & = & (& Q'' & = & l : Label \to \left(\bigcap_{\{l' \in Label \mid R(l')=l\}} .F_S(l')\right), \\ & & & A'' & = & l : Label \times F_A(l, i, t) \\ & & & i'' & = & (i \circ R) \\ & & & t'' & = & \lambda q_1, a, q_2.t(q_1 \circ R, a, q_2 \circ R)). \end{array}$$

This definition induces a renaming operation on state predicates P, providing the following formal meta-theorem:

Theorem 3 *For any automaton M, renaming function R, and state predicate P, if $M \models$ always P, then (M, renaming variables v to $R(v)$) $\models$ always$(\lambda q.P(q \circ R))$.*

5.5 Specifying Ensemble Virtual Synchrony

To demonstrate the use of our new version of IO, we present the specification of Ensemble Virtual Synchrony (EVS). In the EVS model, processes join together to form *views*, which are sets of processes that vary over time as processes join and leave. Views are thought of informally as active multicast domains; when a process fails, or when the network becomes partitioned, a view may be split into several smaller views. When processes are created, or when the network heals, multiple views may merge into one. Each process has its own version of the view it is in. When a process replaces its view $view_1$ with a new view $view_2$, we say the process *installs* view $view_2$. Virtual synchrony provides the following informal properties on *views* and messages:

EVSsingle At any time a process belongs to exactly one view.

EVSself If a process installs a view, it belongs to the view.

EVSvieworder At any process, views are installed in increasing order of view identifier.

EVSnonoverlap If two processes install the same view, their previous views are either the same or they are disjoint.

EVSviewmessage All delivered messages are delivered in the view in which they were sent.

EVSfifo Messages between any two processes in a view are delivered in FIFO order.

EVSsync Any two process that install a view v_2, both with preceding view v_1, deliver the same messages in view v_1.

We can categorize these properties in three parts: message delivery (EVSfifo, EVSviewmessage), view properties (EVSsingle, EVSself, EVSvieworder, EVSnonoverlap), and message/view properties (EVSsync).

We can specify the message delivery properties using the FIFO automaton. Let $VID \subseteq Label$ be the type of views, and let $PID \subseteq Label$ be the type of processes. We implement the *Label* type as a recursive type including names and closed under pairing (which we used for subscripting by process and view), to get the following automaton:

$$\text{EVS\_FIFO} = \bigcap_{v \in VID} \bigcap_{p,q \in PID} . (\text{FIFO} \begin{array}{l} \text{renaming} \\ \text{action SEND}(m) \text{ to EVS-SEND}_{p,v}(m) \\ \text{action RECV}(m) \text{ to EVS-RECV}_{q,p,v}(m) \\ \text{variable } sent \text{ to } sent_{p,v} \\ \text{variable } received \text{ to } received_{q,p,v}). \end{array} \quad (3)$$

The EVSfifo property follows trivially from the FIFO automaton. The EVSviewmessage property follows because FIFO channels are only established within views (they do not cross views).

For the *view* properties, we introduce a new action EVS-NEWVIEW$_p(v)$, which delivers the view $v \in VID \times PID\ Set$ to process $p \in PID$. We refer to the view identifier as $v.id$ and the set of processes that belong to the view as $v.set$. We also need to introduce a history variable *all-viewids*$_p$, for each process $p \in PID$, containing the set of views ever delivered to process p. Several derived variables are defined in terms of *all-views*$_p$:

- *current-view*$_p$ is the view in *all-views*$_p$ with the largest identifier,
- *pred-view*$_{p,v}$ is the view in *all-views*$_p$ with identifier strictly smaller than $v.id$ if such a view exists, otherwise $\perp$, where $\perp \notin VID$ is a constant.

Given these definitions the view part of EVS is shown below.

EVS_VIEW
State: for each $p \in PID$:
all-viewids$_p \in View\ Set$, initially $\{v_p\}$
EVS-NEWVIEW$_p(v)$
Pre: let $v' = $ *current-view*$_p$ in
$v.id > v'.id$ ①
$p \in v.set$ ②
$\forall q \in v.set.$ ③
if *pred-view*$_{q,v} \neq \perp$ then
pred-view$_{q,v} = v' \vee$ *pred-view*$_{q,v}.set \cap v'.set = \{\}$
Eff: *all-views*$_p$ = *all-views*$_p \cup \{v\}$

The precondition for EVS-NEWVIEW$(v)_p$ has several parts, one for each of the view properties. Part ① guarantees that views are delivered in ascending order (EVSvieworder), and the definition of *current-view*$_p$ defines exactly one current view per process (EVSsingle). Part ② ensures that a process belongs to all its view (EVSself). Part ③ sets up the condition on previous views: if another process q has installed view v, then it either has the same previous view, or its previous view was disjoint from v (EVSnonoverlap).

The final part of EVS relates views and message ordering. For this automaton, we need to express the relation between the FIFO and VIEW automata, and we include state variables *received*$_{q,p,v}$ and *all-views*$_p$. The VIEW_MSG automaton is shown below.

VIEW_MSG
State: for $p, q \in PID$, $v \in View$:
received$_{p,q,v} \in \mathcal{M}\ List$
for $p \in PID$:
all-views$_p \in View\ Set$
EVS-NEWVIEW$_p(v)$
Pre: let $v' = $ *current-view*$_p$ in
$\forall q \in v.set.$
$\forall r \in v'.set.$ if *pred-view*$_{q,v} = v'$ then
received$_{r,p,v'.id}$ = *received*$_{r,q,v'.id}$

The VIEW_MSG automaton introduces a new precondition for delivering a view: each process q with the same preceeding view v' receives exactly the same messages from each process $r \in v'.set$ (they EVSsync property).

These three automata specify the properties of EVS individually. The final step is combine them into the complete specification of EVS.

$$EVS \equiv \text{GROUP\_FIFO} \cap \text{VIEW} \cap \text{VIEW\_MSG}. \tag{4}$$

This construction identifies the *received*$_{p,q,v}$ variables of the GROUP_FIFO and VIEW_MSG automata, and the *all-views*$_p$ variables of the VIEW and VIEW_MSG automata. The properties of EVS are the conjunction of the properties of the three parts, forming a complete specification of EVS.

Abadi and Lamport [1] have explored composition in TLA using *assume-guarantee* specifications. We describe our systems with automata, rather than a temporal *logic* like TLA, because we can use a single language to represent both programs and specifications. However, our formalism shares the same problem space with TLA. In fact, our safety theorem $(A \models \mathit{always}\, P) \Rightarrow (A \cap B \models \mathit{always}\, P)$ is currently too weak: while the intersection $A \cap B$ has the safety properties of both A and B, additional safety properties may hold because of interference between the two automata. It is likely that we can use the assume-guarantee style of reasoning to extend our framework with a more complete result.

6 Conclusion

6.1 Objects

Class theory is only one aspect of the type system for object-oriented programming. It is possible to extend these ideas to account for other aspects of objects. Karl Crary has written "Simple, Efficient Object Encoding Using Intersection Types"[16], available at his web page, and the second author has written a draft article available at his web page, "A Predicative Type-Theoretic Interpretation of Objects." In addition Pavel Naumov has shown, in his PhD thesis, how to define Java's recursive types in Nuprl, *Formalizing Reference Types in Nuprl* [33].

Other aspects of Java's class theory can easily be expressed in our type theory. For example, we can include specific methods in a class by specifying that a field names a specific function. To define classes with specific methods we constrain elements of a type to a particular function, for example $\{x : T; x\_def : x = t\}$ for t a particular element of T. In this setting, method override is just a function from records to records.

For example, if the records defined by $Sig : Label \rightarrow Type$, then a map $F : (Label \rightarrow Type) \rightarrow (Label \rightarrow Type)$ can define an override. Let $\{Sig\}$ be the record $i : Label \rightarrow Sig(i)$, then $\{F(Sig)\}$ is the new class. For example, we could update the method t to t', perhaps writing this as: $\{x : T; x\_def : x = t\}\ [x := t]$.

Java has many restrictions dictated by the need to compile efficiently. For example, a class can have only one superclass, and abstract classes cannot be instantiated. Also the primative classes look like our types. It is pleasing to see how class theory can be developed without the restrictions of current compiler technology. This article has given a glimpse of such a theory.

6.2 Ludics

At the Marktoberdorf summer school of 1999, Jean-Yves Girard introduced a new logic called Ludics in which he took into account an analysis of space. It turns out that there is a strong connection to our class theory based on the following points of agreement. Girard also introduces an intersection type with logical meaning, he can define with it as a type like our Top in the same way, $\cap\, x : void.x$. He also uses a subtyping relation that agrees with ours. Finally, and most significantly, he introduces a naming mechanism, like our Labels, that allows naming objects. He says that objects with names are *located.* He uses localization to show how to define $A \times B$ from intersection. This turns out to be exactly these abbreviations:

$$\{x : A\} \cap \{y : B\} = \{x : A; y : B\} \quad \text{if} \quad x \neq y, \text{ and this is isomorphic to } A \times B$$

$$\{x : A\} \cap \{y : B\} = \{x : A \cap B\} \quad \text{if} \quad x = y, \text{ and this is isomorphic to } A \cap B.$$

Duality is important in Girard's theory, and intersection has a dual, namely union. We have defined a union type as well, $A \cup B$, but it did not play a role in this article. The type $A \cup B$ consists of the elements of A and the elements of B, and we say $a = b$ in $A \cup B$ when $a = b$ in A or when $a = b$ in B or when there is a c such that $a = c$ in A and $c = b$ in B.

A Appendix: Automata in NuPRL Type Theory

Mark Bickford, Odyssey Research Associates, Ithaca, NY, USA

A.1 Introduction

The aim of this appendix is to present some of the definitions and theorems of our NuPRL IO-automata theory as they appear in the NuPRL library. The IO-automata theory has two parts. The first part defines the semantic domain of automata, which we call state-machines, and operations on them and theorems about them. The second part defines a syntax for IO-automata and infinitary logic and a meaning function that maps the syntactic forms, which we call automata, to the semantic state-machines. In this appendix we present only some parts of the first part of the theory, the definitions of the state-machine type and operations on it.

We use a "bottom-up" style of presentation, giving the basic concepts first and progressing to the complex. The basics of NuPRL type theory, in particular, an understanding of dependent function, dependent product, intersection type, and set type, are assumed.

A.2 Patterns and Labels

We need a basic type of labels that includes strings and integers and is closed under pairing so that we can form labels like `sent[p]` and x_5. In order to define operations like matching and substitution on our labels we make a more general type of patterns that also includes pattern variables. The labels are then the subtype of "ground" patterns.

These two NuPRL abstractions

```
ptn_con(T) ==  Atom + ℤ + Atom + T × T
Pattern ==  rec(T.ptn_con(T))
```

make the type `Pattern` a recursive type that satisfies

```
Pattern ==  Atom + ℤ + Atom + Pattern × Pattern
```

The first two components of `Pattern` represent the atomic strings and integers that we want as labels. The third component represents the pattern variables, and the fourth component represents the label-pairs, which we write as `x[y]`.

Then we define the ground patterns as the ones that do not mention varaibles.

```
ground_ptn(p) == Case(p)
                   Case ptn_var(v) => ff
                   Case ptn_pr(<x, y>) =>
                     ground_ptn(x) ∧b ground_ptn(y)
                   Default => tt
∀p:Pattern. ground_ptn(p) ∈ 𝔹
Label ==  {p:Pattern| ground_ptn(p)}
```

A.3 Declarations and Records

A declaration is an assignment of types to labels.

```
Decl ==  Label → 𝕌
```

The empty declaration assigns the type `Top` to every label; the base declaration `x:T` assigns `T` to `x` and `Top` to the rest; and we can combine declarations by using type intersection.

```
     ==  λx.Top
x:T  ==  λa.if a = x then T else Top fi
d1;d2 ==  λx.d1 x ∩ d2 x
(D[i] for i ∈ I) ==  λx.(∩i:I.D[i] x)
```

A renaming is a map `f` of type `Label ⟶ Label`. If declaration `d` assigns `T` to `x` and if `f x = z`, then the renamed declaration, `d o f`, should assign `T` to `z`. Rather than restrict renamings to be one to one we also handle the case of many to one renamings. If declaration `d` assigns `T1` to `x` and `T2` to `y`, and if `f x = f y = z`, then the renamed declaration, `d o f`, should assign `T1 ∩ T2` to `z`. So, we define the renaming operation on declarations as follows

```
d o f ==  λx.(∩y:Label.if x = f y then d y else Top fi )
```

The record `{d}` defined by declaration `d` is the dependent function

```
{d} ==  l:Label ⟶ d l
```

and record selection is just application

```
r.l ==  r l
```

If `f` is a renaming and `r` is a record, then `r o f`, where the operation is the usual function composition, is another record. We have the following theorem about record types and renaming

```
∀d:Decl. ∀f:Label ⟶ Label.   ∀r:{d o f}.  r o f ∈ {d}
```

A.4 Sigma types

A dual to the record type is the "sigma" type. It is a dependent product defined by a declaration `d`. Members of this type are pairs of a kind and a value where the type of the value depends on the kind.

```
(Σd) ==  l:Label × d l
kind(a) ==  a.1
value(a) ==  a.2
```

The renaming theorem for sigma types is

```
∀d:Decl. ∀f:Label ⟶ Label.   ∀a:(Σd o f). ∀l:Label.
    f l = kind(a) ⇒ <l, value(a)> ∈ (Σd)
```

A.5 State Machines

Our state machines are labeled transition systems. They are parameterized by two declarations, `da` and `ds`. Declaration `ds`, declares the types of the state varaibles, and the state of the machine is a member of the corresponding record type `{ds}`. Declaration `da` declares the types of the actions that label the transitions. Each action is a kind-value pair in the sigma type `(Σda)` corresponding to `da`. The value components of the actions represent input values.

```
SM ==  da:Decl × ds:Decl ×
       init:({ds} → ℙ) ×
       ({ds} → (Σda) → {ds}   → ℙ)
```

A state machine M ∈SM thus has four components, its two declaration parameters, an initial state predicate and a labeled transition relation. It also has its corresponding state and action types.

```
M.da ==  M.1
M.ds ==  M.2.1
M.init ==  M.2.2.1
M.trans ==  M.2.2.2
M.state ==  {M.ds}
M.action ==  (ΣM.da)
```

A.6 State Machine Composition

Using the combinators already defined for declarations, we can define the composition of two state machines and the composition of and indexed family of state machines.

```
(A ∩ B) ==
      <A.da;B.da, A.ds;B.ds,
       λs.A.init s ∧ B.init s,
       λs1,act,s2.A.trans s1 act s2 ∧ B.trans s1 act s2>
∩i:I. M[i] ==
      <M[i].da for i ∈ I, M[i].ds for i ∈ I,
       λs.∀i:I. M[i].init s,
       λs1,a,s2.∀i:I. M[i].trans s1 a s2>
```

A.7 State Machine Renaming

We define separate operations for renaming of state variables, which we write as (M o f), and for renaming of actions, which we write as (f o M)

```
(M o f) ==
   <M.da, M.ds o f,
    λs.M.init (s o f),
    λs1,a,s2.M.trans (s1 o f) a (s2 o f)>

(f o M) ==
    <M.da o f, M.ds,
     M.init,
     λs1,a,s2.
     ∃l:Label. (kind(a) = f l) c∧
                  (M.trans s1 <l, value(a)> s2)>
```

A.8 Preservation of Invariants

We define the notion of invariant in the usual way

```
n_reachable(M;n;x) ==
  if (n =z 0) then M.init x
```

```
  else ∃x':M.state ∃a:M.action
       n_reachable(M;n - 1;x')
      ∧ M.trans x' a x

reachable(M;x) ==  ∃n:ℕ. n_reachable(M;n;x)
M |= always s.(I[s]) ==  ∀s:M.state. reachable(M;s)      ⇒ I[s]
```

Then we have the following preservation theorems for the composition and renaming operators.

```
∀A,B:SM. ∀Inv1:A.state → ℙ.     ∀Inv2:B.state → ℙ.
A |= always s.(Inv1[s])
⇒ B |= always s.(Inv2[s])
⇒ (A ∩ B) |= always s.(Inv1[s] ∧ Inv2[s])

∀I:𝕌. ∀M:I → SM. ∀Inv:i:I   → M[i].state → ℙ.
(∀i:I. M[i] |= always s.(Inv[i;s]))
⇒ (∩i:I.M[i]) |= always s.(∀i:I. Inv[i;s])

∀M:SM. ∀f:Label → Label.    ∀I:M.state → ℙ.
M |= always s.(I[s]) ⇒ (M o f) |= always s.(I[s o f])

∀M:SM. ∀f:Label → Label.    ∀I:M.state → ℙ.
M |= always s.(I[s]) ⇒ (f o M) |= always s.(I[s])
```

A.9 Refinement

To define a refinment relation between state machines, we need a more detailed definition of reachability, the reachable-from relation.

```
n_reachable_from(M;n;s;x) ==
 if (n =z 0) then x = s
 else ∃x':M.state. ∃a:M.action
   n_reachable_from(M;n - 1;s;x') ∧ M.trans x' a x

 s --M→ x ==  ∃n:ℕ.    n_reachable_from(M;n;s;x)
```

Then we define the refinement of B by A via relartion R as follows

```
A ≤ B via s,s'.R[s; s'] ==
(∀s:A.state. A.init s
  ⇒ (∃s':B.state. reachable(B;s') ∧ R[s; s']))
  ∧
(∀s1,s2:A.state. ∀a:A.action. ∀s1':B.state
  reachable(A;s1)
 ⇒ A.trans s1 a s2
 ⇒ R[s1; s1']
 ⇒ (∃s2':B.state. s1' --B→   s2' ∧ R[s2; s2']))
```

The preservation theorem for refinement is

```
∀A,B:SM. ∀R:A.state → B.state     → ℙ. ∀I:B.state → ℙ.
 B |= always s.(I[s])
⇒ A ≤ B via s,s'.R[s;s']
⇒ A |= always s.(∃s':B.state. R[s;s'] ∧ I[s'])
```

References

[1] Martin Abadi and Leslie Lamport. Conjoining specifications. *ACM Toplas*, 17(3), May 1995.

[2] Stuart F. Allen. A Non-type-theoretic Definition of Martin-Löf's Types. In *Proceedings of the Second Symposium on Logic in Computer Science*, pages 215–224. IEEE, June 1987.

[3] J. L. Bates and Robert L. Constable. Proofs as programs. *ACM Transactions on Programming Languages and Systems*, 7(1):53–71, 1985.

[4] Paul Bernays and A. A. Fraenkel. *Axiomatic Set Theory.* North-Holland Publishing Company, Amsterdam, 1958.

[5] Gustavo Betarte and Alvaro Tasistro. *Extension of Martin Löf's type theory with record types and subtyping* chapter 2, pages 21–39, in Twenty-Five Years of Constructive Type Theory. Oxford Science Publications, 1999.

[6] Mark Bickford and Jason Hickey. An object-oriented approach to verifying group communication systems. Department of Computer Science, Cornell University, 1998.

[7] N. Bourbaki. *Elements of Mathematics, Algebra, Volume 1.* Addison-Wesley, Reading, MA, 1968.

[8] Luca Cardelli. Extensible records in a pure calculus of subtyping. In Carl. A. Gunter and John C. Mitchell, editors, *Theoretical Aspects of Object-Oriented Programming: Types, Semantics and Language Design.* MIT Press, 1994. A preliminary version appeared as SRC Research Report No. 81, 1992.

[9] Robert L. Constable. Experience using type theory as a foundation for computer science. In *Proceedings of the Tenth Annual IEEE Symposium on Logic in Computer Science*, pages 266–279. LICS, June 1995.

[10] Robert. L. Constable. The structure of Nuprl's type theory. In Helmut Schwichtenberg, editor, *Logic of Computation*, volume 157 of *Series F: Computer and Systems Sciences*, pages 123–156, Berlin, 1997. NATO Advanced Study Institute, International Summer School held in Marktoberdorf, Germany, July 25–August 6, 1995, Springer.

[11] Robert L. Constable. Types in logic, mathematics and programming. In S. R. Buss, editor, *Handbook of Proof Theory*, chapter X, pages 683–786. Elsevier Science B.V., 1998.

[12] Robert L. Constable, Stuart F. Allen, H. M. Bromley, W. R. Cleaveland, J. F. Cremer, R. W. Harper, Douglas J. Howe, T. B. Knoblock, N. P. Mendler, P. Panangaden, James T. Sasaki, and Scott F. Smith. *Implementing Mathematics with the Nuprl Development System.* Prentice-Hall, NJ, 1986.

[13] Robert L. Constable, Paul B. Jackson, Pavel Naumov, and Juan Uribe. Constructively formalizing automata. In *Proof, Language and Interaction: Essays in Honour of Robin Milner.* MIT Press, Cambridge, 1998.

[14] Robert L. Constable and D.R. Zlatin. The type theory of PL/CV3. *ACM Transactions on Programming Languages and Systems*, 6(1):94–117, January 1984.

[15] Karl Crary. Foundations for the implementation of higher-order subtyping. In *1997 ACM SIGPLAN International Conference on Functional Programming*, Amsterdam, June 1997. to appear.

[16] Karl Crary. Simple, efficient object encoding using intersection types. Technical Report TR98-1675, Department of Computer Science, Cornell University, April 1998.

[17] Karl Crary. *Type-Theoretic methodology for practical programming languages.* PhD thesis, Cornell University, August 1998.

[18] H. B. Curry and R. Feys. *Combinatory Logic, Volume I.* North-Holland, 1958.

[19] J-Y. Girard. On the meaning of the logical rules I: syntax vs semantics. Institut de Math, Marseille, 1998.

[20] Robert Harper and Mark Lillibridge. A type-theoretic approach to higher-order modules with sharing. *Twenty-First ACM SIGACT-SIGPLAN Symposium on Principles of Programming Languages*, pages 123–137, January 1994.

[21] Robert Harper and John C. Mitchell. On the type structure of standard ml. *ACM Transactions on Programming Languages and Systems*, 15(2):211–252, April 1993.

[22] Jason J. Hickey. Formal objects in type theory using very dependent types. Available through FOOL 3 web set on `www.cs.williams.edu`.

[23] C. A. R. Hoare. Notes on data structuring. In *Structured Programming.* Academic Press, New York, 1972.

[24] W. Howard. The formulas-as-types notion of construction. In *To H.B. Curry: Essays on Combinatory Logic, Lambda-Calculus and Formalism*, pages 479–490. Academic Press, NY, 1980.

[25] Douglas J. Howe. Importing mathematics from HOL into Nuprl. In J. von Wright, J. Grundy, and J. Harrison, editors, *Theorem Proving in Higher Order Logics*, volume 1125, of Lecture Notes in Computer Science, pages 267–282. Springer-Verlag, Berlin, 1996.

[26] Douglas J. Howe. Semantic foundations for embedding HOL in Nuprl. In Martin Wirsing and Maurice Nivat, editors, *Algebraic Methodology and Software Technology*, volume 1101 of Lecture Notes in Computer Science, pages 85–101. Springer-Verlag, Berlin, 1996.

[27] Xiaoming Liu, Christoph Kreitz, Robbert van Renesse, Jason Hickey, Mark Hayden, Ken Birman, and Robert Constable. Building reliable, high-performance communication systems from components. *Proc. of the 17th ACM Symposium on Operating System Principles*, pages 80–92, December 1999.

[28] Nancy Lynch. *Distributed Algorithms.* Morgan Kaufmann Publishers, San Mateo, CA, 1996.

[29] Nancy Lynch and Mark Tuttle. An introduction to Input/Output automata. *Centrum voor Wiskunde en Informatica*, 2(3):219–246, September 1989.

[30] Per Martin-Löf. An intuitionistic theory of types: Predicative part. In *Logic Colloquium '73*, pages 73–118. North-Holland, Amsterdam, 1973.

[31] Per Martin-Löf. Constructive mathematics and computer programming. In *Proceedings of the Sixth International Congress for Logic, Methodology, and Philosophy of Science*, pages 153–175, Amsterdam, 1982. North Holland.

[32] Per Martin-Löf. *Intuitionistic Type Theory, Studies in Proof Theory, Lecture Notes.* Bibliopolis, Napoli, 1984.

[33] P. Naumov. *Formalizing Reference Types in NuPRL.* PhD thesis, Cornell University, August 1998.

[34] Douglas R. Smith. Constructing specification morphisms. *Journal of symbolic Computation, Special Issue on Automatic Programming*, 16(5-6):571–606, 1993.

[35] Douglas R. Smith. Toward a classification approach to design. *Proceedings of the Fiftieth International Conference on Algebraic Methodology and Software Technology, AMAST'96, LNCS*, pages 62–84, 1996. Springer Verlag.

[36] Scott F. Smith and Robert L. Constable. Partial objects in constructive type theory. In *Proceedings of Second Symposium on Logic in Comp. Sci.*, pages 183–93. IEEE, Washington, D.C., 1987.

Foundations of Secure Computation
F.L. Bauer and R. Steinbrüggen (Eds.)
IOS Press, 2000

μJava: Embedding a Programming Language in a Theorem Prover

Tobias Nipkow and David von Oheimb and Cornelia Pusch
Institut für Informatik
Technische Universität München
80290 München, Germany
`http://www.in.tum.de/~{nipkow,oheimb,pusch}`

Abstract. This paper introduces the subset μJava of Java, essentially by omitting everything but classes. The type system and semantics of this language (and a corresponding abstract Machine μJVM) are formalized in the theorem prover Isabelle/HOL. Type safety both of μJava and the μJVM are mechanically verified.

To make the paper self-contained, it begins with introductions to Isabelle/HOL and the art of embedding languages in theorem provers.

1 Introduction

Embedding a programming language in a theorem prover means to describe (parts of) the language in the logic of the theorem prover, for example the abstract syntax, the semantics, the type system, a Hoare logic, a compiler, etc. One could call this *applied machine-checked semantics.*

Why should we want to do this? We have to distinguish two possible applications:

- Proving theorems about programs. This is usually called *program analysis* or *verification* and will not concern us very much in this paper.

- Proving theorems about the programming language. This is meta-theory and could be called *language analysis.* It is the very focus of our work.

Since programming languages are complex entities, the machine, i.e. the theorem prover, helps us to stay honest and also forces us to look for the simplest possible formalization of all concepts.

The purpose of this paper is to describe a particular such embedding, namely the definition of μJava, a fragment of Java, in the theorem prover Isabelle/HOL which is based on higher-order logic. The main analysis that we discuss is the proof of type safety, i.e. the absence of (unchecked) run-time type errors.

The plan of the paper is as follows. In the first third, we survey the necessary background information: after a few general remarks about higher-order logic (§2) we introduce the theorem prover Isabelle/HOL (§3) and discuss the main principles of language embeddings (§4). The other two thirds are dedicated to μJava and the corresponding virtual machine, the μJVM. For both levels, the type system and semantics of the language are presented and type safety is proved. Discussion of related work is found in the individual sections.

2 Higher-order logic

The term *higher-order logic* traditionally means a typed logic that permits quantification over functions or sets. A very specific example of such a logic is Church's *simple theory of types* [Chu40, And86]. In the theorem proving community, higher-order logic is often abbreviated to HOL and refers to the simple theory of types. We follow this convention which is due to one of the first theorem provers for this logic, Mike Gordon's HOL system [Gor85, GM93], a descendant of LCF [Pau87].

The work reported in this paper has been conducted with the help of Isabelle/HOL: Isabelle [Pau94] is a generic interactive theorem prover, and Isabelle/HOL an instance supporting HOL. There are many other systems supporting HOL, and many other higher-order logics. Mike Gordon's HOL system has spawned many closely related implementations. There is even an automatic theorem prover for HOL, the TPS system [ABI+96]—most other theorem provers for higher-order logics are interactive. Then there is the area of *type theories*, which are constructive higher-order logics with sophisticated type systems. This area is marked by its proliferation of different although related logics, many of which are supported by their own theorem prover. The most prominent of these provers are Coq [BBC+97], Nuprl [C+86] and Lego [Pol94]. Also based on type theory are the Elf and Twelf systems [Pfe91, PS99]. Strictly speaking the latter are not fully fledged theorem provers but logical frameworks specifically designed for prototyping but also (automatic) reasoning about deductive systems, in particular operational descriptions of programming languages.

3 Modeling and proving in Isabelle/HOL

What is HOL? In a nutshell, it is a classical (i.e. two-valued) logic with equality and total polymorphic higher-order functions. Therefore familiarity with classical predicate logic and functional programming is all one needs when reading this paper, since we will not be concerned with the low level details in proofs. The system Isabelle/HOL is more than just a theorem prover for HOL, it is a fully fledged specification and programming language. Coming from a programming perspective, one could characterize Isabelle/HOL as combination of functional programming, logic programming and quantifiers. The remainder of this section describes the main features of Isabelle/HOL from an abstract perspective. For more details see the Isabelle/HOL tutorial [Nip99a].

3.1 Terms, types, formulae and theories

The type system is similar to that of typed functional programming languages like ML, Haskell and Gofer. There are basic types like *bool*, *nat* and *int*, and type constructors (written postfix) like $(\tau)list$ and $(\tau)set$ (where τ is the argument type). Function types are written $\tau_1 \Rightarrow \tau_2$ and represent the type of all *total* functions. Type variables, which are used to express polymorphism, are written α, β etc.

Terms are formed as in λ-calculus by application and abstraction. The constructions $\mathsf{let}\ x = e_1\ \mathsf{in}\ e_2$, $\mathsf{if}\ b\ \mathsf{then}\ e_1\ \mathsf{else}\ e_2$ and $\mathsf{case}\ e\ \mathsf{of}\ p_1 \rightarrow e_1 \mid \ldots$ familiar from functional programming are also supported.

Formulae are terms of type *bool*. HOL offers the usual logical vocabulary. The notation

$$\frac{A_1 \quad \ldots \quad A_n}{C}$$

means $A_1 \wedge \ldots \wedge A_n \longrightarrow C$.

Modules in Isabelle/HOL are called *theories* to emphasize their mathematical content. They contain collections of declarations and definitions of types and constants (which include functions). You could also call them specifications or programs, depending on your point of view. Although you can in principle add new axioms as well, this is strongly discouraged because of the following variant of Murphy's law:

What can be inconsistent will be inconsistent.

Therefore the HOL dogma (going back to Gordon's HOL system) is never to add new axioms, only definitions, because the latter preserve consistency. However, working only with basic non-recursive definitions of the form

$$name \equiv term$$

can be very cumbersome. Therefore Isabelle/HOL additionally provides several derived application-oriented definition principles: recursive datatypes, recursive functions and inductively defined sets. We discuss them in turn.

3.2 Functional programming

Functional programming is supported by constructs for the definition of recursive datatypes and recursive functions. A simple example is the theory of lists:

datatype α *list* = Nil ([])
| Cons α (α *list*) (**infixr** #)

consts app :: α *list* $\to$ α *list* $\to$ α *list* (**infixr** @)

primrec
$[]$ @ $ys = ys$
$(x$ # $xs)$ @ $ys = x$ # $(xs$ @ $ys)$

It defines the recursive datatype of lists together with some syntactic sugar (Nil can be written [] and Cons x xs can be written x#xs), declares a function *app* (with infix syntax @), and defines *app* by primitive recursion. The key proof technique in this setting is structural induction on datatypes. For example, associativity of @

$$(xs \mathbin{@} ys) \mathbin{@} zs = xs \mathbin{@} (ys \mathbin{@} zs)$$

is proved by (structural) induction on xs:

Nil: $([] \mathbin{@} ys) \mathbin{@} zs = ys \mathbin{@} zs = [] \mathbin{@} (ys \mathbin{@} zs)$

Cons: $((x \mathbin{\#} xs) \mathbin{@} ys) \mathbin{@} zs = (x \mathbin{\#} (xs \mathbin{@} ys)) \mathbin{@} zs =$
$x \mathbin{\#} ((xs \mathbin{@} ys) \mathbin{@} zs) = x \mathbin{\#} (xs \mathbin{@} (ys \mathbin{@} zs)) = (x\#xs) \mathbin{@} (ys \mathbin{@} zs)$

Such proofs are performed automatically by Isabelle/HOL.

More complex recursion patterns can be expressed by *well-founded recursion*, which requires a termination ordering to convince Isabelle/HOL of the totality of the defined function. More precisely, the ordering is used in a non-recursive definition of the function from which the desired recursion equations are proved as theorems. For details see the work by Slind [Sli96, Sli97, Sli99].

Totality is always the key requirement when defining a function in HOL since HOL is a logic of total functions, and the introduction of a truly partial function would cause an inconsistency.

3.3 Inductively defined sets

Isabelle/HOL comes with a type $(\tau)set$ of (finite and infinite) sets over type τ and together with the usual operations. Set comprehension is written $\{x\ .\ P\}$ instead of $\{x \mid P\}$.

Sets can be defined inductively in Isabelle/HOL, for example the set of even numbers:

consts even :: *nat set*

inductive

$$0 \in \mathsf{even} \qquad \frac{n \in \mathsf{even}}{n{+}2 \in \mathsf{even}}$$

The importance of this mechanism cannot be overestimated because computer science abounds with inductive processes.

In general, an inductive definition looks like this

consts M :: τ *set*

inductive

$$\frac{t_1 \in \mathsf{M} \quad \dots \quad t_n \in \mathsf{M}}{t \in \mathsf{M}}$$

and defines M as the *least* subset of τ which satisfies the given rules. There can be any finite number of rules of the given format. In fact, a more general rule format is supported, but this one suffices for our purposes.

Leastness is the mathematical way of saying that the given rules are the only rules that define M. From a programmer's perspective, inductive definitions can be seen as providing logic programming with closed world assumption. This gives rise to the principle of *rule induction.* For example,

$$n \in \mathsf{even} \longrightarrow n{+}n \in \mathsf{even}$$

is proved by induction on the derivation of $n \in \mathsf{even}$:

rule 1: $0{+}0 \in \mathsf{even}$

rule 2: $n{+}n \in \mathsf{even} \longrightarrow n{+}n{+}2 \in \mathsf{even} \longrightarrow n{+}n{+}2{+}2 \in \mathsf{even} \longrightarrow (n{+}2){+}(n{+}2) \in \mathsf{even}$

In general, $x \in \mathsf{M} \longrightarrow P(x)$ is proved by rule induction on $x \in \mathsf{M}$, i.e. by showing that P is preserved by every rule:

$$\frac{P(t_1) \quad \dots \quad P(t_n)}{P(t)}$$

In fact, one may also assume $t_i \in M$ for all $i = 1, \dots, n$. Isabelle/HOL supports proof by rule induction.

3.4 Peeking at the library

The formalization of Java, as any large project, makes use of many predefined theories. We quickly summarize the most important ones.

3.4.1 Cartesian products

The type $\tau_1 \times \tau_2$ of Cartesian products of τ_1 and τ_2 comes with projection functions $\mathsf{fst} :: \alpha \times \beta \rightarrow \alpha$ and $\mathsf{snd} :: \alpha \times \beta \rightarrow \beta$, and with (postfix) operations for constructing the transitive closure R^+ and transitive reflexive closure R^* of a relation $R :: (\alpha \times \alpha)set$.

3.4.2 Lists

In addition to the basic list constructs shown above, the list library contains the following relevant functions:

$$
\begin{array}{ll}
\mathsf{length} & :: \alpha\ list \to nat \\
\mathsf{set} & :: \alpha\ list \to \alpha\ set \\
\mathsf{map} & :: (\alpha \to \beta) \to \alpha\ list \to \beta\ list \\
\mathsf{zip} & :: \alpha\ list \to \beta\ list \to (\alpha \times \beta) list \\
\mathsf{nodups} & :: \alpha\ list \to bool \\
\mathsf{nth} & :: \alpha\ list \to nat \to \alpha
\end{array}
$$

The meaning of length, set, map and zip should be obvious; nodups xs is true iff xs contains no duplicates, and nth xs i selects the i-th element (starting from 0) and is abbreviated by $xs!i$. The usual notation $[x,y,z]$ instead of $x\#y\#z\#[]$ is also supported.

3.4.3 Options

The datatype of optional values

datatype $\alpha\ option\ =\ \mathsf{None}\ |\ \mathsf{Some}\ \alpha$

consts $\mathsf{the} :: \alpha\ option \to \alpha$

primrec $\mathsf{the}\ (\mathsf{Some}\ x) = x$
$\mathsf{the}\ \mathsf{None} = \ldots$

is used to add a new element None to a type and wrap the remaining elements up in Some; function the unwraps them again; on None it can be defined arbitrarily.

3.4.4 Mappings

One frequently needs partial functions where one can determine if an entry is defined or not. We call them mappings and define them as functions with optional range type:

types $\alpha \leadsto \beta\ =\ \alpha \to \beta\ option$

Typical applications are symbol tables (where declared names are mapped to some information) or heap storage (where allocated addresses are mapped to their content).

For the convenient manipulation of mappings the following functions are provided:

$$
\begin{array}{ll}
\mathsf{empty} & :: \alpha \leadsto \beta \\
\_(\_\mapsto\_) & :: (\alpha \leadsto \beta) \to \alpha \to \beta \to (\alpha \leadsto \beta) \\
\_(\_[\mapsto]\_) & :: (\alpha \leadsto \beta) \to \alpha\ list \to \beta\ list \to (\alpha \leadsto \beta) \\
\_\oplus\_ & :: (\alpha \leadsto \beta) \to (\alpha \leadsto \beta) \to (\alpha \leadsto \beta) \\
\mathsf{map\_of} & :: (\alpha{\times}\beta)\ list \to (\alpha \leadsto \beta)
\end{array}
$$

They represent the empty mapping, updating in one place and in a list of places, overwriting of one map with another, and turning an association list into a mapping. The definitions are unsurprising:

$$
\begin{array}{ll}
\mathsf{empty} & \equiv \lambda k.\ \mathsf{None} \\
m(x \mapsto y) & \equiv \lambda k.\ \mathsf{if}\ k{=}x\ \mathsf{then\ Some}\ y\ \mathsf{else}\ m\ k \\
s \oplus t & \equiv \lambda k.\ \mathsf{case}\ t\ k\ \mathsf{of\ None} \to s\ k\ |\ \mathsf{Some}\ y \to \mathsf{Some}\ y \\
\mathsf{map\_of}\ [] & = \mathsf{empty} \\
\mathsf{map\_of}\ ((x,y)\#l) & = (\mathsf{map\_of}\ l)(x \mapsto y) \\
m([]\ [\mapsto]\ []) & = m \\
m(a\#as[\mapsto]b\#bs) & = m(a{\mapsto}b)(as[\mapsto]bs)
\end{array}
$$

4 The basics of programming language embeddings

Historically, this work has its roots in research on generating programming environments, especially compilers and interpreters, from formal language descriptions. Prominent systems of this kind are PSG [Sne85] (based on denotational semantics), ASF+SDF [Kli93] (based on algebraic specifications) and Centaur [BCD⁺88]. Centaur is quite close to our framework because it is based on operational semantics expressed by inference rules, a connection that has already been exploited by Bertot and Fraer [BF95].

However, the first embedding of a semantics in a theorem prover is due to Gordon [Gor89], who defined the semantics of a simple `while`-language in the HOL system and derived the rules of Hoare logic as theorems. The attractiveness of this approach soon lead other researchers to embed various programming languages in various theorem provers: CCS [Nes94], CSP [TW97], Java [Sym99, ON99, JHvB⁺98], JVM [Coh97, Pus99], ML [Sym94, VG94, MG94], UNITY [APP94, Pra95, HC96, Pau99] and Hoare logics [Nip98, Kle98, Ohe99]. This is just a random selection and not a complete list. We will now discuss the basic principles of language embeddings.

The literature [BGG⁺92] distinguishes two different kinds of embeddings:

deep embeddings represent the abstract syntax of the language as a separate datatype and define the semantics using the syntax (for example as a function from syntax to semantics).

shallow embeddings define the semantics directly, i.e. each construct in the language is represented directly by some function on a semantic domain.

The difference is best explained by an example.

Assume we want to embed boolean expressions consisting of variables, conjunctions and disjunctions in Isabelle/HOL. Let us call them *positive boolean expressions*. The semantics of a boolean expression is a function from environments to boolean values, where environments map variables (we assume we are given a type *var* of variables) to boolean values:

types $env = var \rightarrow bool$
$\quad\quad sem = env \rightarrow bool$

A shallow embedding represents the semantics only, i.e. it identifies the positive boolean expressions with type *sem*. Each language construct is directly defined in terms of semantics:

$$\mathsf{var}\ p \equiv \lambda e.\ e\ p, \qquad \mathsf{and}\ b_1\ b_2 \equiv \lambda e.\ b_1\ e \wedge b_2\ e, \qquad \mathsf{or}\ b_1\ b_2 \equiv \lambda e.\ b_1\ e \vee b_2\ e$$

Thus the boolean expression "$p \wedge q$" (where p and q are variables) is represented directly by the HOL function $\lambda e.\ e(p) \wedge e(q)$ of type *sem*.

A deep embedding requires a definition of the syntax, usually as an inductive type:

datatype $pbex = \mathsf{Var}\ var \mid \mathsf{And}\ pbex\ pbex \mid \mathsf{Or}\ pbex\ pbex$

The semantics is defined by an explicit function $eval :: pbex \rightarrow sem$:

$$\begin{aligned}
\mathsf{eval}\ (\mathsf{Var}\ p) &= \lambda e.\ e(p)\\
\mathsf{eval}\ (\mathsf{And}\ b_1\ b_2) &= \lambda e.\ (\mathsf{eval}\ b_1\ e \wedge \mathsf{eval}\ b_2\ e)\\
\mathsf{eval}\ (\mathsf{Or}\ b_1\ b_2) &= \lambda e.\ (\mathsf{eval}\ b_1\ e \vee \mathsf{eval}\ b_2\ e)
\end{aligned}$$

The boolean expression "$p \wedge q$" is represented by And (Var p) (Var p) and applying *eval* to it yields its semantics $\lambda e.\ e(p) \wedge e(q)$.

Both embeddings allow proofs about individual boolean expressions, for example "$p \wedge p = p$". In a shallow embedding this reduces (via extensionality of functions) to the idempotence of $\wedge$ in HOL:

$$((\lambda e.\ e(p) \wedge e(p)) = (\lambda e.\ e(p))) \quad = \quad (e(p) \wedge e(p) = e(p)) \quad = \quad \mathsf{True}$$

The deep embedding has to be reduced to the shallow one first before the truth emerges:

$$(\mathsf{eval}(\mathsf{And}\ (\mathsf{Var}\ p)\ (\mathsf{Var}\ p)) = \mathsf{eval}(\mathsf{Var}\ p)) \quad = \quad ((\lambda e.\ e(p) \wedge e(p)) = (\lambda e.\ e(p))) \quad = \quad \mathsf{True}$$

This indicates that deep embeddings are often harder to work with than shallow ones because the syntax has to be translated into semantics first.

However, the tide turns against shallow embeddings when we consider general statements about the embedded language as a whole, i.e. meta-theory. For example, we would like to prove monotonicity of positive boolean expressions. To this end we order *bool* and *env* in the canonical way, i.e. False < True and *env* is ordered pointwise:

$$x \leq y \quad \equiv \quad x \longrightarrow y$$
$$e_1 \leq_e e_2 \equiv \quad \forall p.\ e_1(p) \leq e_2(p)$$

In the deep embedding, monotonicity of pb :: *pbex* is expressed as

$$e_1 \leq_e e_2 \quad \longrightarrow \quad \mathsf{eval}\ pb\ e_1 \leq \mathsf{eval}\ pb\ e_2$$

and proved by induction on pb. The Var-case is straightforward by assumption:

$$\mathsf{eval}\ (\mathsf{Var}\ p)\ e_1 = e_1(p) \leq e_2(p) = \mathsf{eval}\ (\mathsf{Var}\ p)\ e_2.$$

The And-case (and similarly the Or-case) follows from the monotonicity of $\wedge$ in HOL using the induction hypotheses:

$$\mathsf{eval}\ (\mathsf{And}\ x\ y)\ e_1 = \mathsf{eval}\ x\ e_1 \wedge \mathsf{eval}\ y\ e_1 \leq \mathsf{eval}\ x\ e_2 \wedge \mathsf{eval}\ y\ e_2 = \mathsf{eval}\ (\mathsf{And}\ x\ y)\ e_2$$

In the shallow embedding however, monotonicity of f :: *sem*, i.e.

$$e_1 \leq_e e_2 \quad \longrightarrow \quad f\ e_1 \leq f\ e_2$$

is not true because *sem* contains the semantics of *all* boolean expressions, not just the positive ones. The restriction to variables, conjunctions and disjunctions is not part of the specification and thus not available for an inductive proof. Hence it is folklore that shallow embeddings do not allow meta-theory. However, this is not true as Felty *et al.* [FHR99] have shown: one can often define the required subset of the semantics via an inductive definition that follows the syntax. In our case we define a subset Pbex of denotations of positive boolean expressions:

consts Pbex :: *sem set*

inductive

$$\frac{}{\mathsf{var}\ p \in \mathsf{Pbex}} \qquad \frac{b_1 \in \mathsf{Pbex} \qquad b_2 \in \mathsf{Pbex}}{\mathsf{and}\ b_1\ b_2 \in \mathsf{Pbex}} \qquad \frac{b_1 \in \mathsf{Pbex} \qquad b_2 \in \mathsf{Pbex}}{\mathsf{or}\ b_1\ b_2 \in \mathsf{Pbex}}$$

Monotonicity of Pbex is expressed as $b \in \mathsf{Pbex} \longrightarrow \ e_1 \leq_e e_2 \longrightarrow \ b\ e_1 \leq b\ e_2$ and proved by rule induction on $b \in \mathsf{Pbex}$. The proof follows the one above for *pbex* very closely.

It should be clear from our discussion that a shallow embedding is advantageous for reasoning about individual elements of the embedded language. For meta-theory a deep embedding is the natural choice, but combining a shallow embedding with an inductive definition may also work. Our Java formalization presented below is a deep embedding because of our interest in meta-theory and also because the semantics is defined operationally rather than denotationally. Thus there is no direct semantic counterpart for each syntactic construct.

5 μJava

This section describes the μJava formalization and one of its applications, a proof of type-safety. After motivating the subset of Java that we chose and giving a short survey of related work, we present the abstract syntax and operational semantics of μJava along with the corresponding well-formedness and well-typedness conditions. Subsequently we introduce the notions required for the type-safety proof and state the main results.

5.1 Why μJava?

Being a general-purpose programming language, Java has (almost) all features a state-of-the-art language is supposed to offer. Formalizing all of them is possible, but the amount of detail and the complexity of several aspects like concurrency would make it involved and difficult to handle. Thus a typical formalization like Bali [ON99] on the one hand tries to cover the main features of Java, but on the other hand intentionally leaves out many bulky but uninteresting details. For didactic purposes, the result is still too involved. So we further reduced Bali to the bare essentials of Java, namely an imperative language with classes: μJava.

5.2 Other approaches to formalizing Java

There are several formalizations of Java, the pioneering one being of Drossopoulou and Eisenbach [DE97]. It gives a transition ("small-step") semantics of the core object-oriented features of Java and a proof of type-safety, which has been extended later [DE99] to include exception handling. Syme has embedded this paper-and-pencil work in his theorem prover DECLARE [Sym99], correcting several flaws that came up thanks to the rigorous machine-checked treatment. In parallel, we have developed the first version of our embedding in Isabelle/HOL [NO98] covering a similar fraction of Java but using an evaluation ("big-step") semantics. Börger and Schulte have formalized (on paper) almost the full Java language as an Abstract State Machine [BS99]. Jacobs el al. translate Java code directly into the PVS higher-order logic (as a shallow embedding) in order to conduct program verification [JHvB+98].

5.3 Design goals

For any formalization, it is important to aim at the following general design goals.

- readability (this is the basic requirement, as otherwise handling and applying the formalization would be severely hampered),
- faithfulness to the original language specification,
- succinctness and simplicity,
- maintainability and extendibility,
- adequacy for applications like theorem proving.

The reader is invited to keep them in mind while reading the subsequent sections and to judge herself how far we have reached them.

5.4 Abstract syntax of μJava

5.4.1 Programs

A key idea of this formalization is to separate declarations from code. Not only is their structure inherently different, they can also be described in isolation from each other. Since furthermore the structures of declarations for μJava and its μJVM are identical (from an abstract point of view), it is profitable to formalize the declarations in a generic style and supplying the actual method bodies (i.e., code) as a parameter.

As a μJava program consists of a series of class declarations, we model with a (parameterized) type that stands for a list of class declarations:

types α *prog* = α *cdecl list*

The parameter α is the type of method bodies. The list representation is not the most abstract one possible, since it retains the immaterial order of the class declarations. Yet its advantages are that it implies a finiteness constraint on the number of declarations and that the canonical conversion to a mapping yields a simple lookup mechanism.

A class declaration consists of the class name (of type *cname* which does not need to be specified further), the name of the superclass (for all classes except `Object`), and the lists of field and method declarations:

types α *cdecl* = *cname* × *cname option* × *fdecl list* × α *mdecl list*

Field declarations simply give the field name and type,

types *fdecl* = *vname* × *ty*

whereas method declarations give the method signature (consisting of the method name and the list of parameter types), the result type, and the method body, which is the parameter motivated above.

types *sig* = *mname* × *ty list*
α *mdecl* = *sig* × *ty* × α

5.4.2 Values and types

The variety of values and their corresponding types in μJava is limited to the most important ones, basically Booleans, integers, and class references:

datatype *val* = Unit
| Bool *bool*
| Intg *int*
| Null
| Addr *loc*

datatype *ty* = `void`
| `boolean`
| `int`
| NT
| Class *cname*

Here NT stands for the null type, i.e. the common type of all Null references. We have invented the type `void` (with the single dummy value Unit) for convenience in modeling the (non-existing) result of void methods.

Function default_val, defined by cases on *ty*, is used for variable initialization. Function typeof (of HOL type (*loc* → *ty option*) → *val* → *ty option*), determining the dynamic type of a value, is used for the definition of conformance in §5.8.2, where the argument *dt* is used to dermine the existence and the (class) types of objects on the heap.

```
primrec default_val void      = Unit
        default_val boolean   = Bool False
        default_val int       = Intg 0
        default_val NT        = Null
        default_val (Class C) = Null
```

```
primrec typeof dt Unit     = Some void
        typeof dt (Bool b) = Some boolean
        typeof dt (Intg i) = Some int
        typeof dt Null     = Some NT
        typeof dt (Addr a) = dt a
```

5.4.3 Looking up method and field declarations

The method lookup function

method :: α *prog* $\times$ *cname* $\rightarrow$ (*sig* $\rightsquigarrow$ *cname* $\times$ *ty* $\times$ α)

serves as a typical example of a definition by well-founded recursion. The intended result of method (Γ, C) sg is Some (D, T, b) where class D is the first class (traversing the subclass hierarchy upwards starting from C) that declares a method with signature sg, which has return type T and body b. Exploiting the fact that the inverse subclass relation (see §5.5.1) is well-founded, the following characteristic equation can be derived from the definition of method:

```
wf ((subcls1 Γ)⁻¹) ⟶
  method (Γ,C) = case map_of Γ C of None → empty
    | Some (sc,fs,ms) →
        (case sc of None → empty | Some D → method (Γ,D)) ⊕
        map_of (map (λ(s,m). (s,C,m)) ms)
```

A similar definition is used for

fields :: α *prog* $\times$ *cname* $\rightarrow$ ((*vname* $\times$ *cname*) $\times$ *ty*) *list*

The formalization given up to here is identical for μJava and our μJVM. Now comes the part of the abstract syntax that is μJava-specific.

5.4.4 μJava statements and expressions

The μJava statements are just the canonical ones for imperative languages, except that any expression may be used as statement and assignments are considered as expressions since they yield a result. Next to literals, local variables and type casts, the μJava expressions contain the actual object-oriented features, namely class creation, field access and assignment, and method call. We model the `this` expression by a special non-assignable local variable of that name. The Isabelle/HOL datatype definition of the abstract syntax intentionally looks pretty much like a BNF specification:

```
datatype  stmt = Skip
               | expr
               | stmt; stmt
               | if (expr) stmt else stmt
               | while (expr) stmt

and       expr = new cname
               | (ty)expr
               | val
               | vname
               | vname := expr
               | {cname}expr.vname
               | {cname}expr.vname := expr
               | expr.mname({ty list}expr list)
```

5.4.5 *Program annotations*

The parts in braces $\{\ldots\}$ in the above definition of expressions are called *type annotations.* Strictly speaking, they are not part of the source language but are normally computed by the compiler during type checking. Their purpose is to serve as auxiliary information that is crucial for the resolution of method overloading and the static binding of fields, with the following meaning:

Static overloading of methods: in the method call *obj.m({formal-param-tys} params)*, *formal-param-tys* stands for the formal parameter types of the maximally specific method applicable w.r.t. the static types of *obj* and *params*. During execution, *(m,formal-param-tys)* is used for method lookup.

Static binding of fields: in $\{C\}obj.f$, C is the class declaring the field f w.r.t. the static type of *obj*. During execution, (C,f) is used for field selection.

In our language embedding, we do not distinguish between the source language and the augmented internal form since this would lead to a considerable amount of redundancy. Instead, we assume that the annotations are added beforehand (by some preprocessing step) and checked by the typing rules given in §5.5.3 below.

5.4.6 *Method bodies*

Finally, the definitions of statements and expressions being available, we can formalize μJava method body declarations. We define them as a tuple of parameter names, local variable declarations, a statement comprising the actual code block, and an expression to be returned—there is no return statement in μJava.

types $java\_mb = vname\ list \times (vname \times ty)\ list \times stmt \times expr$

5.5 *Type system of μJava*

The type system consists of the types already introduced, some basic relations between types (in particular, classes) and the actual typing rules for expressions and statements.

5.5.1 *Type relations*

Being an object-oriented language, μJava of course features the subclass relation, which is extracted w.r.t. a given program Γ:

- $\mathsf{subcls1}\ \Gamma \equiv \{(C,D)\ .\ \exists r.\ (C,\mathsf{Some}\ D,r) \in \mathsf{set}\ \Gamma\}$
- $\Gamma\vdash C \preceq_{\mathsf{c}} D \equiv (C,D) \in (\mathsf{subcls1}\ \Gamma)^*$

Built on the subclass relation we define the important *widening* relation, where $\Gamma\vdash S \preceq T$ means that in the context Γ value of type S may be used in a place where a value of type T is expected. We give this relation via an inductive definition:

inductive

$$\frac{}{\Gamma\vdash T \preceq T} \qquad \frac{}{\Gamma\vdash \mathsf{NT} \preceq \mathsf{Class}\ C} \qquad \frac{\Gamma\vdash C \preceq_{\mathsf{c}} D}{\Gamma\vdash \mathsf{Class}\ C \preceq \mathsf{Class}\ D}$$

5.5.2 Typing judgments

There are three forms of typing judgments, namely for well-typed statements, expressions, and expression lists:
$java\_mb\ env \vdash stmt\ \surd$
$java\_mb\ env \vdash expr :: ty$
$java\_mb\ env \vdash expr\ list\ [::]\ ty\ list$

The judgments include a context called *environment* that consists of the program and type bindings for local variables currently in scope:

types $\alpha\ env = \alpha\ prog \times (vname \rightsquigarrow ty)$

The actual type parameter for μJava environments is $java\_mb$.

5.5.3 Typing rules

The typing rules for most μJava terms are straightforward, thus we give only one typical example, namely the well-typedness of `while` loops:

$$\frac{E \vdash e :: \texttt{boolean} \qquad E \vdash s\ \surd}{E \vdash \texttt{while}\ (e)\ s\ \surd}$$

More interesting are the rules for field access and method call.

The field access rule enables static binding by calculating the annotation C with the help of the auxiliary function $\mathsf{field} \equiv \mathsf{map\_of} \circ (\mathsf{map}\ (\lambda((fn,fd),ft).\ (fn,(fd,ft)))) \circ \mathsf{fields}$ as follows:

$$\frac{\begin{array}{c}E \vdash a :: \mathsf{Class}\ D \\ \mathsf{field}\ (\mathsf{fst}\ E,D)\ fn = \mathsf{Some}\ (C,fT)\end{array}}{E \vdash \{C\}a.fn :: fT}$$

In a similar fashion, method overloading is resolved in the method call rule. This involves the requirement that the max_spec auxiliary function (given below) yields a most specific applicable method.

$$\frac{\begin{array}{c}E \vdash e :: \mathsf{Class}\ C \qquad E \vdash ps\ [::]\ pTs \\ \mathsf{max\_spec}\ (\mathsf{fst}\ E)\ C\ (mn,pTs) = \{((\_,rT),fpTs)\}\end{array}}{E \vdash e.mn(\{fpTs\}ps) :: rT}$$

5.5.4 Maximally specific methods

Following the involved definition in the Java specification, $\mathsf{max\_spec}\ \Gamma\ C\ sig$ determines the set of all maximally specific applicable methods of signature sig available for class C in program Γ: $\mathsf{max\_spec}\ \Gamma\ C\ sig \equiv$
$\{m.\ m \in \mathsf{appl\_methds}\ \Gamma\ C\ sig \wedge (\forall m' {\in} \mathsf{appl\_methds}\ \Gamma\ C\ sig.\ \mathsf{more\_spec}\ \Gamma\ m'\ m \longrightarrow m'{=}m)\}$

The partial order on methods used for max_spec is given by the relation $\mathsf{more\_spec}\ \Gamma$, which states that the defining classes as well as all parameter types are (pointwise) in widening relation:

$\mathsf{more\_spec}\ \Gamma\ ((d,\_),pTs)\ ((d',\_),pTs') \equiv \Gamma \vdash d \preceq d' \wedge \mathsf{list\_all2}\ (\lambda T\ T'.\ \Gamma \vdash T \preceq T')\ pTs\ pTs'$
$\mathsf{list\_all2}\ P\ xs\ ys \equiv \mathsf{length}\ xs = \mathsf{length}\ ys \wedge (\forall (x,y) {\in} \mathsf{zip}\ xs\ ys.\ P\ x\ y)$

The set of methods (available for class C in program Γ) applicable for signature (mn,pTs) are those with name mn and fitting parameter types:

$\mathsf{appl\_methds}\ \Gamma\ C\ (mn,pTs) \equiv \{((\mathsf{Class}\ D,rT),pTs').$
$\quad \mathsf{method}\ (\Gamma,C)\ (mn,pTs') = \mathsf{Some}\ (D,rT,\_) \wedge$
$\quad \mathsf{list\_all2}\ (\lambda T\ T'.\ \Gamma \vdash T \preceq T')\ pTs\ pTs'\}$

5.6 Well-formedness of both μJava and μJVM programs

Now we are equipped to express the well-formedness conditions on programs, which are part of the static checks performed by the compiler.

5.6.1 Programs

A program is well-formed iff it contains class `Object` (for simplicity, we model this class as if it were user-defined) and all class declarations are well-formed and no class is declared twice:

$$\begin{array}{l}\mathsf{wf\_prog}\ \mathit{wf\_mb}\ \Gamma \equiv \mathsf{ObjectDecl} \in \mathsf{set}\ \Gamma\ \wedge \\ \qquad\qquad (\forall c{\in}\mathsf{set}\ \Gamma.\ \mathsf{wf\_cdecl}\ \mathit{wf\_mb}\ \Gamma\ c) \wedge \mathsf{nodups}\ (\mathsf{map}\ \mathsf{fst}\ \Gamma) \\ \mathsf{ObjectDecl} \equiv (\mathtt{Object},\ (\mathsf{None},\ [],\ []))\end{array}$$

Note that this definition is parameterized with *wf_mb*, which is aimed to be the well-formedness predicate for method bodies (given in §5.6.3 below).

A class declaration (C,sc,fs,ms) is well-formed (in Γ) iff

- all types in the field declarations *fs* are legal,
- no field is declared twice,
- all method declarations in *ms* are well-formed,
- no method is declared twice,
- only class `Object` has no superclass,
- if C extends D then
  - D must be declared in Γ,
  - D must not be a subclass of C, and
  - if a method in *ms* overwrites one higher up, its return type must widen to the return type higher up.

Formally:

$$\begin{array}{l}\mathsf{wf\_cdecl}\ \mathit{wf\_mb}\ \Gamma\ (C,sc,fs,ms) \equiv \\ \quad (\forall(\_,T){\in}\mathsf{set}\ fs.\ \mathsf{is\_type}\ \Gamma\ T)\ \wedge \\ \quad \mathsf{nodups}\ (\mathsf{map}\ \mathsf{fst}\ fs)\ \wedge \\ \quad (\forall m{\in}\mathsf{set}\ ms.\ \mathsf{wf\_mdecl}\ \mathit{wf\_mb}\ \Gamma\ C\ m)\ \wedge \\ \quad \mathsf{nodups}\ (\mathsf{map}\ \mathsf{fst}\ ms)\ \wedge \\ \quad \mathsf{case}\ sc\ \mathsf{of}\ \mathsf{None} \rightarrow C = \mathtt{Object} \\ \quad\ \mid \mathsf{Some}\ D \rightarrow D \in \mathsf{set}\ (\mathsf{map}\ \mathsf{fst}\ \Gamma)\ \wedge \\ \qquad\qquad\qquad \neg\ \Gamma{\vdash}D{\preceq_{\mathsf{c}}}C\ \wedge \\ \qquad\qquad\qquad \forall(sg,T,\_){\in}\mathsf{set}\ ms.\ \forall T'.\ \mathsf{method}(\Gamma,D)\ sg = \mathsf{Some}(\_,T',\_) \longrightarrow \Gamma{\vdash}T \preceq T'\end{array}$$

5.6.2 Methods (both μJava and μJVM)

The definition of well-formed classes relies on the well-formedness conditions for method declarations, which in turn rely on the well-formedness of method heads, the well-formedness parameter for method bodies, and the simple is_type predicate testing the existence of a class:

$$\begin{array}{l}\mathsf{wf\_mdecl}\ \mathit{wf\_mb}\ \Gamma\ C\ (sig,rT,b) \equiv \mathsf{wf\_mhead}\ \Gamma\ sig\ rT \wedge \mathit{wf\_mb}\ \Gamma\ C\ (sig,rT,b) \\ \mathsf{wf\_mhead}\ \Gamma\ (mn,pTs)\ rT \quad \equiv (\forall T{\in}\mathsf{set}\ pTs.\ \mathsf{is\_type}\ \Gamma\ T) \wedge \mathsf{is\_type}\ \Gamma\ rT \\ \mathsf{is\_type}\ \Gamma\ T \equiv \mathsf{case}\ T\ \mathsf{of}\ \mathsf{Class}\ C \rightarrow C \in \mathsf{set}\ (\mathsf{map}\ \mathsf{fst}\ \Gamma)\ \mid\ \_ \rightarrow \mathsf{True}\end{array}$$

5.6.3 Method bodies (μJava)

A method with signature (*mn*,*pTs*), return type *rT*, and body (*pns*,*lvars*,*blk*,*res*) is well-formed within class *C* in Γ iff

- there are as many parameter names *pns* as parameter types *pTs*,
- the names of parameters and local variables are unique and do not clash,
- all types of the local variables *lvars* are legal,
- in the context of Γ, the local variables and the current class *C*, the code block *blk* is well-typed and the type of the result expression *res* widens to *rT*.

Formally:

$$
\begin{array}{l}
\mathsf{wf\_java\_mdecl}\ \Gamma\ C\ ((mn,pTs),rT,(pns,lvars,blk,res)) \equiv \\
\quad \mathsf{length}\ pns = \mathsf{length}\ pTs\ \wedge \\
\quad \mathsf{nodups}\ pns\ \wedge\ \mathsf{nodups}\ (\mathsf{map\ fst}\ lvars)\ \wedge \\
\quad (\forall pn{\in}\mathsf{set}\ pns.\ \mathsf{map\_of}\ lvars\ pn = \mathsf{None})\ \wedge \\
\quad (\forall (vn,T){\in}\mathsf{set}\ lvars.\ \mathsf{is\_type}\ \Gamma\ T)\ \wedge \\
\quad \mathsf{let}\ E = (\Gamma,\mathsf{map\_of}\ lvars(pns[\mapsto]pTs)(\mathtt{this}{\mapsto}\mathsf{Class}\ C)) \\
\quad \mathsf{in}\ E{\vdash}blk\ \surd\ \wedge\ (\exists T.\ E{\vdash}res{::}T\ \wedge\ \Gamma{\vdash}T{\preceq}rT)
\end{array}
$$

Note that in contrast to Java, it is not required that local variables are initialized explicitly: the operational semantics does so implicitly upon method invocation.

Predicate wf_java_mdecl serves as actual parameter of wf_prog for μJava programs:

$$\mathsf{wf\_java\_prog}\ \Gamma \equiv \mathsf{wf\_prog}\ \mathsf{wf\_java\_mdecl}\ \Gamma$$

5.7 Operational semantics of μJava

For the semantics of μJava we use an operational description, as this style is the same as the original specification of Java [GJS96], easy to understand, and almost immediately executable.

5.7.1 Program state

A μJava state consists of the local variables and the heap, where the heap is a mapping from locations to objects, where objects consist of a class name and the instance variables.

$$
\begin{array}{lll}
\textbf{types}\ obj & = & cname \times (vname \rightsquigarrow val) \\
\quad heap & = & loc \rightsquigarrow obj \\
\quad locals & = & vname \rightsquigarrow val \\
\quad state & = & heap \times locals
\end{array}
$$

An extended state is augmented with an optional exception. Here we need only a few of the language-defined exceptions of Java.

$$\textbf{types}\quad xstate = xcpt\ option \times state$$

$$
\begin{array}{lll}
\textbf{datatype}\ xcpt & = & \mathtt{NullPointer} \\
 & \mid & \mathtt{ClassCast} \\
 & \mid & \mathtt{OutOfMemory}
\end{array}
$$

Usually the meta-variables σ and *s* are of type *state* and *xstate* respectively.

5.7.2 Evaluation judgments

We deliberately chose an evaluation semantics as opposed to a transition semantics, since it is more abstract, less verbose and more convenient for proofs.

Analogously to typing judgments, there are three forms of evaluation judgments: statements transform an initial state to a final one, expressions additionally yield a value, and expression lists yield a list of values.

$$\begin{array}{ll} java\_mb\ prog \vdash xstate\ -stmt\rightarrow & xstate \\ java\_mb\ prog \vdash xstate\ -expr\succ val\rightarrow & xstate \\ java\_mb\ prog \vdash xstate\ -expr\ list[\succ]val\ list\rightarrow & xstate \end{array}$$

5.7.3 Evaluation rules and exception propagation

For each form of judgment, there is a general rule stating that exceptions propagate, e.g.

$$\Gamma\vdash(\mathsf{Some}\ xc,\sigma)\ -c\rightarrow\ (\mathsf{Some}\ xc,\sigma)$$

All other rules assume that the initial state is exception-free, but any further (intermediate) states may be exceptional, like s_1 and s_2 in the (otherwise trivial) composition rule:

$$\frac{\Gamma\vdash(\mathsf{None},\sigma)\ -c_1\rightarrow\ s_1 \quad \Gamma\vdash s_1\ -c_2\rightarrow\ s_2}{\Gamma\vdash(\mathsf{None},\sigma)\ -c_1;\ c_2\rightarrow\ s_2}$$

5.7.4 Method call rule

Most of the evaluation rules are more or less straightforward and are omitted here. The most complex rule is that for method calls:

$$\frac{\begin{array}{c}\Gamma\vdash(\mathsf{None},\sigma)\ -e\succ a\rightarrow\ s_1 \quad \Gamma\vdash s_1\ -ps[\succ]pvs\rightarrow\ (x,h,l) \\ dynT = \mathsf{fst}\ (\mathsf{the}\ (h\ (\mathsf{the\_Addr}\ a))) \\ (\_,\_,pns,lvars,blk,res) = \mathsf{the}\ (\mathsf{method}\ (\Gamma,dynT)\ (mn,pTs)) \\ \Gamma\vdash(\mathsf{np}\ a\ x,\ h,\ (\mathsf{init\_vars}\ lvars)(pns[\mapsto]pvs)(\mathtt{this}\mapsto a))\ -blk\rightarrow\ s_3 \\ \Gamma\vdash s_3\ -res\succ v\rightarrow\ (x_4,h_4,\_)\end{array}}{\Gamma\vdash(\mathsf{None},\sigma)\ -e.mn(\{pTs\}ps)\succ v\rightarrow\ (x_4,h_4,l)}$$

where

$\mathsf{the\_Addr}(\mathsf{Addr}\ l) = l$
$\mathsf{np}\ v\ x \equiv \mathsf{if}\ \ v = \mathsf{Null} \wedge x = \mathsf{None}\ \ \mathsf{then}\ \ \mathsf{Some}\ \mathtt{NullPointer}\ \ \mathsf{else}\ \ x$
$\mathsf{init\_vars} \equiv \mathsf{map\_of} \circ \mathsf{map}\ (\lambda(n,T).\ (n,\mathsf{default\_val}\ T))$

Note that local variables are initialized with their default values, in contrast to Java, where the programmer must initialize them explicitly.

5.8 Type-safety

5.8.1 The notion of type-safety

A programming language is *type-safe* iff its type system prevents type mismatches, i.e. situations where dynamically produced values do not conform to the corresponding statically determined types. A language may be not type-safe if it has no type system at all (e.g., Smalltalk) or the type system is unsound (e.g., Eiffel). A consequence of type-safety for object-oriented languages is that method calls always find an applicable method. Note that type-safety (usually) does not cover division by zero, nontermination, etc.

5.8.2 Conformance of values to types

Central to the proof of type-safety is an invariant stating that all (run-time) values *conform* to their declared types, i.e. the types of the values are subtypes of the declared types. This notion is lifted pointwise from single values to maps of values and further to the whole state conforming to a type environment. The conformance judgments have the form

$$\begin{array}{lll} \alpha\ prog,heap\vdash & val ::\preceq & ty \\ \alpha\ prog,heap\vdash(\beta \leadsto & val)[::\preceq](\beta \leadsto ty) & \\ \quad state & ::\preceq\ java\_mb\ env & \end{array}$$

and the definitions

$$\begin{array}{ll} \mathsf{obj\_ty}\ o & \equiv \mathsf{case}\ o\ \mathsf{of\ None} \to \mathsf{None} \mid \mathsf{Some}\ (C,fm) \to \mathsf{Some}\ C \\ \Gamma,h\vdash v::\preceq T & \equiv \exists S.\ \mathsf{typeof}\ (\mathsf{obj\_ty} \circ h)\ v = \mathsf{Some}\ S \wedge \Gamma\vdash S\preceq T \\ \Gamma,h\vdash vm[::\preceq]Tm & \equiv \forall n\ T.\ Tm\ n = \mathsf{Some}\ T \longrightarrow (\exists v.\ vm\ n = \mathsf{Some}\ v \wedge \Gamma,h\vdash v::\preceq T) \\ (h,l)::\preceq(\Gamma,lT) & \equiv (\forall a\ C\ fm.\ h\ a = \mathsf{Some}(C,fm) \longrightarrow \Gamma,h\vdash fm\ [::\preceq]\ \mathsf{map\_of(fields(}\Gamma,C))) \wedge \\ & \quad \Gamma,h\vdash\ l\ [::\preceq]\ lT \end{array}$$

5.8.3 Proof of type-safety

A simple but important lemma for type-safety (not considering garbage collection) is the invariant that during execution any object once created is never lost and retains its type. This is formalized as the heap extension relation

$$h\trianglelefteq h' \equiv \forall a\ C\ fm.\ h\ a = \mathsf{Some}(C,fm) \longrightarrow (\exists fm'.\ h'\ a = \mathsf{Some}(C,fm'))$$

The invariant is proved by simultaneous rule induction, such that the proof goal is

$$\begin{array}{l} (\Gamma\vdash(x,h,l)\ -\ c \quad\ \to (x',h',l') \longrightarrow h\trianglelefteq h' \quad \wedge \\ (\Gamma\vdash(x,h,l)\ -\ e \succ v \to (x',h',l') \longrightarrow h\trianglelefteq h' \quad \wedge \\ (\Gamma\vdash(x,h,l)\ -es[\succ]vs\to (x',h',l') \longrightarrow h\trianglelefteq h' \end{array}$$

The main theorem states that for well-formed programs, execution of well-typed statements and expression preserves conformance:

$$\begin{array}{l} \mathsf{wf\_java\_prog}\ \Gamma \longrightarrow \\ (\Gamma\vdash(x,\sigma)\ -c\to (x',\sigma') \longrightarrow \\ \quad \forall lT.\ \sigma::\preceq(\Gamma,lT) \longrightarrow (\Gamma,lT)\vdash c\surd \longrightarrow \\ \qquad \sigma'::\preceq(\Gamma,lT)) \quad \wedge \\ (\Gamma\vdash(x,\sigma)\ -e\succ v\to (x',\sigma') \longrightarrow \\ \quad \forall lT.\ \sigma::\preceq(\Gamma,lT) \longrightarrow \forall T.\ (\Gamma,lT)\vdash e::T \longrightarrow \\ \qquad \sigma'::\preceq(\Gamma,lT) \wedge (x' = \mathsf{None} \longrightarrow \Gamma,\mathsf{fst}\ \sigma'\vdash v::\preceq T)) \quad \wedge \\ (\Gamma\vdash(x,\sigma)\ -es[\succ]vs\to (x',\sigma') \longrightarrow \\ \quad \forall lT.\ \sigma::\preceq(\Gamma,lT) \longrightarrow \forall Ts.\ (\Gamma,lT)\vdash es[::]Ts \longrightarrow \\ \qquad \sigma'::\preceq(\Gamma,lT) \wedge (x' = \mathsf{None} \longrightarrow \mathsf{list\_all2}\ (\lambda v\ T.\ G,\mathsf{fst}\ \sigma'\vdash v::\preceq T)\ vs\ Ts)) \end{array}$$

This theorem is proved again by simultaneous rule induction and requires a large amount of auxiliary lemmas. The part concerning statements may be re-phrased in a more readable form as

$$\mathsf{wf\_java\_prog}\ \Gamma\ \wedge\ E = (\Gamma,lT)\ \wedge\ E\vdash c\ \surd\ \wedge\ \Gamma\vdash(\_,\sigma)\ -c\to (\_,\sigma')\ \wedge\ \sigma ::\preceq E \longrightarrow \sigma' ::\preceq E$$

An almost direct consequence is that "method not understood" run-time errors cannot occur.

6 μJVM

6.1 The μJava Virtual Machine

The source language Java comes with an abstract machine known as the *Java Virtual Machine* (*JVM*) [LY96]. Its instruction set is a high-level assembly language specifically tailored for Java. It is meant to be the standard target language for Java compilers. In this subsection we present the μJVM, an abstract version of the JVM geared towards μJava. The main simplification in our approach is the use of μJava program skeletons for holding μJVM instruction sequences. This is the reason why type *prog* in §5.4.1 above is defined in a generic way and is parameterized by the actual method code. As a result, we can avoid the specialized file formats ("class files") described in the JVM specification [LY96]. Their main purpose is to record the type information present in the source programs.

6.1.1 Related work

There are a number of operational definitions of variants of the JVM. Our model is based on the work of Pusch [Pus99] which in turn is based on the work of Qian [Qia99]. Hartel *et al.* [HBL99] independently arrive at a similar formalization. A description based on Abstract State Machines is given by Börger and Schulte [BS98].

6.1.2 μJVM instructions

The μJVM is a stack machine. For each method invocation there is an operand stack for expression evaluation and a list of local variables (which includes the parameters). The formal model is described in §6.1.3.

Following the JVM specification [LY96], we have structured the instructions into several groups of related instructions, describing each by its own execution function. This makes the operational semantics easier to understand, since every function only works on the parameters that are needed for the corresponding group of instructions:

datatype *instr* = LS *load_and_store*
| CO *create_object*
| MO *manipulate_object*
| CH *check_object*
| MI *meth_inv*
| MR *meth_ret*
| OS *op_stack*
| BR *branch*

We will now discuss these groups briefly. Instruction names mostly follow the JVM nomenclature.

- **datatype** *load_and_store* = Load *nat* | Store *nat* | Bipush *int* | Aconst_null
  Load *n* pushes the contents of local variable *n* on the stack. Store *n* pops the top from the stack and puts it into local variable *n*. Bipush *i* pushes integer *i* on the stack. Aconst_null pushes the null reference on the stack.

- **datatype** *create_object* = New *cname*
  New *C* creates a new object of class *C* and initializes its fields according with their default values.

- **datatype** *manipulate_object* = Getfield *vname cname* | Putfield *vname cname*
  Getfield x C uses the top of the stack as the address of an object of class C and replaces that address with the value of field x of the object; Putfield x C expects both a value and an address on the stack, puts the value into field x of the object and pops both value and address from the stack.

- **datatype** *check_object* = Checkcast *cname*
  Checkcast C checks if the top of the stack is a reference to an object of class C (or a subclass of C) and throws an exception if not.

- **datatype** *meth_inv* = Invoke *mname* (*ty list*)
  Invoke *mn ts* interprets the top of the stack as a reference to an object and calls the method determined by the class of that object and the signature (*mn*,*ts*).

- **datatype** *meth_ret* = Return
  Return returns from a method invocation. The result value is the top of the stack.

- **datatype** *op_stack* = Pop | Dup | Swap
  The instructions pop, duplicate and swap the top of the stack.

- **datatype** *branch* = Goto *int* | Ifcmpeq *int*
  Goto is unconditional, whereas Ifcmpeq compares and pops the two top elements of the stack and only performs the jump if they are equal. The integer argument is added to the current program counter.

This is just a representative sample of instructions which is sufficient to serve as a target language for μJava. Because some features are missing (e.g. arrays and interfaces) and because we have restricted the instruction set to the essentials, some groups have become singletons. Type conversion instructions have disappeared altogether because we have only one numeric type, *int*. Arithmetic is missing (as in μJava) but would be trivial to include. There are also some subtle differences to the corresponding JVM instructions:

- A number of instructions such as Load, Store and Return are overloaded, i.e. they work for all types. This streamlines the instruction set without, as we shall see, compromising type-safety.

- Invoke does not carry the name of the class defining the invoked method. This complicates the proof of type-safety, as discussed in §6.3.

6.1.3 Operational semantics of μJVM instructions

As discussed above, a μJVM program is simply a μJava program where the method bodies consist of instruction sequences. Thus we instantiate our program skeleton type *prog* once more:

types *bytecode* = *instr list*
    jvm_prog = (*nat* × *bytecode*) *prog*

The natural number in the method body simply says how many local variable this method has (which could be computed by scanning the bytecode). It is used when allocating stack space upon method invocation. The JVM also records the maximum stack size, which we have chosen to leave open.

The μJVM state is formalized as a triple consisting of an optional exception, the heap, and the frame stack. This is just like in μJava's *xstate*, except that the local variables are replaced by the frame stack. For each active method invocation, there exists a frame containing its own operand stack, a list of local variables, the name of the current class, the signature of the current method, and the program counter:

types *jvm_state* = *xcpt option* × *heap* × *frame list*
frame = *opstack* × *locvars* × *cname* × *sig* × *nat*
opstack = *val list*
locvars = *val list*

Note that *xcpt*, *val* and *heap* are inherited from μJava. The local variables are laid out in the format [*this,p1,..,pm,l1,..,ln*], where *this* is the value of `this`, *p1* through *pm* are the parameters of the method, and *l1* through *ln* are the remaining local variables.

Execution of a μJVM instruction transforms the machine state. A raised exception or an empty frame stack means the μJVM is in a final state—remember that there is no exception handling. If the machine has not yet reached a final state, function exec performs a single execution step: it calls an appropriate execution function (e.g. exec_mo) and incorporates the result in the new machine state. To model the distinction between final and non-final states, the result type of exec is *jvm_state option*: None is returned if there is no successor state.

```
exec :: jvm_prog × jvm_state → jvm_state option

exec(Γ, (None, hp, (stk,loc,C,sig,pc)#frs)) =
  Some (case snd(snd(snd(the(method (Γ,C) sig)))) ! pc of
          MO ins →
           let (xp',hp',stk',pc') = exec_mo ins hp stk pc
           in (xp',hp',(stk',loc,C,sig,pc')#frs)
        | ... → ...)
exec(Γ, (xp, hp, [])) = None
exec(Γ, (Some xp, hp, frs)) = None
```

For example, the operational semantics of Getfield looks like this:

```
exec_mo :: manipulate_object → heap → opstack → nat →
           (xcpt option × heap × opstack × nat)

exec_mo (Getfield F C) hp stk pc =
  let oref    = hd stk;
      xp'     = if oref=Null then Some NullPointer else None;
      (oc,fs) = the(hp(the_Addr oref));
      stk'    = if xp'=None then the(fs(F,C))#(tl stk) else tl stk
  in (xp', hp, stk', pc+1)
```

F is a field name and *C* the defining class of the field. The top of the operand stack *stk* should contain a reference to a class instance stored on the heap *hp*. In case of a null reference an exception is thrown. Otherwise, the fields *fs* are extracted from the referenced object. The content of the field determined by (*F,C*) is pushed on the operand stack. Finally, the program counter *pc* is incremented.

But what if the stack is empty upon execution of Getfield? The JVM specification describes the operational semantics for each instruction in the context of a JVM state where several constraints hold, e.g. there must be an appropriate number of arguments on the operand stack, or the operands must be of a certain type. If the constraints are not satisfied, the behavior of the JVM is undefined. In our approach, we formalize the behavior of μJVM instructions with total functions. If a state does not satisfy the constraints of the current instruction, the result is defined but we don't know what it is. For example, the top of an empty operand stack is hd [], but the definition of hd (which we have not shown) only says that hd [] is some arbitrary but fixed value.

Finally, execution of the entire code consists of repeated application of exec as long as the result is not None. The relation $\Gamma \vdash s \stackrel{jvm}{\longrightarrow} t$ should be read as "In the context of a μJVM program Γ, the execution starting with state s leads to t in finitely many steps". Its definition uses the reflexive transitive closure of successful execution steps:

$$\Gamma \vdash s \stackrel{jvm}{\longrightarrow} t \;\equiv\; (s,t) \in \{(s,s').\ \mathsf{exec}(\Gamma,s) = \mathsf{Some}\ s'\}^*$$

6.2 The Bytecode Verifier

An essential part of the JVM is the *bytecode verifier* that statically checks several safety-relevant constraints before execution of the code. One main aspect of the bytecode verifier is to statically derive the types of all runtime data and check that all instructions will receive arguments of the correct type. Hence the bytecode verifier can be seen as a type checker (more precisely: a type reconstructor) for the JVM. Therefore it has become customary to separate the bytecode verifier into a specification in terms of a type system and an implementation as a data flow analyzer. Thus the correctness argument for bytecode verification is split in two parts: a type safety proof relating the type system and the operational semantics, and an implementation proof relating the type system and the data flow analyzer.

6.2.1 Related work

Our approach for the proof of type-safety builds on the work of Qian [Qia99] who covers a considerably larger subset of the JVM. Closely related is the work by Stata and Abadi [SA98], who treat subroutines, and the work by Freund and Mitchell [FM98], who treat object initialization. The correctness of the data flow analyzer is analyzed by Goldberg [Gol98] and, more abstractly, Nipkow [Nip99b]. An unorthodox approach to bytecode verification via model checking is reported by Basin *et al.* [BFPV99].

6.2.2 Types and type relations

The static types for the μJVM are the same as for μJava, i.e. of type *ty*. Thus we can reuse a number of concepts from the μJava level. The main distinction is that the JVM allows the type of local variables to change during execution. If at a particular instruction a local variable may hold values from either of two incompatible types (because two execution paths lead to this instruction), this local variable will have type "unusable" at this point. In our formalization we work with the HOL type *ty option*, which is either None, representing the unusable type, or Some T, representing type T. We call these types *static types* because they are the result of a static analysis of the program.

The subtype relation is lifted from types to static types as follows: any static type is a subtype of None (because None represents the set of all types), and otherwise the subtype relation on *ty* is simply lifted:

$$
\begin{array}{lll}
\_ \vdash \_ \preceq_o \_ :: \mathit{jvm\_prog} \to \mathit{ty\ option} \to \mathit{ty\ option} \to \mathit{bool} & & \\
(\Gamma \vdash \_ \qquad \preceq_o \mathsf{None}) & = & \mathsf{True} \\
(\Gamma \vdash \mathsf{None} \quad \preceq_o \mathsf{Some}\ T) & = & \mathsf{False} \\
(\Gamma \vdash \mathsf{Some}\ T \preceq_o \mathsf{Some}\ T') & = & (\Gamma \vdash T \preceq T')
\end{array}
$$

A *state type* contains type information for all local variables and the operand stack at a certain program point. The local variables may contain unusable values, whereas on the operand stack only usable values may be stored.

$$\begin{array}{ll} locvars\_type & = ty\ option\ list \\ opstack\_type & = ty\ list \\ state\_type & = opstack\_type \times locvars\_type \end{array}$$

We extend the predicate $\preceq_o$ in two steps to state types:

$$\begin{array}{ll} \_ \vdash \_ \preceq_l \_ & :: jvm\_prog \to locvars\_type \to locvars\_type \to bool \\ \Gamma \vdash LT \preceq_l LT' & \equiv \mathsf{length}\ LT = \mathsf{length}\ LT' \wedge (\forall (t,t') \in \mathsf{set}\ (\mathsf{zip}\ LT\ LT').\ \Gamma \vdash t \preceq_o t') \end{array}$$

$$\begin{array}{ll} \_ \vdash \_ \preceq_s \_ & :: jvm\_prog \to state\_type \to state\_type \to bool \\ \Gamma \vdash s \preceq_s s' & \equiv \Gamma \vdash \mathsf{map\ Some\ (fst}\ s) \preceq_l \mathsf{map\ Some\ (fst}\ s') \wedge \Gamma \vdash \mathsf{snd}\ s \preceq_l \mathsf{snd}\ s' \end{array}$$

Type information for the entire code of a method is collected in a value of *method type*. A value of *class type* maps a method signature to a value of method type, and a value of *program type* maps a class name to a value of class type:

$$\begin{array}{ll} method\_type & = state\_type\ list \\ class\_type & = sig \to method\_type \\ prog\_type & = cname \to class\_type \end{array}$$

6.2.3 Static well-typedness

Given some instruction sequence, the bytecode verifier has to infer type information for each instruction, i.e. a method type, such that the whole sequence is well-typed. We concentrate on what well-typedness means and ignore the computation of the method type. Let us start by looking at an example of a well-typed instruction sequence.

instruction	stack	local variables
Load 0	[]	[Some(Class B), Some(int)]
Dup	[Class A]	[Some(Class B), None]
Store 1	[Class A, Class A]	[Some(Class B), None]
Invoke m []	[Class A]	[Some(Class B), Some(Class A)]
Goto -3	[Class A]	[Some(Class B), Some(Class A)]

On the left the instructions are shown and on the right the type of the stack elements and the local variables (*opstack_type* and *locvars_type* above). The type information attached to an instruction characterizes the state *before* execution of that instruction. We assume that class B is a subclass of A and that A defines a method m which takes no arguments and returns a value of type A.

Execution starts with an empty stack and the two local variables hold a reference to an object of class B and an integer. The first instruction loads local variable 0, a reference to a B object, on the stack. The type information associated with following instruction may puzzle at first sight: it says that a reference to an A object is on the stack, and that local variable 1 has become unusable. This means the type information has become less precise but is still correct: a B object is also an A object, and an integer is now classified as unusable. Formally: Class $B \preceq$ Class A and Some(int) $\preceq_o$ None. The reason for these more general types is that the predecessor of the Dup instruction may have either been Load 0 or Goto -3. Since there exist different execution paths to reach Dup, the type information of the two paths has to be "merged". The type of the second local variable is either int or Class A, which are incompatible, i.e. the only common supertype is None.

Apart from this complication, the type of the stack elements and the local variables changes as expected. It now remains to specify formally when an instruction sequence is well-typed w.r.t. a method type.

We start by defining a predicate that checks whether an instruction at a certain program point is well-typed with respect to a given method type. Additionally, it checks several other constraints, e.g. an index to a local variable must not be greater than the number of local variables and the program counter must remain within the current method. These constraints are indispensable to carry out the soundness proof for the bytecode verifier. The type-checking predicate makes a case distinction over the instruction to be executed at the current program point. We only show the Load case:

$$\begin{array}{l}
\mathsf{wt_instr} :: \mathit{instr} \to \mathit{jvm_prog} \to \mathit{ty} \to \mathit{method_type} \to \mathit{nat} \to \mathit{nat} \to \mathit{bool} \\
\mathsf{wt_instr}\ (\mathsf{LS}(\mathsf{Load}\ i))\ \Gamma\ _\ \mathit{sts}\ \mathit{max_pc}\ \mathit{pc} = \\
\quad \mathsf{let}\ (\mathit{ST},\mathit{LT}) = \mathit{sts}!\mathit{pc} \\
\quad \mathsf{in}\quad \mathit{pc}+1 < \mathit{max_pc}\ \wedge\ i < \mathsf{length}\ \mathit{LT}\ \wedge \\
\qquad\quad (\exists T.\ \mathit{LT}!i = \mathsf{Some}\ T\ \wedge \Gamma \vdash (T\#\mathit{ST}\ ,\ \mathit{LT})\ \preceq_s\ \mathit{sts}!(\mathit{pc}+1))
\end{array}$$

The above predicate enforces that there is a next instruction ($pc+1 < max\_pc$), that the local variable to be loaded exists ($i <$ length LT) and is usable ($LT!i =$ Some T), and that the new state type ($T\#ST, LT$) is a subtype of the state type associated with the successor instruction. We cannot ask for equality here because that next instruction can have other predecessors as well.

The well-typedness checks for all instructions except Return follow the above schema: there are some instruction-specific conditions and the general requirement that for each successor instruction pc' and corresponding successor state st' both $pc' < max\_pc$ and $\Gamma \vdash st' \preceq_s sts!pc'$ hold.

Step by step, we now extend the notion of well-typedness to methods, classes, and programs. At the start of the execution of a method, the operand stack must be empty, and the local variables must contain values according to the type of the current class C (local variable 0 holds `this`), the parameter types pTs of the current method, and None for all other local variables, because the μJVM (as the JVM) does not initialize the other local variables automatically (replicate i x produces a list of i copies of x):

$$\begin{array}{l}
\mathsf{wt_start} :: \mathit{jvm_prog} \to \mathit{cname} \to \mathit{ty\ list} \to \mathit{nat} \to \mathit{method_type} \to \mathit{bool} \\
\mathsf{wt_start}\ \Gamma\ \ C\ pTs\ mxl\ \Delta \equiv \\
\quad \Gamma \vdash ([],\ \mathsf{Some}(\mathsf{Class}\ C)\#(\mathsf{map\ Some}\ pTs)@(\mathsf{replicate}\ mxl\ \mathsf{None}))\ \preceq_s\ \Delta!0
\end{array}$$

The body of a method must be non-empty. A method is well-typed with respect to a method type Δ, if it is well-typed at the beginning of the method body, and if for every program point in the method body the instruction is well-typed:

$$\begin{array}{l}
\mathsf{wt_method} :: \mathit{jvm_prog} \to \mathit{cname} \to \mathit{ty\ list} \to \mathit{ty} \to \mathit{nat} \to \mathit{instr\ list} \to \mathit{method_type} \to \mathit{bool} \\
\mathsf{wt_method}\ \Gamma\ \ C\ pTs\ rT\ mxl\ ins\ \Delta \equiv \\
\qquad \mathsf{let}\ \mathit{max_pc} = \mathsf{length}\ \mathit{ins} \\
\qquad \mathsf{in}\ 0 < \mathit{max_pc}\ \wedge\ \mathsf{wt_start}\ \Gamma\ \ C\ pTs\ mxl\ \Delta\ \wedge \\
\qquad\quad (\forall pc{<}\mathit{max_pc}.\ \mathsf{wt_instr}\ (\mathit{ins}!pc)\ \Gamma\ rT\ \Delta\ \mathit{max_pc}\ pc)
\end{array}$$

As jvm_prog is an instance of the parameterized type $prog$ of program skeletons, well-typedness of μJVM programs is defined with the help of the parameterized well-formedness predicate wf_prog for program skeletons (see §5.6.1). We simply feed a suitably instantiated version of wt_method to wf_prog:

$$\begin{array}{l}
\mathsf{wt_jvm_prog} :: \mathit{jvm_prog} \to \mathit{prog_type} \to \mathit{bool} \\
\mathsf{wt_jvm_prog}\ \Gamma\ \Phi \equiv \\
\qquad \mathsf{wf_prog}\ (\lambda\Gamma\ \ C\ (sig,rT,maxl,b).\ \mathsf{wt_method}\ \Gamma\ \ C\ (\mathsf{snd}\ sig)\ rT\ maxl\ b\ (\Phi\ \ C\ sig))\ \Gamma
\end{array}$$

This is in complete analogy with the definition of wf_java_prog in §5.6.3.

6.3 The proof of type-safety

A bytecode verifier (or more abstractly: a type system) statically determines the types of all runtime data. A type system is sound if the statically predicted type gives a correct approximation of the runtime value produced during execution. Thus we first need to define this approximation relationship for the various runtime data and types in the μJVM. This means lifting the relation $::\preceq$ already defined at the μJava level (see §5.8.2) to complex data structures containing values and types.

The unusable type None approximates any value; a static type Some T approximates value v if v conforms to T:

$$\begin{array}{l}
\mathsf{approx_val} :: \mathit{jvm_prog} \rightarrow \mathit{heap} \rightarrow \mathit{val} \rightarrow \mathit{ty\ option} \rightarrow \mathit{bool} \\
\mathsf{approx_val}\ \Gamma\ h\ v\ \ \mathsf{None} \qquad = \mathsf{True} \\
\mathsf{approx_val}\ \Gamma\ h\ v\ (\mathsf{Some}\ T)\ = (\Gamma,h \vdash v::\preceq T)
\end{array}$$

This relation is lifted pointwise to local variables and the operand stack:

$$\begin{array}{l}
\mathsf{approx_loc} :: \mathit{jvm_prog} \rightarrow \mathit{heap} \rightarrow \mathit{val\ list} \rightarrow \mathit{locvars_type} \rightarrow \mathit{bool} \\
\mathsf{approx_loc}\ \Gamma\ \mathit{hp}\ \mathit{loc}\ \mathit{LT} \equiv \mathsf{length}\ \mathit{loc} = \mathsf{length}\ \mathit{LT}\ \wedge \\
\qquad\qquad (\forall(\mathit{val},t)\in\mathsf{set}(\mathsf{zip}\ \mathit{loc}\ \mathit{LT}).\ \mathsf{approx_val}\ \Gamma\ \mathit{hp}\ \mathit{val}\ t)
\end{array}$$

$$\begin{array}{l}
\mathsf{approx_stk} :: \mathit{jvm_prog} \rightarrow \mathit{heap} \rightarrow \mathit{opstack} \rightarrow \mathit{opstack_type} \rightarrow \mathit{bool} \\
\mathsf{approx_stk}\ \Gamma\ \mathit{hp}\ \mathit{stk}\ \mathit{ST} \equiv \mathsf{approx_loc}\ \Gamma\ \mathit{hp}\ \mathit{stk}\ (\mathsf{map\ Some}\ \mathit{ST})
\end{array}$$

The proof of type-safety follows the same pattern as the one for μJava: we show that if we start in a correct state and execute an instruction of a well-typed program, we again end up in a correct state. A correct state is one where the program type approximates all the runtime data in the state. Unfortunately, this notion of a correct state is too weak to make the above implication true—a typical example of an invariant that needs strengthening. One has to take into account that the frames on the frame stack are not unrelated but look roughly like this: the top element is the currently executing frame, which can be at any program point, but the remaining frames are all snapshots taken directly after an Invoke instruction. If we do not take this property into account, it becomes impossible to show that the Return instruction preserves correctness of states. Because of this difference between the top frame and the rest, correctness of a state treats the top frame separately:

$$\begin{array}{l}
\mathsf{correct_state} :: \mathit{jvm_prog} \rightarrow \mathit{prog_type} \rightarrow \mathit{jvm_state} \rightarrow \mathit{bool} \\
\mathsf{correct_state}\ \Gamma\ \Phi\ (\mathsf{None},\mathit{hp},f\#\mathit{fs}) = \Gamma \vdash_h \mathit{hp}\surd \wedge (\mathsf{let}\ (\mathit{stk},\mathit{loc},C,\mathit{sig},\mathit{pc}) = f \\
\quad \mathsf{in}\ \exists rT\ \mathit{maxl}\ \mathit{ins}.\ \mathsf{method}\ (\Gamma,C)\ \mathit{sig} = \mathsf{Some}(C,rT,(\mathit{maxl},\mathit{ins}))\ \wedge \\
\qquad \mathsf{correct_frame}\ \Gamma\ \mathit{hp}\ ((\Phi\ C\ \mathit{sig})!\mathit{pc})\ \mathit{maxl}\ \mathit{ins}\ f \wedge \mathsf{correct_frames}\ \Gamma\ \mathit{hp}\ \Phi\ rT\ \mathit{sig}\ \mathit{fs}) \\
\mathsf{correct_state}\ \Gamma\ \Phi\ (\mathsf{None}\quad ,\mathit{hp},[]) = \mathsf{True} \\
\mathsf{correct_state}\ \Gamma\ \Phi\ (\mathsf{Some}\ x,\mathit{hp},\mathit{fs}) = \mathsf{True}
\end{array}$$

Correctness of a single frame requires the stack and heap data to be approximated by the corresponding state type. Additionally, the program counter should point at a valid instruction and the actual number of local variables should be as described by the method definition:

$$\begin{array}{l}
\mathsf{correct_frame} :: \mathit{jvm_prog} \rightarrow \mathit{heap} \rightarrow \mathit{state_type} \rightarrow \mathit{nat} \rightarrow \mathit{bytecode} \rightarrow \mathit{frame} \rightarrow \mathit{bool} \\
\mathsf{correct_frame}\ \Gamma\ \mathit{hp}\ (\mathit{ST},\mathit{LT})\ \mathit{maxl}\ \mathit{ins}\ (\mathit{stk},\mathit{loc},C,\mathit{sig},\mathit{pc}) \equiv \\
\quad \mathsf{approx_stk}\ \Gamma\ \mathit{hp}\ \mathit{stk}\ \mathit{ST}\ \wedge \mathsf{approx_loc}\ \Gamma\ \mathit{hp}\ \mathit{loc}\ \mathit{LT}\ \wedge \\
\quad \mathit{pc} < \mathsf{length}\ \mathit{ins} \wedge \mathsf{length}\ \mathit{loc} = \mathsf{length}\ (\mathsf{snd}\ \mathit{sig}) + \mathit{maxl} + 1
\end{array}$$

Predicate correct_frames, which checks the correctness of a stack of pending frames, takes as an argument the return type and the signature of the method executing in the frame directly above, in order to check that it matches the information in the pending frame below. This check is performed recursively through the frame stack:

```
correct_frames :: jvm_prog → heap → prog_type → ty → sig → frame list → bool
correct_frames Γ hp Φ rT0 sig0 [] = True
correct_frames Γ hp Φ rT0 sig0 (f#frs) =
   let (stk,loc,C,sig,pc) = f;
       (ST,LT) = (Φ C sig) ! pc
   in
   (∃rT maxl ins. method (Γ,C) sig = Some(C,rT,(maxl,ins)) ∧
   (∃mn pTs k. pc = k+1 ∧ ins!k = MI(Invoke mn pTs) ∧ (mn,pTs) = sig0 ∧
   (∃apTs D ST'. fst((Φ C sig)!k) = (rev apTs) @ (Class D) # ST' ∧
   length apTs = length pTs ∧
   (∃D' rT' maxl' ins'. method (Γ,D) sig0 = Some(D',rT',(maxl',ins')) ∧ Γ ⊢ rT0≼rT') ∧
   correct_frame  Γ hp (tl ST, LT) maxl ins f ∧
   correct_frames Γ hp Φ rT sig frs)))
```

This predicate needs some explanation. We discuss its body step by step. It requires that:

- a method with signature *sig* is defined in class *C*;
- the instruction to be executed is preceded by an Invoke instruction which invokes a method with signature *sig0* (from the frame above);
- the *opstack_type*-part of the state type for the Invoke instruction consists of a list of actual argument types *apTs* in reverse order, followed by a class *D* and some remaining stack type;
- the length of the actual and the formal parameter lists agree;
- a method with signature *sig0* (executing in the frame above) is defined in some class *D'* above *D* with a return type that is a supertype of the return type of the actual method executing in the frame above;
- the frame itself is correct, as are the frames below. The current frame is checked against tl *ST* because its operand stack does not yet contain the return value of the method it invoked.

This is more complicated than the corresponding predicate in [Pus99] because the Invoke instruction does not carry around the defining class of the method any more. This loss of static information (wt_instr) requires the invariant (correct_frames) to be strengthened.

Now we can prove the following main type-safety theorem, the preservation of the invariant correct_state:

```
wt_jvm_prog Γ Φ ∧ correct_state Γ Φ s ∧ exec(Γ,s) = Some s' ⟶ correct_state Γ Φ s'
```

It is shown by a case distinction over the instructions. Most instructions are routine and many are proved automatically (once the necessary lemmas have been identified!). Invoke, however, requires fairly subtle reasoning involving key properties of the type system. The final corollary follows easily:

$$\text{wt\_jvm\_prog}\ \Gamma\ \Phi \wedge \text{correct\_state}\ \Gamma\ \Phi\ s \wedge \Gamma \vdash s \stackrel{jvm}{\longrightarrow} t \longrightarrow \text{correct\_state}\ \Gamma\ \Phi\ t$$

7 Conclusion

We have given the reader a guided tour of a formal definition of μJava and the μJVM, their type safety proofs and the supporting theorem proving technology. Although μJava is a very impoverished version of Java, it should have convinced the reader of the main claim, that theorem provers are suitable tools for the analysis of programming language semantics. Further aspects of Java (a compiler and a Hoare logic—see [Ohe99] for a preliminary report) have been formalized as well, thus making μJava a non-trivial example of a formalized programming language. We believe that any serious programming language deserves such formal definition and analysis.

References

[ABI+96] Peter B. Andrews, Matthew Bishop, Sunil Issar, Dan Nesmith, Frank Pfenning, and Hongwei Xi. TPS: A theorem proving system for classical type theory. *J. Automated Reasoning*, 16:321–353, 1996.

[And86] Peter Andrews. *An Introduction to Mathematical Logic and Type Theory: to Truth through Proof.* Computer Science and Applied Mathematics. Academic Press, 1986.

[APP94] F. Andersen, K.D. Petersen, and J.S. Pettersson. Program verification using HOL-UNITY. In J. Joyce and C. Seger, editors, *Higher Order Logic Theorem Proving and Its Applications*, volume 780 of *Lect. Notes in Comp. Sci.*, pages 1–15. Springer-Verlag, 1994.

[BBC+97] B. Barras, S. Boutin, C. Cornes, J. Courant, J.C. Filliatre, E. Giménez, H. Herbelin, G. Huet, C. Muñoz, C. Murthy, C. Parent, C. Paulin, A. Saïbi, and B. Werner. The Coq Proof Assistant Reference Manual — Version V6.1. Technical Report 0203, INRIA, August 1997.

[BCD+88] Patrick Borras, Dominique Clément, Thierry Despeyroux, Janet Incerpi, Gilles Kahn, Bernard Lang, and Valérie Pascual. Centaur: the system. In *Third Symposium on Software Development Environments*, 1988. (Also appears as INRIA Report no. 777).

[BF95] Yves Bertot and Ranan Fraer. Reasoning with executable specifications. In *TAPSOFT '95: Theory and Practice of Software Development*, volume 915 of *Lect. Notes in Comp. Sci.*, pages 531–545. Springer-Verlag, 1995.

[BFPV99] David Basin, Stefan Friedrich, Joachim Posegga, and Harald Vogt. Java bytecode verification by model checking. System abstract. In N. Halbwachs and D. Peled, editors, *Computer Aided Verification (CAV'99)*, volume 1633 of *Lect. Notes in Comp. Sci.*, pages 491–494. Springer-Verlag, 1999.

[BGG+92] Richard Boulton, Andrew Gordon, Mike Gordon, John Harrison, John Herbert, and John Van Tassel. Experience with embedding hardware description languages in HOL. In V. Stavridou, T.F. Melham, and R.T. Boute, editors, *Theorem Provers in Circuit Design*, pages 129–156. North-Holland, 1992.

[BS98] Egon Börger and Wolfram Schulte. Defining the Java Virtual Machine as platform for provably correct Java compilation. In L. Brim, J. Gruska, and J. Zlatuska, editors, *Mathematical Foundations of Computer Science (MFCS'98)*, volume 1450 of *Lect. Notes in Comp. Sci.*, pages 17–35. Springer-Verlag, 1998.

[BS99] Egon Börger and Wolfram Schulte. A programmer friendly modular definition of the semantics of Java. In J. Alves-Foss, editor, *Formal Syntax and Semantics of Java*, volume 1523 of *Lect. Notes in Comp. Sci.*, pages 353–404. Springer-Verlag, 1999.

[C+86] Robert L. Constable et al. *Implementing Mathematics with the Nuprl Proof Development System.* Prentice-Hall, 1986.

[Chu40] Alonzo Church. A formulation of the simple theory of types. *J. Symbolic Logic*, 5:56–68, 1940.

[Coh97] Richard M. Cohen. The defensive Java Virtual Machine specification. Technical report, Computational Logic Inc., 1997. Draft version.

[DE97] Sophia Drossopoulou and Susan Eisenbach. Is the Java type system sound? In *Proc. 4th Int. Workshop Foundations of Object-Oriented Languages*, January 1997.

[DE99] Sophia Drossopoulou and Susan Eisenbach. Describing the semantics of Java and proving type soundness. In J. Alves-Foss, editor, *Formal Syntax and Semantics of Java*, volume 1523 of *Lect. Notes in Comp. Sci.*, pages 41–82. Springer-Verlag, 1999.

[FHR99] Amy Felty, Douglas Howe, and Abhik Roychoudhury. Formal metatheory using implicit syntax, and an application to data abstraction for asynchronous systems. In H. Ganzinger, editor, *Automated Deduction — CADE-16*, volume 1632 of *Lect. Notes in Comp. Sci.*, pages 237–251. Springer-Verlag, 1999.

[FM98] Stephen N. Freund and John C. Mitchell. A type system for object initialization in the Java bytecode language. In *ACM Conf. Object-Oriented Programming: Systems, Languages and Applications*, 1998.

[GJS96] James Gosling, Bill Joy, and Guy Steele. *The Java Language Specification.* Addison-Wesley, 1996.

[GM93] M.J.C. Gordon and T.F. Melham, editors. *Introduction to HOL: a theorem-proving environment for higher order logic.* Cambridge University Press, 1993.

[Gol98] Allen Goldberg. A specification of Java loading and bytecode verification. In *Proc. 5th ACM Conf. Computer and Communications Security*, 1998.

[Gor85] M.C.J. Gordon. HOL — a machine oriented formulation of higher-order logic. Technical Report 68, University of Cambridge, Computer Laboratory, 1985.

[Gor89] M.C.J. Gordon. Mechanizing programming logics in higher order logic. In G. Birtwistle and P.A. Subrahmanyam, editors, *Current Trends in Hardware Verification and Automated Theorem Proving.* Springer-Verlag, 1989.

[HBL99] Pieter Hartel, Michael Butler, and Moshe Levy. The operational semantics of a Java secure processor. In J. Alves-Foss, editor, *Formal Syntax and Semantics of Java*, volume 1523 of *Lect. Notes in Comp. Sci.*, pages 313–352. Springer-Verlag, 1999.

[HC96] Barbara Heyd and Pierre Crégut. A modular coding of Unity in Coq. In J. von Wright, J. Grundy, and J. Harrison, editors, *Theorem Proving in Higher Order Logics*, volume 1125 of *Lect. Notes in Comp. Sci.*, pages 251–266. Springer-Verlag, 1996.

[JHvB+98] B. Jacobs, M. Huisman, M. van Berkum, U. Hensel, and H. Tews. Reasoning about Java classes (preliminary report). In *ACM Conf. Object-Oriented Programming: Systems, Languages and Applications*, pages 329–340, 1998.

[JS94] J. Joyce and C. Seger, editors. *Higher Order Logic Theorem Proving and Its Applications*, volume 780 of *Lect. Notes in Comp. Sci.* Springer-Verlag, 1994.

[Kle98] Thomas Kleymann. *Hoare Logic and VDM: Machine-Checked Soundness and Completeness Proofs.* PhD thesis, Department of Computer Seience, University of Edinburgh, 1998. Report ECS-LFCS-98-392.

[Kli93] Paul Klint. A meta-environment for generating programming environments. *ACM Transactions on Software Engineering and Methodology*, 2(2):176–201, 1993.

[LY96] Tim Lindholm and Frank Yellin. *The Java Virtual Machine Specification.* Addison-Wesley, 1996.

[MG94] Savitri Maharaj and Elsa Gunter. Studying the ml module system in hol. In T.F. Melham and J. Camilleri, editors, *Higher Order Logic Theorem Proving and its Applications*, volume 859 of *Lect. Notes in Comp. Sci.*, pages 269–284. Springer-Verlag, 1994.

[Nes94] Monica Nesi. Value-passing CCS in HOL. In J. Joyce and C. Seger, editors, *Higher Order Logic Theorem Proving and Its Applications*, volume 780 of *Lect. Notes in Comp. Sci.*, pages 352–365. Springer-Verlag, 1994.

[Nip98] Tobias Nipkow. Winskel is (almost) right: Towards a mechanized semantics textbook. *Formal Aspects of Computing*, 10:171–186, 1998.

[Nip99a] Tobias Nipkow. *Isabelle/HOL. The Tutorial*, 1999. Unpublished Manuscript. Available at `http://isabelle.in.tum.de/doc/tutorial.pdf`.

[Nip99b] Tobias Nipkow. Towards verified bytecode verifiers. Submitted for publication, 1999.

[NO98] Tobias Nipkow and David von Oheimb. Java$_{\ell ight}$ is type-safe — definitely. In *Proc. 25th ACM Symp. Principles of Programming Languages*, pages 161–170. ACM Press, 1998.

[Ohe99] David von Oheimb. Hoare logic for mutual recursion and local variables. In C. Pandu Rangan, V. Raman, and R. Ramanujam, editors, *Foundations of Software Technology and Theoretical Computer Science (FST&TCS)*, volume 1738 of *Lect. Notes in Comp. Sci.*, pages 168–180. Springer-Verlag, 1999.

[ON99] David von Oheimb and Tobias Nipkow. Machine-checking the Java specification: Proving type-safety. In J. Alves-Foss, editor, *Formal Syntax and Semantics of Java*, volume 1523 of *Lect. Notes in Comp. Sci.*, pages 119–156. Springer-Verlag, 1999.

[Pau87] Lawrence C. Paulson. *Logic and Computation.* Cambridge University Press, 1987.

[Pau94] Lawrence C. Paulson. *Isabelle: A Generic Theorem Prover*, volume 828 of *Lect. Notes in Comp. Sci.* Springer-Verlag, 1994. Isabelle home page: `http://isabelle.in.tum.de/`.

[Pau99] Lawrence C. Paulson. Mechanizing UNITY in Isabelle. Technical Report 467, University of Cambridge, Computer Laboratory, May 1999. To appear in ACM Trans. Computational Logic.

[Pfe91] Frank Pfenning. Logic programming in the LF Logical Framework. In Gérard Huet and Gordon Plotkin, editors, *Logical Frameworks*, pages 66–78. Cambridge University Press, 1991.

[Pol94] Robert Pollack. *The Theory of LEGO: A Proof Checker for the Extended Calculus of Constructions.* PhD thesis, University of Edinburgh, 1994.

[Pra95] Wishnu Prasetya. *Mechanically Supported Design of Self-stabilising Algorithms.* PhD thesis, University of Utrecht, 1995.

[PS99] Frank Pfenning and Carsten Schürmann. System description: Twelf — a meta-logical framework for deductive systems. In H. Ganzinger, editor, *Automated Deduction — CADE-16*, volume 1632 of *Lect. Notes in Comp. Sci.*, pages 202–206. Springer-Verlag, 1999.

[Pus99] Cornelia Pusch. Proving the soundness of a Java bytecode verifier specification in Isabelle/HOL. In W.R. Cleaveland, editor, *Tools and Algorithms for the Construction and Analysis of Systems (TACAS'99)*, volume 1579 of *Lect. Notes in Comp. Sci.*, pages 89–103. Springer-Verlag, 1999.

[Qia99] Zhenyu Qian. A formal specification of Java Virtual Machine instructions for objects, methods and subroutines. In J. Alves-Foss, editor, *Formal Syntax and Semantics of Java*, volume 1523 of *Lect. Notes in Comp. Sci.*, pages 271–311. Springer-Verlag, 1999.

[SA98] Raymie Stata and Martín Abadi. A type system for Java bytecode subroutines. In *Proc. 25th ACM Symp. Principles of Programming Languages*, pages 149–161. ACM Press, 1998.

[Sli96] Konrad Slind. Function definition in higher order logic. In J. von Wright, J. Grundy, and J. Harrison, editors, *Theorem Proving in Higher Order Logics*, volume 1125 of *Lect. Notes in Comp. Sci.*, pages 381–397. Springer-Verlag, 1996.

[Sli97] Konrad Slind. Derivation and use of induction schemes in higher-order logic. In E. Gunter and A. Felty, editors, *Theorem Proving in Higher Order Logics*, volume 1275 of *Lect. Notes in Comp. Sci.*, pages 275–290. Springer-Verlag, 1997.

[Sli99] Konrad Slind. *Reasoning about Terminating Functional Programs.* PhD thesis, Institut für Informatik, TU München, 1999.

[Sne85] Gregor Snelting. Experiences with the PSG — Programming System Generator. In H. Ehrig, C. Floyd, M. Nivat, and J. Thatcher, editors, *Formal Methods and Software Development (TAPSOFT '85, Vol. 2)*, volume 186 of *Lect. Notes in Comp. Sci.*, pages 148–162. Springer-Verlag, 1985.

[Sym94] D. Syme. Reasoning with the formal definition of Standard ML in HOL. In Joyce and Seger [JS94], pages 43–58.

[Sym99] Donald Syme. Proving Java type soundness. In J. Alves-Foss, editor, *Formal Syntax and Semantics of Java*, volume 1523 of *Lect. Notes in Comp. Sci.*, pages 83–118. Springer-Verlag, 1999.

[TW97] Haykal Tej and Burkhart Wolff. A corrected failure-divergence model for CSP in Isabelle/HOL. In J. Fitzgerald, C.B. Jones, and P. Lucas, editors, *FME '97: Industrial Applications and Strengthened Foundations of Formal Methods*, volume 1313 of *Lect. Notes in Comp. Sci.*, pages 318–337. Springer-Verlag, 1997.

[VG94] M. VanInwegen and E. Gunter. HOL-ML. In Joyce and Seger [JS94], pages 59–72.

Part 2
Extraction and Realizability

H. Schwichtenberg

S. Abramsky

2. The NCKC Hauptsatz

Non-transitivity of 

⇒ Constructive version: see extra slide

⇒ Classical verion:

Suppose  is transitive.

Axiom: kangaroos are curious.

⇒ they take part in MOD Summer School ∨ jump around in Bavarian mountains

[Philosophical aside (orally):]

⇒ visiting MOD Summer School would result in meta-meta-meta-...-jumps (bouncism), which they could not stand.

How to get to Bavarian mountains:

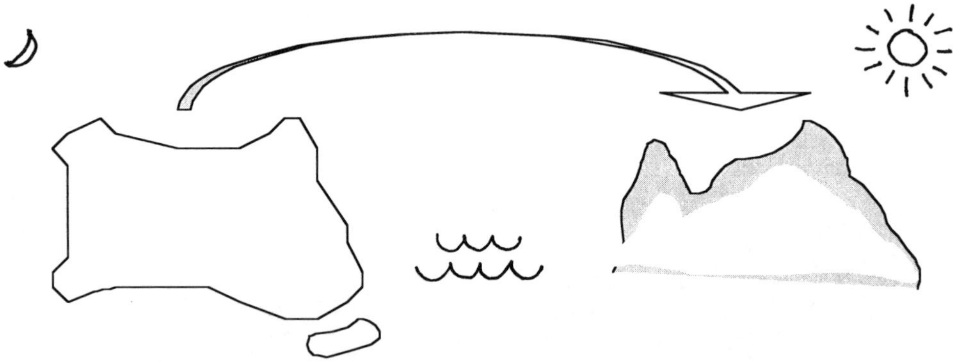

But: no kangaroos found in Bavarian mountains

↯, q.e.d.

Foundations of Secure Computation
F.L. Bauer and R. Steinbrüggen (Eds.)
IOS Press, 2000

Refined Program Extraction from Classical Proofs: Some Case Studies

Helmut Schwichtenberg*

1 Introduction

It is well known that it is undecidable in general whether a given program meets its specification. In contrast, it can be checked easily by a machine whether a formal proof is correct, and from a constructive proof one can automatically extract a corresponding program, which by its very construction is correct as well. This – at least in principle – opens a way to produce correct software, e.g. for safety-critical applications. Moreover, programs obtained from proofs are "commented" in a rather extreme sense. Therefore it is easy to maintain them, and also to adapt them to particular situations.

We will concentrate on the question of classical versus constructive proofs. It is well known that any classical proof of a specification of the form $\forall x \exists y B$ with B quantifier-free can be transformed into a constructive proof of the same formula (for particularly simple proofs, cf. Friedman [5] or Leivant [7]). However, when it comes to extraction of a program from a proof obtained in this way, one easily ends up with a mess. Therefore, some refinements of the standard transformation are necessary.

In the present paper we make use of a refined method of extracting programs from classical proofs; it is developed in detail in [1]. We demonstrate its use with two rather detailed case studies. Specifically, we extract programs from classical proofs of the existence of

- integer square roots, and
- integer coefficients to linearly combine the greatest common divisor of two numbers from these numbers,

The latter example has already been treated in [2]; here we show how it can be dealt with in the present form of the theory. It turns out that the algorithm does not change; however, the method of how to extract a program from this classical proof becomes more perspicious.

Other interesting examples of program extraction from classical proofs have been studied by Murthy [8], the group around Coquand (see e.g. [3]) in a type theoretic context and by Kohlenbach [6] using a Dialectica-interpretation.

The paper is organized as follows. In section 2 the general background is developed. We start in 2.1 with a short exposition of Gödel's system T. Tait's proof of termination for the simply typed λ-calculus is presented in detail, and is then extended to T. In 2.2 we fix our version of intuitionistic arithmetic for functionals, and recall how classical arithmetic can be seen as a subsystem. Subsection 2.3 develops the basic machinery of modified realizability, and contains a detailed proof of the soundness theorem. The

*Mathematisches Institut der Universität München, Theresienstraße 39, D-80333 München, Germany. Phone +49 89 2394 4413, Fax +49 89 280 5248, `schwicht@rz.mathematik.uni-muenchen.de`

main part of the paper is section 3. There definite and goal formulas are defined, and the main theorem on program extraction from classical proofs (Theorem 3.2) is stated; for the proof we have to refer to [1]. Subsections 3.2 and 3.3 then develop the two case studies mentioned above.

Acknowledgements The proof of termination for Gödel's system T uses ideas from Ulrich Berger, Holger Benl, Ralph Matthes and Thorsten Altenkirch. Monika Seisenberger and Felix Joachimski have contributed a lot to the MINLOG system, particularly to the implementation of the translation of classical proofs into constructive ones.

2 General Background

2.1 Gödel's System T

We introduce Gödel's system T of primitive recursive functionals of finite type, formulated as a simply typed lambda calculus with higher type recursion constants.

Types are as for the simply typed lambda calculus, but with concrete ground types ι for the natural numbers and o for the boolean objects *true* and *false*.

$$\iota \mid o \mid \rho \times \sigma \mid \rho \to \sigma.$$

The *constants* are

$$\mathit{true}^o \mid \mathit{false}^o \mid 0^\iota \mid \mathrm{S}^{\iota\to\iota} \mid \mathcal{R}_{o,\rho} \mid \mathcal{R}_{\iota,\rho}.$$

$\mathcal{R}_{\iota,\rho}$ is the *primitive recursion operator* of type $\rho \to (\iota \to \rho \to \rho) \to \iota \to \rho$. $\mathcal{R}_{o,\rho}$ is of type $\rho \to \rho \to o \to \rho$ and represents *boolean induction*, i.e. definition by cases. Instead of $\mathcal{R}_{o,\rho}MNK$ we will often write **if** K **then** M **else** N.

Terms are

$$x^\rho \mid c^\rho \ (c^\rho \text{ a constant}) \mid \langle M, N\rangle \mid \pi_0(M) \mid \pi_1(M) \mid \lambda x^\rho M \mid MN$$

with the usual typing rules. The *conversions* are those for the simply typed lambda calculus, plus some new ones for the recursion operators. We write $K+1$ for SK.

$$\begin{array}{rcl} \mathcal{R}_{o,\rho}MN\,\mathit{true} & \mapsto_{\mathcal{R}} & M \\ \mathcal{R}_{o,\rho}MN\,\mathit{false} & \mapsto_{\mathcal{R}} & N \\ \mathcal{R}_{\iota,\rho}MN0 & \mapsto_{\mathcal{R}} & M \\ \mathcal{R}_{\iota,\rho}MN(K+1) & \mapsto_{\mathcal{R}} & NK(\mathcal{R}_{\iota,\rho}MNK) \end{array}$$

We will prove that for this system of terms every term strongly normalizes. Since the normal form is uniquely determined, the relation $M =_{\beta\mathcal{R}} N$ is decidable (by normalizing M and N). By identifying $=_{\beta\mathcal{R}}$-equal terms (i.e. treating equations on the meta level) we can greatly simplify many formal derivations.

Tait's Proof of Termination for the Simply Typed Lambda Calculus

We first give a well-known proof of *termination* of the simply typed lambda calculus, using method due to W.W. Tait. This proof will later be extended to Gödel's system T.

Tait's proof rests on defining so-called *strong computability predicates*. We present the proof here in a form which avoids intuitive arguments concerning reduction sequences and therefore is suitable for formalization in a theory of inductive definitions.

We begin with a definition of *strongly normalizable terms*, by a strictly positive induction.

If all M' such that $M \longrightarrow_\beta M'$ are strongly normalizable (sn), then so is M.

Obviously M is sn if and only if every reduction sequence starting with M terminates after a finite number of steps. This can be seen as follows. $\Longrightarrow$. Induction on the definition of "strongly normalizable". Consider a reduction sequence starting with M and therein the first reduct M'. The IH for M' yields the assertion. $\Longleftarrow$. By induction on the length of the longest reduction sequence (König's lemma).

We note a number of the properties of the notion "strongly normalizable", to be used below.

$$\text{If all terms } \vec{M} \text{ are sn, then so is } x\vec{M}. \tag{1}$$

Proof. Induction on the definition of sn for $\vec{M}$. Let $x\vec{M} \longrightarrow_\beta N$ be given. It suffices to show that N is sn. From $x\vec{M} \longrightarrow_\beta N$ it follows that $N = x\vec{M}'$, where $\vec{M}'$ arises by substitution of M_i by M_i' with $M_i \longrightarrow_\beta M_i'$. It is to be proved that $x\vec{M}'$ is sn. This follows from the IH for $\vec{M}'$. □

$$\text{If } Mx \text{ is sn, then so is } M. \tag{2}$$

Proof. Induction on the definition of sn for Mx. Let $M \longrightarrow_\beta M'$ be given. It suffices to show that M' is sn. From $M \longrightarrow_\beta M'$ we get $Mx \longrightarrow_\beta M'x$. The IH for $M'x$ then yields that M' is sn. □

We now define when a term M^ρ is strongly computable (sc), by induction on the type ρ.

- M^ι is sc if M^ι is sn.
- $M^{\rho\to\sigma}$ is sc if for every sc N^ρ also $(MN)^\sigma$ is sc.

A term M is called *strongly computable under substitution* if for any sc terms $\vec{N}$ also $M[\vec{x} := \vec{N}]$ is sc.

We note a property of the notion "strongly computable" which will be used below.

$$M \text{ is sc if and only if } M\vec{N} \text{ is sc for all sc } \vec{N}. \tag{3}$$

Proof. Induction on the length of $\vec{N}$. □

Lemma 2.1 *a. Every sc term M^ρ is sn.*

b. If $\vec{M}$ are sn, then $(x\vec{M})^\rho$ is sc.

Proof. By simultaneous induction on the type ρ. *Case* ι. a. By definition. b. By (1).

Case $\rho \to \sigma$ a. Let $M^{\rho\to\sigma}$ be sc. By IHb (with $\vec{M}$ empty) and the definition of strong computability $(Mx)^\sigma$ is sc. By IHa Mx then is sn. By (2) M is sn too. b. Consider $(x\vec{M})^{\rho\to\sigma}$ with $\vec{M}$ sn. Let N^ρ be sc. We have to show that $(x\vec{M}N)^\sigma$ is sc. By IHa N is sn, hence $x\vec{M}N$ is sc by IHb. □

If $M \longrightarrow_\beta M'$ and M is sn, then by the definition of strong normalizability also M' is sn. We now show that the corresponding assertion is also valid for strong computability.

Lemma 2.2 *If $M \longrightarrow_\beta M'$ and M is sc, then so is M'.*

Proof. We use (3). Let $\vec{N}$ be a list of sc terms such that $M\vec{N}$ is of ground type. Then $M\vec{N}$ is sc by (3), hence also sn. Furthermore we have $M\vec{N} \longrightarrow_\beta M'\vec{N}$. By definition of strong normalizablility $M'\vec{N}$ is sn. Thus by (3) M' is sc. □

Lemma 2.3 *Let N be sn. If $M[x := N]\vec{L}$ is sn and of a ground type, then so is $(\lambda x\, M)N\vec{L}$.*

Proof. By induction on the strong normalizability for N and $M[x := N]\vec{L}$. So we consider all the reducts K of $(\lambda x\, M)N\vec{L}$. Clearly it suffices to show that every such K is sn.

Case $K = M[x := N]\vec{L}$, i.e. we have an outer β-conversion. Hence K is sn by assumption.

Case $K = (\lambda x\, M')N\vec{L}$ with $M \longrightarrow_\beta M'$. Then we have $M[x := N]\vec{L} \longrightarrow_\beta M'[x := N]\vec{L}$. By definition of strong normalizability $M'[x := N]\vec{L}$ is sn. Hence by IH K is sn.

Case $K = (\lambda x\, M)N'\vec{L}$ with $N \longrightarrow_\beta N'$. Then we have $M[x := N]\vec{L} \longrightarrow_\beta^* M[x := N']\vec{L}$. By definition of strong normalizability $M[x := N']\vec{L}$ and N' are sn. Hence by IH K is sn.

Case $K = (\lambda x\, M)N\vec{L}'$ with $L_i \longrightarrow_\beta L_i'$ for i and $L_j = L_j'$ for $j \neq i$. Then we have $M[x := N]\vec{L} \longrightarrow_\beta M[x := N]\vec{L}'$. By definition of strong normalizability $M[x := N]\vec{L}'$ is sn. Hence by IH K is sn. □

Corollary 2.4 *If $M[x := N]$ is sc for all sc N, then also $\lambda x\, M$ is sc.*

Proof. Let $M[x := N]$ be sc for all sc N. We have to show that $\lambda x\, M$ is sc. So let N and $\vec{L}$ be sc such that $(\lambda x\, M)N\vec{L}$ is of ground type. We must show that $(\lambda x\, M)N\vec{L}$ is sc. Since $M[x := N]$ is sc by assumption, $M[x := N]\vec{L}$ is sc too and hence also sn. Since by lemma 2.1a N is also sn, by lemma 2.3 it follows that $(\lambda x\, M)N\vec{L}$ is sn and hence also sc. □

Lemma 2.5 *Every term M is sc under substitution.*

Proof. By induction on M. *Case* x. The claim follows from lemma 2.1b or by assumption.

Case MN. $\vec{K}$ be sc. We have to show that $M[\vec{x} := \vec{K}]N[\vec{x} := \vec{K}]$ are sc. This clearly holds, since by IH $M[\vec{x} := \vec{K}]$ as well as $N[\vec{x} := \vec{K}]$ are sc.

Case $\lambda x\, M$. $\vec{K}$ be sc. We have to show that $\lambda x\,(M[\vec{x} := \vec{K}])$ is sc. We now apply corollary 2.4. Let N be sc. By IH for M also $M[x, \vec{x} := N, \vec{K}]$ is sc. Hence by corollary 2.4 the claim follows. □

From lemma 2.5 and lemma 2.1 we directly get

Theorem 2.6 *$\longrightarrow_\beta$ is terminating, i.e. every term M is sn.*

Extension of the Termination Proof to Gödel's System T

This proof can easily be extended to terms with pairing $\langle M_0, M_1\rangle$ and projections $\pi_0(M)$, $\pi_1(M)$. We now show that addition of the conversion rules above for $\mathcal{R}$ does not destroy termination.

We first change the definition of sc for the ground type ι. It is not defined just to be sn (as before), but now is defined inductively, as follows.

Definition 2.7 *M is sc, if*

- *all M' such that $M \longrightarrow_\beta M'$ are sc, and in addition*
- *if $M = \mathrm{S}M_0$, then M_0 is sc.*

Theorem 2.8 *$\longrightarrow_{\beta\mathcal{R}}$ is terminating.*

Proof. We extend the argument above. Clearly it suffices to show that the constants $\mathcal{R}_{\iota,\rho}$ and $\mathcal{R}_{o,\rho}$ are sc. We restrict ourselves to $\mathcal{R}_{\iota,\rho}$; for $\mathcal{R}_{o,\rho}$ the argument is similar (and simpler). So let M, N, K be sc. We must show that $\mathcal{R}MNK$ is sc.

The proof is by induction on sn for M, N and on sc for K. So let $\vec{L}$ be sc. We must show that $\mathcal{R}MNK\vec{L}$ is sc. Since this term is not of the form $\mathrm{S}M_0$, it suffices to consider all reducts Q of $\mathcal{R}MNK\vec{L}$ and to show that every such reduct Q is sc.

Case $K = K_0+1$, $Q = NK_0(\mathcal{R}MNK_0)\vec{L}$. We first show that $\mathcal{R}MNK_0$ is sc. So let $\vec{L}'$ be sc. Since $K = K_0 + 1$ is sc, by definition also K_0 is. So by induction hypothesis $\mathcal{R}MNK_0$ is sc, and we obtain that Q is sc.

If the reduction takes place within a subterm $M, N, K, \vec{L}$ the claim follows by induction hypothesis (here we need that strong computability is preserved under conversion steps; cf. lemma 2.2). Since the case $K = 0$, $Q = M\vec{L}$ is trivial this proves the claim. □

Now we can conclude via Newman's Lemma [9] that the normal form is uniquely determined. For simplicity we identify terms with the same $\beta\mathcal{R}$-normal form. Hence every closed term of type ι is identified with a term of the form $S(S(S\ldots(S0)\ldots))$ and every closed term of type o is identified with either *true* or *false*. Such terms are denoted by $\underline{n}$ and called *numerals* (even if they are of type o).

2.2 Intuitionistic Arithmetic for Functionals

The system we consider is essentially Heyting's intuitionistic arithmetic in finite types HA^ω as described e.g. in [4]. It is based on Gödel's system T and just adds the corresponding logical and arithmetical apparatus to it. Classical arithmetic is obtained by restriction to formulas without the constructive existential quantifier $\exists^*$ but using the classical definition $\exists = \neg\forall\neg$ instead. Equations are treated on the meta level by identifying terms with the same normal form.

We now write $r, s, t, \ldots$ for (object) terms, and reserve $M, N, K, \ldots$ for derivation terms.

Arithmetic: Predicate symbols and atomic formulas

Every predicate symbol P now has a fixed arity, which is a tupel of types $(\rho_1, \dots, \rho_k)$. So atomic formulas are of the form $P(r_1^{\rho_1}, \dots, r_k^{\rho_k})$. The choice of the predicate symbols depends on the particular problem under consideration. In most cases there will be the predicate symbols $\bot$ (falsity) of arity $()$ and *atom* of arity (o). The intended interpretation of *atom* is the set $\{true\}$. Hence "$atom(t)$" means "$t = true$". Every decidable relation (i.e., every relation given by a term t of type o), can then be written in the form $atom(t)$. If confusion is unlikely, we will write t instead of $atom(t)$. So formulas are

$$P(r_1^{\rho_1}, \dots, r_k^{\rho_k}) \mid A \wedge B \mid A \to B \mid \forall x^\rho A \mid \exists^* x^\rho A.$$

To accomodate the specific ground types ι and o, we need an induction scheme for both types, and in addition a "truth axiom" .

$$\begin{array}{rl} Ind_{p,A}: & A[p := true] \to A[p := false] \to \forall p A \\ Ind_{n,A}: & A[n := 0] \to (\forall n. A \to A[n := n+1]) \to \forall n A \\ T: & atom(true) \end{array}$$

We also need $\exists^*$-axioms:

$$\begin{array}{rll} \exists^{*+}_{x,A}: & \forall x. A \to \exists^* x A & \\ \exists^{*-}_{x,A,B}: & \exists^* x^\rho A \to (\forall x^\rho. A \to B) \to B & (x \notin FV(B)) \end{array}$$

Derivations are within minimal logic. They are written in natural deduction style, i.e. as typed λ-terms via the well-known Curry-Howard correspondence.

$$\begin{array}{l} u^B \quad \text{(assumptions)} \mid \text{axioms} \mid \\ \langle M^A, N^B \rangle^{A \wedge B} \mid \pi_i(M^{A_0 \wedge A_1})^{A_i} \mid \\ (\lambda u^A M^B)^{A \to B} \mid (M^{A \to B} N^A)^B \mid \\ (\lambda x^\rho M^A)^{\forall x^\rho A} \mid (M^{\forall x^\rho A} t^\rho)^{A[x^\rho := t^\rho]} \end{array}$$

where in the $\forall$-introduction $\lambda x M^A$, x must not be free in any B with $u^B \in FA(M)$.

Classical logic

Assume that *atom* is the only predicate symbol, and replace $\bot$ by $atom(false)$. Then we have

$$\begin{array}{rl} \neg A & := A \to atom(false) \\ \exists x A & := \neg \forall x \neg A, \end{array}$$

and stability $\neg\neg A \to A$ is provable for all $\exists^*$-free formulas A, using boolean induction for the case $atom(t)$. Hence classical arithmetic (in all finite types) is a subsystem of our present system based on minimal logic.

So for $\exists^*$-free formulas (no restriction from a classical point of view) we have full classical logic.

Note also that for quantifier-free formulas B built from prime formulas of the form $atom(t)$ we can easily construct a boolean term $t_B\colon o$ such that

$$atom(t_B) \leftrightarrow B$$

is derivable. Therefore we can use boolean induction to derive *case distinction* for quantifier-free formulas.

2.3 Program Extraction from Constructive Proofs

We now come back to the full system, and assign to every formula A an object $\tau(A)$ (a type or the symbol $*$). $\tau(A)$ is intended to be the type of the program to be extracted from a proof of A. In case $\tau(A) = *$ proofs of A have no computational content; such formulas A are called *Harrop formulas*.

$$\begin{aligned}
\tau(P(\vec{s})) &:= * \\
\tau(\exists^* x^\rho A) &:= \begin{cases} \rho & \text{if } \tau(A) = * \\ \rho \times \tau(A) & \text{otherwise} \end{cases} \\
\tau(\forall x^\rho A) &:= \begin{cases} * & \text{if } \tau(A) = * \\ \rho \to \tau(A) & \text{otherwise} \end{cases} \\
\tau(A_0 \wedge A_1) &:= \begin{cases} \tau(A_i) & \text{if } \tau(A_{1-i}) = * \\ \tau(A_0) \times \tau(A_1) & \text{otherwise} \end{cases} \\
\tau(A \to B) &:= \begin{cases} \tau(B) & \text{if } \tau(A) = * \\ * & \text{if } \tau(B) = * \\ \tau(A) \to \tau(B) & \text{otherwise} \end{cases}
\end{aligned}$$

We now define, for a given derivation M of a formula A with $\tau(A) \neq *$, its *extracted program* $[\![M]\!]$ of type $\tau(A)$.

$$\begin{aligned}
[\![u^A]\!] &:= x_u^{\tau(A)} \quad (x_u^{\tau(A)} \text{ uniquely associated with } u^A) \\
[\![\lambda u^A M]\!] &:= \begin{cases} [\![M]\!] & \text{if } \tau(A) = * \\ \lambda x_u^{\tau(A)} [\![M]\!] & \text{otherwise} \end{cases} \\
[\![M^{A \to B} N]\!] &:= \begin{cases} [\![M]\!] & \text{if } \tau(A) = * \\ [\![M]\!][\![N]\!] & \text{otherwise} \end{cases} \\
[\![\langle M_0^{A_0}, M_1^{A_1} \rangle]\!] &:= \begin{cases} [\![M_i]\!] & \text{if } \tau(A_{1-i}) = * \\ \langle [\![M_0]\!], [\![M_1]\!] \rangle & \text{otherwise} \end{cases} \\
[\![\pi_i(M^{A_0 \wedge A_1})]\!] &:= \begin{cases} [\![M]\!] & \text{if } \tau(A_{1-i}) = * \\ \pi_i [\![M]\!] & \text{otherwise} \end{cases} \\
[\![\lambda x^\rho M]\!] &:= \lambda x^\rho [\![M]\!] \\
[\![Mt]\!] &:= [\![M]\!] t
\end{aligned}$$

We also need extracted programs for induction and $\exists^*$-axioms. For the induction scheme $Ind_{n,A}\colon A[n := 0] \to (\forall n.A \to A[n := n+1]) \to \forall n A$ let

$$[\![Ind_{n,A}]\!] := \mathcal{R}_{\iota,\rho}\colon \rho \to (\iota \to \rho \to \rho) \to \iota \to \rho,$$

where $\rho = \tau(A)$. Similarly boolean induction is realized by $\mathcal{R}_{o,\rho}$.

For the $\exists^*$-axioms we set

$$\begin{aligned}
[\![\exists^{*+}_{x^\rho, A}]\!] &:= \begin{cases} \lambda x^\rho x & \text{if } \tau(A) = * \\ \lambda x^\rho \lambda y^{\tau(A)} \langle x, y \rangle & \text{otherwise} \end{cases} \\
[\![\exists^{*-}_{x^\rho, A, B}]\!] &:= \begin{cases} \lambda x^\rho \lambda f^{\rho \to \tau(B)} f x & \text{if } \tau(A) = * \\ \lambda z^{\rho \times \tau(A)} \lambda f^{\rho \to \tau(A) \to \tau(B)}. f \pi_0(z) \pi_1(z) & \text{otherwise} \end{cases}
\end{aligned}$$

For derivations M^A where $\tau(A) = *$ (i.e. A is a Harrop-formula) we define $[\![M]\!] := \varepsilon$ (ε some new symbol). This applies in particular if A is $\exists^*$-free.

Finally we define the notion of *modified realizability*. More precisely, we define formulas r **mr** A, where A is a formula and r is either a term of type $\tau(A)$ if the latter is a type, or the symbol ε if $\tau(A) = *$.

$$\begin{aligned}
\varepsilon \mathbf{\ mr\ } P(\vec{s}) &= P(\vec{s}) \\
r \mathbf{\ mr\ } (\exists^* x A) &= \begin{cases} \varepsilon \mathbf{\ mr\ } A[x := r] & \text{if } \tau(A) = * \\ \pi_1(r) \mathbf{\ mr\ } A[x := \pi_0(r)] & \text{otherwise} \end{cases} \\
r \mathbf{\ mr\ } (\forall x A) &= \begin{cases} \forall x. \varepsilon \mathbf{\ mr\ } A & \text{if } \tau(A) = * \\ \forall x. rx \mathbf{\ mr\ } A & \text{otherwise} \end{cases} \\
r \mathbf{\ mr\ } (A \to B) &= \begin{cases} \varepsilon \mathbf{\ mr\ } A \to r \mathbf{\ mr\ } B & \text{if } \tau(A) = * \\ \forall x. x \mathbf{\ mr\ } A \to \varepsilon \mathbf{\ mr\ } B & \text{if } \tau(A) \neq * = \tau(B) \\ \forall x. x \mathbf{\ mr\ } A \to rx \mathbf{\ mr\ } B & \text{otherwise} \end{cases} \\
r \mathbf{\ mr\ } (A_0 \wedge A_1) &= \begin{cases} \varepsilon \mathbf{\ mr\ } A_0 \wedge r \mathbf{\ mr\ } A_1 & \text{if } \tau(A_0) = * \\ r \mathbf{\ mr\ } A_0 \wedge \varepsilon \mathbf{\ mr\ } A_1 & \text{if } \tau(A_1) = * \\ \pi_0(r) \mathbf{\ mr\ } A_0 \wedge \pi_1(r) \mathbf{\ mr\ } A_1 & \text{otherwise} \end{cases}
\end{aligned}$$

Note that for A $\exists^*$-free we have $\tau(A) = *$ and $\varepsilon \mathbf{\ mr\ } A = A$. For the formulation of the soundness theorem below it will be useful to let $x_u := \varepsilon$ if u^A is an assumption variable with a Harrop-formula A.

Theorem 2.9 (Soundness) *If M is a derivation of a formula B, then there is a derivation $\mu(M)$ of $[\![M]\!] \mathbf{\ mr\ } B$ from $\{ x_u \mathbf{\ mr\ } C \mid u^C \in FA(M) \}$.*

Proof. Induction on M. *Case* $u: A$. Then we have $\bar{u}: x_u \mathbf{\ mr\ } A$. Let $\mu(u) := \bar{u}$. *Case* $\lambda u^A M^B$. We must find a derivation $\mu(\lambda u M)$ of

$$[\![\lambda u M]\!] \mathbf{\ mr\ } (A \to B).$$

Subcase $\tau(A) = *$. Then we have $[\![\lambda u M]\!] = [\![M]\!]$, hence

$$[\![\lambda u M]\!] \mathbf{\ mr\ } (A \to B) \quad = \quad \varepsilon \mathbf{\ mr\ } A \to [\![M]\!] \mathbf{\ mr\ } B.$$

By induction hypothesis we can define $\mu(\lambda u M) := \lambda \bar{u} \mu(M)$ with $\bar{u}: \varepsilon \mathbf{\ mr\ } A$. *Subcase* $\tau(A) \neq * = \tau(B)$. Then we have $[\![\lambda u M]\!] = \varepsilon$ and

$$[\![\lambda u M]\!] \mathbf{\ mr\ } (A \to B) \quad = \quad \forall x. x \mathbf{\ mr\ } A \to \varepsilon \mathbf{\ mr\ } B.$$

By induction hypothesis define $\mu(\lambda u M) := \lambda x_u \lambda \bar{u} \mu(M)$ with $\bar{u}: x_u \mathbf{\ mr\ } A$. *Subcase* $\tau(A) \neq * \neq \tau(B)$. Then we have

$$[\![\lambda u M]\!] \mathbf{\ mr\ } (A \to B) \quad = \quad \forall x. x \mathbf{\ mr\ } A \to [\![\lambda u M]\!] x \mathbf{\ mr\ } B$$

Because of $[\![\lambda u M]\!] = \lambda x_u [\![M]\!]$ and since we identify terms with the same β-normal form, by induction hypothesis we can define $\mu(\lambda u M) := \lambda x_u \lambda \bar{u} \mu(M)$.

Case $M^{A \to B} N^A$. We must find a derivation $\mu(MN)$ of $[\![MN]\!] \mathbf{\ mr\ } B$. *Subcase* $\tau(A) = *$. Then we have $[\![MN]\!] = [\![M]\!]$. By induction hypothesis we have derivations $\mu(M)$ of

$$[\![M]\!] \mathbf{\ mr\ } (A \to B) \quad = \quad \varepsilon \mathbf{\ mr\ } A \to [\![M]\!] \mathbf{\ mr\ } B$$

and $\mu(N)$ of $\varepsilon \mathbf{\ mr\ } A$; hence we can define $\mu(MN) := \mu(M)\mu(N)$. *Subcase* $\tau(A) \neq * = \tau(B)$. Then we have $[\![MN]\!] = \varepsilon$. By induction hypothesis we have derivations $\mu(M)$ of

$$[\![M]\!] \mathbf{\ mr\ } (A \to B) \quad = \quad \forall x. x \mathbf{\ mr\ } A \to \varepsilon \mathbf{\ mr\ } B$$

and $\mu(N)$ of $[\![N]\!] \mathbf{\ mr\ } A$; hence we can define $\mu(MN) := \mu(M)[\![N]\!]\mu(N)$. *Subcase* $\tau(A) \neq * \neq \tau(B)$. Then we have $[\![MN]\!] = [\![M]\!][\![N]\!]$. By induction hypothesis we have derivations $\mu(M)$ of

$$[\![M]\!] \mathbf{\ mr\ } (A \to B) \quad = \quad \forall x. x \mathbf{\ mr\ } A \to [\![M]\!] x \mathbf{\ mr\ } B$$

and $\mu(N)$ of $[\![N]\!]$ **mr** A; hence we can define $\mu(MN) := \mu(M)[\![N]\!]\mu(N)$.

Case $\langle M_0^{A_0}, M_1^{A_1}\rangle$. We must find a derivation $\mu(\langle M_0, M_1\rangle)$ of

$$[\![\langle M_0, M_1\rangle]\!] \textbf{ mr } (A_0 \wedge A_1).$$

Subcase $\tau(A_0) = * = \tau(A_1)$. Then we have $[\![\langle M_0, M_1\rangle]\!] = \varepsilon$, hence

$$[\![\langle M_0, M_1\rangle]\!] \textbf{ mr } (A_0 \wedge A_1) \quad = \quad \varepsilon \textbf{ mr } A_0 \ \wedge \ \varepsilon \textbf{ mr } A_1$$

and by induction hypothesis we can define $\mu(\langle M_0, M_1\rangle) := \langle \mu(M_0), \mu(M_1)\rangle$. *Subcase* $\tau(A_0) = * \neq \tau(A_1)$. Then we have $[\![\langle M_0, M_1\rangle]\!] = [\![M_1]\!]$, hence

$$[\![\langle M_0, M_1\rangle]\!] \textbf{ mr } (A_0 \wedge A_1) \quad = \quad \varepsilon \textbf{ mr } A_0 \ \wedge \ [\![M_1]\!] \textbf{ mr } A_1$$

and by induction hypothesis we can define $\mu(\langle M_0, M_1\rangle) := \langle \mu(M_0), \mu(M_1)\rangle$. *Subcase* $\tau(A_0) \neq * = \tau(A_1)$. Similar. *Subcase* $\tau(A_0) \neq * \neq \tau(A_1)$. Then we have $[\![\langle M_0, M_1\rangle]\!] = \langle [\![M_0]\!], [\![M_1]\!]\rangle$, hence

$$[\![\langle M_0, M_1\rangle]\!] \textbf{ mr } (A_0 \wedge A_1) \quad = \quad [\![M_0]\!] \textbf{ mr } A_0 \ \wedge \ [\![M_1]\!] \textbf{ mr } A_1$$

and by induction hypothesis we can define $\mu(\langle M_0, M_1\rangle) := \langle \mu(M_i), \mu(M_{1-i})\rangle$.

Case $\pi_0(M^{A_0 \wedge A_1})$. We must find a derivation $\mu(\pi_0(M))$ of

$$[\![\pi_0(M)]\!] \textbf{ mr } A_0.$$

Subcase $\tau(A_1) = *$. Then we have $[\![\pi_0(M)]\!] = [\![M]\!]$. by induction hypothesis we have a derivation $\mu(M)$ of

$$[\![M]\!] \textbf{ mr } (A_0 \wedge A_1) \quad = \quad [\![M]\!] \textbf{ mr } A_0 \ \wedge \ \varepsilon \textbf{ mr } A_1.$$

hence we can define $\mu(\pi_0(M)) := \pi_0(\mu(M))$. *Subcase* $\tau(A_0) = * \neq \tau(A_1)$. Then we have $[\![\pi_0(M)]\!] = \varepsilon$. by induction hypothesis we have a derivation $\mu(M)$ of

$$[\![M]\!] \textbf{ mr } (A_0 \wedge A_1) \quad = \quad \varepsilon \textbf{ mr } A_0 \ \wedge \ [\![M]\!] \textbf{ mr } A_1.$$

hence we can define $\mu(\pi_0(M)) := \pi_0(\mu(M))$. *Subcase* $\tau(A_0) \neq * \neq \tau(A_1)$. Similar; we can define $\mu(\langle M_0, M_1\rangle) := \langle \mu(M_0), \mu(M_1)\rangle$.

Case $\pi_1(M^{A_0 \wedge A_1})$. Similar.

Case $\lambda z M^A$. We must find a derivation $\mu(\lambda z M)$ of $[\![\lambda z M]\!]$ **mr** $\forall z A$. By definition $[\![\lambda z M]\!] = \lambda z [\![M]\!]$. *Subcase* $\tau(A) = *$. Then we have

$$\lambda z[\![M]\!] \textbf{ mr } \forall z A \quad = \quad \forall z.\varepsilon \textbf{ mr } A$$

and by induction hypothesis we can define $\mu(\lambda z M) := \lambda z \mu(M)$. The variable condition is satisfied, since $\lambda z M^A$ is a derivation term, and hence z does not occur free in any assumption variable $u\colon B$ free in M^A, hence also does not occur free in the free assumption $\bar{u}\colon x_u$ **mr** B. *Subcase* $\tau(A) \neq *$. Then we have

$$\lambda z[\![M]\!] \textbf{ mr } \forall z A \quad = \quad \forall z.(\lambda z[\![M]\!])z \textbf{ mr } A.$$

Since we identify terms with the same β-normal form, by induction hypothesis we again can define $\mu(\lambda z M) := \lambda z \mu(M)$. As before one can see that the variable condition is satisfied.

Case $M^{\forall z A} t$. We must find a derivation $\mu(Mt)$ of $[\![Mt]\!]\ \mathbf{mr}\ A[x := t]$. By definition we have $[\![Mt]\!] = [\![M]\!]t$. *Subcase* $\tau(A) = *$. By induction hypothesis we have a derivation of

$$[\![M]\!]\ \mathbf{mr}\ \forall z A \quad = \quad \forall z.\varepsilon\ \mathbf{mr}\ A$$

hence we can define $\mu(Mt) := \mu(M)t$. *Subcase* $\tau(A) \neq *$. By induction hypothesis we have a derivation of

$$[\![M]\!]\ \mathbf{mr}\ \forall z A \quad = \quad \forall z.[\![M]\!]z\ \mathbf{mr}\ A,$$

hence we again can define $\mu(Mt) := \mu(M)t$.

Case $\exists^{*+}_{x,A}\colon \forall \vec{x} \forall x.A \to \exists^* x^\rho A$. We must find a derivation $\mu(\exists^{*+}_{x,A})$ of

$$[\![\exists^{*+}_{x,A}]\!]\ \mathbf{mr}\ \forall \vec{x} \forall x.A \to \exists^* x^\rho A.$$

Subcase $\tau(A) = *$. Then we have $\exists^{*+}_{x,A} = \lambda\vec{x}\lambda x x$ and we obtain

$$\begin{aligned}(\lambda\vec{x}\lambda x x)\ \mathbf{mr}\ \forall\vec{x}\forall x.A \to \exists^* x A &= \forall\vec{x}\forall x.x\ \mathbf{mr}\ (A \to \exists^* x A)\\ &= \forall\vec{x}\forall x.\varepsilon\ \mathbf{mr}\ A \to x\ \mathbf{mr}\ \exists^* x A\\ &= \forall\vec{x}\forall x.\varepsilon\ \mathbf{mr}\ A \to \varepsilon\ \mathbf{mr}\ A.\end{aligned}$$

Hence we can define $\mu(\exists^{*+}_{x,A}) = \lambda\vec{x}\lambda x\lambda u u$. *Subcase* $\tau(A) \neq *$. Then we have $\exists^{*+}_{x,A} = \lambda\vec{x}\lambda x\lambda y\langle x, y\rangle$ and we obtain

$$\begin{aligned}&\lambda\vec{x}\lambda x\lambda y\langle x, y\rangle\ \mathbf{mr}\ \forall\vec{x}\forall x.A \to \exists^* x A\\ &= \forall\vec{x}\forall x\forall y.y\ \mathbf{mr}\ A \to \langle x, y\rangle\ \mathbf{mr}\ \exists^* x A\\ &= \forall\vec{x}\forall x\forall y.y\ \mathbf{mr}\ A \to y\ \mathbf{mr}\ A\end{aligned}$$

Hence we can define $\mu(\exists^{*+}_{x,A}) = \lambda\vec{x}\lambda x\lambda y\lambda u u$.

Case $\exists^{*-}_{x,A,B}\colon \forall\vec{x}[\exists^* x A \to (\forall x.A \to B) \to B]$ with $x \notin FV(B)$. We must find a derivation $\mu(\exists^{*-}_{x,A,B})$ of $\forall\vec{x}[\exists^* x A \to (\forall x.A \to B) \to B]$. *Subcase* $\tau(A) = * = \tau(B)$. Then we have $[\![\exists^{*-}_{x,A,B}]\!] = \varepsilon$ and we obtain

$$\begin{aligned}&\varepsilon\ \mathbf{mr}\ \forall\vec{x}[\exists^* x A \to (\forall x.A \to B) \to B]\\ &= \forall\vec{x}\forall x.x\ \mathbf{mr}\ \exists^* x A \to \varepsilon\ \mathbf{mr}\ ((\forall x.A \to B) \to B)\\ &= \forall\vec{x}\forall x.\varepsilon\ \mathbf{mr}\ A \to \varepsilon\ \mathbf{mr}\ (\forall x.A \to B) \to \varepsilon\ \mathbf{mr}\ B\\ &= \forall\vec{x}\forall x.\varepsilon\ \mathbf{mr}\ A \to \forall x\, \varepsilon\ \mathbf{mr}\ (A \to B) \to \varepsilon\ \mathbf{mr}\ B\\ &= \forall\vec{x}\forall x.\varepsilon\ \mathbf{mr}\ A \to (\forall x.\varepsilon\ \mathbf{mr}\ A \to \varepsilon\ \mathbf{mr}\ B) \to \varepsilon\ \mathbf{mr}\ B.\end{aligned}$$

Hence we can define $\mu(\exists^{*-}_{x,A,B}) = \lambda\vec{x}\lambda x\lambda u\lambda v.vxu$. *Subcase* $\tau(A) \neq * = \tau(B)$. Then we again have $[\![\exists^{*-}_{x,A,B}]\!] = \varepsilon$ and we obtain

$$\begin{aligned}&\varepsilon\ \mathbf{mr}\ \forall\vec{x}[\exists^* x A \to (\forall x.A \to B) \to B]\\ &= \forall\vec{x}\forall x.x\ \mathbf{mr}\ \exists^* x A \to \varepsilon\ \mathbf{mr}\ ((\forall x.A \to B) \to B)\\ &= \forall\vec{x}\forall x.\pi_1(x)\ \mathbf{mr}\ A[x := \pi_0(x)] \to \varepsilon\ \mathbf{mr}\ (\forall x.A \to B) \to \varepsilon\ \mathbf{mr}\ B\\ &= \forall\vec{x}\forall x.\pi_1(x)\ \mathbf{mr}\ A[x := \pi_0(x)] \to \forall x\, \varepsilon\ \mathbf{mr}\ (A \to B) \to \varepsilon\ \mathbf{mr}\ B\\ &= \forall\vec{x}\forall x.\pi_1(x)\ \mathbf{mr}\ A[x := \pi_0(x)] \to \forall x\forall y(y\ \mathbf{mr}\ A \to \varepsilon\ \mathbf{mr}\ B) \to \varepsilon\ \mathbf{mr}\ B.\end{aligned}$$

Hence we can define $\mu(\exists^{*-}_{x,A,B}) = \lambda\vec{x}\lambda x\lambda u\lambda v.v\pi_0(x)\pi_1(x)u$. *Subcase* $\tau(A) = * \neq \tau(B)$. Then we have $[\![\exists^{*-}_{x,A,B}]\!] = \lambda\vec{x}\lambda x\lambda z(zx)$ and we obtain

$$\begin{aligned}&\lambda\vec{x}\lambda x\lambda z(zx)\ \mathbf{mr}\ \forall\vec{x}[\exists^* x A \to (\forall x.A \to B) \to B]\\ &= \forall\vec{x}\forall x.x\ \mathbf{mr}\ \exists^* x A \to \lambda z(zx)\ \mathbf{mr}\ ((\forall x.A \to B) \to B)\\ &= \forall\vec{x}\forall x.\varepsilon\ \mathbf{mr}\ A \to \forall z.z\ \mathbf{mr}\ (\forall x.A \to B) \to zx\ \mathbf{mr}\ B\\ &= \forall\vec{x}\forall x.\varepsilon\ \mathbf{mr}\ A \to \forall z.\forall x\, zx\ \mathbf{mr}\ (A \to B) \to zx\ \mathbf{mr}\ B\\ &= \forall\vec{x}\forall x.\varepsilon\ \mathbf{mr}\ A \to \forall z.(\forall x.\varepsilon\ \mathbf{mr}\ A \to zx\ \mathbf{mr}\ B) \to zx\ \mathbf{mr}\ B.\end{aligned}$$

Hence we can define $\mu(\exists^{*-}_{x,A,B}) = \lambda\vec{x}\lambda x\lambda u\lambda v.vxu$. *Subcase* $\tau(A) \neq * \neq \tau(B)$. Then we have $[\![\exists^{*-}_{x,A,B}]\!] = \lambda\vec{x}\lambda x\lambda z(z\pi_0(x)\pi_1(x))$ and we obtain

$$\begin{aligned}
&\lambda\vec{x}\lambda x\lambda z(z\pi_0(x)\pi_1(x)) \mathbf{\ mr\ } \forall\vec{x}[\exists^* xA \to (\forall x.A \to B) \to B] \\
&= \forall\vec{x}\forall x.x \mathbf{\ mr\ } \exists^* xA \to \lambda z(z\pi_0(x)\pi_1(x)) \mathbf{\ mr\ } ((\forall x.A \to B) \to B) \\
&= \forall\vec{x}\forall x.\pi_1(x) \mathbf{\ mr\ } A[x := \pi_0(x)] \to \\
&\qquad \forall z.z \mathbf{\ mr\ } (\forall x.A \to B) \to z\pi_0(x)\pi_1(x) \mathbf{\ mr\ } B \\
&= \forall\vec{x}\forall x.\pi_1(x) \mathbf{\ mr\ } A[x := \pi_0(x)] \to \\
&\qquad \forall z.\forall x\forall y(y \mathbf{\ mr\ } A \to zxy \mathbf{\ mr\ } B) \to z\pi_0(x)\pi_1(x) \mathbf{\ mr\ } B.
\end{aligned}$$

Hence we can define $\mu(\exists^{*-}_{x,A,B}) = \lambda\vec{x}\lambda x\lambda u\lambda z\lambda v.v\pi_0(x)\pi_1(x)u$. □

If B is $\exists^*$-free, then $\varepsilon \mathbf{\ mr\ } B = B$. Hence for $\forall x^\rho\exists^* y^\sigma B$ with $\exists^*$-free B we have $\tau(\forall x\exists y^* B) = \rho \to \sigma$ and

$$t \mathbf{\ mr\ } \forall x\exists^* yB = \forall xB[y := tx].$$

Then as a corollary to the soundness theorem we obtain the extraction theorem

Theorem 2.10 *From a derivation* $M{:}\,\forall x^\rho\exists^* y^\sigma B$ *with* B $\exists^*$*-free from* $\exists^*$*-free assumptions* Γ *one can extract a closed term* $[\![M]\!]^{\rho\to\sigma}$ *such that the formula* $\forall xB[y := [\![M]\!]x]$ *is provable from* Γ.

Here Γ should be viewed as lemmata, i.e. true formulas (proved separately, to keep M short). The theorem says that the extracted program is independent of how this shortcut is achieved.

3 Computational Content of Classical Proofs

3.1 Definite and Goal Formulas

For simplicity we only treat formulas in the $\to\forall$ fragment; this is not an essential restriction, since conjunctions can be easily removed.

A formula is *relevant* if it "ends" with $\bot$. More precisely, relevant formulas are defined inductively by the clauses

- $\bot$ is relevant,
- if C is relevant and B is an arbitrary formula, then $B \to C$ is relevant, and
- if C is relevant, then $\forall xC$ is relevant.

A formula which is not relevant is called *irrelevant*.

We define *goal formulas* G and *definite formulas* D inductively. These notions are related to similar ones common under the same name in the context of extensions of logic programming. Let P range over atoms (including $\bot$).

$$\begin{array}{lllll}
G & := & P & \mid D \to G & \text{provided } D \text{ irrelevant} \Rightarrow D \text{ quantifier-free} \\
 & & & \mid \forall xG & \text{provided } G \text{ irrelevant} \\
D & := & P & \mid G \to D & \text{provided } D \text{ irrelevant} \Rightarrow G \text{ irrelevant} \\
 & & & \mid \forall xD &
\end{array}$$

Lemma 3.1 *For definite formulas D, relevant goal formulas G and an arbitrary formula A we have derivations*

$$\begin{aligned} N_D^A &: D \to D^A \\ H_G^A &: G^A \to \neg G \to A \end{aligned}$$

The proof is by induction on definite and goal formulas; it is necessary to prove several additional claims simultaneously, to get the induction through. For details we refer to [1].

Theorem 3.2 *Let $D_1, \dots, D_l$ be relevant and $D_{l+1}, \dots, D_n$ irrelevant definite formulas, and $G_1, \dots, G_k$ be relevant quantifier-free and $G_{k+1}, \dots, G_m$ irrelevant goal formulas. Let $A := \exists^* y \vec{G}$ and*

$$t := \lambda y, \vec{x}.\mathbf{if}\ \neg G_1\ \mathbf{then}\ [\![H_{G_1}^A]\!](x_1)\ \mathbf{else}\ \dots\ \mathbf{if}\ \neg G_k\ \mathbf{then}\ [\![H_{G_k}^A]\!](x_k)\ \mathbf{else}\ y.$$

Assume that we have a derivation

$$M \colon \vec{D} \to (\forall y.\vec{G} \to \bot) \to \bot.$$

Let M^A denote the result of substituting $\bot$ by A everywhere in M. Then we can derive

$$\vec{D} \to [\![M^A]\!][\![N_{D_1}^A]\!] \dots [\![N_{D_l}^A]\!] t\ \mathbf{mr}\ \exists^* y \vec{G}.$$

The proof uses the soundness theorem 2.9 and lemma 3.1. For details we again have to refer to [1].

3.2 Example: Integer Square Roots

Let $f \colon \iota \to \iota$ be unbounded with $f0 = 0$; think of f as the square function $f(n) = n^2$. We want to prove that integer square roots always exist, or more precisely a general form of this proposition, using only the two properties of f above. We specify our problem as follows. Here f, g, n are parameters; g is used as an explicit witness of the unboundedness of f.

$$\forall n\, \neg n<f0 \to \forall n\, n<f(gn) \to (\forall m.\neg n<fm \to n<f(m+1) \to \bot) \to \bot$$

Clearly

$\forall n\, \neg n<f0$	is a relevant definite formula
$\forall n\, n<f(gn)$	is an irrelevant definite formula
$\neg n<fm$	is a relevant goal formula
$n<f(m+1)$	is an irrelevant goal formula,

hence theorem 3.2 can be applied without inserting any double negations.

To construct a derivation, assume

$$\begin{aligned} v_1 &: \forall n\, \neg n<f0, \\ v_2 &: \forall n\, n<f(gn), \\ u &: \forall m.\neg n<fm \to n<f(m+1) \to \bot. \end{aligned}$$

Our goal is $\bot$. From v_1 and u we inductively get $\forall m\, \neg n<fm$. For $m := gn$ this yields a contradiction to v_2. The derivation is

$$\cfrac{\cfrac{\cfrac{\mathit{Ind} \quad \neg n<f0 \quad \forall m.\neg n<fm \to \neg n<f(m+1)}{\forall m \neg n<fm} \quad gn}{\neg n<f(gn)} \quad n<f(gn)}{\bot}$$

with derivation term

$$M := \lambda v_1 \lambda v_2 \lambda u.Ind_{m,\neg n<fm} n(v_1 n)u(gn)(v_2 n),$$

Now let $A := \exists^* m.\neg n<fm \wedge n<f(m+1)$, hence

$$M^A = \lambda v_1^{\forall n.n<f0 \to A} \lambda v_2^{\forall n n<f(gn)} \lambda u^{\forall m.(n<fm \to A) \to n<f(m+1) \to A}. Ind_{m,n<fm \to A} n(v_1 n)u(gn)(v_2 n)$$

and therefore

$$[\![M^A]\!] =_\beta \lambda x_{v_1}^{\iota \to \iota} \lambda x_u^{\iota \to \iota \to \iota}.\mathcal{R}_\iota (x_{v_1} n) x_u (gn)$$

From the proof of theorem 3.2 we generally know $D \to [\![N_D^A]\!]$ **mr** D^A for every relevant definite formula D. In our case, with $D = \forall n.\neg n<f0$, we can derive directly

$$(\forall n.n<f0 \to \bot) \to (\lambda n0) \textbf{ mr } \forall n.n<f0 \to A,$$

since we can use ex-falso. So we may assume $[\![N_D^A]\!] = \lambda n0$. Also, from the proof of theorem 3.2 we generally know x **mr** $G^A \to \neg G \to [\![H_G^A]\!](x)$ **mr** A for every relevant goal formula G. In our case, with $G = \neg n<fm$, we can derive directly

$$(x \textbf{ mr } n<fm \to A) \to \neg\neg n<fm \to x \textbf{ mr } A.$$

So we may assume $[\![H_G^A]\!] = \lambda x x$. Now let

$$\begin{aligned} t: &= \lambda m \lambda x.\textbf{if } \neg G_1 \textbf{ then } [\![H_{G_1}^A]\!](x) \textbf{ else } m \\ &= \lambda m \lambda x.\textbf{if } n<fm \textbf{ then } x \textbf{ else } m. \end{aligned}$$

Then the extracted term according to theorem 3.2 is

$$\begin{aligned} [\![M^A]\!][\![N_D^A]\!]t &= \big(\lambda x_{v_1}^{\iota \to \iota} \lambda x_u^{\iota \to \iota \to \iota}.\mathcal{R}_\iota (x_{v_1} n) x_u (gn)\big)(\lambda n0)t \\ &=_\beta \mathcal{R}_\iota 0 t(gn) \\ &= \mathcal{R}_\iota 0(\lambda n \lambda x \textbf{if } n<fm \textbf{ then } x \textbf{ else } m)(gn). \end{aligned}$$

Informally, the algorithm can be written in the form $h(gn)$ where $h\colon \iota \to \iota$ is such that

$$h(0) = 0,$$
$$h(m+1) = \begin{cases} h(m) & \text{if } n<f(m) \\ m & \text{else} \end{cases}$$

3.3 Example: The Greatest Common Divisor

Yiannis Moschovakis suggested the following example of a classical existence proof with a quantifier-free kernel which does not obviously contain an algorithm: the gcd of two natural numbers a_1 and a_2 is a linear combination of the two. Here we treat that example as a case study for program extraction from classical proofs. In the original treatment in [2] we identified one of the predicate symbols as critical (the divisibility relation $\cdot|\cdot$). Here we show how this example can be treated in the present form of the theory, with definite and goal formulas. It turns out that the algorithm does not change; however, the method of how to extract a program from this classical proof becomes more perspicious.

Let $a, b, c, i, j, k, \ell, m, n, q, r$ denote natural numbers. Our language is determined by the constants $0, 1, +, *$, function symbols for the quotient and the remainder denoted by $q(a,c)$ and $r(a,c)$, a 4-ary function denoted by $abs(k_1a_1 - k_2a_2)$ whose intended meaning is clear from the notation and an auxiliary 5-ary function f which will be defined later. We will express the intended meaning of these function symbols by stating some properties (lemmata) $v_1, \dots, v_6$ of them; these will be formulated as we need them.

Theorem 3.3 *For natural numbers* a_1, a_2 *with* $0 < a_2$

$$\exists k_1, k_2.abs(k_1a_1 - k_2a_2)|a_1 \wedge abs(k_1a_1 - k_2a_2)|a_2 \wedge 0 < abs(k_1a_1 - k_2a_2).$$

Proof. Let a_1, a_2 be given and assume $0 < a_2$. The ideal (a_1, a_2) generated from a_1, a_2 has a least positive element c, since $0 < a_2$. This element has a representation $c = abs(k_1a_1 - k_2a_2)$ with $k_1, k_2 \in \mathbb{N}$. It is a common divisor of a_1 and a_2 since otherwise the remainder $r(a_i, c)$ would be a smaller positive element of the ideal.

The number $c \in (a_1, a_2)$ dividing a_1 and a_2 is the greatest common divisor since any common divisor of a_1 and a_2 must also be a divisor of c. □

The minimum principle and course-of-values induction.

In order to formally write out the proof above we need to make explicit the instance of the induction scheme used implicitly in the minimum principle. The minimum principle w.r.t. a measure μ says

$$\exists \vec{k} R(\vec{k}) \to \exists \vec{k}.R(\vec{k}) \wedge \forall \vec{\ell}.\mu(\vec{\ell}) < \mu(\vec{k}) \to R(\vec{\ell}) \to \bot$$

(in our example $R(k_1, k_2) \equiv 0 < abs(k_1a_1 - k_2a_2)$ and $\mu(k_1, k_2) \equiv abs(k_1a_1 - k_2a_2)$). In order to reduce this to the induction scheme we use the fact that the formula above is classically equivalent to

$$(\forall \vec{k}.R(\vec{k}) \to [\forall \vec{\ell}.\mu(\vec{\ell}) < \mu(\vec{k}) \to R(\vec{\ell}) \to \bot] \to \bot) \to \forall \vec{k}.R(\vec{k}) \to \bot,$$

i.e. the principle of *course-of-values induction* for $R(\vec{k}) \to \bot$ w.r.t. the measure $\mu(\vec{k})$. We can write this as

$$Prog \to \forall \vec{k}.R(\vec{k}) \to \bot,$$

where

$$Prog := \forall \vec{k}.[\forall \vec{\ell}.\mu(\vec{\ell}) < \mu(\vec{k}) \to R(\vec{\ell}) \to \bot] \to R(\vec{k}) \to \bot.$$

In the formal treatment of our example it will be more convenient to use the minimum principle in the form of course-of-values induction.

To prove course-of-values induction assume w_1: *Prog* and prove $\forall \vec{k}.R(\vec{k}) \to \bot$. This is achieved by proving $\forall n B$, where

$$B := \forall \vec{k}.\mu(\vec{k}) < n \to R(\vec{k}) \to \bot,$$

and using B with $n := \mu(\vec{k}) + 1$. We prove $\forall n B$ by (zero-successor) induction.

Base. $B[n := 0]$ follows easily from the lemma

$$v_1 \colon \forall m.m < 0 \to \bot.$$

Step. Let n be given and assume $w_2 \colon B$. To show $B[n := n+1]$ let $\vec{k}$ be given and assume $w_3 \colon \mu(\vec{k}) < n + 1$. We will derive $R(\vec{k}) \to \bot$ by using w_1: *Prog* at $\vec{k}$. Hence we have to prove

$$\forall \vec{\ell}.\mu(\vec{\ell}) < \mu(\vec{k}) \to R(\vec{\ell}) \to \bot.$$

So, let $\vec{\ell}$ be given and assume further $w_4 \colon \mu(\vec{\ell}) < \mu(\vec{k})$. From w_4 and $w_3 \colon \mu(\vec{k}) < n + 1$ we infer $\mu(\vec{\ell}) < n$ (using an arithmetical lemma). Hence, by induction hypothesis $w_2 \colon B$ at $\vec{\ell}$ we get $R(\vec{\ell}) \to \bot$.

Detailed proof of the theorem

Now we repeat the proof of the theorem in some more detail using course-of-values induction. As always in classical logic, we may view the proof as an indirect one, deriving a contradiction from the assumption that the claim is false. So let a_1, a_2 be given and assume $v_0\colon 0 < a_2$ and

$$u\colon \forall k_1, k_2. abs(k_1 a_1 - k_2 a_2)|a_1 \to abs(k_1 a_1 - k_2 a_2)|a_2 \to \\ 0 < abs(k_1 a_1 - k_2 a_2) \to \bot.$$

We have to prove $\bot$ which will be achieved by proving $\forall k_1, k_2. 0 < abs(k_1 a_1 - k_2 a_2) \to \bot$ by course-of-values induction and then specializing this formula to $k_1, k_2 = 0, 1$ and using the assumption $v_0\colon 0 < a_2$ $(= abs(0a_1 - 1a_2))$.

The principle of course-of-values induction is used with

$$N(k_1, k_2) := 0 < abs(k_1 a_1 - k_2 a_2) \to \bot \quad \text{and} \quad \mu(k_1, k_2) := abs(k_1 a_1 - k_2 a_2).$$

We have to show that N is progressive. To this end let k_1, k_2 be given and assume

$$u_1\colon \forall \ell_1, \ell_2. \mu(\ell_1, \ell_2) < \mu(k_1, k_2) \to N(\ell_1, \ell_2).$$

We have to prove $N(k_1, k_2)$. So, assume $u_2\colon 0 < \mu(k_1, k_2)$. We have to show $\bot$. This will be achieved by using the (false) assumption u at k_1, k_2. We have to prove $\mu(k_1, k_2)|a_1$ and $\mu(k_1, k_2)|a_2$. Informally, one would argue "if, say, $\mu(k_1, k_2) \not| a_1$ then the remainder $r_1 := r(a_1, \mu(k_1, k_2))$ is positive and less than $\mu(k_1, k_2)$. Furthermore we can find ℓ_1, ℓ_2 such that $r_1 = \mu(\ell_1, \ell_2)$. Altogether this contradicts the assumption u_1". More formally, to prove $\mu(k_1, k_2)|a_1$ we use the lemma

$$v_2\colon \forall a, q, c, r. a = qc + r \to (0 < r \to \bot) \to c|a$$

at a_1, $q_1 := q(a_1, \mu(k_1, k_2))$ (the quotient), $\mu(k_1, k_2)$ and r_1. We have to prove the premises

$$a_1 = q_1 \mu(k_1, k_2) + r_1 \quad \text{and} \quad 0 < r_1 \to \bot$$

of the instantiated lemma v_2. Here we need the lemmata

$$v_3\colon \forall a, c. 0 < c \to a = q(a, c)c + r(a, c),$$
$$v_4\colon \forall a, c. 0 < c \to r(a, c) < c$$

specifying the functions quotient and remainder. Now the first premise follows immediately from lemma v_3 and $u_2\colon 0 < \mu(k_1, k_2)$. To prove the second premise, $0 < r_1 \to \bot$, we assume $u_3\colon 0 < r_1$ and show $\bot$. First we compute ℓ_1, ℓ_2 such that $r_1 = \mu(\ell_1, \ell_2)$. This is done by some auxiliary function f, defined by

$$f(a_1, a_2, k_1, k_2, q) := \begin{cases} qk_1 - 1, & \text{if } k_2 a_2 < k_1 a_1 \text{ and } 0 < q; \\ qk_1 + 1, & \text{otherwise.} \end{cases}$$

f satisfies the lemma

$$v_5\colon \forall a_1, a_2, k_1, k_2, q, r. a_1 = q \cdot \mu(k_1, k_2) + r \to r = \mu(f(a_1, a_2, k_1, k_2, q), qk_2).$$

Hence we let $\ell_1 := f(a_1, a_2, k_1, k_2, q_1)$ and $\ell_2 := q_1 k_2$. Now we have $\mu(\ell_1, \ell_2) = r_1 < \mu(k_1, k_2)$ by v_5, u_2 and v_4, as well as $0 < r_1 = \mu(\ell_1, \ell_2)$ by u_3 and v_5. Therefore, we get $\bot$ by u_1 at ℓ_1, ℓ_2 (using some equality lemmata). This completes the proof of $\mu(k_1, k_2)|a_1$. $\mu(k_1, k_2)|a_2$ is proved similarly using the lemma

$$v_6\colon \forall a_1, a_2, k_1, k_2, q, r. a_2 = q \cdot \mu(k_1, k_2) + r \to r = \mu(qk_1, f(a_2, a_1, k_2, k_1, q)).$$

Turning the lemmata and the claim into definite and goal formulas

In order to make our general theory applicable to the present example we have to make sure that the lemmata assert definite formulas and the claim is given by goal formulas. This is almost the case already, with the sole exeption of

$$v_2 \colon \forall a, q, c, r. a = qc + r \to (0 < r \to \bot) \to c|a,$$

which is not definite (we have concluded something positive, i.e. $c|a$, from something negative, i.e. $0 < r \to \bot$). We now make it definite by inserting a double negation in front of the final conclusion $c|a$, i.e. we replace the formula of v_2 by

$$\forall a, q, c, r. a = qc + r \to (0 < r \to \bot) \to (c|a \to \bot) \to \bot.$$

Clearly this will not affect our proof in any essential way; however, it will make a difference when it comes to extract the program.

Formal proof

The proof of the principle of course-of-values induction and the proof of the theorem were given in such a detail that it is now easy to formalize them completely. Only some arguments concerning $<$ and $=$ were left implicit, but since these will be irrelevant formulas we don't need to worry about these omissions.

$$\begin{aligned}
M := \; & \lambda v_0^{0<a_2} \\
& \lambda v_1^{\forall m. m<0\to\bot} \\
& \lambda v_2^{\forall a,q,c,r. a=qc+r\to(0<r\to\bot)\to(c|a\to\bot)\to\bot} \\
& \lambda v_3^{\forall a,c. 0<c\to a=q(a,c)c+r(a,c)} \\
& \lambda v_4^{\forall a,c. 0<c\to r(a,c)<c} \\
& \lambda v_5^{\forall a_1,a_2,k_1,k_2,q,r. a_1=q\cdot\mu(k_1,k_2)+r\to r=\mu(f(a_1,a_2,k_1,k_2,q),qk_2)} \\
& \lambda v_6^{\forall a_1,a_2,k_1,k_2,q,r. a_2=q\cdot\mu(k_1,k_2)+r\to r=\mu(qk_1,f(a_2,a_1,k_2,k_1,q))} \\
& \lambda u^{\forall \vec{k}. \mu(\vec{k})|a_1\to\mu(\vec{k})|a_2\to 0<\mu(\vec{k})\to\bot}. \\
& M_{\mathrm{cvind}}^{Prog\to\forall\vec{k}.0<\mu(\vec{k})\to\bot} M_{\mathrm{prog}} 01 (L^{0<\mu(0,1)}[v_0])
\end{aligned}$$

where

$$\begin{aligned}
M_{\mathrm{cvind}} &= \lambda w_1^{Prog} \lambda\vec{k}. Ind_{n,B} M_{\mathrm{base}} M_{\mathrm{step}} (\mu(\vec{k})+1)\vec{k} L^{\mu(\vec{k})<\mu(\vec{k})+1}, \\
M_{\mathrm{base}} &= \lambda\vec{k}\lambda w_0^{\mu(\vec{k})<0} \lambda\tilde{w}_0^{0<\mu(\vec{k})}. v_1 \mu(\vec{k}) w_0, \\
M_{\mathrm{step}} &= \lambda n \lambda w_2^B \lambda\vec{k}\lambda w_3^{\mu(\vec{k})<n+1}. w_1\vec{k}(\lambda\vec{\ell}\lambda w_4^{\mu(\vec{\ell})<\mu(\vec{k})}. w_2\vec{\ell}(L^{\mu(\vec{\ell})<n}[w_4, w_3])), \\
\\
M_{\mathrm{prog}} &= \lambda\vec{k}\lambda u_1^{\forall\vec{\ell}.\mu(\vec{\ell})<\mu(\vec{k})\to 0<\mu(\vec{\ell})\to\bot} \lambda u_2^{0<\mu(\vec{k})}. \\
&\qquad M_{\mathrm{div}_2}^{(\mu(\vec{k})|a_2\to\bot)\to\bot} \lambda u_3^{\mu(\vec{k})|a_2}. M_{\mathrm{div}_1}^{(\mu(\vec{k})|a_1\to\bot)\to\bot} \lambda u_4^{\mu(\vec{k})|a_1}. u\vec{k}u_4u_3u_2, \\
M_{\mathrm{div}_i} &= v_2 a_i q_i(\vec{k})\mu(\vec{k}) r_i(\vec{k}) (L^{a_i=q_i(\vec{k})\mu(\vec{k})+r_i(\vec{k})}[v_3, u_2]) M_{\not<_i}^{0<r_i(\vec{k})\to\bot}, \\
M_{\not<_i} &= \lambda u_{3,i}^{0<r_i(\vec{k})}. u_1 \vec{\ell}_i(\vec{k}) \\
&\qquad (L^{\mu(\vec{\ell}_i(\vec{k}))<\mu(\vec{k})}[v_{4+i}, v_3, u_2, v_4])(L^{0<\mu(\vec{\ell}_i(\vec{k}))}[u_{3,i}, v_{4+i}, v_3, u_2]).
\end{aligned}$$

Here we have used the abbreviations

$$\begin{aligned}
Prog &= \forall\vec{k}.[\forall\vec{\ell}.\mu(\vec{\ell}) < \mu(\vec{k}) \to 0 < \mu(\vec{\ell}) \to \bot] \to 0 < \mu(\vec{k}) \to \bot \\
B &= \forall\vec{k}.\mu(\vec{k}) < n \to 0 < \mu(\vec{k}) \to \bot
\end{aligned}$$

Term extraction

Let

$$A := \exists^* \vec{k}.\mu(\vec{k})|a_1 \wedge \mu(\vec{k})|a_2 \wedge 0 < \mu(\vec{k}),$$

so $\tau(A) = \vec{\iota} := \iota \times \iota$. Let $C^A := C[\bot := A]$, hence

$$\tau(\mathrm{Prog}^A) = \vec{\iota} \to (\vec{\iota} \to \vec{\iota}) \to \vec{\iota},$$
$$\tau(B^A) = \vec{\iota} \to \vec{\iota}.$$

Furthermore recall $[\![Ind_{n,B^A}]\!] = \mathcal{R}_{\iota,\vec{\iota}\to\vec{\iota}}$ where

$$\mathcal{R}_{\iota,\vec{\iota}\to\vec{\iota}} \colon (\vec{\iota} \to \vec{\iota}) \to (\iota \to (\vec{\iota} \to \vec{\iota}) \to (\vec{\iota} \to \vec{\iota})) \to \iota \to (\vec{\iota} \to \vec{\iota})$$

Note that $\mathcal{R}_{\iota,\vec{\iota}\to\vec{\iota}}$ may be viewed as simultaneous primitive recursion operators $\vec{\mathcal{R}} = (\mathcal{R}_1, \mathcal{R}_2)$ with

$$\mathcal{R}_i \vec{y} \vec{f} 0 = y_i,$$
$$\mathcal{R}_i \vec{y} \vec{f} (z+1) = f_i z (\mathcal{R}_1 \vec{y} \vec{f} z)(\mathcal{R}_2 \vec{y} \vec{f} z).$$

Now we are prepared to compute the extracted term. Let M^A denote the result of replacing every formula C in the derivation M by C^A (note that M^A generally does *not* derive A).

$$[\![M^A]\!] = \lambda x_{v_1}^{\iota\to\vec{\iota}} \lambda x_{v_2}^{\iota^4\to\vec{\iota}\to\vec{\iota}\to\vec{\iota}} \lambda x_u^{\vec{\iota}\to\vec{\iota}}.[\![M^A_{\text{cvind}}]\!][\![M^A_{\text{prog}}]\!]01$$

where

$$\begin{aligned}
[\![M^A_{\text{cvind}}]\!] &= \lambda x_{w_1}^{\vec{\iota}\to(\vec{\iota}\to\vec{\iota})\to\vec{\iota}} \lambda \vec{k}.\mathcal{R}[\![M^A_{\text{base}}]\!][\![M^A_{\text{step}}]\!](\mu(\vec{k})+1)\vec{k} \\
[\![M^A_{\text{base}}]\!] &= \lambda \vec{k}.x_{v_1}\mu(\vec{k}) \\
[\![M^A_{\text{step}}]\!] &= \lambda n \lambda x_{w_2}^{\vec{\iota}\to\vec{\iota}} \lambda \vec{k}.x_{w_1}\vec{k}(\lambda \vec{\ell}.x_{w_2}\vec{\ell}),
\end{aligned}$$

$$\begin{aligned}
[\![M^A_{\text{prog}}]\!] &= \lambda \vec{k} \lambda x_{u_1}^{\vec{\iota}\to\vec{\iota}}.[\![M^A_{\text{div}_2}]\!]([\![M^A_{\text{div}_1}]\!](x_u \vec{k})) \\
[\![M^A_{\text{div}_i}]\!] &= x_{v_2} a_i q_i(\vec{k})\mu(\vec{k}) r_i(\vec{k})[\![M^A_{\not{k}_i}]\!] \\
[\![M^A_{\not{k}_i}]\!] &= x_{u_1}\vec{\ell}_i(\vec{k}).
\end{aligned}$$

From the proof of theorem 3.2 we generally know $D \to [\![N^A_D]\!]$ **mr** D^A for every relevant definite formula D. In our case for $D_1 = \forall m.m < 0 \to \bot$ we can derive directly

$$(\forall m.m < 0 \to \bot) \to (\lambda n 0) \ \mathbf{mr}\ \forall m.m < 0 \to A,$$

since we can use ex-falso. So we may assume $[\![N^A_{D_1}]\!] = \lambda n 0$. Similarly for

$$\begin{aligned}
D_2 &= \forall a,q,c,r.a = qc + r \to (0 < r \to \bot) \to (c|a \to \bot) \to \bot \qquad \text{we have} \\
D_2^A &= \forall a,q,c,r.a = qc + r \to (0 < r \to A) \to (c|a \to A) \to A.
\end{aligned}$$

Now an informal proof of $D_2 \to D_2^A$ runs as follows. Assume the hypotheses. We prove A by cases on $0 < r$. In case $0 < r$ the hypothesis $0 < r \to A$ yields A. In case $0 < r \to \bot$ we obtain $(c|a \to \bot) \to \bot$ and hence $c|a$. Now the hypothesis $c|a \to A$ yields A.

From this proof we can derive directly

$$D_2 \to (\lambda a \lambda q \lambda c \lambda r \lambda \vec{x} \lambda \vec{y}.\mathbf{if}\ 0 < r\ \mathbf{then}\ \vec{x}\ \mathbf{else}\ \vec{y})\ \mathbf{mr}\ D_2^A.$$

So we may assume $[\![N^A_{D_2}]\!] = \lambda a \lambda q \lambda c \lambda r \lambda \vec{x} \lambda \vec{y}.\mathbf{if}\ 0 < r\ \mathbf{then}\ \vec{x}\ \mathbf{else}\ \vec{y}$.

Moreover, there is no relevant goal formula, hence $t = \lambda\vec{y}\vec{y}$. Then the extracted term according to theorem 3.2 is

$$[\![M^A]\!][\![N^A_{D_1}]\!][\![N^A_{D_2}]\!]t =_\beta [\![M^A_{\text{cvind}}]\!]'[\![M^A_{\text{prog}}]\!]'01$$

where $'$ indicates substitution of $[\![N^A_{D_1}]\!]$, $[\![N^A_{D_2}]\!]$, t for x_{v_1}, x_{v_2}, x_u, so

$$\begin{aligned}
[\![M^A_{\text{cvind}}]\!]' &=_{\beta\eta} \lambda x_{w_1}^{\vec{\iota}\to(\vec{\iota}\to\vec{\iota})\to\vec{\iota}}\lambda\vec{k}'.\mathcal{R}(\lambda\vec{k}.\vec{0})(\lambda n\lambda x_{w_2}\lambda\vec{k}.x_{w_1}\vec{k}x_{w_2})(\mu(\vec{k}')+1)\vec{k}',\\
[\![M^A_{\text{prog}}]\!]' &=_\beta \lambda\vec{k}\lambda x_{u_1}^{\vec{\iota}\to\vec{\iota}}.[\![M^A_{\text{div}_2}]\!]'([\![M^A_{\text{div}_1}]\!]'\vec{k}),\\
[\![M^A_{\text{div}_i}]\!]' &=_\beta (\lambda\vec{x}\lambda\vec{y}.\textbf{if } 0 < \vec{r}_i(\vec{k}) \textbf{ then } \vec{x} \textbf{ else } \vec{y})(x_{u_1}\vec{\ell}_i(\vec{k}))
\end{aligned}$$

and hence

$$\begin{aligned}
[\![M^A_{\text{prog}}]\!]' =_\beta \lambda\vec{k}\lambda x_{u_1}. &\ \textbf{if } 0 < r_2(\vec{k}) \textbf{ then } x_{u_1}\vec{\ell}_2(\vec{k}) \textbf{ else}\\
&(\ \textbf{if } 0 < r_1(\vec{k}) \textbf{ then } x_{u_1}\vec{\ell}_1(\vec{k}) \textbf{ else } \vec{k})
\end{aligned}$$

Therefore we obtain as extracted algorithm, using the fact that $\mu(0,1) = a_2$,

$$\begin{aligned}
[\![M^A]\!][\![N^A_{D_1}]\!][\![N^A_{D_2}]\!]t =_\beta\ & \mathcal{R}(\lambda\vec{k}.\vec{0})\\
& (\lambda n\lambda x_{w_2}^{\vec{\iota}\to\vec{\iota}}\lambda\vec{k}.\textbf{if } 0 < r_2(\vec{k}) \textbf{ then } x_{w_2}\vec{\ell}_2(\vec{k}) \textbf{ else}\\
& \qquad\qquad \textbf{if } 0 < r_1(\vec{k}) \textbf{ then } x_{w_2}\vec{\ell}_1(\vec{k}) \textbf{ else } \vec{k})\\
& (a_2+1)01
\end{aligned}$$

To make this algorithm more readable we may write $[\![M^A]\!][\![N^A_{D_1}]\!][\![N^A_{D_2}]\!]t = h(a_2+1, 0, 1)$, where

$$\begin{aligned}
h(0,\vec{k}) &:= \vec{0},\\
h(n+1,\vec{k}) &:= \textbf{if } 0 < r_2(\vec{k}) \textbf{ then } h(n, \vec{\ell}_2(\vec{k})) \textbf{ else}\\
&\quad\ (\textbf{if } 0 < r_1(\vec{k}) \textbf{ then } h(n, \vec{\ell}_1(\vec{k})) \textbf{ else } \vec{k})
\end{aligned}$$

Example

Let us use the extracted algorithm to compute coefficients k_1, k_2 such that $\gcd(66, 27) = |k_1 \cdot 66 - k_2 \cdot 27|$.

$$
\begin{array}{ll}
h(28,0,1) & \mu(0,1) = 27 \\
 & 0 < r_1 = 12 \quad q_1 = 2 \\
 & \underbrace{q_1 k_1}_{0} \pm 1, \quad \underbrace{q_1 k_2}_{2} \qquad -1, \text{ if } k_2 a_2 < \underbrace{k_1 a_1}_{0} \quad \text{No} \\
 & 1, \quad 2 \\
h(27,1,2) & \mu(1,2) = 12 \\
 & 0 < r_1 = 6 \quad q_1 = 5 \\
 & \underbrace{q_1 k_1}_{5\cdot 1} \pm 1, \quad \underbrace{q_1 k_2}_{5\cdot 2} \qquad -1, \text{ if } \underbrace{k_2 a_2}_{2\cdot 27} < \underbrace{k_1 a_1}_{1\cdot 66} \quad \text{Yes} \\
 & 4, \quad 10 \\
h(26,4,10) & \mu(4,10) = |4 \cdot 66 - 10 \cdot 27| = |264 - 270| = 6 \\
 & 6|66 \\
 & 0 < r_2 = 3 \quad q_2 = 4 \\
 & \underbrace{q_2 k_1}_{4\cdot 4}, \quad \underbrace{q_2 k_2}_{4\cdot 10} \pm 1 \qquad -1, \text{ if } \underbrace{k_1 a_1}_{4\cdot 66=264} < \underbrace{k_2 a_2}_{10\cdot 27=270} \quad \text{Yes} \\
 & 16, \quad 39 \\
h(25,16,39) & \mu(16,39) = |16 \cdot 66 - 39 \cdot 27| = |1056 - 1053| = 3 \\
 & 3|66 \\
 & 3|27 \\
 & \text{Result: } 16, 39
\end{array}
$$

Note that, although $3 = |16 \cdot 66 - 39 \cdot 27|$ is the least positive element of the ideal $(66, 27)$, the coefficients 16, 39 are not minimal. The minimal coefficients are 2, 5.

Remarks

1. As one sees from this example the recursion parameter n is not really used in the computation but just serves as a counter or more precisely as an upper bound for the number of steps until both remainders are zero. This will always happen if the induction principle is used only in the form of the minimum principle (or, equivalently, course-of-values induction). Because then in the extracted terms of course-of-values induction, the step $[\![M^A_{\mathrm{step}}]\!] = \lambda n \lambda x^{\vec{\imath}\to\vec{\imath}}_{w_2} \lambda \vec{k} . x_{w_1} \vec{k}(\lambda \vec{\ell} . x_{w_2} \vec{\ell})$ has in its kernel no free occurrence of n.

2. If one removes n according to the previous remark it becomes clear that our gcd algorithm is similar to Euclid's. The only difference lies in the fact that we have kept a_1, a_2 fixed in our proof whereas Euclid changes a_1 to a_2 and a_2 to $r(a_1, a_2)$ provided $r(a_1, a_2) > 0$ (using the fact that this doesn't change the ideal).

Implementation

The gcd example has been implemented in the interactive proof system MINLOG. We show the term which was extracted automatically from a derivation of the theorem.

```
(lambda (a1)
 (lambda (a2)
  ((((((nat-rec-at '(arrow nat (arrow nat (star nat nat))))
```

```
     (lambda (k1) (lambda (k2) (cons n000 n000))))
    (lambda (n)
     (lambda (w)
      (lambda (k1)
       (lambda (k2)
        ((((if-at '(star nat nat))
           ((<-strict-nat 0) r2))
          ((w l21) l22))
          ((((if-at '(star nat nat))
            ((<-strict-nat 0) r1))
            ((w l11) l12))
           (cons k1 k2))))))))
  ((plus-nat a2) 1))
 0)
1)))
```

We have manually introduced `r1, r2, l11, l12, l21, l22` for somewhat lengthy terms corresponding to our abbreviations r_i, $\vec{\ell_i}$. The unbound variable `n000` appearing in the base case is a dummy variable used by the system when it is asked to produce a realizing term for the instance $\bot \to \exists k A(k)$ of ex-falso-quodlibet. In our case, when the existential quantifier is of type ι one might as well pick the constant 0 (as we did in the text).

References

[1] Ulrich Berger, Wilfried Buchholz, and Helmut Schwichtenberg. Refined program extraction from classical proofs. In preparation.

[2] Ulrich Berger and Helmut Schwichtenberg. The greatest common divisor: a case study for program extraction from classical proofs. In S. Berardi and M. Coppo, editors, *Types for Proofs and Programs. International Workshop TYPES '95, Torino, Italy, June 1995. Selected Papers*, volume 1158 of *Lecture Notes in Computer Science*, pages 36–46. Springer Verlag, Berlin, Heidelberg, New York, 1996.

[3] Thierry Coquand and Hendrik Persson. Gröbner Bases in Type Theory. In T. Altenkirch, W. Naraschewski, and B. Reus, editors, *Types for Proofs and Programs*, volume 1657 of *Lecture Notes in Computer Science*. Springer Verlag, Berlin, Heidelberg, New York, 1999.

[4] Anne S. Troelstra (editor). *Metamathematical Investigation of Intuitionistic Arithmetic and Analysis*, volume 344 of *Lecture Notes in Mathematics*. Springer Verlag, Berlin, Heidelberg, New York, 1973.

[5] Harvey Friedman. Classically and intuitionistically provably recursive functions. In D.S. Scott and G.H. Müller, editors, *Higher Set Theory*, volume 669 of *Lecture Notes in Mathematics*, pages 21–28. Springer Verlag, Berlin, Heidelberg, New York, 1978.

[6] Ulrich Kohlenbach. Analyzing proofs in analysis. In W. Hodges, M. Hyland, C. Steinhorn, and J. Truss, editors, *Logic: from Foundations to Applications. European Logic Colloquium (Keele, 1993)*, pages 225–260. Oxford University Press, 1996.

[7] Daniel Leivant. Syntactic translations and provably recursive functions. *The Journal of Symbolic Logic*, 50(3):682–688, September 1985.

[8] Chetan Murthy. Extracting constructive content from classical proofs. Technical Report 90–1151, Dep.of Comp.Science, Cornell Univ., Ithaca, New York, 1990. PhD thesis.

[9] M.H.A. Newman. On theories with a combinatorial definition of "equivalence". *Annals of Mathematics*, 43(2):223–243, 1942.

Foundations of Secure Computation
F.L. Bauer and R. Steinbrüggen (Eds.)
IOS Press, 2000

Process Realizability

Samson Abramsky

1 Introduction

Realizability has proved to be a fruitful approach to the semantics of computation, see e.g. [AL91, Cro93, Lon95, AC98]. The *scope* of realizability methods has been limited to *Intuitionistic Logic* (with some extensions to Classical Logic), on the logical side, and to *functional computation* on the computational side. Our aim in the present work is to explore the possibilities for broadening the scope of realizability:

- beyond Intuitionistic Logic, to Classical Linear Logic, and more;
- beyond functional computation, to encompass concurrent and non-deterministic computation.

Why do this? We shall mention just one, fairly concrete motivation. Consider the well-established paradigm of extracting *functional programs* from (Intuitionistic or Classical) *proofs*, using the Curry-Howard isomorphism or realizability [GLT89, BS94]. Can we analogously find a suitable combination of a logic and a realizability universe such that we can extract interesting *concurrent programs*—communication protocols, distributed algorithms, security protocols—from proofs of their specifications?

Two important caveats should be registered here. The first is that we don't envisage the extraction of programs from proofs as a practical programming methodology. However, in the case of functional computation, the well-understood paradigm of program extraction from proofs is a key component of our foundational understanding of functional programming; the objective here is to attain a comparably well-founded paradigm for concurrent programming. The second caveat is that we don't—as yet—claim to be able to extract *interesting* concurrent programs, in the above sense, from proofs. However, we *do* see the ideas which we shall now put forward as a step in this direction.

Note to the reader This paper aims to give a readable and reasonably accessible account of some ideas linking the currently still largely separate worlds of concurrency theory and process algebra, on the one hand, and type theory, categorical models and realizability on the other. Background in process algebra may be found in standard texts such as [Hoa85, Hen88, Mil89, Ros97]; while background in realizability, categorical models etc. is provided by texts such as [GLT89, AL91, Cro93, AC98, BW99]. A modest background in either or both of these fields should suffice to understand the main ideas. Most of the detailed verification of properties of the formal definitions we will present is left as a series of exercises. The diligent reader who attempts a number of these should get some feeling for the interplay between concrete process-theoretic notions, and more abstract logical and categorical ideas, which is characteristic of this topic. It is this interplay which makes the topic a fascinating one for the author; I hope this brief introduction, to a field which is still wide open for further development, succeeds in conveying something of this fascination to the reader.

2 CCS with simultaneous actions

Our universe of realizers will be a minor extension of one of the most standard and widely-used process calculi, namely Milner's CCS [Mil89]. The extension is to allow "compound" actions, consisting of the simultaneous performance of several "atomic" actions. This idea of compound actions is present in the synchronous process calculus SCCS [Mil89]; the point here is to introduce this as an extension of the asynchronous calculus CCS. Our reason for using this extension is that it will allow us to realize identities and other canonical isomorphisms as "wires", with typical behaviour

$$\alpha \underline{\qquad} \beta$$

in which two signals are propagated simultaneously, at the two "ends of the wire", so to speak. This extension is not new; it was introduced in the present author's work on asynchronous interaction categories [Abr94a, AGN96], for similar reasons. Much of what we will do here can be seen as a recasting of the work on interaction categories into a realizability framework. Indeed, the essential ideas on the process interpretation of proofs go back to a 1991 lecture on "Proofs as Processes" (see [Abr94b]).

2.1 Names, co-names and actions

As usual with CCS, we introduce two disjoint, countable sets $\mathcal{N}$ of *names*, and $\bar{\mathcal{N}}$ of *co-names*, with a bijection $\bar{(\,)} : \mathcal{N} \xrightarrow{\cong} \bar{\mathcal{N}}$, which we extend to an involution

$$\bar{(\,)} : \mathcal{N} + \bar{\mathcal{N}} \xrightarrow{\cong} \bar{\mathcal{N}} + \mathcal{N}.$$

We use α, β, γ to range over names, and write $\bar{\alpha}$, $\bar{\beta}$, $\bar{\gamma}$ for the corresponding co-names, with $\bar{\bar{\alpha}} = \alpha$ etc. We write $\mathcal{L} = \mathcal{N} \cup \bar{\mathcal{N}}$ for the set of *labels*, ranged over by λ, μ, ν. An *action* will be a finite set of labels. We write Act for the set of actions, ranged over by a, b, c. In particular, we write τ for the empty set $\varnothing$. The interpretation of an action $a = \{\lambda_1, \ldots, \lambda_n\}$ is that the simultaneous performance of the actions in a is observed; thus τ can be viewed as a "silent" or "unobservable" or "internal" action. The involution $\bar{(\,)}$ is extended pointwise to actions:

$$\bar{a} = \{\bar{\lambda} \mid \lambda \in a\}.$$

Note that $\bar{\bar{a}} = a$, and that $\bar{\tau} = \tau$.

2.2 Guarded Terms

We now introduce a class of *guarded* process terms, with the following syntax.

$$P \;::=\; a.P \mid \Sigma_{i \in I} a_i.P_i \; (\forall i \in I.\, a_i \neq \tau) \mid P \mid Q \mid G \backslash L \mid G[f] \mid X \mid \mathsf{rec}\,\mathsf{X}.\,\mathsf{P}.$$

Here I ranges over countable index sets, L ranges over subsets of $\mathcal{L}$ (*i.e. sorts*), X ranges over a set of process variables, and f over *renamings*, i.e. $\bar{(\,)}$-preserving injective functions on $\mathcal{L}$. (In fact, we shall allow *partial* injective functions as renamings, with the proviso that the *sort* of the process to which the renaming is applied is contained in the domain of the function. For details—which are easy and standard—see [Mil89]). Renamings are extended pointwise to actions. As usual, the empty sum is written as 0, and the binary case as $a.P + b.Q$.

2.3 Transitions

We define the labelled transitions $\xrightarrow{a}$, $(a \in \mathsf{Act})$ by the following inductive definition.

$$\frac{}{a.P \xrightarrow{a} P} \qquad \frac{}{\Sigma_{i \in I} a_i.P_i \xrightarrow{a_j} P_j \ (j \in I)}$$

$$\frac{P \xrightarrow{a} Q}{P\backslash L \xrightarrow{a} Q\backslash L} \ (a \cap (L \cup \bar{L}) = \varnothing) \qquad \frac{P \xrightarrow{a} Q}{P[f] \xrightarrow{f(a)} Q[f]}$$

$$\frac{P[\mathsf{rec}\,\mathsf{X}.\,\mathsf{P}/\mathsf{X}] \xrightarrow{\mathsf{a}} \mathsf{Q}}{\mathsf{rec}\,\mathsf{X}.\,\mathsf{P} \xrightarrow{\mathsf{a}} \mathsf{Q}}$$

$$\frac{P \xrightarrow{a} P'}{P \mid Q \xrightarrow{a} P' \mid Q} \qquad \frac{Q \xrightarrow{a} Q'}{P \mid Q \xrightarrow{a} P \mid Q'}$$

$$\frac{P \xrightarrow{a \dot{\cup} b} P' \quad Q \xrightarrow{\bar{b} \dot{\cup} c} Q'}{P \mid Q \xrightarrow{a \dot{\cup} c} P' \mid Q'}$$

Here $a \mathbin{\dot{\cup}} b$ means that a and b are disjoint; this, together with $b \mathbin{\dot{\cup}} c$ and $a \mathbin{\dot{\cup}} c$ should be viewed as *constraints* on the applicability of the rule. These rules are completely standard, except for the last, which generalizes the usual rule

$$\frac{P \xrightarrow{\lambda} P' \quad Q \xrightarrow{\bar{\lambda}} Q'}{P \mid Q \xrightarrow{\tau} P' \mid Q'}$$

(Take $a = c = \varnothing$, $b = \{\lambda\}$).

Note that we can define the wire $W_{\lambda,\mu}$ which repeatedly performs the compound action

$$\lambda \underline{\qquad} \beta$$

as the term

$$W_{\lambda,\mu} \triangleq \mathsf{rec}\,\mathsf{X}.\,\{\lambda, \mu\}.\mathsf{X}.$$

2.4 Failures Equivalence

Let Act_+ be the set of non-empty actions. We define the observable transition relations $\overset{a}{\Longrightarrow}$, for $a \in \mathsf{Act}_+$, as $\xrightarrow{\tau}^{\star}\xrightarrow{a}\xrightarrow{\tau}^{\star}$, and extend this to $\overset{s}{\Longrightarrow}$ for strings $s \in \mathsf{Act}_+^{\star}$ in the usual fashion. We define the set of *failures* of a process P by

$$\mathcal{F}(P) = \{(s, X) \mid s \in \mathsf{Act}_+^{\star} \wedge X \subseteq \mathsf{Act}_+ \wedge \exists Q.\,(P \overset{s}{\Longrightarrow} Q \wedge \forall a \in X.\, Q \overset{a}{\not\Longrightarrow})\}.$$

We define failures equivalence by

$$P \approx_f Q \overset{\Delta}{\iff} \mathcal{F}(P) = \mathcal{F}(Q).$$

Proposition 2.1 *Failures equivalence is a congruence on guarded terms.*

Discussion Our reason for working with failures equivalence ([BHR84, BR83]) is that it, or one of its variants such as the testing equivalences of Hennessy and De Nicola [DNH83], or the Failures-Divergences model of Brookes and Roscoe [BR84], seem to be the finest equivalences which will suffice for our purposes. In particular, the realizability for the additive connectives of Linear Logic will not work in a fully satisfactory way if we use a finer equivalence such as weak congruence or weak bisimulation. It is worth noting that failures equivalence (or more accurately, the refined Failures-Divergences equivalence) is the standard equivalence for CSP, the other widely used process calculus.

Our reason for using guarded sums is to give a slightly simplified treatment of non-determinism. We could equally well have introduced the usual external and internal choice constructs as in [Hoa85, Hen88, Ros97].

The representation of processes in terms of their failures gives rise to a fully abstract model for failures equivalence, on which the process operations can be defined in a denotational, compositional fashion [BHR84, Ros97]. We have presented the semantics in an operational style to be concrete and simple, but in many ways the denotational presentation is more elegant and illuminating. It is also worth noting that we could equally well work with CSP as our process calculus rather than CCS, using the same underlying denotational model.

2.5 Some basic combinators

Since processes are untyped, we will build a type-free universe of realizers. As usual, this will require a little coding (*cf.* the Kleene algebra K_0 [Kle45], graph models [Sco76] etc.), but in our setting this will take a very simple form. We simply split the set of names into two infinite disjoint sets

$$\mathcal{N} = \mathcal{N}_l \mathbin{\dot{\cup}} \mathcal{N}_r$$

and fix bijections

$$\mathtt{l} : \mathcal{N} \xrightarrow{\cong} \mathcal{N}_l \qquad \mathtt{r} : \mathcal{N} \xrightarrow{\cong} \mathcal{N}_r$$

and extend these in a $(\bar{\ })$-respecting way to the set of labels:

$$\mathcal{L} = \mathcal{L}_l \mathbin{\dot{\cup}} \mathcal{L}_r$$

$$\mathtt{l} : \mathcal{L} \xrightarrow{\cong} \mathcal{L}_l \qquad \mathtt{r} : \mathcal{L} \xrightarrow{\cong} \mathcal{L}_r.$$

This means that we can view an arbitrary process P as having its interface to its environment split into two disjoint parts:

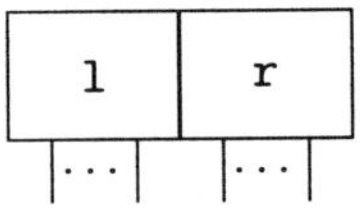

We can use this splitting of the name space to define some combinators which will play a fundamental role in our notion of process realizability.

Firstly, we have a tensor product which will express *disjoint (non-communicating) parallel composition*:

$$P \otimes Q \triangleq P[\mathtt{l}] \mid Q[\mathtt{r}].$$

The use of the relabelling functions *forces* the two processes to be disjoint:

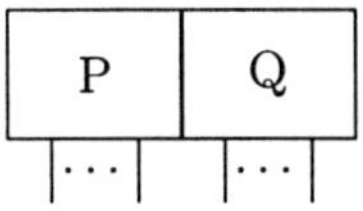

Secondly, we can define a notion of *application*. As usual in a type-free setting, we have to be able to see arbitrary elements of our universe either as "functions" or as "arguments", as required. The basic splitting of our name space allows us to see P as a "function" in *two, entirely symmetrical ways.* We can see the left part of the name space as the "attachment point" for an argument, with the right part left free to communicate the "result"; or we can attach on the right and transmit the result through the left.

The first view leads to a *left* (or *forwards*) application:

$$\langle Q|P \triangleq ((Q[\mathtt{l}] \mid P)\backslash\mathcal{L}_l)[\mathtt{r}^{-1}]$$

which we can visualize as follows:

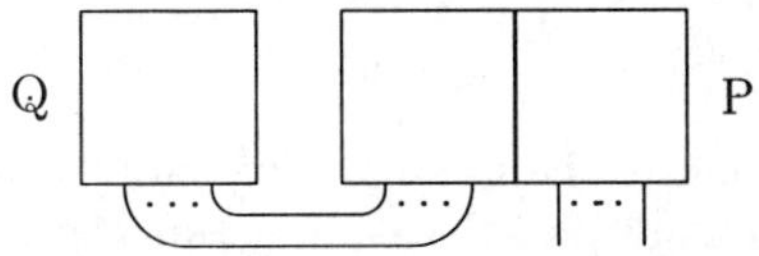

We use a Dirac-style bra-ket notation (*cf.* [Dir67]) to denote the left application of P to Q. The idea is that Q is relabelled into the left part of P's name space, and we then restrict on the left name space so that P and Q are forced to interact there; the resulting observable behaviour is purely that produced by P in the right part of its name space. Finally, we "normalize" by relabelling back into the global name space, using the inverse of the bijection $\mathtt{r}$.

Symmetrically, we can define a *right* (or *reverse*) application:

$$P|R\rangle \triangleq ((P \mid R[\mathtt{r}])\backslash\mathcal{L}_r)[\mathtt{l}^{-1}]$$

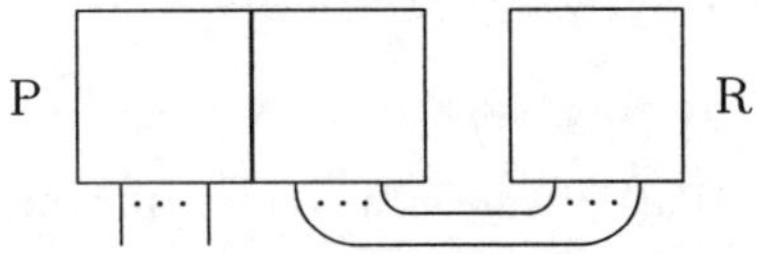

3 Realizability

We will now define a notion of realizability for formulas built from the propositional connectives of (Classical) Linear Logic: the multiplicatives $\otimes$ and $\invamp$, the additives & and $\oplus$, and the exponentials ! and ?. More precisely, we shall define two relations

$$P \Vdash_+ A \quad \text{and} \quad P \Vdash_- A$$

between process terms P and formulas A, by induction on the construction of A. We shall read $P \Vdash_+ A$ as: "P is a realizer/strategy/proof of A", or "P is a value of type A"; and $P \Vdash_- A$ as: "P is a counter-realizer/counter-strategy/refutation of A", or "P is an A-consuming context". This builds a classical (involutive) duality, and specifically an interpretation of the Linear negation $(\_)^\perp$, into our realizability interpretation. In particular, we will have:

$$P \Vdash_+ A^\perp \equiv P \Vdash_- A$$
$$P \Vdash_- A^\perp \equiv P \Vdash_+ A.$$

3.1 Multiplicatives

For each connective, we must define both the positive and negative notions of realizability. However, once this is done for one connective, the notions for the de Morgan duals are also determined.
The definitions for the tensor product are as follows:

$$P \Vdash_{+} A \otimes B \ \equiv\ P \approx_f P_1 \otimes P_2 \ \wedge\ P_1 \Vdash_{+} A \ \wedge\ P_2 \Vdash_{+} B.$$

Note that, because of the disjoint relabelling in the definition of the tensor combinator on processes:

$$P_1 \otimes P_2 \approx_f Q_1 \otimes Q_2 \implies P_1 \approx_f Q_1 \ \wedge\ P_2 \approx_f Q_2$$

so the decomposition in the above clause is unique up to failures equivalence (in fact, up to weak bisimulation).

$$P \Vdash_{-} A \otimes B \ \equiv\ \forall Q.\,(Q \Vdash_{+} A \Rightarrow \langle Q|P \Vdash_{-} B) \ \wedge\ \forall R.\,(R \Vdash_{+} B \Rightarrow P|R\rangle \Vdash_{-} A).$$

This is a symmetrized version of the familiar "logical relations" or realizability condition. P counter-realizes the multiplicative conjunction $A \otimes B$ if it carries every realizer of A, under forwards application, to a counter-realizer for B, and every realizer of B, under reverse application, to a counter-realizer for A.
Applying de Morgan duality, this yields the more familiar-looking definition for linear implication:

$$A \multimap B \ \triangleq\ A^{\perp} \mathbin{⅋} B \ \triangleq\ (A \otimes B^{\perp})^{\perp}.$$

$$P \Vdash_{+} A \multimap B \ \equiv\ \forall Q.\,(Q \Vdash_{+} A \Rightarrow \langle Q|P \Vdash_{+} B) \ \wedge\ \forall R.\,(R \Vdash_{-} B \Rightarrow P|R\rangle \Vdash_{-} A).$$

P realizes the linear implication $A \multimap B$ if it carries realizers of A to realizers of B, and counter-realizers of B to counter-realizers of A.

The reading of the clause for negative realizability for the linear implication is also interesting:

$$P \Vdash_{-} A \multimap B \ \equiv\ P \approx_f Q \otimes R \ \wedge\ Q \Vdash_{+} A \ \wedge\ R \Vdash_{-} B.$$

This can be read as saying that P realizes a context for consuming a "linear function" f of type $A \multimap B$ if it decomposes as an input of type A to be plugged into f, and a context of type B for consuming the corresponding output.

It is interesting to note that the combinators $\otimes$, $\langle\cdot|\cdot$ and $\cdot|\cdot\rangle$ which we introduced in order to realize the multiplicative connectives are defined purely in terms of the *static* operators of CCS in Milner's classification [Mil89], namely parallel composition, restriction and relabelling. As we shall now see, the additive connectives will be realized using only the *dynamic* operators of CCS (prefixing and summation), while the exponentials will require a combination of the two, together with recursion.

3.2 Additives

Firstly, we fix once and for all two distinct names, say α and β. These will be used to distinguish the left and right cases in the additive choice constructs $A\&B$ and $A \oplus B$. For the additive product or conjunction $A\&B$, the Opponent or Environment will make the choice, and the realizers for $A\&B$ will have the form $\alpha.P+\beta.Q$, where P is a realizer for A and Q is a realizer for B. For the additive sum or disjunction $A \oplus B$, Player or System makes the choice, and realizers for $A \oplus B$ either have the form $\bar{\alpha}.R$, where R is a realizer for A, or $\bar{\beta}.S$, where S is a realizer for B.

This leads to the following formal definitions:

$$
\begin{array}{lcl}
P \Vdash_{+} A\&B & \equiv & P \approx_{f} \alpha.Q + \beta.R \;\wedge\; Q \Vdash_{+} A \;\wedge\; R \Vdash_{+} B \\
P \Vdash_{-} A\&B & \equiv & (P \approx_{f} \bar{\alpha}.Q \;\wedge\; Q \Vdash_{-} A) \vee (P \approx_{f} \bar{\beta}.R \;\wedge\; R \Vdash_{-} B) \\
P \Vdash_{+} A \oplus B & \equiv & (P \approx_{f} \bar{\alpha}.Q \;\wedge\; Q \Vdash_{+} A) \vee (P \approx_{f} \bar{\beta}.R \;\wedge\; R \Vdash_{+} B) \\
P \Vdash_{-} A \oplus B & \equiv & P \approx_{f} \alpha.Q + \beta.R \;\wedge\; Q \Vdash_{-} A \;\wedge\; R \Vdash_{-} B.
\end{array}
$$

3.3 Exponentials

As already indicated, to interpret the exponentials we combine additive and multiplicative features with recursion on processes, and also induction to define the realizability relation. This use of recursion and induction will be set in a more general context in our later discussion of inductive and coinductive types.
As for the additives, we fix some global names: ω (for weakening), δ (dereliction) and γ (contraction). We define a process combinator

$$!P \;\triangleq\; \mathsf{rec}\,\mathsf{X}.\,\omega.0 + \delta.\mathsf{P} + \gamma.(\mathsf{X}[\mathtt{l}] \mid \mathsf{X}[\mathtt{r}]).$$

We can then define positive realizability for !:

$$P \Vdash_{+} !A \;\equiv\; P \approx_{f} !Q \;\wedge\; Q \Vdash_{+} A.$$

We can think of $!P$ as a process which the environment can request to:

- deliver one copy of P (dereliction)
- be discarded (weakening)
- make two copies of itself (contraction).

The negative realizability for $!A$ can be defined as follows.

$$
\begin{array}{ll}
P \Vdash_{-} !A \equiv & (P \approx_{f} \omega.0) \vee (P \approx_{f} \bar{\delta}.Q \;\wedge\; Q \Vdash_{-} A) \\
& \vee\; (P \approx_{f} \bar{\gamma}.Q \;\wedge\; (\forall R \Vdash_{+} A.\, \langle !R \,|\, Q \Vdash_{-} !A \;\wedge\; Q \,|\, !R\rangle \Vdash_{-} !A)).
\end{array}
$$

Note that for the first time, the realizability relation is not being defined purely by structural induction on the formula. Rather, $P \Vdash_{-} !A$ is being defined inductively, as the least fixed point of the evident monotone operator on sets of processes which can be extracted from the above definition, keeping $!A$ fixed. Note, however, that the universal quantifier $\forall R \Vdash_{+} A$ is ranging over realizers for A, which we *can* take to be already defined by structural induction on $!A$. This is crucial for monotonicity.

The realizability relation for the dual connective ? is defined by De Morgan duality from that for !, since $?A = (!A^{\perp})^{\perp}$. To understand the inductive definition, think of it as defining the set of all $!A$-consuming contexts, which request a number of copies of a realizer for A, and then consume these copies. Recall that $?A$ is the "⅋-monoid generated by A", just as $!A$ is the "$\otimes$-comonoid cogenerated by A". Thus the inductive clause for contraction parallels that for Par, just as the case for contraction in the recursive definition of $!P$ parallels that for Tensor. This also says that there is no communication between the copies of P in $!P$, while the counter-realizers for $!A$ can use the information obtained from each copy in interacting with the others, as for Par.

3.4 Interpretation of Proofs

We now show how to assign a realizer for A to each proof of A in Linear Logic. We will then be able to extract concurrent processes as realizers from proofs.

We extend realizability to sequents $\Gamma = A_1, \ldots, A_k$, treating Γ as $\invamp \Gamma$ in the obvious fashion. We now indicate how to assign realizers to sequent proofs in Linear Logic.

3.4.1 Identity Axioms

$$\overline{\vdash A^{\perp}, A}$$

All instances of the Identity Axioms are realized by the process

$$I \triangleq \mathsf{rec}\,\mathsf{X}.\ \sum_{\mathsf{a}\in\mathsf{Act}_+} (\mathtt{l}(\mathsf{a}) \cup \overline{\mathtt{r}(\mathsf{a})}).\mathsf{X}$$

This behaves like a wire for any choice of actions

$$a \,\underline{\qquad}\, \bar{a}$$

where the action at the left hand end of the wire corresponds to $\mathtt{l}(a)$, and that on the right to $\overline{\mathtt{r}(a)} = \mathtt{r}(\bar{a})$. To check that I is indeed a realizer for $A^{\perp} \invamp A = A \multimap A$ amounts to verifying the process-algebraic fact that

$$\forall P.\, \langle P|I \approx_f P \approx_f I|P \rangle.$$

Exercise Verify!

3.4.2 Cut Rule

$$\frac{P \Vdash_+ \Gamma, A \qquad Q \Vdash_+ A^{\perp}, \Delta}{P; Q \Vdash_+ \Gamma, \Delta}$$

Here we are inductively assuming that we have already assigned a (positive) realizer P to the proof of Γ, A, and a realizer Q to the proof of $A^{\perp}, \Delta$. We must construct a realizer $P; Q$ for Γ, Δ. This composition combinator will simultaneously generalize the left and right application combinators we have previously introduced.
We fix a three-fold decomposition of the name space:

$$\mathcal{N} = \mathcal{N}_1 \,\dot{\cup}\, \mathcal{N}_2 \,\dot{\cup}\, \mathcal{N}_3$$

with bijections $\phi_{i,j} : \mathcal{N} \xrightarrow{\cong} \mathcal{N}_i \,\dot{\cup}\, \mathcal{N}_j$ such that $\phi_{i,j}(\mathcal{N}_l) = \mathcal{N}_i$, $\phi_{i,j}(\mathcal{N}_r) = \mathcal{N}_j$. We can then define

$$P; Q \triangleq ((P[\phi_{1,2}] \mid Q[\phi_{2,3}]) \backslash \mathcal{N}_2)[\phi^{-1}_{1,3}].$$

The picture is

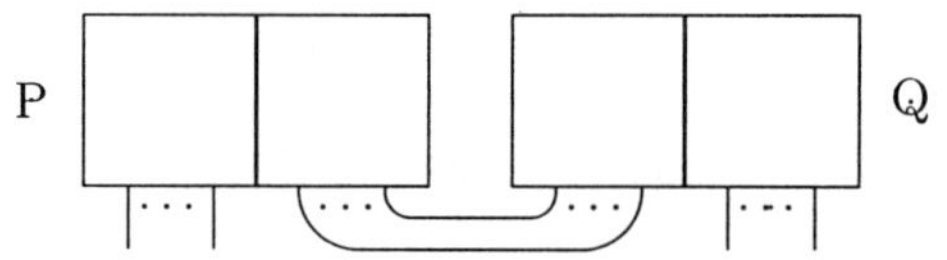

The key process-algebraic facts are

$$\begin{array}{lcl} (P;Q);R & \approx_f & P;(Q;R) \\ P;I & \approx_f & P \\ I;P & \approx_f & P \\ \langle P|(Q;R) & \approx_f & \langle\langle P|Q|R \\ (P;Q)|R\rangle & \approx_f & P|Q|R\rangle\rangle \end{array}$$

Exercise Verify!

From these, the fact that $P;Q$ realizes Γ, Δ follows easily. For example, suppose that $R \Vdash_- \Gamma$. We must show that $\langle R|P;Q \Vdash_+ \Delta$. But

$$P \Vdash_+ \Gamma, A \implies \langle R|P \Vdash_+ A$$

$$Q \Vdash_+ A^\perp, \Delta \implies \langle\langle R|P|Q \Vdash_+ \Delta$$

and the result follows since

$$\langle R|P;Q \approx_f \langle\langle R|P|Q.$$

This last step uses the fact that, as already stated, we are taking processes modulo failures equivalence as our realizers. In fact, all the equivalences stated so far are valid with respect to much finer notions, in particular for weak bisimulation.

3.4.3 Multiplicatives

The construction of realizers for the multiplicative rules requires nothing more than renaming.

$$\frac{P \Vdash_+ \Gamma, A \quad Q \Vdash_+ \Delta, B}{P \otimes Q[\phi] \Vdash_+ \Gamma, \Delta, A \otimes B} \qquad \frac{P \Vdash_+ \Gamma, A, B}{P[\psi] \Vdash_+ \Gamma, A \parr B}$$

for suitable renamings ϕ, ψ.

Exercise Define ϕ and ψ, and verify that the required realizability relations do hold.

3.4.4 Additives

$$\frac{P \Vdash_+ \Gamma, A \quad Q \Vdash_+ \Gamma, B}{\mathtt{r}(\alpha).P + \mathtt{r}(\beta).Q \Vdash_+ \Gamma, A \& B}$$

$$\frac{P \Vdash_+ \Gamma, A}{\overline{\mathtt{r}(\alpha)}.P \Vdash_+ \Gamma, A \oplus B} \qquad \frac{Q \Vdash_+ \Delta, B}{\overline{\mathtt{r}(\beta)}.Q \Vdash_+ \Delta, A \oplus B}.$$

We can define the process combinators

$$\langle P, Q\rangle \triangleq \mathtt{r}(\alpha).P + \mathtt{l}(\beta).Q.$$

$$\mathtt{l}(P) \triangleq \overline{\mathtt{l}(\alpha)}.P \quad \mathtt{r}(Q) \triangleq \overline{\mathtt{r}(\beta)}.Q.$$

The key process algebraic facts we need to show the soundness of the above rules are

$$\begin{array}{lcl} \langle P, Q\rangle; \mathtt{l}(R) & \approx_f & P;R \\ \langle P, Q\rangle; \mathtt{r}(S) & \approx_f & Q;S \\ \langle R|\langle P, Q\rangle & \approx_f & \langle\langle R|P, \langle R|Q\rangle. \end{array}$$

Exercise Verify these equations. Show that the first two hold with respect to weak bisimulation, but the third does not. Validating this last equation is one main reason for working with failures equivalence in this paper. (Those familiar with the failures-divergences model will note that this equation only holds in that model on the assumption that R is not the immediately divergent process. It is possible to adapt our treatment to accomodate divergences. We have not done so here to simplify the presentation.)

Exercise Using the above equations, show the soundness of the realizability assignments for the additive rules.

Exercise Work out the realizability assignments for the exponentials ! and ? of Linear Logic, and prove their soundness.

3.5 Cut-Elimination

Thus for each sequent proof Π in Linear Logic, we can assign a process term $[\![\Pi]\!]$. Moreover, we have the following result expressing the soundness of our assignment with respect to Cut Elimination.

Proposition 3.1 *If Π reduces to Π' under cut-elimination, then $[\![\Pi]\!] \approx_f [\![\Pi']\!]$.*

By virtue of these results, we can claim to have modelled Cut-elimination by process interaction. We can also prove that Cut-elimination *terminates* in our model. We outline the argument. For a detailed account in the interaction categories setting, see [AGN99].

Firstly, we say that a process P *diverges*, written $P\Uparrow$, if there is a sequence $(P_n \mid n \in \omega)$ with $P = P_0$ and $P_n \xrightarrow{\tau} P_{n+1}$ for all $n \in \omega$. We say that P is *convergent*, written $P\Downarrow$, if it does not diverge.
Now we define

$$P \perp Q \stackrel{\Delta}{\Longleftrightarrow} ((P \mid Q)\backslash\mathcal{N})\Downarrow.$$

Thus if we "close the system", so that P and Q can only interact with each other, there must be no possible divergences.
We say that a formula A is *total* if

$$\forall P \Vdash_{+} A.\ \forall Q \Vdash_{-} A.\ P \perp Q,$$

and that it is *inhabited* if it has both positive and negative realizers. Note that a realizer for a total and inhabited type is convergent.

Proposition 3.2 *If A and B are total and inhabited, then so are $A^{\perp}$, $A \otimes B$, $A \& B$, $!A$ (and hence also the other connectives).*

This means that if we start from total and inhabited interpretations of the atomic formulas, then the process we extract from any proof will be convergent. The key case is Cut, where the totality condition plays an analogous role to the computability predicate in a Tait-style proof of strong normalization [Tai67, GLT89]. The fact that our process realizers are convergent is analogous to the fact that a functional realizer extracted by standard realizability from a proof say in second-order logic will compute a total functional.

4 The Realizability Category

We now turn to a more semantic view of process realizability, in the same general spirit as the by now standard idea of constructing categories of assemblies or realizability toposes (for which see *e.g.* [AL91, Cro93, Lon95, AC98]).

For each formula A, we can define

$$\begin{array}{rcl} S_A & = & \{P \mid P \Vdash_+ A\} \\ S_A^* & = & \{Q \mid Q \Vdash_- A\} \end{array}$$

We can then define the "realizability semantics" for a formula A as

$$[\![A]\!] = (S_A, S_A^*).$$

The advantage of this point of view is that we can now abstract to consider *any* pair (S, S^*) of sets of processes as a "type" of realizers and counter-realizers, and define the action of the various Linear connectives over these types. Thus for example

$$(S, S^*)^\perp = (S^*, S)$$

while $(S, S^*) \multimap (T, T^*)$ is the pair

$$(\{P \mid \forall Q \in S. \langle Q|P \in T \ \wedge \ \forall R \in T^*. P|R\rangle \in S^*\}, \{P \otimes Q \mid P \in S \ \wedge \ Q \in T^*\})$$

etc. This idea needs to be refined slightly to yield a satisfactory result. In particular, in order to build in a suitable "modulus of extensionality", we shall work with *partial equivalence relations* on processes, rather than simply sets of processes. Recall that a partial equivalence relation is a symmetric, transitive relation.

We shall take a type to be a pair (E, E^*) of partial equivalence relations on processes, where processes are identified up to failures equivalence. The interpretations of the linear connectives lift to operations on partial equivalence relations in a straightforward manner. For example, $E_{A \multimap B}$ consists of all pairs (P, Q) such that

$$\forall (R, S) \in E_A. (\langle R|P, \langle S|Q) \in E_B \ \wedge \ \forall (T, U) \in E_B^*. (P|T\rangle, Q|U\rangle) \in E_A^*.$$

We proceed to define a realizability category $\mathcal{C}$. The objects

$$A = (E_A, E_A^*)$$

are pairs of partial equivalence relations on processes. A morphism $f : A \to B$ is a partial equivalence class $[P]$ of $E_{A \multimap B}$. This partial equivalence class induces a pair of maps (f^+, f^-), where f maps partial equivalence classes of E_A to partial equivalence classes of E_B, and f^- maps partial equivalence classes of E_B^* to partial equivalence classes of E_A^*:

$$f^+([Q]) = [\langle Q|P], \quad f^-([R]) = [P|R\rangle].$$

Conversely, any such pair of maps which is "tracked" by a process P in this way determines a unique partial equivalence class of $E_{A \multimap B}$.

The further structure of the category unfolds as essentially a recapitulation of our account of realizability for linear proofs. For example, identities and composition are realized as for Axiom and Cut. Our constructions for $\otimes$ and $\multimap$ give $\mathcal{C}$ the structure of a symmetric monoidal closed category. There is a duality

$$\frac{f : A \to B}{f^\perp : B^\perp \to A^\perp}$$

where if $f = (f^+, f^-)$, $f^\perp = (f^-, f^+)$. At the process level, the duality just amounts to interchanging the left-right partition of the name space

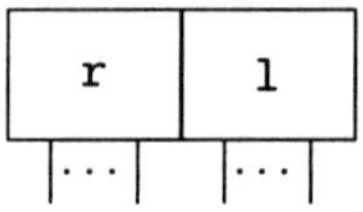

The additive connectives &, $\oplus$ give products and coproducts in $\mathcal{C}$, and in fact $\mathcal{C}$ has all (countable) limits and colimits. $!A$ gives the cofree cocommutative comonoid on A.

Proposition 4.1 *$\mathcal{C}$ is a model of Linear Logic.*

Exercise Verify some of this structure. For example, show that & gives the categorical product in $\mathcal{C}$.

4.1 Quantifiers

This construction is easily extended to yield a model of second-order Linear Logic.

A formula $A[X]$ with a second-order propositional variable X can be interpreted as a function F_A on the objects of $\mathcal{C}$ in the obvious fashion. We then define

$$E_{\forall X.\, A[X]} = \bigcap \{E_{F_A(B)} \mid B \in \mathsf{Ob}\,\mathcal{C}\}$$

$$E^*_{\forall X.\, A[X]} = (\bigcup \{E^*_{F_A(B)} \mid B \in \mathsf{Ob}\,\mathcal{C}\})^+.$$

The clause for the negative realizers is really for the second-order existential:

$$(\forall X.\, A[X])^\perp = \exists X.\, A[X]^\perp.$$

The transitive closure is used, since the union of a family of per's need not be transitive. This "information loss" is typical of the behaviour of second-order existentials.

First-order quantifiers are handled nicely by value-passing at the process algebra level. We take the set $\mathcal{V}$ of values to be the domain of quantification. The realizability definitions are similar to those for the additives. We fix an atomic name σ.

$$P \Vdash_+ \forall x.\, A \;\equiv\; P \approx_f \sigma x.\, Q \;\wedge\; \forall v \in \mathcal{V}.\, Q[v/x] \Vdash_+ A[v/x]$$

$$P \Vdash_- \forall x.\, A \;\equiv\; P \approx_f \bar{\sigma} v.R \;\wedge\; R \Vdash_- A[v/x].$$

In terms of operations on partial equivalence relations:

$$E_{\forall x.\, A} = \{(\sigma x.P, \sigma x.Q) \mid \forall v \in \mathcal{V}.\, (P[v/x], Q[v/x]) \in E_{A[v/x]}\}$$

$$E^*_{\forall x.\, A} = \{(\bar{\sigma} v.P, \bar{\sigma} v.Q) \mid (P, Q) \in E^*_{A[v/x]}\}.$$

4.2 Inductive and Co-inductive types

Inductive and coinductive types can be canonically interpreted in $\mathcal{C}$ as initial T-algebras and final T-coalgebras for endofuctors $T : \mathcal{C} \to \mathcal{C}$. We look at a basic example by way of illustration. Firstly, we define a unit type I with

$$E_I = E^*_I = \{(0, 0)\}.$$

We fix a type A, and define a type of A-lists by

$$L = \mu X.\, I \oplus (A \otimes X).$$

What are the realizers for L? The empty list is realized by $\bar{\alpha}.0$. Given a realizer P for A, which may be taken as realizing the "value" $v = [P]$, the unit list $[v]$ is realized by $\bar{\beta}.(P \otimes \bar{\alpha}.0)$. Inductively, if an A-list l is realized by Q, and an A-value v is realized by P, then the list $v :: l$ is realized by $\bar{\beta}.(P \otimes Q)$. Thus we get an inductive definition of the positive realizers for L, which may be compared to that for $?A$. It is worth noting that these lists are truly *linear*—to "read" them (by interacting with the process realizing the list) is to consume them.

What of the counter-realizers for L? These will be the A-list consuming contexts. Such a context can be defined as follows. Let $(Q_n \mid n \in \omega)$ be a family of processes, with

$$Q_n \Vdash_{-} \underbrace{A \otimes \cdots \otimes A}_{n}, \quad (n \in \omega).$$

Define a family $(P_n \mid n \in \omega)$ by simultaneous recursion:

$$P_i = \alpha.Q_i + \beta.P_{i+1} \quad (i \in \omega).$$

Then P_0 is a counter-realizer for L.

Exercise Work out the details of this example, to give an explicit description of the initial T-algebra for the endofunctor

$$TX = I \oplus (A \otimes X).$$

Exercise Similarly, analyze the coinductive type of A-streams:

$$S = \nu X. I \,\&\, (A \otimes X).$$

We can use the example of lists to give a useful intuition for the symmetric condition on realizers for the linear implication. Consider a morphism

$$f : \mathsf{List(A)} \to \mathsf{List(B)}.$$

This means that we have a realizer P for a pair of maps (f^+, f^-). In the forwards direction, P induces a function f^+ mapping A-lists to B-lists. In the backwards direction, P induces a *context-transformer* f^- mapping contexts whch consume B-lists to contexts which consume A-lists. E.g. given the definition

$$\begin{array}{lcl} \mathtt{f}\,[\,] & = & [\,] \\ \mathtt{f}\ \mathsf{a} :: \mathsf{b} :: \mathtt{xs} & = & (a+b) :: xs \end{array}$$

we have the usual function

$$f^+([1,2]) = [3]$$

and also

$$f^-(\mathsf{hd}([\cdot]) = \mathsf{hd}(\mathsf{hd}[\cdot]).$$

The context-transformer part of the interpretation of f in our realizability semantics is *intensional* information about the behaviour of f as an *algorithm*, rather than merely a set-theoretical function. This opens up the possibility of accurate realizability models for non-functional languages.

References

[Abr94a] S. Abramsky. Interaction Categories and Communicating Sequential Processes. In *A Classical Mind. Essays in Honour of C. A. R. Hoare*, ed. A. W. Roscoe, 1–16. Prentice Hall 1994.

[Abr94b] S. Abramsky. Proofs as Processes. *TCS* vol. 135, 5–9, 1994.

[AGN96] S. Abramsky, S. J. Gay and R. Nagarajan. Interaction Categories and the Foundations of Typed Concurrent Programming. In M. Broy, ed. *Deductive Program Design: Proceedings of the 1994 Marktoberdorf Summer School*, 35–113. Springer, 1996.

[AGN99] S. Abramsky, S. J. Gay and R. Nagarajan. A specification structure for deadlock-freedom of synchronous processes. *TCS*, vol. 222, 1–53, 1999.

[AC98] R. Amadio and P.-L. Curien. *Domains and Lambda-Calculi*. Cambridge University Press, 1998.

[AL91] A. Asperti and G. Longo. *Categories, Types and Structures*. MIT Press, 1991.

[BW99] M. Barr and C. Wells. *Category Theory for Computing Science. Third Edition*. Les Publications CRM, Montreal, 1999.

[BR83] S. Brookes and W. Rounds. Behavioural Equivalences induced by Programming Logics. In *Proceedings of ICALP '83*, Springer Lecture Notes in Computer Science vol. 154, 97–108, 1983.

[BHR84] S. Brookes, C. A. R. Hoare and A. W. Roscoe. A Theory of Communicating Sequential Processes. *JACM* vol. 31, no. 7, 560–599, 1984.

[BR84] S. Brookes and A. W. Roscoe. An Improved Failures Model for Communicating Processes. In Springer Lecture Notes in Computer Science vol. 197, 281–305, 1984.

[Cro93] R. L. Crole. *Categories for Types*. Cambridge University Press, 1993.

[DNH83] R. DeNicola and M. Hennessy. Testing Equivalence for Processes. *TCS* vol. 34, 83–133, 1983.

[Dir67] P. A. M. Dirac. *Principles of Quantum Mechanics*. Oxford University Press, 1967.

[GLT89] J.-Y. Girard, Y. Lafont and P. Taylor. *Proofs and Types*. Cambridge University Press, 1989.

[Hen88] M. Hennessy. *Algebraic Theory of Processes*. MIT Press, 1988.

[Hoa85] C. A. R. Hoare. *Communicating Sequential Processes*. Prentice Hall, 1985.

[Kle45] S. C. Kleene. On the interpretation of intuitionistic number theory. *JSL* vol. 10, 1945.

[Lon95] J. R. Longley. *Realizability Toposes and Language Semantics*. Ph.D. thesis, Department of Computer Science, University of Edinburgh, 1995.

[Mil89] R. Milner. *Communication and Concurrency*. Prentice Hall, 1989.

[Ros97] A. W. Roscoe. *The Theory and Practice of Concurrency*. Prentice Hall, 1997.

[BS94] U. Berger and H. Schwichtenberg. Program extraction from classical proofs. In D. Leivant, ed. *Logic and Computational Complexity*, Springer Lecture Notes in Computer Science vol. 960, 77–97, 1995.

[Sco76] D. S. Scott. Data Types as Lattices. *SIAM J. on Computing*, vol. 5, 522–587, 1976.

[Tai67] W. W. Tait. Intensional interpretation of functionals of finite type I. *JSL* vol. 32, 198–212, 1967.

Part 3
Logic and Domains

J.-Y. Girard

V. Stoltenberg-Hansen

3. Bounded Bang

$!\_ \twoheadrightarrow \_ : \mathbb{K} \times \mathbb{K} \rightarrow \mathbb{K} \times \mathbb{K} \times \wp(\mathbb{K})$

complex operational semantics (in, out, etc.)

 $\leftarrow$ P
$\leftarrow$ O

[17 side conditions]

$!\,P \twoheadrightarrow O \quad \xrightarrow{?} \quad P \parallel O \parallel d \qquad d \in \wp(\mathbb{P} \lozenge \mathbb{O})$ descendants $\leftarrow$ non-determinism

tricky safety & security aspects, left as exercise!

[hint: exchange protocol for private keys,
with continuously realistic non-alphabetic domains]

Observation: $\mathbb{K} = \mathbb{P} \oplus \mathbb{O}$

as ($!\_ \twoheadrightarrow \_$) is not associative, two-party operation,
interchange of roles $P \leftrightarrow O$ is not allowed
$\Rightarrow$ refinement: $!\_\rightarrow\_ : \mathbb{P} \times \mathbb{O} \rightarrow \mathbb{P} \times \mathbb{O} \times \wp(\mathbb{P} \lozenge \mathbb{O})$

Future work: conversion operator
$\_^{\perp} : \mathbb{K} \rightarrow \mathbb{K}$
Specification: $K^{\perp\perp} = K$, $P^{\perp} = O$, $O^{\perp} = P$
Implementations (so far): non-constructive ☹

Foundations of Secure Computation
F.L. Bauer and R. Steinbrüggen (Eds.)
IOS Press, 2000

On the Meaning of Logical Rules II : Multiplicatives and Additives

Jean-Yves Girard
Institut de Mathématiques de Luminy, UPR 9016 - CNRS
163, Avenue de Luminy, Case 930, F-13288 Marseille Cedex 09, France

girard@iml.univ-mrs.fr

Abstract. *El método inicial que imaginó era relativamente sencillo. Conocer bien el español, recuperar la fe católica, guerrear contra los moros o contra el turco, olvidar la historia de Europa entre los años de 1602 y de 1918,* ser *Miguel de Cervantes. Pierre Ménard estudió ese procedimiento (sé que logró un manejo bastante fiel del español del siglo diecisiete), pero lo descartó por fácil. [...] Mi complaciente precursor no rehusó la colaboración del azar : iba componiendo la obra inmortal un poco* à la diable, *llevado por inercias del lenguaje y de la invención. Yo he contraído el misterioso deber de reconstruir literalmente su obra espontánea. Mi solitario juego está gobernado por dos leyes polares. La primera me permite ensayar variantes de tipo formal o psicológico ; la segunda me obliga a sacrificarlas al texto « original » y a razonar de un modo irrefutable esa aniquilación.*

J. L. Borges *Pierre Ménard autor del Quijote*, 1939.

The paper expounds the solution to our search for meaning [3] in a particular case : the fragment of logic built from the neutral elements $\bot, \top, \mathbf{1}, \mathbf{0}$ by means of the connectives $⅋, \&, \otimes, \oplus$.

As explained in the previous paper and summarized in the abstract, the task is to produce a trivial meet between syntax and semantics, but in a non-trivial way. Typically, we cannot content ourselves with a plain game-theoretic paraphrases of logic ; we have to deconstruct familiar syntax and to reconstruct it in another way. But, as in the case of Ménard reconstructing the *Quijote*, the synthesis is absolutely prior to the analysis... in particular the presentation analysis/synthesis that we follow is completely alien to the very spirit of the work.

We shall organize a sort of tunnel between syntax and semantics, with a meet in between : the analysis will replace syntax with a game-theoretic variant, and synthesis will elaborate an abstract notion of game, which can be specialized to our fragment and yield exactly the same games as those obtained by the analysis.

Analysis We shall modify the extant sequent calculus into a *hypersequentialized* version **HC**, which has internalized the alternation positive/negative to the extent that even negative formulas disappear... the usual connectives being replaced with *synthetic connectives*. The configurations of **HC** can be fully analyzed by means of various game-theoretic artefacts. Moreover, **HC** admits wrong logical rules (*paralogisms*[1]), which are essential to prove the basic equivalences between usual logic and its game-theoretic version in **HC**. These paralogisms have a heavy price :

[1] To avoid misunderstandings : the mistakes are *volontary*, nothing to do with —say— « abduction » and other non-monotonic « logics ».

who uses them loses, and we end with a complete equivalence between usual logic and *winning strategies* in a sort of analytic game.

Synthesis We can, starting with the geometrical idea of iterated division of space, build a universal game. The *disputes* (i.e. the plays) of this game are equipped with a (sort of) structure of coherent space. Then cliques in this coherent space may be seen as *designs* (i.e. a very specific sort of strategy), and when a design is *orthogonal* to a counterdesign, the unique dispute they share has at most one winner. If we define a *behavior* as a set of designs equal to its biorthogonal, then logical formulas are interpreted as behaviors. Then it is a matter of care to translate a design within a logical behavior into a paraproof of the corresponding formula, and a winning design into a real proof. By the way, losing corresponds to giving up or making a deliberate mistake to annoy the enemy, what is called here a *dog's move*, whose basic meaning (besides the fact that it might also make your opponent lose) is that of an artificial obstruction : this is the geometrical meaning of paralogisms.

Technically speaking, our interpretation is based on seven pillars, that we distinguish by different fonts/styles, namely :

- **Fingers** (in French : *doigts* ; intuition : *subformula index*) $i, j, k, \ldots$
- **Hands** (in French : *mains* ; intuition : *formula*) $\sigma, \xi, \eta, \ldots$
- **Blokes** (in French : *gonzes* ; intuition : *sequent*) $\Xi \vdash \Sigma$, or $\mathbf{a}, \mathbf{b}, \mathbf{c}, \ldots$
- **Mauls** (in French : *mêlées* ; intuition : *proof of the empty sequent*) $\mathfrak{m}, \mathfrak{n}, \mathfrak{p}, \ldots$
- **Disputes** (in French : *disputes* ; intuition : *process of normalization*) $[\mathfrak{m}_o, \ldots, \mathfrak{m}_n]$ or $\mathfrak{D}, \mathfrak{E}, \mathfrak{F}, \ldots$
- **Designs** (in French : *desseins* ; intuition : *proofs and paraproofs*) $\mathcal{S}, \mathcal{T}, \mathcal{R}, \ldots$
- **Behaviors** (in French : *comportements* ; intuition : *the meaning of a formula*) $\mathbf{G}, \mathbf{H}, \mathbf{K}, \ldots$

Indeed this is not the last word, and the general constraints coming from the missing logical primitives (essentially the exponentials) induce some modifications of this pattern, the main avenues remaining unchanged ; the final solution, called *ludics*, is only available (November 1999) through a draft in French, [4]. It strongly reacts against the Tarskian schizophrenia which consists in presenting logical artefacts by means of pairs (syntax,semantics) : ludics is not dealing with syntax or semantics, it is just dealing with plain logic, if something of the like exists !

Many thanks to Alexandra Bac and Claudia Faggian for their careful reading of the first version of this paper.

1 The Hypersequentialized Calculus

We recall that formulas are classified according to their *polarity* :

- $\mathbf{1}, \mathbf{0}$ and formulas starting with $\otimes, \oplus$ are *positive*.
- $\bot, \top$ and formulas starting with $⅋, \&$ are *negative*.

We shall later introduce the atom $\mathbf{0}^\flat$ (positive), the *boot*. As usual we should pay attention to repetitions of formulas, i.e. the phenomenon of *occurrences*. But there is a very radical way to do so, namely to have infinitely many constants —say $\mathbf{0}_i^\flat, \mathbf{0}_i$— and to systematically use fresh constants.

1.1 Synthetic Connectives

Take a formula, say positive ; then we can decompose it into its subformulas, and go on until we stop, either because we reach an atom like $\mathbf{0}$, or a negative formula. Then our formula looks like $P = \psi[N_1, \ldots, N_k]$, where ϕ is a *cluster* of positive connectives and the N_i are negative. We can rewrite this as $P = \phi[P_1, \ldots, P_k]$, where the P_i are the negations of the N_i. Typically $L \oplus (M \otimes N)$ will appear as a ternary operation $\phi[P, Q, R] = P^\perp \oplus (Q^\perp \otimes R^\perp)$. The major property of these new connectives is that they lead from positive to positive, i.e. that there is no longer any negative formula. This is made technically possible by the *focalization property* of Andreoli [1], which states the possibility of handling a cluster of connectives of the same polarity as a single connective, see also [3], annex F.

PROPOSITION 1
If X is a finite coherent space, then the following are equivalent :

- *X is series/parallel, i.e. it can be built from the coherent space* $\mathbf{1}$ *by means of the constructions & (series) and $\oplus$ (parallel).*
- *X harbors no* horseshoe, *i.e. no 4-element subgraph such that $a \frown b \frown c \frown d$ and $b \smile d \smile a \smile c$.*
- *X can be contracted into one point by iteration of the operation : if x, y are undiscernible, i.e. $\forall z \neq x, y \quad (z \frown x \Leftrightarrow z \frown y)$, then remove one of x, y.*

Such an X is called contractile. *If $X \neq \emptyset$ and C is a maximal clique in X and D is a maximal anticlique in X, then $C \cap D \neq \emptyset$.*

Proof : Folkloric. □

DEFINITION 1
A n-ary synthetic connective *$\mathfrak{X}$ is a finite set of propositional variables $\{p_1, \ldots, p_n\}$ equipped with a structure of contractile coherent space.*

Typically :

1. The empty coherent space (corresponding to the constant $\mathbf{0}$ of linear logic)
2. The binary connective $p_1 \frown p_2$, which corresponds to the connective ${p_1}^\perp \otimes {p_2}^\perp$ of linear logic.
3. The binary connective $p_1 \smile p_2$, which corresponds to the connective ${p_1}^\perp \oplus {p_2}^\perp$ of linear logic.

4. The unary connective p (one point space), which corresponds to the positivization of negation, i.e. $\uparrow p$ is $p^{\perp}$ made positive[2]. Later on, we shall use $\downarrow$ to denote the same operation (one dummy move) but without the negation, so that $\uparrow p = \downarrow p^{\perp}$.

5. There is no synthetic connective corresponding to the constant $\mathbf{1}$; in fact the only reasonable candidate would be the empty set which already takes care of the constant $\mathbf{0}$. The constant $\mathbf{1}$ will therefore be $\uparrow \mathbf{0}^{\flat} = \downarrow(\mathbf{0}^{\flat\perp})$, where $\mathbf{0}^{\flat}$ is a new constant specific of **HC**. By the way, interpreting $\mathbf{1}$ as $\emptyset$ would force $\mathbf{1} \oplus \mathbf{1}$ to be empty as well, but this would cause a degeneracy of the interpretation, since $\mathbf{1} \oplus \mathbf{1}$ is a reasonable interpretation of booleans.

DEFINITION 2
Let $\phi[N_1, \ldots, N_k, \mathbf{1}_1, \ldots, \mathbf{1}_l]$ be a positive formula built on the formulas $N_1, \ldots, N_k$ (negative) and $\mathbf{1}_1, \ldots, \mathbf{1}_l$ (occurrences of $\mathbf{1}$), by means of $\mathbf{0}$, $\oplus$, $\otimes$. Let $\mathbf{0}^{\flat}_1, \ldots, \mathbf{0}^{\flat}_l$ be occurrences of the (positive) atom $\mathbf{0}^{\flat}$. Then we construct a synthetic connective $\mathfrak{X}$ on a subset of the positive atoms $N_1{}^{\perp}, \ldots, N_k{}^{\perp}, \mathbf{0}^{\flat}_1, \ldots, \mathbf{0}^{\flat}_l$:

1. *If $\phi = \mathbf{0}$, then $\mathfrak{X}$ is the empty coherent space.*

2. *If $\phi = \mathbf{1}_i$ (resp. N_i) then $\mathfrak{X}$ is the unit coherent space on the atom $\mathbf{0}^{\flat}_i$ (resp. $N_i{}^{\perp}$).*

3. *If $\phi = \phi_1 \oplus \phi_2$, then $\mathfrak{X} = \mathfrak{X}_1 \oplus \mathfrak{X}_2$ (i.e. the parallel sum of the coherent spaces $\mathfrak{X}_i$)*

4. *If $\phi = \phi_1 \otimes \phi_2$, then $\mathfrak{X} = \mathfrak{X}_1 \,\&\, \mathfrak{X}_2$ (i.e. the series sum of the coherent spaces $\mathfrak{X}_i$), except if one of the $\mathfrak{X}_i$ is empty, in which case $\mathfrak{X}$ is empty as well.*

PROPOSITION 2
Let ϕ, $\mathfrak{X}$ be as above, and let X be a non-empty maximal clique in $\mathfrak{X}$; then

1. *$\mathfrak{X}$ cannot be empty, i.e. if $\phi = \mathbf{0}$, there is no such X.*
2. *If ϕ is $\mathbf{1}_i$ or N_i, then X is the unique singleton clique of $\mathfrak{X}$.*
3. *If ϕ is $\phi_1 \oplus \phi_2$, then X is either a maximal non-empty clique in $\mathfrak{X}_1$ or (exclusive or) in $\mathfrak{X}_2$.*
4. *If ϕ is $\phi_1 \otimes \phi_2$, then X is the union of a non empty maximal clique in $\mathfrak{X}_1$ and a non-empty maximal clique in $\mathfrak{X}_2$: this excludes the case where one of $\mathfrak{X}_1, \mathfrak{X}_2$ is empty.*

Proof : Obvious ; the proposition explains the peculiarities of definition 2. □

1.2 The Syntax of HC

DEFINITION 3
The formulas in **HC** *are defined inductively by :*

1. *The atom $\mathbf{0}^{\flat}$ is a formula.*

2. *If $\mathfrak{X}$ is a synthetic connective on the variables $p_1, \ldots, p_n$ and if $P_1, \ldots, P_n$ are formulas, then $\mathfrak{X}P_1, \ldots, P_n$ is a formula.*

[2] In terms of games, a positive formula corresponds to « I start », and negation is the interchange between players ; $\uparrow p$ is still positive, i.e. a dummy first move being added : $\uparrow$ is not involutive, since doing it twice will produce the same plays, but with two additional dummy moves, which do matter !

From what precedes, one can associate to any positive formula P written in the fragment $\mathbf{1}, \mathbf{0}, \perp, \top, \otimes, \oplus, \parr, \&$, a unique formula of **HC** : one writes P as $\phi[N_1, \ldots, N_k, 1_1, 1_l]$, where ϕ is purely positive and the N_i are negative, and one replaces ϕ with the appropriate $\mathfrak{X}$, applied to some of the $N_i{}^\perp, \mathbf{0}^\flat_j$; the $\mathbf{0}^\flat_j$ are just occurrences of $\mathbf{0}^\flat$ whereas the $N_i{}^\perp$ can in turn be analyzed in the same way. Observe that $\mathbf{0}^\flat$ does not correspond to anything in linear logic, in particular one should not imagine that $\mathbf{0}^\flat$ is a missing constant of LL (expressions like $\mathbf{0}^\flat \oplus P$ do not seem to make sense in LL).

1.3 The Calculus HC : Cut-Free Part

DEFINITION 4
A sequent $\Xi \vdash \Sigma$ consists in two multisets of formulas Ξ, Σ ; there must be at least one formula in $\Xi \cup \Sigma$ and at most one formula in Ξ. A sequent with Ξ empty is said to be major, *a sequent $\xi \vdash \Sigma$ is said to be* minor. *We shall consider that we are working with sets, i.e. that we are indeed dealing with occurrences.*

DEFINITION 5
The rules of the (cut-free) sequent calculus **HC** *are defined below ; some of them will be considered as* paralogisms, *and therefore the other rules will be considered as* correct.

1. *The hypothesis $\vdash \Sigma$ for any major sequent (paralogism) ; the expression* hypothesis *means that the proof-tree is not quite well-founded, i.e. that something is missing.*

2. *The axiom $\mathbf{0}^\flat \vdash \Sigma$ (paralogism, unless Σ only consists in occurrences of $\mathbf{0}^\flat$).*

3. *Let $\mathfrak{X}P_1, \ldots, P_n$ be a formula, and let X be a non-empty maximal clique of $\mathfrak{X}$, e.g. $X = \{p_{i_1}, \ldots, p_{i_k}\}$. Then we are allowed to use the following rule : from $P_{i_1} \vdash \Sigma_1, \ldots, P_{i_k} \vdash \Sigma_k$ deduce $\vdash \mathfrak{X}P_1, \ldots, P_n, \Sigma_1, \ldots, \Sigma_k$.*

4. *Let $\mathfrak{X}P_1, \ldots, P_n$ be a formula ; for each non-empty maximal clique X of $\mathfrak{X}$, e.g. $X = \{p_{i_1}, \ldots, p_{i_k}\}$, let us introduce $\Upsilon_X = P_{i_1}, \ldots, P_{i_k}$. Then we are allowed to use the following rule : from $\vdash \Upsilon_X, \Sigma$ for each X, deduce $\mathfrak{X}P_1, \ldots, P_n \vdash \Sigma$.*

A paraproof *is anything generated by these rules ; a* proof *is a paraproof without paralogism.*

Our distinction between axiom and hypothesis comes from the fact that in 1. Σ is major, and that a rule introducing a major sequent should have at least one premise. This is not the case for minor sequents, which have a well-defined rule introducing them, which may be without premise ; this is why 2. is called axiom. By the way, the case $\mathfrak{X} = \emptyset$ (i.e. $\mathbf{0}$) produces an axiom too, see below. It is quite easy to see that :

1. When $\mathfrak{X}$ is empty, then there is no rule introducing $\mathfrak{X}$ to the right, but $\mathfrak{X} \vdash \Sigma$ is an axiom : this corresponds to the connective $\mathbf{0}$.

2. The rules of $\mathfrak{X}[P_1, P_2]$ will correspond to the rules for the tensor $P_1{}^\perp \otimes P_2{}^\perp$ (if $P_1 \frown P_2$) or the sum $P_1{}^\perp \oplus P_2{}^\perp$ (if $P_1 \smile P_2$).

3. The constant $\mathbf{1}$ is represented by $\uparrow\mathbf{0}^\flat$, but the situation is more complex :

(a) Since the only correct axioms are of the form $\mathbf{0}^\flat \vdash \mathbf{0}^\flat, \ldots, \mathbf{0}^\flat$, a real proof of a sequent involving $\uparrow\mathbf{0}^\flat$ to the right must somewhere use the right rule for $\uparrow$, i.e. derive some $\vdash \Sigma, \uparrow\mathbf{0}^\flat$ from $\mathbf{0}^\flat \vdash \Sigma$, whose only real proof consists in an axiom, but Σ must then consist of occurrences of $\mathbf{0}^\flat$. This corresponds to the « derived axiom » $\vdash \mathbf{1}, \mathbf{0}^\flat, \ldots, \mathbf{0}^\flat$.

(b) Now given any paraproof of $\Xi \vdash \Sigma$, one can produce a « weakened » paraproof of $\Xi \vdash \Sigma, \mathbf{0}^\flat$, by adding some $\mathbf{0}^\flat$ to the right of all sequents of the paraproof. Moreover, this operation preserves correctness. This indeed justifies the derived rule « From $\vdash \Sigma$ derive $1 \vdash \Sigma$ », which is weakening.

(c) We therefore see that the rules for $\mathbf{1}$ and $\perp$ are faithfully represented. However the case of weakening is awfully non deterministic : typically, in the case of $\vdash \mathfrak{X}PQ$, where $\mathfrak{X}$ means $p^\perp \otimes q^\perp$, the addition of $\mathbf{0}^\flat$ to get $\vdash \mathfrak{X}PQ, \mathbf{0}^\flat$ will involve a choice between P and Q, e.g. to modify the premises $P \vdash$ and $Q \vdash$ into $P \vdash \mathbf{0}^\flat$ and $Q \vdash$. In other terms, we rediscover the absence of satisfactory proof-nets for the multiplicative neutrals, that we shall formulate in a more drastic way : the multiplicative neutrals are not quite neutral, at least in the present setting. In the next paper [4], they will be neutral. But we refuse to introduce the full setting corresponding to exponentials for such a marginal issue.

From this it is quite easy to prove a correspondence between (real) cut-free proofs in **HC** and cut-free proofs in the fragment of linear logic under study. Let us for instance look at the less trivial part, i.e. how we can translate a proof of a sequent $\vdash A$ in our fragment into a **HC**-proof.

1. We write the final sequent as $\vdash A$ if A is positive, or $A^\perp \vdash$ if A is negative. We also modify the proof so as to use no identity axiom : « reverse η-conversion ».

2. We are iteratively led to the more general situation of a cut-free proof of a sequent $\Xi \vdash \Sigma$, made of positive formulas, and with at most one formula in Ξ. Moreover the proof does not use the identity axiom of linear logic.

3. If $\Xi = P$, then, by appropriate permutations of rules, we can make sure that the last rule of the proof introduces P to the left, typically $P = A \otimes B$, then the premise is $A, B \vdash \Sigma$, and in case one of A, B is not negative, we iterate the process. Eventually we get a portion of proof using only left rules, and starting with sequents $\Theta_i \vdash \Sigma$, where the Θ_i are non-empty multisets of negative formulas. Indeed I can put the Θ_i to the right by negating them, and I can produce a bijection $f : \Theta_{f(X)}{}^\perp = \Upsilon_X$ so that the sequents $\vdash \Sigma, \Upsilon_X$, are exactly the premises of the left rule of the appropriate synthetic connective.

4. If $\Xi = \emptyset$, then we can apply focalization, i.e. that —up to permutation of rules— one of the formulas of $\vdash \Sigma$, say P, is such that a cluster of right rules has been applied, up to the negative constituants of P ; the premises of the cluster are of the form $\vdash \Sigma_i, N_i$, and if we replace them by $N_i{}^\perp \vdash \Sigma_i$ we are in the position to apply one of the right rules of the appropriate synthetic connective. Observe that, due to the possibility of alternative focalizations, several distinct **HC**-proofs can arise in this way.

5. One should be slightly more precise with $\mathbf{1}, \perp$, but this is a minor pedantic issue.

6. Last but not least : no paralogism is used in the translation.

1.4 The Full HC

The consideration of cut forces one to use some proof-net technology, i.e. boxes and cut-links, see [3].

DEFINITION 6
By a box *we mean a sequent, together with a* justification. *The justification can be —at this stage— rather arbitrary, i.e. boxes interact through the formulas of the sequent, which are the* doors *of the box ; observe that a box has at most one* main door, *i.e. the formula which is on the left-hand side of the sequent, the others being* auxiliary *; the main door P is indicated by $P \vdash$ —after all the turnstile is a sort of door. Given boxes $\mathcal{B}_0, \ldots, \mathcal{B}_n$, we can produce a cut-net, by means of only two links :*

- *The boxes, seen as generalized axioms (conclusions : the formulas of the sequent, but the main door is understood « negatively »).*
- *The cut-link, which links a main door with an auxiliary door, which are occurrences of the same formula. The cut-link has therefore two premises, no conclusion, and the premises cannot be reused for another link.*

Moreover the graph induced by the cut-net should be connected and acyclic.
The conclusion *of the cut-net is $\Xi \vdash \Sigma$, where Ξ, Σ consist of all formulas that are not used as premises of cut-links, Ξ listing the main doors and Σ listing the auxiliary doors. It is easy to see that Ξ consists of at most one formula. However we cannot claim that the conclusions form a sequent, since both Ξ and Σ might be empty... and this is indeed the most important case ! When we want to allow $\vdash$ we speak of an* extended *sequent.*

The calculus with cuts is defined inductively as follows : a paraproof of a (n extended) sequent consists in a cut-net with this sequent as conclusion, and whose boxes are justified as follows :

1. A box with conclusions $\vdash \Sigma$ *can* be justified by the magical expression *hypothesis*.
2. A box with conclusions $\mathbf{0}^\flat \vdash \Sigma$ *must* be justified by the expression *axiom*.
3. A box with conclusions $\vdash \mathfrak{X}P_1, \ldots, P_n, \Sigma_1, \ldots, \Sigma_k$ *can* be justified by means of a non-empty maximal clique of $\mathfrak{X}$, e.g. $X = \{p_{i_1}, \ldots, p_{i_k}\}$, together with cut-nets whose respective conclusions are $P_{i_1} \vdash \Sigma_1, \ldots, P_{i_k} \vdash \Sigma_k$.
4. A box with conclusions $\mathfrak{X}P_1, \ldots, P_n \vdash \Sigma$ *must* be justified by the data, for any non-empty maximal clique X of $\mathfrak{X}$, e.g. $X = \{p_{i_1}, \ldots, p_{i_k}\}$, of a cut-net whose conclusions are $\vdash \Upsilon_X, \Sigma$, with $\Upsilon_X = P_{i_1}, \ldots, P_{i_k}$.

Observe the difference between « must » (minor sequents) and « can » (major sequents). Remember the distinction between cut-nets (with unjustified boxes), and paraproofs (where the boxes are in turn justified by cut-nets).
The cut-free calculus is the particuliar case where all cut-nets which hereditarily occur are indeed boxes.

1.5 Cut-Elimination : Eager Version

In this process, all cuts will be eliminated. It is done as follows : we select a cut-link anywhere (including in the hereditary justifications of the boxes) and then we proceed according to the case. We now assume that our cut is between two occurrences of ξ, one being an auxiliary door of a box $\mathcal{B}$ ending with the conclusions $\Xi \vdash \Sigma, \xi$ and the other the main door of a box $\mathcal{B}'$ whose conclusions are $\xi \vdash \Sigma'$. The idea is to produce a cut-net whose conclusions are $\Xi \vdash \Sigma, \Sigma'$ and to replace the configuration « Two boxes and the cut-link » with it. In all the minor cases, the cut-net is indeed a box, but in the main case it is a non-trivial cut-net, i.e. some destruction of boxes has been performed.

hypothesis If $\Xi = \emptyset$ and $\mathcal{B}$ is justified as a hypothesis, then we just replace the two boxes with a single one (conclusions $\vdash \Sigma, \Sigma'$), justified as a hypothesis.

axiom If $\Xi = \mathbf{0}^\flat$, then $\mathcal{B}$ is justified as an axiom ; then we just replace the two boxes with a single one (conclusions $\mathbf{0}^\flat \vdash \Sigma, \Sigma'$), justified as an axiom ; observe that, in case our proof was a real one, correctness is respected.

negative commutation If $\Xi = \mathfrak{X}P_1, \ldots, P_n$, then $\mathcal{B}$ is justified by cut-nets $\mathbf{n}_X$, where X varies through all maximal non-empty cliques of $\mathfrak{X}$. Each of these boxes $\mathbf{n}_X$ has a conclusion $\vdash \Sigma, \Upsilon_X, \xi$ and we can enlarge $\mathbf{n}_X$ by means of a cut with the box $\mathcal{B}'$: this yields a cut-net $\mathbf{n}'_X$ whose conclusions are now $\vdash \Sigma, \Upsilon_X, \Sigma'$. Then from the $\mathbf{n}'_X$ we form a box $\mathcal{B}''$ whose conclusions are $\Xi \vdash \Sigma, \Sigma'$, which replaces the previous configuration.

positive commutation If $\Xi = \emptyset$ and $\mathcal{B}$ is justified by cut-nets $\mathbf{n}_1, \ldots, \mathbf{n}_k$, but not with the rule introducing ξ to the right, then one of the $\mathbf{n}_i$ has ξ among its conclusions, say $i = 1$. We cut $\mathbf{n}_1$ with $\mathcal{B}'$, so as to get a cut-net $\mathbf{n}'_1$; then we can form a box with $\mathbf{n}'_1, \mathbf{n}_2, \ldots, \mathbf{n}'_k$, say $\mathcal{B}''$, which replaces the previous configuration.

main case If $\Xi = \emptyset$ and $\mathcal{B}$ is justified by cut-nets $\mathbf{n}_1, \ldots, \mathbf{n}_k$, corresponding to a rule introducing ξ to the right and assume that the respective conclusions of $\mathbf{n}_1, \ldots, \mathbf{n}_k$ are $P_{i_1} \vdash \Sigma_1, \ldots, P_{i_k} \vdash \Sigma_k$, and let $X = \{i_1, \ldots, ß_k\}$. Now $\mathcal{B}'$ is justified by a bunch of cut-nets, including one for X, say $\mathbf{n}'$, whose conclusions are $\vdash \Sigma', \Upsilon_X$. Υ_X is equal to $P_{i_1}, \ldots, P_{i_k}$, hence we can link the cut-nets $\mathbf{n}_1, \ldots, \mathbf{n}_k$ with $\mathbf{n}'$, yielding a cut-net $\mathbf{n}$" : this cut-net replaces our configuration.

THEOREM 1

The procedure just described induces a deterministic full cut-elimination (strong normalization).

Proof : It would be out of proportion to prove such an easy result in full details. Let us just give some hints as to the proof :

1. The first thing to check is that all operations preserve the property of being a cut-net : immediate.

2. All possibilities of cut have been considered, so if the algorithm converges, all cuts will be eliminated.

3. The small normalization theorem of [2] can be mimicked : associate a *size* to each box and cut-net, namely :

(a) $s(\mathcal{B}) = 2$ when $\mathcal{B}$ is axiom or hypothesis.

(b) $s(\mathcal{B}) = 1 + \sum s(\mathbf{n}_X)$ when $\mathcal{B}$ is obtained by a « left rule ».

(c) $s(\mathcal{B}) = 1 + (s(\mathbf{n}_{i_1}) + \cdots + s(\mathbf{n}_{i_k}))$, when $\mathcal{B}$ is obtained by a « right rule ».

(d) $s(\mathbf{n}) = \prod s(\mathcal{B}_i)$, when $\mathbf{n}$ is obtained from boxes $\mathcal{B}_i$ by means of cut-links.

It is easy to see that each step makes the size stricly decrease.

4. The last point is Church-Rosser, i.e. the determinism of the computation. This must be obvious to people familiar with general proof-nets [2] or with interaction nets [6].

□

2 Game-Theoretic Interpretation of HC

2.1 Cut-Elimination : Lazy Case

Since the theorem is based on the decreasing of the size, we can investigate a *lazy* version, namely not to use all our transformations. It will converge, i.e. stop, but not on a cut-free paraproof, especially if we restrict our transformations to the main case, and do not even allow to work inside boxes ; in that case, we can drastically simplify the size as :

1. $s(\mathcal{B}) = 0$ when $\mathcal{B}$ is axiom or hypothesis.

2. $s(\mathcal{B}) = 1 + \sup s(\mathbf{n}_X)$ when $\mathcal{B}$ is obtained by a « left rule ».

3. $s(\mathcal{B}) = 1 + (s(\mathbf{n}_{i_1}) + \ldots + s(\mathbf{n}_{i_k}))$, when $\mathcal{B}$ is obtained by a « right rule ».

4. $s(\mathcal{B}) = \sum s(\mathcal{B}_i)$, when $\mathcal{B}$ is obtained from boxes $\mathcal{B}_i$ by means of cut-links.

and we rediscover the familiar linearity of lazy evaluation in the absence of exponentials. But the question is to determine whether this is still interesting. For this we shall only consider cut-nets with an empty conclusion $\vdash$. The main point is that in such a cut-net, at most one cut-link can be simplified : indeed there is exactly one (external) box which has no main door, say $\vdash \Sigma$, and this box is a hypothesis or it is justified by a right introduction of $\xi = \mathfrak{X}P_1, \ldots, P_n$ in which case this formula ξ is linked with a main door of a box $\mathfrak{X}P_1, \ldots, P_n \vdash \Sigma'$, which is also justified by a (here : left) introduction of the same ξ. Then the main case applies, and we are left with a similar configuration... this procedure is purely sequential, i.e. only one transformation can be performed at each step. When the procedure stops, this is always because the major sequent is badly justified (hypothesis) : otherwise, the formula ξ introduced to the right is distinct from $\mathbf{0}^\flat$, hence we are in the main case.
Now we decide to consider the cut-elimination steps as the moves in a particular play. Our first concern is to individuate the players's moves. For this, let us start with the simplest case of a cut between $P \vdash$ and $\vdash P$. After the first step we shall get —say— three boxes ($\vdash P_1, P_5$; $P_1 \vdash$ and $P_5 \vdash$) with two cut-links, P_1, P_5 being immediate subformulas of P. After the second step one of the P_i, say P_5 will be split into —say— three immediate subformulas, say P_{52}, P_{55}, P_{57}, and the cut-net will now consist of five

boxes ($P_{52} \vdash$; $P_{55} \vdash$; $P_{57} \vdash P_1$; $P_1 \vdash$; $\vdash P_{52}, P_{55}, P_{57}$) with four cut-links... Now associate a *parity* to all the hereditary subformulas of P, so that P is even, P_5 is odd, P_{57} is even etc., i.e. the parity of the depth of the subformula. Then one checks that :

1. Each sequent occurring at any stage in the process (i.e. any external box) has the property that the right-hand side has a definite parity, which is opposite to the parity of the left-hand side (if this makes sens). From this we can define a parity for any sequent, e.g. $P_{52} \vdash$ is odd as well as $P_{57} \vdash P_1$ and $\vdash P_1, P_5$, whereas $\vdash P$ and $\vdash P_{52}, P_{55}, P_{57}$ are even.

2. Each of the external cut-nets has a unique major sequent, and we observe that the parity alternates. The first position is even, the second is odd, the third is even etc. We can therefore see the process as the result of a *dispute* between the players *Even* and *Odd*.

3. If one the players stops, i.e. if cut-elimination cannot proceed further, it must be because one of the players didn't play, and this corresponds to a hypothesis. Clearly this player loses. But what about the axiom for $\mathbf{0}^\flat$? Indeed a configuration $\mathbf{0}^\flat \vdash \Sigma_i$ can be created by an appropriate move from a configuration $\vdash \Sigma, Q$, and Σ_i is now captive, in the sense that, since $\mathbf{0}^\flat$ cannot be activated, (remember : there is no right rule for $\mathbf{0}^\flat$!), it will never be possible to proceed further. Thus the fact of giving part of the context Σ to $\mathbf{0}^\flat$ is approximately the same as erasing Σ_i, and of course, erasing Σ_i may help a lot. This is why this move is considered as *unfair*, more precisely to be a *dog's move*. There is however one exception : if Σ_i only consists of occurrences of $\mathbf{0}^\flat$, we can hardly say that some damage has been caused, since this part of the context was already frozen for ever. We can summarize this by declaring that there two ways of losing :

   give up Just stop playing (hypothesis).

   dog's move When playing, create a sequent $\mathbf{0}^\flat \vdash \Sigma, P$, with $P \neq \mathbf{0}^\flat$.

2.2 Soundness

This is not yet the real thing, but just the remark that :

- A paraproof **n** of $\vdash P$ and a paraproof **m** of $P \vdash$ generate a finite dispute, noted **nm**, or **mn** (we prefer not to distinguish in this notation between *Even* and *Odd*).
- If —say— **n** uses no paralogism, then *Even* wins the dispute **nm**.

As expected, soundness is basically a reformulation of cut-elimination.

2.3 Open your Box, Sir !

But we shall have some difficulty to prove a corresponding first approximation to completeness. We ask for something very weak indeed : given a paraproof **n** of a sequent —say $\vdash P$—, is it possible to recover it from all disputes **nm**, when **m** varies through all paraproofs of $P \vdash$? The difficulty is with unopened boxes : if a player can force his opponent to open his boxes in the right way, then he is done.
Assume that *Even* plays following the paraproof **n**, and that *Odd* wants to reconstruct it.

- *Even* replaces $\vdash P$ with $P_1 \vdash$, $P_5 \vdash$, and *Odd*, obeying *perinde ac cadaver* replaces his own $P \vdash$ with $\vdash P_1, P_5$. *Odd* now must decide to check the paraproof above $P_1 \vdash$ or $P_5 \vdash$.

- He decides to see $P_5 \vdash$; he knows that anyway the last rule of *Even* is the rule of a specific connective $\mathfrak{X}$, whose premises are of the form $\vdash \Upsilon_X$. He decides to check above a specific $\vdash \Upsilon_X$, and he chooses —say— $X = \{2, 5, 7\}$. Then *Even* obeys in turn like a Jesuit and the new major sequent $\vdash P_{52}, P_{55}, P_{57}$ is created...

- Then *Even* must play or give up. If he plays, then *Odd* goes on as before.

- Eventually, a full branch of the tree will be explored.

Indeed, the exploration just described corresponds to a specific **nm** : the paraproof **m** starts with a left-introduction rule, corresponding to a specific synthetic connective, it must have a certain number of premises, including $\vdash \Upsilon_{\{1,5\}}$, that we have actually used... but what about the premise —say— $\vdash \Upsilon_{\{4,6,9\}}$, if such a premise is needed ? This is simple, *Odd* gives up (admits it as a hypothesis). In other terms, *Odd* can explore paraproofs only because there are enough paralogisms, here « give up ».
Then the full structure can be reconstructed by allowing *Odd* to make other trials, i.e. the paraproof **n** can been reconstructed from the disputes **nm**. But there is still a pending question : if *Even* wins all disputes **nm**, does this mean that **n** is a real (i.e. correct) proof ? In fact a strange phenomenon might perhaps happen when *Odd* explores a branch : at some moment he couldn't choose a move (i.e. a right introduction) corresponding to the formula Q he would like to explore, to the effect that *Even* would win, but perhaps only for bad reasons. In fact there could only be two possibilities :

1. Q begins with $\mathfrak{X}$, but there is no rule at all introducing Q to the right : we are in the case of the constant $\mathbf{0}$, the synthetic 0-ary connective. *Odd* would like to question $\mathbf{0} \vdash \Sigma$ in **n**, he cannot, but anyway this sequent is provable by a left introduction (no premise at all).

2. Q is $\mathbf{0}^\flat$ and remember that there is no rule introducing $\mathbf{0}^\flat$ to the right. But in this case, *Odd* wants to check something like $\mathbf{0}^\flat \vdash \Sigma$ in **n**. But the presence of such a sequent in **n** can only be attributed to dog's play, unless Σ is made of occurrences of $\mathbf{0}^\flat$. In other terms, either *Even* has already lost and *Odd* is wasting his time, or $\mathbf{0}^\flat \vdash \Sigma$ is a correct axiom.

Since our potential objection didn't work, **n** is a real proof as an easy consequence of the additional remark that **n** is finite.
Let us reflect a little more on dog's play : assume that *Even* wants to prove $\perp \otimes \perp$. Then he starts splitting the tensor, and we get the configuration $P \vdash$, $Q \vdash$ (for *Even*) against $\vdash P, Q$ (for *Odd*), with $P = Q = \mathbf{1}$. Now if the poor *Odd* cannot play the dog, he must give up, and *Even* has won too easily. So *Odd* will be allowed to play —say— $\mathbf{0}^\flat \vdash P$ and *Even* will receive $\vdash \mathbf{0}^\flat$, on which he must give up, hence he loses. Now it would be excessive to give the victory to *Odd* : since he « killed P » he loses too.
Dog's play is not quite using a wrong rule, but using a rule in such a way that one premise cannot be decently proven : typically, prove $\vdash P^\perp \otimes \mathbf{1}, \mathbf{1}$ from $P \vdash$ and $\mathbf{0}^\flat \vdash \mathbf{1}$ is using a correct rule... but introducing an « impossible » premise.

2.4 Projection

We now come to the syntactical aspect of the most important artefact, namely *projection.*

Assume for instance that our starting configuration is $P \vdash$, $Q \vdash$ (for *Even*) against $\vdash P, Q$ (for *Odd*). Now the dispute proceeds ; but would it be possible to produce a relativized dispute, i.e. a dispute between $P \vdash$, and $\vdash P$?. The answer is YES.

Let $\mathfrak{m}$ be one of the configurations of the dispute ; the formulas occurring in $\mathfrak{m}$ are either subformulas of P or subformulas of Q. We decide to eliminate all subformulas $\mathbf{q}$ of Q as follows : if we find two boxes $\Xi \vdash \Sigma, \mathbf{q}$ and $\mathbf{q} \vdash \Sigma'$, we replace them with $\Xi \vdash \Sigma, \Sigma'$. We do this *ad nauseam* until we get a configuration made only of subformulas of P : these configurations are the *projections* on P of the original ones.

Now consider any move, making us pass from a configuration to another. They fall into 4 classes, for which we indicate what happens to the respective projections of the initial and final configurations.

P-Even (active) *Even* plays, with the focus in a subformula of P. Then this can mimicked by the same move.

Q-Even (passive) *Even* plays, with the focus in a subformula of Q. This leaves no trace on the projections.

Q-Odd (passive) *Odd* plays, with the focus in a subformula of Q. This move is not visible on the projection.

P-Odd (active) *Odd* plays, with the focus on a subformula of P. Then it is possible to find a move of *Odd*, with the same focus etc., which acts in the right way on the projections.

In other terms a dispute can be projected as a dispute.

Projection is associative : if we had started with $P \vdash$ and $Q \vdash$ and $R \vdash$ (for *Even*) against $\vdash P, Q, R$ (for *Odd*), then we could have projected on P in three ways, either directly, or by first projecting on P, Q or on P, R : the three methods yield the same projection.

Projection is indeed the only convincing way to explain eager cut-elimination :

THEOREM 2

Let $\mathbf{l}, \mathbf{n}, \mathbf{m}$ *be respective cut-free paraproofs of* $\vdash P, Q$ *and* $P \vdash$ *and* $Q \vdash$ *; then we can consider on one side the dispute* $\mathbf{lnm}$ *obtained by means of two cut-links, and project it on* P*, so as to get a dispute* $\mathbf{lnm}\lceil P$*. We can also make a single cut-link on* Q *and obtain through eager cut-elimination, a cut-free paraproof* $\mathbf{l}(\mathbf{m})$ *of* $\vdash P$*, and we can therefore produce a dispute* $\mathbf{l}(\mathbf{m})\mathbf{n}$*. Then*

$$\mathbf{lnm}\lceil P = \mathbf{l}(\mathbf{m})\mathbf{n}$$

Proof : Straightforward. □

2.5 The Game-Theoretic Translation

We are almost done with this side of the tunnel. The ultimate thing is to remove syntax : for this we decide to specialize our construction w.r.t. a formula P of **HC**, and our results —completeness, soundness— will refer to paraproofs of $\vdash P$ or $P \vdash$.
We now consider the full tree of finite sequences of integers : I represent each subformula of P by an element of the tree, typically $P = < 0 >$. If a subformula $Q = \mathfrak{X}R_1 \ldots R_n$ is represented by s, then we choose distinct indices $i_1, \ldots, i_n$, and represent R_1 by $s * i_1$, R_n by $s * i_n$. The parity will correspond to the length of the sequence, i.e. $< i_0, \ldots, i_n >$ has the parity of n.
In fact we are not completely free in the choice of the indices : we must first split $\mathbb{N}$ into two infinite subsets (even numbers and odd numbers if you want, but call them « simple » and « multiple »). Now, i_k will be chosen simple when $R_k \neq \mathbf{0}^\flat$, multiple otherwise.
Now our analysis led us to the point when the disputes **nm** can be described as particular plays in a game involving this tree. Our problem is now to find an alternative description of the same thing.

3 Disputes

3.1 Fingers, Hands and Blokes

DEFINITION 7
Fingers are the elements of a denumerable set, say $\mathbb{N}$ *; we distinguish between* simple *and* multiple *fingers, i.e. by writing* $\mathbb{N}$ *as the union of two infinite disjoint subsets, e.g. even and odd numbers.*
$\mathbb{H}$ *is the tree of all finite sequences* $<x_0, \ldots, x_{n-1}>$*, where* $x_i \in \mathbb{N}$ *are fingers. The elements of* $\mathbb{H}$ *of length* $\neq 0$ *are called* hands *; according to the parity of* $n-1$ *a hand is* even *or* odd*. If we use « $*$ » for concatenation, then* $\sigma * \tau \leqslant \sigma$ *defines an order, the* subhand *relation : if* $\tau \neq <>$ *one speaks of a strict subhand, if* $\tau = <i>$*, of an immediate subhand ; in that case parity alternates, e.g. an immediate subhand* $\sigma * i$ *of an even hand* σ *is odd.*
The hands $s*i$ *with* i *simple are* simple*, whereas hands* $s*i$ *with* i *multiple are* multiple.

DEFINITION 8
A bloke $\Xi \vdash \Sigma$ *consists in :*

1. *Two finite sets of hands* Ξ, Σ *; these hands must be pairwise incomparable and* $\Xi \cup \Sigma$ *must be non-empty*
2. *The hands in* Σ *have the same parity ;*
3. Ξ *is either empty or consists of a single hand* ξ *of parity opposite to* Σ *(if non empty) ; in the first case the bloke is* major*, otherwise it is* minor *; the hand* ξ *of the minor bloke* $\mathfrak{b} = \xi \vdash \Sigma$ *is the* tutor *of* $\mathfrak{b}$.

The common parity of Σ *and/or the parity opposite to* Ξ *is the* parity *of the bloke ; there are therefore* even *blokes and* odd *blokes.*
A bloke $\xi \vdash \Sigma$ *with* ξ *multiple is said to be* multiple *; other blokes are* simple*. A bloke is* schizoid *when it is multiple, but its right-hand side contains at least one simple hand.*

We shall use the familiar conventions of sequent calculus, e.g. Σ, Σ' for (disjoint) union, σ instead of $\{\sigma\}$, so that we can write $\vdash \Sigma, \sigma$ or $\xi \vdash \Sigma, \sigma$ etc.

3.2 Mauls

DEFINITION 9
The full maul $\mathbb{M}$ *consists in all finite sequences of hands* $<\sigma_0, \ldots, \sigma_{n-1}>$. *This tree is ordered as usual by :* $<\sigma_0, \ldots, \sigma_{n+m-1}> \leqslant <\sigma_0, \ldots, \sigma_{n-1}>$.

DEFINITION 10
An even maul $\mathfrak{m}$ *is a finite subtree of* $\mathbb{M}$ *such that :*

1. *$\mathfrak{m}$ is non-trivial, i.e. non restricted to its root* $<>$
2. *If a hand σ occurs in $\mathfrak{m}$, i.e. belongs to some* $<\sigma_0, \ldots, \sigma_{n-1}, \sigma> \in \mathfrak{m}$, *then its parity is equal to the parity of n.*
3. *The hands occurring in $\mathfrak{m}$ are pairwise incomparable, in particular there is at most one sequence* $<\sigma_0, \ldots, \sigma_{n-1}, \sigma> \in \mathfrak{m}$ *ending with σ.*

An odd maul is defined in the same way, except that the parity of σ such that $<\sigma_0, \ldots, \sigma_{n-1}, \sigma> \in \mathfrak{m}$ *is opposite to the parity of n.*

We can associate blokes to a maul $\mathfrak{m}$, namely :

1. The bloke $\vdash \Sigma$, with $\Sigma = \{\sigma; <\sigma> \in \mathfrak{m}\}$; this bloke is the unique *major bloke* of $\mathfrak{m}$. The *parity* of $\mathfrak{m}$ is equal to the parity of its major bloke.
2. For each ξ occurring in $\mathfrak{m}$ through the sequence $\ell = <\sigma_0, \ldots, \sigma_{n-1}, \xi> \in \mathfrak{m}$, the bloke $\xi \vdash \Sigma$, with $\Sigma = \{\sigma; \ell * \sigma \in \mathfrak{m}\}$. These are the *minor blokes* of $\mathfrak{m}$.

Conversely, observe that a maul $\mathfrak{m}$ can be recovered from its blokes : $<\sigma_0, \ldots, \sigma_n> \in \mathfrak{m}$ iff σ_0 belongs to the major bloke of $\mathfrak{m}$ and for each $i < n$ there is a minor bloke $\sigma_i \vdash \Sigma$ in $\mathfrak{m}$ with $\sigma_{i+1} \in \Sigma$.

EXAMPLE 3.2.1
Given a bloke $\Xi \vdash \Sigma$ we can form a maul by adding the atomic blokes $\sigma \vdash$ (for $\sigma \in \Sigma$) and $\vdash \xi$ (for $\xi \in \Xi$). This maul is the *standard maul* associated with $\Xi \vdash \Sigma$, and we shall abusively note it $\Xi \vdash \Sigma$.

REMARK 3.2.1
An alternative presentation of a maul is a forest of hands (a *forest* is a partial order such that for each x the set of points greater than x is linearily ordered). In that case the major bloke is the set of maximal elements of the forest, whereas the minor bloke $\xi \vdash \Sigma$ gives the set Σ of immediate predecessors of ξ.

It is sometimes convenient to introduce the *unproper maul*, namely the trivial tree reduced to its root.

3.3 Actions and Disputes

DEFINITION 11
Let $\mathfrak{m}$ *be a maul, with major bloke* $\vdash \Sigma$; *an* action κ *in* $\mathfrak{m}$ *consists in the following data :*

1. *A hand* $\xi \in \Sigma$, *the* focus *of the action ; we can therefore write* $\Sigma = \Sigma', \xi$
2. *A non-empty finite subset* I *of* $\mathbb{N}$; *let* $\Xi = \{\xi * i; i \in I\}$
3. *For each* $i \in I$ *a bloke* $\xi * i \vdash \Sigma_i$; *we require* Σ' *to be the disjoint union of the* Σ_i.

DEFINITION 12
The result $\mathfrak{m}' = \kappa(\mathfrak{m})$ *of the action* κ *is obtained as follows :* $\mathfrak{m}$ *has a unique bloke of the form* $\xi \vdash \Upsilon$; *then* $\kappa(\mathfrak{m})$ *has exactly the same blokes as* $\mathfrak{m}$, *except that* $\vdash \Sigma$ *is replaced with the* $\xi * i \vdash \Sigma_i$ *and* $\xi \vdash \Upsilon$ *is replaced with* $\vdash \Upsilon, \Xi$.

A direct description of $\mathfrak{m}'$ is the set of :

1. For any sequence $<\xi, \sigma_1, \ldots, \sigma_n> \in \mathfrak{m}$, the sequence $<\sigma_1, \ldots, \sigma_n>$
2. For any sequence $<\sigma_0, \ldots, \sigma_n> \in \mathfrak{m}$, with $\sigma_0 \in \Sigma_i$, the sequence $<\xi_i, \sigma_0, \ldots, \sigma_n>$.

An action changes the parity of the maul. In images, if $\mathfrak{m}$ is even, then *Even* acts, and produces $\mathfrak{m}'$ which is odd ; then *Odd* may act etc.

DEFINITION 13
A dispute *is a finite sequence* $[\mathfrak{m}_0, \ldots, \mathfrak{m}_p]$, *such that* $\mathfrak{m}_{i+1} = \kappa_i(\mathfrak{m}_i)$ *for appropriate actions* κ_i.
$\mathfrak{m}_0$ *is the* initial *maul of the action,* $\mathfrak{m}_p$ *its* final *maul ;* p *is the* length *(duration ?) of the dispute.*

The sequence of actions can be recovered from the sequence of mauls : this is why we never indicate the actions of a dispute.

3.4 Output of a Dispute

DEFINITION 14
A dispute $\mathfrak{D}$ *is* lost *by* Odd *when one of the following holds :*

schizoid bloke *One of the odd blokes is of the form* $\xi \vdash \Sigma, \eta$, *with* ξ *multiple and* η *simple.*

give up *The last maul is odd.*

We define similarly the notion of a dispute lost by Even. *A dispute has necessarily at least one loser, and by complement, at most one* winner.

In general the starting maul is simple and contains no multiple hand. Then a schizoid odd bloke $\xi \vdash \Sigma, \eta$, with ξ multiple and η simple must have been created by an action of *Odd*, what we call a *dog's move.*
In order to win, *Even* must always be fair play, and should not give up, i.e. must be the last to play. Of course unfair play will often be the only way to avoid giving up, at the price of a draw. This is why we speak of « dog's move », see [3].

3.5 Projections

DEFINITION 15
Let $X, Y \subset \mathbb{H}$ be two disjoint sets of hands closed under the subhand relation. X, Y is said to realize an even splitting *of a maul $\mathfrak{m}$ when the following holds :*

1. *Every hand occurring in $\mathfrak{m}$ belongs to $X \cup Y$*
2. *If an even bloke of $\mathfrak{m}$ contains a hand of X, then all hands of the bloke are included in X. Odd splittings are defined in the same way.*

A splitting is non-trivial *when both X and Y meet $\mathfrak{m}$.*

EXAMPLE 3.5.1
An even bloke of $\mathfrak{m}$ determines an even splitting : let X be the set of subhands of the bloke and Y be the set of subhands of the other even blokes.

DEFINITION 16
To any sequence in $\ell \in \mathfrak{m}$ we associate the projected *sequence $\ell \upharpoonright X$ in which only the elements of X remain. Then the* projection *of the maul $\mathfrak{m}$ on X is defined as $\mathfrak{m} \upharpoonright X = \{\ell \upharpoonright X; \ell \in \mathfrak{m}\}$. Particular cases : projection on a bloke $\mathfrak{b}$ of $\mathfrak{m}$, noted $\mathfrak{m} \upharpoonright \mathfrak{b}$, and in case of an atomic bloke $\xi \vdash$ or $\vdash \xi$ of $\mathfrak{m}$, projection on the hand ξ, noted $\mathfrak{m}$, $\mathfrak{m} \upharpoonright \xi$.*

Another description of projection is by iterated removals, i.e. « use of cut » : removing one hand σ from a maul consists in replacing the two blokes containing σ, i.e. $\Xi \vdash \Sigma, \sigma$ and $\sigma \vdash \Upsilon$ by $\Xi \vdash \Sigma, \Upsilon$ (which need not be a bloke since it might be empty or have no definite parity). Removing several hands is the iteration of the previous algorithm ; the result does not depend on the order of the removals. Projecting $\mathfrak{m}$ on X consists in removing all hands which do not belong to X.

PROPOSITION 3
Assume that X, Y realize a non-trivial splitting (even or odd) of $\mathfrak{m}$; then $\mathfrak{m} \upharpoonright X$ is a maul. Indeed $\mathfrak{m} \upharpoonright X$ has the same parity as $\mathfrak{m}$ except when $\mathfrak{m}$ is even and the major bloke of $\mathfrak{m}$ is in Y, in which case $\mathfrak{m} \upharpoonright X$ is odd.

Proof : The splitting condition ensures that, whenever σ disappears, then a full bloke containing σ disappears too. The result therefore follows from the fact that the removal of a full bloke $\Xi \vdash \Sigma$ preserves the fact of being a maul (maybe unproper) ; in fact all blokes containing one of the hands of the —say— even bloke $\Xi \vdash \Sigma$ are replaced with an odd bloke. If the splitting is non-trivial, we get a proper maul. The checking of the parities offers no difficulty. □

PROPOSITION 4
Assume that X, Y realize a non-trivial splitting (even or odd) of $\mathfrak{m}$, and let $\mathfrak{m}' = \mathfrak{m} \upharpoonright X$. Then one can define for each hand ξ occurring in $\mathfrak{m}$ a finite set $X(\xi)$ of hands of X with the following property : if we extend the map to sets of hands by $X(\Sigma) = \bigcup_{\sigma \in \Sigma} X(\sigma)$, then

1. *If $\vdash \Sigma$ is the major bloke of $\mathfrak{m}$ then $\vdash X(\Sigma)$ is the major bloke of $\mathfrak{m}'$*
2. *If $\xi \in X$ and $\xi \vdash \Sigma$ is a minor bloke in $\mathfrak{m}$, then $\xi \vdash X(\Sigma)$ is a minor bloke in $\mathfrak{m}'$*
3. *If $\xi \notin X$ and $\xi \vdash \Sigma$ is a minor bloke in $\mathfrak{m}$, then $X(\xi) = X(\Sigma)$*

Proof : If $\ell * \xi \in \mathfrak{m}$, then we can consider all its extensions $\ell * \xi * \cdots * \sigma \in \mathfrak{m}$ such that $\sigma \in X$ and which are maximal, i.e. such that no subextension ends in X ; $X(\xi)$ is defined as the set of the hands σ obtained in this way. The properties are obvious. □

EXAMPLE 3.5.2
If $\xi \in X$, then $X(\xi) = \{\xi\}$.

PROPOSITION 5
If X, Y realize an even splitting of $\mathfrak{m}$ and $\mathfrak{m}'$ is the result of an action from $\mathfrak{m}$, then X, Y realize an even splitting of $\mathfrak{m}'$.

Proof : Each new bloke in $\mathfrak{m}'$ is made of « subblokes » of a bloke of $\mathfrak{m}$ with the same parity. This is enough for the result. □

We investigate the behavior of an action $\kappa = (\xi, \Sigma_i)$ under non-trivial projection :

X-Even If the focus ξ of κ is in X and $\mathfrak{m}$ is even, then the major bloke of $\mathfrak{m}$ is included in X and $\mathfrak{m}' \upharpoonright X = \kappa(\mathfrak{m} \upharpoonright X)$

X-Odd If the focus ξ of κ is in X and $\mathfrak{m}$ is odd, then projection replaces the major bloke $\vdash \Sigma', \xi$ by $\vdash X(\Sigma'), \xi$. If κ' is the action with the same focus, the same I, but with $X(\Sigma_i)$ instead of Σ_i, then clearly $\mathfrak{m}' \upharpoonright X = \kappa'(\mathfrak{m} \upharpoonright X)$.

Y-Even If the focus of κ is not in X and $\mathfrak{m}$ is even, then $\mathfrak{m}' \upharpoonright X = \mathfrak{m} \upharpoonright X$ and the action induces nothing.

Y-Odd If the focus of κ is not in X and $\mathfrak{m}$ is odd : as above, nothing.

In other terms an action κ is *projected* into $\kappa \upharpoonright X$, which is either an action or nothing. In case of consecutive actions, observe that, due to alternation of parities, cases *X-Even* or *Y-Even* can only be followed by cases *X-Odd* or *Y-Odd* ; conversely case *X-Odd* can only be followed by case *X-Even*, and case *Y-Odd* can only be followed by case *Y-Even*. Let $\mathfrak{D} = [\mathfrak{m}_0, \ldots, \mathfrak{m}_p]$ be a dispute and assume that X, Y realize a non-trivial splitting (—say even—) of the initial maul ; then we can consider $[\mathfrak{m}_0 \upharpoonright X, \ldots, \mathfrak{m}_p \upharpoonright X]$ which is a sequence of mauls. Each $\kappa_i \upharpoonright X$ is either an action or nothing ; and let $i_1, \ldots, i_k$ is the increasing list of those which are actions. Then, between two consecutive mauls of the sequence $[\mathfrak{m}_0 \upharpoonright X, \mathfrak{m}_{i_1+1} \upharpoonright X, \ldots, \mathfrak{m}_{i_k+1} \upharpoonright X]$, only action κ_k matters ; this sequence is therefore a dispute, and we have indeed proved the :

PROPOSITION 6
The sequence $[\mathfrak{m}_0 \upharpoonright X, \mathfrak{m}_{i_1+1} \upharpoonright X, \ldots, \mathfrak{m}_{i_k+1} \upharpoonright X]$, where $i_1, \ldots, i_k$ is the subsequence made of those i such that the focus of κ_i belongs to X, is a dispute, called the projection *of $[\mathfrak{m}_0, \ldots, \mathfrak{m}_p]$. Notation : $[\mathfrak{m}_0, \ldots, \mathfrak{m}_p] \upharpoonright X$. Particular case : projection on a bloke of $\mathfrak{m}_0$, on a hand etc.*

THEOREM 3
Let $\mathfrak{D}$ be a dispute, let X, Y realize a non-trivial even splitting of its initial maul $\mathfrak{m}$ and let $\mathfrak{E}$, $\mathfrak{F}$ be the respective projections of the disputes on X and Y then :

1. *If* Even *wins $\mathfrak{D}$, then it wins both $\mathfrak{E}$ and $\mathfrak{F}$.*
2. *If* Even *wins both $\mathfrak{E}$ and $\mathfrak{F}$, then it wins $\mathfrak{D}$.*

3. *If* Odd *wins* $\mathfrak{D}$ *and* Even *wins the projection* $\mathfrak{E}$, *then* Odd *wins the projection* $\mathfrak{F}$.

Proof : 1. Since *Even* wins, all even blokes are fair ; moreover, in the projected dispute, even blokes disappear or remain the same. Let us now look at the last maul of the projected dispute : if it is even, then its major bloke is in X and it comes from an even maul (proposition 3) in the original dispute, i.e. a kind *X-Even*, but since *Even* wins, it cannot be the final maul of the original dispute.

2. Similar argument.

3. An odd bloke in $\mathfrak{F}$ comes from an odd bloke in the original dispute. Assume this bloke to be unfair : then it is of the form $\xi \vdash \Sigma, \eta$, with ξ multiple and η simple, and it has been obtained by iterated cuts, starting with an odd bloke $\xi \vdash \Sigma'$, with even blokes (but located in X) and other odd blokes. Since *Even* wins the projection on X, all these blokes are fair, i.e. the result of the cuts is fair. If the last maul of the dispute $\mathfrak{F}$ is odd, then it comes from an odd maul in the original dispute (proposition 3) (impossible, since it is won by *Odd*) or from an even maul with major bloke in X (impossible, since *Even* wins the projection on X).

□

4 Designs and Behaviors

4.1 Chronicles and Agendas

Our basic idea is to present a strategy $\mathcal{S}$ as the set of all disputes $\mathcal{ST}$ generated by a counterstrategy $\mathcal{T}$. For this we shall equip disputes with a structure of coherent space, and try to define a strategy as any *clique* of the space ; since a clique and an anticlique intersect on at most one point, this seems to be promising. Now what could be the notion of coherence ? This is simple : if two disputes are distinct, it is because one the two players made a different action, and even coherence should correspond to the case where *Odd* was the first one to change his mind. This notion has the nice property of defining an unambiguous first action, in case the initial maul is even... But it doesn't work : the notion is not compatible with projection. To understand this essential point, take the example of two disputes $\mathfrak{D}, \mathfrak{E}$, which first differ on an action of type *Odd* ; when I project them on X, this part cannot be seen (the view ?, see below), which shows that *Even* cannot take this as a pretext to play different actions of kind *X-Even* afterwards. This is why the notion of coherence must be localized, and this leads to chronicles and agendas. By the way we are not quite producing a coherent space, since $\mathfrak{D}, \mathfrak{E}$ might be neither evenly or oddly coherent.
The notions defined below are presumably related to the *views* of « H^2O-games » introduced by **H**anno Nickau [7] and **H**yland & **O**ng [5].

DEFINITION 17
Let $\mathfrak{D} = [\mathfrak{m}_0, \ldots, \mathfrak{m}_p]$ *be a dispute, and let* $\mathbf{b}$ *be a bloke in* $\mathfrak{m}_{i+1}$ *which is not in* $\mathfrak{m}_i$ *(there is at most one such* i*), then* $\mathbf{b}$ *has a well-defined* father *in* $\mathfrak{m}_i$, *namely a bloke* $\mathbf{a}$ *of the same parity (*$\mathbf{b}$ *is said to be a* son *of* $\mathbf{a}$*) : with the notation of definition 12 for the action* κ_i

1. *If* $\mathbf{b}$ *is* $\vdash \Upsilon, \Xi$, $\mathbf{a}$ *is* $\xi \vdash \Upsilon$

2. *If* $\mathbf{b}$ *is* $\xi_i \vdash \Sigma_i$, $\mathbf{a}$ *is* $\vdash \Sigma, \xi$

A chronicle *is a sequence* $<\mathbf{a}_0; \ldots; \mathbf{a}_{k-1}>$ *of blokes such that* $\mathbf{a}_i$ *is the father of* $\mathbf{a}_{i+1}$ *for each* $i < k-2$, *and such that, in case* $k \neq 0$, $\mathbf{a}_0$ *is a bloke of* $\mathfrak{m}_0$, *in which case it is called the chronicle of* $\mathbf{a}_{k-1}$. *Each non-zero chronicle has a well-defined parity, and we decide to give both parities to the empty chronicle.*
The even agenda *of* $\mathfrak{D}$ *is the tree of its even chronicles. The odd agenda is defined in the same way.*

PROPOSITION 7

A dispute is completely determined by its agendas (both of them are needed).

Proof : The chronicles of length 1 give the blokes of $\mathfrak{m}_0$; then if the initial maul is —say odd—, with major bloke $\mathbf{a}$, there is a first action exactly when there is a chronicle of length 2, $<\mathbf{a}; \xi * i \vdash \Sigma_i>$, in which case we know the focus ξ of this rule. Consider all other chronicles of length 2 starting with $\mathbf{a}$; they are of the form $<\mathbf{a}; \xi * j \vdash \Sigma_j>$, which completely determines the first action, etc. □

4.2 Coherence

DEFINITION 18

Two disputes $\mathfrak{D} = [\mathfrak{n}_0, \ldots, \mathfrak{n}_p]$ *and* $\mathfrak{E} = [\mathfrak{n}_0 = \mathfrak{m}_0, \ldots, \mathfrak{m}_q]$ *are* evenly coherent *when the following holds :* $\mathfrak{n}_0 = \mathfrak{m}_0$ *and whenever an even bloke* $\vdash \Sigma$ *occurs in both disputes with the same chronicle, then it has the same sons in both disputes. Odd coherence is defined in a similar way.*

PROPOSITION 8

If two disputes $[\mathfrak{n}_0, \ldots, \mathfrak{n}_p]$ *and* $[\mathfrak{m}_0, \ldots, \mathfrak{m}_q]$ *share the same initial action* κ, *i.e.*
$\mathfrak{n}_1 = \mathfrak{m}_1$, *then they are evenly coherent iff their continuations* $[\mathfrak{n}_1, \ldots, \mathfrak{n}_p]$ *and* $[\mathfrak{m}_1, \ldots, \mathfrak{m}_q]$ *are evenly coherent.*

Proof : Immediate. □

PROPOSITION 9

If two disputes $\mathfrak{D}$ *and* $\mathfrak{E}$ *start with an even maul and are evenly coherent, then either they are both of length* 0, *or they share the same first action.*

Proof : If $\mathfrak{D}$ has a first action κ, then its even agenda contains all chronicles $<\vdash \Sigma, \xi; \xi * i \vdash \Sigma_i>$ corresponding to κ, and since the even agenda of $\mathfrak{E}$ contains $<\vdash \Sigma, \xi>$, all these chronicles must belong to the even agenda of $\mathfrak{E}$. This forces the existence of a first action in $\mathfrak{E}$, with the same focus ξ, etc. □

COROLLARY 3.1

Two disputes are both evenly and oddly coherent iff they are equal.

PROPOSITION 10

If two disputes $\mathfrak{D}$ *and* $\mathfrak{E} = [\mathfrak{m}_0, \ldots, \mathfrak{m}_p]$ *are evenly coherent and* $q < p$ *is such that* $\mathfrak{m}_q$ *is odd, then* $\mathfrak{D}$ *and* $\mathfrak{F} = [\mathfrak{m}_0, \ldots, \mathfrak{m}_q]$ *are evenly coherent.*

Proof : The restriction to q means that some chronicles of $\mathfrak{E}$ are shortened. So let us consider a bloke $\mathbf{a} = \vdash \Sigma$ whose chronicles belongs to the even agendas of $\mathfrak{D}$ and $\mathfrak{F}$; then it has the same sons in the even agendas of $\mathfrak{D}$ and $\mathfrak{E}$. If $\mathbf{a}$ has a son in the even agenda of $\mathfrak{E}$, observe that the action producing this son must be done without delay, i.e. it is a κ_r with $r \leqslant q$, and since $r = q$ is impossible for questions of parity, the son is still in the agenda of $\mathfrak{F}$. □

COROLLARY 3.2

If $\mathfrak{m}$ is even, then the trivial dispute « give up » $[\mathfrak{m}]$ is evenly coherent only with itself ; if $\mathfrak{m}$ is odd, it is evenly coherent with anybody.

The next result expounds the behavior of coherence under projection.

THEOREM 4

Let $\mathfrak{D} = [\mathfrak{n}_0, \ldots, \mathfrak{n}_p]$ and $\mathfrak{E} = [\mathfrak{m}_0, \ldots, \mathfrak{m}_q]$ be two disputes with the same initial maul $\mathfrak{n}_0 = \mathfrak{m}_0 = \mathfrak{m}$. Assume that X, Y realizes a non-trivial even splitting of $\mathfrak{m}$, and let $\mathfrak{D}'$, $\mathfrak{D}''$, $\mathfrak{E}'$ and $\mathfrak{E}''$ be the projections $\mathfrak{D} \upharpoonright X$, $\mathfrak{D} \upharpoonright Y$, $\mathfrak{E} \upharpoonright X$, $\mathfrak{E} \upharpoonright Y$. Then :

1. *If $\mathfrak{D}$ and $\mathfrak{E}$ are evenly coherent, so are $\mathfrak{D}'$ and $\mathfrak{E}'$.*
2. *Conversely if $\mathfrak{D}'$ and $\mathfrak{E}'$ are evenly coherent, as well as $\mathfrak{D}''$ and $\mathfrak{E}''$, so are $\mathfrak{D}$ and $\mathfrak{E}$.*
3. *If $\mathfrak{D}$ and $\mathfrak{E}$ are oddly coherent, if $\mathfrak{D}'$ and $\mathfrak{E}'$ are evenly coherent, then $\mathfrak{D}''$ and $\mathfrak{E}''$ are oddly coherent.*
4. *Moreover, in case 3, if $\mathfrak{D}$ and $\mathfrak{E}$ are distinct so are their projections $\mathfrak{D}''$ and $\mathfrak{E}''$.*

Proof : All proofs are by induction on $\inf(p, q)$:

1. Due to splitting, the even agendas of the projections on X are just the subtrees containing only the chronicles starting with a bloke in X.
2. Similar argument.
3. We consider several cases, according to the type of the first action :
   (a) If $\mathfrak{m} \upharpoonright Y$ is odd and $\mathfrak{m}$ is odd as well, then $\mathfrak{D}, \mathfrak{E}$ have a common initial action, leading to $\mathfrak{m}' = \mathfrak{n}_1 = \mathfrak{m}_1$; then the continuations $[\mathfrak{n}_1, \ldots, \mathfrak{n}_p]$ and $[\mathfrak{m}_1, \ldots, \mathfrak{m}_q]$ are oddly coherent, and we can apply the induction hypothesis.
   (b) If $\mathfrak{m}$ is even and its major bloke is in X, then by even coherence of $\mathfrak{D}', \mathfrak{E}'$, we can deduce that the two disputes share the same initial action, and conclude as above.
   (c) If $\mathfrak{m} \upharpoonright Y$ is even, then $\mathfrak{m}$ is even, with a major bloke in Y.
      - We first consider the case where $\mathfrak{m} \upharpoonright Y$ has only one odd bloke $\mathbf{a} = \xi \vdash \Sigma$. Due to even splitting, all even blokes located in Y are atomic. Therefore the major bloke of $\mathfrak{m} \upharpoonright Y$ is $\vdash \xi$ and the initial actions can be reconstructed from the odd agendas : the odd agendas of $\mathfrak{D}''$, $\mathfrak{E}''$ respectively contain $\langle \mathbf{a}; \vdash \Sigma, \Upsilon \rangle, \langle \mathbf{a}; \vdash \Sigma, \Upsilon' \rangle$, for appropriate Υ, Υ' which do define the first actions. If $\Upsilon = \Upsilon'$, then we can conclude as above. Otherwise, $\langle \mathbf{a} \rangle$ is the chronicle in both agendas, we conclude that $\mathfrak{D}''$, $\mathfrak{E}''$ are oddly coherent.

- Otherwise, we use part 2 of the theorem : $\mathfrak{D}'', \mathfrak{E}''$ are coherent iff for any odd bloke $\mathbf{a}$ in $\mathfrak{m} \upharpoonright Y$, $\mathfrak{D}'' \upharpoonright \mathbf{a}$ and $\mathfrak{E}'' \upharpoonright \mathbf{a}$ are oddly coherent. So let us select such an $\mathbf{a}$. $\mathbf{a}$ is obtained from odd blokes $\mathbf{b}_1, \ldots, \mathbf{b}_k$ of $\mathfrak{m}$, and we can consider all even blokes $\mathbf{c}_1, \ldots, \mathbf{c}_l$ which shake a hand of X with some $\mathbf{b}_i$: if we take all hands occurring in some $\mathbf{c}_i$ or $\mathbf{b}_j$ and their « subhands », we get a set Z part of an odd splitting Z, T of $\mathfrak{m}$ such that the only hands in $Z \cap Y$ occur in $\mathbf{a}$ and whenever an even bloke meets $Z \cap X$ it is contained in it. In fact $(\mathfrak{m} \upharpoonright Y) \upharpoonright \mathbf{a} = (\mathfrak{m} \upharpoonright Z) \upharpoonright Z \cap Y$ and $(\mathfrak{m} \upharpoonright Z) \upharpoonright Z \cap X = \mathfrak{m} \upharpoonright Z \cap X = (\mathfrak{m} \upharpoonright X) \upharpoonright Z \cap X$.
  From this we see that the disputes projected on Z, and the even splitting $X \cap Z, Y \cap Z$, enjoy the hypotheses of the theorem ; moreover $(\mathfrak{m} \upharpoonright Z) \upharpoonright Z \cap Y$ has a unique odd bloke, and we have reduced the problem to the case already treated, whereas $\inf(p, q)$ remains unchanged, but this case has already been treated.

4. If $\mathfrak{D}'' = \mathfrak{E}''$, they are evenly coherent and since $\mathfrak{D}'$ and $\mathfrak{E}'$ are evenly coherent the two disputes are evenly coherent. So they are equal.

□

4.3 Designs

DEFINITION 19
An even design, *is a non-empty set $\mathcal{S}$ of disputes which are pairwise evenly coherent, and which is closed under odd restrictions : if $[\mathfrak{m}_0, \ldots, \mathfrak{m}_p] \in \mathcal{S}$ and $q < p$ is such that $\mathfrak{m}_q$ is odd, then $[\mathfrak{m}_0, \ldots, \mathfrak{m}_q] \in \mathcal{S}$. Observe that the maul $\mathfrak{m}_0$ is common to all $[\mathfrak{m}_0, \ldots, \mathfrak{m}_p] \in \mathcal{S}$: this is the* initial maul *of $\mathcal{S}$.*
Besides the parity (odd/even) of a design, we may consider its polarity *(positive/negative) :*

1. *$\mathcal{S}$ is positive when its parity is the same as the parity of $\mathfrak{m}$*
2. *$\mathcal{S}$ is negative when its parity is opposite to the parity of $\mathfrak{m}$*

A design is a sort of strategy for the player, *Even* or *Odd*, corresponding to its parity ; styling it positive means that this player actually starts (or at least should start) ; styling it negative means that this player cannot start.

DEFINITION 20
An even design is winning *when its disputes are won by* Even. *Odd winning designs are defined similarly.*

The definitions make sense because even coherence is closed under odd restrictions, as well as even winning.

4.4 Orthogonality

We assume in what follows that initial maul of all disputes is fixed.
A positive design and a negative design have at most one dispute in common, since two disputes in the intersection must be both evenly and oddly coherent ; if they actually meet, the common dispute cannot be won by both disputers, hence at most one of the designs can be winning.

DEFINITION 21
Let $\mathcal{S}, \mathcal{T}$ be even and odd designs ; we say that $\mathcal{S}, \mathcal{T}$ are orthogonal *when they intersect. Given a set* $\mathbf{G}$ *of even designs we define its* orthogonal $\mathbf{G}^\perp$ *as the set of all odd designs which are orthogonal to all designs in* $\mathbf{G}$. *We define in a similar way the orthogonal of a set of odd designs. As usual* $\mathbf{G} \subset \mathbf{G}^{\perp\perp}$ *and* $\mathbf{G}^{\perp\perp\perp} = \mathbf{G}^\perp$.

PROPOSITION 11
Orthogonals are never empty, namely :

1. *If* $\mathbf{G}$ *is positive, then* $\mathbf{G}^\perp$ *contains the design* $\mathbf{triv}^-$ *made of all disputes of length one and of the trivial dispute* $[\mathfrak{m}]$.
2. *If* $\mathbf{G}$ *is negative, then* $\mathbf{G}^\perp$ *contains the design* $\mathbf{triv}^+$ *reduced to the trivial dispute* $[\mathfrak{m}]$.

Proof : Let us assume that $\mathfrak{m}$ is even ; then :

1. All disputes in $\mathbf{triv}^-$ are oddly coherent, and the presence of the trivial dispute ensures closure under even restriction. Take a design $\mathcal{S} \in \mathbf{G}$, and a dispute in $\mathcal{S}$, then it is either of length zero, or can be restricted to a dispute of length one, still in $\mathcal{S}$ by odd restriction : in both cases it contains an element of our design.
2. Take a design $\mathcal{S}$ in $\mathbf{G}$, then it contains by even restriction the trivial dispute $[\mathfrak{m}]$, i.e. meets the design $\mathbf{triv}^+$.

□

The two designs of our proposition are called the *trivial* designs of $\mathbf{G}^\perp$. Of course none of them is winning : indeed they are both based on giving up, the only difference being that $\mathbf{triv}^+$ directly commits suicide, whereas $\mathbf{triv}^-$ can only do this provided his opponent didn't commit suicide before him.

4.5 Behaviors

DEFINITION 22
An even behavior $\mathbf{G}$ *is a set of even designs equal to its biorthogonal ; its orthogonal, which is a set of odd designs equal to its biorthogonal, is an* odd behavior. *The* extension $|\mathbf{G}|$ *of* $\mathbf{G}$ *(which is also the extension of* $\mathbf{G}^\perp$*) is the set of disputes which occur both in a design of* $\mathbf{G}$ *and a design of* $\mathbf{G}^\perp$. *The* polarity, *positive, or negative, of a behavior, is defined as for designs.*

REMARK 4.5.1
We shall sometimes prefer to see a behavior as the pair $\mathbf{G}, \mathbf{G}^\perp$, in which case $\mathbf{G}$ (identified with $\mathbf{G}^\perp$) contains positive and negative designs, or even and odd designs. This may help to simplify notations and the statement of results.

PROPOSITION 12
The extension of $\mathbf{G}$ *is closed under restriction.*

Proof : Assume that $\mathbf{G}$ is even. If $[\mathfrak{m}_0, \ldots, \mathfrak{m}_p] \in |\mathbf{G}|$ then $[\mathfrak{m}_0, \ldots, \mathfrak{m}_p] \in \mathcal{S} \cap \mathcal{T}$, with $\mathcal{S}, \mathcal{T}$ designs in $\mathbf{G}, \mathbf{G}^\perp$ respectively. If $q < p$ is such that $\mathfrak{m}_q$ is odd, then $[\mathfrak{m}_0, \ldots, \mathfrak{m}_q] \in \mathcal{S}$. The only disputes in $\mathcal{T}$ that are no longer oddly coherent with $[\mathfrak{m}_0, \ldots, \mathfrak{m}_q]$ are of the form $\mathfrak{D} = [\mathfrak{n}_0, \ldots, \mathfrak{n}_i, \ldots, \mathfrak{n}_r]$ where $\mathfrak{m}_q, \mathfrak{n}_i$ have the same major bloke, with the same odd chronicle : so we replace any such dispute by its restriction $[\mathfrak{n}_0, \ldots, \mathfrak{n}_i]$. The set $\mathcal{T}'$ thus defined is indeed a design. Now if $\mathcal{S}' \in \mathbf{G}$, $\mathcal{S}'$ meets $\mathcal{T}$; if it happens that the meeting occurs in $\mathcal{T}-\mathcal{T}'$, then the restriction at length i of the common dispute belongs to $\mathcal{S}' \cap \mathcal{T}'$: from this $\mathcal{T}'$ belongs to $\mathbf{G}^\perp$ and $[\mathfrak{m}_0, \ldots, \mathfrak{m}_q] \in |\mathbf{G}|$. □

PROPOSITION 13

Let us order designs by inclusion. Then if $\mathcal{S}$ is a subdesign of $\mathcal{T}$ and $\mathcal{S}$ is in the behavior $\mathbf{G}$, so is $\mathcal{T}$. Conversely, any intersection of designs of $\mathbf{G}$ is still a design of $\mathbf{G}$, provided their union is a design. In particular any design $\mathcal{S}$ of $\mathbf{G}$ contains a minimum subdesign, still in $\mathbf{G}$.

Proof : Immediate. The minimum subdesign of $\mathcal{S}$ is indeed $\mathcal{S} \cap |\mathbf{G}|$. □

DEFINITION 23

The extension *of $\mathcal{S}$ is defined as $\mathcal{S} \cap |\mathbf{G}|$. A design equal to its extension will be called* clean. *A* useful part *of a behavior $\mathbf{G}$ is a subset $\mathbf{G}' \subset \mathbf{G}$ such that the designs $\mathcal{T} \cap |\mathbf{G}|$; $\mathcal{T} \in \mathbf{G}'$ are exactly the clean designs of $\mathbf{G}$.*

REMARK 4.5.2

The extension of $\mathcal{S}$ is what can be « observed » if we follow the behavior. But, as in real life, designs may take into account impossible disputes (i.e. we overestimate our opponent). In practice it is much simpler to work with unclean designs : typically, if $\mathbf{G}, \mathbf{H}$ are negative, then a design for $\mathbf{G} \,\&\, \mathbf{H}$ is also a design for $\mathbf{G}$, and this will enable one to write $\mathbf{G} \,\&\, \mathbf{H}$ as $\mathbf{G} \cap \mathbf{H}$. In some sense, the fact that the extension of a design varies with the behavior is a form of *polymorphism*, analogous to the fact that a pure λ-expression may receive several types.

4.6 Embeddings

DEFINITION 24

An embedding *is an injective map Φ from $\mathbb{H}$ to itself which preserves the relation « to be an immediate subhand », and the fact of being simple or multiple. Therefore an embedding is either* even *which means that $\Phi(\xi)$ has the parity of ξ, or* odd *which means that $\Phi(\xi)$ has a parity opposite to ξ.*

If Φ is an embedding, then it is extended in the usual way to arbitrary sets of hands, and therefore to blokes, by means of $\Phi(\Xi \vdash \Sigma) = \Phi(\Xi) \vdash \Phi(\Sigma)$. If $\mathfrak{m}$ is a maul, the maul $\Phi(\mathfrak{m})$ is defined as the tree $\{<\Phi(\sigma_0), \ldots, \Phi(\sigma_{n-1})>; <\sigma_0, \ldots, \sigma_{n-1}> \in \mathfrak{m}\}$. Finally, if $[\mathfrak{m}_0, \ldots, \mathfrak{m}_p]$ is a dispute, then the sequence $\Phi([\mathfrak{m}_0, \ldots, \mathfrak{m}_p]) = [\Phi(\mathfrak{m}_0), \ldots, \Phi(\mathfrak{m}_p)]$ is easily seen to be a dispute.
An embedding can also be applied to a design, and to a behavior : $\Phi(\mathbf{G}) = \mathbf{K}^{\perp\perp}$, with $\mathbf{K} = \{\Phi(\mathcal{S}) ; \mathcal{S} \in \mathbf{G}\}$; indeed $\mathbf{K}$ is a useful part of $\Phi(\mathbf{G})$. Using embeddings, it is not difficult to define the notion of *equivalent* behaviors, and of course an even behavior may be equivalent to an odd behavior.

4.7 Basic Examples

Take an *atomic* maul $\mathfrak{m}$, consisting of $\vdash \xi$ and $\xi \vdash$; then $\mathbf{G} = \{\mathbf{triv}^+\}$ defines a positive behavior, whose orthogonal consists in all negative designs starting with $\mathfrak{m}$. The behavior $\mathbf{G}$ is noted $\mathbf{0}$ (and then its orthogonal is noted $\top$) when ξ is simple, and

$\mathbf{0}^\flat$ when ξ is multiple. (To be precise, we should indicate ξ in the notation, but any two choices can be related by appropriate embeddings).

5 Behavioral Connectives

We shall now combine behaviors to produce new ones ; these ways will correspond to the connectives (multiplicative and additive) of linear logic. There is no particular difficulty, except that the same definition may take up to three different forms :

analytic Usual binary connectives, e.g. $\oplus, \otimes$. Since the polarity of the constituent behaviors in —say $\mathbf{G} \oplus \mathbf{G}'$— does matter, it is wiser to consider these operations as mapping positive behaviors to positive behaviors, and to add a special unary connective for the change of polarity.

synthetic Synthetic connectives ; here, given positive behaviors $\mathbf{G}_1, \ldots, \mathbf{G}_n$, we construct a new positive behavior $\mathfrak{X}\mathbf{G}_1 \ldots \mathbf{G}_n$, e.g. $\mathbf{G}_1{}^\perp \otimes (\mathbf{G}_2{}^\perp \oplus \mathbf{G}_3{}^\perp)$.

sequential Given a sequent $\vdash \mathbf{G}_1, \ldots, \mathbf{G}_n$ or $\mathbf{G}_0 \vdash \mathbf{G}_1, \ldots, \mathbf{G}_n$ of positive behaviors, define a new behavior.

5.1 Sequents of Behaviors

Let $\Xi \vdash \Sigma$ be an even bloke ; we shall (abusively) identify it with the corresponding standard maul, see example 3.2.1.

PROPOSITION 14

projection *If $\mathcal{T}$ is an odd design with starting maul $\Xi \vdash \Sigma$, and $\eta \in \Sigma, \Xi$, then the set $\mathcal{T} \lceil \eta$ of the projections on η of all disputes of $\mathcal{T}$ is an odd design with starting maul η.*

tensorization *Given odd designs $\mathcal{T}_\eta$ with starting mauls $\vdash \eta$ for all $\eta \in \Sigma, \Xi$, then the set $\bigotimes_\eta \mathcal{T}_\eta$ consisting of all disputes with starting maul $\Xi \vdash \Sigma$ whose respective projections on the η belong to $\mathcal{T}_\eta$, is an odd design.*

application *Given $\nu \in \Sigma, \Xi$, together with an even design $\mathcal{S}$ with starting maul $\Xi \vdash \Sigma$ and odd designs $\mathcal{T}_\eta$ with starting mauls $\vdash \eta$ for all $\eta \in \Sigma, \Xi$, $\eta \neq \nu$ (notation : $\mathcal{T}_\Upsilon$), then one can define the set $\mathcal{S}(\mathcal{T}_\Upsilon)$, as the set of all $\mathfrak{D} \lceil \nu$ such that $\mathfrak{D} \in \mathcal{S}$ and $\mathfrak{D} \lceil \eta \in \mathcal{T}_\eta$ for all $\eta \in \Sigma, \Xi$, $\eta \neq \nu$. $\mathcal{S}(\mathcal{T}_\Upsilon)$ is an even design.*

focalization $(\mathcal{S} \cap \bigotimes_\eta \mathcal{T}_\eta) \lceil \nu = \mathcal{S}(\mathcal{T}_\Upsilon) \cap \mathcal{T}_\nu$.

Proof : The result is almost immediate from theorem 4, projection coming from 1, tensorization from 2, and application from 3. Focalization is essentially trivial. □

DEFINITION 25

Let $\Xi \vdash \Sigma$ be an —say— even bloke, and let $\mathbf{G}_\eta$ be, for each $\eta \in \Sigma, \Xi$, a positive behavior with starting maul $\vdash \eta$; we assume that $\mathbf{G}_\eta$ is even for $\eta \in \Sigma$ and odd for $\eta \in \Xi$. We define a new behavior $\mathbf{H} = \mathbf{G}_\Xi \vdash \mathbf{G}_\Sigma$, as $\mathbf{K}^\perp$, where $\mathbf{K}$ is the set of all designs $\bigotimes_\eta \mathcal{T}_\eta$ where the $\mathcal{T}_\eta$ are odd designs (see the remark following definition 22 : if $\mathbf{G}_\eta$ is even, by an odd design in $\mathbf{G}_\eta$ I mean a design in $\mathbf{G}_\eta{}^\perp$) in $\mathbf{G}_\eta$ for $\eta \in \Sigma, \Xi$. This behavior is positive exactly when Ξ is empty.

THEOREM 5

With the notations of definition 25 let $\mathbf{H} = \mathbf{G}_\Xi \vdash \mathbf{G}_\Sigma = \mathbf{K}^\perp$ *; then :*

1. *Let us focalize on some* $\nu \in \Sigma, \Xi$ *; then* $\mathbf{H}$ *consists in those even designs* $\mathcal{S}$ *such that for all odd designs* $\mathcal{T}_\eta$ *in* $\mathbf{G}_\eta$ *(*$\eta \in \Sigma, \Xi$*,* $\eta \neq \nu$*),* $\mathcal{S}(\mathcal{T}_\Upsilon)$ *is an even design of* $\mathbf{G}_\nu$.
2. $\mathbf{K}$ *is a useful part of* $\mathbf{K}^{\perp\perp}$.

Proof : 1. This is an immediate application of focalization : $(\mathcal{S} \cap \bigotimes_\eta \mathcal{T}_\eta) \upharpoonright \nu = \mathcal{S}(\mathcal{T}_\Upsilon) \cap \mathcal{T}_\nu$.

2. We first prove a lemma, which is an essential application of dog's moves.

LEMME 5.1

Let $\nu \in \Sigma, \Xi$ *and let* $\mathcal{S}_\nu$ *be an even design in* $\mathbf{G}_\nu$*. Then one can build an even design* $\check{\mathcal{S}}_\nu \in \mathbf{G}_\Xi \vdash \mathbf{G}_\Sigma$ *such that* $\check{\mathcal{S}}_\nu \upharpoonright \nu = \mathcal{S}_\nu$.

Proof : We consider three cases :

(a) If $\nu \in \Xi$, let $\check{\mathcal{S}}_\nu$ be the set of all disputes starting with the maul $\Xi \vdash \Sigma$ and whose succession of actions correspond to a dispute of $\mathcal{S}_\nu$.

(b) If $\Xi = \emptyset$, let $\check{\mathcal{S}}_\nu$ be the set of all disputes starting with the maul $\Xi \vdash \Sigma$ and whose succession of actions correspond to a dispute of $\mathcal{S}_\nu$, except for the first one : the common action $(\nu, I, (\emptyset_i)$ is replaced with a fixed action $(\nu, I, (\Sigma_i)$, where (Σ_i) is the partition of $\Sigma - \nu$, such that all Σ_i are empty but the one of smallest index.

(c) If $\nu \notin \Xi \neq \emptyset$, then $\check{\mathcal{S}}_\nu$ is the set of all disputes starting with any action focusing on ξ, then resuming as above, i.e. as a dispute of $\mathcal{S}_\nu$, whose first move is inflated as above (this inflation is precisely the dog's move).

Now we can apply what we just proved : focus on ν, and choose the $\mathcal{T}_\eta$ to be trivial designs $\mathbf{triv}_\eta$ (positive when $\eta \in \Sigma$, negative for $\eta \in \Xi$) ; it is immediate that $\check{\mathcal{S}}_\nu(\mathbf{triv}_\Upsilon) = \mathcal{S}_\nu$. □

Take $\mathcal{U} \in \mathbf{K}^{\perp\perp}$, $\nu \in \Xi \vdash \Sigma$ and let $\mathcal{U}_\nu = \mathcal{U} \upharpoonright \nu$. Let $\mathcal{S}_\nu$ be an even design in $\mathbf{G}_\nu$. By lemma 5.1, $\check{\mathcal{S}}_\nu \in \mathbf{K}^\perp$. So $\check{\mathcal{S}}_\nu \cap \mathcal{U} \neq \emptyset$ and $(\check{\mathcal{S}} \cap \mathcal{U})_\nu \subset \mathcal{S}_\nu \cap \mathcal{U}_\nu \neq \emptyset$. From this it follows that $\mathcal{U}_\nu \in \mathbf{G}_\nu$, so $\otimes_\eta \mathcal{U}_\eta \in \mathbf{K}$ and contains $\mathcal{U}$: they have therefore the same extension.

□

REMARK 5.1.1

The basic use of the theorem is as follows : given a sequent of behaviors $\mathbf{G}_\Xi \vdash \mathbf{G}_\Sigma$, it enables one to *focalize* on some $\mathbf{G}_\nu$, i.e. to work with $\mathcal{S}(\mathcal{T}_\Upsilon)$ instead of $\mathcal{S}$, and then to come back to $\mathcal{S}$.

5.2 Synthetic Connectives

DEFINITION 26
Let ξ be a simple hand, of —say— even parity. If $\mathfrak{D}$ is any dispute with an initial maul $\mathfrak{m}$ of the form $\vdash \xi * i_0, \ldots, \xi * i_k$, let $\downarrow\mathfrak{D}$ be the dispute $[\vdash \xi, \mathfrak{D}]$, to which a first action has been added. If $\mathcal{S}$ is any design with starting maul $\mathfrak{m}$, then $\downarrow\mathcal{S}$ is the set of all $\downarrow\mathfrak{D}$, when $\mathfrak{D} \in \mathcal{S}$: it is a design of the same parity and opposite polarity.

PROPOSITION 15
If $\mathbf{G}$ is any behavior with starting maul $\mathfrak{m}$ then the set consisting of the trivial design and of all $\downarrow\mathcal{S}$, where $\mathcal{S} \in \mathbf{G}$, is a useful part of a behavior $\downarrow\mathbf{G}$, with starting maul $\vdash \xi$. $\downarrow\mathbf{G}$ has the same parity as $\mathbf{G}$ and opposite polarity. Moreover $\downarrow(\mathbf{G}^\perp) = (\downarrow\mathbf{G})^\perp$.

Proof : Obvious. It basically consists in changing the first player, and adding a dummy action. □

DEFINITION 27
Let ξ be a simple hand, of —say— even parity. Let $F = \{i_1, \ldots, i_n\}$ be a finite set of fingers ; for each $i \in F$ let $\mathbf{G}_i$ be an odd positive behavior with starting maul $\vdash \xi * i$. If $\mathfrak{X}$ is a synthetic connective of arity n, then we define the even positive behavior $\mathbf{H} = \mathfrak{X}\mathbf{G}_{i_1}, \ldots, \mathbf{G}_{i_n}$, with starting maul $\vdash \xi$ as $\mathbf{K}^{\perp\perp}$, where $\mathbf{K}$ consists in the following designs :

- *The trivial positive design $\mathbf{triv}^+$.*
- *For each maximal non-empty clique $I \in \mathfrak{X}$, for each negative (i.e. even) design $\mathcal{S} \in (\vdash \mathbf{G}_I)^\perp$ the design $\downarrow\mathcal{S}$. (Concretely, we add a first action, which is a splitting of ξ along I.)*

PROPOSITION 16
1. *$\mathbf{H} = \mathbf{K}$.*
2. *$\mathbf{H}^\perp = \bigcap_I \downarrow(\vdash \mathbf{G}_I)$, the intersection being taken over all maximal non-empty cliques of $\mathfrak{X}$.*

Proof : Almost obvious ; notice the extreme simplicity of the formulation. □

5.3 Analytic Connectives

If we turn our attention towards connectives like $\oplus, \otimes$, then the situation is complex, since we must take into account the polarity of the components. But there is an immediate simplification, namely to use $\downarrow$ to change polarity, so that we need to define $\mathbf{G} \oplus \mathbf{H}$ and $\mathbf{G} \otimes \mathbf{H}$ only when $\mathbf{G}, \mathbf{H}$ are positive behaviors distinct from $\mathbf{0}^\flat$, with the same starting mauls, say $\vdash \xi$.
Then one needs two embeddings $\mathbb{F} \rightsquigarrow \mathbb{F}$, so as to make disjoint the first respective actions in the two behaviors. Once the behaviors have been modified in this way, then the additives take a nice form, typically $\mathbf{G}^\perp \,\&\, \mathbf{H}^\perp = \mathbf{G}^\perp \cap \mathbf{H}^\perp$, etc.
One can observe that we don't know how to define $\mathbf{G} \oplus \mathbf{0}^\flat$; of course this construction is not needed, since it corresponds to nothing in **HC**, neither in usual syntax. This is a small mystery...

5.4 Isomorphisms

Basic isomorphisms (associativity, commutativity, neutrality, distributivity, absorbtion) are easily obtained, e.g. $\mathbf{G} \otimes \mathbf{0} \simeq \mathbf{0}$. They are basically contained in proposition 16. Moreover these isomorphisms are *inner* ones, i.e. can be obtained as proofs of logical equivalence, see below. There is only one exception, namely the neutrality of $\mathbf{1}$ (and dually $\perp$) : there are definitely more designs in $\vdash \mathbf{G} \otimes \mathbf{1}, \mathbf{H}$ than in $\vdash \mathbf{G}, \mathbf{H}$. This will be fixed in the next paper, remember that $\mathbf{1}$ is an exponential.
To make things precise, we first define what is a morphism of —say— positive behaviors :

DEFINITION 28
Let $\mathbf{G}, \mathbf{H}, \mathbf{K}$ be positive behaviors. Assume that $\mathbf{G}$ has starting maul η and $\mathbf{H}$ has starting maul ξ with η, ξ icmprarable and of opposite parities (what we shall note $\eta >< \xi$). A morphism φ from $\mathbf{G}$ to $\mathbf{H}$ is a design in $\mathbf{G} \vdash \mathbf{H}$.
Assume that $\mathbf{H}$ has a starting maul η and choose an involutive embedding Φ such that $\eta >< \Phi(\eta)$. Then consider all disputes with starting maul $\eta \vdash \Phi(\eta)$ defined as follows : (one easily checks that, throughout such disputes, in each odd maul of the dispute the even blokes are all of the form $\xi \vdash \Phi(\xi)$). The only constraint on such disputes is that Even *reacts to any action $(\xi, I, (\Sigma_i)$ with the action $(\Phi(\xi), I, \{\xi * i\})$. These disputes of even length are evenly coherent. Indeed they form a morphism from $\mathbf{H}$ to itself, the* identity *or* copycat *design, written $\iota_{\mathbf{H}}$.*
Composition is defined as follows : assume that the three behaviors have been assigned starting mauls, say ν for $\mathbf{G}$, η and $\Phi(\eta)$ for $\mathbf{H}$, ζ for $\mathbf{K}$, and that the starting mauls are pairwise incomparable, with alternating parities between $\nu, \eta, \Phi(\eta)$, ζ. Assumle that $\varphi \in \mathbf{G} \vdash \mathbf{H}$ and $\psi \in \mathbf{H} \vdash \mathbf{K}$. Then $\psi\varphi$ is the set of all projections $\mathfrak{E} \upharpoonright (\nu \vdash \zeta)$ which project as follows, where $\mathfrak{E}$ is a dispute with starting maul
$\{\vdash \nu; \nu \vdash \eta; \eta \vdash \Phi(\eta); \Phi(\eta) \vdash \zeta; \zeta \vdash\}$ *which projects :*

1. *As a dispute of φ on $\nu \vdash \eta$.*

2. *As a dispute of ψ on $\Phi(\eta) \vdash \zeta$.*

3. *As a dispute of $\iota_{\mathbf{H}}$ on $\eta \vdash \Phi(\eta)$.*

PROPOSITION 17

1. *The identity is a morphism and composition maps morphisms to morphisms.*

2. *Composition is associative, and the identity is neutral on both sides.*

Proof : Obvious. Notice that the identity is just the imitation strategy discussed in [3]. □

THEOREM 6

We anticipate on next section, i.e. we assume that we know how to translate proofs into designs ; then :

1. *The identity of $\mathbf{P} \vdash \mathbf{P}$ is the interpretation of the (η-expanded version of) the identity axiom $P \vdash P$.*

2. *Composition corresponds to eager cut-elimination.*

Proof : This result might be boring to prove, hence we quail before this task. Anyway it is is a straightforward consequence of theorems 2 and 5 and of corollary 7.1 (completeness). □

From this, it is easy to produce the take the canoical proofs of —say— $P \otimes (Q \oplus R) \vdash P \otimes Q \oplus P \otimes R$ and $P \otimes Q \oplus P \otimes R \vdash P \otimes (Q \oplus R)$, and to show that their interpretations φ and ψ are inverse one of the other.
So what is wrong with $\mathbf{P} \simeq \mathbf{P} \otimes \mathbf{1}$ (only for $\mathbf{P}$ positive) ? The two behaviors are isomorphic, but the isomorphism is not unique. In other terms, when *Odd* starts, splitting ξ into the $\xi * i$, including a multiple $\xi * j$ for $\mathbf{1}$, and then *Even* will react by imitation, but he must give $\xi * j$ to some $\Phi(\xi * i)$, with $i \neq j$. These various isomorphisms induce the same map, but when they are used in a functorial way, i.e. in a context, « intensionality » —to take an expression often used to compensate for the want of real structure— strikes back.

6 Adequation

We shall now look at the main results, completeness and soundness (in this order). For this we shall start with a sequent $\vdash P$ (or $P \vdash$) where P is a formula of **HC** and write the tree of its subformulas, as explained in subsection 2.5. We just pay attention to give simple fingers to usual formulas, and multiple fingers to subformulas of the form $\mathbf{0}^\flat$.
The tree is finite and we can therefore, starting with the minimal subformulas, associate a behavior $\boldsymbol{\Xi} \vdash \boldsymbol{\Sigma}$ to any sequent $\Xi \vdash \Sigma$, with starting maul $\Xi \vdash \Sigma$ (if we identify abusively a maul with a sequent).
Now, given a paraproof $\mathbf{n}$ of $\vdash P$ and a paraproof $\mathbf{m}$ of $P \vdash$, we can construct, as in subsection 2.2 a finite dispute $\mathbf{nm}$, which is indeed a dispute in the technical sense we introduced later. Now each $\mathbf{n}$ can therefore be interpreted as a design, namely the set of all $\mathbf{nm}$, when $\mathbf{m}$ varies trough the paraproofs of $P \vdash$.

6.1 Completeness

Take a sequent $\Xi \vdash \Sigma$ of **HC**, and let $\boldsymbol{\Xi} \vdash \boldsymbol{\Sigma}$, be the appropriate sequent of behaviors, that we shall call $\mathbf{G}$.

THEOREM 7

1. *If $\mathbf{G}$ is negative and $\mathcal{S} \in \mathbf{G}$ is clean, then :*
   - (a) *If $\Xi = \mathbf{0}^\flat$, then $\mathcal{S}$ is reduced to the trivial dispute.*
   - (b) *If $\Xi = \xi = \mathfrak{X} P_1 \ldots P_n$, let I be a non-empty maximal clique of $\mathfrak{X}$, and let $\vdash \Sigma, \Upsilon(I)$ be the result of the corresponding first action. Then*

     $$\mathcal{S}_I = \{\mathfrak{D}; [\xi \vdash \Sigma, \mathfrak{D}] \in \mathcal{S} \text{ and the initial maul of } \mathfrak{D} \text{ is } \vdash \Sigma, \Upsilon(I)\}$$

     is a design of $\vdash \boldsymbol{\Sigma}, \Upsilon(I)$. Furthermore, $\mathcal{S}$ is the intersection of the $\downarrow\mathcal{S}_I$ and of the trivial dispute.
2. *If $\mathbf{G}$ is positive i.e. if $\Xi = \emptyset$, and if $\mathcal{S} \in \mathbf{G}$, then :*
   - (a) *Either $\mathcal{S}$ is the trivial design.*

(b) *Or there is some $\xi \in \Sigma$, and a first action $\xi * i, \Sigma_i \,; i \in I$ common to all disputes of $\mathcal{S}$, which can therefore be written $\{[\Xi \vdash \Sigma; \mathfrak{D}] \,; \mathfrak{D} \in \mathcal{T}\}$, for a certain design $\mathcal{T}$. Moreover, ξ corresponds to a formula $\mathfrak{X}P_{i_1} \ldots P_{i_n}$, and I is a maximal clique in $\mathfrak{X}$. Finally, given $i \in I$, and let $\Xi_i = \xi * i$; then the projection of $\mathcal{T}$ on $\Xi_i \vdash \Sigma_i$ belongs to the behavior $\mathbf{\Xi}_i \vdash \mathbf{\Sigma}_i$.*

Proof : We assume that the starting maul is even.

1. In case $\xi = \mathbf{0}^\flat$, then *Odd* cannot start, since his first action should project into an action inside the behavior $\mathbf{0}^\flat$. From this we see that the extension of $\mathcal{S}$ is reduced to the trivial dispute.
   Otherwise, one first establishes the result when $\Sigma = \emptyset$: this is exactly proposition 16, 2. Then by a back and forth focalization on ξ we get the general case.

2. By proposition 9, $\mathcal{S}$ is either reduced to the trivial dispute, or all the disputes in $\mathcal{S}$ share the same initial action, $\xi * i, \Sigma_i \,; i \in I$. In a first step we treat the case where $\Sigma = \emptyset$, which is basically definition 26 and proposition 16, 1. Then, we apply a back and forth focalization on ξ to get the general case.

□

COROLLARY 7.1
Let $\mathcal{S} \in \mathbf{\Xi} \vdash \mathbf{\Sigma}$, $\mathcal{S}$ clean. Then $\mathcal{S}$ is the interpretation of a paraproof of **HC**. *Moreover in case $\mathcal{S}$ is winning, the proof is a real one, i.e. is correct.*

Proof : We iterate the previous theorem, and remark that all cases correspond to a rule of **HC** : 1.(a) corresponds to the axiom for $\mathbf{0}^\flat$, 1.(b) corresponds to the left rule for $\mathfrak{X}$, 2.(a) corresponds to the hypothesis, 2.(b) corresponds to one of the right rules for $\mathfrak{X}$. From this we can reconstruct a paraproof in **HC** from below, and an obvious finiteness argument makes the paraproof finite. Now in case $\mathcal{S}$ is winning, no paralogism can be used, i.e. the paraproof is correct. □

6.2 Soundness

We assume that $\Xi \vdash \Sigma$ contains exactly one formula. Observe that, due to completeness, any design $\mathcal{T}$ in $\mathbf{G}^\perp$ comes indeed from a paraproof $\mathbf{m}$ in **HC**. Now, if $\mathcal{S}$ is the interpretation of a paraproof $\mathbf{n}$ of $\Xi \vdash \Sigma$, and if $\mathcal{T} \in \mathbf{G}^\perp$, then $\mathcal{S} \cap \mathcal{T}$ is nonempty : it contains $\mathbf{nm}$. This shows that $\mathcal{S} \in \mathbf{G}$. Finally, if $\mathcal{S}$ is winning, then all disputes $\mathbf{nm}$ are won by the side of $\mathbf{n}$, and from this we know that $\mathbf{n}$ is an actual proof, see subsection 2.3. We just proved the :

THEOREM 8
If $\mathcal{S}$ is the interpretation of a paraproof **n** *of $\Xi \vdash \Sigma$, then $\mathcal{S} \in \mathbf{\Xi} \vdash \mathbf{\Sigma}$; moreover, if* **n** *is a real proof, $\mathcal{S}$ is a winning design.*

References

[1] J.-M. Andreoli and R. Pareschi. **Linear objects: logical processes with built-in inheritance.** *New Generation Computing*, 9(3–4):445–473, 1991.

[2] J.-Y. Girard. **Linear logic.** *Theoretical Computer Science*, 50:1–102, 1987.

[3] J.-Y. Girard. **On the meaning of logical rules I : syntax vs. semantics.** In U. Berger and H. Schwichtenberg, editors, *Computational Logic*, Heidelberg, 1999. *Springer Verlag.* NATO series F 165.

[4] J.-Y. Girard. **Locus Solus.** *Manuscrit*, Institut de Mathématiques de Luminy, Marseille, 1999.

[5] J. M. E. Hyland and C.-H. L. Ong. **Π-calculus, dialogue games and PCF.** In *Proc. 7th* ACM *Conf. Functional Prog. Lang. Comp. Architecture*, pages 96 – 107. ACM Press, 1995.

[6] Y. Lafont. **From proof-nets to interaction nets.** In Girard, Lafont, and Regnier, editors, *Advances in Linear Logic*, Cambridge, 1995. *Cambridge University Press.*

[7] H. Nickau. **Hereditarily Sequential Functionals.** In Anil Nerode and Yu. V. Matiyasevich, editors, *Proc. Symp. Logical Foundations of Computer Science: Logic at St. Petersburg*, volume 813 of *Lecture Notes in Computer Science*, pages 253–264. Springer-Verlag, 1994.

Foundations of Secure Computation
F.L. Bauer and R. Steinbrüggen (Eds.)
IOS Press, 2000

Effective Domains and Concrete Computability: A survey

Viggo Stoltenberg-Hansen*
Department of Mathematics, Uppsala University, Box 480,
S-751 06 Uppsala, Sweden

1 Introduction

We take as our starting point the following problem. Suppose we want to compute on a possibly uncountable structure such as the field $\mathbb{R}$ of real numbers. The elements of $\mathbb{R}$ are in general truly infinite objects (Cauchy sequences or Dedekind cuts) with no finite description. However, *real* computations, that is computations that can in principle be performed by a digital computer or Turing machine, must operate on 'concrete' objects. By an element being concrete we mean (at least) that it is finitely describable or, equivalently, coded by a natural number. In particular, the structure on which the computations are performed must be countable. Therefore it is not possible to compute directly on $\mathbb{R}$, we can at best compute on concrete approximations of elements in $\mathbb{R}$. If the approximations are such that each real number is a limit of its concrete approximations then we can extend a computation to $\mathbb{R}$ by interpreting a computation on a real number as the 'limit' of the computations on its approximations, where such a limit exists. This is the technique used in recursive analysis, see e.g. Pour-El and Richards [19].

Is there a general method or a general class of structures which captures computations via approximations as in the example of the reals $\mathbb{R}$? More precisely, is there a uniform method to study concrete computability on topological algebras? We claim that the use of domains, or *domain representability*, is one such method.

Domain theory is a theory of approximation and carries a satisfactory computability theory. Classes of domains useful in this context are the continuous and algebraic cpos. A cpo D is continuous if it has a basis B_D. The basis B_D is considered as the set of concrete approximations. Each element $x \in D$ is completely determined by its set of concrete approximations $\mathrm{approx}_{B_D}(x)$ and x is the limit of $\mathrm{approx}_{B_D}(x)$. Thus D is a structure which has the pleasing property that it contains both the elements we are primarily interested in *and* their approximations. We say that the approximations of elements in D are *explicit* in D. This allows for a simple theory of effective approximations.

*email: viggo@math.uu.se

The method of domain representability goes roughly as follows. Given a topological algebra A we find an effective domain D (continuous or algebraic cpo) which contains (representations of elements in) A and also approximations of all elements in A. Then the computability or effectivity of D induces computability and effectivity on A via the representations.

This paper is an exposition of material covered in lectures given by the author at the Marktoberdorf Summer School 1999. Section 2 provides a succinct review of basic domain theory including an account of domains with partial equivalence relations (or domains with totalities). Section 3 gives a detailed account of central parts of the effective theory of continuous and algebraic domains. Section 4 contains the basic material on domain representability. In particular it considers the problem of representing non-continuous functions, such as (characteristic functions of) relations. Then, in Section 5, the effective theory of domains is tied up with domain representability showing that domain representations do provide a uniform method to study effectivity on topological algebras.

2 Basic theory of domains

Domain theory is by now a rather large mathematical theory with applications in many areas such as denotational semantics, type theory and recursive mathematics. In this paper we concentrate on its use in the latter.

The axioms for algebraic and also continuous cpos are easily derived from an elementary analysis of approximations, e.g. via approximation structures as in [20, 25]. Here, however, we will only review some basic notions and results to make our presentation self-contained. For thorough accounts of domain theory we refer to [21] and [1].

2.1 *Complete partial orders*

Let $D = (D, \sqsubseteq)$ be a partial order and let $A \subseteq D$. We will use the notation $\uparrow A$ to denote the set $\{y \in D : (\exists x \in A)(x \sqsubseteq y)\}$. The set $\uparrow\{x\}$ is abbreviated by $\uparrow x$. We define $\downarrow A$ and $\downarrow x$ dually. A is *directed* if $A \neq \emptyset$ and whenever $x, y \in A$ then there is $z \in A$ such that $x \sqsubseteq z$ and $y \sqsubseteq z$. An *ideal* is a directed set which is downwards closed. The supremum, or least upper bound, of A (if it exists) is denoted by $\bigsqcup A$. As usual we write $x \sqcup y$ instead of $\bigsqcup\{x, y\}$.

The notions of a directed set and ideal make sense for any (transitive) relation $\sqsubseteq$.

A *complete partial order*, abbreviated *cpo*, is a partial order with least element $D = (D; \sqsubseteq, \bot)$, such that any directed set $A \subseteq D$ has a supremum $\bigsqcup A$ in D. It is not always required in the literature that a cpo has a least element $\bot$. For our considerations, however, it is natural to do so.

Let D and E be cpos. A function $f: D \to E$ is *continuous* if f is monotone and

$$f(\bigsqcup A) = \bigsqcup f[A]$$

for any directed set $A \subseteq D$.

The topology corresponding to the above order theoretic notion of continuity is the Scott topology:

Definition 2.1. Let $D = (D; \sqsubseteq, \bot)$ be a cpo. Then $U \subseteq D$ is *open* if

(i) whenever $A \subseteq D$ is directed and $\bigsqcup A \in U$ then $A \cap U \neq \emptyset$; and

(ii) if $x \in U$ and $x \sqsubseteq y$ then $y \in U$.

A directed set A should be thought of as a generalised sequence and $\bigsqcup A$ as its limit, thus making the notions of continuity and open set natural.

For cpos D and E we define the *function space* $[D \to E]$ of D and E by

$$[D \to E] = \{f \colon D \to E \mid f \text{ continuous}\}.$$

We order $[D \to E]$ by

$$f \sqsubseteq g \iff (\forall x \in D)(f(x) \sqsubseteq g(x)).$$

It is easy to see that $[D \to E]$ is a cpo where for a directed set $\mathcal{F} \subseteq [D \to E]$ and $x \in D$,

$$(\bigsqcup \mathcal{F})(x) = \bigsqcup \{f(x) : f \in \mathcal{F}\}.$$

The Scott topology on $[D \to E]$ is known as the *topology of pointwise convergence.* It is the subspace topology of the Tychonoff topology on E^D, the set of *all* functions from D to E. The Tychonoff topology on E^D considers D only as an index set and hence does not depend on the topology on D. Thus we obtain the terminology of pointwise convergence, which also should be apparent from the equation above.

We form a category $\mathbf{CPO}_\perp$ whose objects are cpos and whose morphisms are continuous functions between cpos. It is well-known and easy to prove that $\mathbf{CPO}_\perp$ is a cartesian closed category, where the product of cpos D and E is given by

$$D \times E = \{(x, y) : x \in D, y \in E\}$$

and ordered by

$$(x, y) \sqsubseteq (z, w) \iff x \sqsubseteq_D z \text{ and } y \sqsubseteq_E w.$$

The exponent of D and E is the function space $[D \to E]$. In particular this means that the corresponding projection functions for the product are continuous. Furthermore eval: $[D \to E] \times D \to E$ defined by

$$\text{eval}(f, x) = f(x)$$

is continuous and curry: $[D \times E \to F] \to [D \to [E \to F]]$ defined by

$$\text{curry}(f)(x)(y) = f(x, y)$$

is continuous.

Each continuous function $f \colon D \to D$ has a least fixed point, which is a crucial fact for the use of cpos in semantics. Furthermore the function fix: $[D \to D] \to D$ defined by

$$\text{fix}(f) = \text{least fixed point of } f$$

is continuous.

2.2 Continuous and algebraic cpos

The appropriate approximation relation on cpos is the way below relation.

Definition 2.2. Let $D = (D; \sqsubseteq, \perp)$ be a cpo and $x, y \in D$.

(i) x is *way below* y, denoted $x \ll y$, if for each directed set $A \subseteq D$,

$$y \sqsubseteq \bigsqcup A \implies (\exists z \in A)(x \sqsubseteq z).$$

(ii) x is *compact* or *finite* if $x \ll x$. The set of compact elements is denoted by D_c.

The way below relation is sometimes called the *approximation relation.* Of course, $\bot$ is always compact.

It is easy to see that $x \ll y \implies x \sqsubseteq y$ and that $z \sqsubseteq x \ll y \sqsubseteq w \implies z \ll w$. In particular $\ll$ is transitive and antisymmetric. But reflexivity does not hold in general; reflexivity is what characterises the compact elements.

A useful notation for sets determined by the way below relation are, for x an element of a cpo D,

$$\Downarrow x = \{y \in D : y \ll x\} \qquad \text{and} \qquad \Uparrow x = \{y \in D : x \ll y\}.$$

Example 2.3. Let $\mathbb{CI} = ([0,1]; \leq, 0)$ where $\leq$ is the usual order. Then

$$x \ll y \iff x < y.$$

Example 2.4. Let $\mathbb{CIR} = \{[x,y] : x, y \in \mathbb{R}, x \leq y\} \cup \{\mathbb{R}\}$ ordered by reverse inclusion. Then

$$[x,y] \ll [z,w] \iff x < z \leq w < y,$$

i.e., $[z,w] \subseteq (x,y)$, the interior of $[x,y]$.

Note the lack of compact elements in these examples.

Definition 2.5. A cpo $D = (D; \sqsubseteq, \bot)$ is *continuous* if for each $x \in D$,

(i) the set $\{y \in D : y \ll x\}$ is directed (w.r.t. $\sqsubseteq$); and

(ii) $x = \bigsqcup\{y \in D : y \ll x\}$.

Continuous cpos satisfy the following crucial *interpolation property.*

Lemma 2.6. *Let D be a continuous cpo. Let $M \subseteq D$ be a finite set and suppose $M \ll y$, i.e., $(\forall z \in M)(z \ll y)$. Then there is $x \in D$ such that $M \ll x \ll y$.*

Proof. (Sketch) Suppose $M \ll y$. Let $A = \{x \in D : \exists x'(x \ll x' \ll y)\}$. Using the continuity of D one shows that A is directed and $\bigsqcup A = y$. Say $M = \{z_1, \ldots, z_n\}$. Then we know from the above that there are $a_i \in A$ such that $z_i \sqsubseteq a_i$ and hence there is $a \in A$ such that $M \sqsubseteq a$. But then, by the definition of A, there is x such that $M \ll x \ll y$. □

It follows that if D is a continuous cpo then $\Downarrow y = \{x \in D : x \ll y\}$ is directed with respect to $\ll$ for each $y \in D$.

Definition 2.7. Let $D = (D; \sqsubseteq, \bot)$ be a cpo. A subset $B \subseteq D$ is a *base* for D if for each $x \in D$,

$$\text{approx}_B(x) = \{y \in B : y \ll x\}$$

is directed and $\bigsqcup \text{approx}_B(x) = x$.

Actually it suffices to require that for each $x \in D$ there is a directed subset $A \subseteq \text{approx}_B(x)$ such that $x = \bigsqcup A$. Note that if B is a base for a cpo D then $D_c \subseteq B$.

The following proposition is an easy exercise.

Proposition 2.8. *A cpo is continuous if, and only if, it has a base.*

A continuous cpo is completely determined by a base. For example, the interpolation property (Lemma 2.6) is such that the witness always can be chosen from a base of D.

Proposition 2.9. *Suppose B is a base for the cpo D. Let $\text{Idl}(B, \ll)$ be the set of ideals of B with respect to the $\ll$ relation, ordered by inclusion. Then $D \cong \text{Idl}(B, \ll)$.*

The continuous functions between continuous cpos are also characterised by their behaviour on bases of the cpos. We leave its easy proof as an exercise.

Proposition 2.10. *Let D and E be continuous cpos with bases B_D and B_E respectively.*

(i) *A function $f: D \to E$ is continuous if, and only if, f is monotone and for each $x \in D$,*
$$(\forall b \in \text{approx}_{B_E}(f(x)))(\exists a \in \text{approx}_{B_D}(x))(b \ll f(a)).$$

(ii) *A monotone function $f: B_D \to E$ has a unique continuous extension $\bar{f}: D \to E$ defined by*
$$\bar{f}(x) = \bigsqcup \{f(a) : a \in \text{approx}_{B_D}(x)\}.$$

The connection with the Scott topology is as follows.

Theorem 2.11. *Let D be a cpo with a base B. Then a topological base for the Scott topology on D is given by the family $\{\twoheaduparrow x : x \in B\}$.*

Proof. First we note that $\twoheaduparrow x$ is open for any $x \in D$. It is clearly upwards closed. Suppose $x \ll \bigsqcup A$ where A is directed. Then, by interpolation, there is y such that $x \ll y \ll \bigsqcup A$. Hence there is $a \in A$ such that $y \sqsubseteq a$, so $x \ll a$.

Suppose $w \in \twoheaduparrow x \cap \twoheaduparrow y$, i.e., $x, y \ll w$. By interpolation we choose $b \in B$ such that $x, y \ll b \ll w$. Thus $w \in \twoheaduparrow b \subseteq \twoheaduparrow x \cap \twoheaduparrow y$. Similarly one shows that for each open $U \subseteq D$,
$$U = \bigcup_{x \in U \cap B} \twoheaduparrow x.$$
□

Definition 2.12. A cpo D is *algebraic* if its set of compact elements D_c is a base for D.

In particular, every algebraic cpo is continuous. The way below relation $\ll$ on an algebraic cpo D is characterised by
$$x \ll y \iff (\exists a \in D_c)(x \sqsubseteq a \sqsubseteq y).$$

Thus $\ll$ on D_c coincides with $\sqsubseteq$. Furthermore for $a \in D_c$, $\twoheaduparrow a = \uparrow a$.

We conclude this section by providing a connection between algebraic cpos and continuous cpos. Let D and E be cpos. Then a pair of functions $e: D \to E$ and $p: E \to D$ is a *projection pair* from D to E if they are continuous and
$$p \circ e = \text{id}_D \quad \text{and} \quad e \circ p \sqsubseteq \text{id}_E$$

where id is the identity function.

Let D be a continuous cpo with a base B and let $E = \mathrm{Idl}(B; \sqsubseteq)$ ordered by inclusion, the *ideal completion* of the partial order $(B; \sqsubseteq)$. It is not hard to prove that E is an algebraic cpo whose compact elements are precisely the principal ideals $\downarrow a$ for $a \in B$. Define $e: D \to E$ and $p: E \to D$ by

$$e(x) = \mathrm{approx}_B(x) = \{y \in B : y \ll x\} \quad \text{and} \quad p(I) = \bigsqcup_D I.$$

Proposition 2.13. *The pair (e, p) is a projection pair from D to E.*

The proof is straightforward, noting that the continuity of e depends on the interpolation property.

2.3 The function space

It is well-known that the classes of continuous and algebraic cpos are not closed under the function space construction. The usual added requirement is the following.

Definition 2.14. Let D be a cpo. Then D is said to be *consistently complete* if whenever $x, y \in D$ are consistent in D (i.e. have a common upper bound) then their supremum $x \sqcup y$ exists in D.

A consistently complete continuous (algebraic) cpo is said to be a continuous (algebraic) *domain.* The categories of continuous domains and algebraic domains *are* cartesian closed and these are the ones most often considered in semantics. However, there are important larger cartesian closed subcategories of the continuous and algebraic cpos. The category of bifinite domains is particularly important. The latter category is essential in connection with the Plotkin power domain construction. Bifinite domains (or a continuous analogue) are also important from the point of view of domain representability. For example, they are used to study the computability of iterated function systems (see [6] and [8]). Nonetheless we restrict ourselves here to the smaller cartesian closed categories of algebraic and continuous domains.

To know the structure of a base for the function space, rather than just its existence, is essential in order to determine the effectivity of the function space. Given cpos D and E, where E is consistently complete, with bases B_D and B_E we want to construct a base for the function space $[D \to E]$. Such a base can be taken as finite suprema of step functions determined from B_D and B_E. Here is the definition of a step function.

Definition 2.15. Let $D = (D; \sqsubseteq, \bot)$ and $E = (E; \sqsubseteq, \bot)$ be cpos. For $a \in D$ and $b \in E$ define $\langle a; b\rangle: D \to E$ by

$$\langle a; b\rangle(x) = \begin{cases} b & \text{if } a \ll x \\ \bot & \text{otherwise.} \end{cases}$$

Note that each step function $\langle a; b\rangle$ is continuous since $\Uparrow a$ is open for each $a \in D$.

Proposition 2.16. *Let D and E be cpos with bases B_D and B_E. Let $a \in D$ and $b \in E$ and suppose $f: D \to E$ is continuous. Then*

(i) $b \ll f(a) \Longrightarrow \langle a; b\rangle \ll f$; *and*

(ii) $f = \bigsqcup\{\langle a; b\rangle : a \in B_D,\ \ b \in B_E,\ \langle a; b\rangle \ll f\}$.

Proof.

(i) Suppose $f \sqsubseteq \bigsqcup \mathcal{F}$ where $\mathcal{F} \subseteq [D \to E]$ is directed and $b \ll f(a)$. Then $f(a) \sqsubseteq \bigsqcup \{g(a) : g \in \mathcal{F}\}$ and hence $b \sqsubseteq g(a)$ for some $g \in \mathcal{F}$, i.e., $\langle a; b \rangle \sqsubseteq g$.

(ii) Suppose $\{\langle a; b \rangle : a \in B_D,\ b \in B_E,\ \langle a; b \rangle \ll f\}$ has g as an upper bound and let $x \in D$. Then $x = \bigsqcup \{a \in B_D : a \ll x\}$ and hence $f(x) = \bigsqcup \{f(a) : a \ll x\}$. For $b \ll f(x)$ we obtain (by interpolation) $a \ll x$ such that $b \ll f(a)$ and hence, by (i), $\langle a; b \rangle \ll f$. Thus $\langle a; b \rangle \sqsubseteq g$. In particular, $b = \langle a; b \rangle(x) \sqsubseteq g(x)$ so $f(x) \sqsubseteq g(x)$.

□

It is clearly not the case that the set in (ii) is directed in general. In order to obtain a directed set we expand it by including suprema of finite subsets of step functions way below f. To obtain such suprema we need something like consistent completeness.

The following characterisation is important when considering the effectivity of the functions space construction.

Proposition 2.17. *Let D be a continuous cpo, E a consistently complete cpo, and let $a_1, \ldots, a_n \in D$ and $b_1, \ldots, b_n \in E$. Then*

$$\{\langle a_1; b_1 \rangle, \ldots, \langle a_n; b_n \rangle\} \quad \textit{is consistent in} \quad [D \to E]$$

if, and only if,

$$\forall I \subseteq \{1, \ldots, n\} (\bigcap_{i \in I} \Uparrow a_i \neq \emptyset \Longrightarrow \{b_i : i \in I\} \quad \textit{consistent}).$$

Proof. The witness in the non-trivial direction is

$$h(x) = \bigsqcup \{b_i : a_i \ll x\}$$

which also is the supremum. □

Using Proposition 2.16 (ii) it is now straightforward to prove that the categories of continuous domains and algebraic domains are cartesian closed.

Theorem 2.18. *Let D and E be continuous cpos with bases B_D and B_E. If E is consistently complete then $[D \to E]$ is continuous and consistently complete, i.e., a continuous domain. A base for $[D \to E]$ is*

$$B_{[D \to E]} = \{\bigsqcup_{i=1}^{n} \langle a_i; b_i \rangle : a_i \in B_D,\ b_i \in B_E,\ \{\langle a_1; b_1 \rangle, \ldots, \langle a_n; b_n \rangle\} \textit{ consistent}\}.$$

For algebraic domains we let the bases be the conditional upper semilattices of compact elements D_c and E_c. For $a \in D_c$ and $b \in E_c$ the step function $\langle a; b \rangle$ is compact. It follows that $B_{[D \to E]}$ is a base for $[D \to E]$ consisting only of compact elements. This shows that $[D \to E]$ is an algebraic domain.

2.4 Domains with partial equivalence relations

The idea that certain elements in a domain are representations of elements of another mathematical structure is captured by the notion of a *partial equivalence relation* (abbreviated *per*). Let D be a continuous domain. A *per* on D is a binary relation $\equiv$ which is symmetric and transitive. We say the the pair $(D, \equiv)$ is a *domain with per.*

Given a domain with per $(D, \equiv)$ we extract the set

$$\bar{D} = \{x \in D : x \equiv x\} = \mathrm{Field}(\equiv).$$

Then the pair $(D, \bar{D})$ is a *domain with totality.* We now take the quotient $\bar{D}/\equiv$ of $\bar{D}$ with $\equiv$, defined by

$$\bar{D}/\equiv\; = \{[x] : x \in \bar{D}\}$$

where $[x] = \{y \in \bar{D} : x \equiv y\}$ is the equivalence class of x, and give it the *quotient topology.* The latter is defined by

$$U \subseteq \bar{D}/\equiv \text{ open} \iff \bigcup U \subseteq \bar{D} \text{ open}$$

where $\bar{D}$ has the subspace topology from the Scott topology on D. Define $\nu: \bar{D} \to \bar{D}/\equiv$ by

$$\nu(x) = [x].$$

Then ν is a *quotient map*, i.e.

$$U \subseteq \bar{D}/\equiv \text{ open} \iff \nu^{-1}(U) \text{ open in } \bar{D}.$$

Let $(D, \equiv_D)$ and $(E, \equiv_E)$ be domains with pers. Then we define a relation $\sim$ on $[D \to E]$ by

$$f \sim g \iff (\forall x, y \in D)(x \equiv_D y \Longrightarrow f(x) \equiv_E g(y)). \tag{1}$$

It is immediate that $\sim$ is a per on $[D \to E]$.

The domains with pers make up a category **PER(Dom)** in the following way. Let **Dom** be a category of domains (continuous or algebraic) with continuous functions as morphisms. An object in **PER(Dom)** is a domain with a per $(D, \equiv_D)$. A morphism from $(D, \equiv_D)$ to $(E, \equiv_E)$ is obtained as follows. Let $\sim$ be the per on $[D \to E]$ defined by (1). For $f \in [D \to E]$ such that $f \sim f$ let $[f]$ be the equivalence class of f w.r.t. $\sim$. Then we say that $[f]: (D, \equiv_D) \to (E, \equiv_E)$ is a morphism. The operation on morphisms is defined by $[f] \circ [g] = [f \circ g]$ and $\mathrm{id}_{(D, \equiv_D)} = [\mathrm{id}_D]$. It is an easy exercise to show, using the equivalence given by (1), that

Proposition 2.19. **PER(Dom)** *is a cartesian closed category.*

3 Effective domains

In this section we will impose and study notions of computability or effectivity on domains. The type of effectivity we consider is based on what may be described as "concrete" computability, i.e., based on computations which may in principle be performed on a digital computer. Put differently, our computability theory is driven by the partial recursive functions. We use the Mal'cev-Ershov-Rabin theory of numberings in order to extend computability from the natural numbers to other structures, such as domains.

The theory is developed for continuous cpos in a rather detailed way. The results are known but, to the author's knowledge, they have not appeared in print in this general form in an easily accessible manner.

We assume some very basic knowledge of recursion theory. This can be found in any text on recursion theory and also in [21]. Here are a few conventions and facts. We denote by $\langle\cdot,\cdot\rangle\colon \omega^2 \to \omega$ a standard recursive pairing function for which there are corresponding recursive projections. Throughout we let $\{W_e\}_{e\in\omega}$ be a standard numbering of the recursively enumerable (r.e.) sets. Let W be an r.e. set. An *enumeration* of W is a total recursive function $\lambda n.W^n$, where W^n is (a canonical index for) a finite set, such that the following hold:

(i) $m \leq n \implies W^m \subseteq W^n$, and

(ii) $W = \bigcup_{n\in\omega} W^n$.

Each r.e. set has an enumeration. In fact, there is a total recursive function $\lambda en.W_e^n$ such that for each e, $\lambda n.W_e^n$ is an enumeration of W_e.

Let A be a set. A *numbering* of A is a surjective function $\alpha\colon \Omega_\alpha \to A$, where $\Omega_\alpha \subseteq \omega$. It should be thought of as a coding of A by natural numbers. In case $\Omega_\alpha = \omega$ we say that a subset $S \subseteq A$ is *α-semidecidable* if $\alpha^{-1}(S)$ is r.e. and S is *α-decidable* if $\alpha^{-1}(S)$ is recursive.

Let B be a set with a numbering $\beta\colon \Omega_\beta \to B$. Then a function $f\colon A \to B$ is said to be *(α,β)-computable* if there is a partial recursive function $\bar{f}$ such that for each $n \in \Omega_\alpha$, $\bar{f}(n)\downarrow$ (i.e. is defined) and

$$f(\alpha(n)) = \beta(\bar{f}(n)).$$

We say that $\bar{f}$ *tracks* f.

We know from Section 2.2 that a continuous cpo is completely determined by a base. Moreover continuous functions between continuous cpos are completely determined by their behaviour on the bases of the cpos (see Proposition 2.10). Thus it suffices to compute on a base of a continuous cpo.

Definition 3.1. A continuous cpo $D = (D; \sqsubseteq, \bot)$ is *weakly effective* if D has a base B for which there is a surjective function

$$\alpha\colon \omega \to B$$

such that the relation $\alpha(n) \ll \alpha(m)$ is an r.e. relation on ω.

We denote a continuous cpo weakly effective under a numbering α by (D,α). Implicit in this notation is a fixed base $B = \alpha[\omega] = \mathrm{Im}(\alpha)$. We will use the notation B_α for such a base. Thus for $x \in D$, we let

$$\mathrm{approx}_\alpha(x) = \{a \in B_\alpha : a \ll x\}$$

the set of approximations of x w.r.t. α. The condition on the numbering in Definition 3.1 is usually stated as $\ll$ is *α-semidecidable.*

Computable elements are those that can be effectively approximated and effective functions are those whose values can be effectively approximated from effective approximations of the arguments.

Definition 3.2. Let (D,α) and (E,β) be weakly effective continuous cpos.

(i) An element $x \in D$ is *α-computable* if the set

$$\{n \in \omega : \alpha(n) \ll x\} = \alpha^{-1}(\text{approx}_\alpha(x))$$

is r.e. An r.e. index for the set $\alpha^{-1}(\text{approx}_\alpha(x))$ is an *index* for x.

(ii) A continuous function $f: D \to E$ is *(α, β)-effective* if the relation

$$\beta(m) \ll f(\alpha(n))$$

is r.e. An r.e. index for the set $\{\langle m, n\rangle : \beta(m) \ll f(\alpha(n))\}$ is an *index* for f.

Note the distinction between (α, β)-effective and (α, β)-computable! The intuition in part (ii) is that the approximations to $f(x)$ are generated simultaneously with the approximations to x.

Notation $D_{k,\alpha} = \{x \in D : x\ \alpha\text{-computable}\}$.

Proposition 3.3. *Let (D, α), (E, β) and (F, γ) be weakly effective continuous cpos and suppose $f: D \to E$ and $g: E \to F$ are (α, β)-effective and (β, γ)-effective, respectively.*

(i) *If $x \in D$ is α-computable then $f(x)$ is β-computable.*

(ii) *$h = g \circ f$ is (α, γ)-effective.*

Proof. (i) Let $W = \{n : \alpha(n) \ll x\}$. Then W is r.e. and

$$\beta(m) \ll f(x) \iff (\exists n \in W)(\beta(m) \ll \alpha(n))$$

by Proposition 2.10. (ii) is proved similarly. □

Observe that the proof is *uniform*. This means there is a total recursive function which given indices for x and f computes an index for $f(x)$. Similarly, there is a recursive function which given indices for f and g computes an index for $g \circ f$.

We now show that $D_{k,\alpha}$ has a natural numbering.

Theorem 3.4. *Let (D, α) be a weakly effective continuous cpo. Then there is a numbering $\bar{\alpha}: \omega \to D_{k,\alpha}$ obtained from α such that*

(i) *the inclusion mapping $\iota: B_\alpha \to D_{k,\alpha}$ is $(\alpha, \bar{\alpha})$-computable; and*

(ii) *the relation $\alpha(n) \ll \bar{\alpha}(m)$ is r.e., i.e.,* $\text{approx}_\alpha(\bar{\alpha}(m))$ *is α-semidecidable uniformly in m.*

Proof. Let $s: \omega \to \omega$ be a total recursive function such that

$$W_{s(e)} = \{n : (\exists m \in W_e)(\alpha(n) \ll \alpha(m))\}$$

and let $\lambda n. \ll^n$ be a recursive enumeration of $\ll$ (or more precisely $\alpha^{-1}(\ll)$).

We define total recursive functions $f(e, n)$ and $r(e, n)$, a recursive relation $R(e, n)$ and a recursive enumeration of finite sets V_e^n. Set $f(e, 0) = n_\perp$, where $\alpha(n_\perp) = \perp$, $r(e, 0) = 0$, and $V_e^0 = \{n_\perp\} = \{f(e, 0)\}$. Let

$$R(e, n) \iff (\exists k \in W_{s(e)}^n)(\alpha[V_e^n \cup W_{s(e)}^{r(e,n)}] \ll^n \alpha(k)).$$

Now define

$$f(e,n+1) = \begin{cases} (\text{some } k \in W^n_{s(e)})(\alpha[V^n_e \cup W^{r(e,n)}_{s(e)}] \ll^n \alpha(k)) & \text{if } R(e,n) \\ f(e,n) & \text{if } \neg R(e,n); \end{cases}$$

$$r(e,n+1) = \begin{cases} r(e,n)+1 & \text{if } R(e,n) \\ r(e,n) & \text{if } \neg R(e,n); \end{cases}$$

and

$$V^{n+1}_e = V^n_e \cup \{f(e,n+1)\}.$$

These functions are clearly recursive. Let $V_e = \bigcup_n V^n_e$. Then V_e is r.e. with an r.e. index computed uniformly from e. Let $t: \omega \to \omega$ be a total recursive function such that

$$W_{t(e)} = \{m \in \omega : (\exists k \in V_e)(\alpha(m) \ll \alpha(k))\}.$$

It is not hard to show, using interpolation when appropriate, that $\alpha[W_{t(e)}]$ is an ideal, that $\alpha[V_e]$ is a $\ll$-chain and that $\bigsqcup \alpha[W_{t(e)}] = \bigsqcup \alpha[V_e]$.

Define $\bar{\alpha}: \omega \to D_{k,\alpha}$ by

$$\bar{\alpha}(e) = \bigsqcup \alpha[W_{t(e)}] = \bigsqcup \alpha[V_e].$$

Then $\bar{\alpha}$ is a surjective numbering of $D_{k,\alpha}$.

Let $\iota: B_\alpha \to D_{k,\alpha}$ be the inclusion mapping and let g be a total recursive function such that $W_{g(n)} = \{m : \alpha(m) \ll \alpha(n)\}$. Then

$$\bar{\alpha}(g(n)) = \bigsqcup \alpha[W_{tg(n)}] = \bigsqcup \alpha[W_{g(n)}] = \alpha(n)$$

since $W_{tg(n)} = W_{g(n)}$. Thus ι is $(\alpha, \bar{\alpha})$-computable.

Finally, it follows that $\alpha(n) \ll \bar{\alpha}(e)$ is r.e. since

$$\alpha(n) \ll \bar{\alpha}(e) = \bigsqcup \alpha[W_{t(e)}] \iff (\exists m \in W_{t(e)})(\alpha(n) \ll \alpha(m)).$$

□

A numbering γ of $D_{k,\alpha}$ satisfying (i) and (ii) of the theorem, as does $\bar{\alpha}$, is said to be a *constructive numbering* of $D_{k,\alpha}$. We say that $\bar{\alpha}$ is the *canonical numbering* of $D_{k,\alpha}$ obtained from α.

¿From the proof of the theorem we easily abstract the following important facts.

Lemma 3.5. *Let (D,α) be a weakly effective continuous cpo and let $\bar{\alpha}$ be the canonical numbering of $D_{k,\alpha}$ obtained from α.*

(i) *There is a total recursive function $t: \omega \to \omega$ such that for each e,*
$W_{t(e)} = \alpha^{-1}(\text{approx}_\alpha(\bar{\alpha}(e)))$ and $\bar{\alpha}(t(e)) = \bar{\alpha}(e)$.

(ii) *For each $x \in D_{k,\alpha}$, $W_e = \alpha^{-1}(\text{approx}_\alpha(x)) \Longrightarrow \bar{\alpha}(e) = x$.*

(iii) *If $\alpha[W_e]$ is directed then $\bar{\alpha}(e) = \bigsqcup \alpha[W_e]$.*

The following approximations will be used later.

Lemma 3.6. *Let (D, α) be a weakly effective continuous cpo. There is a function $\tilde{\alpha}: \omega^2 \to B_\alpha$ and a total recursive function $p: \omega^2 \to \omega$ such that for each $e \in \omega$,*

(i) $m \leq n \Longrightarrow \tilde{\alpha}(e,m) \ll \tilde{\alpha}(e,n)$;

(ii) $\bar{\alpha}(e) = \bigsqcup_n \tilde{\alpha}(e,n)$; *and*

(iii) $\tilde{\alpha}(e,n) = \alpha(p(e,n))$.

Proof. We use the notation in the proof of Theorem 3.4. The function $r(t(e), n)$ is unbounded so we define a recursive function q by $q(0) = 0$ and

$$q(n+1) = (\text{least } k > q(n)) R(t(e), k).$$

Let $p(e,n) = f(t(e), q(n))$ and $\tilde{\alpha}(e,n) = \alpha(p(e,n))$. □

Definition 3.7. Let (D, α) be a weakly effective continuous cpo. A constructive numbering γ of $D_{k,\alpha}$ is *recursively complete* if there is a total recursive function h such that for each e,

$$\gamma[W_e] \text{ directed} \quad \Longrightarrow \gamma h(e) = \bigsqcup \gamma[W_e].$$

Theorem 3.8. *Let (D, α) be a weakly effective continuous cpo.*

(i) $\bar{\alpha}$ *is recursively complete.*

(ii) *If γ is a recursively complete constructive numbering of $D_{k,\alpha}$ then* id: $D_{k,\alpha} \to D_{k,\alpha}$ *is $(\bar{\alpha}, \gamma)$-computable and $(\gamma, \bar{\alpha})$-computable.*

Part (ii) of the theorem says that $\bar{\alpha}$ and γ are equivalent as numberings of $D_{k,\alpha}$, i.e., $D_{k,\alpha}$ is *stable* with respect to recursively complete numberings.

Proof. (i) Let W_e be r.e. such that $\bar{\alpha}[W_e]$ is directed. Then

$$\alpha(n) \ll \bigsqcup \bar{\alpha}[W_e] \Longleftrightarrow (\exists k \in W_e)(\alpha(n) \ll \bar{\alpha}(k)).$$

Thus there is a total recursive function h such that

$$W_{h(e)} = \{n : (\exists k \in W_e)(\alpha(n) \ll \bar{\alpha}(k))\},$$

since $\bar{\alpha}$ is constructive. By Lemma 3.5, $\bar{\alpha}(h(e)) = \bigsqcup \bar{\alpha}[W_e]$.

The proof of (ii) is similar, again using Lemma 3.5. □

If (D, α) is a weakly effective flat domain. Then $D_{k,\alpha} = D$. Let $\mathcal{P}$ be the domain of all partial functions from $\mathbb{N}$ into $\mathbb{N}$ ordered by graph inclusion and let α be a standard numbering of the set $\mathcal{P}_c$ of finite functions. Then $\mathcal{P}_{k,\alpha}$ is the set of partial recursive functions. The numbering $\bar{\alpha}$ is a standard numbering of the partial recursive functions satisfying the universal property and the s-m-n theorem. Finally if $\wp(\omega)$ is the domain of subsets of ω ordered by inclusion and α is the canonical numbering of the finite subsets of ω then $\wp(\omega)_{k,\alpha}$ is the family of r.e. sets.

We are now going to consider the equivalence of a function between weakly effective continuous cpos being computable and being effective in the sense of Definition 3.2. One direction is simple.

Proposition 3.9. *Let (D, α) and (E, β) be weakly effective continuous cpo. If $f: D \to E$ is (α, β)-effective then $f|_{D_{k,\alpha}}: D_{k,\alpha} \to E_{k,\beta}$ is $(\bar{\alpha}, \bar{\beta})$-computable.*

Proof. Considering the functions from Lemma 3.6 we have

$$f(\bar{\alpha}(e)) = f(\bigsqcup_{n\in\omega} \tilde{\alpha}(e,n)) = \bigsqcup_{n\in\omega} f\tilde{\alpha}(e,n).$$

But $\tilde{\alpha}(e,n) = \alpha(p(e,n))$ where p is total recursive, so

$$\beta^{-1}(\text{approx}_\beta(f\bar{\alpha}(e))) = \{m : \exists n(\beta(m) \ll f(\alpha(p(e,n))))\}.$$

The right hand side is r.e. uniformly in e so there is a total recursive function g such that $W_{g(e)} = \{m : \exists n(\beta(m) \ll f(\alpha(p(e,n))))\}$. But then

$$\bar{\beta}(g(e)) = f\bar{\alpha}(e),$$

i.e., g recursively tracks $f|_{D_{k,\alpha}}$. □

Note that an index for g is obtained uniformly from an index for f.

We are now going to show the converse of the above proposition. We are, however, going to show something stronger, namely, that each $(\bar{\alpha}, \bar{\beta})$-computable function $f: D_{k,\alpha} \to E_{k,\beta}$ has an (α, β)-effective (and hence continuous) extension $\bar{f}: D \to E$.

First we need a recursion theoretic lemma, a consequence of the second recursion theorem.

Lemma 3.10. (Berger) *Let V and W be r.e. sets such that W contains all r.e. indices for V. Let r be a total recursive function and let $\lambda q.V^q$ be a recursive enumeration of V. Then there is $e \in W$ and $q \in \omega$ such that*

$$W_e = V^q \cup W_{r(q)}.$$

In other words, if W contains all r.e. indices for V then W also contains an index for $W_{r(q)}$ for some q, modulo a finite subset of V.

Proof. Let $\lambda q.W^q$ be an enumeration of W such that $W^0 = \emptyset$. Define W_e using the second recursion theorem by

$$x \in W_e \iff \exists q[(x \in V^q \wedge e \notin W^q) \vee (x \in W_{r(q)} \wedge e \in W^{q+1} - W^q)].$$

Suppose $e \notin W$. Then

$$x \in W_e \iff \exists q(x \in V^q) \iff x \in V,$$

i.e., $W_e = V$. But then $e \in W$ by assumption, so we conclude $e \in W$. Let q be such that $e \in W^{q+1} - W^q$. Then

$$x \in W_e \iff x \in V^q \vee x \in W_{r(q)}.$$

□

We now connect effectivity with the Scott topology.

Definition 3.11. Let (D, α) be a weakly effective continuous cpo.

(i) $U \subseteq D$ is *α-effectively open* if there is an r.e. set W such that

$$U = \bigcup_{e\in W} \Uparrow\alpha(e).$$

An r.e. index for W is an *α-index* for U as an effectively open set.

(ii) $U \subseteq D_{k,\alpha}$ is *α-effectively open* in $D_{k,\alpha}$ if there is an α-effectively open set V such that $U = D_{k,\alpha} \cap V$.

Theorem 3.12. (Ershov) *Let (D, α) be a weakly effective continuous cpo. Then $U \subseteq D_{k,\alpha}$ is $\bar{\alpha}$-semidecidable if, and only if, U is α-effectively open in $D_{k,\alpha}$.*

Proof. Suppose U is α-effectively open and let W be an r.e. set such that $U = \bigcup_{e \in W}(D_{k,\alpha} \cap \Uparrow\alpha(e))$. Then

$$\bar{\alpha}(n) \in U \Longleftrightarrow (\exists e \in W)(\alpha(e) \ll \bar{\alpha}(n))$$

so U is $\bar{\alpha}$-semidecidable.

For the converse suppose $U \subseteq D_{k,\alpha}$ is $\bar{\alpha}$-semidecidable and consider $W = \{e \in \omega : \alpha(e) \in U\}$. Note that W is r.e. since the inclusion $\iota: B_\alpha \to D_{k,\alpha}$ is $(\alpha, \bar{\alpha})$-computable and U is $\bar{\alpha}$-semidecidable. Suppose we have shown

(i) U is upwards closed with respect to $\ll$ in $D_{k,\alpha}$, and

(ii) for each $x \in U$ there is $a \in B_\alpha \cap U$ such that $a \ll x$.

Then $U = \bigcup_{e \in W}(D_{k,\alpha} \cap \Uparrow\alpha(e))$, i.e., U is α-effectively open.

To prove (i) we show

$$x \in U, y \in D_{k,\alpha} \text{ and } x \sqsubseteq y \implies y \in U.$$

Suppose $x = \bar{\alpha}(m)$ and $y = \bar{\alpha}(n)$ and let $W = \bar{\alpha}^{-1}(U)$. We assume $m \in W$ and $x \sqsubseteq y$ and we show $n \in W$. Let t be the total recursive function from Lemma 3.5 and consider $W_{t(m)} = \alpha^{-1}(\text{approx}_\alpha(x))$. Suppose $W_e = W_{t(m)}$. Then

$$\bar{\alpha}(e) = \bar{\alpha}(t(m)) = \bar{\alpha}(m) = x \in U,$$

i.e., $e \in W$. Thus W contains all r.e. indices for $W_{t(m)}$. Let $r(q)$ be the constant function with value $t(n)$. Then by Lemma 3.10, there are numbers e and q such that $e \in W$ and $W_e = W^q_{t(m)} \cup W_{t(n)}$. But

$$W_{t(m)} = \alpha^{-1}(\text{approx}_\alpha(x)) \subseteq \alpha^{-1}(\text{approx}_\alpha(y)) = W_{t(n)}$$

so $W_e = W_{t(n)}$. Again by Lemma 3.5

$$y = \bar{\alpha}(n) = \bar{\alpha}(t(n)) = \bar{\alpha}(e)$$

and $e \in W$, so $y \in U$.

To prove (ii) we again let $W = \bar{\alpha}^{-1}(U)$ and $x = \bar{\alpha}(m) \in U$. Let p be the total recursive function from Lemma 3.6 and let r be a total recursive function such that $W_{r(q)} = \{p(t(m), q)\}$ for $q \in \omega$. Let

$$W^q_{t(m)} = \{k \leq q : \alpha(k) \ll^q \alpha(p(t(m), q))\}.$$

By the properties of t and p, we see that $\lambda q.W^q_{t(m)}$ is a recursive enumeration of $W_{t(m)}$. By Lemma 3.10 there is $e \in W$ and $q \in \omega$ such that

$$W_e = W^q_{t(m)} \cup W_{r(q)} = W^q_{t(m)} \cup \{p(t(m), q)\}.$$

But $\alpha(p(t(m), q))$ is top element in $\alpha[W_e]$. In particular $\alpha[W_e]$ is directed and hence

$$\bar{\alpha}(e) = \bigsqcup \alpha[W_e] = \alpha(p(t(m), q)) = \tilde{\alpha}(t(m), q) \ll \bar{\alpha}(t(m)) = \bar{\alpha}(m) = x.$$

By the above, $\bar{\alpha}(e)$ is the sought element. □

Note that the proof of the theorem is uniform.

Remark 3.13. The Rice-Shapiro theorem follows from the theorem above when applied to the algebraic domain $\wp(\omega)$.

Definition 3.14. Let (D, α) and (E, β) be weakly effective continuous cpos and let $D' \subseteq D$ and $E' \subseteq E$. Then a function $f: D' \to E'$ is *effectively continuous* if there is a total recursive function $g: \omega \to \omega$ such that

$$f^{-1}[E' \cap \Uparrow\beta(e)] = \bigcup_{m \in W_{g(e)}} (D' \cap \Uparrow\alpha(m)).$$

The following proposition is straight forward.

Proposition 3.15. *Let (D, α) and (E, β) be weakly effective continuous cpos and let $D' \subseteq D$ and $E' \subseteq E$ containing the bases determined by α and β. Suppose $f: D' \to E'$ is continuous.*

(i) *f is effectively continuous if, and only if, the relation $\beta(m) \ll f(\alpha(n))$ is r.e.*

(ii) *f has a unique continuous extension to $\bar{f}: D \to E$ and $\bar{f}$ is (α, β)-effective if, and only if, f is effectively continuous.*

Here follows a generalisation of the Myhill-Shepherdson theorem.

Theorem 3.16. *Let (D, α) and (E, β) be weakly effective continuous cpos and let $f: D_{k,\alpha} \to E_{k,\beta}$. Then f is $(\bar{\alpha}, \bar{\beta})$-computable if, and only if, there is an (α, β)-effective function $\bar{f}: D \to E$ such that $\bar{f}|_{D_{k,\alpha}} = f$.*

Proof. One direction is Proposition 3.9. For the other direction we assume $f: D_{k,\alpha} \to E_{k,\beta}$ is $(\bar{\alpha}, \bar{\beta})$-computable. Let $\hat{f}$ be the total recursive function tracking f. Then

$$\bar{\alpha}(n) \in f^{-1}(\Uparrow\beta(m) \cap E_{k,\beta}) \iff \beta(m) \ll f(\bar{\alpha}(n)) \iff \beta(m) \ll \bar{\beta}\hat{f}(n).$$

The latter relation is r.e. since $\bar{\beta}$ is a constructive numbering. Thus the set $f^{-1}(\Uparrow\beta(m) \cap E_{k,\beta})$ is open by Theorem 3.12. By the uniformity of that theorem we compute an index for the open set from m, i.e., f is effectively continuous. Now the result follows from Proposition 3.15. □

We see from the above theorem that the rather weak hypothesis that the way below relation $\ll$ is semidecidable nonetheless suffices to obtain strong results. However, we cannot build effective type structures even for domains. For this we need a stronger notion of effectivity. Here we give one such notion, for simplicity restricting ourselves to consistently complete algebraic cpos, i.e., algebraic domains.

Definition 3.17. An algebraic domain $D = (D; \sqsubseteq, \bot)$ is *effective* if there is a numbering $\alpha: \omega \to D_c$ such that the following relations are recursive:

(i) $\alpha(m) \sqsubseteq \alpha(n)$;

(ii) $\exists k(\alpha(m), \alpha(n) \sqsubseteq \alpha(k))$; and

(iii) $\alpha(m) \sqcup \alpha(n) = \alpha(k)$.

An effective algebraic domain is a pair (D, α) where D is an algebraic domain and α is an effective numbering of D_c in the above sense.

Let **EADOM** be the category of effective algebraic domains whose morphism set from (D, α) to (E, β) consists of the (α, β)-effective functions from D to E.

Theorem 3.18. *The category* **EADOM** *is cartesian closed.*

Proof. Straightforward from the results in Section 2.3 □

We close by stating some important results about effective domains with partial equivalence relations.

Let $(D, \equiv)$ be a domain with per and let $\bar{D} = \text{Field}(\equiv)$. We say that $\equiv$ is *dense* in D if $\bar{D}$ is dense in D, i.e., $\bar{D} \cap U \neq \emptyset$ for each non-empty open set $U \subseteq D$. The per $\equiv$ is *local* if whenever $x \equiv y$ then x and y are consistent, and $\equiv$ is *upwards closed* if $\bar{D}$ is upwards closed.

Let **EPER(Dom)** be the category whose objects are $(D, \equiv, \alpha)$, where (D, α) is an effective domain and $\equiv$ is a per on D. The morphisms are those morphisms in **PER(Dom)** with an effective representative. It is easily verified that **EPER(Dom)** is cartesian closed.

Let $(D, \equiv_D, \alpha)$ be an effective domain with a per, let $\bar{D} = \text{Field}(\equiv_D)$ and let $\Omega_{\equiv_D} = \bar{\alpha}^{-1}(\bar{D} \cap D_{k,\alpha})$. Then $\bar{\alpha}|_{\Omega_{\equiv_D}} : \Omega_{\equiv_D} \to D_{k,\alpha} \cap \bar{D}$ is a numbering. Note that $\Omega_{\equiv_D}$ is not r.e. in general. Let also $(E, \equiv_E, \beta)$ be an effective domain with per. Then by $f: \bar{D} \cap D_{k,\alpha} \to \bar{E} \cap E_{k,\beta}$ being $(\bar{\alpha}, \bar{\beta})$-computable we mean that f is computable with respect to these numberings.

The following theorem is due to Berger [2]. It will be used later to derive a form of Ceitin's theorem [7].

Theorem 3.19. *Let $(D, \equiv_D, \alpha)$ and $(E, \equiv_E, \beta)$ be effective algebraic domains with pers such that $\equiv_D$ is dense and $\equiv_E$ is local and upwards closed. Let*

$$f: \bar{D} \cap D_{k,\alpha} \to \bar{E} \cap E_{k,\beta}$$

be $(\bar{\alpha}, \bar{\beta})$-computable. Then there is an (α, β)-effective $\bar{f}: D \to E$ such that for each $x \in \bar{D}$, $f(x) \sqsubseteq \bar{f}(x)$.

Let $\mathcal{P}$ be the domain of partial functions on $\mathbb{N}$ and let $\mathcal{R}$ be the total recursive functions. Then, using a standard numbering of $\mathcal{P}$ and letting $\equiv$ be the equality relation on $\mathcal{R}$, Berger's theorem yields that any computable function from $\mathcal{R}$ to $\mathcal{R}$ (i.e. any recursive operator on $\mathcal{R}$) has an effective extension to all of $\mathcal{P}$. This is the Kreisel-Lacombe-Shoenfield theorem [12].

4 Domain representability

In this section we describe how large classes of topological algebras can be given natural domain representations which later will be shown to satisfactorily model concrete computations on the algebras. To a topological algebra A is associated a domain (of some kind) D_A from which a subset D_A^R is selected to make a representation of A via a surjective quotient map $\nu: D_A^R \to A$. Also the operations on A must be tracked by continuous operations on D, i.e., D must be a Σ-domain when representing a topological Σ-algebra.

The notion of effective domain representability for topological algebras was, as far as we know, first made explicit in [22] where it was used to study the effective content of the completion of a computable Noetherian local ring. It was further extended to ultrametric spaces and locally compact regular spaces in [23, 24, 25] and to metric spaces in the thesis [3].

However, it was clear from the beginning of the development of domain theory that domain theory is a theory of approximation and computation. For example, this was exploited in [9] where Ershov gave a domain representation of the Kleene-Kreisel continuous functionals. An effective and adequate domain model of Martin-Löf partial type theory is given in [18] which has been extended in [27] to provide a domain representation of Martin-Löf total type theory (see also [2, 17]). Also related to domain representability is [28] where embeddings of metric spaces into complete partial orders equipped with weight and distance are considered.

The work on domain representability referred to above use algebraic domains. Extensive related work on domain representability using continuous (most often non-algebraic) domains has been pursued by Edalat and his group; for a survey and further references of their work, which includes many interesting applications, see [8].

4.1 Basic definitions

The concepts below are valid both for continuous domains and algebraic domains. Therefore in this section we simply use the term *domain* to mean continuous domain or, if the reader so desires, algebraic domain. For D a domain we use the notation B_D for a base of D. In case D is algebraic the reader should read D_c for B_D. Recall the definitions of quotient map and quotient topology from Section 2.4.

Definition 4.1. Let X be a topological space, let D be a domain and D^R a subset of D. Then (D, D^R, ν) is a *domain representation* of X in case $\nu: D^R \to X$ is a surjective quotient map when D^R is given the (relativised) Scott topology.

¿From a domain representation (D, D^R, ν) of X we define a partial equivalence relation $\equiv$ on D by $x \equiv y \iff \nu(x) = \nu(y)$. Then $D^R = \mathrm{Field}(\equiv)$ and $D^R/\!\equiv\, \cong X$. Thus a domain representation (D, D^R, ν) of a space X is *upwards closed* if whenever $x \in D^R$ and $x \sqsubseteq y$ then $y \in D^R$ and $\nu(x) = \nu(y)$. It is *dense* if for each $a \in B_D$, $\uparrow a \cap D^R \neq \emptyset$, and it is *local* if $(\forall x, y \in D^R)(\nu(x) = \nu(y) \implies x$ and y are consistent$)$.

Upwards closed domain representations (D, D^R, ν) are natural when regarding the ordering $\sqsubseteq$ on D as an information ordering. If $x \in D^R$ completely determines $\nu(x) \in X$ and $x \sqsubseteq y$ then y contains all the information of x and hence also completely determines $\nu(x)$. Note that if the represented space X is T_1 then the condition $\nu(x) = \nu(y)$ is redundant.

We also distinguish between domain representations by putting further requirements on the quotient map ν. We say that a domain representation (D, D^R, ν) of X is a *retract representation* if ν is a retract, i.e., if there is a continuous function $e: X \to D$ such that $\nu \circ e = \mathrm{id}_X$. It is a *homeomorphic representation* if ν is a homeomorphism. For a thorough study of various kinds of domain representations we refer to [5].

Domain representations are uniformly closed under most of the usual constructions, such as retracts, quotients, disjoint sums and direct limits. However, perhaps surprisingly, domain representations are not uniformly closed under products. That is, if (D, D^R, ν) and (E, E^R, μ) are domain representations of X and Y respectively, then $\nu \times \mu: D^R \times E^R \to X \times Y$ need not be a quotient map (see [5]). Retract representations are uniformly closed under (arbitrary) products.

The next step is to represent continuous functions between topological spaces.

Definition 4.2. Let (D, D^R, ν) and (E, E^R, μ) be domain representations of X and Y respectively. A function $f: X \to Y$ is *represented* by (or *lifts* to) a continuous function $\bar{f}: D \to E$ if $\bar{f}[D^R] \subseteq E^R$ and $\mu(\bar{f}(x)) = f(\nu(x))$, for all $x \in D^R$.

Let (D, D^R, ν) and (E, E^R, μ) be domain representations of X and Y respectively. Suppose $\bar{f}: D \to E$ is such that $\bar{f}[D^R] \subseteq E^R$ and such that $\nu(x) = \nu(y) \implies \mu(\bar{f}(x)) = \mu(\bar{f}(y))$. Then $\bar{f}$ induces a unique function $f: X \to Y$ defined by $f(\nu(x)) = \mu(\bar{f}(x))$. In the terminology above, f is represented by $\bar{f}$.

Observe that if (D, D^R, ν) is local and upwards closed and (E, E^R, μ) is upwards closed then every continuous function $\bar{f}: D \to E$ such that $\bar{f}[D^R] \subseteq E^R$ induces a unique function $f: X \to Y$.

Proposition 4.3. *If $f: X \to Y$ is represented by a continuous $\bar{f}: D \to E$ then f is continuous.*

The proof is simple and depends on the fact that ν is assumed to be a quotient (only continuity of μ is required). It is a topological result and has nothing to do with the special case of domains. The problematic part is the converse.

Question: When does a continuous function $f: X \to Y$ have a lifting $\bar{f}: D \to E$?

Now let (D, D^R, ν) and (E, E^R, μ) be domain representations of X and Y respectively and let $\equiv_D$ and $\equiv_E$ be the induced pers. Suppose $f: X \to Y$ is represented by $\bar{f}: D \to E$. Then it is immediate from Definitions 4.1 and 4.2 that for each $x, y \in D$,

$$x \equiv_D y \Longrightarrow \bar{f}(x) \equiv_E \bar{f}(y). \tag{2}$$

If $\bar{g}: D \to E$ is another lifting of f then

$$(\forall x, y \in D)(x \equiv_D y \Longrightarrow \bar{f}(x) \equiv_E \bar{g}(y)). \tag{3}$$

Conversely, if $\bar{f}: D \to E$ is a continuous function satisfying (2) then $\bar{f}$ is the lifting of a continuous function $f: X \to Y$ by Proposition 4.3.

We have shown that an equivalent alternative to domain representability is the use of domains with pers. By Proposition 2.19 this means that we can build type structures in a natural way over a domain representable space X.

We now extend domain representability to topological algebras. Let Σ be a (finite) signature. Recall that a *topological* Σ-*algebra* A is a structure $A = (A; \sigma_1, \ldots, \sigma_k)$ where A is a topological space and the operations $\sigma_i: A^{n_i} \to A$ are continuous. The signature Σ gives k and the arity of each σ_i. (A constant is regarded as a 0-ary operation.)

A structure $D = (D; \sqsubseteq, \bot; \psi_1, \ldots, \psi_k)$ is a *structured domain* or Σ-*domain* for a signature Σ if $(D; \sqsubseteq, \bot)$ is a domain and each ψ_j is a continuous n_j-ary operation on D, that is $\psi_j : D^{n_j} \to D$ is continuous, where D^{n_j} is given the product topology, and k and the arities n_j are given by Σ.

Definition 4.4. A topological Σ-algebra $A = (A; \sigma_1, \ldots, \sigma_k)$ is *domain representable by* a Σ-domain $D = (D; \sqsubseteq, \bot; \hat{\sigma}_1, \ldots, \hat{\sigma}_k)$ if there is a Σ-substructure $D_A = (D_A; \hat{\sigma}_1, \ldots, \hat{\sigma}_k)$ of D and a Σ-epimorphism

$$\nu_A : D_A \to A$$

which is a quotient map with respect to the subspace topology of D_A. The triple (D, D_A, ν_A) is a *domain representation* of A.

We say that a topological Σ-algebra A is *domain representable* if A is representable by some Σ-domain D.

4.2 Standard algebraic representations

In this section we will describe a method to obtain *algebraic* domain representations which covers all regular Hausdorff algebras. We could as well use continuous (non-algebraic) domain representations. Each approach has its advantage. A continuous domain representation can usually be obtained as a homeomorphic representation where the representing elements form a subset of the maximal elements. On the other hand non-algebraic domains are more complicated structures than the algebraic ones.

For algebraic domains we have the following restriction.

Theorem 4.5. (Blanck [5]) *A compact topological space X has an algebraic homeomorphic representation by maximal elements if, and only if, X is totally disconnected.*

It follows that we have nice algebraic representations for, e.g., ultrametric algebras. Variants of the above result show that if we want to represent spaces more often used in analysis, such as the reals $\mathbb{R}$, we will obtain algebraic domain representations (D, D^R, ν) where by necessity the quotient $D^R/\equiv_\nu$ is non-trivial. From a computational point of view the latter is not as problematic as it may seem since computations are performed on the representation and are only induced on the quotient structure.

¿From Proposition 2.13 we see that every continuous domain has an algebraic dense retract domain representation. It follows that every space X representable by a continuous domain is also representable by an algebraic domain. Thus the choice is mainly a matter of convenience. Here we will pursue an algebraic representation.

We choose a set P of approximations for a topological space X, a family of subsets of X. Then the domain representing X will be the ideal completion $\bar{P}$ of P.

Definition 4.6. Let X be a topological space. Then a family P of non-empty subsets of X is a *neighbourhood system* if $X \in P$ and

(i) if $F, G \in P$ and $F \cap G \neq \emptyset$ then $F \cap G \in P$; and

(ii) if $x \in U$, where U is open, then $(\exists F \in P)(x \in F^\circ \subseteq \bar{F} \subseteq U)$.

Some remarks on notation and concepts. For $F \subseteq X$, F° denotes the *interior* of F, i.e., $F^\circ = \bigcup\{U : U \subseteq F \text{ and } U \text{ open}\}$. Similarly, $\bar{F}$ denotes the *closure* of F, i.e., $\bar{F} = \bigcap\{H : F \subseteq H \text{ and } H \text{ closed}\}$.

A Hausdorff space X is said to be *regular* if whenever $x \in U$, where U is open, there is V open such that $x \in V \subseteq \bar{V} \subseteq U$. Condition (ii) above implies that a Hausdorff space with a neighbourhood system is regular.

Here are some examples of neighbourhood systems for X.

Example 4.7.

(i) A topological base $\mathcal{B}$ for a regular space X closed under intersection.

(ii) The set P of all non-empty compact sets (and X) for a locally compact regular space X.

(iii) The set P of all non-empty closed subsets of a regular space.

Of course, there is no need generally to take *all* compact or closed sets in Example 4.7. It is enough to take sufficiently many. This is crucial from a computational point of view.

Example 4.8. For $\mathbb{R}$ we have the following natural neighbourhood systems.

(i) $P_1 = \{(a,b) : a < b, a, b \in \mathbb{Q}\} \cup \{\mathbb{R}\}$;

(ii) $P_2 = \{[a,b] : a \leq b, a, b \in \mathbb{Q}\} \cup \{\mathbb{R}\}$.

Note that P_1 is a neighbourhood system of type (i) in Example 4.7 whereas P_2 is of type (ii) and type (iii). Perhaps surprisingly, the neighbourhood system P_2 will turn out to be preferable to P_1.

Let P be a neighbourhood system for X. Then $P = (P; \supseteq, X)$ is a *conditional upper semilattice*, or *cusl*. Let $\bar{P} = \mathrm{Idl}(P; \supseteq)$, the ideal completion of P. Then it is easy to see that $\bar{P} = (\bar{P}; \subseteq, \{X\})$ is an algebraic domain whose cusl of compact elements are the principal ideals $\downarrow F$ for $F \in P$. (We identify $\downarrow F$ with F).

Definition 4.9. An ideal $I \in \bar{P}$ *converges* to a point $x \in X$ if for every open set U containing x there is $F \in I$ such that $x \in F \subseteq U$. I converges to x is denoted by $I \to x$.

Let X be a Hausdorff space and let $\bar{P}^R = \{I \in \bar{P} : I \text{ convergent}\}$. Define $\nu \colon \bar{P}^R \to X$ by

$$\nu(I) = x \Longleftrightarrow I \to x.$$

For $x \in X$ we define the important ideal

$$I_x = \{F \in P : x \in F^\circ\}.$$

Note that $I_x \to x$ and that $J \to x \Longleftrightarrow I_x \subseteq J$.

Theorem 4.10. *Let X be a Hausdorff space and P a neighbourhood system for X. Then $(\bar{P}, \bar{P}^R, \nu)$ is an algebraic retract representation of X which is upwards closed.*

Proof. Suppose $U \subseteq X$ is open and $\nu(I) = x \in U$. By Definition 4.6 (ii) there is $F \in P$ such that $x \in F^\circ \subseteq \bar{F} \subseteq U$. Thus $F \in I_x$ and hence $F \in I$. Suppose $J \in \bar{P}^R$ and $F \in J$. Then, clearly $\nu(J) \in \bar{F}$, i.e., $\uparrow F \subseteq U$. Thus ν is continuous.

Define $\eta \colon X \to \bar{P}^R$ by $\eta(x) = I_x$. Then $\nu \circ \eta = \mathrm{id}_X$. Furthermore η is continuous since for $F \in P$,

$$\eta^{-1}(\uparrow F \cap \bar{P}^R) = \{x \in X : F \in I_x\} = \{x \in X : x \in F^\circ\} = F^\circ.$$

The representation is upwards closed since I_x is the smallest ideal converging to x. □

Note that the domain representation of $\mathbb{R}$ obtained from P_1 in Example 4.8 is not local, whereas the one obtained from P_2 is local. This is one indication why open neighbourhood systems such as P_1 may not be as useful as closed neighbourhood systems.

Suppose P is a neighbourhood system for X consisting of only closed sets. Then for $x \in X$,

$$I^x = \{F \in P : x \in F\}$$

is an ideal, $I^x \to x$, and I^x is the largest ideal converging to x.

Theorem 4.11. *Every regular Hausdorff space X has an algebraic retract representation which is upwards closed, dense and local.*

Proof. Choose the neighbourhood system P consisting of all non-empty closed subsets of X. Then the representation $(\bar{P}, \bar{P}^R, \nu)$ is dense since for $F \in P$ there is $x \in F$ and hence $F \in I^x$, i.e., $I^x \in \uparrow F$. The representation is local since I^x is the largest ideal converging to x. □

A domain representation of X obtained from a neighbourhood system is said to be a *standard algebraic representation* of X.

The following theorem says that if a space X has an upwards closed algebraic retract domain representation then X has a standard algebraic representation.

Theorem 4.12. (Blanck [5]) *A topological space X has an upwards closed algebraic retract domain representation if, and only if, X is a regular Hausdorff space.*

Next we consider the problem of lifting continuous functions to the representing domains.

Theorem 4.13. *Let X and Y be regular Hausdorff spaces with neighbourhood systems P and Q, respectively. Let $(\bar{P}, \bar{P}^R, \nu)$ and $(\bar{Q}, \bar{Q}^R, \mu)$ be the standard domain representations of X and Y obtained from P and Q. Then every continuous function $f: X \to Y$ has a continuous lifting $\bar{f}: \bar{P} \to \bar{Q}$.*

Proof. Given continuous $f: X \to Y$ define $\bar{f}: P \to \bar{Q}$ by

$$\bar{f}(F) = \{G \in Q : f[F] \subseteq G^\circ\}.$$

It is easily verified that $\bar{f}(F)$ is an ideal and that $\bar{f}$ is monotone. We also denote by $\bar{f}$ its unique continuous extension to all of $\bar{P}$. In fact for $I \in \bar{P}$,

$$\bar{f}(I) = \{G \in Q : (\exists F \in I)(f[F] \subseteq G^\circ)\}.$$

Suppose $I \in \bar{P}^R$ and $\nu(I) = x$. Then $I_x \subseteq I$ and hence $\bar{f}(I_x) \subseteq \bar{f}(I)$. Thus it suffices to show that $I_{f(x)} \subseteq \bar{f}(I_x)$.

Let $G \in I_{f(x)}$. Then $f(x) \in G^\circ$ and $x \in f^{-1}[G^\circ]$. But then there is $F \in I_x$ such that $F \subseteq f^{-1}[G^\circ]$. This shows that $G \in \bar{f}(I_x)$. □

Corollary 4.14. *Let $A = (A; \sigma_1, \dots, \sigma_k)$ be a topological Σ-algebra and suppose A is a regular Hausdorff space. Then A has an algebraic retract domain representation which is upwards closed, dense and total.*

Proof. This follows from the theorem since if P is a neighbourhood system for A then P^n is a neighbourhood system for A^n. □

The ring operations on $\mathbb{R}$ are continuous so the ring of real numbers has a nice domain representation. In Section 5 we will show that the domain representation for the ring $\mathbb{R}$ obtained from P_2 in Example 4.8 is effective. We denote this representation of $\mathbb{R}$ by $\mathcal{R}$.

Domains and (ultra-)metric spaces have both been successfully used in denotational semantics despite the fact that they satisfy drastically different separation properties. A perhaps naive explanation for this coincidence is that each metric space has a domain representation. Furthermore the Banach fixed point theorem, which is crucial for semantics with metric spaces, corresponds in a precise and concrete way to the fixed point theorem over the representing domains. (See [21, 4].)

4.3 Representing relations and non-continuous functions

In this section we briefly consider the problem of representing relations. For example, how do we represent the $\leq$ relation on $\mathbb{R}$ over its domain representation $\mathcal{R}$? The problem is that relations in terms of their characteristic functions are often not continuous and such functions have no continuous representation by Proposition 4.3. The more general problem is then how to represent non-continuous functions.

Let X be a topological space and let $\mathbb{B} = \{\text{true}, \text{false}\}$ be the discrete boolean space. An n-ary relation P on X is identified with its *characteristic function* $c_P : X \to \mathbb{B}$ defined by

$$c_P(a_1, \ldots, a_n) = \begin{cases} \text{true}, & \text{if } P(a_1, \ldots, a_n); \\ \text{false}, & \text{if } \neg P(a_1, \ldots, a_n). \end{cases}$$

The idea is to represent the possibly non-continuous characteristic function continuously in such a way that it gives exact values at points of continuity and only proper approximations at points of discontinuity.

Let (D, D^R, ν) be an algebraic domain representation of X and let P be an n-ary relation on X. Define $\bar{c}_P : D_c^n \to \mathbb{B}_\bot$ by

$$\bar{c}_P(\vec{a}) = \begin{cases} \text{true}, & \text{if } (\forall \vec{x} \in (D^R)^n)(\vec{a} \sqsubseteq \vec{x} \implies P(\nu(\vec{x}))); \\ \text{false}, & \text{if } (\forall \vec{x} \in (D^R)^n)(\vec{a} \sqsubseteq \vec{x} \implies \neg P(\nu(\vec{x}))); \\ \bot, & \text{otherwise.} \end{cases}$$

$\bar{c}_P$ is clearly monotone and hence extends uniquely to a continuous function

$$\bar{c}_P : D^n \to \mathbb{B}_\bot.$$

We say that $\bar{c}_P$ *represents* c_P or P *approximately.*

Example 4.15. Consider the standard closed interval representation $\mathcal{R}$ of the reals $\mathbb{R}$ and the relation $\leq$. Then

$$\bar{c}_\leq([a, b], [c, d]) = \begin{cases} \text{true}, & \text{if } b \leq c; \\ \text{false}, & \text{if } d < a; \\ \bot, & \text{otherwise.} \end{cases}$$

If $x < y$ in $\mathbb{R}$ then $\bar{c}_\leq(I_x, I_y) = \text{true}$ and if $y < x$ in $\mathbb{R}$ then $\bar{c}_\leq(I_x, I_y) = \text{false}$. In case $x = y$ then $\bar{c}_\leq(I_x, I_x) = \bot$.

The function $c_\leq : \mathbb{R}^2 \to \mathbb{B}$ is continuous on

$$\{(x, y) : x \neq y\} \subseteq \mathbb{R}^2,$$

and discontinuous on the diagonal. Thus $\bar{c}_\leq$ represents $c_\leq$ exactly on points of continuity. At points of discontinuity $\bar{c}_\leq$ only provides the trivial approximation of the value of $c_\leq$.

We generalise the above to obtain continuous representations of non-continuous functions.

Definition 4.16. Let (D, D^R, ν_X) and (E, E^R, ν_Y) be domain representations of the topological spaces X and Y, respectively. Then a function $f : X \to Y$ (not necessarily continuous) is said to be *represented approximately* by (or *lifts approximately* to) $\bar{f} : D \to E$ if

(i) $\bar{f}$ is continuous,

(ii) $(\forall x \in D^R)(f$ continuous at $\nu_X(x) \implies \bar{f}(x) \in E^R$ and $f\nu_X(x) = \nu_Y \bar{f}(x))$, and

(iii) $(\forall x \in D^R)(f$ not continuous at $\nu_X(x) \implies (\exists y \in \nu_Y^{-1}[f\nu_X(x)])(\bar{f}(x) \sqsubseteq y))$.

We show that under rather general conditions there is a best continuous approximate representation of an arbitrary function, if there is one at all.

Theorem 4.17. *Let (D, D^R, ν_X) and (E, E^R, ν_Y) be domain representations of X and Y, respectively. Assume that D^R is dense in D, and that (E, E^R, ν_Y) is upwards closed and local. Let $f: X \to Y$ be a function and assume that f has one approximate representation in $[D \to E]$. Then f has a best approximate representation $\bar{f} \in [D \to E]$ in the sense of the domain ordering.*

Proof. Let $\mathcal{A}_f = \{\bar{f} \in [D \to E] : \bar{f}$ represents f approximately$\}$. We show that $\mathcal{A}_f$ is directed. $\mathcal{A}_f \neq \emptyset$ by assumption. Suppose $\bar{f}_1, \bar{f}_2 \in \mathcal{A}_f$. We first show that $\bar{f}_1$ and $\bar{f}_2$ are consistent. For this it suffices by the density of D^R to show that $\bar{f}_1(x)$ and $\bar{f}_2(x)$ are consistent for each $x \in D^R$.

Fix $x \in D^R$ and assume f is continuous at $\nu_X(x)$. Thus $\bar{f}_1(x), \bar{f}_2(x) \in E^R$ and

$$\nu_Y(\bar{f}_1(x)) = \nu_Y(\bar{f}_2(x)) = f(\nu_X(x)).$$

But by the hypotheses on (E, E^R, ν_Y) the supremum $\bar{f}_1(x) \sqcup \bar{f}_2(x)$ exists and

$$\nu_Y(\bar{f}_1(x) \sqcup \bar{f}_2(x)) = f(\nu_X(x)).$$

Now assume f is discontinuous at $\nu_X(x)$. Then there are $y_1, y_2 \in E^R$ such that $\nu_Y(y_1) = \nu_Y(y_2) = f(\nu_X(x))$ and $\bar{f}_1(x) \sqsubseteq y_1$ and $\bar{f}_2(x) \sqsubseteq y_2$. Again, by the assumptions on (E, E^R, ν_Y),

$$\bar{f}_1(x) \sqcup \bar{f}_2(x) \sqsubseteq y_1 \sqcup y_2 \in E^R$$

and $\nu(y_1 \sqcup y_2) = f(\nu_X(x))$. We conclude that $\bar{f}_1$ and $\bar{f}_2$ are consistent and $\bar{f}_1 \sqcup \bar{f}_2 \in \mathcal{A}_f$, that is, $\mathcal{A}_f$ is directed.

Let $\bar{f} = \bigsqcup \mathcal{A}_f$. We need to show that $\bar{f} \in \mathcal{A}_f$. Let $x \in D^R$ be such that f is continuous at $\nu_X(x)$ and let $\bar{g} \in \mathcal{A}_f$. Then $\bar{g}(x) \sqsubseteq \bar{f}(x)$ and $\bar{g}(x) \in E^R$ so $\bar{f}(x) \in E^R$ and

$$\nu_Y(\bar{f}(x)) = \nu_Y(\bar{g}(x)) = f(\nu_X(x)).$$

Now suppose f is discontinuous at $\nu_X(x)$. Let $\bar{y} \in E^R$ be the maximal element such that $\nu_Y(\bar{y}) = f(\nu_X(x))$. The assumptions on (E, E^R, ν_Y) imply that such $\bar{y}$ exists. Thus $\bar{g}(x) \sqsubseteq \bar{y}$ and hence

$$\bar{f}(x) = \bigsqcup\{\bar{g}(x) : \bar{g} \in \mathcal{A}_f\} \sqsubseteq \bar{y},$$

proving that $\bar{f} \in \mathcal{A}_f$. □

An important example from computer science is the theory of streams. Let us model streams as functions from time to data. What is interesting from our point of view is that we allow continuous time which we model by the real numbers $\mathbb{R}$ or a final segment of $\mathbb{R}$. If the set of data is discrete, i.e. has the discrete topology, then the only continuous streams are the constant streams. Thus to model streams from continuous time such as signals and study their computability we need to be able to model non-continuous functions.

Theorem 4.18. *Let A be a metric space with a standard domain representation (D_A, D_A^R, ν_A) and let $\mathcal{R}$ be the standard closed interval representation of $\mathbb{R}$. Then each function $f: \mathbb{R} \to A$ has a continuous approximate representation $\bar{f}: \mathcal{R} \to D_A$.*

Proof. Let $f: \mathbb{R} \to A$ be a function. We define $\bar{f}: \mathcal{R}_c \to D_A$ by

$$\bar{f}([a,b]) = \{F \in (D_A)_c : f([a,b]) \subseteq F^\circ\},$$

where F° denotes the interior of F. Then $\bar{f}$ is monotone and extends uniquely to a continuous function $\bar{f}: \mathcal{R} \to D_A$. In fact,

$$\bar{f}(I) = \{F \in (D_A)_c : (\exists [a,b] \in I)(f([a,b]) \subseteq F^\circ)\}.$$

Suppose f is continuous at the point $x \in \mathbb{R}$ and consider the ideal $I_x = \{[a,b] : a < x < b\} \in \mathcal{R}^R$. Recall that I_x is the smallest ideal representing x. Let $J = \bar{f}(I_x)$. We need to show that $J \in D_A^R$ and that $\nu_A(J) = f(x)$. Put differently, we need to show that $\bigcap J = \{f(x)\}$. Obviously $f(x) \in \bigcap J$. Given $\varepsilon > 0$, take $F \in (D_A)_c$ such that

$$f(x) \in F^\circ \subseteq F \subseteq B(f(x), \varepsilon),$$

where the latter is the open ε-ball around $f(x)$. Since f is continuous at x and F° is open there are $a', b' \in \mathbb{Q}$, $a' < x < b'$ and $f[(a', b')] \subseteq F^\circ$. But then there is $[a,b] \in I_x$ such that

$$f[\,[a,b]\,] \subseteq f[(a',b')] \subseteq F^\circ,$$

i.e., $F \in J$. But $\mathrm{diam}(F) < \varepsilon$ and ε was arbitrary. It follows that $\bigcap J = \{f(x)\}$.

Now suppose $x \in \mathbb{R}$ is a point of discontinuity of f. It suffices to show

$$I \supseteq I_x \implies \bar{f}(I) \sqsubseteq I_{f(x)}.$$

But this follows directly from the definition of $\bar{f}$. □

The theorem shows that the domain of continuous functions $[\mathcal{R} \to D_A]$ contains representations of all streams from $\mathbb{R}$ to A. The representations are, however, only approximate on points of discontinuity. From a computational point of view this is quite reasonable. We cannot compute exactly on continuous data types, including continuous time, we can only compute on approximations of data. At points of continuity we obtain approximations of arbitrary precision. At points of discontinuity we can only expect proper approximations. However, with an appropriate choice of domain representation this may nonetheless produce important information.

Corollary 4.19. *Each function $f: \mathbb{R} \to A$ has a best representation $\bar{f}$ in $[\mathcal{R} \to D_A]$.*

Proof. The hypotheses of Theorem 4.17 are satisfied for standard representations. □

¿From an approximate domain representation of the complete stream space $(\mathbb{R} \to A)$ we define an equivalence relation $\sim$ on $(\mathbb{R} \to A)$ by saying that $f \sim g$ if they have the same best approximation. Thus we obtain a domain representation in the sense of Definition 4.1 of $(\mathbb{R} \to A)/\sim$.

5 Effective domain representations

Our motivation for the study of domain representability was its use together with the theory of effective domains in investigating in a uniform way the effective content of topological algebras. In this final section we survey some results of this approach indicating that it is a general method. A further conclusion is that various notions of computability via "concrete" computations coincide, thus showing that the theory of "concrete" computability is stable (see [26]).

5.1 *Effective topological algebras*

The general method we pursue to study the effective properties of a generally uncountable topological algebra A is to find an *effective* domain D representing A in the sense of Definition 4.1 and then measure the effectivity of A by means of the effectivity of the representing domain D. Thus the effectivity of A is dependent on the domain representation D and its effectivity.

Definition 5.1. Let A be a topological Σ-algebra. Then A is *(weakly) effectively domain representable* by (D, D_A, ν, α) if (D, D_A, ν) is a domain representation of A and (D, α) is a (weakly) effective Σ-domain.

Next we consider the set of computable elements of a weakly effectively domain representable algebra A, analogous to the set $D_{k,\alpha}$ of computable elements in a weakly effective domain (D, α).

Definition 5.2. Let A be a topological Σ-algebra weakly effectively domain representable by (D, D_A, ν, α). Then the set $A_{k,\alpha}$ of (D, D_A, ν, α)*-computable elements* of A is the set

$$A_{k,\alpha} = \{x \in A : \nu^{-1}(x) \cap D_{k,\alpha} \neq \emptyset\}.$$

We suppress the reference to (D, D_A, ν, α) whenever possible and simply write $A_{k,\alpha}$ for the set of computable elements.

A Σ-algebra A is said to have a *numbering with recursive operations* if there is a numbering $\beta : \Omega \to A$ such that each operation in A is β-computable. We say that (A, β) is a *numbered algebra with recursive operations.* Note that we put *no* requirement on the complexity of the code set Ω nor on the (relative) complexity of the equality relation.

Proposition 5.3. *Let $(A; \sigma_1, \ldots, \sigma_q)$ be a topological Σ-algebra weakly effectively domain representable by (D, D_A, ν, α).*

(i) *$A_{k,\alpha}$ is a subalgebra of A.*

(ii) *$A_{k,\alpha}$ is a numbered algebra with recursive operations by a numbering $\tilde{\alpha}$ induced by α.*

Proof. Let $\bar{\alpha}: \omega \to D_{k,\alpha}$ be the canonical constructive numbering of $D_{k,\alpha}$ obtained from α. Let $\Omega_A = \bar{\alpha}^{-1}(D_{k,\alpha} \cap D_A)$ and define $\tilde{\alpha}: \Omega_A \to A_{k.\alpha}$ by

$$\tilde{\alpha}(n) = \nu(\bar{\alpha}(n)).$$

Then $\tilde{\alpha}$ is a surjective numbering of $A_{k,\alpha}$.

Now (i) follows immediately from Proposition 3.3 (i). For the proof of (ii) let σ be an m-ary operation tracked by the effective operation $\hat{\sigma}$ on D. Then by Proposition 3.9 there is a recursive function $f: \omega^m \to \omega$ tracking $\hat{\sigma}$ on $D_{k,\alpha}$. Thus for each $n_1, \ldots, n_m \in \Omega_A$,

$$\begin{aligned} \sigma(\tilde{\alpha}(n_1), \ldots, \tilde{\alpha}(n_m)) &= \nu(\hat{\sigma}(\bar{\alpha}(n_1), \ldots, \bar{\alpha}(n_m))) \\ &= \nu(\bar{\alpha}(f(n_1, \ldots, n_m))) \\ &= \tilde{\alpha}(f(n_1, \ldots, n_m)), \end{aligned}$$

showing that f also tracks σ with respect to $\tilde{\alpha}$. □

Definition 5.4. Let A and B be topological spaces, weakly effectively domain representable by (D, D_A, ν_A, α) and (E, E_B, ν_B, β), respectively. Then a function $f: A \to B$ is said to be (α, β)-*effective* if there is an (α, β)-effective continuous function $\bar{f} : D \to E$ representing f.

It is an easy exercise using Proposition 3.9 to show that if $f: A \to B$ is (α, β)-effective then $f|_{A_{k,\alpha}} : A_{k,\alpha} \to B_{k,\beta}$ is $(\tilde{\alpha}, \tilde{\beta})$-computable. The converse lifting is a much more delicate problem (see Theorem 5.18).

5.2 Locally compact Hausdorff spaces

In this section we analyse the effectivity of standard algebraic domain representations from Section 4.2 for locally compact Hausdorff (and hence regular) spaces. We restrict our attention to effective domain representations. The reader is invited to make a similar analysis of weakly effective domain representations using continuous domains or using the technique described in [26].

Let X be a locally compact Hausdorff space and let P be a neighbourhood system for X in the sense of Definition 4.6 consisting of compact sets (except possibly X). We call such a P for a *compact neighbourhood system.*

A compact neighbourhood system is said to be α-*computable* if α is a numbering of P satisfying the conditions in Definition 3.17. It follows that if P is α-computable then $\bar{P}$, the ideal completion of P, is an effective domain under α (identifying elements of P with their principal ideals).

The extra hypothesis on a computable compact neighbourhood system needed in order to obtain a smooth theory is that the relation $F \subseteq G^\circ$ must be α-semidecidable.

A first observation is that the ideals I_x play an important role.

Lemma 5.5. *Suppose the relation* $F \subseteq G^\circ$ *is* α*-semidecidable for* $F, G \in P$. *Let* $f: \bar{P} \to \bar{P}$ *be the function defined by*

$$f(I) = \{G \in P : (\exists F \in I)(F \subseteq G^\circ)\}.$$

(i) f *is a continuous* (α, α)*-effective function and* $f[\bar{P}^R] \subseteq \bar{P}^R$.

(ii) f *restricted to* $\bar{P}^R_{k,\alpha}$ *is* $\bar{\alpha}$*-computable.*

Proof. The proof of (i) is immediate using the added hypothesis. Part (ii) follows from Proposition 3.9 □

Corollary 5.6. *Suppose the relation* $F \subseteq G^\circ$ *is* α*-semidecidable for* $F, G \in P$. *Then* $x \in X_{k,\alpha}$ *if, and only if, the ideal* $I_x = \{G \in P : x \in G^\circ\} \in \bar{P}_{k,\alpha}$.

Proof. For the non-trivial direction assume $x \in X_{k,\alpha}$. Let $I \in \bar{P}^R$ be an α-computable ideal and let f be the effective function from Lemma 5.5. Then $f(I) = I_x$ and hence I_x is computable by the effectivity of f. □

Next we give a sufficient condition for continuous functions between locally compact Hausdorff spaces to be effective. The crucial condition is the semidecidability of whether, for given compact sets, the image of one is contained in the interior of the other.

Proposition 5.7. *Let X and Y be locally compact Hausdorff spaces with cusls P and Q of compact neighbourhood systems, respectively. Suppose P is α-computable and Q is β-computable. Let $f: X \to Y$ be a continuous function such that the relation*

$$f[F] \subseteq G^\circ$$

is (α, β)-semidecidable for all (compact) $F \in P$ and $G \in Q$. Then f is (α, β)-effective.

Proof. Let $\bar{f}: \bar{P} \to \bar{Q}$ be the continuous function representing f, defined in the proof of Theorem 4.13. Thus, for compact $F \in P$,

$$\bar{f}(F) = \{G \in Q : f[F] \subseteq G^\circ\},$$

that is $\downarrow G \sqsubseteq \bar{f}(F) \Longleftrightarrow f[F] \subseteq G^\circ$, which is (α, β)-semidecidable by assumption. □

In the remaining part of this section we consider the effective content of the ring of real numbers $\mathbb{R}$. The set P_2 of Example 4.8 is a compact neighbourhood system for $\mathbb{R}$. Let $\mathcal{R} = \bar{P}_2$, the ideal completion, and let α be a standard numbering of P_2 making $\mathcal{R}$ into en effective domain. Then $(\mathcal{R}, \mathcal{R}^R, \nu, \alpha)$ is the standard domain representation of $\mathbb{R}$ that we consider.

The effective theory of $\mathbb{R}$ has been much studied and is well understood. Our purpose here is to show that the standard effective theory of $\mathbb{R}$ is equivalent with that obtained from domain representability. A nice general reference for recursive analysis is [19].

Definition 5.8. An element $x \in \mathbb{R}$ is a *computable real* if there is a computable sequence of rational numbers (r_n) such that for each n,

$$|r_n - x| < 2^{-n}.$$

Proposition 5.9. *The set $\mathbb{R}_{k,\alpha}$ is precisely the set of computable reals.*

Proof. Suppose $x \in \mathbb{R}$ is a computable real. Let (r_n) be a computable sequence of rationals converging to x with the modulus prescribed by Definition 5.8. For each n, let $F_n = [r_n - 2^{-n}, r_n + 2^{-n}]$. Then $x \in F_n^\circ$ and the set $\{F_n : n \in \omega\}$ generates a computable ideal, in fact I_x. Thus $x \in \mathbb{R}_{k,\alpha}$.

For the converse inclusion suppose $x \in \mathbb{R}_{k,\alpha}$. Then an $\tilde{\alpha}$-index for x is an $\bar{\alpha}$-index for some ideal $I \in \mathcal{R}^R$ such that $\bigcap I = \{x\}$. By Lemma 3.5 we uniformly obtain an r.e. index for $\alpha^{-1}[I]$. For each n we effectively search through I and find $[a_n, b_n] \in I$ such that $b_n - a_n < 2^{-n}$, and set $r_n = (b_n + a_n)/2$. Then (r_n) is a computable sequence of rational numbers witnessing that x is a computable real. □

An index for a computable real x is an index for a computable sequence (r_n) of rationals converging to x in the manner prescribed by Definition 5.8. Thus we obtain a numbering

$$\beta : \Omega \to \mathbb{R}_{k,\alpha}$$

where Ω is the set of such indices. The above proof is uniform in the sense that given a β-index for a computable real x then we can compute an $\tilde{\alpha}$-index for x, and conversely. To be precise, there are partial recursive functions f and g such that if e is a β-index for a computable real x then $f(e)$ is defined and $f(e)$ is an $\tilde{\alpha}$-index for x. Similarly, if e is an $\tilde{\alpha}$-index for x then $g(e)$ is defined and $g(e)$ is a β-index for x. Of course, it is not recursively decidable whether or not a number e is an index of a computable real. In fact, Ω is a $\prod_2^0$ set.

We now proceed to show that a function on $\mathbb{R}$ is computable in the sense of recursive analysis if, and only if, it is effective in our sense.

The notion of a *computable* or *recursive* function in recursive analysis is a sensitive one. Here we consider the generally accepted notion, originally due to Grzegorczyk [10] and Lacombe [14].

We say that a sequence (x_n) of real numbers is *computable* if there is a computable double sequence (r_{nk}) of rational numbers such that $|r_{nk} - x_n| \leq 2^{-k}$ for all k and n.

Definition 5.10. A function $f: \mathbb{R} \to \mathbb{R}$ is *computable* if the following hold.

(i) If (x_n) is a computable sequence of real numbers then $(f(x_n))$ is a computable sequence.

(ii) There is a recursive function $d: \omega^2 \to \omega$ such that for all natural numbers N and M and for each $x, y \in [-M, M]$,

$$|x - y| < \frac{1}{d(M, N)} \implies |f(x) - f(y)| < 2^{-N}.$$

Condition (ii) assures that a computable function on $\mathbb{R}$ is continuous. Thus, in order to show that such a function f is effective, it suffices by Proposition 5.7 to show that the relation $f[[a, b]] \subseteq [c, d]^\circ$ is α-semidecidable, where $f[[a, b]]$ denotes the image of $[a, b]$ under f. Of course, $f[[a, b]]$ is again a compact interval by continuity.

Lemma 5.11. *Let $f: \mathbb{R} \to \mathbb{R}$ be a computable function. Then f is (α, α)-effective.*

Proof. We sketch the argument. It is well-known from recursive analysis that given recursive real numbers $a \leq b$ we can compute indices for recursive real numbers $m \leq M$ such that $f[[a, b]] = [m, M]$. (Note, however, that one cannot in general compute where a maximum or minimum is taken.) It is also well-known and easy to see that the $<$ relation on the recursive reals is semidecidable. It follows that for $[a, b], [c, d] \in \mathcal{R}_c$ the relation

$$f[[a, b]] \subseteq [c, d]^\circ$$

is α-semidecidable, and hence that f is (α, α)-effective. □

Now assume that $f: \mathbb{R} \to \mathbb{R}$ is effective. Thus f is represented by an effective continuous function $\bar{f}: \mathcal{R} \to \mathcal{R}$. By Lemma 5.5 we may assume that $\bar{f}(I) = I_{f(x)}$ whenever I is a total ideal representing x. We shall show that f is computable.

To prove condition (i) let (x_n) be a computable sequence of reals and let (w_{nk}) be an associated computable double sequence of rationals such that $|w_{nk} - x_n| < 2^{-k}$ for each n and k. Then the ideal I_{x_n} is computable, uniformly in n, since it is generated by

$$[w_{nk} - 2^{-k}, w_{nk} + 2^{-k}] \quad \text{for } k \in \omega.$$

By the effectivity of $\bar{f}$, the ideal $I_{f(x_n)} = \bar{f}(I_{x_n})$ is computable, uniformly in n. Thus, given a number t, we search effectively for $[c,d] \in I_{f(x_n)}$ such that $|d-c| < 2^{-t}$. In this way we obtain a computable double sequnce (s_{nt}) by letting

$$s_{nt} = (c+d)/2.$$

Clearly $|s_{nt} - f(x_n)| < 2^{-t}$ for each n and t, so $(f(x_n))$ is a computable sequence.

It remains to prove the existence of a recursive modulus function for f. Suppose we are given positive natural numbers M and N. For each $k \in \omega$, partition $[-M,M]$ into k subintervals

$$[a_{ki}, a_{ki+1}] \quad i = 0, \ldots, k-1$$

of equal length.

Claim. There is k such that for each $i = 0, \ldots, k-1$ there is $[c,d] \in \bar{f}([a_{ki}, a_{ki+1}])$ such that $|d-c| < 2^{-N}$.

Suppose the claim is false for N. Then for each k we choose i_k, $0 \leq i_k \leq k-1$, such that

$$[c,d] \in \bar{f}([a_{ki_k}, a_{ki_k+1}]) \implies |d-c| \geq 2^{-N}.$$

Choose $x_k \in [a_{ki_k}, a_{ki_k+1}]$. Then, by compactness, the set $\{x_k : k \in \omega\}$ has a limit point x in $[-M,M]$. Suppose first that $x \neq \pm M$. Choose $[c,d] \in I_{f(x)} = \bar{f}(I_x)$ such that $|d-c| < 2^{-N}$. Thus for some $[a,b] \in I_x$, $[c,d] \in \bar{f}([a,b])$. But then there is k sufficiently large so that $[a_{ki_k}, a_{ki_k+1}] \subseteq [a,b]$ and hence

$$[c,d] \in \bar{f}([a_{ki_k}, a_{ki_k+1}])$$

which is a contradiction. In case $x = M$ we consider the ideal I_x^L, generated by $\{[a,M] : a < M\}$, in place of I_x to obtain a contradiction. The case $x = -M$ is handled similarly, completing the proof of the claim.

Given M and N we compute a number k which witnesses the claim. The computation is performed by an effective search, using the effectivity of $\bar{f}$. Then we define $d: \omega^2 \to \omega$ by

$$d(M,N) = \text{ least number} > k/2M.$$

Thus d is a total recursive function with an index obtained uniformly from an index of $\bar{f}$.

Suppose $x, y \in [-M,M]$ and $|x-y| < 1/d(M,N)$. Then for the k computed above, $|x-y| < 2M/k$ so there is i such that

$$|x - a_{ki}| < 2M/k \quad \text{and} \quad |y - a_{ki}| < 2M/k.$$

Say, without loss of generality, that $x \in [a_{ki}, a_{ki+1}]$. Then there is $[c,d] \in \bar{f}([a_{ki}, a_{ki+1}])$ such that $|d-c| < 2^{-N}$. It is easy to see that

$$f[[a_{ki}, a_{ki+1}]] \subseteq [c,d]$$

so $|f(x) - f(a_{ki})| < 2^{-N}$. The same holds for y and hence we have

$$|f(x) - f(y)| \leq |f(x) - f(a_{ki})| + |f(a_{ki}) - f(y)| < 2^{-N} + 2^{-N} = 2^{-N+1}.$$

We have proved the following theorem.

Theorem 5.12. *A function $f: \mathbb{R} \to \mathbb{R}$ is computable in the sense of recursive analysis if, and only if, f is effective.*

5.3 Metric spaces

Some early analysis of the effective content of metric spaces are [14] and [16]. There is also an important constructive analysis of metric spaces in [7].

Definition 5.13. A metric space (X, d) is *recursive* in the sense of Moschovakis if

(i) there is a surjective numbering $\alpha: \Omega_\alpha \to X$, where $\Omega_\alpha \subseteq \omega$;

(ii) $d: X \times X \to \mathbb{R}_k$, where $\mathbb{R}_k$ is the set of recursive real numbers; and

(iii) the distance function d is (α, ρ)-computable, where $\rho: \Omega_\rho \to \mathbb{R}_k$ is a standard numbering.

This is a very general definition. Its weak point is that calculations with distances are limited to those possible with recursive reals. Nonetheless it is possible to give a weakly effective domain representation to (the completion of) a recursive metric space along the lines given below. We shall not pursue this here. Instead we give an alternate more restrictive definition that strengthens the computability of the space and which is still appropriate for examples.

By an ordered field K we mean a field $K = (K; +, -, \times, 0, 1, \leq)$. The field K is *computable* if there is a numbering of K from ω such that all the operations and the relation $\leq$ (and hence $=$) are recursive. It is known that if K is a computable ordered field then its real closure is computable as an ordered field. Furthermore, if K is archimedian then K is computably embedded into $\mathbb{R}_k$ (see [15, 13]).

Definition 5.14. A metric space (X, d) is *computable* if

(i) there is a numbering $\alpha: \omega \to X$ with decidable equality;

(ii) $d: X \times X \to K$, for some computable archimedian ordered field K;

(iii) the distance function d is (α, γ)-computable, where $\gamma: \omega \to K$ is a computable numbering of K.

These two definitions determine two general definitions of effective metric spaces.

Definition 5.15.

(i) A metric space (X, d) is *weakly effective* if there exists a dense subspace A of X such that (A, d) is recursive in the sense of Moschovakis.

(ii) A metric space (X, d) is *effective* if there exists a dense subspace A of X such that (A, d) is computable.

The majority of examples of interest are effective metric spaces (rather than weakly effective metric spaces), including: (i) the Euclidean spaces $\mathbb{R}^n$; (ii) the space $C[0, 1]$ of continuous functions $[0, 1] \to \mathbb{R}$ with the sup norm; and (iii) L^p spaces for rational $p \geq 1$.

The existence of a recursive or computable dense subset A of X allows us to define the *computable elements* of the metric space; these are the elements of X that can be approximated by computable Cauchy sequences of elements from A with computable modulus functions. To define the set X_k of computable elements of X we embed the space X in the metric completion A^* of A. So we may assume that $A \subseteq X \subseteq A^*$. From the numbering $\alpha: \Omega_\alpha \to A$ we construct a canonical numbering $\alpha_k: \Omega_{\alpha_k} \to A_k$ of the set A_k of computable elements in the completion A^*. Then we set $X_k = X \cap A_k$, and give it the numbering α_k restricted to $\alpha_k^{-1}(X_k)$.

We now describe how to obtain an effective algebraic domain representation of an effective metric space. Our development follows [4].

Let (X, d) be a metric space with a dense subset A. A *formal closed ball* is a "notation" $F_{a,r}$, where $a \in A$ and $r \in \mathbb{Q}_+$, the set of non-negative rational numbers. The formal ball is a name or syntax for a closed ball and we may write it semantically by

$$F_{a,r} = \{x \in X : d(a, x) \leq r\}.$$

Two formal balls are *consistent*,

$$F_{a,r} \uparrow F_{b,s} \quad \text{if } d(a, b) \leq r + s.$$

We say that $F_{b,s}$ is *formally contained* in $F_{a,r}$,

$$F_{a,r} \sqsubseteq F_{b,s} \quad \text{if } d(a, b) + s \leq r.$$

A set $\{F_{a_1,r_1}, \ldots, F_{a_n,r_n}\}$ of formal balls is *permissible* if the balls are pairwise consistent and no ball is contained within another, i.e., for $1 \leq i \leq j \leq n$, $F_{a_i,r_i} \uparrow F_{a_j,r_j}$ and it is not the case that $F_{a_i,r_i} \sqsubseteq F_{a_j,r_j}$ or $F_{a_j,r_j} \sqsubseteq F_{a_i,r_i}$. We use the notation σ, τ for permissible sets.

Let P be the set of all permissible sets of formal balls. We need to extend the relation $\sqsubseteq$ to permissible sets:

$$\sigma \sqsubseteq \tau \iff (\forall F_{a,r} \in \sigma)(\exists F_{b,s} \in \tau)(F_{a,r} \sqsubseteq F_{b,s}).$$

We note that consistency is characterised by

$$\sigma \uparrow \tau \iff (\forall F_{a,r} \in \sigma)(\forall F_{b,s} \in \tau)(F_{a,r} \uparrow F_{b,s}).$$

Given consistent permissible sets σ and τ, the supremum $\sigma \sqcup \tau = g(\sigma, \tau)$ where g removes those formal balls in $\sigma \cup \tau$ properly contained in others.

The following is immediate from the construction above. But note that we need to consider sets of formal balls in order to be able to compute the supremum operation.

Lemma 5.16. *If (A, d) is a computable metric space then the obtained structure $P = (P; \sqsubseteq, \uparrow, \sqcup, \perp)$ is a computable cusl with a numbering α obtained from the numbering of A.*

We now let $D = \bar{P}$, the ideal completion of P. Thus (D, α) is an effective domain.

An ideal $I \in D$ is *converging* if for any $\varepsilon > 0$ there exists $\{F_{a,r}\} \in I$ such that $r < \varepsilon$. We define $x \in A^*$ to be *approximated* by the ideal I if $(\forall \sigma \in I)(\forall F_{a,r} \in \sigma)(x \in F_{a,r})$. A convergent ideal I approximates exactly one element x in A^*; we write $I \to x$. Let $D_X = \{I \in D : I \to x \in X\}$. The function $\nu_X: D_X \to X$ defined by

$$\nu_X(I) = x \iff I \to x$$

is a quotient mapping. Using this construction one may now verify

Theorem 5.17. *Each effective metric space X has an effective domain representation (D, α) such that the computable elements X_k obtained from the metric coincides uniformly with the computable elements induced by (D, α), i.e., $X_k = X_{k,\alpha}$.*

The situation with computable functions is more difficult. We just state the following theorem which is, essentially, Theorem 3.4.33 in [3]. By a semieffective domain we mean an effective domain except that the consistency relation on the compact elements need not be decidable.

Theorem 5.18. *Let X and Y be effective metric spaces. Then there exists a semieffective domain representation $D = (D, D_X, \nu_X, \alpha)$ of X consisting of permissible sets of formal balls such that together with a standard effective formal ball representation $E = (E, E_Y, \nu_Y, \beta)$ of Y, the following are equivalent for any function $f: X_{k,\alpha} \to Y_{k,\beta}$:*

(i) *the function $f: X_{k,\alpha} \to Y_{k,\beta}$ is $(\tilde{\alpha}, \tilde{\beta})$-computable; and*

(ii) *there is a continuous extension of f to $\bar{f}: X \to Y$ which is (α, β)-effective.*

The proof is an application of Theorem 3.19. However some work is necessary. It is not the case in general that a standard effective formal ball representation of X is dense, which is (seemingly) a necessary condition in that theorem. First we need to take a dense part of the standard effective formal ball representation of X, thus obtaining a semieffective domain representation, and observe that Theorem 3.19 is still valid.

The implication (i) implies (ii) has a form of Ceitin's Theorem as a corollary, showing that functions on metric spaces computable under reasonable numberings are continuous.

References

[1] S. Abramsky and A. Jung, Domain theory, in *Handbook of Logic in Computer Science*, volume 3, (S. Abramsky, D. Gabbay, and T. S. E. Maibaum, editors), Oxford University Press, Oxford, 1995, 1 – 168.

[2] U. Berger, Total sets and objects in domain theory, *Annals of Pure and Applied Logic* 60 (1993), 91 – 117.

[3] J. Blanck,Computability on topological spaces by effective domain representations, Uppsala Dissertations in Mathematics, vol. 7, 1997.

[4] J. Blanck, Domain-representability of metric spaces, *Annals of Pure and Applied Logic* 83 (1997), 225 – 247.

[5] J. Blanck, Domain representations of topological spaces, *Electronic Notes in Theoretical Computer Science* 13 (1998).

[6] J. Blanck, Effective domain representation of $\mathcal{H}(X)$, the space of compact subsets, *Theoretical Computer Science* 219 (1999), 19 – 48.

[7] G. S. Ceitin, Algorithmic operators in constructive complete separable metric spaces, *Doklady Akademii Nauk SSSR* 128, 49 – 52, 1959.

[8] A. Edalat, Domains for computation in mathematics, physics and exact real arithmetic, *Bulletin of Symbolic Logic* 3 (1997), 401 – 452.

[9] Yu. Ershov, The model C of the partial continuous functionals, in *Logic Colloquium 76*, (R. O. Gandy and J. M. E. Hyland editors), North-Holland, Amsterdam, 1977, 455 – 467.

[10] A. Grzegorczyk, Computable functionals, *Fundamenta Mathematicae* 42 (1955), 168 – 202.

[11] A. GRZEGORCZYK, On the definitions of computable real continuous functions, *Fundamenta Mathematicae* 44 (1957), 61 - 71.

[12] G. KREISEL, D. LACOMBE, AND J. R. SHOENFIELD, Partial recursive functionals and effective operations, in *Constructivity in Mathematics*, (A. Heyting editor), North-Holland, Amsterdam, 195 - 207.

[13] A. H. LACHLAN AND E. W. MADISON, Computable fields and arithmetically definable ordered fields, *Proceedings of the American Mathematical Society* 24 (1970), 803 - 807.

[14] D. LACOMBE, Extension de la notion de fonction récursive aux fonctions d'une ou plusieurs variables réelles, I, II, III. Comptes Rendus 240, 241 (1955), 2478 - 2480, 13 - 14, 151 - 155.

[15] E. W. MADISON, A note on computable real fields, *Journal of Symbolic Logic* 35 (1970), 239 - 241.

[16] Y. N. MOSCHOVAKIS, Recursive metric spaces, *Fundamenta Mathematicae* 55 (1964), 215 - 238.

[17] D. NORMANN, A hierarchy of domains with totality but without density, in *Computability, enumerability, unsolvability*, (B. Cooper, T. Slaman and S. S. Wainer editors), Cambridge University Press, 1996, 233 - 257.

[18] E. PALMGREN AND V. STOLTENBERG-HANSEN, Domain interpretations of Martin-Löf's partial type theory, *Annals of Pure and Applied Logic* 48 (1990), 135 - 196.

[19] M. B. POUR-EL AND J. I. RICHARDS, *Computability in Analysis and Physics*, Perspectives in Mathematical Logic, Springer-Verlag, Berlin, 1989.

[20] V. STOLTENBERG-HANSEN, Mathematical theory of domains (Notes for Marktoberdorf 1999), U.U.D.M Lecture Notes, 1999:4

[21] V. STOLTENBERG-HANSEN, I. LINDSTRÖM AND E. R. GRIFFOR, *Mathematical Theory of Domains*, Cambridge University Press, 1994.

[22] V. STOLTENBERG-HANSEN AND J. V. TUCKER, Complete local rings as domains, *Journal of Symbolic Logic* 53 (1988), 603 - 624.

[23] V. STOLTENBERG-HANSEN AND J. V. TUCKER, Algebraic equations and fixed-point equations in inverse limits, *Theoretical Computer Science* 87 (1991), 1 - 24.

[24] V. STOLTENBERG-HANSEN AND J. V. TUCKER, Infinite systems of equations over inverse limits and infinite synchronous concurrent algorithms, in *Semantics – Foundations and Applications*, Lecture Notes in Computer Science vol. 666, Springer Verlag, Berlin, 1993, 531 - 562.

[25] V. STOLTENBERG-HANSEN AND J. V. TUCKER, Effective algebra, in *Handbook of Logic in Computer Science*, volume 4, (S. Abramsky, D. Gabbay, and T. S. E. Maibaum, editors), Oxford University Press,1995, 357 - 526.

[26] V. STOLTENBERG-HANSEN AND J. V. TUCKER, Concrete models of computation for topological algebras, *Theoretical Computer Science* 219 (1999), 347 - 378.

[27] G. WAAGBØ, Denotational semantics for intuitionistic type theory using a hierarchy of domains with totality, *Archive for Mathematical Logic* 38 (1999), 19 - 60.

[28] K. WEIHRAUCH AND U. SCHREIBER Embedding metric spaces into cpo's, *Theoretical Computer Science* 16 (1981), 5 - 24.

Part 4
Complexity and Feasibility

S. S. Wainer

O. Danvy

4. *Lochness in NCκC [technical aside]*

Current research in the Scottisch Highlands on
proof burden of Bouncing Confluence in NCκC

Lochness Categories

Current Obstacles:

- Higher-Order Abstract Kangaroos
- Abundant existence of joeys
- ...

(proof theory)$^{\omega}$ $\vdash$  $\geq O(p(n))$

Joey [oz slang] $=_{\text{def}}$ partially evaluated Kangaroo

Exact format of a joey: see handout

(which I must have left on my mattress)

Foundations of Secure Computation
F.L. Bauer and R. Steinbrüggen (Eds.)
IOS Press, 2000

Proof Theoretic Complexity of Low Subrecursive Classes

Naim ÇAĞMAN
Dept. of Mathematics, University of Gaziosmanpaşa, Tokat, 60100, Turkey

Geoffrey E. OSTRIN
Dept. of Mathematics, University of Lisbon, Lisbon, 1700, Portugal

Stanley S. WAINER
School of Mathematics, University of Leeds, Leeds, LS2 9JT, UK

Abstract. A two-sorted version of Peano Arithmetic is developed, with proof-rules corresponding to the normal/safe recursion schemes of Bellantoni and Cook. Classical methods of proof theory still apply, but now the provably recursive functions are brought down to more computationally realistic levels than in the single-sorted case, since the bounding functions turn out to be "*slow growing*" rather than "*fast growing*". Results very similar to earlier ones of Leivant are obtained characterizing Grzegorczyk's classes $\mathcal{E}^2$ (in the existential fragment) and $\mathcal{E}^3$ (in the full theory).

1 Introduction

We describe joint work[1] on the proof theory of low sub-recursive classes, between Grzegorczyk's $\mathcal{E}^2$ and $\mathcal{E}^3$. The main underlying idea is supplied by Bellantoni and Cook [2] who showed that an amazingly simple and natural two-sorted re-interpretation of the usual primitive recursion schemes characterizes polynomially bounded computation. We carry this idea over to a first-order proof theoretic context by showing that, if Peano Arithmetic (PA) is instead formulated in this two-sorted fashion – with quantification allowed only over one sort ("*safe*" or "*output*" variables) and induction allowed only over the other sort ("*normal*" or "*input*" variables) – then the provably recursive functions are exactly the $\mathcal{E}^3$ (elementary) functions. Furthermore, the Σ_1-inductive fragment of this theory corresponds to the $\mathcal{E}^2$ (linear space) functions, analogous to the classical result that in the single-sorted case, the provably recursive functions of Σ_1-induction are exactly the primitive recursive ones. The work is clearly related to earlier results of (among others) Buss [5], Bellantoni [3], Beckmann and Weiermann [1], and especially Leivant [12] who already proved results of this kind in a somewhat different context, but precise connections remain to be investigated. The main novelty here is that the work illustrates nicely the applicability of classical ordinal analysis techniques even at

[1]The present paper is a condensation of parts of the Ph.D. theses [6] and [14] of the first two authors, written at Leeds under the supervision of the third.

the low sub-recursive level. The difference with classical (single-sorted) PA is that the separation of induction from quantification means that the bounding functions are now "*Slow Growing*" rather then "*Fast Growing*". Below ϵ_0 the Slow Growing hierarchy gives only elementary bounds – hence the result.

Definition 1.1 (BCu). The Bellantoni and Cook *normal/safe* recursion schemes, BC, are formulated by taking the *primitive recursive* function schemes and separating the variables into two sorts, depending on their computational roles:

Input or *normal* variables denoted $x, y, z, \ldots$ with or without subscripts.

Output or *safe* variables denoted $a, b, c, \ldots$ with or without subscripts.

To formalise this distinction, in any formula the input variables will always be listed first and followed immediately by a semi-colon to distinguish them from the remaining output variables (if any). We think of $f(x; a)$ as denoting a function of type $I \times O \to O$, taking an input argument x and an output argument a to an output value.

The class BC was formulated with numbers represented in a binary notation. We present a unary version BCu (see Handley and Wainer [10] for background).

BCu is the smallest class which contains the following five initial functions:

(a) *Zero*, $Z \in BCu^{0,0}$, where $Z(;) = 0$

(b) *Successor*, $S \in BCu^{0,1}$, where $S(;a) = a + 1$.

(c) *Predecessor*, $P \in BCu^{0,1}$, where $P(;a) = max(a-1, 0)$.

(d) *Projections*, $U_i^m \in BCu^{0,m}$, where $U_i^m(;\vec{a}) = a_i, \ 1 \le i \le m$

(e) *Cases*, $C(;a,b,c) \in BCu^{0,3}$, where $C(;a,b,c) = \begin{cases} b & if \ \ a = 0 \\ c & if \ \ a \neq 0. \end{cases}$

and is closed under the following two schemes

• *BCu-Composition.* It is only allowed over output variables. If $h_1, \ldots, h_l \in BCu^{n,m}$, $g \in BCu^{k,l}$, $\{i_1, \ldots, i_k\} \subseteq \{1, 2, \ldots, n\}$, then $f \in BCu^{n,m}$ is defined by BCu-composition

$$f(\vec{x}; \vec{a}) = g(x_{i_1}, \ldots, x_{i_k}; h_1(\vec{x}; \vec{a}), \ldots, h_l(\vec{x}; \vec{a}))$$

• *BCu-Recursion.* It is only allowed over input variables. If $g \in BCu^{n,m}$, $h \in BCu^{n+1,m+1}$, then $f \in BCu^{n+1,m}$ is defined by BCu-recursion

$$\begin{cases} f(0, \vec{x}; \vec{a}) & = g(\vec{x}; \vec{a}), \\ f(z+1, \vec{x}; \vec{a}) & = h(z, \vec{x}; \vec{a}, f(z, \vec{x}; \vec{a})), \end{cases}$$

and we have also *simultaneous* BCu recursion defining $\vec{f} = f_1, \ldots, f_m$ together. See Leivant [13].

Thus $f \in BCu^{n,m}$ if it is of arity $I^n \times O^m$. Hence we can define

$$BCu_{normal} = \bigcup_{n \in \mathbb{N}} BCu^{n,0}$$

and it is these functions from I^n into O that we are ultimately concerned with.

Remark 1.2. The BCu-composition and BCu-recursion are essentially the so-called *safe composition* and *safe recursion* schemes of Bellantoni and Cook [2]. We have made one adaptation to the original Bellantoni-Cook composition scheme, since they also allow a form of restricted substitution into the normal positions. As it turns out, the same class of functions is still obtained whether we include this or not. We will choose the more restrictive formulation since it emphasises a clear typing format for the BCu functions. If we look at the conclusion to our formulation of output induction in section 3 we see this generalization of *normal substitution* beginning to emerge.

Definition 1.3 ($\mathcal{E}^2$). Grzegorczyk's class $\mathcal{E}^2$ is the smallest class of functions containing the zero, successor and projections functions and closed under *compositions* and *polynomially-limited primitive recursion* as follows:

• If g and h are functions which have been introduced previously in the class, and p is any polynomial, then we define a new function f from g, h, p by limited primitive recursion thus

$$\begin{cases} f(0,\vec{x}) &= g(\vec{x}) \\ f(y+1,\vec{x}) &= h(y, f(y,\vec{x}),\vec{x}) \\ f(y,\vec{x}) &\leq p(y,\vec{x}) \end{cases}$$

Definition 1.4 ($\mathcal{E}^3$). If we allow limited recursion bounded by exponential polynomials p, then we obtain Grzegorczyk's class $\mathcal{E}^3$. This class coincides with the class of elementary functions which was first introduced by Kalmar [11] and Csillag [7]. See also Rose [16].

We have the following basic facts:

$$BCu_{normal} = \mathcal{E}^2$$

which coincides with (i) the class of functions computable on a register machine in time bounded by a polynomial of the (unary) input, and (ii) the class of functions computable on a Turing Machine in space bounded by a linear function of the binary length of the input. See Handley-Wainer [10]. $\mathcal{E}^3$ coincides with the class of functions computable in time or space bounded by an exponential polynomial.

2 $PA(;)$, its Fragment $\Sigma_1(;) - IND$, and $\mathcal{E}^2$

In this chapter we shall obtain a new logical theory, two-sorted Peano Arithmetic $PA(;)$, from the formal proof system of single-sorted Peano Arithmetic, PA, by using the Bellantoni-Cook variable separation. In $PA(;)$, quantification is exclusively applied over output variables whereas induction is formulated only over input variables, which remain free throughout. We then obtain the theory of $\Sigma_1(;) - IND$ from $PA(;)$ by restricting the induction rule to apply only to $\Sigma_1(;)$-formulas, and get the result that the provably terminating functions of $\Sigma_1(;) - IND$ are exactly the functions of BCu.

2.1 $PA(;)$

Definition 2.1 (Variables). The variables in the language of $PA(;)$ are distinguished into two-sorts as in BCu, both intended to range over natural numbers.

The *input* variables which are called *I-variables* denoted by $x, y, z, \ldots$.

The *output* variables which are called *O-variables* denoted by $a, b, c, \ldots$.

Definition 2.2 (Basic Terms). The *basic terms* are defined by

(a) 0 is a basic term.

(b) Either sort of variable is a basic term.

(c) If t is a basic term, then St and Pt are basic terms.

Where S and P are the *successor* and *predecessor* function-symbols.

Definition 2.3 (Terms). More general *terms* are denoted by $s, t, r, ...$ constructed from basic terms with use of function symbols, $f, g, h, ...$, standing for (primitive) recursive functions, formulated over either sort of variables. These are given by their regular (primitive) recursive definitions which will be assumed as axioms.

Definition 2.4 (Formulas). $PA(;)$ is formulated here classically in the style of Tait [19] with finite sets of formulas for sequences. The *judgements* will be of the form

$$PA(;) \vdash \Gamma, A(x_1, ..., x_n; a_1, ..., a_m)$$

where A is a formula, built out of atomic formulas $R(\vec{x}; \vec{a})$ and their complements $\bar{R}(\vec{x}; \vec{a})$ by applying the logical connectives; $\vee$ (or), $\wedge$ (and), $\exists$ (some) and $\forall$ (all). It is sometimes convenient to display the free variables occurring in A by writing $A(x_1, ..., x_n; a_1, ..., a_m)$. Here the semi-colon is not part of the official syntax, we still use it to clarify the separation of the input variables from the output variables. The Γ denotes finite sets of formulas, $\{A_1, ..., A_n\}$, the intending meaning being A_1 or A_2 or ... or A_n. Furthermore Γ, A denotes $\Gamma \cup \{A\}$.

Note that *negation* $\neg$ and *implication* $\rightarrow$ are not included as basic logical symbols. The negation is defined by De Morgan's Laws:

$$\neg R \equiv \bar{R} \qquad \neg(A \vee B) \equiv \neg A \wedge \neg B \qquad \neg(\exists a A(;a)) \equiv \forall a \neg A(;a)$$
$$\neg \bar{R} \equiv R \qquad \neg(A \wedge B) \equiv \neg A \vee \neg B \qquad \neg(\forall a A(;a)) \equiv \exists a \neg A(;a)$$

The implication is defined by

$$A \rightarrow B \equiv \neg A \vee B$$

The reason for presenting logic in this way is merely one of choice, but it makes it possible to exploit the duality between $\vee$ and $\wedge$, and between $\exists$ and $\forall$ for the purposes of simple cut-reduction.

Definition 2.5 (Axioms and Rules). For any Γ the arithmetical axioms and logical rules are highlighted in the following list.

- *Arithmetical Axioms.* All the substitution-instances of

(a) $\vdash \Gamma,\ u = v,\ u \neq v$

(b) $\vdash \Gamma,\ u < v,\ u \not< v$

(c) $\vdash \Gamma,\ Su \neq 0$

(d) $\vdash \Gamma,\ Su \neq Sv,\ u = v$

(e) $\vdash \Gamma,\ P0 = 0$

(f) $\vdash \Gamma,\ u = 0,\ S(Pu) = u$

(g) $\vdash \Gamma,\ P(Su) = u$

(h) $\vdash \Gamma,\ u = u$

(i) $\vdash \Gamma,\ u \neq v,\ v = u$

(j) $\vdash \Gamma,\ u \neq v,\ v \neq w,\ u = w$

(k) $\vdash \Gamma,\ u \not< 0$

(l) $\vdash \Gamma,\ u < Su$

(m) $\vdash \Gamma,\ u \not< Sv,\ u < v,\ u = v$

(n) $\vdash \Gamma,\ u \not< u$

(o) $\vdash \Gamma,\ u \not< v,\ v \not< w,\ u < w$

(p) $\vdash \Gamma,\ u < v,\ u = v,\ v < u$

(q) $\vdash \Gamma,\ u \neq v,\ \neg A(u),\ A(v)$ with A atomic.

Where to simplify the list, both variables safe and normal are represented by u, v, w, and $A(u)$ means appropriate $A(u;)$ or $A(;u)$ in arithmetical axioms. From (q) one can easily derive $\Gamma,\ u \neq v,\ \neg A(u),\ A(v)$ for all formulas A.

• *Recursion Axioms.* For each primitive recursive function f defined over input or output variables, we add its defining equations as new axioms. These new primitive recursive function-symbols can be used to generate arbitrary terms in the normal way. But these are not basic terms. For each defining equation $f(\vec{x};\vec{a}) = t$, the corresponding axiom is,

$$\vdash \Gamma, f(\vec{x};\vec{a}) = t$$

• *Further Arithmetical Axioms* are added, expressing the associativity, commutativity and distributivity of addition, multiplication, and the usual index laws of exponentiation.

• *Logical Rules.*

(∨) $$\frac{\vdash \Gamma, A_i}{\vdash \Gamma, (A_0 \vee A_1)}$$ where $i = 0$ or 1.

(∧) $$\frac{\vdash \Gamma, A_0 \qquad \vdash \Gamma, A_1}{\Gamma, (A_0 \wedge A_1)}$$

(∃) $$\frac{\vdash \Gamma, A(;t)}{\vdash \Gamma, \exists a A(;a)}$$ where t is a basic term.

(∀) $$\frac{\vdash \Gamma, A(;b)}{\vdash \Gamma, \forall a A(;a)}$$ where b is not free in Γ.

(*Cut*) $$\frac{\vdash \Gamma, A \qquad \vdash \Gamma, \neg A}{\vdash \Gamma}$$ where A is the "cut formula".

(*Ind*) $$\frac{\vdash \Gamma, A(0;) \qquad \vdash \Gamma, \neg A(x;), A(x+1;)}{\vdash \Gamma, A(t;)}$$ where x is not free in Γ.

In the induction rule, we do not quantify the variable in the conclusion, and t *is any basic term over an input variable* and A is said to be the induction formula. We have to point out that

Quantification is exclusively over output variables.

Induction is formulated over input variables.

We are allowed to introduce any function or term, but writing the defining schemes down is not enough. To use the function, we must first prove that it terminates.

Definition 2.6 (Defined Term). Apart from the variable separation another major difference between this arithmetic and the more usual formulations of *single-sorted* Peano Arithmetic is the non-standard existential rule. Whereas in PA we allow any term to act as a witness for an existential rule, (similar for the conclusion of an induction), here we restrict our witnesses to be only *basic terms.* On the other hand, we can obtain such a rule for more general witnessing terms, the only proviso being that we must first prove

$$\vdash \exists b(t = b)$$

In such circumstances we call such a term *defined* and often we will use the shorthand

$$t \downarrow$$

Remarks 2.7. If t is a basic term, then we can prove $t \downarrow$ immediately by applying the $\exists$-rule to the axiom $t = t$.

Furthermore, from the equality axiom

$$t = b \rightarrow A(t) \rightarrow A(b)$$

we easily obtain (since the term b is basic)

$$t \downarrow \rightarrow A(t) \rightarrow \exists b A(b)$$

In other words we can only use provably-defined terms to witness existential formulas, that is

$$(\exists \downarrow) \qquad \frac{\Gamma, t \downarrow \qquad \Gamma, A(t)}{\Gamma, \exists b A(b)}$$

Lemma 2.8 (**$\forall$-inversion**). *Assume that* $\vdash \Gamma, \forall a A(x; a)$ *where* $\forall a A(x; a)$ *is nowhere used as an induction formula. Then* $\vdash \Gamma, A(x; b)$, *and the height of the new proof is not increased.*

Examples 2.9.

1. Let us consider the following axioms which describe the (primitive) recursion of $+ : I \times O \rightarrow O$. Note that all our functions give values which we consider as output.

   $$\vdash 0 + a = a \qquad \vdash (x + 1) + a = (x + a) + 1$$

   Through cuts with appropriate equality axioms we obtain,

   $$\vdash 0 + a = a \qquad \vdash x + a \neq c,\ (x + 1) + a = c + 1$$

   Since a and $c + 1$ are basic terms we can use them as a witness for existential quantifications. Following this up with a universal quantification we have,

   $$\vdash \exists c.0 + a = c \qquad \vdash \forall c.x + a \neq c,\ \exists c.(x + 1) + a = c$$

   Now we can apply an induction over the input variable x to obtain,

   $$\vdash \exists c.x + a = c$$

   This final sequent tells us that $x + a$ is defined. In other words we have proved that the function $+$, of this particular arity, is terminating.

2. Now let us use this function to demonstrate the $(\exists\ \downarrow)$ rule in proving multiplication, of arity $I \times I \to O$, terminating. Following as above we arrive with,

$$\vdash 0.y = 0 \qquad \vdash x.y \neq c,\ (x+1).y = c+y$$

Here we cannot directly use the existential rule, as the witnessing term $c+y$ is not basic. On the other hand the previous example gave this term to be defined, hence we can existentially quantify but now we are applying the derived rule $(\exists\ \downarrow)$. In completing the remainder of this proof we follow exactly the proof as given above for addition.

3. Finally let us consider an addition, but now formulated over two output variables, $+ : O \times O \to O$.

$$\vdash 0 + a = a \qquad \vdash b + a \neq c,\ (b+1) + a = c+1$$

We start by following the quantifications of the first example, until we have,

$$\vdash \exists c.0 + a = c \qquad \vdash \forall c.b + a \neq c,\ \exists c.(b+1) + a = c$$

Whereas before we would apply an induction, here we cannot do this since the active variable, b, is an output. Hence, if addition is formulated over two outputs then the termination proof breaks down.

2.2 $\Sigma_1(;) - IND$

In this section, we obtain the two-sorted fragment $\Sigma_1(;) - IND$ from $PA(;)$ by restricting induction formulas to being $\Sigma_1(;)$-formulas.

Definition 2.10 ($\Sigma_1(;)$-formula). Two-sorted $\Sigma_1(;)$-formulas $A(\vec{x};\vec{b})$ will be of the form

$$\exists\vec{a}A'(\vec{x};\vec{a},\vec{b})$$

where A' is a quantifier free formula.

Definition 2.11 (Truth). A $\Sigma_1(;)$-formula $\exists\vec{a}A'(\vec{x};\vec{a},\vec{b})$ is *true*, if there are selection functions $\vec{f}(\vec{x};\vec{b}) = f_1(\vec{x};\vec{b}),\dots,f_m(\vec{x};\vec{b})$ such that for all $\vec{x}$ and $\vec{b}$ the formula $A'(\vec{x};\vec{f}(\vec{x},\vec{b}),\vec{b})$ is true in the standard model. We often denote this as

$$\vec{f}(\vec{x};\vec{b}) \models \exists\vec{a}A'(\vec{x};\vec{a},\vec{b})$$

In general, if $\Gamma(\vec{x},\vec{b}) = \{A_1(\vec{x},\vec{b}),\dots,A_k(\vec{x},\vec{b})\}$ is a set of $\Sigma_1(;)$-formulas, then we also have $\vec{f}(\vec{x},\vec{b}) \models \bigvee_{i=1,\dots,k} A_i(\vec{x},\vec{b})$. Then we write simply

$$\vec{f} \models \Gamma$$

Definition 2.12 (Provably Terminating). Let a function f be defined by a primitive recursive program. Then we say that it is *provably terminating* or *provably recursive* in a two-sorted theory, if we have derivation of

$$\vdash \exists c.f(\vec{x};\vec{a}) = c$$

We ask how is a proof of $\exists\vec{a}A'(\vec{x};\vec{a},\vec{b})$ related to the complexity of the selection function $\vec{f}(\vec{x},\vec{b})$? It is an old and classical result of logic that the primitive recursive functions are exactly those which are provably terminating in the fragment $\Sigma_1 - IND$ of PA. Below we investigate the two-sorted analogue of this result.

2.3 Provable Functions of $\Sigma_1(;) - IND$ same as BCu

In this section, we want to prove that if a two-sorted function $f(x;a)$ is provably terminating in $\Sigma_1(;)-IND$, then f is definable in BCu, and vice versa. It gives us that the provable functions of $\Sigma_1(;)-IND$ are the same as the functions of $\mathcal{E}^2$ since $BCu = \mathcal{E}^2$.

Lemma 2.13. *Assume that* $\Sigma_1(;)-IND \vdash \Gamma$ *where* Γ *is a set of* $\Sigma_1(;)$*-formulas. Then there are* BCu *functions* $\vec{f}(\vec{x};\vec{b})$ *such that*

$$\vec{f} \vDash \Gamma$$

Proof. The lemma says that for every $\Sigma_1(;)$-formula provable in the theory of $\Sigma_1(;) - IND$, there are BCu functions $\vec{f}(\vec{x};\vec{b})$ such that $A'(\vec{x};\vec{f}(\vec{x};\vec{b}),\vec{b})$ is true for every x and b.

Let $\Gamma = \{\ \exists \vec{a}_i A'_i(\vec{x};\vec{a}_i,\vec{b})\ \}_{i=1,\ldots,k}$ be the set of $\Sigma_1(;)$-formulas. Then we proceed by induction on the height of the derivation in $\Sigma_1(;) - IND$.

Note that a standard "*free cut*" elimination argument shows that any $\Sigma_1(;)-IND$ derivation can be transformed into one with only $\Sigma_1(;)$ cut formulas.

Case (Axs). The axioms are true and quantifier-free, so any BCu function f will do for them.

Case $(\vee),(\wedge)$. The $(\vee)$ and $(\wedge)$-rules respectively

$$\frac{\Gamma, A_0}{\Gamma,(A_0 \vee A_1)} \qquad \frac{\Gamma, A_0 \qquad \Gamma, A_1}{\Gamma,(A_0 \wedge A_1)}$$

They are trivial since Γ contains only $\Sigma_1(;)$-formulas and A_0 and A_1 must be quantifier free otherwise $A_0 \vee A_1$ and $A_0 \wedge A_1$ can not be $\Sigma_1(;)$-formula. We are therefore concerned merely that their truth is preserved.

Case $(\exists)$. The $(\exists)$-rule

$$\frac{\Gamma, A(\vec{x};t,\vec{b})}{\Gamma, \exists d A(\vec{x};d,\vec{b})} \qquad t \text{ is a basic term}$$

where $A(\vec{x};t,\vec{b}) \equiv \exists \vec{a} A'(\vec{x};\vec{a},t,\vec{b})$ and $\exists d A(\vec{x};d,\vec{b}) \equiv \exists d \exists \vec{a} A'(\vec{x};\vec{a},d,\vec{b})$. Then the $(\exists)$-rule will be

$$\frac{\Gamma, \exists \vec{a} A'(\vec{x};\vec{a},t,\vec{b})}{\Gamma, \exists d \exists \vec{a} A'(\vec{x};\vec{a},d,\vec{b})}$$

Applying the induction hypothesis we have BCu functions $\vec{f}(\vec{x};\vec{b})$ such that for all $\vec{x}$ and $\vec{b}$

$$\vDash \Gamma, A'(\vec{x};\vec{f}(\vec{x};\vec{b}),t,\vec{b})$$

where t is a basic term, so we have a BCu function $g(\vec{x};\vec{b})$ such that for all $\vec{x},\vec{b}$

$$g(\vec{x};\vec{b}) = t$$

Now we define BCu functions $\vec{h}(\vec{x};\vec{b})$ such that for all $\vec{x},\vec{b}$

$$\vDash \Gamma, A'(\vec{x};\vec{h}(\vec{x};\vec{b}),h_{k+1}(\vec{x};\vec{b}),\vec{b})$$

where $h_i(\vec{x};\vec{b}) = f_i(\vec{x};\vec{b})$, i=1,...,k, and $h_{k+1}(\vec{x};\vec{b}) = g(\vec{x};\vec{b})$. This completes the proof of this case.

Case (∀). The (∀)-rule

$$\frac{\Gamma, A(\vec{x}; b)}{\Gamma, \forall d A(\vec{x}; d)} \qquad b \text{ is not free in } \Gamma$$

which is not applicable since in conclusion $\forall d A(\vec{x}; d)$ can not be $\Sigma_1(;)$-formula because it contains universal quantifier $\forall d$.

Case (Cut). The (Cut)-rule

$$\frac{\Gamma, A \qquad\qquad \Gamma, \neg A}{\Gamma}$$

where we can crucially assume that the (Cut)-formula A is in $\Sigma_1(;)$-form, say $A \equiv \exists \vec{a} A'(\vec{x}; \vec{a}, \vec{b})$, then $\neg A \equiv \forall \vec{a} \neg A'(\vec{x}; \vec{a}, \vec{b})$. But the right premise now contains a $\forall \vec{a}$ which must be removed in order to continue the proof. $\forall$-inversion allows the proof of $\Gamma, \forall \vec{a} \neg A'(\vec{x}; \vec{a}, \vec{b})$ to be replaced by a proof of $\Gamma, \neg A'(\vec{x}; \vec{c}, \vec{b})$ but containing new variables $\vec{c}$. So the application of (Cut) will be

$$\frac{\Gamma, \exists \vec{a} A'(\vec{x}; \vec{a}, \vec{b}) \qquad\qquad \Gamma, \neg A'(\vec{x}; \vec{c}, \vec{b})}{\Gamma}$$

Applying the induction hypothesis to left premise, we have BCu functions $\vec{f_1}(\vec{x}; \vec{b})$, ..., $\vec{f_k}(\vec{x}; \vec{b}), \vec{f}_{k+1}(\vec{x}; \vec{b})$ such that

$$\models \{\ A'_i(\vec{x}; \vec{f_i}(\vec{x}; \vec{b}), \vec{b})\ \}_{i=1,\dots,k}, A'(\vec{x}; \vec{f}_{k+1}(\vec{x}; \vec{b}), \vec{b}) \tag{1}$$

and from right premise, we have BCu functions $\vec{g_1}(\vec{x}; \vec{c}, \vec{b}), \dots, \vec{g_k}(\vec{x}; \vec{c}, \vec{b})$ such that

$$\models \{\ A'_i(\vec{x}; \vec{g_i}(\vec{x}; \vec{c}, \vec{b}), \vec{b})\ \}_{i=1,\dots,k}, \neg A'(\vec{x}; \vec{c}, \vec{b}) \tag{2}$$

Now we define BCu functions $\vec{h_1}(\vec{x}; \vec{b}), \dots, \vec{h_k}(\vec{x}; \vec{b})$ from $\vec{f}$ and $\vec{g}$;

$$\vec{h_i}(\vec{x}; \vec{b}) := \begin{cases} \vec{f_i}(\vec{x}; \vec{b}) & \text{if } A'_i(\vec{x}; \vec{f_i}(\vec{x}; \vec{b}), \vec{b}) \text{ is true,} \\ \vec{g_i}(\vec{x}; \vec{f}_{k+1}(\vec{x}; \vec{b}), \vec{b}) & \text{otherwise} \end{cases}$$

such that

$$\models \{\ A'_i(\vec{x}; \vec{h_i}(\vec{x}; \vec{b}), \vec{b})\ \}_{i=1,\dots,k}$$

To check this, in (1), either one of the formulas $\{\ A'_i(\vec{x}; \vec{f_i}(\vec{x}; \vec{b}), \vec{b})\ \}_{i=1,\dots,k}$ is true or $A'(\vec{x}; \vec{f}_{k+1}(\vec{x}; \vec{b}), \vec{b})$ is true. Suppose $\{\ A'_i(\vec{x}; \vec{f_i}(\vec{x}; \vec{b}), \vec{b})\ \}_{i=1,\dots,k}$ is true, then for some i we have

$$\vec{h_i}(\vec{x}; \vec{b}) := \vec{f_i}(\vec{x}; \vec{b})$$

Otherwise $A'(\vec{x}; \vec{f}_{k+1}(\vec{x}; \vec{b}), \vec{b})$ is true. Now we chose $\vec{c} = \vec{f}_{k+1}(\vec{x}; \vec{b})$. In (2) we have just $\{\ A'_i(\vec{x}; \vec{g_i}(\vec{x}; \vec{c}, \vec{b}), \vec{b})\ \}_{i=1,\dots,k}$ which is true because $\neg A'(\vec{x}; \vec{c}, \vec{b})$ is false. Then $\vec{h} \models \Gamma$ since

$$\vec{h_i}(\vec{x}; \vec{b}) := \vec{g_i}(\vec{x}; \vec{f}_{k+1}(\vec{x}, \vec{b}), \vec{b})$$

Case (Ind). The (Ind)-rule

$$\frac{\Gamma, A(0,\vec{x};\vec{b}) \qquad \Gamma, \neg A(z,\vec{x};\vec{b}), A(z+1,\vec{x};\vec{b})}{\Gamma, A(y,\vec{x};\vec{b})}$$

where z not free in Γ. The A is in $\Sigma_1(;)$-form, $A(z,\vec{x};\vec{b}) \equiv \exists\vec{a}A'(z,\vec{x};\vec{a},\vec{b})$ and $\neg A(z,\vec{x};\vec{b}) \equiv \forall\vec{a}\neg A'(z,\vec{x};\vec{a},\vec{b})$. In order to continue the proof $\forall\vec{a}$ must be removed. $\forall$-inversion allows the formula to be replaced by $\neg A'(z,\vec{x};\vec{c},\vec{b})$ but containing new variables $\vec{c}$. The (Ind)-rule becomes

$$\frac{\exists\vec{a}A'(0,\vec{x};\vec{a},\vec{b}) \qquad \neg A'(z,\vec{x};\vec{c},\vec{b}), \exists\vec{a}A'(z+1,\vec{x};\vec{a},\vec{b})}{\exists\vec{a}A'(y,\vec{x};\vec{a},\vec{b})}$$

where we ignored the Γ for the sake of brevity since it does not change the proof. Applying the induction hypothesis to left premise, we have BCu functions $\vec{f}(\vec{x};\vec{b})$, such that for all $\vec{x},\vec{b}$

$$\models A'(0,\vec{x};\vec{f}(\vec{x};\vec{b}),\vec{b}) \tag{3}$$

and applying the induction hypothesis to right premise, we have BCu functions $\vec{g}(\vec{x};\vec{c},\vec{b})$, such that for $\vec{x},\vec{b},\vec{c}$

$$\models \neg A'(z,\vec{x};\vec{c},\vec{b}), A'(z+1,\vec{x};\vec{g}(\vec{x};\vec{c},\vec{b}),\vec{b}) \tag{4}$$

Now we define BCu functions $\vec{h}(z,\vec{x};\vec{b})$ by simultaneous primitive recursion from $\vec{f}$ and $\vec{g}$ by

$$\begin{cases} \vec{h}(0,\vec{x};\vec{b}) & = \vec{f}(\vec{x};\vec{b}) \\ \vec{h}(z',\vec{x};\vec{b}) & = \vec{g}(\vec{x};\vec{h}(z,\vec{x};\vec{b}),\vec{b}) \end{cases}$$

such that $\models A'(z,\vec{x};\vec{h}(z,\vec{x};\vec{b}),\vec{b})$ for every z. We can prove this by induction on z.

□

Corollary 2.14. *All provably terminating recursive functions of $\Sigma_1(;)-IND$ are BCu definable.*

Lemma 2.15. *If $f(\vec{x};\vec{b}) \in BCu$, then*

$$\Sigma_1(;) - IND \vdash \exists a(f(\vec{x};\vec{b}) = a)$$

Proof. It can be proved by induction on the length of the BCu definition:

Case (Initial Functions). Suppose f is one of the five initial functions respectively,

(a) $\Sigma_1(;) - IND \vdash \exists a(Z(\vec{x};\vec{b}) = a)$ with basic witness $a = 0$,

(b) $\Sigma_1(;) - IND \vdash \exists a(S(\vec{x};b) = a)$ with basic witness $a = S(;b)$,

(c) $\Sigma_1(;) - IND \vdash \exists a(P(\vec{x};b) = a)$ with basic witness $a = P(;b)$,

(d) $\Sigma_1(;) - IND \vdash \exists a(U_i(\vec{x};\vec{b}) = a)$ with basic witness $a = b_i$,

(e) $\Sigma_1(;)-IND \vdash \exists a(C(\vec{x};b,c,d)=a)$. Since $b=0 \vee b=S(P(b))$ is an axiom, and $C(\vec{x};0,c,d)=c$ and $C(\vec{x};S(P(b)),c,d)=d$, so by logic

$$\vdash \exists a(C(\vec{x};b,c,d)=a)$$

Case (BCu-composition). Suppose $f,g,h \in BCu$ and f is defined explicitly from g and h by

$$f(\vec{x};\vec{b}) = g(\vec{x};h(\vec{x};\vec{b}),\vec{b}) \tag{5}$$

where it is already assumed that

$$\Sigma_1(;)-IND \vdash \exists c(h(\vec{x};\vec{b})=c)$$
$$\Sigma_1(;)-IND \vdash \exists a(g(\vec{x};c,\vec{b})=a)$$

We have to show that $\Sigma_1(;)-IND \vdash \exists a(f(\vec{x};\vec{b})=a)$. Axiom (q) of $PA(;)$ gives

$$\vdash h(\vec{x};\vec{b}) \neq c, \neg\exists a(g(\vec{x};c,\vec{b})=a), \exists a(g(\vec{x};h(\vec{x};\vec{b}),\vec{b})=a)$$

and by using (5) we obtain

$$\vdash h(\vec{x};\vec{b}) \neq c, \neg\exists a(g(\vec{x};c,\vec{b})=a), \exists a(f(\vec{x};\vec{b})=a)$$

hence

$$\dfrac{\exists c(h(\vec{x};\vec{b})=c) \qquad \dfrac{\dfrac{\dfrac{\exists a(g(\vec{x};c,\vec{b})=a) \qquad h(\vec{x};\vec{b}) \neq c, \neg\exists a(g(\vec{x};c,\vec{b})=a), \exists a(f(\vec{x};\vec{b})=a)}{h(\vec{x};\vec{b}) \neq c, \exists a(f(\vec{x};\vec{b})=a)}\,(Cut)}{\forall c\neg(h(\vec{x};\vec{b})=c), \exists a(f(\vec{x};\vec{b})=a)}\,(\forall)}{\neg\exists c(h(\vec{x};\vec{b})=c), \exists a(f(\vec{x};\vec{b})=a)}}{\exists a(f(\vec{x};\vec{b})=a)}\,(Cut)$$

Case (BCu-recursion). Suppose $f,g,h \in BCu$ and f is defined recursively from g and h by

$$f(0,\vec{x};\vec{b}) = g(\vec{x};\vec{b}) \tag{6}$$
$$f(z',\vec{x};\vec{b}) = h(\vec{x};f(z,\vec{x};\vec{b}),\vec{b}) \tag{7}$$

where g and h are already assumed terminating:

$$\Sigma_1(;)-IND \vdash \exists a(g(\vec{x};\vec{b})=a)$$
$$\Sigma_1(;)-IND \vdash \exists a(h(\vec{x};c,\vec{b})=a)$$

First using (6) and first assumption we get

$$\vdash \exists a(f(0,\vec{x};\vec{b})=a)$$

Now we have to show that $\Sigma_1(;)-IND \vdash \exists a(f(z,\vec{x};\vec{b})=a)$. Axiom (q) of $PA(;)$ gives

$$\vdash f(z,\vec{x};\vec{b}) \neq c, \neg\exists a(h(\vec{x};c,\vec{b})=a), \exists a(h(\vec{x};f(z,\vec{x};\vec{b}),\vec{b})=a)$$

and by using (7) we obtain

$$\vdash f(z,\vec{x};\vec{b}) \neq c, \neg\exists a(h(\vec{x};c,\vec{b})=a), \exists a(f(z',\vec{x};\vec{b})=a)$$

hence

$$\dfrac{\exists a(f(0,\vec{x};\vec{b})=a) \quad \dfrac{\dfrac{\dfrac{\exists a(h(\vec{x};c,\vec{b})=a) \quad f(z,\vec{x};\vec{b})\neq c, \neg\exists a(h(\vec{x};c,\vec{b})=a), \exists a(f(z',\vec{x};\vec{b})=a)}{f(z,\vec{x};\vec{b})\neq c, \exists a(f(z',\vec{x};\vec{b})=a)}\,(Cut)}{\forall a\neg(f(z,\vec{x};\vec{b})=a]), \exists a(f(z',\vec{x};\vec{b})=a)}\,(\forall)}{\neg\exists a(f(z,\vec{x};\vec{b})=a), \exists a(f(z',\vec{x};\vec{b})=a)}}{\exists a(f(z,\vec{x};\vec{b})=a)}\,(Ind)$$

Simultaneous recursion can be handled similarly. □

Theorem 2.16. *The functions of input arguments only which are provably recursive in $\Sigma_1(;)-IND$ are exactly the $\mathcal{E}^2$ functions.*

Proof. The one way the Lemma 2.13 shows that all provable terminating recursive functions of $\Sigma_1(;)-IND$ are BCu function. The other way the Lemma 2.15 shows that all BCu functions are provable terminating recursive functions of $\Sigma_1(;)-IND$. But $BCu_{normal}=\mathcal{E}^2$ from the introduction. □

3 Output Induction

In this section we use a fundamental method of Gentzen to show that all $\mathcal{E}^3$ functions are provably terminating in $PA(;)$.

Definition 3.1 (Progressive). We say that a formula A is *progressive*, $ProgA$, to express

$$A(;0)\wedge\forall d.(A(;d)\rightarrow A(;d+1))$$

Definition 3.2. Given a formula A, with a distinguished free output variable, define the formula A^o as follows:

$$A^o(x;c):=\forall b.(A(;b)\rightarrow b+x^c\downarrow\wedge A(;b+x^c))$$

Lemma 3.3.

$$\vdash ProgA\rightarrow ProgA^o$$

Proof. We want to prove $ProgA^o$ which is,

$$A^o(;0)\wedge\forall d.(A^o(;d)\rightarrow A^o(;d+1))$$

The first conjunct comes directly from the assumption $ProgA$, since $b+x^0=b+1$. For the second conjunct we prove $A^o(x;c+1)$ given the assumption $A^o(x;c)$. We start by inverting the universal quantifier, witnessing at $b+x^c.z$, which we will further assume is defined. This gives,

$$b+x^c.z\downarrow\rightarrow(A(;b+x^c.z)\rightarrow(b+x^c.z+x^c\downarrow\wedge A(;b+x^c.z+x^c)))$$

This can be re-expressed as,

$$(b+x^c.z\downarrow\wedge A(;b+x^c.z))\rightarrow(b+x^c.(z+1)\downarrow\wedge A(;b+x^c.(z+1)))$$

This is an induction step over the input variable z. All that remains is to show the zero case which is easily obtained from the axiom $\vdash b+x^c.0=b$. Hence by induction

$$A(;b)\rightarrow b+x^c.x\downarrow\wedge A(;b+x^c.x)$$

Since $x^c.x=x^{c+1}$, upon inspection this last line gives $A^o(x;c+1)$. Hence we have the second conjunct thus completing the proof. □

Definition 3.4 (Output Induction). We define the formula, $OInd$, which represents the notion of *Output Induction*, over a formula A up to a term t as follows,

$$OInd(A, t) := ProgA \rightarrow A(;t)$$

Lemma 3.5.

$$OInd(A^{\circ}, t) \rightarrow OInd(A, x^{t})$$

Proof. Given the assumption $OInd(A^{\circ}, t)$ this means we have $ProgA^{\circ} \rightarrow A^{\circ}(x;t)$. Inverting the universal quantifier in the definition of A°, witnessing at 0, obtains,

$$ProgA^{\circ} \rightarrow (A(x;0) \rightarrow A(x;x^{t}))$$

We obtain $A(x;0)$ from the assumption $ProgA$. Further, from this same assumption and an application of Lemma 3.3 we obtain $ProgA^{\circ}$. Thus we have,

$$ProgA \rightarrow A(x;x^{t})$$

which is our conclusion $OInd(A, x^{t})$. □

Definition 3.6 (Exponential Stacks). *Exponential stacks* exp_x^n are terms constructed from input variables defined inductively as follows,

$$\begin{cases} exp_x^0 & = & 1 \\ exp_x^{n+1} & = & x^{exp_x^n} \end{cases}$$

Thus the term exp_x^n represents a stack of n many x's. We say that n measures the exponential height of the term.

Theorem 3.7. *For any formula A, and any exponential stack exp_x^n, there is a derivation in $PA(;)$ of the following,*

$$\vdash OInd(A, exp_x^n)$$

Proof. The proof of this is by an outer induction over the stack height n. For when n is zero the exponential stack is 1 and the proof is trivial. The induction hypothesis is a direct application of Lemma 3.5. □

Corollary 3.8. *All exponential stacks are defined.*

Proof. This result is proved directly from the previous theorem where the formula $A(;c)$ represents $\exists d.c = d$. All we need show is that this formula is progressive, an easy fact to demonstrate. □

Theorem 3.9. *Every $\mathcal{E}^3$-function is provably terminating in $PA(;)$.*

Proof. Every $\mathcal{E}^3$-function f is computable by a register machine in time bounded by some exponential stack of height say k. Furthermore, as in e.g. Börger [4], there is an $\mathcal{E}^2$ (in fact BCu)-function U such that $U(x, s)$ gives the output of the computation at step s, and the formula $U(x, s) \downarrow$ is progressive in the variable s. So by output induction,

$$PA(;) \vdash U(x, exp_x^k \downarrow)$$

We can define f by $f(x) = U(x, exp_x^k)$ and therefore $PA(;) \vdash f(x) \downarrow$. □

4 The Functional Interpretation of $PA(;)$

The aim of this section is to develop a Gödel dialectica style interpretion of the full theory of $PA(;)$, using a BCu-version of higher type primitive recursive functionals. Our system of two-sorted higher-type Gödel primitive recursive functionals, is denoted $T(;)$, and the result is that every provably recursive function of $PA(;)$ is definable in $T(;)$. The converse, that every function definable in $T(;)$ is elementary, will be dealt with in the next section.

4.1 Gödel's System $T(;)$

The Gödel primitive recursive functionals were first given by Gödel in [9]. We now define two-sorted higher-type Gödel primitive recursive functionals by using the variable separation and in fact we follow closely the development by Shoenfield [17]. This two-sorted Gödel system is denoted by $T(;)$ and has two crucial distinctions

- The composition is exclusively over output variables.
- The recursion is formulated over input variables.

as in $PA(;)$.

Definition 4.1 (Types). The types fall into two classes; *input* and *output.* They are generated from two ground-types ι (input) and o (output) using "$\rightarrow$", according to the following inductive definition:

(a) o is an output type, and ι is the only input type.

(b) If τ and σ are output types, then $\sigma \rightarrow \tau$ and $\iota \rightarrow \tau$ output types.

Definition 4.2 (Functionals). A functional of type $\sigma \rightarrow \tau$ is any mapping from the set of functionals of type σ into the set of functionals of type τ. The objects of type ι and o are natural numbers. These functionals constitute the *maximal* type-structure over $\mathbb{N}$.

A *functional* will mean function of some type. We shall not always give the type of a functional explicitly, but it is to be understood that whatever *functionals* we write are properly typed, and context should make the typing clear.

We have three function constants: *Successor* S of type $o \rightarrow o$, *Predecessor* P of type $o \rightarrow o$, *Cases function* C of type $o \rightarrow o \rightarrow o \rightarrow o$.

Definition 4.3 (Terms). The *terms* of $T(;)$ fall into two classes:

• *I-terms.* The only terms of type ι are those built up from I-variables and the constant 0 by (repeated) application of $+1$ or $\dot{-}\,1$. For notational convenience we shall often denote an I-term simply x (although strictly-speaking it is an I-variable).

• *O-terms.* The output variables of type σ are called *O-variables*, denoted by u^σ, v^σ, ... with or without subscripts. The *O-terms*, denoted by r, s, t with or without subscripts, are defined by the generalised inductive definition:

(a) Every *O-variable* is an O-term.

(b) The *constants* 0, S, P, C are O-terms of type o, $o \rightarrow o$, $o \rightarrow o$, $o \rightarrow o \rightarrow o \rightarrow o$ respectively.

(c) If t_1 and t_2 are O-terms of type $\sigma \to \tau$ and τ respectively, then the *application* $t_1 t_2$ is an O-term of type τ.

(d) If t is an O-term of type τ all of whose variables occur among I-variables $x_1, ..., x_n$ and O-variables $v_1, ..., v_m$ of type $\sigma_1, ..., \sigma_m$, then we introduce a new constant O-term f of type $\iota \to ... \to \iota \to \sigma_1 \to ... \to \sigma_m \to \tau$ with the defining equation:

$$fx_1...x_n v_1...v_m = t$$

(e) If g and h are constant O-terms of type τ and $\iota \to \tau \to \tau$ respectively, then we introduce a new constant O-term f of type $\iota \to \tau$ by the *primitive recursion*

$$\begin{cases} f0 &= g \\ f(x+1) &= h(x; fx) \end{cases}$$

Notations 4.4. We shall adopt the following notations whenever the context makes the arguments clear.

1. $T(;)$-*terms* will be used for either I-*terms* or O-*terms* whenever there is no confusion.

2. Denote the type of a term t by writing $t : \sigma$ or sometimes t^σ.

3. Parentheses will be omitted from types and terms according to the usual conventions, by association to the right for types and association to the left for terms. For examples,

$$\begin{aligned} \rho \to \sigma \to \tau &= (\rho \to (\sigma \to \tau)) \\ tsr &= ((ts)r) \end{aligned}$$

4. We shall write $\sigma_1, ..., \sigma_n \to \tau$ for $\sigma_1 \to ... \to \sigma_n \to \tau$ which will also be abbreviated by $\vec{\sigma} \to \tau$. Hence $\vec{t} : \vec{\sigma}$ will mean $\vec{t} = t_1, ..., t_n$ are of types $\sigma_1, ..., \sigma_n$ respectively.

5. We shall omit to write the types with terms whenever the context makes the arguments clear. In such a case every term, of course, has an appropriate type. We shall do this just for the sake of brevity.

4.2 Two-sorted Generalised Formulas

The *two-sorted generalised formulas* are to be viewed as higher-type extensions of $\Sigma_1(;)$-formulas in $PA(;)$.

Definition 4.5 (Generalised Formulas). To each arithmetical formula $A(\vec{x}; \vec{a})$ is associated a *generalised formula*

$$A^D = \forall \vec{u} \exists \vec{v} A'(\vec{x}; \vec{a}, \vec{u}, \vec{v})$$

where A' is quantifier free, and where $\vec{u}, \vec{v}$ are now lists of higher-type variables.

Let $B(\vec{x}; \vec{a})$, $C(\vec{x}; \vec{a_1})$ be any arithmetical formulas with generalised formulas $B^D = \forall \vec{u} \exists \vec{v} B'(\vec{x}; \vec{a}, \vec{u}, \vec{v})$, $C^D = \forall \vec{u_1} \exists \vec{v_1} C'(\vec{x}; \vec{a_1}, \vec{u_1}, \vec{v_1})$ respectively. Then the definition of A^D is by induction over the logical structure of the $PA(;)$-formula A, as follows:

(a) A is atomic $\Rightarrow$ $A^D = A$

(b) $A = \neg B$ $\Rightarrow$ $A^D = \forall \vec{f} \exists \vec{u} \neg B'(\vec{x}; \vec{a}, \vec{u}, \vec{f}\vec{u})$

(c) $A = B \vee C$ $\Rightarrow$ $A^D = \forall \vec{u}\vec{u_1} \exists \vec{v}\vec{v_1} (B'(\vec{x}; \vec{a}, \vec{u}, \vec{v}) \vee C'(\vec{x}; \vec{a_1}, \vec{u_1}, \vec{v_1}))$

(d) $A = \forall b B$ $\Rightarrow$ $A^D = \forall b \vec{u} \exists \vec{v} B'(\vec{x}; \vec{a}, b, \vec{u}, \vec{v})$

Where in clause (b), $(\neg B)^D$ can be shown by using skolemization

$$\begin{aligned}
(\neg B)^D &\equiv \neg B^D \\
&\equiv \neg(\forall \vec{u} \exists \vec{v} B'(\vec{x}; \vec{a}, \vec{u}, \vec{v})) \\
&\equiv \neg(\exists \vec{f} \forall \vec{u} B'(\vec{x}; \vec{a}, \vec{u}, \vec{f}\vec{u})) \\
&\equiv \forall \vec{f} \exists \vec{u} \neg B'(\vec{x}; \vec{a}, \vec{u}, \vec{f}\vec{u})
\end{aligned}$$

where $\vec{f}$ is a sequence of new variables of the appropriate types and $\vec{f}\vec{u}$ denotes the finite list $f_1\vec{u}, f_2\vec{u}, ..., f_k\vec{u}$ where k is the length of the list $\vec{v}$.

We therefore also can obtain $(B \to C)^D$ classically as

$$\begin{aligned}
(B \to C)^D &\equiv (\neg B \vee C)^D \\
&\equiv (\neg B)^D \vee C^D \\
&\equiv \forall \vec{f} \exists \vec{u} \neg B'(\vec{x}; \vec{a}, \vec{u}, \vec{f}\vec{u}) \vee \forall \vec{u_1} \exists \vec{v_1} C'(\vec{x}; \vec{a_1}, \vec{u_1}, \vec{v_1}) \\
&\equiv \forall \vec{f} \forall \vec{u_1} \exists \vec{u}\vec{v_1} (\neg B'(\vec{x}; \vec{a}, \vec{u}, \vec{f}\vec{u}) \vee C'(\vec{x}; \vec{a_1}, \vec{u_1}, \vec{v_1})) \\
&\equiv \forall \vec{f} \forall \vec{u_1} \exists \vec{u}\vec{v_1} (B'(\vec{x}; \vec{a}, \vec{u}, \vec{f}\vec{u}) \to C'(\vec{x}; \vec{a_1}, \vec{u_1}, \vec{v_1}))
\end{aligned}$$

Note that $\forall \vec{a}\vec{b}\vec{c}$ ... means $\forall \vec{a} \forall \vec{b} \forall \vec{b}$ ..., similarly $\exists \vec{a}\vec{b}\vec{c}$ ... means $\exists \vec{a} \exists \vec{b} \exists \vec{c}$ ... .

Definition 4.6 (Valid). We say that a generalised formula $\forall \vec{u} \exists \vec{v} A'(\vec{x}; \vec{a}, \vec{u}, \vec{v})$ is *valid*, if there are selection functionals $\vec{F}$ of the appropriate types such that for all $\vec{x}, \vec{a}$ and $\vec{u}$, the formula $A'(\vec{x}; \vec{a}, \vec{u}, \vec{F}\vec{x}\vec{a}\vec{u})$ is true, when interpreted in the maximal type-structure as explained in Definition 4.2.
It is *valid in* $T(;)$ if the selection functionals $\vec{F}$ can be chosen so as to be definable in $T(;)$.

Directly from Shoenfield [17] we obtain:

Theorem 4.7. *Assume that* $PA(;) \vdash A(\vec{x}; \vec{a})$. *Then the generalised formula* $A^D = \forall \vec{u} \exists \vec{v} A'(\vec{x}; \vec{a}, \vec{u}, \vec{v})$ *is valid in* $T(;)$.

Corollary 4.8. *If* $f(\vec{x}; \vec{a})$ *is a provably recursive or provably terminating function of* $PA(;)$, *i.e.*

$$PA(;) \vdash \forall \vec{a} \exists b (f(\vec{x}; \vec{a}) = b)$$

then (since the generalised formula of $\forall \vec{a} \exists b (f(\vec{x}; \vec{a}) = b)$ *is equivalent to itself) there is a selection function* g *definable in* $T(;)$ *such that for all* $\vec{x}, \vec{a}$

$$f(\vec{x}; \vec{a}) = g(\vec{x}; \vec{a})$$

Thus f *is itself definable in* $T(;)$.

5 Definable Functions in $T(;)$ are Elementary

In this section we wish to prove the converse of the result of the previous chapter, that is: every definable function in $T(;)$ is elementary. This will be proved by using normalisation and transfinite "bounding" by means of infinite terms.

5.1 Infinitary λ-calculus

In order to analyse the complexity of the Gödel system $T(;)$ we are going to embed it in an infinitary λ-calculus, denoted by $T^\infty(;)$, due originally to Tait [18], which allows us systematically to unravel the primitive recursions.

The infinite terms of $T^\infty(;)$ are obtained from $T(;)$ by three changes:

1. The substitution is replaced by λ-abstraction.
2. The primitive recursion is replaced by "infinite sequencing".
3. The finite lists $\vec{F} = F_1, ..., F_l$ are replaced by cartesian products $(F_1, ..., F_l)$.

Definition 5.1 (Types). In our new infinitary λ-calculus $T^\infty(;)$, the *types* are as in $T(;)$, except that here we add the *product types.* An object of product type $\sigma \times \tau$ is an ordered pair consisting of an object of type σ and an object of type τ. Here again, the input type is only ι which is also input ground type as in $T(;)$, and the output types are generated from two ground-types ι and output ground type o using "$\rightarrow$" and "$\times$", according to the following inductive definition:

(a) o is an output type, and ι is the only input type.

(b) If τ and σ are output types, then $\sigma \rightarrow \tau$ and $\iota \rightarrow \tau$ are output types.

(c) If τ and σ are output types, then $\sigma \times \tau$ is an output type.

Definition 5.2 (Type Level). The *level* of a type σ, denoted by $L(\sigma)$, is defined as in $T(;)$, but here we have an extra clause for product type. It is inductively defined by

(a) $L(o) = L(\iota) = 0$

(b) $L(\sigma \rightarrow \tau) = max(L(\sigma) + 1, L(\tau))$

(c) $L(\sigma \times \tau) = max(L(\sigma), L(\tau))$

Definition 5.3 (Infinite Terms). In $T^\infty(;)$, the *variables* and *constants* are the same as in $T(;)$. The terms of the system $T^\infty(;)$ are, of course, of two-sorts:

• I^∞*-terms.* The *input* terms of $T^\infty(;)$ of type ι are called I^∞*-terms* and are defined as in $T(;)$.

• O^∞*-terms.* The *output* terms of $T^\infty(;)$ are called O^∞*-terms* and are defined inductively as follows:

(a) Any O^∞*-variables* and *constants* are O^∞-terms.

(b) If t and s are O^∞-terms of types $\sigma \rightarrow \tau$ and σ respectively, then the *application* ts is an O^∞-term of type τ.

(c) If t is an O^∞-term of type τ and v is an O^∞- variable of type σ, then the *abstraction* $\lambda v.t$ is an O^∞-term of type $\sigma \to \tau$.

(d) If x is a I^∞-term of type ι and t_i is an O^∞-term of type σ for each $i \in \mathbb{N}$, then the *infinite sequence* $< t_i >_{i \in \mathbb{N}} x$ is an O^∞-term of type σ. (Note the occurrence of the free input-term x here).

(e) If t_1 and t_2 are O^∞-terms of type σ and τ respectively, then the *pair* (t_1, t_2) is an O^∞-term of type $\sigma \times \tau$.

(f) For each σ_1 and σ_2, the new constants *first projection* π_1 of type $\sigma_1 \times \sigma_2 \to \sigma_1$ and *second projection* π_2 of type $\sigma_1 \times \sigma_2 \to \sigma_2$ are O^∞-terms.

Notations 5.4. Whenever there is no confusion we shall use the following apprevia-tions.

1. $T^\infty(;)$-*terms* will be used for either I^∞-*terms* or O^∞-*terms*.
2. $< t_i > x$ will be used for $< t_i >_{i \in \mathbb{N}} x$ dropping the subscripts $i \in \mathbb{N}$.
3. $< t_i >_x$ will be used for $< t_i > x$.
4. π_j will be used to denote either π_1 or π_2.

Definition 5.5 (Finite Sequence). A *finite sequence* $(t_1, ..., t_l)$ is abbreviated by $\vec{t}$ which can be defined by the *pair* using the following convention of parenthesis

$$(t_1, t_2, ..., t_l) := (((t_1, t_2), t_2)...), t_l)$$

Therefore the first projection π_1 and second projection π_2 applied to a finite sequence give

$$\begin{aligned} \pi_1 \vec{t} &:= (t_1, t_2, ..., t_{l-1}) \\ \pi_2 \vec{t} &:= t_l \end{aligned}$$

So t_i can be obtained for each $i = 1, 2, ..., l$ by

$$t_1 = \pi_1^{l-1} \vec{t} \quad \text{and} \quad t_i = \pi_2(\pi_1^{l-i} \vec{t}) \quad \text{for } 2 \le i \le l$$

where π_j^l is the l-times iterate of π_j.

Definition 5.6 (Valuation Function). Suppose that t is any $T^\infty(;)$-term of type σ, containing free variables $u_1, ..., u_k$ of types $\sigma_1, ..., \sigma_k$ respectively. Then given any assignment of functionals $f_1, ..., f_k$ (in the maximal type structure) to the free variables $\vec{u}$, we define the *value* of $t(\vec{u})$

$$\mathcal{V}t[\vec{u} := \vec{f}]$$

by induction over the build up of t as follows:

(a) $t = v \quad \Rightarrow \quad \mathcal{V}v[\vec{u} := \vec{f}] = f_i$

(b) $t = c \quad \Rightarrow \quad \mathcal{V}c[\vec{u} := \vec{f}] = c$ where c is any constant

(c) $t = t_0 t_1 \quad \Rightarrow \quad \mathcal{V}(t_0 t_1)[\vec{u} := \vec{f}] = \mathcal{V}t_0[\vec{u} := \vec{f}](\mathcal{V}t_1[\vec{u} := \vec{f}])$

(d) $t = < t_i >_x \Rightarrow \mathcal{V}(< t_i >_x)[x =: n, \vec{u} := \vec{f}] = \mathcal{V}t_n[x := n, \vec{u} := \vec{f}]$

(e) $t = \lambda v.r \Rightarrow \mathcal{V}(\lambda v.r)[\vec{u} := \vec{f}] = F$ where $F(g) := \mathcal{V}r[\vec{u} := \vec{f}, v := g]$.

(f) $t = (t_0, t_1) \Rightarrow \mathcal{V}(t_0, t_1)[\vec{u} := \vec{f}] = (\mathcal{V}t_0[\vec{u} := \vec{f}], \mathcal{V}t_1[\vec{u} := \vec{f}])$

Definition 5.7 (Substitution). The formulation $t[s/v]$ denotes the result of substituting s for v in t, assuming that v and s have same type.

5.2 Normalisation

In this section we shall first define a reduction mechanism whereby every term of $T^{\infty}(;)$ reduces to another term by reducing the rank of the term by at least one. We then show that every term of finite rank reduces to a normal form with rank 0.

Definition 5.8 (Term Level). The *level of a term* t is the level of type of the term t, denoted by $L(t)$, that is

$$t : \sigma \quad \Rightarrow \quad L(t) = L(\sigma)$$

Lemma 5.9. *If* $t = \lambda v.r$, *then we have the following*

$$L(v) < L(t)$$

Proof. If $v : \sigma$ and $r : \tau$, then $t : \sigma \to \tau$. Hence

$$\begin{aligned} L(v) &= L(\sigma) && \text{by Def. 5.8} \\ &< L(\sigma) + 1 \\ &\leq max(L(\sigma) + 1, L(\tau)) \\ &= L(\sigma \to \tau) && \text{by Def. 5.2} \\ &= L(t) && \text{by Def. 5.8} \end{aligned}$$

Definition 5.10 (Redexes). The *redexes* are certain kinds of application terms as defined by

(I) *Abstraction-redex,* $(\lambda v.t)s$

(II) *Sequence-redex,* $< t_i >_x s$

(III) *Projection-redexes,* $\pi_j(t_1, t_2)$ or $\pi_j < t_i >_x$

Definition 5.11 (Rank). The *rank* of $T^{\infty}(;)$-term t, denoted by $R(t)$, is defined to be the supremum of type levels of all sub-terms of the form

$$\begin{array}{rlll} \lambda v.r & \text{in context} & (\lambda v.r)s & \text{or} \\ < t_i >_x & \text{in context} & < t_i >_x s & \text{or} \\ \pi_j & \text{in context} & \pi_j(t_1, t_2) & \text{or} \quad \pi_j < t_i >_x \end{array}$$

So the *rank function* R is defined from terms into numbers recursively by the following properties:

(a) $R(t) = 0$ if t is a variable or a constant

(b) $R(\lambda v.r) = R(r)$

(c) $R(t_1t_2) = \begin{cases} max(R(t_1), R(t_2), L(t_1)) & \text{if } t_1t_2 \text{ is a redex} \\ max(R(t_1), R(t_2)) & \text{otherwise} \end{cases}$

(d) $R(< t_i >_x) = sup(R(t_i))$

(e) $R((t_1, t_2)) = max(R(t_1), R(t_2))$

Definition 5.12 (Rank-Reduction). A *rank-reduced* term t' is obtained from t (with a reduction in the rank of the term by at least one) by the *rank-reduction*. The rank-reduction operator $t \mapsto t'$ is defined recursively as follows:

(a) t is a variable or constant $\Rightarrow$ $t' = t$

(b) $t = \lambda v.r$ $\Rightarrow$ $t' = \lambda v.r'$

(c) $t =< r_i >_x$ $\Rightarrow$ $t' =< r'_i >_x$

(d) $t = rs$ $\Rightarrow$ $t' = (r's')^*$

(e) $t = (r_1, r_2)$ $\Rightarrow$ $t' = (r'_1, r'_2)$

The operation $(\ )^*$ in (d) is defined below.

Definition 5.13. The notation $(ts)^*$ is defined by

(a) $(ts)^* = ts$ if ts is not a redex

(b) $((\lambda v.r)s)^* = r[s/v]$

(c) $(< r_i >_x s)^* =< (r_is)^* >_x$

(d) $(\pi_j s)^* = \begin{cases} s_j & \text{if } s = (s_1, s_2) \\ < (\pi_j s_i)^* >_x & \text{if } s =< s_i >_x \end{cases}$

Definition 5.14 (Normal). A term is said to be *normal* or to be in *normal form*, if it does not contain any kind of redex. Thus if a term t contains no redex its rank is 0.

If a term t reduces to a normal form $t^{''\cdots'}$ after k-many times application of rank-reduction, then this normal form of t is abbreviated by $t^{[k]}$.

Lemma 5.15. *Let t_1, t_2 be any terms with positive finite rank and let v be a variable in $T^\infty(;)$. Then if $max(R(t_1), R(t_2), L(v)) = k$ we have the following property*

$$R(t_1[t_2/v]) \leq k$$

Proof. The proof is by induction on construction of t_1, and is quite standard. □

Lemma 5.16. *Let t_1, t_2 be any $T^\infty(;)$-terms of finite rank and suppose the application term t_1t_2 is a redex. Then if $R(t_1t_2) = k + 1$ where $R(t_1) \leq k$ and $R(t_2) \leq k$ we have*

$$R((t_1t_2)^*) \leq k$$

Proof. Before starting proof we have to point out that since t_1t_2 is a redex we have

$$R(t_1t_2) = max(R(t_1), R(t_2), L(t_1)) \qquad \text{by Def. 5.11} - (c)$$

which means $L(t_1) = k + 1$. Hence the proof runs by induction on construction of the term t_1:

Case 1. It t_1 is a variable or a constant (except π_j), then t_1t_2 can not be redex. If $t_1 = \pi_j$, then t_1t_2 can be a projection-redex whenever t_2 is either a pair or a sequence. So there are two sub-cases to consider:

1.1. If $t_2 = (r_1, r_2)$, then

$$\begin{array}{rcll} R((\pi_j(r_1,r_2))^*) & = & R(r_j) & \text{by Def. } 5.13-(d) \\ & \leq & max(R(r_1),R(r_2)) & \\ & = & R(t_2) & \text{by Def. } 5.11-(e) \\ & \leq & k & \text{given} \end{array}$$

1.2. If $t_2 =< r_i >_x$, then by a sub-induction over sub-terms of t_2,

$$\begin{array}{rcll} R((\pi_j < r_i >_x)^*) & = & R(< (\pi_j r_i)^* >_x) & \text{by Def. } 5.13-(c) \\ & = & sup(R((\pi_j r_i)^*)) & \text{by Def. } 5.13-(d) \\ & \leq & k & \end{array}$$

since $R((\pi_j r_i)^*) \leq k$ whether the application term $\pi_j r_i$ is a redex or not.

Case 2. If $t_1 = \lambda v.r$, then t_1t_2 is an abstraction-redex. So

$$\begin{array}{rcll} R(((\lambda v.r)t_2)^*) & = & R(r[t_2/v]) & \text{by Def. } 5.13-(b) \\ & \leq & k & \text{by Lemma 5.15} \end{array}$$

where $max(R(r), R(t_2), L(v)) \leq k$ because $R(r) \leq k$ since $R(r) = R(t_1)$ by Definition 5.11-(b), and $L(v) \leq k$ since $L(t_1) = k+1$ and $L(v) \leq k$ since $L(v) < L(t_1)$ by Lemma 5.9.

Case 3. If $t_1 =< r_i >_x$, then t_1t_2 is a sequence-redex.

$$\begin{array}{rcll} R((< r_i >_x t_2)^*) & = & R(< (r_i t_2)^* >_x) & \text{by Def. } 5.13-(b) \\ & = & sup(R(r_i t_2)^*)) & \text{by Def. } 5.13-(d) \\ & \leq & k & \end{array}$$

since by the induction hypothesis $R((r_i t_2)^*) \leq k$ whether the application term $r_i t_2$ is a redex or not.

Case 4. If $t_1 = (r_1, r_2)$, then t_1t_2 can not be a redex.

□

Lemma 5.17. *Let t be any $T^\infty(;)$-term with a positive finite rank $k+1$. In that case, if t rank-reduces to t' as in Definition 5.12, then*

$$R(t') < R(t)$$

Proof. The proof goes by induction on the construction of t: the only non-trivial case is that if $t = t_1t_2$, then

$$\begin{array}{rcll} R((t_1t_2)') & = & R((t_1't_2')^*) & \text{by Def. } 5.12-(d) \\ & < & R(t_1t_2) & \text{by Lemma 5.16} \end{array}$$

□

Theorem 5.18 (Normalisation). *Every $T^\infty(;)$-term of finite rank reduces to a normal form.*

Proof. Let t be any $T^\infty(;)$-term. If we continue the procedure of Lemma 5.17, then $R(t)$ strictly decreases and then we must eventually obtain a normal form. □

5.3 Ordinal Notations

A knowledge of some of the theory of ordinals is required to examine the proof complexity. In this section we wish to introduce some fundamental notions of the theory of *countable tree-ordinals* $< \epsilon_0$, *not set-theoretic ordinals*. We shall use the lower case Greek letters $\alpha, \beta, \gamma, \ldots, \lambda, \ldots$ with or without subscripts to denote the ordinals, and $i, j, k, l, m, n, \ldots$ to denote ordinals $< \omega$ or natural numbers.

For a more thorough analysis of tree ordinals see Fairtlough and Wainer [8].

Definition 5.19 (Tree Ordinal). The *set of countable tree-ordinals*, Ω, is generated inductively according to the following rules:

$$(a) \quad 0 \in \Omega$$

$$(b) \quad \alpha \in \Omega \quad \Rightarrow \quad \alpha + 1 := \alpha \cup \{\alpha\} \in \Omega$$

$$(c) \quad \lambda \text{ is a function from } \mathbb{N} \text{ to } \Omega \quad \Rightarrow \quad \sup_{n \in \mathbb{N}}(\lambda_n) := \lambda \in \Omega$$

Where $\alpha + 1$ is called *successor* of α, and λ is called a *limit.*

Notations 5.20. Whenever there is no confusion we shall adopt the following:

1. In the sequel we shall only be dealing with *countable tree ordinals*, and we shall refer to them as *ordinals.*
2. We usually use $sup(\alpha_n)$ for $\sup_{n \in \mathbb{N}}(\alpha_n)$by dropping off the subscripts $n \in \mathbb{N}$ whenever it is possible.

Definition 5.21 (Ordinal Arithmetic). We would like to define arithmetical operations *addition, multiplication* and *exponentiation* on the ordinals by recursion, as follows.

$$\textit{(Add)} \quad \alpha + 0 = \alpha, \quad \alpha + (\beta + 1) = (\alpha + \beta) + 1, \quad \alpha + \lambda = sup(\alpha + \lambda_n)$$

$$\textit{(Mlt)} \quad \alpha \cdot 0 = 0, \quad \alpha \cdot (\beta + 1) = \alpha \cdot \beta + \alpha, \quad \alpha \cdot \lambda = sup(\alpha \cdot \lambda_n)$$

$$\textit{(Exp)} \quad \alpha^0 = 1, \quad \alpha^{\beta+1} = \alpha^\beta \cdot \alpha, \quad \alpha^\lambda = sup(\alpha^{\lambda_n})$$

Note that for all the above, it is straightforward to prove that *associativity* and *left-handed distributivity*

$$\alpha \cdot (\beta + \gamma) = \alpha \cdot \beta + \alpha \cdot \gamma$$

for every α, β and γ, holds, but *right-side distributivity* does not. Furthermore, they are not commutative.

Definition 5.22 (Sub-Tree Ordering). For $k \in \mathbb{N}$, the *sub-tree ordering* $\prec_k$ is the transitive closure of the following two rules for any tree ordinal α

$$(a) \quad \alpha \prec_k \alpha + 1$$

$$(b) \quad \alpha_k \prec_k \alpha \qquad \text{where} \quad \alpha = sup(\alpha_n)$$

Note that we are going to write $\alpha \preccurlyeq_k \beta$ to mean $\alpha = \beta$ or $\alpha \prec_k \beta$. Note also that for all $n, m \in \mathbb{N}$ we have that

$$m \prec_k n \Longleftrightarrow m < n$$

Definition 5.23 (Ordinal Height). The set-theoretical-*height* of tree ordinal α, denoted by $|\alpha|$, is defined inductively by

(a) $|0| = 0$

(b) $|\alpha + 1| = |\alpha| + 1$

(c) $|\lambda| = sup(|\lambda_n| + 1)$

Note that for the ordinal numbers α and β we have that

$$\alpha \prec_k \beta \Rightarrow |\alpha| < |\beta|$$

Definition 5.24 (Slow-Growing Function). Let $G_n(\alpha)$ be cardinality of the set $\{\beta : \beta + 1 \preccurlyeq_n \alpha\}$. Then we immediately get the *Slow-Growing function* $G_n : \Omega \to \mathbb{N}$ by the transfinite recursion

$$\begin{cases} G_n(0) & = 0 \\ G_n(\alpha + 1) & = G_n(\alpha) + 1 \\ G_n(\lambda) & = G_n(\lambda_n) \end{cases}$$

for each fixed $n \in \mathbb{N}$.

Lemma 5.25. *We have the following arithmetical relations for each fixed $n \in \mathbb{N}$*

(i) $G_n(\alpha + \beta) = G_n(\alpha) + G(\beta)$

(ii) $G_n(\alpha \cdot \beta) = G_n(\alpha) \cdot G(\beta)$

(iii) $G_n(\alpha^\beta) = (G_n(\alpha))^{G_n(\beta)}$

Proof. All easily prove by induction on β. □

Remark 5.26. For each countable ordinal there are many $\prec_k$-incomparable tree ordinals with the same set-theoretic height. (If we take the ordinal $\alpha_f = sup(f(x))$ for each increasing function $f : \mathbb{N} \to \mathbb{N}$, then $G_{\alpha_f} = f$ and hence every such function already crops up at the first limit level in Ω). Of course, each tree ordinal has a set-theoretic ordinal-height. For instance, the tree ordinals ω, $1 + \omega$, 2^ω are incomparable but they have the same set-theoretic height ω. Some of these are more natural then others, the most natural being $\omega_0 = sup(n)$ and $\omega = sup(n+1)$. Set theoretically they are the same but in the context of tree ordinals they are different, and they are also incomparable under the relation $\prec_n$.

In this work we will be concerned with those ordinals which can be constructed from

$$\omega = sup(n + 1)$$

by addition, multiplication and exponentiation. It means that we chose $\{n + 1\}$ as the fundamental sequence for ω.

Lemma 5.27. *If β is "structured tree-ordinal" in the sense that for every limit sub-tree λ of β*

$$\forall m, n.(m < n \Rightarrow \lambda_m + 1 \prec_n \lambda)$$

then

$$\alpha \prec_k \beta \quad \Rightarrow \quad \forall n > k(G_n(\alpha) < G_n(\beta))$$

Proof. For all $n > k$, we can prove it by induction on β:

Case 1. If $\beta = 0$, it is trivial.

Case 2. If β is a successor, then $\beta = \beta' + 1$. So $\alpha \preccurlyeq_k \beta'$ and we have

$$\begin{array}{rcll} G_n(\alpha) & \leq & G_n(\beta') & \text{by ind. hyp.} \\ & < & G_n(\beta') + 1 & \\ & = & G_n(\beta' + 1) & \text{by Def. 5.24} \\ & = & G_n(\beta) & \end{array}$$

Case 3. If β is a limit, then $\beta_k \prec_k \beta$. So $\alpha \preccurlyeq_k \beta_k$ and we have

$$\begin{array}{rcll} G_n(\alpha) & \leq & G_n(\beta_k) & \text{by ind. hyp.} \\ & < & G_n(\beta_k + 1) & \\ & \leq & G_n(\beta_n) & \text{since} \quad \beta_k + 1 \preccurlyeq_n \beta_n \\ & = & G_n(\beta) & \text{by Def. 5.24} \end{array}$$

□

Note that from now on all the tree-ordinals we construct will be "*structured tree-ordinal*" as in this Lemma.

Definition 5.28 (Step-Down Relation). The *step-down relation* is the relation $\alpha \prec_o \beta$. It is defined inductively by

(*a*) $\alpha \prec_o \alpha + 1$ for any α

(*b*) $\alpha_0 \prec_o \alpha$ where $\alpha = sup(\alpha_n)$

(*c*) $\gamma \prec_o \alpha,\ \alpha \prec_o \beta \quad \Rightarrow \quad \gamma \prec_o \beta$

Note that our work is based on this special *sub-tree ordering* $\prec_o$, the reason is that from the above Lemma 5.27 we get

$$\begin{array}{llll} \alpha \prec_o \beta & \Rightarrow & G_n(\alpha) < G_n(\beta) & \text{for all} \quad n > 0 \\ \alpha \preccurlyeq_o \beta & \Rightarrow & G_n(\alpha) \leq G_n(\beta) & \text{for all} \quad n \geq 0 \end{array}$$

Lemma 5.29. *Let α, β, γ be ordinals and let k be a natural number. Then the following are true*

(*i*) $\alpha \preccurlyeq_o \beta \quad \Rightarrow \quad \gamma + \alpha \preccurlyeq_o \gamma + \beta$

(*ii*) $\alpha \preccurlyeq_o \beta \quad \Rightarrow \quad k \cdot \alpha \preccurlyeq_o k \cdot \beta$

In particular,

(i') $\gamma \preccurlyeq_o \gamma + \beta$ with $\alpha = 0 \preccurlyeq_o \beta$ in (i)

(ii') $k \preccurlyeq_o k \cdot \beta$ with $\alpha = 1 \preccurlyeq_o \beta$ in (ii)

Definition 5.30 (Ordinal Function φ). The *ordinal function* φ on the tree-ordinals is defined recursively as follows:

$$\begin{cases} \varphi(0) &= 1 \\ \varphi(\alpha+1) &= \varphi(\alpha) + 2 \cdot \varphi(\alpha) + 2 \cdot \varphi(\alpha) \\ \varphi(\lambda) &= sup\ \varphi(\lambda_i) \end{cases}$$

The reason for this somewhat strange-looking function will become clear in Theorem 5.38. It is an abstract form of exponentiation.

Lemma 5.31. *Let φ be the function above. Then the following are true*

(i) $1 \preccurlyeq_o \varphi(\alpha)$ *for every α.*

(ii) $\varphi(\alpha) + 1 \prec_o \varphi(\alpha + 1)$

(iii) *α is a limit* $\Rightarrow$ $\varphi(\alpha_i) \prec_i \varphi(\alpha)$ *for every i*

(iv) $\alpha \preccurlyeq_o \beta$ $\Rightarrow$ $\varphi(\alpha) \preccurlyeq_o \varphi(\beta)$

Proofs.

(i). It is trivial.

(ii). For any α the proof directly is as follows

$$\begin{array}{rcll} \varphi(\alpha)+1 & \prec_o & \varphi(\alpha)+2 & \text{by Def. 5.28} - (a) \\ & \preccurlyeq_o & \varphi(\alpha) + 2\cdot\varphi(\alpha) & \text{by Lemmas 5.29} - (ii) \\ & \preccurlyeq_o & \varphi(\alpha) + 2\cdot\varphi(\alpha) + 2\cdot\varphi(\alpha) & \text{by Lemma 5.29} - (i) \\ & = & \varphi(\alpha+1) & \text{by Def. 5.30} \end{array}$$

(iii). It is trivial.

(iv). If $\alpha = \beta$ the proof is trivial. If $\alpha \prec_o \beta$ it proves by induction on β:

Case 1. If $\beta = 0$, it is trivial.

Case 2. If β is a successor, then $\beta = \beta' + 1$. So $\alpha \preccurlyeq_o \beta'$ and we have

$$\begin{array}{rcll} \varphi(\alpha) & \preccurlyeq_o & \varphi(\beta') & \text{by ind. hyp.} \\ & \prec_o & \varphi(\beta')+1 & \text{by Def. 5.28} - (a) \\ & \prec_o & \varphi(\beta'+1) & \text{by } (ii) \\ & = & \varphi(\beta) & \text{by Def. 5.30} \end{array}$$

Case 3. If β is a limit, then $\beta_0 \prec_o \beta$. So $\alpha \preccurlyeq_o \beta_0$ and we have

$$\begin{array}{rcll} \varphi(\alpha) & \preccurlyeq_o & \varphi(\beta_0) & \text{by ind. hyp.} \\ & \preccurlyeq_o & \varphi(\beta) & \text{by } (iii) \end{array}$$

□

Lemma 5.32. *Let G_n be the slow-growing function, and let φ be as in the Definition 5.30. Then for every α we have*

$$G_n(\varphi(\alpha)) = 5^{G_n(\alpha)}$$

Proof. By induction on α:

Case 1. If $\alpha = 0$, it is trivial.

Case 2. If α is a successor, then $\alpha = \alpha' + 1$. So

$$\begin{array}{lll} & G_n(\varphi(\alpha'+1)) & \\ = & G_n(\varphi(\alpha') + 2\cdot\varphi(\alpha') + 2\cdot\varphi(\alpha')) & \text{by Def. 5.30} \\ = & G_n(\varphi(\alpha')) + G_n(2\cdot\varphi(\alpha')) + G_n(2\cdot\varphi(\alpha')) & \text{by Lemma 5.25} - (i) \\ = & 5^{G_n(\alpha')} + 2\cdot 5^{G_n(\alpha')} + 2\cdot 5^{G_n(\alpha')} & \text{by ind. hyp.} \\ = & 5\cdot 5^{G_n(\alpha')} & \text{on natural numbers} \\ = & 5^{G_n(\alpha')+1} & \text{on natural numbers} \\ = & 5^{G_n(\alpha'+1)} & \text{by Def. 5.24} \end{array}$$

Case 3. If α is a limit, then $\alpha = sup\ (\alpha_n)$. So

$$\begin{array}{rcll} G_n(\varphi(sup(\alpha_n))) & = & G_n(\varphi(\alpha_n)) & \text{by Def. 5.24} \\ & = & 5^{G_n(\alpha_n)} & \text{by ind. hyp.} \\ & = & 5^{G_n(\alpha)} & \text{by Def. 5.24} \end{array}$$

□

5.4 Embedding

The aim of this section is to prove that every functional of $T(;)$ is represented by a term of $T^\infty(;)$ with an ordinal bound of set-theoretic height below ω^2.

In this section the types will not be written for sake of brevity, through of course, each term has an appropriate type.

Definition 5.33 (Majorization Relation). Let t be a term of $T^\infty(;)$ and α be a tree ordinal. The *majorization relation* $t \lhd \alpha$, reading "*t is majorized by α*", is defined inductively as follows:

(a) t is a variable or constant $\Rightarrow$ $t \lhd 0$

(b) $t_1 \lhd \alpha_1,\ t_2 \lhd \alpha_2,\ \alpha_1 \preccurlyeq_o \alpha_2 \Rightarrow t_1 t_2 \lhd \alpha_2 + 1$

(c) $r \lhd \beta \Rightarrow \lambda v.r \lhd \beta + 1$

(d) $\forall i \exists \beta (t_i \lhd \beta \land \beta + 1 \preccurlyeq_o \gamma_i) \Rightarrow\ < t_i > x \lhd \gamma$, where $\gamma = sup(\gamma_i)$

(e) $t_1 \lhd \alpha,\ t_2 \lhd \alpha \Rightarrow (t_1, t_2) \lhd \alpha$

(f) $t \lhd \beta,\ \beta \prec_o \alpha \Rightarrow t \lhd \alpha$

Lemma 5.34. *Let α and β be ordinals and let k be a positive natural number. Then for a $T^\infty(;)$-term t the following are true*

(i) $t \lhd \alpha \Rightarrow t \lhd \alpha + \beta$

$(ii) \qquad t \lhd \alpha \quad \Rightarrow \quad t \lhd \beta + \alpha$

$(iii) \qquad t \lhd \alpha \quad \Rightarrow \quad t \lhd k \cdot \alpha$

Proof. (i) is streightforward since $\alpha \preccurlyeq_o \alpha + \beta$, and (ii), (iii) are proven by induction on α. □

Theorem 5.35. *For every finite list of functionals $\vec{F} = F_1, ..., F_l$ definable in $T(;)$ there is a term $t_{\vec{F}} = (t_{F_1}, ..., t_{F_l})$ of $T^\infty(;)$ such that for each $i = 1, ..., l$, the term t_{F_i} represents functional F_i (the value of t_{F_i} is same as value of F_i) and*

$$t_{\vec{F}} \lhd (k \cdot \omega) \cdot m$$

for some positive integers k and m. Here k is any number greater than or equal to twice the maximum length of any list of functionals defined, and m is the finite number of the different definitions in the program of $T(;)$ defining $\vec{F}$.

Proof. We are going to prove it by induction on the definition of functionals of $T(;)$. When we get the system $T^\infty(;)$ from $T(;)$, we replace the substitution and primitive recursion by λ-abstraction application and infinite sequence respectively. So it is enough to show that the *substitution* and *recursion* in $T(;)$ are definable in $T^\infty(;)$. The other clauses of definition of $T(;)$ are clearly representable.

Case (Substitution). Let $\vec{r} = (r_1, ..., r_l)$ be a sequence of $T(;)$-terms all of whose variables occur among I-variables $x_1, ..., x_p$ and O-variables $u_1, ..., u_q$. Then a new sequence of constants $\vec{F}$ is defined by *simultaneous explicit definition*

$$\vec{F}(x_1, ..., x_p; u_1, ..., u_q) = \vec{r}$$

i.e. $F_i(x_1, ..., x_p; u_1, ..., u_q) = r_i$ for each $i = 1, 2, ..., l$. If $\vec{r}$ is represented by $t_{\vec{r}}$, then $\vec{F}$ is represented by $T^\infty(;)$-term $t_{\vec{F}} = (t_{F_1}, ..., t_{F_l})$ which will be as follows by means of *λ-abstraction*

$$t_{F_i} = \lambda u_1 ... u_q . t_{r_i}$$

for each $i = 1, ..., l$. Where the t_i may be obtained by repeated *application* of previously defined constant, called K, each of which is already assumed to be represented by a $T^\infty(;)$-term t_K with $t_K \lhd (k \cdot \omega) \cdot m_K$ for some fixed m_K. Hence when translated into $T^\infty(;)$ we will have $t_{q_i} \lhd (k \cdot \omega) \cdot m$. Then for each $i = 1, 2, ..., l$

$$\begin{array}{lll} \lambda u_q . t_{r_i} & \lhd \; (k \cdot \omega) \cdot m + 1 & \text{by Def. 5.33-(c)} \\ & \prec_o \; (k \cdot \omega) \cdot m + k \cdot \omega & \text{since } 1 \prec_o k \cdot \omega \end{array}$$

thus using this procedure for $u_{q-1}, ..., u_1, x_p, ..., x_1$ we get that

$$\lambda u_1 ... u_q . t_{r_i} \lhd (k \cdot \omega) \cdot (m + q + p)$$

So if we change m to $m + q + p$ we get the result as it is required

$$t_{F_i} \lhd (k \cdot \omega) \cdot m$$

Case (Recursion). Let I-variable x and $T(;)$-terms $\vec{G}$ and $\vec{H}$ be given. Then a new sequence of constants $\vec{F}$ is defined by *simultaneous primitive recursion*

$$\begin{cases} \vec{F}(0) &= \vec{G} \\ \vec{F}(x+1) &= \vec{H}x(\vec{F}x) \end{cases}$$

i.e. for each $i = 1, ..., l$

$$\begin{cases} F_i(0) &= G_i \\ F_i(x+1) &= H_i x(F_1 x F_2 x ... F_l x) \end{cases}$$

We assume that $\vec{G}$ and $\vec{H}$ are represented by the $T^\infty(;)$-terms $t_{\vec{G}}$ and $t_{\vec{H}}$ respectively with $t_{G_i} \lhd (k \cdot \omega) \cdot m_G$, $t_{H_i} \lhd (k \cdot \omega) \cdot m_H$ where $m = max(m_G, m_H)$.

We now define $T^\infty(;)$-terms $\vec{s}_n = (s_{1,n}, ..., s_{l,n})$ recursively as follows for each $i = 1, ..., l$

$$\begin{cases} s_{i,0} &= t_{G_i} \\ s_{i,n+1} &= t_{H_i}\bar{n}(s_{1,n})(s_{2,n})...(s_{l,n}) \end{cases}$$

The $s_{1,n}, s_{2,n}, ..., s_{l,n}$ can be obtained from $\vec{s}_n$. Hence we get

$$\begin{cases} \vec{s}_0 &= t_{\vec{G}} \\ \vec{s}_{n+1} &= t_{\vec{H}}\bar{n}(\pi_1^{l-1}\vec{s}_n)(\pi_2(\pi_1^{l-2}\vec{s}_n))...(\pi_2(\pi_1^0\vec{s}_n)) \end{cases}$$

Then $\vec{F}x = (F_1 x, ..., F_l x)$ is represented by the infinite term

$$t_{\vec{F}x} = < \vec{s}_n > x$$

by means of *infinite sequencing.* Now we shall find an ordinal which majorizes the $\vec{s}_n$. The proof runs by induction on n.

- *Base case,* $n = 0$. Then $\vec{s}_0 \lhd (k \cdot \omega) \cdot m$ since $\vec{s}_0 = t_{\vec{G}}$ and $m_G \leq m$.
- *Induction case,* assume that $s_{i,n} \lhd (k \cdot \omega) \cdot m + 2ln$. Then we first get the following

  $$\begin{array}{ll} \vec{s}_n \lhd (k \cdot \omega) \cdot m + 2ln & \text{by Def. 5.33-(e)} \\ \pi_i^l \vec{s}_n \lhd (k \cdot \omega) \cdot m + 2ln + l & \text{by Def. 5.33-(b)} \\ S \lhd 0, \quad 0 \lhd 0 & \text{by Def. 5.33-(a)} \\ \bar{n} = \underbrace{SS...S}_{n} 0 \lhd n \preccurlyeq_o (k \cdot \omega) \cdot m + 2ln & \text{by Def. 5.33-(b)} \end{array}$$

  Hence we now can majorize $\vec{s}_{n+1}$ as follows

  $$t_{\vec{H}}\bar{n} \quad \lhd \quad (k \cdot \omega) \cdot m + 2ln + 1 \qquad \text{by Def. 5.33-(b)}$$

  and then by Definition 5.33-(b)

  $$\begin{array}{rcl} t_{\vec{H}}\bar{n}(\pi_1^{l-1}\vec{s}_n) & \lhd & (k \cdot \omega) \cdot m + 2ln + l + 1 \\ t_{\vec{H}}\bar{n}(\pi_1^{l-1}\vec{s}_n)(\pi_2(\pi_1^{l-2}\vec{s}_n)) & \lhd & (k \cdot \omega) \cdot m + 2ln + l + 2 \\ & \vdots & \\ t_{\vec{H}}\bar{n}(\pi_1^{l-1}\vec{s}_n)(\pi_2(\pi_1^{l-2}\vec{s}_n))...(\pi_2(\pi_1^0\vec{s}_n)) & \lhd & (k \cdot \omega) \cdot m + 2ln + l + l \end{array}$$

  that is, we have got $\vec{s}_{n+1} \lhd (k \cdot \omega) \cdot m + 2l(n+1)$.

Therefore by induction on n we have $\vec{s}_n \lhd (k \cdot \omega) \cdot m + 2ln$ where by the Definition 5.28

$$\begin{aligned}(k \cdot \omega) \cdot m + 2ln &\preccurlyeq_o (k \cdot \omega) \cdot m + 2ln + 1 \\ &\preccurlyeq_o (k \cdot \omega) \cdot m + 2ln + 2l\end{aligned}$$

we chose that $\omega = sup(n+1)$, then

$$sup((k \cdot \omega) \cdot m + 2l(n+1)) = (k \cdot \omega) \cdot m + 2l \cdot \omega$$

If we change k to $2l$ we get

$$< \vec{s}_n > x \quad \lhd \quad (k \cdot \omega) \cdot (m+1) \qquad \text{by Def. } 5.33 - (d)$$

So if we also change m to $m+1$ we get the result as it is required

$$t_{\vec{F}_x} \lhd (k \cdot \omega) \cdot m$$

which completes the proof.

□

5.5 Ordinal Bounding

In this section we shall prove that the complexity of normalisation is super-exponential.

Lemma 5.36. *Let t_1, t_2 be $T^\infty(;)$-terms such that $t_1 \lhd \alpha_1$ and $t_2 \lhd \alpha_2$. Then*

$$t_1[t_2/v] \lhd \alpha_2 + \alpha_1$$

Proof. By induction on the construction of t_1. □

Lemma 5.37. *Let t_1, t_2 be $T^\infty(;)$-terms with $t_1 \lhd \alpha_1$ and $t_2 \lhd \alpha_2$. Then if $t_1 t_2$ is a redex we have*

$$(t_1 t_2)^* \lhd 2 \cdot \alpha_2 + 2 \cdot \alpha_1$$

Proof. We shall prove it by induction on the construction of t_1. Since $t_1 t_2$ is a redex, there are just three main cases:

Case 1. If $t_1 = \pi_j$ where $j = 1, 2$, then $t_1 t_2$ is a projection-redex. So there are two subcases to consider, and we deal with them by sub-induction on t_2:

1.1. If $t_2 = (r_1, r_2)$ with $r_j \lhd \beta$ where $j = 1, 2$ and $\beta \preccurlyeq_o \alpha_2$, then

$$\begin{aligned}(\pi_j(r_1, r_2))^* &= r_j && \text{by Def. } 5.13 - (d) \\ &\lhd \beta && \text{given} \\ (\pi_j(r_1, r_2))^* &\lhd \alpha_2 && \text{since } \beta \preccurlyeq_o \alpha_2 \\ (\pi_j(r_1, r_2))^* &\lhd 2 \cdot \alpha_2 && \text{Lemma } 5.34 - (iii) \\ &\preccurlyeq_o 2 \cdot \alpha_2 + 2 \cdot \alpha_1 && \text{by Def. } 5.33 - (f)\end{aligned}$$

1.2. If $t_2 =< r_i >_x$ with $\forall i \exists \beta (r_i \lhd \beta \wedge \beta + 1 \preccurlyeq_o \gamma_i)$ where γ is a limit and $\gamma \preccurlyeq_o \alpha_2$, then

$$(\pi_j < r_i >_x)^* =< (\pi_j r_i)^* >_x \qquad \text{by Def. 5.13} - (c)$$

where the term $\pi_j r_i$ is a redex or not, for $j = 1, 2$ and for every $i \in \mathbb{N}$.

– If it is a redex, then

$$\begin{array}{rcll} (\pi_j r_i)^* & \lhd & 2 \cdot \beta + 2 \cdot 0 & \text{by ind. hyp.} \\ & \prec_o & 2 \cdot \beta + 1 & \text{by Def. 5.28} - (a) \end{array}$$

– If it is not a redex, then we get

$$(\pi_j r_i)^* = \pi_j r_i \qquad \text{by Def. 5.13}$$

where

$$\begin{array}{rcll} \pi_j & \lhd & 0 & \text{by Def. 5.28} - (a) \\ \pi_j & \lhd & 2 \cdot \beta & \text{by Lemma 5.34} - (iii) \end{array}$$

and

$$\begin{array}{rcll} r_i & \lhd & \beta & \text{given} \\ r_i & \lhd & 2 \cdot \beta & \text{by Lemma 5.34} - (iii) \end{array}$$

then

$$\pi_j r_i \lhd 2 \cdot \beta + 1 \qquad \text{by Def. 5.28} - (b)$$

So for the both sub-cases, we get that $(\pi_j r_i)^* \lhd 2 \cdot \beta + 1$. Here $2 \cdot \beta + 1 + 1 = 2 \cdot (\beta + 1) \preccurlyeq_o 2 \cdot \gamma_i$, and $sup(2 \cdot \gamma_i) = 2 \cdot \gamma$. Then

$$\begin{array}{rcll} < (\pi_j r_i)^* >_x & \lhd & 2 \cdot \gamma & \text{by Def. 5.28} - (b) \\ & \preccurlyeq_o & 2 \cdot \alpha_2 & \text{since } \gamma \preccurlyeq_o \alpha_2 \\ & \preccurlyeq_o & 2 \cdot \alpha_2 + 2 \cdot \alpha_1 & \text{Lemma 5.29} - (i) \end{array}$$

Case 2. If $t_1 = \lambda v.r$ with $r \lhd \beta$ where $\beta + 1 \preccurlyeq_o \alpha_1$, then $t_1 t_2$ is an abstraction-redex.

$$\begin{array}{rcll} ((\lambda v.r)t_2)^* & = & r[t_2/v] & \text{by Def. 5.13} - (b) \\ ((\lambda v.r)t_2)^* & \lhd & 2 \cdot \alpha_2 + 2 \cdot \beta & \text{by Lemma 5.29} - (ii) \\ & \prec_o & 2 \cdot \alpha_2 + 2 \cdot \beta + 2 & \text{by Def. 5.28} - (a) \\ & = & 2 \cdot \alpha_2 + 2 \cdot (\beta + 1) & \\ & \preccurlyeq_o & 2 \cdot \alpha_2 + 2 \cdot \alpha_1 & \text{since } \beta + 1 \preccurlyeq_o \alpha_1 \end{array}$$

Case 3. If $t_1 =< r_i >_x$ with $\forall i \exists \beta (r_i \lhd \beta \wedge \beta + 1 \preccurlyeq_o \gamma_i)$ where γ is a limit and $\gamma \preccurlyeq_o \alpha_1$, then $t_1 t_2$ is a sequence-redex.

$$(< r_i >_x t_2)^* =< (r_i t_2)^* >_x \qquad \text{by Def. 5.13} - (c)$$

In this case, we shall look at whether the term $r_i t_2$ is a redex or not, for $j = 1, 2$ and for every $i \in \mathbb{N}$.

– If it is a redex, then

$$\begin{array}{rcll} (r_i t_2)^* & \lhd & 2 \cdot \alpha_2 + 2 \cdot \beta & \text{by ind. hyp.} \\ & \prec_o & 2 \cdot \alpha_2 + 2 \cdot \beta + 1 & \text{by Def.5.28} - (a) \end{array}$$

– If it is not a redex, then

$$(r_i t_2)^* = r_i t_2 \qquad \text{by Def. 5.13}$$

where

$$\begin{array}{lll} r_i & \lhd & \beta & \text{by Def. 5.28} - (a) \\ r_i & \lhd & 2\cdot\beta & \text{by Lemma 5.34} - (iii) \\ r_i & \lhd & 2\cdot\alpha_2 + 2\cdot\beta & \text{by Lemma 5.34} - (ii) \end{array}$$

and

$$\begin{array}{lll} t_2 & \lhd & \alpha_2 & \text{given} \\ t_2 & \lhd & 2\cdot\alpha_2 & \text{by Lemma 5.34} - (iii) \\ & \preccurlyeq_o & 2\cdot\alpha_2 + 2\cdot\beta & \text{by Lemma 5.29} - (ii) \end{array}$$

then

$$r_i t_2 \lhd 2\cdot\alpha_2 + 2\cdot\beta + 1 \qquad \text{by Def. 5.28} - (b)$$

So for the both sub-cases, we get that $(r_i t_2)^* \lhd 2\cdot\alpha_2 + 2\cdot\beta + 1$. Here $2\cdot\alpha_2 + 2\cdot\beta + 1 + 1 = 2\cdot\alpha_2 + 2\cdot(\beta+1) \preccurlyeq_o 2\cdot\alpha_2 + 2\cdot\gamma_i$, and $sup(2\cdot\alpha_2 + 2\cdot\gamma_i) = 2\cdot\alpha_2 + 2\cdot\gamma$. Then

$$\begin{array}{llll} <(r_i t_2)^*>_x & \lhd & 2\cdot\alpha_2 + 2\cdot\gamma & \text{by Def. 5.28} - (b) \\ & \preccurlyeq_o & 2\cdot\alpha_2 + 2\cdot\alpha_1 & \text{since } \gamma \preccurlyeq_o \alpha_1 \end{array}$$

□

Theorem 5.38 (Ordinal Bounding). *Let t be any $T^\infty(;)$-term with positive finite rank such that $t \lhd \alpha$. Then $t \mapsto t'$ where the rank of t' is at least one less then the rank of t, and the following result holds*

$$t' \lhd \varphi(\alpha)$$

where φ is the function defined in Definition 5.30.

Proof. We can prove it by induction over the construction of t:

Case 1. If t is a variable or constant where $0 \preccurlyeq_o \alpha$, then

$$\begin{array}{llll} t' & = & t & \text{by Def. 5.12} - (a) \\ & \lhd & 0 & \text{by Def. 5.33} - (a) \\ & \prec_o & \varphi(\alpha) & \text{by Remark 5.26} - 2 \end{array}$$

Case 2. If $t = \lambda v.s$ with $s \lhd \beta$ where $\beta + 1 \preccurlyeq_o \alpha$, then

$$t' = \lambda v.s' \qquad \text{by Def. 5.12} - (b)$$

where

$$s' \lhd \varphi(\beta) \qquad \text{by ind. hyp.}$$

Hence

$$\begin{array}{llll} \lambda v.s' & \lhd & \varphi(\beta) + 1 & \text{by Def. 5.33} - (c) \\ & \prec_o & \varphi(\beta + 1) & \text{by Lemma 5.31} - (ii) \\ & \preccurlyeq_o & \varphi(\alpha) & \text{by Lemma 5.31} - (iv) \end{array}$$

Case 3. If $t = < r_i >_x$ with $\forall i \exists \beta (r_i \lhd \beta \wedge \beta + 1 \preccurlyeq_o \gamma_i)$ where γ is a limit and $\gamma \preccurlyeq_o \alpha$, then

$$t' = < r'_i > x \qquad \text{by Def. } 5.12 - (c)$$

where for every i,

$$r'_i \lhd \varphi(\beta) \qquad \text{by ind. hyp.}$$

and

$$\begin{aligned} \varphi(\beta) + 1 &\prec_o \varphi(\beta + 1) && \text{by Lemma } 5.31 - (ii) \\ &\preccurlyeq_o \varphi(\gamma_i) && \text{by Lemma } 5.31 - (iv) \end{aligned}$$

and

$$sup\, \varphi(\gamma_i) = \varphi(\gamma) \qquad \text{by Def. } 5.21$$

Hence

$$\begin{aligned} < r'_i > x &\lhd \varphi(\gamma) && \text{by Def. } 5.33 - (d) \\ &\preccurlyeq_o \varphi(\alpha) && \text{by Lemma } 5.31 - (iv) \end{aligned}$$

Case 4. If $t = t_1 t_2$ with $t_1 \lhd \beta_1, \ t_2 \lhd \beta_2, \ \ \beta_1 \preccurlyeq_o \beta_2$ where $\beta_2 + 1 \preccurlyeq_o \alpha$, then

$$t' = (t'_1 t'_2)^* \qquad \text{by Def. } 5.12 - (d)$$

where

$$t'_1 \lhd \varphi(\beta_1), \ \ t'_2 \lhd \varphi(\beta_2) \qquad \text{by ind. hyp.}$$

Hence

$$\begin{aligned} (t'_1 t'_2)^* &\lhd 2 \cdot \varphi(\beta_2) + 2 \cdot \varphi(\beta_1) && \text{by Lemma } 5.37 \\ &\preccurlyeq_o 2 \cdot \varphi(\beta_2) + 2 \cdot \varphi(\beta_2) && \text{since } \ \varphi(\beta_1) \preccurlyeq_o \varphi(\beta_2) \\ (t'_1 t'_2)^* &\lhd \varphi(\beta_2) + 2 \cdot \varphi(\beta_2) + 2 \cdot \varphi(\beta_2) && \text{by Lemma } 5.29 - (ii) \\ &= \varphi(\beta_2 + 1) && \text{by Def. } 5.30 \\ &\preccurlyeq_o \varphi(\alpha) && \text{by Lemma } 5.31 - (iv) \end{aligned}$$

Case 5. If $t = (t_1, t_2)$ with $t_i \lhd \beta$ for each $i = 1, 2$, where $\beta \preccurlyeq_o \alpha$, then

$$t' = (t'_1, t'_2) \qquad \text{by Def. } 5.12 - (d)$$

where for each $i = 1, 2$

$$t'_i \lhd \varphi(\beta) \qquad \text{by ind. hyp.}$$

Hence

$$\begin{aligned} (t'_1, t'_2) &\lhd \varphi(\beta) && \text{by Def. } 5.33 - (e) \\ &\preccurlyeq_o \varphi(\alpha) && \text{by Lemma } 5.31 - (iv) \end{aligned}$$

□

Theorem 5.39. *Assume that t be any $T^\infty(;)$-term which has a positive finite rank k and majorized by ordinal α. If the term t reduces to a normal form $t^{[k]}$ after k-many times application of rank-reduction, then the complexity of normalisation is super-exponential*

$$t^{[k]} \lhd \varphi^k(\alpha)$$

Proof. By the definition of rank-reduction, each reduction reduces the rank by at least one, and by Lemma 5.17 one more application of φ is needed to majorize it. □

5.6 Complexity

In this final section we shall prove that every $T(;)$-definable function is bounded by a super-exponential function exp_5^k for some fixed k. We then get the result that every $T(;)$-definable function is elementary. This follows from the embedding of $T(;)$ into $T^\infty(;)$ and the normalisation of $T^\infty(;)$-terms.

Lemma 5.40. *Suppose that $t(\vec{x};\vec{a})$ is a normal term of type o in $T^\infty(;)$ which contains only free variables $\vec{x}$ of ground type ι and $\vec{a}$ of ground type o. Then the term t must have one of the following forms:*

(*I*) *A variable a or the constant* 0

(*II*) *Applications: St_0 or Pt_0 or $Ct_0t_1t_2$*

(*III*) *An infinite sequence $< t_i >_x$*

where $t_0, t_1, ..., t_i, ...$ are themselves normal form of type o.

Proof. By induction on construction of term t of type o.

Case 1. If t is a variable a of type o or the constant 0 of type o, then we obtain the form (I). But t can not be variable x of type ι and can not be the constants S or P or C or π_j because their types are wrong.

Case 2. The term t can not be an abstraction $\lambda v.s$ because the type is wrong.

Case 3. If t be an infinite sequence $< t_i >_x$ of type o, then we obtain the form (III).

Case 4. The term t can not be a pair (t_1, t_2) because the type is wrong.

Case 5. If t is an application $t_0t_1t_2...t_n$ of type o where t_0 not an application, then we shall look at the following *sub-cases* by induction on the construction of term t_0:

5.1. The term t_0 must have function-type. So t_0 can not be a variable because t contains no variables of function-type. However t_0 might be S or P or C. So we obtain the terms St_1, Pt_1 and $Ct_1t_2t_3$ which gives the form (II).

5.2. The term t_0 can not be an abstraction $\lambda v.s$ because then t would not be normal.

5.3. The term t_0 can not be an infinite sequence $< t_i >_x$ because then t would not be normal.

5.4. The term t_0 can not be a pair (r_1, r_2) because the type is wrong.

5.5. It remains to show that why t_0 can not be a constant π. Here the π stands for either π_1 or π_2. If $t_0 = \pi$, then we have to look at t_1.

The term t_1 can not be a pair or a sequence because then t would not be normal; and can not be a constant or a variable or λ-abstraction because the type would be wrong. The only possibility is that t_1 is also an application term $s_0s_1s_3...s_m$ of product-type where $m > 0$ as before and s_0 is not an application. We have to continue the procedure by induction on the construction of term s_0.

Again, there is only one possibility, namely $s_0 = \pi$. Then by the same argument, s_1 must be an application beginning with a π. We can thus continue indefinitely, contradicting the well foundedness of the term t.

□

Remark 5.41. Any function $f : \mathbb{N} \to \mathbb{N}$ is representable by a normal term of $T^\infty(;)$ of type o. We already embedded $T(;)$ into $T^\infty(;)$. Here we consider the computable subsystem of $T^\infty(;)$ arising from this embedding.

Definition 5.42 (Computation Function). Let $t(\vec{x};\vec{a})$ be such a computable term as in the previous Lemma 5.40. Then the *valuation function* $\mathcal{V}t[\vec{x} := \vec{n}; \vec{a} := \vec{m}]$ needs a certain number of steps to compute, say by a register machine. This number of steps, denoted $\#t(\vec{n};\vec{m})$ can be defined by induction over the build up of the term.

(a) $t = 0$ or $a_i \quad \Rightarrow \quad \#t(\vec{n};\vec{m}) = 1$

(b) $t = St_0$ or $Pt_0 \quad \Rightarrow \quad \#t(\vec{n};\vec{m}) = \#t_0(\vec{n};\vec{m}) + 1$

(c) $t = Ct_0t_1t_2 \quad \Rightarrow \quad \#t(\vec{n};\vec{m}) = \#t_0(\vec{n};\vec{m}) + max(\#t_1(\vec{n};\vec{m}), \#t_2(\vec{n};\vec{m})) + 1$

(d) $t = < t_i >_{x_j} \quad \Rightarrow \quad \#t(\vec{n};\vec{m}) = \#t_{n_j}(\vec{n};\vec{m}) + 1$

Definition 5.43 (φ-Majorization Relation). Let t be a term of $T^\infty(;)$ and let φ be as in Definition 5.30. Then the *φ-majorization relation* $t \lhd_\varphi \varphi(\alpha)$ is defined inductively as follows:

(a) t is a variable or constant $\quad \Rightarrow \quad t \lhd_\varphi \varphi(\alpha)$ for any α.

(b) $r \lhd_\varphi \varphi(\beta), \quad \beta + 1 \preccurlyeq_o \alpha \quad \Rightarrow \quad \lambda v.r \lhd_\varphi \varphi(\alpha)$

(c) $t_1 \lhd_\varphi \varphi(\alpha_1), \quad t_2 \lhd_\varphi \varphi(\alpha_2), \quad \alpha_1 \preccurlyeq_o \alpha_2 \prec_o \alpha_2 + 1 \preccurlyeq_o \alpha \quad \Rightarrow \quad t_1t_2 \lhd_\varphi \varphi(\alpha)$

(d) $\forall i \exists \beta (t_i \lhd_\varphi \varphi(\beta) \wedge \beta + 1 \preccurlyeq_o \gamma_i), \quad \gamma \preccurlyeq_o \alpha \quad \Rightarrow \quad < t_i > x \lhd_\varphi \varphi(\alpha)$

(e) $t_k \lhd_\varphi \varphi(\alpha), \quad k = 1,2 \quad \Rightarrow \quad (t_1, t_2) \lhd_\varphi \varphi(\alpha)$

Note 5.44. The proof of the Lemma 5.38 actually gives that

$$t \lhd \alpha \quad \Rightarrow \quad t' \lhd_\varphi \varphi(\alpha)$$

Theorem 5.45 (Complexity Theorem). *Let $t(\vec{x};\vec{a})$ be a normal computable term of type o as in the Definition 5.42, let G_n be the slow-growing function, and let $n = max(\vec{n})$. Then*

$$t \lhd_\varphi \varphi(\alpha) \quad \Rightarrow \quad \#t(\vec{n};\vec{m}) \leq G_n(\varphi(\alpha))$$

Proof. By the Lemma 5.40 the term t is built up from one of the following forms: $a, \quad 0, \quad St_0, \quad Pt_0, \quad Ct_0t_1t_2, \quad < t_i >_x$. So it is enough to consider these forms:

Case 1. If $t = 0$ or a_i, then

$$\begin{aligned} \#t(\vec{n};\vec{m}) &= 1 && \text{by Def. 5.42-(a)} \\ &\leq G_n(\varphi(\alpha)) \end{aligned}$$

Case 2. If $t = St_0$ or Pt_0 where $t_0 \lhd_\varphi \varphi(\beta)$ and $\beta + 1 \preccurlyeq_o \alpha$, then

$$\begin{array}{rcll} \#t(\vec{n};\vec{m}) & = & \#t_0(\vec{n};\vec{m}) + 1 & \text{by Def. 5.42} - (b) \\ & \leq & G_n(\varphi(\beta)) + 1 & \text{by ind. hyp.} \\ & = & G_n(\varphi(\beta) + 1) & \text{by Def. 5.24} \\ & \leq & G_n(\varphi(\beta + 1)) & \text{by Lemma 5.31} - (ii) \\ & \leq & G_n(\varphi(\alpha)) & \text{since} \quad \beta + 1 \preccurlyeq_o \alpha \end{array}$$

Case 3. If $t = Ct_0t_1t_2$ where $t_k \lhd_\varphi \varphi(\beta)$ for each $k = 0, 1, 2$ and $\beta + 1 \preccurlyeq_o \alpha$, then

$$\begin{array}{cll} & \#t(\vec{n};\vec{m}) & \\ = & \#t_0(\vec{n};\vec{m}) + max(\#t_1(\vec{n};\vec{m}), \#t_2(\vec{n};\vec{m})) + 1 & \text{by Def. 5.42} - (c) \\ \leq & G_n(\varphi(\beta)) + G_n(\varphi(\beta)) + 1 & \text{by ind. hyp.} \\ \leq & G_n(\varphi(\beta)) + 2 \cdot G_n(\varphi(\beta)) + 2 \cdot G_n(\varphi(\beta)) & \\ = & G_n(\varphi(\beta) + 2 \cdot \varphi(\beta) + 2 \cdot \varphi(\beta)) & \text{by Def. 5.24} \\ = & G_n(\varphi(\beta + 1)) & \text{by Def. 5.30} \\ \leq & G_n(\varphi(\alpha)) & \text{since} \quad \beta + 1 \preccurlyeq_o \alpha \end{array}$$

Case 4. Let $t = < t_i >_{x_j}$ where $\forall i \exists \beta (t_i \lhd_\varphi \varphi(\beta) \wedge \beta + 1 \preccurlyeq_o \gamma_i)$ where γ is a limit and $\gamma \preccurlyeq_o \alpha$, then for $i = n_j$,

$$\begin{array}{rcll} \#t(\vec{n};\vec{m}) & = & \#t_{n_j}(\vec{n};\vec{m}) + 1 & \text{by Def.5.42} - (d) \\ & \leq & G_n(\varphi(\beta)) + 1 & \text{by ind. hyp.} \\ & = & G_n(\varphi(\beta) + 1) & \text{by Def. 5.24} \\ & \leq & G_n(\varphi(\beta + 1)) & \text{by Lemma 5.31} - (ii) \\ & \leq & G_n(\varphi(\gamma_{n_j})) & \text{since} \quad \beta + 1 \preccurlyeq_o \gamma_{n_j} \\ & \leq & G_n(\varphi(\gamma)) & \text{since} \quad n_j \leq n \\ & \leq & G_n(\varphi(\alpha)) & \text{since} \quad \varphi(\gamma) \preccurlyeq_o \varphi(\alpha) \end{array}$$

□

Corollary 5.46. *Assume that $t(\vec{x};\vec{a})$ is computable and let $n = max(\vec{n})$ and $m = max(\vec{m})$. Then*

$$t \lhd_\varphi \varphi(\alpha) \quad \Rightarrow \quad \mathcal{V}t[\vec{x} := \vec{n}; \vec{a} := \vec{m}] \leq m + G_n(\varphi(\alpha))$$

Theorem 5.47. *Every number-theoretic function f definable in $T(;)$ is elementary.*

Proof. Putting all the foregoing work together, we obtain a $T^\infty(;)$-term t and then a normal $t^{[k]}$ representing $f(\vec{n}, \vec{m})$ such that

Step 1. $t \lhd (p \cdot \omega) \cdot q$ — by Embedding Theorem 5.35.

Step 2. $t \mapsto t' \quad \Rightarrow \quad t' \lhd \varphi((p \cdot \omega) \cdot q)$ — by Ordinal Bounding Theorem 5.38.

Step 3. $t \mapsto t^{[k]}$, $t^{[k]}$ is a normal term, — by Normalisation Theorem 5.18.

Step 4. $t^{[k]} \lhd \varphi^k((p \cdot \omega) \cdot q)$ — by Theorem 5.39, where $k = R(t)$.

Step 5. $\#t^{[k]}(\vec{n};\vec{m}) \leq G_n(\varphi^k(\alpha))$ where $\alpha = (p \cdot \omega) \cdot q$. — by Complexity Theorem 5.45,

Then $f(\vec{n},\vec{m})$ is computable with in a number of steps bounded by

$$G_n(\varphi^k((p\cdot\omega)\cdot q)) = 5^{5^{\cdot^{\cdot^{\cdot^{5^{(p(n+1)q)}}}}}} \qquad (\ k \text{ many } 5)$$

which is an elementary function of $\vec{n}$. Since every function computable in an elementary-bounded number of steps is itself elementary, we therefore have

$$f \in \mathcal{E}^3.$$

□

Corollary 5.48. *Every function provably recursive in $PA(;)$ is elementary.*

References

[1] A. Beckmann and A. Weiermann, Characterizing the elementary recursive functions by a fragment of Gödel's T, *to appear.*

[2] S. J. Bellantoni and S. Cook, A new recursion-theoretic characterization of the polytime functions, *Computational Complexity* **2** (1992) 97-110.

[3] S. J. Bellantoni, *Predicative recursion and computational complexity*, PhD thesis, Department of Computer Science, University of Toronto, 1992.

[4] E. Börger, *Computability, Complexity, Logic*, Elsevier, N-Holland Studies in Logic, Vol. 128, 1989.

[5] S. R. Buss, *Bounded Arithmetic*, Bibliopolis, Naples, 1986.

[6] N. Çağman, *Tiered Arithmetic, its Functional Interpretation and Slow Growing Bounds*, PhD thesis, Department of Pure Mathematics, University of Leeds, 2000.

[7] P. Csillag, Eine Bemerkung zur Auflosung der eingeschachtelten Recursion, *Acta Sci. Math. Szeged*, **11** (1947) 169-173.

[8] M. Fairtlough and S.S. Wainer, Hierarchies of provably recursive functions. In: S. R. Buss (ed.), *Handbook of Proof Theory*, Elsevier Science, 1998, pp. 149-207.

[9] K. Gödel, Über eine bisher noch nicht benutzte Erweiterung des finiten Standplunktes, *Dialectica* **12** (1958) 280-287. (also appears, with English translation, in: S.Feferman, et al (eds.), Kurd Gödel: Collected works, Vol 2, Oxford University Press, 1990.)

[10] W. G. Handley and S. S. Wainer, Complexity of primitive recursion In: U. Berger and H. Schwichtenberg (eds.), *Computational Logic*, Springer, NATO ISI Series F, Vol. 165, 1999, pp. 273-300.

[11] L. Kalmar, Egyszerü példa eldönthetetlen aritmetikai problémára, Mates és Fizikai Lapok **50** (1943) 1-23.

[12] D. Leivant, Intrinsic theories and computational complexity, In: D. Leivant (ed.), *Logic and Computational Complexity*, Springer, LNCS, Vol. 960, 1995, pp. 177-194.

[13] D. Leivant, Ramified recursion and computational complexity, In: P. Clote and J. Remmel (eds.), *Feasible Mathematics II*, Birkhauser, 1995, pp. 320-345.

[14] G. E. Ostrin, *Proof Theories of Low Sub-recursive Classes*, PhD thesis, Department of Pure Mathematics, University of Leeds, 1999.

[15] D. Rödding, Klassen rekursiven Funktionen, In: M. H. Löb (ed.), *Springer Lecture Notes in Mathematics 70*, 1968, pp. 159-222.

[16] H. E. Rose, *Subrecursion*, Clarendon Press, Oxford, 1984.

[17] J. R. Shoenfield, *Mathematical Logic*, Addion-Wesley Publishing Company, 1967.

[18] W. W. Tait, Infinitely long terms of transfinite type, In: J. N. Crossley and M. Dummett (eds.), Formal Siytems and Recursive Fuinctions, North Holland, 1965, pp. 176-185.

[19] W. W. Tait, Normal derivability in classical logic, In: J. Barwise (ed.), *Springer Lecture Notes in Mathematics 72*, 1968, pp. 204-236.

Foundations of Secure Computation
F.L. Bauer and R. Steinbrüggen (Eds.)
IOS Press, 2000

Programming Techniques for Partial Evaluation *

Olivier Danvy

BRICS †
Department of Computer Science,
University of Aarhus, Denmark ‡

Abstract. These lecture notes describe how to write generating extensions, i.e., dedicated program specializers. The focus is on compositional programs and their associated fold functions. Each generating extension is expressed as an instance of this fold function. A number of examples are considered and pointers to related work are provided.

1 Introduction

Partial evaluation is a program-transformation method for specializing programs with respect to part of their data. It is motivated by the fact that dedicated programs operate more efficiently than general-purpose ones. To specialize programs, one typically uses techniques also found in optimizing compilers: constant propagation, constant folding, call unfolding / inlining, dead-code elimination, memoization, folding, etc. A wide variety of literature on partial evaluation is available today, including a textbook by Neil Jones, Carsten Gomard, and Peter Sestoft [31], a number of overviews [8, 24, 30], at least three encyclopedia entries [14, 35, 36], the ACM SIGPLAN PEPM series,[1] several special issues of journals [15, 12, 29, 37], and the proceedings of occasional meetings and summer schools [4, 11, 20, 27]. More information is available at the web site of the PEPT mailing list.[2]

The goal of these lecture notes is to document the programming techniques for writing *generating extensions* (a term due to Andrei P. Ershov). A generating extension for a program p is a program p' which, given some data s, (1) performs the operations of p that depend on s and (2) constructs residual code for the remaining operations. Running p' on s thus returns a version of p that is specialized with respect to s.

Correctness criterion for specialization

Given a program p and its generating extension p', running p' on some data s yields a residual program p_s such that running p_s on the remaining data d yields the same result as running p on both s and d, provided p', p_s, and p all terminate.

---

*Extended version available in the BRICS lecture note series.

†Basic Research in Computer Science (`http://www.brics.dk/`), Centre of the Danish National Research Foundation.

‡Building 540, Ny Munkegade, DK-8000 Aarhus C, Denmark.
Phone: (+45) 89 42 33 69. Fax: (+45) 89 42 32 55. E-mail: `danvy@brics.dk`
Home page: `http://www.brics.dk/~danvy/`

[1] `http://www.acm.org/pubs/contents/proceedings/series/pepm/`

[2] `http://www.yl.is.s.u-tokyo.ac.jp/~sumii/pept/`

The means of these lecture notes are fairly minimal: rather than relying on an existing partial evaluator, we have chosen to use the code-generating facilities of Scheme. To this end, the reader is provided with a handful of vanilla Scheme functions. We choose to use the Scheme language for its simplicity and the Petite Chez Scheme implementation for its availability and excellence.[3] All the following Scheme programs are available online from the author's home page, together with sample solutions for the exercises.

For the purpose of these lecture notes, we focus on compositional programs performing a recursive descent over their known input. To enforce this requirement, we express these programs with the fold function associated with the known input. The generating extension is thus obtained by passing code-generating functions to each fold function. The lecture notes are composed as a series of simple examples, setting up themes and inviting the reader to exercise some variations.

1.1 Prerequisites and notation

A passing familiarity with Scheme and quasiquotation will definitely help the reader. The most up-to-date reference for Scheme is the R^{5}RS [32]. Alan Bawden presented a survey of quasiquotation in Scheme at PEPM'99 [2]. Further information is available in Kent Dybvig's textbook [18] and in the Chez Scheme user's guide [19]. All these documents are freely available online.

In the rest of these notes, all efficiency measurements are carried out with Chez Scheme's timing facilities [19, Section 10.6]. Occasionally, to illustrate a point or an exercise, we display the transcript of an interactive Scheme session. In such sessions, "> " is the interactive prompt, preceding an expression to be evaluated; what follows is the result of the evaluation.

Throughout, we only consider exact integers [32], and occasionally, we rely on a simple record facility. We use `define-record` to define a new record and `case-record` to dispatch among possible records, much like the pattern matching of ML.

We also assume a basic familiarity with fold, as can be gathered from Graham Hutton's recent tutorial [28].

1.2 Overview

The rest of these lecture notes is organized as follows. We first describe a simple toolkit for program-generating programs in Scheme (Section 2) and then treat the power function, which is a canonical example in partial evaluation (Sections 3 and 4). We then consider a multiplication function (Section 5), the Euclidean algorithm (Section 6), and regular expressions (Section 7), before concluding (Section 8).

2 A Toolkit for Program-Generating Programs

We want to write programs that construct other programs. In Scheme, where programs are represented as S-expressions, constructing a residual program boils down to constructing an S-expression conforming to the syntax of Scheme. The rest of this section addresses the issue of fresh names (Section 2.1), common idioms for block structure and predefined functions (Section 2.2), advanced idioms (Section 2.3), and common errors (Section 2.4).

[3]Petite Chez Scheme is freely available at `http://www.scheme.com/`.

2.1 Fresh names

We want to generate residual programs with scope. Therefore it is essential that no name clashes occur. A name clash occurs if a residual program attempts to use the same variable with more than one purpose in the same scope. Names clashes are traditionally avoided by systematically generating fresh variables during the construction of residual programs, using a generator of new symbols (traditionally named "gensym"). We adopt this solution here, since alternatives such as combinators, de Bruijn indices, or de Bruijn levels are not as practical.

For readability as well as for debugging purposes, we parameterize the gensym function with a name stub. We also reset the gensym function prior to any specialization, so that performing the same specialization several times yields the same textual result.

2.2 Standard idioms

Let us review how to construct the usual syntactic forms of Scheme: function application, function declaration, conditional expressions, and lexical blocks.

Constructing a residual application is straightforward: given the operator and the operands, simply construct a flat list. We choose to inline this construction everywhere. However, we factor out the construction of residual applications of a predefined function when this function may give rise to algebraic simplifications (Section 2.2.1).

Constructing residual lambda-abstractions requires fresh names. The same goes for constructing residual let- or letrec-expressions. We choose to factor out these constructions (Sections 2.2.2 and 2.2.3).

Residual programs typically include nested let-expressions (`let` in Scheme), which can be written more concisely using the sequential `let*` construct of Scheme. We thus provide the corresponding syntax constructor (Section 2.2.4).

2.2.1 Residualizing versions of predefined functions

Let us consider multiplication. Its simplest residualizing version takes two residual expressions and constructs the corresponding residual multiplication:

```
(define mk-*
  (lambda (x y)
    `(* ,x ,y)))
```

This simple residualizing function can be refined, since multiplying any number by 1 yields that number unchanged. A more refined version thus reads as follows:

```
(define mk-*
  (lambda (x y)
    (cond
      [(equal? x 1)
       y]
      [(equal? y 1)
       x]
      [else
       `(* ,x ,y)])))
```

Exercise 2.1: One might be tempted to further refine `mk-*` by taking into account that multiplying any number by 0 yields 0. Is this a good idea in general?

Hint—the non-zero argument may represent a non-trivial computation. □

Exercise 2.2: What happens if `mk-*` is applied to two residual literals? Does this suggest yet another refinement? □

Other residualizing functions can be found in the appendix.

2.2.2 Bindings

Constructing residual lambda-abstractions requires gensym. We factor it out in constructors such as `mk-lambda` and `mk-lambda2`. Given a name stub and a function expecting a fresh name and yielding a residual expression, `mk-lambda` constructs a unary residual lambda-abstraction.

Example 2.3:

```
> (mk-lambda "x" (lambda (x)
                   (mk-* x 100)))
(lambda (x0)
  (* x0 100))
```

□

Similarly, `mk-lambda2` constructs a binary residual lambda-abstraction, given two name stubs and a function expecting two fresh names and yielding a residual expression.

Example 2.4:

```
> (mk-lambda2 "x" "k" (lambda (x k)
                        `(,k ,x)))
(lambda (x0 k1)
  (k1 x0))
```

□

`mk-lambda` and `mk-lambda2` are defined in the appendix.

2.2.3 Block structure

Constructing residual blocks (`let` and `letrec`) also requires gensym. Similarly, we factor it out in two constructors `mk-let` and `mk-letrec`. Given a name stub, a residual expression, and a function expecting a fresh name and yielding a residual expression, `mk-let` constructs a unary residual let-expression.

Example 2.5:

```
> (mk-lambda "f"
             (lambda (f)
               (mk-let "x"
                       `(,f 1000)
                       (lambda (x)
                         (mk-let "y"
                                 `(,f 2000)
                                 (lambda (y)
                                   (mk-* x y)))))))
(lambda (f0)
  (let ([x1 (f0 1000)])
    (let ([y2 (f0 2000)])
      (* x1 y2))))
```

□

Similarly, `mk-letrec` constructs a unary residual letrec-expression, given a name stub, a function expecting a fresh name and yielding a residual lambda-abstraction, and a function expecting a fresh name and yielding a residual expression.

`mk-let` and `mk-letrec` are defined in the appendix.

2.2.4 Naming and sequentialization

The previous example is typical of residual code: it contains nested let-expressions, which would be more concisely expressed with one sequential let-expression. Such a let-expression is obtained using the `mk-let*` constructor defined in the appendix. Using `mk-let*` instead of `mk-let` in the previous example yields the following residual expression:

```
(lambda (f0)
  (let* ([x1 (f0 1000)]
         [y2 (f0 2000)])
    (* x1 y2)))
```

For simplicity, we define `mk-let` to be `mk-let*` in the rest of these lecture notes.

2.3 Advanced idioms

Higher-order program-generating programs typically require one to write functions mapping residual expressions to residual expressions. Two particular cases stand out.

2.3.1 Reflection: from expressions to functions

Let us go back to the first version of `mk-*` from Section 2.2.1. In essence, it maps two residual expressions (the operands of a residual multiplication) into another residual expression (a residual multiplication). This idiom recurs frequently, in that it will appear in the definition of every residualizing function where there is no opportunity to simplify.

Let us abstract this idiom:

```
(define reflect-fun  ;;; exp -> (exp -> exp)
  (lambda (e)
    (lambda (x)
      `(,e ,x))))

(define reflect-fun2 ;;; exp -> (exp * exp -> exp)
  (lambda (e)
    (lambda (x y)
      `(,e ,x ,y))))
```

We can now instantiate it at will:

```
> ((reflect-fun2 '*) 'a 'b)
(* a b)
> ((reflect-fun 'car) '...)
(car ...)
```

2.3.2 Reification: from functions to expressions

Symmetrically, one often needs to residualize a function mapping an expression to an expression—for example, a function obtained by reflection.

The corresponding idiom is abstracted as follows:

```
(define reify-fun     ;;; (exp -> exp) -> exp
  (lambda (f)
    (mk-lambda "x" f)))

(define reify-fun2    ;;; (exp * exp -> exp) -> exp
  (lambda (f)
    (mk-lambda2 "x" "x" f)))
```

For example, we can reify the residualizing version of multiplication:

```
> (reify-fun2 mk-*)
(lambda (x0 x1)
  (* x0 x1))
```

We can also reify the identity function:

```
> (reify-fun (lambda (x) x))
(lambda (x0)
  x0)
```

2.3.3 Summary and conclusion

We have described two functions arising frequently in higher-order generating extensions: `reflect-fun` and `reify-fun`.

- `reflect-fun` maps a residual expression to a residualizing function.
- `reify-fun` maps a residualizing function into a residual expression.

Further applications of reification and reflection are mentioned in Section 8.1.

2.4 Common errors

The following two common errors often arise when one programs with quasiquote and unquote in general and often with `reify-fun` and `reflect-fun` in particular:

- An expression is used as a value (e.g., an integer or a function), making Scheme signal a run-time error.
- A compound value (such as a Scheme closure) is used as an expression, yielding an ill-formed residual program.

These type errors would be detected earlier in a statically typed language such as ML or Haskell.

2.5 Summary and conclusion

We have briefly presented a toolkit for program-generating programs using Scheme, using quasiquote and unquote and factoring out the generation of fresh names. In the rest of these lecture notes, we occasionally use the Scheme function `eval` to evaluate residual programs. This function essentially provides a form of run-time code generation.

Exercise 2.6: Write a similar toolkit in ML or in Haskell.

Hint #1—define a datatype of residual expressions, and use a pretty-printer to obtain a residual program in concrete syntax.

Hint #2—to evaluate a residual program, one can either cut and paste it at the toplevel loop, or save it in a file and load this file. □

3 The Power Function

We begin with a canonical example of partial evaluation: the power function (Section 3.1). We first consider its naive generating extension (Section 3.2). The power function, however, implicitly uses the fold function for natural numbers (Section 3.3). We thus revisit both the power function (Section 3.4) and its generating extension (Section 3.5) using this fold function. We then consider how the fold function makes it possible to stage specialization (Section 3.6). Finally, we assess the overall approach of specializing the power function (Section 3.7).

3.1 The power function

We consider the linear power function. (A logarithmic version is considered in Section 4.)

```
(define power (lambda (x n)
                (letrec ([walk (lambda (n)
                                 (if (zero? n)
                                     1
                                     (* x (walk (- n 1)))))])
                  (walk n))))
```

3.2 Specializing the power function

Specializing `power` with respect to a given value for its induction variable makes it possible to unroll all the recursive calls, leaving a trail of residual multiplications. To this end, one instruments the power function by (1) making it generate a residual lambda-abstraction, and (2) using a residualizing multiplication.

```
(define power-gen
  (lambda (n)
    (mk-lambda "x" (lambda (x)
                     (letrec ([walk (lambda (n)
                                      (if (zero? n)
                                          1
                                          (mk-* x (walk (- n 1)))))])
                       (walk n))))))
```

And indeed applying `power-gen` to `5` yields the following simplified and non-recursive residual program:

```
(lambda (x0)
  (* x0 (* x0 (* x0 (* x0 x0)))))
```

The correctness criterion of partial evaluation reads as follows here: applying the function denoted by this residual program to any number x yields the same result as applying `power` to x and `5`.

For all `x` and `n`,

`((eval (power-gen n)) x)` = `(power x n)`

Exercise 3.1: Modify `power-gen` so that passing it `5` yields the following residual program:

```
(lambda (x0)
  (let* ([v1 (* x0 x0)]
         [v2 (* x0 v1)]
         [v3 (* x0 v2)])
    (* x0 v3)))
```

Hint—equip `walk` with a continuation. □

3.3 A fold function for the power function

There is nothing magical, however, about the power function. It is an instance of the following fold function for natural numbers:

```
(define nat
  (lambda (bc is)
    (letrec ([walk (lambda (n)
                     (if (zero? n)
                         bc
                         (is (walk (- n 1)))))])
      walk)))
```

`nat` corresponds to primitive iteration. It is parameterized with two functions: one for the base case and one for the induction step. We can instantiate `nat` to define the power function (Section 3.4) and its generating extension (Section 3.5). Conversely, we can specialize `nat` with respect to a natural number prior to instantiating it for obtaining a specialized power function or a specialized generating extension (Section 3.6).

3.4 The power function, revisited

We express the power function in terms of `nat` as follows. For the base case, we pass it the literal `1`,[4] and for the induction step, we pass it a curried multiplication function, partially applied to the number to exponentiate.

```
(define power-alt
  (lambda (x n)
    ((nat 1 (lambda (a) (* x a))) n)))
```

For all `x` and `n`,

`(power-alt x n)` = `(power x n)`

3.5 Specializing the power function, revisited

Similarly, we can express the generating extension of the power function in terms of `nat` as follows. For the base case, we pass it the residual literal `1`,[4] and for the induction step, we pass it a code-generating function residualizing a multiplication:

[4] In Scheme, the literal `1` and the residual literal `1` coincide, but that would not be the case in ML or Haskell: one would have an integer type, and the other would have the type of residual expressions.

```
(define power-gen-alt
  (lambda (n)
    (mk-lambda "x" (lambda (x)
                     ((nat 1 (lambda (a) (mk-* x a))) n)))))
```

And indeed applying `power-gen-alt` to `5` yields the same residual program as in Section 3.2.

> For all `n`,
>
> `(power-gen-alt n)` = `(power-gen n)`

Exercise 3.2: Modify `power-gen-alt` so that passing it `5` yields the same residual program as in Exercise 3.1. □

3.6 A generating extension for the fold function

Sections 3.4 and 3.5 make it clear that both the power function and its generating extension are instances of the fold function for natural numbers. Therefore, we can shift perspectives: instead of instantiating the fold function prior to specialization, we can specialize it prior to instantiation. To this end, let us write the corresponding generating extension. This generating extension is given a natural number and invokes the fold function with code-generating functions.

```
(define nat-gen
  (lambda (n)
    (mk-lambda2 "bc" "is" (lambda (bc is)
                            ((nat bc (reflect-fun is)) n)))))
```

N.B. In the definition of `nat-gen`, `reflect-fun` maps the residual identifier denoted by `is` into a residualizing function.

For example, applying `nat-gen` to `5` yields the following residual program:

```
(lambda (bc0 is1)
  (is1 (is1 (is1 (is1 (is1 bc0))))))
```

This residual program can be instantiated either to compute the power function (as in Section 3.4) or to specialize it (as in Section 3.5) with an exponent fixed to be `5`. We come back to this point in Section 6.4.

> For all `n`, `bc`, and `is`,
>
> `((eval (nat-gen n)) bc is)` = `((nat bc is) n)`

Exercise 3.3: Write an alternative version of `nat-gen` so that applying it to `4` yields the following residual program:

```
(lambda (bc0 is1)
  (let* ([v2 (is1 bc0)]
         [v3 (is1 v2)]
         [v4 (is1 v3)]
         [v5 (is1 v4)])
    (is1 v5)))
```

Hint—instantiate `nat` with continuation-passing functions. □

3.7 A critical assessment

Let us now compare the efficiency of the power function and of its specialized instances. In Petite Chez Scheme, the arithmetic operators are overloaded in that they work in two modes: over fixed numbers (represented as simple data objects and thus incurring a fixed allocation cost) and over big numbers (represented as heap-allocated "bignums" and thus incurring a variable allocation cost). We are thus led to distinguish two cases:

For fixed numbers:

- The specialized instances consume virtually no space whereas the original function does.
- The specialized instances are about twice as fast as the original function.

For big numbers: there is no perceptible difference between the original function and its specialized instances.

The second item indicates that the real cost of the power function is not the interpretive overhead of the exponent, but the cost of the multiplications over bignums. The linear power function is thus mostly a pedagogical example of partial evaluation.

3.8 Summary and conclusion

We have treated the power function, which is a canonical example in partial evaluation. Specializing it with respect to a given exponent amounts to unrolling all its recursive calls and to constructing residual multiplications. We have shown that this specialization strategy is not ad hoc: it is an instance of the fold function for natural numbers, like the power function itself. This observation makes it clear that the generating extension, like the power function, terminates. It also suggests that one can specialize the fold function prior to instantiating it. Finally, we have measured the effect of partial evaluation on the linear power function in Scheme, and found it to be minor.

4 The Binary Power Function

We continue with the power function in its Russian-peasant form, taking the same steps as in Section 3, but in the form of exercises.

4.1 *The power function*

This version of the power function works by dividing the exponent by two rather than decrementing it. (N.B. We have short-cut one recursive call in the odd case, compared to traditional presentations of the Russian-peasant algorithm.)

```
(define power2
  (lambda (x n)
    (letrec ([walk (lambda (n)
                     (cond
                       [(zero? n)
                        1]
                       [(even? n)
                        (sqr (walk (quotient n 2)))]
                       [else
                        (* x (sqr (walk (quotient n 2))))]))])
      (walk n))))

(define sqr
  (lambda (x)
    (* x x)))
```

4.2 *Specializing the power function*

Exercise 4.1: As in Section 3.2, instrument the power function and write a function `power2-gen` such that (1) it generates a residual lambda-abstraction, and (2) it uses a residualizing multiplication and a residualizing squaring function. □

Question 4.2: Suppose that the residualizing squaring function is defined in terms of the residualizing multiplication:

```
(define mk-sqr
  (lambda (x)
    (mk-* x x)))
```

What is the effect of this change on the residual code? □

Exercise 4.3: As in Section 3.2, modify `power2-gen` to make it generate residual let-expressions. □

Question 4.4: If `power2-gen` generates residual let-expressions, does it matter that the residualizing squaring function is defined in terms of the residualizing multiplication? □

4.3 A fold function for the power function

Again, there is nothing magical about the binary power function. It is an instance of the following binary fold function for natural numbers:

```
(define nat2
  (lambda (bc ec oc)
    (letrec ([walk (lambda (n)
                     (cond
                       [(zero? n)
                        bc]
                       [(even? n)
                        (ec (walk (quotient n 2)))]
                       [else
                        (oc (walk (quotient n 2)))]))])
      walk)))
```

4.4 The power function, revisited

Exercise 4.5: As in Section 3.4, write a function `power2-alt` using the binary fold function defined just above. □

4.5 Specializing the power function, revisited

Exercise 4.6: As in Section 3.5, write a function `power2-alt-gen` using the binary fold function. □

4.6 A generating extension for the fold function

Exercise 4.7: As in Section 3.6, write a function `nat2-gen` using the binary fold function, and test it to compute the binary power function and to specialize it with respect to a fixed exponent. □

4.7 A critical assessment

Exercise 4.8: As in Section 3.7, compare the efficiency of the binary power function and of its specialized instances. □

4.8 Summary and conclusion

We have visited the binary power function, which is another canonical example in partial evaluation. Specializing it with respect to a given exponent amounts to unrolling all its recursive calls and to constructing residual multiplications and squaring functions. As in Section 3, we have shown that this specialization strategy is not ad hoc either: it is an instance of a fold function for natural numbers, like the power function itself. Therefore specialization, like the power function, terminates.

5 The Multiplication Function (Outline)

The goal of this section is to specialize the multiplication function into a combination of left-shifts and additions, given one of its arguments. For example, `left-shift` could be defined as follows:

```
(define left-shift
  (lambda (n x)
    (* x (expt 2 n))))
```

Usually, though, `left-shift` is implemented more efficiently (cf. `fxsll` in Petite Chez Scheme).

Exercise 5.1: Define the multiplication function so that specializing it with respect to 25 yields the following residual program:

```
(lambda (y0)
  (+ y0 (left-shift 3 (+ y0 (left-shift 1 y0)))))
```

□

Exercise 5.2: Define the multiplication function so that specializing it with respect to 25 yields the following residual program:

```
(lambda (y0)
  (let* ([v1 (left-shift 1 y0)]
         [v2 (+ y0 v1)]
         [v3 (left-shift 3 v2)])
    (+ y0 v3)))
```

Hint—use continuation-passing style. □

6 The Euclidean Algorithm

We consider the gcd function because of its interesting recursion pattern. At each recursive call, its two arguments are intertwined so that, unlike in the power function, there is no clear binding-time separation between these two arguments, making it a challenge to specialize the gcd function with respect to either of them (Section 6.1). The gcd function is an instance of the Euclidean algorithm. We review a few other such instances (Section 6.2) before turning to the fold function associated to the Euclidean algorithm (Section 6.3). We then stage its various instantiations (Section 6.4).

6.1 The Euclidean algorithm

The gcd function is standard, and presented, e.g., in Knuth's Volume 2 [33, Section 4.5.2]. We name it `gcd-std` rather than `gcd` in order not to redefine the resident gcd function in Petite Chez Scheme.

```
(define gcd-std
  (lambda (i j)
    (letrec ([walk (lambda (i j)
                     (if (zero? i)
                         j
                         (walk (remainder j i) i)))])
      (walk i j))))
```

In Sections 3 and 4, the induction variable of the power functions denotes a natural number. In the gcd function, however, it denotes a pair of integers, which presents the following challenge for partial evaluation.

Say that we want to specialize the gcd function with respect to one of its two arguments. This knowledge may enable us to unfold one recursive call. However, and in contrast to the power function, the zero test cannot be resolved. Therefore, short of speculative evaluation across both branches of the if, we are stuck. (Besides, should we wish to evaluate speculatively, how could we ensure that unfolding terminates?) Fortunately, either argument of gcd actually determines an upper bound on the number of recursive calls [33, page 360]. This upper bound makes it possible to unroll all the recursive calls [3, 13, 34].

Let us first write the gcd function in terms of the fold function `nat` defined in Section 3.3, using Finck's upper bound:

```
(define upper-bound
  (lambda (n)
    (if (< n 2)
        2
        (+ 1 (inexact->exact (ceiling (* 2 (log n))))))))
```

The upper bound provides the number of iterations. Since the base-case function should never be reached, we define it as an error-raising function. The induction-step function, which is naturally continuation-passing, carries out an iteration step.

```
(define nat-gcd
  (lambda (i j)
    (((nat (lambda (i j)
             (error 'nat-gcd "out of steam"))
           (lambda (k)
             (lambda (i j)
               (if (zero? i)
                   j
                   (k (remainder j i) i)))))
      (upper-bound (min i j)))
     i j)))
```

Like the power function in Section 3.5, we can obtain a generating extension of the gcd function using the same fold function. For the base case, we pass it a constant residual function raising an error, and for the induction step, we pass it a code-generating function residualizing an iteration step.

```
(define nat-gcd-gen
  (lambda (i)
    (mk-lambda "j" (lambda (j)
                     (((nat (lambda (i j)
                              (mk-error 'nat-gcd "out of steam"))
                            (lambda (k)
                              (lambda (i j)
                                (mk-if (mk-zero? i)
                                       j
                                       (mk-let "r"
                                               (mk-remainder j i)
                                               (lambda (r)
                                                 (k r i)))))))
                       (upper-bound i))
                      i j)))))
```

The outcome is straightforward: all the iteration steps are unrolled. Here is a sample result:

```
> (nat-gcd-gen 4)
(lambda (j0)
  (let ([r1 (remainder j0 5)])
    (if (zero? r1)
        5
        (let ([r2 (remainder 5 r1)])
          (if (zero? r2)
              r1
              (let ([r3 (remainder r1 r2)])
                (if (zero? r3)
                    r2
                    (let ([r4 (remainder r2 r3)])
                      (error 'nat-gcd "out of steam")))))))))
```

The usefulness of the residual let-expressions is now plain, since the result of each remainder (except the innermost one) may be used twice.

> For all `i` and `j`,
> `((eval (nat-gcd-gen i)) j)` = `((eval (nat-gcd-gen j)) i)` = `(gcd-std i j)`

Exercise 6.1: Compare the efficiency of `gcd-std` and of its specialized versions. Does it match your expectations? □

6.2 Instances of the Euclidean algorithm

We consider three more instances of the Euclidean algorithm: computing the partial quotients of a rational number (Section 6.2.1), computing the Euclidean coefficients recursively (Section 6.2.2), and computing them iteratively (Section 6.2.3).

6.2.1 Finite simple continued fractions

The partial quotients q_0, q_1, q_2, ..., q_n of a rational number i/j are defined by the following equality:

$$\frac{i}{j} = q_0 + \frac{1}{q_1 + \frac{1}{q_2 + \dots \frac{1}{q_n}}}$$

They can be computed by the following variant of the Euclidean algorithm [33, Section 4.5.3]:

```
(define pq
  (lambda (i j)
    (letrec ([walk (lambda (i j)
                     (if (zero? i)
                         '()
                         (cons (quotient j i)
                               (walk (remainder j i) i))))])
      (walk i j))))
```

Given two natural numbers representing the numerator and the denominator of a rational number, `pq` constructs a list of its partial quotients.

6.2.2 *The Euclidean coefficients (a recursive solution)*

The Euclidean coefficients of any natural numbers i and j are two integers a and b such that $ai + bj = \gcd(i, j)$. Let us calculate two such ones.[5]

Base case: if $i = 0$ then $a = 0$ and $b = 1$ since, by definition of gcd, $\gcd(0, j) = j = 0i + 1j$.

Induction case: if $i \neq 0$ then by definition of gcd, $\gcd(i, j) = \gcd(j \,\mathrm{rem}\, i, i)$. By induction hypothesis, two integers a and b exist such that $\gcd(j \,\mathrm{rem}\, i, i) = a(j \,\mathrm{rem}\, i) + bi$. Therefore we are looking for two integers a' and b' such that $a'i + b'j = a(j \,\mathrm{rem}\, i) + bi$.

Since $i(j \,\mathrm{quo}\, i) + (j \,\mathrm{rem}\, i) = j$ a simple calculation leads one to $a(j \,\mathrm{rem}\, i) + bi = (b - a(j \,\mathrm{quo}\, i))i + aj$. Therefore $a' = b - a(j \,\mathrm{quo}\, i)$ and $b' = a$.

The Euclidean coefficients are thus computed as follows:

```
(define gcd-coeff
  (lambda (i j)
    (letrec ([walk (lambda (i j)
                     (if (zero? i)
                         '(0 . 1)
                         (let ([p (walk (remainder j i) i)])
                           (let ([a (car p)]
                                 [b (cdr p)])
                             (cons (- b (* a (quotient j i)))
                                   a)))))])
      (walk i j))))
```

6.2.3 *The Euclidean coefficients (an iterative solution)*

In Section 6.2.2, `gcd-coeff` is recursive: `walk` dives to the base case and computes a series of intermediate pairs all the way back. An iterative solution, however, exists, based on the observation that the intermediate pairs are obtained by a linear transformation. Such a transformation is canonically represented by a 2×2 matrix, and multiplying this (easily calculated) matrix with an intermediate pair yields the next pair in the series:

$$\begin{pmatrix} a' \\ b' \end{pmatrix} = \begin{bmatrix} -(j \,\mathrm{quo}\, i) & 1 \\ 1 & 0 \end{bmatrix} \begin{pmatrix} a \\ b \end{pmatrix}$$

Since matrix multiplication is associative, we can write an iterative version of `gcd-coeff` using an accumulator initialized to the identity matrix. The result reads as follows:

```
(define gcd-coeff-acc
  (lambda (i j)
    (letrec ([walk (lambda (i j x11 x12 x21 x22)
                     (if (zero? i)
                         (cons x12 x22)
                         (let ([q (quotient j i)])
                           (walk (remainder j i)
                                 i
                                 (- x12 (* x11 q))
                                 x11
                                 (- x22 (* x21 q))
                                 x21))))])
      (walk i j 1 0 0 1))))
```

[5]Euclidean coefficients are not unique, but this issue is out of the scope of these lecture notes.

6.3 A fold function for the Euclidean algorithm

Along the same lines as Sections 3 and 4, let us now turn to a fold function associated to the Euclidean algorithm. The fold function we consider here is parameterized with two functions: one for the base case and one for the induction step.

```
(define euclid
  (lambda (bc is)
    (letrec ([walk (lambda (i j)
                     (if (zero? i)
                         (bc j)
                         (is i j (walk (remainder j i) i))))])
      walk)))
```

During its course of values, `euclid` passes intermediate values to `bc` and `is`. It is thus more akin to primitive recursion than to primitive iteration.

Exercise 6.2: Write a function `gcd-std-alt` computing the gcd function, in terms of `euclid`. □

Exercise 6.3: Write a function `gcd-noi` computing the number of iterations of the Euclidean algorithm, in terms of `euclid`. □

Exercise 6.4: Write a function `pq-alt` computing the partial quotients of a rational number represented as a pair of integers, in terms of `euclid`. □

Exercise 6.5: Write a function `gcd-coeff-alt` computing the Euclidean coefficients recursively, in terms of `euclid`. □

Exercise 6.6: Write a function `gcd-coeff-acc-alt` computing the Euclidean coefficients iteratively, in terms of `euclid`. □

Exercise 6.7: Write a generating extension `euclid-gen` for `euclid`. □

Example 6.8: Evaluating `(euclid-gen 5 8)` yields

```
(lambda (bc0 is1)
  (is1 5 8 (is1 3 5 (is1 2 3 (is1 1 2 (bc0 1))))))
```

This residual program illustrates the course of values of the Euclidean algorithm for the two Fibonacci numbers 5 and 8. □

For all `i`, `j`, `bc`, and `is`,

```
((eval (euclid-gen i j)) bc is) = ((euclid bc is) i j)
```

We are now in position to stage the Euclidean algorithm, following the same approach used to stage the power function in Section 3.6.

6.4 Staging the Euclidean algorithm

When performing a Euclidean computation, we now have the choice of doing it either directly, as in Section 6.2, or generically through a fold function, as in Section 6.3. This section compares the performance of non-unfolded, dedicated code such as

```
(gcd-coeff 5 8)
```

with unfolded, non-dedicated code such as

```
(euclid-5-8 (lambda (d) ...) (lambda (i j) ...))
```

where `euclid-5-8` denotes the value of

```
(lambda (bc0 is1)
  (is1 5 8 (is1 3 5 (is1 2 3 (is1 1 2 (bc0 1))))))
```

which is the result of evaluating `(euclid-gen 5 8)`.

The purpose of this comparison is only pedagogical, since we disregard the cost of evaluating `(euclid-gen 5 8)` and its result.

6.4.1 Experiments

We conduct five comparisons, corresponding to the exercises of Section 6.3:

GCD-STD: calculating the gcd of two numbers. This is the base experiment: we compare the non-unfolded, dedicated code and the unfolded, non-dedicated code (where the result is already computed).

GCD-NOI: calculating the number of iterations of the Euclidean algorithm. This is a witness experiment.

- The non-unfolded, dedicated code iterates and increments an integer.
- The unfolded, non-dedicated code instantiates the base case and the induction step; at each induction step, it increments an integer.

PQ: calculating the partial quotients of a rational number.

- The non-unfolded, dedicated code iterates and computes a quotient and a remainder at each iteration.
- The unfolded, non-dedicated code instantiates the base case and the induction step; at each induction step, it computes one quotient.

GCD-COEFF: calculating Euclidean coefficients, recursively.

- The non-unfolded, dedicated code computes a remainder at each call; at each return, it computes a quotient and allocates a pair.
- The unfolded, non-dedicated code instantiates the base case and the induction step; at each induction step, it computes one quotient and allocates one pair.

GCD-COEFF-ACC: calculating Euclidean coefficients, iteratively.

- The non-unfolded, dedicated code iterates and computes a quotient, a remainder, two subtractions, and two multiplications at each iteration.
- The unfolded, non-dedicated code instantiates the base case and the induction step; at each induction step, it computes one quotient, one subtraction, and one multiplication.

We chose to use the Chez Scheme compiler instead of the Petite Chez Scheme interpreter, to avoid interpretive noise. The measurements were conducted on a Pentium 150MHz running Linux. In each case, we performed 5000 runs of the non-unfolded, dedicated code and 5000 runs of the unfolded, non-dedicated code, and we measured their performance with Chez Scheme's `time` function [19, Section 10.6]. Throughout, the Chez Scheme process occupied a handful of megabytes and thus incurred no swapping costs.

6.4.2 Analysis of the results

Figures 1 and 2 display the results. The left columns correspond to CPU time, including garbage collection, and the right columns correspond to allocated memory. Each line groups two graphs and corresponds to one experiment (GCD-STD, GCD-NOI, PQ, GCD-COEFF, and GCD-COEFF-ACC).

In each graph, the horizontal axis accounts for the number of iterations of the Euclidean algorithm, and the vertical axis accounts for time (left column) and space (right column). Figure 1 displays up to 50 iterations and Figure 2 displays up to 250 iterations. (Further experiments up to 500 iterations yield curves that are similar to the ones in Figure 2.)

Each graph contains two curves: one for an unfolded, non-dedicated function and one for a non-unfolded, dedicated function.

GCD-STD and GCD-NOI: as could be expected, the unfolded, non-dedicated code incurs essentially no cost in time and space, whereas the non-unfolded, dedicated code pays for iterating and computing quotients.

PQ: Up to 45 iterations, the unfolded, non-dedicated code is about twice as fast as the non-unfolded, dedicated code, for about the same memory usage. Beyond this threshold, the curves diverge, reflecting the increased costs of bignum calculations. The PQ figures match the GCD-STD figures in that adding the GCD-STD curve to the lower PQ curve yields the higher PQ curve.

GCD-COEFF: Up to 45 iterations, the time and space curves essentially match. Beyond this threshold, the curves diverge: the unfolded, non-dedicated code is about 50% faster than the non-unfolded, dedicated code, while allocating about 70% less memory.

GCD-COEFF-ACC: Up to 45 iterations, the time curves essentially match, but the non-unfolded, dedicated code allocates virtually no space, probably reflecting a better register-allocation policy of the accumulator. Beyond this threshold, the memory usages essentially match, while the unfolded, non-dedicated code slowly gets to be faster than the non-unfolded, dedicated code.

Both the memory curve and the time curve suggest that the threshold between fixed-number and big-number arithmetic is reached after about 45 iterations.

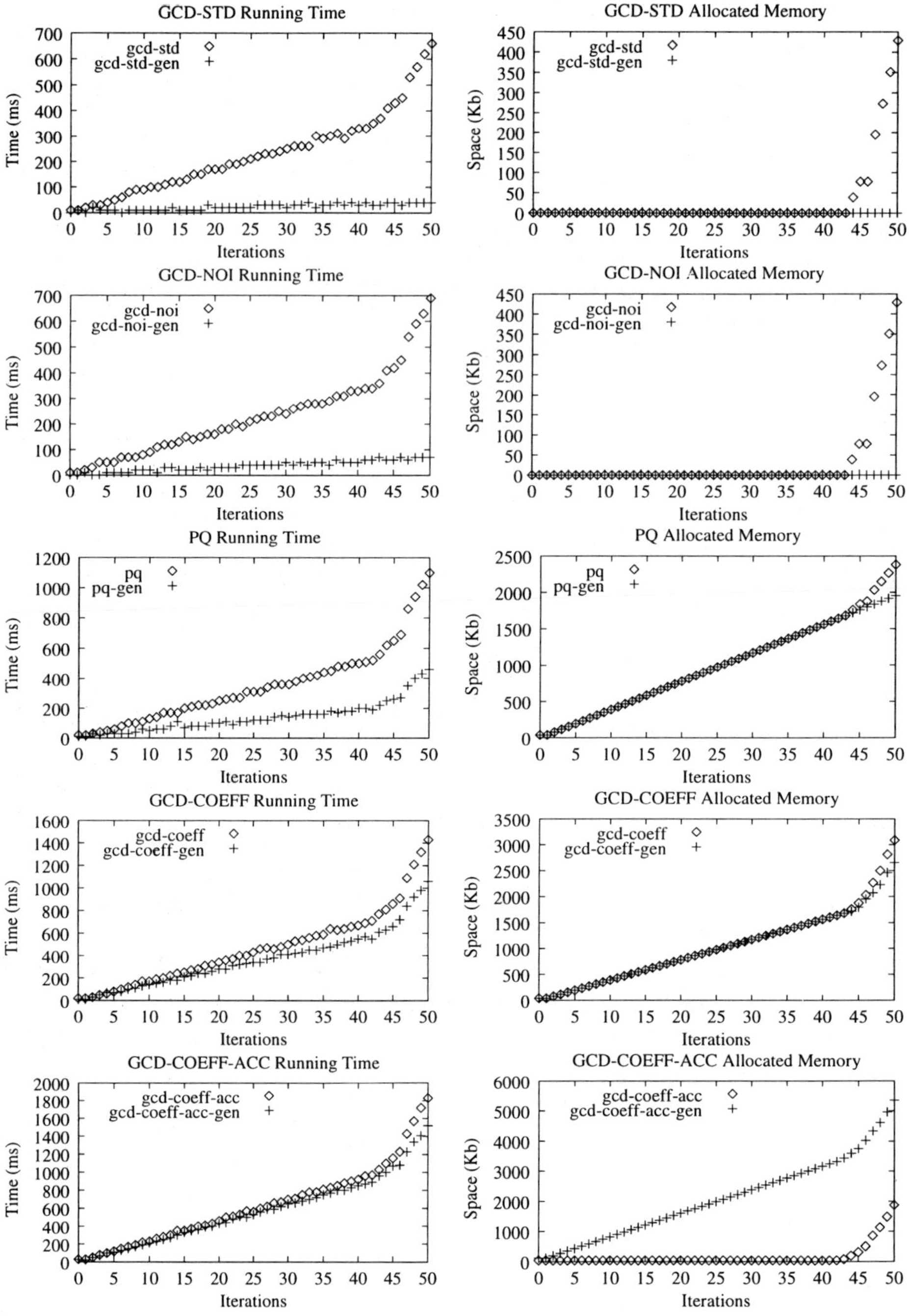

Figure 1: Benchmarks (up to 50 iterations)

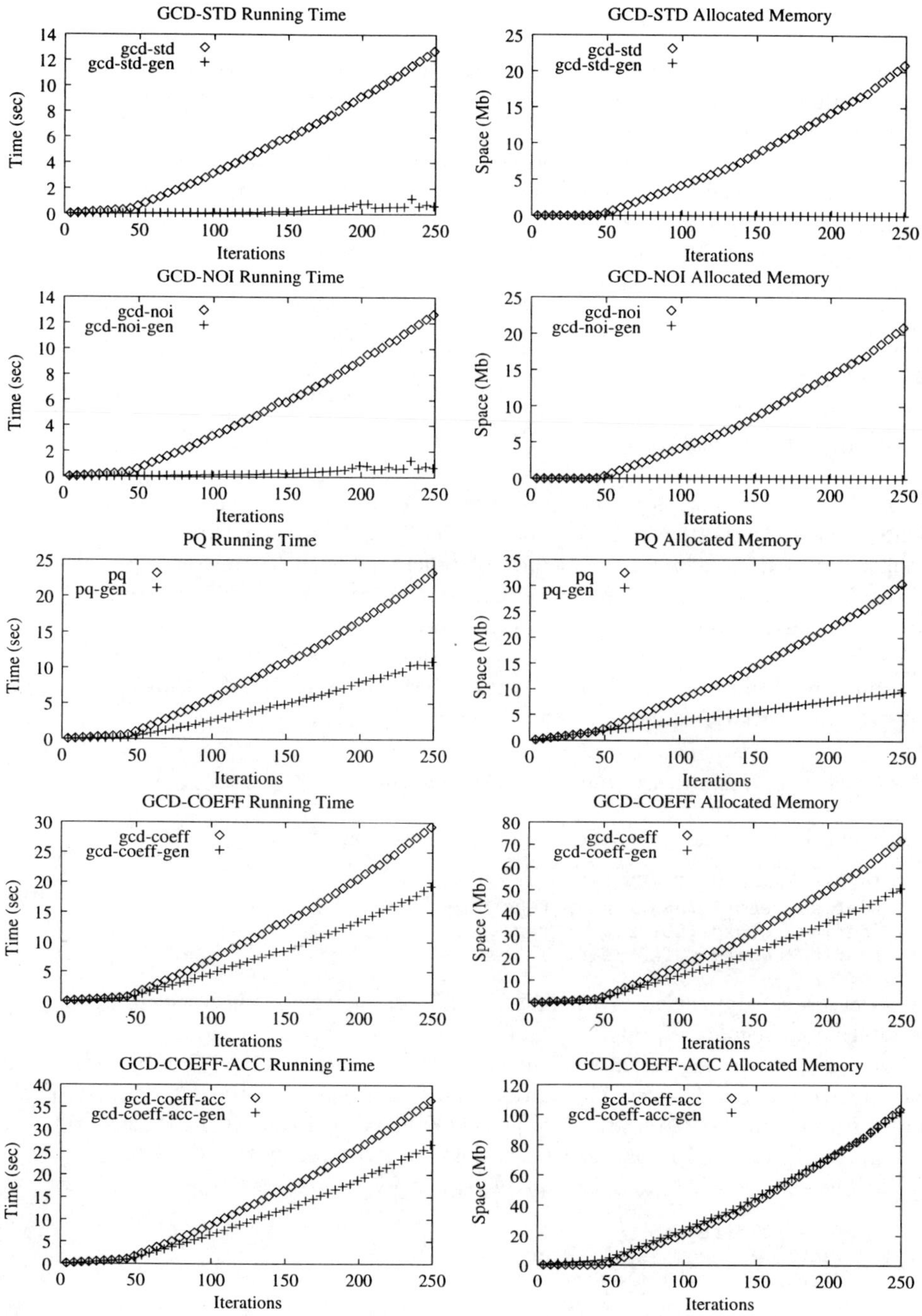

Figure 2: Benchmarks (up to 250 iterations)

6.5 Summary and conclusion

Somewhat recreationally, we have explored the Euclidean algorithm in the light of partial evaluation, unfolding it given an upper bound on the number of iterations, and writing it generically and unfolding the generic version prior to instantiating it. We also have measured the relative performances of unfolded, non-dedicated code and non-unfolded, dedicated code; as contrived as the overall experiment may be—the Euclidean algorithm is already very efficient and we are using Chez Scheme's bignum arithmetic off-the-shelf—the results are as could be expected, showing that unfolding calls and propagating and folding constants can pay off.

Exercise 6.9: Write the fold function associated to the binary Euclidean algorithm [33, page 338]. □

7 Regular Expressions

The goal of this section is to write an interpreter for regular expressions and its associated generating extension. The interpreter takes a regular expression and a list of tokens, and decides whether the list of tokens belongs to the set represented by the regular expression. The generating extension compiles a regular expression into a dedicated decision procedure written in Scheme.

We first define the regular expressions considered here (Section 7.1), and then the corresponding interpreter (Section 7.2) and generating extension (Section 7.3). We also consider some variations and extensions (Section 7.4).

7.1 Regular expressions and the associated fold function

The regular expressions we consider here have four constructors:

```
(define-record (TOKEN token))
(define-record (SEQ regexp regexp))
(define-record (ALT regexp regexp))
(define-record (STAR regexp))
```

`TOKEN` defines a fixed token, `SEQ` defines a sequence of regular expressions, `ALT` defines two alternative regular expressions, and `STAR` defines a Kleene closure.

For example, writing `TOKEN` without tag, `SEQ` with infix $\cdot$, `ALT` with infix $|$, and `STAR` with superscripted $*$, the regular expression $10 \cdot 20$ represents the set {`(10 20)`}; the regular expression $10 \cdot (20 \mid 30) \cdot 40$ represents the set {`(10 20 40)`, `(10 30 40)`}; and the regular expression $10^* \cdot 20$ represents the set {`(20)`, `(10 20)`, `(10 10 20)`, ...}.

The fold function for the data type of regular expressions is defined as follows.

```
(define fold-regexp
  (lambda (token seq alt star)
    (letrec ([walk (lambda (e)
                     (case-record e
                       [(TOKEN s)
                        (token s)]
                       [(SEQ e1 e2)
                        (seq (walk e1) (walk e2))]
                       [(ALT e1 e2)
                        (alt (walk e1) (walk e2))]
                       [(STAR e)
                        (star (walk e))]
```

```
                              [else
                               (error 'fold-regexp "not a regexp ~s" e)]))])
      walk)))
```

7.2 An interpreter for regular expressions

An interpreter for regular expressions takes a regular expression and a list of tokens, and determines whether the list belongs to the set represented by the regular expression. If it does, then we say that the regular expression 'accepts' the list, and otherwise that it 'rejects' it.

Exercise 7.1: Write an interpreter `ire` for regular expressions using `fold-regexp`. The interpreter should return `#t` if the list is accepted, and `#f` otherwise.

Hint—the type of the instance of `walk`, in `fold-regexp`, should be as follows:

```
regexp -> list-of-tokens * (list-of-tokens -> boolean) -> boolean
```

For example, here is a continuation-passing function for testing the first element of a list of tokens. If the test is positive, the rest of the list is sent to the continuation.

```
(define test-token
  (lambda (a ts k)
    (and (not (null? ts))
         (equal? a (car ts))
         (k (cdr ts)))))
```

N.B. Section 7.3 provides some hints about how to write `ire`. □

7.3 A generating extension for regular expressions

Exercise 7.2: Write a generating extension `ire-gen` for regular expressions using `fold-regexp`. The generating extension should take a regular expression and compile it into Scheme code, and this Scheme code should satisfy the correctness criterion of specialization.

> For all `re` and `ts`,
>
> `((eval (ire-gen re)) ts)` = `(ire re ts)`

For example, using the same convention as above, $10 \cdot 20$ could be compiled into:

```
(lambda (ts0)
  (test-token 10 ts0 (lambda (ts1)
                       (test-token 20 ts1 (lambda (ts2)
                                            (null? ts2))))))
```

Similarly, $10 \cdot (20 \mid 30) \cdot 40$ could be compiled into:

```
(lambda (ts0)
  (test-token 10 ts0 (lambda (ts1)
                       (let ([k4 (lambda (ts2)
                                   (test-token 40 ts2 (lambda (ts3)
                                                        (null? ts3))))])
                        (or (test-token 20 ts1 (lambda (ts5)
                                                 (k4 ts5)))
                            (test-token 30 ts1 (lambda (ts6)
                                                 (k4 ts6))))))))
```

And finally, $10^* \cdot 20$ could be compiled into:

```
(lambda (ts0)
  (letrec ([star1
            (lambda (ts2)
              (or (test-token 20 ts2 (lambda (ts3)
                                       (null? ts3)))
                  (test-token 10 ts2 (lambda (ts4)
                                       (star1 ts4)))))])
    (star1 ts0)))
```

N.B. $(42^*)^*$ should be compiled into a non-diverging residual program such as the following one:

```
(lambda (ts0)
  (letrec ([star1
            (lambda (ts2)
              (or (null? ts2)
                  (letrec ([star3
                            (lambda (ts4)
                              (or (and (not (equal? ts2 ts4))
                                       (star1 ts4))
                                  (test-token 42
                                              ts4
                                              (lambda (ts5)
                                                (star3 ts5)))))])
                    (star3 ts2))))])
    (star1 ts0)))
```

□

Question 7.3: The second example suggests that the compiler should name the continuation of an `ALT` expression. Why? □

Exercise 7.4: Observing that the compiled regular expressions contain many eta-redexes, how could `mk-lambda` be modified to avoid them? For example, $10^* \cdot (20 \mid 30)$ could be compiled into:

```
(lambda (ts0)
  (letrec ([star1 (lambda (ts2)
                    (or (or (test-token 20 ts2 null?)
                            (test-token 30 ts2 null?))
                        (test-token 10 ts2 star1)))])
    (star1 ts0)))
```

□

Question 7.5: In Scheme, or-expressions can take arbitrarily many arguments, not just two. How could this be used so that the compiled code just above reads instead as follows?

```
(lambda (ts0)
  (letrec ([star1 (lambda (ts2)
                    (or (test-token 20 ts2 null?)
                        (test-token 30 ts2 null?)
                        (test-token 10 ts2 star1)))])
    (star1 ts0)))
```

□

7.4 *Variations and extensions*

7.4.1 *Efficiency*

The compiled version of $(10 \cdot 20) \mid (10 \cdot 30)$, or of $10 \mid 10$ for that matter, is sub-optimal, since the token `10` is tested repeatedly.

Food for thought 7.6: How could the situation be improved?

Hint—think of the *nullable*, *firstpos* and *followpos* functions in the Dragon book [1, page 135]. □

7.4.2 *A wild card*

Let us extend the language of regular expressions with a wild card, i.e., a constructor that matches any token.

```
(define-record (ANY))
```

Exercise 7.7: Extend the fold function, the interpreter, and its generating extension to cater for this new constructor.

Hint—define a variant of `test-token`. □

7.4.3 *Variables*

Let us extend the language of regular expressions with non-linear variables, i.e., with a constructor introducing a variable such that all other occurrences of this variable must match the same token.

```
(define-record (VAR symbol))
```

For example, the regular expression $x \cdot 20 \cdot x$ accepts all the lists `(v1 v2 v3)` such that `v2` = 20 and `v1` = `v3`.

The goal of this section is to extend the interpreter and its generating extension to cater for this new constructor. For example, given a function for variables such as the following one,

```
(define name-token
  (lambda (ts k)
    (and (not (null? ts))
         (k (car ts) (cdr ts)))))
```

the regular expression $x \cdot 20 \cdot x$ could be compiled into the following residual code:

```
(lambda (ts0)
  (name-token ts0 (lambda (v1 ts2)
                    (test-token 20 ts2 (lambda (ts3)
                                         (test-token v1 ts3 null?))))))
```

The key point of this residual code is that the first element of the list of tokens is named `v1`, using `name-token`, and the second call to `test-token` checks whether `v1` and the third element of the list denote the same token.

Exercise 7.8: Extend the interpreter to handle variables. To this end, equip it with an *environment* mapping variables to tokens. □

Exercise 7.9: Extend the generating extension to handle variables, so that all references to the environment are resolved at compile time. (Indeed, there is no track of any environment in the example just above.) □

Food for thought 7.10: Alternatively, the interpreter could be equipped with a run-time stack of tokens. Named tokens would be pushed on that stack and the environment, which would live at compile time, would map compile-time variables to run-time stack offsets. □

7.4.4 Accepting prefixes

Suppose that we want to check whether the *prefix* of a list of tokens (instead of the whole list) is accepted by a regular expression.

Exercise 7.11: Modify the interpreter so that it yields either a rejection value or the suffix of the input list of tokens, using the two following records to distinguish between failure and success:

```
(define-record (ACCEPT list-of-tokens))
(define-record (REJECT))
```

Hint—start by modifying `test-token`. □

7.4.5 Multiple answers

There may be several ways for a list of tokens to be accepted by a regular expression.

Exercise 7.12: Modify the interpreter so that it yields the number of ways in which a regular expression accepts a list of tokens—0 signifying failure. □

7.4.6 Collecting suffixes

Building on Sections 7.4.4 and 7.4.5, we want to construct the list of suffixes of the input list of tokens such that the prefix of each of these lists is accepted by the regular expression.

Exercise 7.13: Modify the interpreter to make it construct a list of accepted suffixes.
Hint—add an extra continuation. □

7.5 Summary and conclusion

We have gone through a classical example of partial evaluation, namely an interpreter for regular expressions. Specializing it with respect to a given regular expression amounts to unrolling all of its recursive calls and constructing residual calls to atomic tests. As in the previous sections, we have shown that this specialization strategy is not ad hoc: the compiler is an instance of a fold function which is defined inductively on the structure of regular expressions and therefore it is guaranteed to terminate.

Further references about interpreters for regular expressions include Neil Jones, Carsten Gomard, and Peter Sestoft's textbook [31], Bob Harper's article on proof-directed debugging [25], and Andrzej Filinski and the author's work on continuations [10].

The programming techniques reviewed in Section 7.4 apply directly to writing programming-language interpreters and specializing them with respect to a program, which is one of the most celebrated applications of partial evaluation. Further references about programming-language interpreters include the above-mentioned textbook, Yoshihiko Futamura's seminal article on self-applicable partial evaluation [23], and the author's joint work on imperative languages [7, 16].

8 Conclusion and Issues

Through a series of examples and exercises, we have illustrated some programming techniques for partial evaluation, focusing on generating extensions and structuring them as instances of fold functions. We conclude these lecture notes with some further issues.

8.1 Type-directed partial evaluation

The functions `reify-fun` and `reflect-fun` of Section 2.3 can be generalized to work at arbitrary type rather than at `exp -> exp`. The resulting type-indexed reify function implements a practical and efficient normalization function for the λ-calculus. This normalization function is efficient because—like the generating extensions considered here—it requires no translation overhead and operates at native speed. It is also practical because, for example, it enables one to obtain the effect of all the generating extensions considered here without writing a single quasiquote and unquote: these are all factored out in the normalization function. More detail and further bibliographic references can be found in the author's 1998 lecture notes on type-directed partial evaluation [9] and in Andrzej Filinski's semantic account [22].

8.2 Sharing residual code

The following observation applies to all the examples considered here: when specializing a compositional program with respect to a given data structure for its induction variable, we map this data structure into the control structure of the residual program, homomorphically. This means that when the data structure is tree-shaped, the control-flow graph of the specialized program is also tree-shaped. In particular, when the source program is recursive rather than inductive over a part of the data structure (e.g., a Kleene star in regular expressions or a while loop in an imperative program), the residual program contains a recursive definition (e.g., an instance of `star` in Section 7).

Exercise 8.1: In this light, revisit how regular expressions are traditionally compiled into finite automata in, e.g., the Dragon Book [1, Sections 3.7, 3.8, and 3.9]. □

DAG-shaped, rather than tree-shaped, residual programs can be obtained as follows.

By construction, each residual program point is a version of a source program point, specialized with respect to some static values. Suppose that we index some source program points with some static values, together with a pointer to the corresponding residual code. This indexing makes it possible, at specialization time, to *share* residual computations. If, later in the specialization, the same source program point needs to be specialized with respect to the same static values, there is no need to duplicate the specialization and the residual code. This strategy is known as *polyvariant program-point specialization*, and has proven instrumental, e.g., to derive Knuth, Morris, and Pratt's linear string matcher out of a naive quadratic one [6]. More detail can be found in Jones, Gomard, and Sestoft's textbook, including a study of the program speedups enabled by partial-evaluation techniques [31].

8.3 Data specialization

There is ample room for variation in the area of partial evaluation. One is *data specialization.* The issue is crystallized in the following example. Rather than generating a residual program such as

```
(lambda (bc0 is1)
  (is1 3 5 (is1 2 3 (is1 1 2 (bc0 1)))))
```

one could store the static values 3, 5, etc. in a residual table and generate a more compact residual program accessing this table at run time. Such data specialization has proven to be practically useful in scientific computing, where it allows one to share and reuse the result of expensive computations. More detail and further bibliographic references can be found in Sandrine Chirokoff, Charles Consel and Renaud Marlet's recent article on program and data specialization [5].

8.4 Binding times

Let us conclude with the following quote from Jerome Feldman's PhD thesis, written in the early sixties.

> "One of the most difficult concepts in translator writing is the distinction between actions done at translation time and those done at run time. Anyone who has mastered this difference has taken the basic step towards gaining an understanding of computer languages." [21]

This quote is visionary in that the issue it raises occurs both in Yoshihiko Futamura's statement of the problem of self-applicable partial evaluation [23] and in Neil Jones's solution [31]. Jones's solution hinges on a *binding-time analysis* occurring prior to specialization and determining which parts of a source program can be safely performed at specialization time and which parts should be reconstructed. This solution spawned the so-called offline approach to partial evaluation, which is a topic of active research today [17].

Feldman's point is as valid today as it was almost 40 years ago: even though binding-time analyses provide automated support to distinguish, e.g., between compile time and run time, this support does not dispense one from understanding personally the distinction between binding times and its consequences for programming.[6] This distinction is the underlying theme of these lecture notes.

Acknowledgments: Grateful thanks to the organizers of Marktoberdorf'99 for the invitation, to the staff, for a friendly and flawless organization, and to the other participants, for the pleasant and studious atmosphere which seems to make Marktoberdorf, year after year, such a successful scientific retreat. I would also like to thank Ralf Steinbrueggen for outstanding editorship, Andrzej Filinski for comments and sound encouragement, Daniel Damian and Morten Rhiger for comments and editorial assistance, Torben Amtoft, Anindya Banerjee, Peter Chang, Charles Consel, Kent Dybvig, Mayer Goldberg, Hanne Gottliebsen, John Hatcliff, Niels O. Jensen, Julia Lawall, Gilles Muller, David Schmidt, Ulrik Schultz, Sebastian Skalberg, Charles Stewart, René Vestergaard, and Oscar Waddell for timely comments, and Sandrine Chirokoff, Irène Danvy, Bernd Grobauer, Karoline Malmkjær, and Zhe Yang for discussions and feedback.

References

[1] Alfred V. Aho, Ravi Sethi, and Jeffrey D. Ullman. *Compilers: Principles, Techniques and Tools.* Addison-Wesley, 1986.

[2] Alan Bawden. Quasiquotation in Lisp. In Olivier Danvy, editor, *Proceedings of the ACM SIGPLAN Workshop on Partial Evaluation and Semantics-Based Program Manipulation*, Technical report BRICS-NS-99-1, University of Aarhus, pages 4–12, San Antonio, Texas, January 1999. Available online at `http://www.brics.dk/~pepm99/programme.html`

[3] Jon Bentley. *Writing Efficient Programs.* Prentice-Hall, 1982.

[4] Dines Bjørner, Andrei P. Ershov, and Neil D. Jones, editors. *Partial Evaluation and Mixed Computation.* North-Holland, 1988.

[5] Sandrine Chirokoff, Charles Consel, and Renaud Marlet. Combining program and data specialization. *Higher-Order and Symbolic Computation*, 12(4):309–335, 1999.

[6] Charles Consel and Olivier Danvy. Partial evaluation of pattern matching in strings. *Information Processing Letters*, 30(2):79–86, January 1989.

[7] Charles Consel and Olivier Danvy. Static and dynamic semantics processing. In Robert (Corky) Cartwright, editor, *Proceedings of the Eighteenth Annual ACM Symposium on Principles of Programming Languages*, pages 14–24, Orlando, Florida, January 1991. ACM Press.

[8] Charles Consel and Olivier Danvy. Tutorial notes on partial evaluation. In Susan L. Graham, editor, *Proceedings of the Twentieth Annual ACM Symposium on Principles of Programming Languages*, pages 493–501, Charleston, South Carolina, January 1993. ACM Press.

[9] Olivier Danvy. Type-directed partial evaluation. In Hatcliff et al. [27], pages 367–411. Extended version available as the lecture notes BRICS LN-98-3.

[10] Olivier Danvy and Andrzej Filinski. Abstracting control. In Mitchell Wand, editor, *Proceedings of the 1990 ACM Conference on Lisp and Functional Programming*, pages 151–160, Nice, France, June 1990. ACM Press.

[11] Olivier Danvy, Robert Glück, and Peter Thiemann, editors. *Partial Evaluation*, number 1110 in Lecture Notes in Computer Science, Dagstuhl, Germany, February 1996. Springer-Verlag.

[6] A similar point can be made for static type-checking.

[12] Olivier Danvy, Robert Glück, and Peter Thiemann, editors. *Symposium on Partial Evaluation*, volume 30, number 3es of *Computing Surveys*. ACM Press, September 1998.

[13] Olivier Danvy and Mayer Goldberg. Partial evaluation of the Euclidean algorithm. *Lisp and Symbolic Computation*, 10(2):101–111, 1997.

[14] Olivier Danvy and John Hatcliff. Partial evaluation. In David Hemmendinger, Anthony Ralston, and Edwin Reilly, editors, *Encyclopedia of Computer Science (Fourth Edition)*. Macmillan Reference/Grove Dictionaries, 1999.

[15] Olivier Danvy and Carolyn L. Talcott, editors. *Special Issue on Partial Evaluation, Part I*, Higher-Order and Symbolic Computation, Vol. 12, No. 4, 1999.

[16] Olivier Danvy and René Vestergaard. Semantics-based compiling: A case study in type-directed partial evaluation. In Herbert Kuchen and Doaitse Swierstra, editors, *Eighth International Symposium on Programming Language Implementation and Logic Programming*, number 1140 in Lecture Notes in Computer Science, pages 182–197, Aachen, Germany, September 1996. Springer-Verlag. Extended version available as the technical report BRICS-RS-96-13.

[17] Rowan Davies and Frank Pfenning. A modal analysis of staged computation. *Journal of the ACM*. To appear.

[18] R. Kent Dybvig. *The Scheme Programming Language, Second Edition*. Prentice Hall, 1996. Available online at `http://www.scheme.com/tspl2d/`.

[19] R. Kent Dybvig. *Chez Scheme User's Guide*. Cadence Research Systems, 1998. Available online at `http://www.scheme.com/csug/`.

[20] Andrei P. Ershov, Dines Bjørner, Yoshihiko Futamura, K. Furukawa, Anders Haraldsson, and William Scherlis, editors. *Special Issue: Selected Papers from the Workshop on Partial Evaluation and Mixed Computation, 1987*, New Generation Computing, Vol. 6, No. 2-3. Ohmsha Ltd. and Springer-Verlag, 1988.

[21] Jerome A. Feldman. *A formal semantics for computer oriented languages*. PhD thesis, Department of Mathematics, Carnegie Institute of Technology, Pittsburgh, Pennsylvania, 1964.

[22] Andrzej Filinski. A semantic account of type-directed partial evaluation. In Gopalan Nadathur, editor, *International Conference on Principles and Practice of Declarative Programming*, number 1702 in Lecture Notes in Computer Science, pages 378–395, Paris, France, September 1999. Springer-Verlag. Extended version available as the technical report BRICS RS-99-17.

[23] Yoshihiko Futamura. Partial evaluation of computation process – an approach to a compiler-compiler. *Higher-Order and Symbolic Computation*, 12(4), 1999. Reprinted from Systems · Computers · Controls 2(5), 1971.

[24] Robert Glück and Neil D. Jones. Automatic program specialization by partial evaluation: an introduction. In W. Mackens and S.M. Rump, editors, *Software Engineering in Scientific Computing*, pages 70–77. Vieweg, 1996.

[25] Robert Harper. Proof-directed debugging. *Journal of Functional Programming*. To appear.

[26] John Hatcliff and Olivier Danvy. A computational formalization for partial evaluation. *Mathematical Structures in Computer Science*, pages 507–541, 1997. Extended version available as the technical report BRICS RS-96-34.

[27] John Hatcliff, Torben Æ. Mogensen, and Peter Thiemann, editors. *Partial Evaluation – Practice and Theory; Proceedings of the 1998 DIKU Summer School*, number 1706 in Lecture Notes in Computer Science, Copenhagen, Denmark, July 1998. Springer-Verlag.

[28] Graham Hutton. A tutorial on the universality and expressiveness of fold. *Journal of Functional Programming*, 9(4):355–372, 1999.

[29] Neil D. Jones, editor. *Special issue on Partial Evaluation*, Journal of Functional Programming, Vol. 3, Part 3, July 1993.

[30] Neil D. Jones. An introduction to partial evaluation. *ACM Computing Surveys*, 28(3):480–504, 1996.

[31] Neil D. Jones, Carsten K. Gomard, and Peter Sestoft. *Partial Evaluation and Automatic Program Generation*. Prentice-Hall International, 1993. Available online at `http://www.dina.kvl.dk/~sestoft/pebook/pebook.html`

[32] Richard Kelsey, William Clinger, and Jonathan Rees, editors. Revised[5] report on the algorithmic language Scheme. *Higher-Order and Symbolic Computation*, 11(1):7–105, 1998. Also appears in ACM SIGPLAN Notices 33(9), September 1998. Available online at http://www.wkap.nl/sampletoc.htm?1388-3690+11+1+1998

[33] Donald E. Knuth. *The Art of Computer Programming, Volume 2: Seminumerical Algorithms – Third Edition.* Addison-Wesley, 1988.

[34] Chin-Soon Lee. Partial evaluation of the Euclidean algorithm, revisited. *Higher-Order and Symbolic Computation*, 12(2):203–212, 1999.

[35] Torben Æ. Mogensen and Peter Sestoft. Partial evaluation. In Allen Kent and James G. Williams, editors, *Encyclopedia of Computer Science and Technology*, volume 37, pages 247–279. Marcel Dekker, 270 Madison Avenue, New York, New York 10016, 1997.

[36] Gilles Muller, Calton Pu, and Charles Consel. Specialization. In J. Urban and P. Dasgupta, editors, *Encyclopedia of Distributed Computing '99*. Kluwer Academic Publisher, 1999.

[37] Peter Sestoft and Harald Søndergaard, editors. *Special issue on partial evaluation*, Lisp and Symbolic Computation, Vol. 8, No. 3, 1993.

A Some residual-code constructors

A.1 Section 2.2.1

```
(define mk-zero?
  (lambda (n)
    (if (number? n)
        (zero? n)
        `(zero? ,n))))

(define mk-if
  (lambda (test then else)
    (if (boolean? test)
        (if test then else)
        `(if ,test ,then ,else))))
```

```
(define mk-error
  (lambda (f s . vs)
    `(error ',f ,s ,@vs)))

(define mk-remainder
  (lambda (i j)
    (if (and (number? i)
             (number? j))
        (remainder i j)
        `(remainder ,i ,j))))
```

Question A.1: Why is this definition of `mk-if` unsatisfying? □

A.2 Section 2.2.2

```
(define mk-lambda
  (lambda (stub f)
    (let ([x (gensym! stub)])
      `(lambda (,x)
         ,(f x)))))
```

```
(define mk-lambda2
  (lambda (stub1 stub2 f)
    (let* ([x1 (gensym! stub1)]
           [x2 (gensym! stub2)])
      `(lambda (,x1 ,x2)
         ,(f x1 x2)))))
```

A.3 Section 2.2.3

```
(define mk-let
  (lambda (stub e f)
    (let ([x (gensym! stub)])
      `(let ([,x ,e])
         ,(f x)))))
```

```
(define mk-letrec
  (lambda (stub header body)
    (let ([x (gensym! stub)])
      `(letrec ([,x ,(header x)])
         ,(body x)))))
```

A.4 Section 2.2.4

```
(define mk-let*
  (lambda (stub e f)
    (let* ([x (gensym! stub)]
           [body (f x)])
      (cond
        [(equal? x body)
         e]
        [(and (pair? body) (equal? (car body) 'let*))
         `(let* ([,x ,e] ,@(cadr body)) ,(caddr body))]
        [else
         `(let* ([,x ,e])
            ,body)]))))

(define mk-let mk-let*)
```

Exercise A.2: Motivate the clause `(equal? x body)` in the definition of `mk-let*`. □

Exercise A.3: What happens if the second argument of `mk-let*` is atomic, i.e., a symbol, a number, a string, or a boolean? Modify `mk-let*` to cater for this case. □

B An alternative to continuations

In several exercises, we have hinted at continuations for constructing flat residual let-expressions. Alternatively, one could modify `mk-let*` to exploit the following equation [26]:

```
(let* ([x (let* ([x1 e1] [x2 e2] ...) e)]) body)
= (let* ([x1 e1] [x2 e2] ... [x e]) body)
```

(This equation is valid if there is no name clash, which is the case here because of gensym.)

Question B.1: What else should be modified in the toolkit to enable this alternative version of `mk-let*`? □

Author Index